AFRICAN POLITICS AND SOCIETY

AFRICAN POLITICS AND SOCIETY

**BASIC ISSUES AND PROBLEMS
OF GOVERNMENT AND DEVELOPMENT**

Irving Leonard Markovitz

THE FREE PRESS, NEW YORK
COLLIER-MACMILLAN LIMITED, LONDON

The Free Press
A Division of The Macmillan Company
866 Third Avenue, New York, New York 10022
Collier-Macmillan Canada Ltd., Toronto, Ontario

Library of Congress Catalog Card Number: 79–88119

Printing Number
1 2 3 4 5 6 7 8 9 10

For my mother and father

CONTENTS

ACKNOWLEDGMENTS

I should like to express my appreciation to Stanley Meisler, Daniel McCall, and Patricia McNees Mancini for their suggestions about the readings. Robert Engler, Solomon Resnick, Michael Walzer, and Harvey Glickman commented on versions of the introduction. Marvin Gettleman stimulated and encouraged the project from its inception, and when it faltered he was quick to offer his support. My wife, Ruth, helped tremendously with the typing. To a large extent, the idea for this book grew out of the teaching necessities of attempting to organize in a meaningful fashion a large amount of material so that it would fit within the confines of an academic course. My students, therefore, have also been participants in this endeavor and have helped shape the many versions of the basic course on African politics from which this volume finally emerged.

CONTRIBUTORS NOTES

SAMIR AMIN, employed as an economist by the United Nations, is currently associated with the *Institut Africain de Developpement Economique et de Plannification* at Dakar. Included among his publications is the study *Trois Experiences Africaines de Developpement: Le Mali, la Guinée et le Ghana.*

DAVID E. APTER, formerly Professor of Political Science and Director of the Institute of International Studies, University of California, Berkeley, is now Professor of Political Science at Yale University. His first of many books, *The Gold Coast in Transition*, stirred the interest of young scholars in an until-then neglected field.

GIOVANNI ARRIGHI was one of nine lecturers from the University College of Rhodesia who were expelled from their jobs and the country in July, 1966. He now teaches in the Department of Economics of the University College, Tanzania.

MARY BENSON, author of many books, including *South Africa: The Struggle for a Birthright*, left South Africa in 1966 after being placed under house arrest under the Suppression of Communism Act.

PAULA BROWN, currently affiliated with the State University of New York at Stony Brook, has written extensively for scholarly journals.

AIMÉ CÉSAIRE, one of the founders of the doctrine of Négritude in the 1930's, as well as philosopher, poet, dramatist, statesman, mayor, and Deputy from Martinique to the French National Assembly, is one of this century's outstanding men of *belles lettres*. Most of his work has not yet been translated into English.

JAMES S. COLEMAN, Director of the Institute for Development Studies, University College, Kenya, was in charge of the African

Studies Program of the University of California, Los Angeles. Among his publications is *Nigeria: Background to Nationalism*, and he has edited several works important for the field of developing areas.

Compagnie d'Études Industrielles et d'Amènagement du Territoire is a private French company largely responsible, in conjunction with the government, for surveying the country's resources and drawing up Senegal's plans for development.

MICHAEL CROWDER, formerly Director of the Institute of African Studies, Fourah Bay College, The University College of Sierra Leone, is the Executive Secretary of the Permanent Bureau of the International Congress of Africanists.

CHEIKH ANTA DIOP has begun a Carbon 14 Dating Laboratory at the *Institut Fondamental d'Afrique Noire* in Dakar. His latest book is *Anteriorité des Civilisations Nègres: Mythe ou Verite Historique*, published by Presence Africaine.

RUPERT EMERSON is professor of government and research associate at the Center for International Affairs at Harvard University. He is the author of *From Empire to Nation* and *Representative Government in South East Asia*.

MAX GLUCKMAN, noted for his path-finding studies, including *Custom and Conflict in Africa*, is professor of Anthropology at the University of Manchester and former Director of the Rhodes-Livingstone Institute for Social Research.

ROBERT F. GRAY is Professor of Anthropology at Tulane and author of numerous articles and several volumes of Africana.

FRED GREENE is a Professor of Political Science at Williams College, Williamstown, Massachusetts, and author of *Dynamics of International Relations* (Holt, Rinehart and Winston, 1964).

FRED L. HADSEL is Director of the Office of Inter-African Affairs, Department of State. A Foreign Service Officer, he has also been Professorial Lecturer at George Washington University, Johns Hopkins University, and Howard University.

ELLEN CONROY KENNEDY was nominated for the National Book Awards in 1969 for her translation of Albert Camus, *Lyrical and Critical Essays*, published by Alfred Knopf. Her articles and reviews of black French-language writings have appeared in many scholarly journals.

COLIN LEGUM is the African correspondent of *The Observer* and the author of many articles and books on African politics.

IRVING LEONARD MARKOVITZ teaches political science at Queens College, the City University of New York, and is the author of *Léopold Sédar Senghor and the Politics of Négritude* published in 1969 by Atheneum.

GICHA MBEE is a farmer and member of the Mbugwe tribe of Northern Tanzania.

TOM MBOYA was the Minister of Economic Planning and Development in the Kenya Government. In 1969 he was felled by a member's bullet.

NORMAN N. MILLER, Associate Professor of Political Science and African Studies, Michigan State University, did research in East Africa during 1964–1966 and 1969.

EDUARDO C. MONDLANE, formerly a Professor at Syracuse University, was President of FRELIMO, the Liberation Movement of Mozambique, before his assassination in Tanzania in 1969.

JEAN-PIERRE N'DIAYE, a young Senegalese sociologist, experienced in survey and interviewing methods at the *Institut Français d'Opinion Publique* and the *Institut de Recherches et de Formation en vue du Developpement,* was the first African to undertake and publish a study of his fellow African students in France.

JOHN NOTTINGHAM, after long administrative experience in Kenya, taught at Makere College in Uganda and the University College of Tanzania. He is currently editor and Director of the East African Publishing House.

JULIUS K. NYERERE is President of Tanzania and Chief Executive Officer of the Tanzania African National Union.

SURENDRA J. PATEL is a member of the secretariat of the United Nations Economic Commission for Africa.

R. CRANFORD PRATT is Chairman of the International Studies Program, The University of Toronto.

CARL G. ROSBERG, JR., who recently spent two years acting as Chairman of the newly established Department of Political Science at the University College of Tanzania, is Professor of Political Science at the University of California, Berkeley.

GEORGE A. SHEPPERSON teaches at the University of Edinburgh and is the author of numerous important works on Africa.

ELLIOTT P. SKINNER, formerly Professor of Anthropology at Columbia is now the United States Ambassador to Upper Volta.

JEAN SURET-CANALE has acted as advisor to several African governments, authored *Afrique Noire, L'Ere Coloniale 1900–1945,* as well as *Afrique Noire Occidentale et Centrale* and co-authored *Histoire de l'Afrique Occidentale.*

SÉKOU TOURÉ is President of the Republic of Guinea and head of the ruling Democratic Party of Guinea.

STANLEY TRAPIDO, formerly of the University of Natal, the Republic of South Africa, now teaches in the Department of Politics, the University of Durham, England.

AFRICA

POLITICAL DIVISIONS

— — — — — —
BOUNDARY REPRESENTATION
IS NOT
NECESSARILY AUTHORITATIVE

o Capital

```
0   MILES   500        1000
0      500   1000
       KILOMETERS
```

Rabat o
Algiers o   o Tunis
TUNISIA   Tripoli
Benghazi

MOROCCO

Sidi Ifni o
IFNI (Sp.)

El Aiún o

SPANISH
SAHARA

ALGERIA

LIBYA

Cairo o

UNITED
ARAB
REPUBLIC

MAURITANIA
o Nouakchott

MALI

NIGER

Khartoum o

THE
GAMBIA   Dakar o SENEGAL
Bissau o   o Bathurst

PORTUGUESE
GUINEA   GUINEA

UPPER
VOLTA   o Niamey
Bamako o   Ouagadougou o

CHAD
Fort-Lamy o

SUDAN

FRENCH
SOMALILAND
o Djibouti

Conakry o
Freetown o
SIERRA LEONE
Monrovia o
LIBERIA   o Abidjan

IVORY
COAST   TOGO
GHANA
Accra o   DAHOMEY   NIGERIA
Lagos o
Lomé o   o Porto Novo

CAMEROON

CENTRAL
AFRICAN REPUBLIC

Addis Ababa o
ETHIOPIA

SOMALIA

Santa Isabel o
FERNANDO PO
RIO MUNI
PRÍNCIPE (Port.)
SÃO TOMÉ

EQUATORIAL
GUINEA
(Sp.)

ANNOBON

o Yaoundé
Bangui o

GABON   CONGO
o Libreville

Brazzaville o

Kinshasa o

DEMOCRATIC
REPUBLIC OF
THE CONGO

UGANDA
o Kampala
Kigali o   KENYA
o Nairobi
RWANDA
Bujumbura o   BURUNDI

Mogadiscio o

PEMBA
ZANZIBAR
Dar es Salaam

TANZANIA

Luanda o

ANGOLA
(Port.)

ZAMBIA   Lusaka o

MALAWI
Zomba o

Tananarive o

SOUTH-WEST
AFRICA
(Rep. of S. Africa)

WALVIS
BAY
(Rep. of S. Africa)

Windhoek o

Salisbury o
SOUTHERN
RHODESIA
BOTSWANA   (U.K.)
Gaberones o
Pretoria o

Mbabane o
Maseru o   SWAZILAND (U.K.)
LESOTHO

MOZAMBIQUE
(Port.)

Lourenço Marques o

MALAGASY REPUBLIC

REPUBLIC OF
SOUTH AFRICA

AFRICAN POLITICS AND SOCIETY

INTRODUCTION: THE THREE STAGES OF AFRICAN POST-COLONIAL DEVELOPMENT

*T*his book focuses upon the dynamics of societies in transition in "sub-Saharan" Africa, from colonial dependency to independence and from traditional tribal units to modern nation states. Rather than an area or country-by-country study, the approach is problem oriented, concentrating on the difficulties of creating viable, stable, and progressive governments. Given the historical, cultural, economic, and social conditions of these countries, a central question examined is the compatibility of democracy and economic development.

To the extent that democracy can exist in the new developing nations, its form and substance may differ radically from that in the West. I wish to guard against the type of ethnocentrism that insists on the absolute universal necessity of particular political and economic forms and institutions (e.g., a parliamentary, two-party system, *laissez-faire* capitalism, etc.). However, my concern for certain values—as well as for a more "scientific" understanding of basic processes—has dictated the fundamental problem areas chosen in this volume. My basic assumption is that within the historical and economic limits of any given society those social and political arrangements are most legitimate which encourage the political participation of the vast majority of the population and maximize the distribution of any fruits of economic development.

In terms of the evolution of African states, on the surface the prospects for stability, let alone development, would not at this moment appear sanguine. The decimation of Biafra, the various military *coups d'état*, the disintegration of the Congo, civil war in the Soudan appear to give credence to those who see Africa as a land of primitivism and barbarism. The rise of one-party states, as well as the failure of a substantial instantaneous rise in the standard of living, have also cruelly disappointed the high hopes and invariably inflated expectations that soared with the advent of self-government. Yet, historically, European societies advanced no more smoothly. The transition of feudal kingdoms of the Middle Ages to technologically sophisticated nation-states involved not only the Industrial Revolution of the nineteenth century, but the religious and civil wars of the seventeenth century.

Clearly, one may already discern an evolutionary process in the political history of Africa's new states. If utopia does not necessarily lie at the end of this evolution, by having some image of these stages of transition in mind we can at least distinguish among developments in Africa and obtain a clearer idea of their significance.

African history before the advent of the European redounded with great kingdoms and glittered with brilliant works of art. Colonial rulers denied this past and imposed the myth of barbarism in justification of their rule. Colonial policies varied, as did African traditional systems, and constituted major factors that vitally affected the development of nationalism.

Today, since the end of the Second World War, almost all African states have passed or are passing through three stages of political development: (1) the achievement of formal independence; (2) the consolidation of power—i.e., the determination of the basic framework and institutions of the new state structures, including the forging of the boundaries of the political arena; and (3) the restructuring of society and the creation of a new bureaucratic apparatus for the purposes of organizing a mental and technical framework for development.

The First Stage: The Struggle for Independence

To understand the evolution of African states, we must first make the fundamental distinction between those countries that are politically independent and those, like the Portuguese colonies, that are not. Political independence is the prerequisite, if not sufficient, condition for the establishment of policies of self-determination.

During the period of the achievement of independence, the social forces striving to control the newly independent states remained undetermined. In many instances, basic agreement on the framework and nature of the state that had to be constructed did not exist.

Once the colonial establishment transferred formal political authority to the territorial state, the new nation had to settle decisively the question of who was to govern and had to determine the structure and essential purposes of the government. This was a time of the consolidation of power.

These two periods of the struggle for independence and the consolidation of power are obviously interrelated: the way in which independence came about crucially affected the determination of the participants of the political arena, as well as their relative positions of power.

Political independence resulted either from the response to some sort of movement involving the mobilization of mass support and entailing or threatening the use of force, or from a simple "hand-over" of government by the imperial power to an African elite because independence had become the political style of the day on the continent, and not because anyone—either the African or the imperial elite—really believed that anything substantial in the colonial relationship would be changed, or that political independence was really important.

This group of African states, which achieved independence in the latter manner, involved virtually all of the French-speaking countries, with the notable exceptions of Guinea, Mali, and now, in certain respects, Congo-Brazzaville. In general, these new governments tended to perpetuate the alliance of forces created under the colonial power as the basis of their own political power and the foundation of their newly independent states. Politics continued essentially an elite affair, dependent on intercession with the populus by traditional chiefs, religious marabouts who are heads of powerful spiritual brotherhoods, conservative intellectuals, doctors, lawyers, and other professional people who were the first to clash, and then to cooperate, with the Europeans.

These elites made little effort to appeal directly to the peasant or urban majorities, to arouse them to participate directly in a course of action or mass community effort. In these countries not only have the peasant and urban majorities not developed a sense of self-consciousness and class grievance, they have yet to participate fully in any meaningful, significant way in the political process, except under the direct aegis of a traditional or conservative elite. Politics in these countries involves a coalition of forces that are often antagonistic—from neofeudal religious chiefs to technocratic social engineers. Faction is pitted against faction in arrangements often so complex that, even to the extent that innovation is desired, it becomes difficult to implement any rapid change without seriously threatening the entire system of mutual allegiances. These complicated allegiances are often buttressed by complex ideologies (e.g., Negritude or African socialism) that add to the difficulty of stimulating popular enthusiasm, and that are not meant to arouse popular mass mobilization.

Without any direct confrontation of opposing social forces, these states attempt to move directly on to the third stage of technical encadrement. Those leaders of this type of state who are sincere in their determination to achieve economic growth rely upon the passage of time to erode the feudal and mystical basis of the traditional leaders' power, and upon the scientific wonders of fertilizer and agronomy to achieve an increased output. They never find it necessary to appeal to the people themselves as instrumental for change.

The Second Stage: The Consolidation of Power
The Weltanschauung Opposition

During the second period of state consolidation, one can distinguish two distinct subphases involving different types of objectives and opposition. First, there is what might be called an *external opposition*, one that is outside the pale of consensus of the governing or major party. Involved here is usually a *Weltanschauung* type of politics, that is, the conflict of world views and opposing class interests, each determined to found different structures of government upon different bases of legitimacy and authority. Opposition is directed at total systems, rather than the authority of a specific government, and, cloaked in an ideology of superhuman causes, it tends to engender an exceptional bitterness. The fact that the boundaries of the political arena are not defined also exacerbates the conflict; the areas of agreement and disagreement are not outlined, nor are the channels and methods for a peaceful resolution of differences known or highly valued.

The overall goal of this period is to achieve national unity and a basic consensus. Some of the specific issues and objectives debated and contested are the promotion of a strong central state versus a weak confederacy; "traditionalism" versus "modernism"; indirect elections versus the principle of one man, one vote; a regional locus of authority versus national loyalty; future versus historical orientation; and so on.

In Ghana, for example, before the coup in 1966, wealthy financiers, anglophile intellectuals, the African bourgeoisie, and tribal and religious leaders formed the basis of a *Weltanschauung* opposition to Nkrumah's modernizing CPP (Convention Peoples Party), an opposition that over a period of years (certainly before 1961) was decisively defeated. Sékou Touré, during the same stage, talked about the struggle against colonial-allied feudal elements.

A *Weltanschauung* opposition need not, however, be only of the "right." In Senegal and in the Cameroons, Marxist-Leninist parties seeking the support of the peasantry and urban workers were stridently put down and outlawed. In Senegal, the bringing to heel of labor unions and the squashing, in 1963, of Mamadou Dia, the President of the governing Council, who sought a more rapid pace of economic development based on certain sections of the administration, were also part of this process.

Interesting variations of this type of development have occurred in Zanzibar where, in 1964, conflict over control of the state involved a revolution of landless African peasants against a predominantly Arab land-owning minority who also controlled the institutions of the government. Here, race was an additional complicating factor. In Rwanda and in Burundi during the same year there were again social revolutions, but this time they were complicated by the factor of caste. In Rwanda, the Tutsi, comprising less than 15 per cent of the population, constituted a ruling class based upon a highly centralized feudal administration, a royal and warrior caste, and a monopoly of all cattle and land. A similar condition existed in Burundi, and it was to abrogate patron-client feudal relations and establish modern states that the revolutions were directed.

Violence during 1965 in Uganda, in which the army destroyed the palace of the Kabaka, the king of the Buganda, must be viewed in the perspective of efforts that go back at least to 1953 to incorporate four of the toughest, most enduring traditional kingdoms into a national secular state. Royalists and associated traditionalists in all four of the kingdoms, in company with prosperous Buganda capitalists, landowners, farmers, and businessmen, were wary of their future in a unified, consolidated socialist state.

The Internal Opposition

The second phase of state consolidation generally takes place when the governing party or interests have established the predominance of their control, and the opposition directs arguments to specific pieces of legislation, rather than against the entire structure of government. Essentially what is involved in this stage are matters of pace and degree. The legitimacy of the system has come to be accepted. During this period the voluntary associations and trade unions are more tightly unified into the governing party or coalition. The government makes advances in creating mechanisms of coercion involving strengthened army and police forces, as well as other administrative agencies. It also develops propaganda media.

Although the goal of national unity has not been completely achieved, more opportunities for economic development are available, which is an objective that becomes increasingly emphasized as pressures grow to satisfy vastly aroused expectations from all sectors of the population.

Three types of opposition are distinguishable in this period:

1. The organized *Weltanschauung* opposition, to the extent that it is not silent or destroyed, cooperates or is co-opted within the newly defined areas of agreement.

2. Other organized opposition parties (sometimes built around outstanding personalities, a particular issue of certain historical moment, or differences or variations of *method* of approach) that did not constitute a fundamental ideological or political threat to the governing party—and were sometimes dubbed "constructive"—often voluntarily combine or merge with the prevailing power.

3. Finally, and most significantly, a new opposition emerges, distinguishable from the others by its spontaneous character and the fact that, in general, it emerges *from within* the governing party or coalition.

This internal opposition can emerge within "radical" or "conservative" regimes, and this phenomenon is evidence of the nonmonolithic character of all African political parties. These spontaneous outbursts demonstrate that even the regimes that are supposedly the most disciplined, rigid, hierarchical, and authoritarian are in reality parties of coalition or reconciliation. The internal opposition does not question the authority of the government, nor even so much desire a change of personnel—although this is a possibility. Instead it disagrees over specific pieces of legislation and particular policies.

The rebellion by the dockworkers and railway and municipal employees in the 1961 strike in Ghana, which was triggered off by specific aspects of the government's austerity program, is one outstanding example of internal opposition. Within more conservative regimes temporary defections have been threatened at different times by various political, religious, or traditional leaders and interests.

In the case of Ghana, strikers and the government arrived at a compromise. By the time such dissatisfactions are manifest, however, there is a possibility that the coercive mechanisms that have continually been reinforced might effectively be turned against the mass internal base of the governing party in a program of systematic, widespread repression. In any event, the tremendous growth of large bureaucracies is a major indication that a new stage of development has been reached.

The Third Stage: Technology, Democracy, and the Problem of Encadrement

Most of the bureaucratic-led *coups d'état* of 1965 and 1966 in Africa were only possible in the post-independence period. This is because (1) the problems involved arose primarily from tensions stemming from national construction and economic development; and (2) the societies involved had become simplified, in the sense that new arenas of political conflict were forged as parochial loyalties diminished in comparison to the dominating rise of governmental bureaucracies.

During the immediate pre- and post-independence era, at an earlier stage in their evolution, the main problems were to create a development bureaucracy and to Africanize it. Now the problem had become—as it still is—to make African bureaucracy work effectively—i.e., rationally and predictably. The fundamental goal of government administration is to develop precise objectives and to work directly towards them, without corruption and insecurity. This goal and the problem of bureaucracy are fundamental aspects of societies wishing to develop. Without a properly functioning bureaucracy, the *encadrement* of the population and economic development would be impossible.

Within the remotest African country there are forces pressing for immediate important increases in the standard of living of the entire population through rapid economic development. The cry arises increasingly from the most diverse factions that something must be done about relieving those pressures for growth, if not for development.

In at least partial response to this rebellion against perpetual, perpetuated, objective misery, almost all underdeveloped countries are either engaged in, or on the verge of doing, two things: (1) creating new administrative structures whose fundamental task is to do something about the problem of development, as well as that of unity, which is its general prerequisite; and (2) converting the population into a type of "framework" for development. *Encadrement* is the word used by the French, who have been foremost in a type of planning that involves not only an organization of productive and/or distributive activities, but also changes in the attitudes of the peasant-producer, as well as the provision of various types of scientific knowledge and technical assistance. The avowed objective of this process is to reconstitute the population into a framework that will make the resources of the society more easily amenable to efficient development.

Virtually all African countries have a plan for development and accept in principle some degree of government direction. However, vital issues and differences exist over the content and the method of the planning, as well as the degree of government control, and the final purpose of the activity. Because some Western commentators have asserted that planning and the entire process of *encadrement* are simply a matter of technology and are politically neutral, it is important to emphasize the choices government leaders can and must make. Among the crucial questions to be answered are the following:

1. Given the fact that foreign private enterprise is to be invited to invest, under what conditions should this be done, and what guarantees and rights should be granted?

2. Should a domestic *bourgeoisie* be allowed to emerge? If so, under what conditions? What role should it play in the economy? in policy-making? What aid should the government give it?

3. What role should the state corporations play? Should the government establish wholly publicly owned and managed industries, or should it buy minority or majority stock in mixed or privately owned companies?

4. Should the government nationalize trade or commerce, or assume monopolies over certain vital commodities, such as rice or millet? In

one-crop economies, is there any reason why the government should not eliminate all middlemen by itself buying and selling the entire crop?

5. Are marketing boards necessary? By what criteria should the price paid to the producer be determined? If there are surpluses, how, where, and for what purposes should they be used?

6. If the government does nationalize an industry, a sector, or a function of the economy, when, why, and how should this be done? Contrary to first impressions, the achievement of "Socialism" need not be the only purpose or result. Taking over onerous, complicated, and unprofitable tasks by the government from business may be actually of great benefit to private enterprise. What therefore is the overall framework and purpose of the government and the direction of the society? Whose interest is to be served?

7. Who is to make the basic decisions of policy, and by what criteria? Who is to propose the hundreds of specific projects that go into the drawing of the plan? Is the plan to be made by technicians, professional planners, politicians, businessmen, peasants? Are the masses even to be consulted, and if so, how? Are there to be local meetings drawing up specific recommendations for criticism? for ratification?

8. How is the plan to be financed—directly? by taxes? Who is to pay? Who is to decide fiscal policy? Who will debate the social consequences of policies of inflation and budget balancing? What about the ramifications of various types of loans and grants?

9. How many civil servants does a country really need? How much should they be paid? Should there be minimum-wage laws? social security legislation? Should aid be given to religious leaders? to traditional chiefs?

10. In terms of percentages, how much of the national income should be spent on primary education, university education, fertilizers, co-operatives, salaries, aid to African business, corporations; and how much for animation of the countryside, sound trucks, the army, a police force, roads, administration buildings, and so on?

11. Are cooperatives to be only agencies for the more efficient marketing of goods? Are they instruments whereby each cooperator can individually realize a great personal profit? or are they to be organizations for the development of a cooperative spirit and communal values that would become the basis for a new socialist society?

The answers given to these questions—which are specific concrete questions involving the hard facts of economic realities—will determine the social organization and content of the new states. Technical criteria alone do not provide a solution to these problems. Political considerations must be involved. In part, this is why the bureaucratically staged *coups* ultimately seem to fall back on, or try to seek out, some form of social base. Tribal identities and the fact that conflicts often assume tribal form, although of the greatest importance, should not obscure these underlying social realities (see Colin Legum on Nigeria, Part IV in the present volume).

Technology and Politics

One common trait of all the leaders of African military *coups d'état* (in Ghana, Nigeria, Togo, Dahomey, etc.) was an intense dislike of politicians.

Unfortunately, one does not have to go far to find corruption, incompetence, and finagling. Yet, the reasons for hatred of politicians went beyond these failings, which are common in any country. Some commentators have likened politicians to adolescents, who are childish in the promulgation of fantasies such as, "Seek ye first the political kingdoms and all other things will be added unto you." (See W. Arthur Lewis, *Politics in West Africa*, Oxford University Press, New York, 1965.) Other critics have alleged that in "mature" societies, administration replaces politics and a trained civil service replaces politicians— as if technicians bore no human failings or that the "philosopher king" had not died. Yet in a situation where the poverty of resources cripples all who would build the future, where bread is scarce and crusts divided, who can be objective about the allocation of goods? Where is the science that is free of personal choices, not guided by *hubris* or worse?

To state that Africa has had its share of bad politicians and bad men would be banal if critics did not simplify so many of the continent's problems down to a consideration of parochial, power-hungry personalities, and go so far as to declare that tendencies towards authoritarianism and one-party systems can be explained by the supposed fact that a personal love for power has been the prime motive of politicians.

Ever since Moses smote the rock with his staff in his haste to satisfy his impatient constituency's demands and was denied access to the Promised Land, who can be totally without sympathy for politicians?

Politicians, whatever the unsavory characteristics of the worst of the profession, act as compromisers and brokers. At their best, they relate the government to the people and vice versa. Relying upon the art of persuasion as a tool of the trade, politicians can avert violence and the unnecessary use of force. Even if they are not wholly *responsible*, politicians do tend to be *responsive* to the wishes of their constituents more than to other interests because of the nature of their occupations and their own concern. The social bases of the politician's support is often more crucial than his own volition.

However, to a large extent many of Africa's new technicians are, as a class, elitist and manipulative in their orientations, if not in their professions, and show no desire or need to mingle or maintain anything but the most superficial relations with the people. In addition, they are not particularly concerned with the articulation of various social interests or the awakening of dormant social classes. And, to the extent that these generalizations are true, there is a tremendous new danger to the democratic evolution of African societies.

Restructuring the countryside, according to these technicians, can be accomplished simply by providing scientific information through organizations that are wholly instrumental and not social or political. The purpose of cooperatives, for example, is not that of grouping a community of men, women, and children as productive participants in a nonexploitative, humanistic society. Cooperatives, in the technical perspective, are simply tools to lower costs, facilitate distribution, or ease some of the tasks of production, and perhaps enable the individual producers who are members to realize a greater personal profit. The peasantry is not to be mobilized, aroused, or shocked into a realization of its collective interests or needs. This might mean a conflict with the government, or even with the civil servants and technicians themselves— why not, for example, cut administrative salaries and put the money into hospitals, wells, or fertilizers? The peasantry is, rather, to be educated, instructed, and manipulated in the latest agronomic techniques.

In Francophone Africa, techniques and politicians talk about the necessity of the peasantry having a *prise de conscience. Prise de conscience* does *not* mean the development of self-consciousness in the Marxist sense (i.e., of a class in itself becoming a class for itself). Instead, it means simply a recognition on the part of the peasant that the world is subject to the laws of Newtonian science and hence controllable.

Insofar as the technicians provide this education and information, they are the masterminds of the whole operation of *encadrement,* as well as the legitimate source of authority. In this perspective, the cooperatives and all the activities of rural reconstruction become simply the planners' instruments to utilize and manipulate. Insofar as this manipulation takes a collective form in an effort so vast as the *encadrement* of the whole rural population, it does so simply because it is technologically possible and desirable. In part, this analysis helps explain the tendency in Africa towards military-led regimes, for the military are technicians *par excellence.*

The Army as the Logical Culmination of Technology

If technology entails the ability to perform a given task with expert, scientific knowledge, combined with the optimum organization and mobilization of men and resources, then the army is one of the best technical instruments, as well as one of the most highly developed bureaucracies. Greater discipline, better training, no corruption, unlimited hours—these are some of the characteristics that might appear to distinguish the military from the civilian bureaucracy with which it shares basically the same rational, instrumental outlook and education.

African leaders are under growing pressures from demands by all levels of society—demands that cannot be met, especially while productivity has not increased. At the same time, the army, having grown tremendously in men and material because of increased attention and appropriations, has shown its strength. Thus, it is not surprising that leaders place greater and greater reliance on the army. This growing dependency can be regarded in many instances as the logical, if not final, culmination of the tendency towards technology.

Dangers of Technology

The question may well arise: What, after all, is wrong with the government and program of the technicians as long as it is scientific and results in economic growth? First, there is the possibility that economic growth will not even occur. Peasants might not be inclined to listen to or follow the advice of functionaries who, by their style of life, speech, and dress, are obviously foreigners. The civil servants themselves, motivated almost solely by their salaries, might not be counted on to do their appointed jobs. Without a force, or *raison majeure*, to motivate all the bureaucratic instruments, there is no guarantee that all of the administrative machinery will not itself break down into chaos and degenerate into corruption.

Secondly, economic growth is not the same as economic development. All the African states are concerned, explicitly or implicitly, not simply with an increase in the gross national product but, at least ultimately—and this is another way to distinguish between them—with the *distribution* of the national incomes. Nothing will guarantee that an increase in productivity under either a technocratic or nontechnocratic regime will, in and of itself, result in a higher standard of living for the disadvantaged peasant producer. Improvements in scientific techniques may result in widening, not diminishing, the gulf between rich and poor.

Mass mobilization of the population, on the other hand, may be advantageous in a number of ways:

1. The more rapid occurrence of a *prise de conscience*. This would enable a quicker, more intensive, and more widespread participation of the population in the Newtonian manipulation of their environment.

2. More democratic participation in the benefits of development.

Instead of a "trickle-down" mechanism for the distribution of benefits, more levels of the population could more directly have greater opportunities for positions of wealth and prestige. The failure of widespread popular recruitment in the governing of the state is especially evident in the present predominantly upper-class, high-caste, urban origin of the civil servants.

3. Shifting the basis of political support from the administration to the peasantry, if possible, would enable the cut-back of salaries and privileges of functionaries, as well as a complete revision of the import and tax structures. For the first time, a true regime of austerity could potentially be undertaken with the availability of additional funds for investment in the rural sector.

4. If the goal is to attain a socialist regime, the dangers of an opposing coalition of the administrative bourgeoisie, political bourgeoisie, religious and traditional leaders, and businessmen could be avoided.

As long as widespread political participation does not exist, it is not unlikely that some combination of religious and traditional leaders, merchants, and technicians inimical to socialist development—possibly to any form of economic development—will emerge out of many of the recent African changes of government.

Hopefully, this volume will aid in clarifying these and some of the other major issues and problems of today's Africa. The following criteria played an important part in the selection of the writings in this volume: readability, continentwide coverage, problem orientation, and a focus on underlying social and economic realities. As a result of this analytic orientation, most of the material included should not soon become dated, in the sense that hopefully it will provide a frame of reference from which to make new data easily understandable. Primarily because of limitations of space, this volume does not cover all the problem areas. Nevertheless, I have not hesitated to use articles reproduced elsewhere if they make an important point better than any others, and if the problem covered is essential to the understanding of the evolution of the stages of African politics as discussed above.

Several authors have taken this opportunity to share with us their most recent thoughts, reassessments, and new information. Most of the material presented here has not been widely available previously. This includes six original translations from the French. Too many people still believe that French literature on Africa is confined to anthropology and linguistics. Hopefully, this volume will serve the auxiliary purpose of providing a glimpse of important contemporary work in the social sciences not available to most Americans.

Part I   *AFRICA'S DUAL HERITAGE:*
IMPERIALISM AND PRECOLONIAL
GREATNESS

Newly independent African states do not come "historically naked into the civilized and self-governing world." Rather, they are heir to two pasts: a history stemming from contact with Western civilization mediated by colonial rule and administration, and a heritage derived from indigenous civilizations thousands of years old. After decades of European tutelage, the school children of this black continent no longer recite the adventures of their "ancestors" who fought on the plains of Runnymede or in the streets of Paris. Rather, they recall the glories of the ancient kingdoms of Dahomey, Benin, Songhai, and Mali.

For an understanding of contemporary African problems, this dual past is important in two respects: first, because of the social forces and processes it inhibits or initiates; and secondly, because of the psychological reactions and attitudes it generates.

Travelers' accounts and oral tradition, coupled with the newest tools of archeology, have established the *fact* of African civilizations. With every discovery and investigation, the myth of savagery is pushed back and the outlines of African history become clearer. Popular images of Africa as the Dark Continent cloaked in a mantle of mystery, a land of exotica and savagery inhabited by primitive peoples hidden behind inaccessible forests, served the colonial myth. This myth alleged that Africans had no history, meaning that they did not change, or progress, or have science, art, or inventions among themselves. The same attitude that led mapmakers of the early nineteenth century to mark the interior of the continent as "uninhabited," meaning that only Africans lived there, decreed that nothing of significance existed before the advent of the European. This alleged lack of a past functioned to justify the colonial intrusion—to Africans as well as to Europeans. The African was ignorant or simple, vicious or barbaric. He needed education, civilization, culture, religion, knowledge, discipline, law, and punishment for his future beneficial development. The colonial establishment could therefore justify itself in its own eyes as well as to the European masses, and lay claim to the "burden" of civilization.

Frantz Fanon speaks of how Africans also long accepted the myth of their own inferiority and were diminished as men. A people must begin to question the legitimacy of an oppressive system before they will revolt. Individuals who identify with the culture and history of an alien power, who feels they possess no past of their own and nowhere else to turn, will tend to be co-opted into the governing system, absorbed and assimilated. Hence, it is important to establish the *fact* of African history, as well as its significance. Cheikh Anta Diop, in a series of studies, most dramatically and controversially enlarged the scope of Africa's contribution to world civilization. Diop stressed the great contributions of Egypt to the origins of culture and science, asserting that Egyptian civilization was of black origin. Diop also challenged the prevailing view that the flow of cultural influence was from the North, the European or Hammitic areas down to the more primitive areas. The *origins* of civilization lay in black Africa, he argued. Although his theses have created a storm of controversy, and scholars have challenged his facts as well as intrepretations, Diop has opened up new paths of exploration, given a new generation redemptive faith in its roots, and presented, if nothing else, a poetic image of greatness that, in its daring, will come closer to truth than his critics, as discovery is piled upon discovery in the unfolding of a new renaissance. In 1966 at Dakar, the World Festival of Negro Arts honored Diop as "the black intellectual who has exercised the most fruitful influence in the twentieth century."

Africa's other past—the colonial era—was marked by both differences and similarities in the objectives and methods of the imperialists in Africa. Before World War II, British policy accepted self-government as its ultimate objective, but had as a basic premise the necessity of a long period of external control under its trusteeship. The colonial establishment considered independence only as a remote possibility for the far future, brought about not by revolution, but by gradually increasing the degree of participation by inhabitants in the political decision-making process. Two somewhat conflicting institutions evolved: (1) the Legislative Council, directed towards the English-educated intelligentsia as parliaments in embryo; and (2) the "Native Authority System" (indirect rule), designed to support traditional authorities "purged of their excesses." The British placed great emphasis on slow change; the ideal systems were those that least disturbed the rural life of the African. In theory, the system of indirect rule sought to maintain the uniqueness of customary society, although in fact it constituted a cheap and effective instrument of rule by having local chiefs govern behind a façade of semiautonomy.

If the British granted a great deal of autonomy to local governors and foresaw each of its colonies evolving along separate lines, the French, during the same period, never considered self-government. In Cartesian fashion, the ministries centralized in Paris promulgated the same rules for all the colonies, in theory countenancing no interference and taking into account no local conditions. The objective was complete political and administrative integration of "overseas France" with metropolitan France and a permanent association was taken for granted. French policy wavered between the principles of "identity" and "assimilation," depending on the nature of the regime in power. Originating from the Age of Enlightenment and the Revolution of 1789, the principle of "Identity" held that, insofar as all men were basically equal in their capacity for Reason, all Africans were to be completely assimilated and made equal citizens of France. The principle of "Association" called for the deliberate creation of an African elite, which would accept the standards of the West and become "associated" with French rulers in the work of colonial development.

Belgium colonial administration was pragmatic and empirical, without a national philosophy of either self-government or eventual political integration. Wholly paternalistic, a policy based on direct rule from Belgium by Belgians left room for neither African local government nor African representation in Belgian institutions. Their objective—which was an efficient, profitable administration free of the financial scandals and the atrocities of the old Leopold regime—accepted completely rapid economic development and its consequences, e.g., the breakdown of the old authority system. The Belgians rejected the *industrial* color bar and trained Africans to do the work of more expensive Europeans because of their single-minded pursuit of profit.

The Portuguese, while promising Africans who possessed the "necessary educational and cultural attainment" equal legal status, in fact practiced the crudest form of direct exploitation, with neither political nor economic development of the country.

Kenneth Robinson has pointed out that, behind the diversity, certain common assumptions and practices characterized pre-World War II colonial policy:

1. The policies of Identity or self-government were myths—promises to be fulfilled so far in the future as to have little meaning.

2. Every regime in practice followed pragmatic policies of differentiation. When the French, for example, came across a strong traditional leader, they tried to incorporate him in their own organization.

3. A subordinate role was clearly established for Africans in relation to Europeans.

4. All regimes emphasized negative duties—the prevention of extortion, the maintenance of law and order—rather than the promotion of large-scale social trends.

After the Second World War, British policy had to change least, because the development of self-government within the Commonwealth was always its declared policy and each territory was treated as a distinct unit with its own laws, budget, public service, and legislative council. In two basic changes, however, the imperial government declared *African* majority rule in the multiracial territories and, secondly, accepted an immense change in the *speed* of the evolution towards independence.

The French enormously expanded suffrage in a brief span, extended representation in the French National Assembly and upper house to all territories, inaugurated local assemblies that were popularly elected, and increased their concern with more rapid economic development. A turning point was the *loi cadre*, or "Framework" Law of 1956 which accepted the objective of autonomy rather than the previous principle of integration. In 1958, only Guinea "opted" for independence in referendums held in all the territories; but in 1960, with France's blessing, all of her overseas territories became independent.

Until the last moment, the Belgians produced no major change, although the beginnings of a new system of local government was instituted, secondary education was expanded, and a new university established.

In the articles of this section, Michael Crowder discusses some of the differences as well as similarities between the British and French systems. Aimé Césaire argues in effect that no matter how different various colonial regimes were, they were alike in their inhumanity and exploitation. Eduardo C. Mondlane, former revolutionary leader of African opposition to colonialism assassinated in Tanzania in 1969, in a statement written not long before his death, points out that colonialism is not a dead issue and focuses on what is happening in Mozambique today.

Cheikh Anta
Diop

THE BIRTH OF THE "NEGRO MYTH"

Egypt had already lost her independence a century previous to the time of Herodotus' visit. From the time Egypt was conquered by the Persians in 525 B.C. she was dominated by foreigners: the Persians were followed by the Macedonians under Alexander, the Romans under Julius Caesar (50 B.C.,), the Arabs in the seventh century, the Turks in the sixteenth century, the French under Napoleon, and then, at the end of the nineteenth century, the English.

Egypt—cradle of civilization for ten thousand years, while the rest of the world wallowed in barbarism—was prostrated by these successive occupations, and never again achieved any political importance. But for hundreds of years after her political decline she continued to initiate young Mediterranean peoples (the Greeks and Romans, among others) into the enlightenments of civilization. Throughout antiquity, Egypt remained the classic land for Mediterranean peoples, the fount of scientific, religious, moral, and social knowledge, the most ancient cultural source that mankind had produced.

Building on the Egyptian model new civilizations successively sprang up around the perimeter of the Mediterranean. These civilizations benefited from the many advantages of their geographical location at the crossroads of the world and developed above all in a material and technological direction as part of an evolution that had its origins in the materialistic genius of the Indo-Europeans, the Greeks, and the Romans.

The pagan spirit that animated Greco-Roman civilization was waning as the fourth century approached. Two new factors, Christianity and the barbarian invasions, intruded upon the already ancient terrain of Western Europe to give birth to a new civilization, one which today, in its turn, shows signs of exhaustion. This newest civilization, which, thanks to uninterrupted contact among its various peoples fell heir to all human progress up to that time, was already sufficiently advanced technologi-

Reprinted from *Nations, Nègres et Cultures,* 2nd ed., *Présence Africaine,* Paris, 1955, pp. 39–48. By permissitn of the author and *Présence Africaine.* Translated from the French by Ellen Conroy Kennedy.

19

cally by the fifteenth century to throw itself into the discovery and conquest of the rest of the world.

From the fifteenth century on, Europeans, led by the Portuguese, made landings along the Atlantic coast of Africa. They established Africa's first contacts with the West of modern times, contacts that have continued uninterrupted since.

What did the Europeans find at this other extremity of Africa? What populations did they meet? Had these people been there since antiquity or had they only recently migrated? What was their cultural level, the degree of their social and political organization, their state of civilization? What impression of people did the Europeans come away with? What did they learn of their intellectual capacity and technical aptitude? What was the nature of the social relationships that would exist from that point on between Europe and Africa? In what sense have these relations constantly evolved?

The answers to these various questions will provide a full explanation of the contemporary myth of the primitive Negro. In order to answer them, one must look to Egypt at the time she came under foreign domination.

The distribution of Negroes on the African continent must have evolved in two principal stages. It is generally agreed that the drying up of the Sahara Desert must have been completed by about 7000 B.C. Equatorial Africa was probably still a region of forests, too dense to be favorable to human life. The last Negroes who lived in the Sahara would have emigrated toward the Upper Nile, except perhaps for a few isolated groups who remained scattered over the rest of the continent, either because they had emigrated southward or had moved north.[1]

The early migrants may perhaps have found an indigenous Negro population in the Upper Nile. Be that as it may, out of this process of adaption to new conditions of life the most ancient civilization the earth has known was born. This civilization, in our time called Egyptian, developed within its primitive cradle for many centuries, then descended slowly along the Nile Valley and radiated outward around the Mediterranean basin. This cycle of civilization, the most protracted in history, must have lasted ten thousand years. This time span represents a compromise between the long chronology of Herodotus and Manetho who, according to the data of Egyptian priests, set its beginnings at 17,000 B.C., and the short chronology of modern scholars, who acknowledge that by 4245 B.C. the Egyptians had invented the calendar, which required calculations presupposing some thousands of years of previous development.

During this long period, Negroes once more spread progressively

1. Discoveries in the Sahara indicate that it was inhabited by Negroes . . . (Th. Monod, *Méharées, exploration au vrai Sahara*, ed. *Je sers*, Paris, 1937, p. 108.)

toward the interior of the continent and constituted nuclei that would later become the centers of new continental civilizations. . . . These African civilizations were destined to be more and more cut off from the rest of the world. Because of the enormous distance that separated them from the access to the Mediterranean, they would tend to exist in isolation. With Egypt's loss of independence, their isolation became complete.

Cut off, then, from the mother country, which had been invaded by foreigners, closed in by the sort of environment that required only the slightest adaptation, yet favored by advantageous economic conditions, the Negroes directed their energies toward developing social and political structures and systems of morality and ethics rather than toward scientific and speculative pursuits that their milieu not only did not encourage, but made impossible.

Adapting to the narrow fertile valley of the Nile, on the other hand, required setting up a sophisticated system of irrigation and dikes. It called for precise calculation in order to predict the floodings of the Nile and to deduce their consequences. In Egypt to invent geometry became a material, practical necessity. Property lines that the floodings of the Nile periodically obliterated had to be demarcated and disputes among cohabitants settled. The long flat bands of terrain dictated the transformation of the paleonigritic hoe into the plough, pulled at first by men, then by animals. Just as this was indispensable to the material survival of the Negro in the valley of the Nile, so also was it superfluous to the new conditions of life in the interior of the continent.

After history had altered his former equilibrium with his environment, the Negro found a new one which differed from the first in that technological skill became irrelevant. The opposite was true of social and political organization and codes of conduct, however. Economic resources were assured by means that did not require continual invention, so the Negro became progressively less interested in material progress.

It was in this new state of civilization that the first modern encounter with Europe occurred. In the fifteenth century, when the first Portuguese, Dutch, English, French, Danish, and Brandenburgian merchantmen began establishing trading posts on the west coast of Africa, the political organization of African states was equal—and often superior—to those of the Europeans. The monarchies were already constitutional, with a people's council in which the different social levels were represented. In these councils the Negro king, contrary to legend, was not and never had been a despot with unlimited powers. Here and there he was chosen by the people, through the intermediary of a prime minister representing free men. His mission was to serve his people wisely, and his authority was a function of his respect for a constitution established in this manner. . . .

The social and moral order were on the same advanced level. For the reasons already indicated, technology was less emphasized than in Europe. The Negro, although he was the first to discover iron, had cast no cannons. The secret of gunpowder was known to Egyptian priests but they utilized it only in religious rites involving the mysteries of Osiris (cf. *Recherches sur les Egyptiens et les Chinois,* by M. de Paw).

Africa was therefore very vulnerable from the technological point of view. It became a tempting prey, irresistible to a West equipped with firearms and long-distance navies.

The economic rise of Renaissance Europe drove her to the rapid conquest of Africa. Europe's intrusion proceeded by stages from coastal trading posts to annexation by means of western international *ententes* to the conquest of the interior by armed means, which Europeans called "pacification."

The discovery of America by Christopher Columbus was part of this same expansionist surge. Peoples from the old continent poured into the new. The rising value of the virgin lands called for cheap labor, and defenseless Africa seemed just the right human reservoir from which such labor could be drawn at minimum risk and cost. Thus, the modern slave trade became an economic necessity and lasted until the middle of the nineteenth century and the coming of the machine age. . . .

The knowledge that a Negro Egypt had once civilized the earth was obscured, lost in the ruins of antiquity or hidden in libraries. It was to be still further obscured in the course of four centuries of slavery. Suffused with their technological superiority, the Europeans developed an *a priori* scorn for the entire Negro world, from which they deigned only to steal. Ignorance of the ancient history of the Negroes, differences in mores and customs, ethnic prejudices between two races who believed that they were meeting face to face for the first time, combined with the economic need to exploit—all these factors predisposed the European mind to distort completely the moral qualities of the Negro as well as his intellectual abilities.

Negro became from that time on a synonym for the primitive being, the inferior one, endowed with a "prelogical mentality." And because human beings are always careful to justify their behavior, the Europeans went further. Their concern to legitimize colonization and the slave trade would engender a whole descriptive literature on the alleged inferior capacities of the Negro. The thinking of several generations of Europeans was thus progressively distorted. Western opinion crystallized in such a way as to instinctively recognize as revealed truth that the word "Negro" was synonymous with "inferior humanity."

An example of cynicism at its height was the formulation of the concept that colonization was a humanitarian duty, the civilizing mission of the Western man upon whom fell the burden of elevating the African to the level of other men. Capitalism could then practice the most ferocious forms of exploitation under the guise of moral pretexts.

At the very most, the Negro was recognized for certain artistic gifts linked to his sensibility as an inferior creature. Such was the opinion of the Frenchman de Gobineau, the nineteenth-century precursor of the Nazi philosophers, who, in his book *On the Inequality of Human Races*, decreed that the artistic sense is inseparable from Negro blood. He reduced art, however, to an inferior manifestation of human nature; the sense of rhythm, in particular, he linked to the emotional aptitudes of the Negro.

Such a climate of alienation had a profound effect on the Negro personality, particularly on the educated Negro, who had the opportunity to see how the rest of the world regarded him and his people. It often happens that the Negro intellectual thus loses confidence in his own potential and that of his race. Often the effect is so crushing that some Negroes, having evidence to the contrary, still find it hard to accept the fact we really were the first to civilize the world.

Frequently, Negroes of great intellectual capacity remain victims of this alienation, going so far as to try to codify Nazi ideas about a presumed duality of the Negro (sensitive emotive, creator of art) and the white man (above all, a creature of rationality). So is it in all sincerity that an African Negro poet, Léopold Sédar Senghor, composed this admirable line of verse:

> "L'émotion est nègre et la raison hellène"
> [Emotion is Negro and reason hellenic.]

Little by little, a literature of Negro complementarity has been created, depicting him as cheerfully childish, puerile, dutiful, passive, sniveling, resigned. This is still the image that many contemporary Westerners carry of the Negro. It reinforces what they believe is their superiority and allows them to indulge in a kind of paternal sensitivity. Even a perfectly executed work of Negro art fails to shake their conviction. The usual response is that it seems pretentious. It is exasperating and for them intolerable to equate it with "art."

Since slavery there has been an effort, in obvious defiance of all historical truth, to fabricate the myth that the Negro has always been slave to the superior white races with whom he lived. This easily explains the presence of Negroes in Egypt or in Mesopotamia or in Arabia, from the most ancient times. Even though such an affirmation is mere dogma, meant to falsify history and known as a falsification by those who advance it, it contributes nonetheless to the alienation of the Negro consciousness. So it was that Aimé Césaire, another great Negro poet, the greatest perhaps of our time, wrote in a poem from *Soleil cou coupé* as follows:

> Dupuis Akkad, depuis Elam, depuis Sumer
> Maître des trois chemins, tu as en face de toi un homme qui a
>   beaucoup marché
> Maître des trois chemins, tu as en face de toi un homme qui a
>   marché sur les mains, marché sur les pieds, marché sur le
>   ventre, marché sur le cul.
> Depuis Elam, depuis Akkad, depuis Sumer.

> [Since Akkad, Since Elam, Since Sumer].

> [Master of the three roads you see before you a man who has walked much
> Master of the three roads, you see before you a man who has walked on
>   his hands, on his feet, on his belly, on his tail.

> Since Elam, since Akkad, since Sumer.]

In another place (the *Cahier d'un retour au pays natal*) he writes of:

> Ceux qui n'ont inventé ni la poudre, ni la boussole,
> Ceux qui n'ont jamais su dompter ni la vapeur, ni l'électricité
> Ceux qui n'ont exploré ni la mer, ni le ciel. . . .

> [Those who invented neither gunpowder nor compass
> Those who never conquered steam or electricity
> Those who explored neither sea nor the heavens. . . .]

In the course of the transformations in Negro-European relations it became more and more difficult, and even incenceivable, to those who were ignorant of his past grandeur—and to Negroes themselves—that Negroes could have been responsible for the very beginnings of the first civilization to spread across the earth, the civilization to which humanity at large owes the very basis of its progress.

From then on, even as proof piled up, people continued to interpret it falsely. They constructed the most implausible theories. *Any* implausible theory seemed more logical to them than a proven historical fact. Before turning to an examination of these contemporary contradictions, which seek to establish at all costs that Egyptians were of the white race, let us point to the astonishment of Volney, a scholar in good faith, imbued with all the prejudices with regard to the Negro of which we have been speaking, who, upon visiting Egypt between 1783 and 1785, made the following observations about the Copts, the very race from which Egypt's Pharoahs were descended:

". . . all have the puffy face, the extended eyes, the flattened nose, the thick lips, in a word, a true mulatto face. I was tempted to attribute this to the climate, when, having been to visit the Sphinx, the look of him gave me the clue to the enigma. Seeing this head, characteristically Negro in all its features, I recalled the remarkable passage in Herodotus, where he says: 'As for me, I think the Colches are a colony of the Egyptians because, like them, they have black skin and frizzy hair.' That is to say, the ancient Egyptians were true Negroes like all those natural to Africa. Since then, their blood, mixed for several centuries with that of the Romans and the Greeks, must have lost the intensity of its original color, while still keeping the imprint of its mold. One can even give this observation larger scope and pose the principle that physiognomy is a kind of monument, in many cases verifying or illuminating the evidence of history on the origin of peoples. . . ."

After illustrating this proposition by citing the case of the Normans who, nine hundred years after the conquest of Normandy, still looked like Danes, Volney added:

"But, getting back to Egypt, the historical fact that it reestablishes suggests some philosophical reflections. What a subject for meditation: to see the present barbarity and ignorance of the Copts, who issued from the alliance of the profound genius of the Egyptians and the brilliant minds of the Greeks; to think that this race of black men, today our slaves and the object of our scorn, is the same race to whom we owe our art, our science, and even the use of words; to imagine, finally, that it is the people who call themselves the greatest friends of liberty and humanity who have sanctioned the most barbarous of slaveries and who today question whether black men have an intelligence of the kind that white men do!"[2]

2. M. C.-F. Volney, *Voyages en Syrie et en Egypte*, Paris, 1787. Vol. I, pp. 74–77.

Michael
Crowder

INDIRECT RULE—FRENCH AND
BRITISH STYLE

*I*n his witty and thought-provoking Lugard Me-
morial Lecture, "Et maintenant, Lord Lugard?" (*Africa*, Vol. 33, No. 4,
1963), Governeur Deschamps has provided us with an excellent general
appraisal of the relative achievements and failures of French and British
"native" administration in Africa. But he does not do full justice to the
fundamental differences between the two systems. Though he hints at
these differences on several occasions in his lecture, he contends that,
far from what is generally supposed, the two were in practice very
similar, since they both reposed on indigenous chiefs.[1] He insists that
"the only difference is that we, unlike you, Lord Lugard, have not tried
to modernize these former states or create embryonic states where they
did not exist"; or ". . . [our administrative practice] only differed from
yours (at least in Black Africa) by a behavior that was more familiar
and by objectives that were less well defined" [Ed. trans.]. This seems
seriously to underestimate the nature of the differences between the two
systems, which were rather those of kind than of degree.[2] M. Deschamps
rightly insists that there has been a tendency on both sides of the
Channel to oversimplify the basic characteristics of systems of colonial
administration in Africa. Nevertheless there were such fundamental
differences between the French and British systems that, even if both

1. In the summary of the lecture in English it is put more explicitly: "Indirect
rule has been practised by local governors at least since the second empire;
from the end of the nineteenth century
the official policy was that of 'association'
—very close to Lugard's ideas." [Editor's
note: The "policy of Association" assumed that a small African elite would
be educated in French values and then,
while maintaining a separate identity, become "associated" with the colonial establishment in raising the standards of the
masses. Historically, associated was a
less liberal policy than "Assimilation,"
which was rooted in the ideals of Equality and Fraternity of the 1789 Revolution and assumed that the ideal objective
of colonial policy was to give Africans
the *same* rights and standard of living as
Frenchmen.]
2. See L. P. Mair, *Native Policies in
Africa*, London, 1936.

Reprinted from *Africa*, Vol. 34, No. 3 (July 1964), 197–205, by
permission of the International African Institute and the author.

26

did make use of "chiefs," it is not possible to place the French system of native administration in the same category as British Indirect Rule. It is true that both powers had little alternative to the use of existing political authorities as a means of governing their vast African empires, and in most cases these authorities were headed by chiefs. What *is* important is the very different way in which these authorities were used. The nature of the position and power of the chief in the two systems was totally different and, as a corollary, so were the relations between the chief and the political officer, who were inspired in each case by very different ideals.

The British in Northern Nigeria, which became the model for indirect rule, believed that it was their task to conserve what was good in indigenous institutions and assist them to develop on their own lines. The relation between the British political officer and the chief was in general that of an adviser who only in extreme circumstances interfered with the chief and the native authority under him. However, where chiefs governed small political units, and in particular where their traditional executive authority was questionable, the political officer found himself interfering in native authority affairs more frequently than ideally he should. This was true in many parts of East Africa and in parts of Yorubaland, where the borderline between "advisory" and "supervisory" in the activities of the political officer was not always clear. Though indirect rule reposed primarily on a chief as executive, its aim was not to preserve the institution of chieftaincy as such, but to encourage local self-government through indigenous political institutions, whether these were headed by a single executive authority, or by a council of elders.[3] In Northern Nigeria a policy of minimal interference with the chiefs and their traditional forms of government was pursued. But Lugard himself had insisted on a reform of the indigenous taxation system and of the administration of native justice when he was Governor of Northern Nigeria and believed that, while the colonial government should repose on the chiefs, their administration should be progressively modernized. And, though his successors left them largely to themselves, Sir Donald Cameron, Governor of Nigeria from 1931 to 1935, who had introduced indirect rule to Tanganyika and held similar beliefs to those of Lugard, was shocked by

---

3. See Sir Philip Mitchell's article on "Indirect Rule," when Governor of Uganda, in the *Uganda Journal*, iv, no. 1, July 1936, where he says that indirect rule is founded on the assumption that "every group of people must possess some form of . . . natural authority, normally, of course symbolized in the person of some individual or individuals." "The administrative system called 'Indirect Rule' endeavours in each place where it is to be applied to ascertain what are the persons or institutions which the people concerned look upon as the natural authority."

the situation in Northern Nigeria, where he felt the emirates were fast developing into Indian-style native states.

Indeed, in the earliest interwar period many emirs and chiefs ruled as "sole native authorities," a position which gave them for practical purposes more power than they had in precolonial days, where they were either subject to control by a council or liable to deposition if they became too unpopular.[4] They were permitted to administer traditional justice, which, in the case of certain emirs, included trying cases of murder for which the death sentence, subject to confirmation by the Governor, could be passed. They administered political units that corresponded to those they would have administered before the arrival of the colonial power. They were elected to office by traditional methods of selection, and only in the case of the election of a patently unsuitable candidate to office would the colonial power refuse recognition. There was thus a minimal undermining of the traditional sources of authority. The main change for the Fulani Emirs of Northern Nigeria, for instance, was that they now owed allegiance to the British Government rather than to the Sultan of Sokoto, and collected taxes on its behalf, though they retained, in most cases, 70 per cent of the amount collected for the administration of their native authority.

This system of indirect rule was, with modifications, practised whereever possible in Britain's colonies in West Africa and in most of her other African territories. There were notable exceptions, especially in Eastern Nigeria where the absence of identifiable executive authority in most communities made indirect rule as practised in Northern Nigeria almost impossible to apply. In such societies, British assiduity in trying to discover chiefs, or invent them, might lend color to M. Deschamps' argument; but, in practice, the goal of ruling through traditional political units on whom local self-government could be devolved was maintained, and after much trial and error a system of democratically elected councils was formulated as most closely corresponding to the traditional methods of delegating authority.

If, taking into account such variations, we use indirect rule in Northern Nigeria as a model, we shall see just how greatly the French system of administration in Black Africa differed from that of the British.

The British system depended on the advisory relationship between the political officer and the native authority, usually a chief, heading a local government unit that corresponded to a precolonial political unit. The French system placed the chief in an entirely subordinate role

4. See P. C. Lloyd's article "Kings, Chief and Local Government," *West Africa,* Saturday, 31 January 1953, where he remarks that the Yoruba kings became much more powerful under the British. "They could only be deposed by the British administration which often tended to protect them against their own people."

to the political officer. M. Deschamps alludes only briefly to the role of the French political officer towards the end of his article, where he hints at the nature of his status as a *roi paternel* or *roi absolu*. But it is important to stress that the chief in relation to the French political officer was a mere agent of the central colonial government with clearly defined duties and powers. He did not head a local government unit, nor did the area which he administered on behalf of the government necessarily correspond to a precolonial political unit. In the interests of conformity the French divided the country up administratively into *cantons* which frequently cut across precolonial political boundaries. Chiefs did not remain chiefs of their old political units but of the new cantons, though sometimes the two coincided. In certain cases the French deliberately broke up the old political units, as in the case of the Futa Jallon where their policy was "the progressive suppression of the chiefs and the parcelling out of their authority."[5] Most important of all, chiefs were not necessarily those who would have been selected according to customary procedures; more often than not they were those who had shown loyalty to the French or had obtained some education. While the British were scrupulous in their respect for traditional methods of selection of chiefs, the French, conceiving of them as agents of the administration, were more concerned with their potential efficiency than their legitimacy. We need not wonder then that as a young French administrator, after serving in Senegal and Dahomey, M. Robert Delavignette should have been astonished, on his way to duty in Niger, to find that the British political officer in Kano actually called on the Emir when he had business with him and paid him the compliment of learning Hausa so that he could speak to him direct. "For the young French administrator, such a manner of administrating had the charm of a tale from *A Thousand and One Nights*."[6] Contrast the position of the Emir of Kano with that of the Alaketu of Ketu in Dahomey. By tradition he was one of the seven most important rulers in Yorubaland, on an equal footing with the Oni of Ife and the Alafin of Oyo. A friend who visited him while Dahomey was still under French rule found him waiting outside the French Chef de Subdivision's office. He mentioned the fact that the King was waiting to see the French administrator, who replied, "So what if he gets used to being abused?" and kept him waiting a little longer.

It is clear, then, that the French explicitly changed the very nature of the powers of the chief and that "his functions were reduced to that

5. *Overall report on the general situation of French Guinea in 1906*, Conakry, 1906, cited by J. Suret-Canale in "Guinea under the Colonial System," *Présence africaine*, No. 29 (English ed.).
6. R. Delavignette in "Lord Lugard et la politique africaine," *Africa*, Vol. 21, No. 3, 1951.

of a mouthpiece for orders emanating from outside."[7] This is brought out clearly, for example, in the *Arrêté of 28th December 1936 on the organisation and regulation of the local indigenous administration in French Equatorial Africa,* in the section dealing with *Chefs de Canton* (or *de Terre* or *de Tribu*).[8]

> The *Chefs de Canton,* etc., are recruited:
> (1) for preference from among the descendants of old families traditionally or customarily destined to command;
> (2) from among notable natives, literate if possible, who have rendered services to the French cause and who are fitted to fill these functions by their authority or influence in the country;
> (3) from among the *Chefs de Canton* (etc.) who have satisfactorily carried out their functions for at least four years;
> (4) from among old soldiers who have completed more than the normal terms of service and who qualify for special treatment;
> (5) from among local civil servants (clerks, interpreters, etc.) who have worked satisfactorily for at least four years in the public service.
>
> The following are the disciplinary measures applicable to *Chefs de Canton,* etc.:
> (1) Reprimand by the *Chef de Département*
> (2) Temporary withholding of salary
> (3) Temporary interdiction
> (4) Reduction of salary
> (5) Dismissal

Since the chiefs did not, except in rare cases, represent traditional authority and, since they were the agents of the colonial power for carrying out its more unpopular measures, such as collecting taxes and recruiting for labour, they were resented in most parts of French West Africa. While they retained no traditional judicial authority such as that of their counterparts in British West Africa in their Native Courts, they were agents of the law, in this case the unpopular system of summary administrative justice known as the *indigénat.*[9] In many areas in the postwar period they became identified with pro-French administra-

---

7. L. P. Mair, *op. cit.,* p. 210. R. L. Buell in his *The Native Problem in Africa* cites Joost Van Vollenhoven, Governor-General of French West Africa, 1912–17, as describing the chiefs as having "no power of their own of any kind. There are not two authorities in the *cercle,* the French authority and the native authority; there is only one."
8. Translated by T. G. Brierly.
9. Concessions were made to customary law prior to 1946, when native penal law was abolished and all inhabitants of French Tropical Africa became subject to the French code. Before that time only those Africans who were French citizens could claim justice under the Code. The vast majority of *sujets* were subject to the *indigénat* already referred to and to customary law. Customary law, however, was not administered by the chief but by the French administrator, who was assisted by two notables of the area who were versed in tradition. These courts could try both penal and civil cases. Now customary law survives in questions of inheritance, marriage, and land.

tive parties, particularly in Soudan (Mali). Hence it was not surprising that when, in 1957, just before the independence of Guinea, Sékou Touré (then Vice-Président du Conseil) decided to do away with chiefs, the operation was effected with remarkably little protest from either the indigenous population or from the French administration that had made use of them. Of the twenty-two Commandants de Cercle, still mostly French, called to Conakry to discuss the proposed removal of the chiefs (from 25 to 27 July) only four felt that the *chefs de canton* had a useful role to fulfil in the territory, and nearly all confirmed that the chiefs no longer possessed political traditional authority and had become mere agents of the administration. As far as the Commandant de Cercle for Labé was concerned: ". . . it doesn't matter if they're there or not."[10] This is a far cry from Nigeria of the day, where in the North the opposition party (NEPU) were trying unsuccessfully to rouse the people against the chiefs and where the Government of Eastern Nigeria, an area in which traditionally most societies did not have chiefs, commissioned a former expatriate administrative officer to "investigate the position, status, and influence of Chiefs and Natural Rulers in the Eastern Region, and make recommendations as to the necessity or otherwise of legislation regulating their appointment, recognition, and deposition."[11] In African countries where the British had imposed chiefs, as in Eastern Nigeria and parts of Uganda, their prestige had in fact gone up, but this has certainly not been true in the former French territories.

In formulating these general models it is once again essential to recognize exceptions to the general rule. For example, the kings of the Mossi in Upper Volta, the Fulani Emirs of the northern provinces of Cameroun, and a number of chiefs in Niger retained some power. But in general the French system of administration deliberately sapped the traditional powers of the chiefs in the interests of uniformity of administrative system, not only within individual territories but throughout the two great federations of West and Equatorial Africa. Thus it seems somewhat of an understatement to describe the French attitude, as Gouverneur Deschamps does, as "our casual practice toward the chieftaincy." Robert Delavignette in *Freedom and Authority in West Africa* (London, 1950) bears this out in his chapter on the Commandant. "The man who really personified the *Cercle* was the Commandant. . . . He was the Chief of a clearly defined country called Damaragam (Zinder in Niger), and chief in everything that concerned that country." Yet

10. *Conférence des commandants de cercle, Imprimerie du gouvernement,* Conakry, 1957.
11. G. I. Jones, *Report on the Position, Status and Influence of Chiefs and Natural Rulers in the Eastern Region of Nigeria.* Government Printer, Enugu (1957–8).

this was the Damaragam once ruled over by the powerful sultans of Zinder, who are now reduced to little more than exotic showpieces of traditional Africa. So too does Geoffrey Gorer in *Africa Dances* (London, 1935), when he writes of the *chefs de canton:* "In theory these local chiefs rule under the guidance of the local administrator: in practice they are the scapegoats who are made responsible for the collection of money and men. While they enjoy the administrator's favour they have certain privileges, usually good houses and land and in a few cases subsidies; but unless they are completely subservient they risk dismissal, prison and exile." Gorer draws attention to a phenomenon that bears out just how much the French had changed the nature of chiefs in West Africa. In Ivory Coast, if a *chef de canton* with no traditional rights to "rule" were imposed by the administration, the people often elected in secret a "real" chief. Delavignette also notes this in *Freedom and Authority in French West Africa.*[12]

Why this great difference in approach by the two powers to the question of native administration, given that both for reasons of economy had to administer their vast African possessions with the aid of "chiefs"? The difference has much to do with difference in national character and political traditions. While few would disagree that the British were inspired by the concept of separate development for their African territories, there is still much debate as to how far the French were inspired by the concept of assimilation even after its formal abandonment as official policy in favour of a *politique d'association* [policy of association]. Only by an examination of the extent of the survival of assimilationist goals in French colonial policy can we understand the reasons for the difference in the two approaches to native administration. This survival showed itself at two levels: as a dominant feature of the *politique d'association* and in the personal ethos of the French political officer.

12. A somewhat extreme point of view with regard to the French attitude to chiefs, which is the exact opposite of that of M. Deschamps, is held by J. Suret-Canale in 'Guinea under the Colonial System,' *Présence Africaine*, no. 29, p. 53 (English edition): "Between 1890 and 1914 the system of 'direct administration' was progressively established. The former sovereigns (including those who had rendered the best service to French penetration) were utterly eliminated and the former political leaders utterly overthrown; ethnic limits, the traditional limits of the former '*diwe*' in the Futa Jallon, all those were carved up and rearranged at the whim of administrative needs or fancies. The political reality was henceforward the Circle, and where appropriate, the Subdivision, commanded by a European administrator, and below them, the canton and the village commanded by African chiefs described as 'traditional' or 'customary.' In reality, these chiefs in their role and in the powers devolved upon them had absolutely nothing traditional or customary; designed to ensure the cheapest execution (under their own responsibility) of the multiple tasks of administration, taxation, forced labour, recruitment etc., they were the exact counterpart of the caids of Algeria, subordinate administrators."

One of the problems here is to define assimilation. M. D. Lewis[13] has drawn attention to the many definitions of assimilation in use: (1) assimilation as the dominant colonial policy of France, i.e., its dominant and continuing characteristics; (2) assimilation as the policy abandoned in favour of association; (3) assimilation as opposed to autonomy, i.e., integration versus devolution; (4) assimilation as a legalistic definition, i.e., representation in the mother of parliaments; (5) assimilation as civilization; (6) assimilation as representing racial equality as against British tendency to the colour bar; and (7) assimilation as a highly centralized form of direct rule of colonies. It is of course difficult to choose any one definition as the satisfactory one. Assimilation as practised in the four communes of Senegal, the only instance of its full-scale application in French Tropical Africa, had the following distinctive features: political assimilation to the metropolitan country through the representation of Senegal in the Chambre des Députés; administrative assimilation by creating a Conseil-Général for Senegal modelled on the Conseils du Département of France, and by the establishment of municipal councils on the French model; the personal assimilation of Senegalese in the communes by according them the status of French citizens, though they were allowed to retain their *statut personnel;* the extension of French educational facilities as part of the French *mission civilisatrice.* This policy was abandoned not so much because men like Lyautey and Jules Harmand advocated Lugardian ideas about the relationship between the colonial power and African peoples, but because, to use Lewis's phrase, the French were "not prepared to undertake the massive work of social transformation which alone could make it a reality." But the *politique d'association* that succeeded it was certainly not that advocated by Jules Harmand, whereby the colonial power would respect the manners, customs, and religion of the natives and follow a policy of mutual assistance rather than exploitation. Rather it was one in which, while recognition was given to the impracticability of applying a full-scale policy of assimilation to African societies, a number of assimilationist characteristics were retained. First, the goal of creating French citizens out of Africans was not abandoned; it was just made more distant and much more difficult of achievement. Second, there was a high degree of administrative centralization on the mother country, which was not compatible with a true *politique d'association.* We have already seen that the French made little concession to indigenous political units in dividing up their African territories for administrative purposes. Third, the French civilizing mission was not abandoned, and though education might be sparse, it was modelled on

13. M. D. Lewis, "The Assimilation Theory in French Colonial Policy," *Comparative Studies in Society and History,* iv, no. 2, January 1962.

the French system. Children spoke French from the day they entered school. No concession was made to teaching in the vernacular as in the British territories. Fourth, individual territories were not considered as having special characters, so that the same administrative organization was imposed on them all. Political officers would be posted from one territory to the other sometimes every other year, which gave them little time to learn the local language or ethnography. On the other hand the British political officer remained in the same territory for a long period of time, and in the case of Nigeria, in the same region; and promotion depended in part on the ability of the political officers to learn indigenous languages. Thus under the French system the one constant for the political officer could only be French culture, while for the British officer every encouragement was given to him to understand the local culture. As a corollary the French did give some encouragement to the formation of a native elite, which was absorbed into the territorial and federal administrative services, albeit not on a very large scale. The British, on the other hand, in the twenties and thirties actively discouraged the formation of a class of Europeanized Africans, particularly at the level of the central colonial administration. Miss Perham in the late thirties was advocating that no African should be appointed to the administrative service, which she regarded as an alien superstructure.[14] Rather they should be encouraged to work with the native administration. Nigeria was, in the words of Sir Hugh Clifford, Governor from 1919 to 1925, a "collection of self-contained and mutually independent Native States" which the educated Nigerian had no more business coordinating than the British administration. Thus Nigerians were by and large excluded from the senior service of government, while a number of French colonials reached high posts in the administration. Professor Lucy Mair writing in 1936[15] about the status of the educated African in the French colonies remarked that "The assumption which governs the whole attitude of France towards native development is that French civilisation is necessarily the best and need only be presented to the intelligent African for him to adopt it. Once he has done so, no avenue is to be closed to him. If he proves himself capable of assimilating French education, he may enter any profession, may rise to the dignity of Under-Secretary for the Colonies, and will be received as an equal by French society. This attitude towards the educated native arouses the bitter envy of his counterpart in neighbouring British colonies." Jean Daniel Meyer in *Desert Doctor* (London, 1960) writes of his experiences in French Soudan in the Army Colonial Medical Service before the Second World War: "My colleague was a full-

14. P. C. Lloyd, "Lugard and Indirect Rule," *Ibadan*, no. 10, 1960.

15. L. P. Mair, *op. cit.*, p. 189.

blooded Senegalese. He had studied medicine in France, attending the Bordeaux Naval School, and had the rank of lieutenant." Fifth, the African colonies were considered economic extensions of the metropolitan country, and as Albert Sarraut insisted in his *La Mise en valeur de nos colonies* (Paris, 1923)[16] that the colonies should provide assistance to France in the form of raw materials for her industry, and, in addition to this, troops in time of war, in return for which the African would benefit from French civilization. Colonial policy in the interwar period was to be "a doctrine of colonisation starting from a conception of power or profit for the metropolis, but instinctively impregnated with altruism."

Finally it was at the level of the political officer himself that the tendency to assimilation so often manifested itself. Whatever official colonial policy may have been concerning the status of chiefs and the necessity to respect indigenous institutions, it is clear that the majority of French political officers believed sincerely in the French civilizing mission and that it was their role to bring "enlightenment" to the African. They certainly did not believe that indigenous culture or institutions had anything of value to offer except as a stop-gap. L. Gray Cowan writing in 1958 observed: "The young *chef de subdivision* in bush is still a proponent of assimilation through the very fact of his education as a Frenchman although it is no longer a part of official policy."[17] The administrator from republican France, particularly in the interwar period, had little time for the notion of chiefs holding power other than that derived from the administration itself. This provides a marked contrast with the average British administrator, who believed sincerely that for Africans their own traditional methods of government were the most suitable, provided they were shorn of certain features that did not correspond to his sense of justice. Coming from a country which still maintained a monarchy that had done little to democratize itself on the lines of the Scandinavian monarchies, he had a basic respect for the institution of kingship and the panoply of ritual that surrounded it. The British officer respected his chief as separate but equal, though certainly not somebody with whom he could establish personal social relations. It was the educated African before whom he felt uneasy. Indeed many political officers openly expressed their contempt for the "savvy boy" or "trousered African." In Nigeria, even as late as 1954, one could hear such epithets used by Northern political officers about Southern politicians. The African's place was in the Emir's court, not at Lincoln's Inn or Oxford.

The French political officer, on the other hand, was able to establish

16. Quoted by L. P. Mair, *op. cit.*, pp. 186–89.

17. L. Gray Cowan, *Local Government in West Africa*, New York, 1958.

relationships with the educated African. M. Delavignette has published in *L'Afrique noire et son destin* (1962) a revealing letter which he received from Ouezzin-Coulibaly, late Prime Minister of Upper Volta, in 1939, concerning his application for French citizenship. Ouezzin-Coulibaly, then a young teacher in Upper Volta, had been friendly with Delavignette at that time for some ten years and expresses his devotion to France and her cause in the war in the warmest terms: "I was at Sindou and it was there that the news of the mobilization reached me on August 29, 1939. In this far-off corner of the bush I was able to admire the affection that the natives had for France. The movement unfolded in silence and with a rapidity that presupposed a certain understanding of duty. I marveled at it, and this is your work: it is the work of all those who have passed through there and inculcated in the native peasant who had been wrongly disappointed the idea of France and Fatherland." It would be difficult to find such an intimate relationship between a British political officer and a Nigerian teacher at that period. Even as late as 1954, such contact would have been rare. It would be interesting to make a comparison of the philosophy of the colonial service training courses of France, which were much longer established, with that of the British Devonshire courses.

In conclusion, the differences between the French and British systems of administration in Africa were not only differences in degree but in kind. Both may have used chiefs, but the position of the chief in each system was radically different. The basis for these differences may be sought in the fact that though assimilation as an official policy was abandoned after the early experiment in Senegal, it continued to be a most important inspiration both for the *politique d'association* and for the political officer charged with carrying it out. An understanding of the nature of these differences is not only essential to an understanding of colonial history in Africa, but also to an appreciation of the differences between the two main language blocks in independent Africa today.

Aimé
Césaire

ON THE NATURE OF
COLONIALISM

Acivilization which appears to be incapable
of resolving the problems which disturb its functioning is a decadent
civilization.

A civilization which chooses to close its eyes to its most crucial
problems is a stricken civilization.

A civilization which plays tricks with its principles is a moribund
civilization.

The fact is that so-called "European" civilization—"Western" civilization as two centuries of bourgeois regimes have made it—is incapable
of resolving the two major problems to which its existence has given
birth—the proletariat problem and the colonial problem. Exempted from
the bar of "reason" as from the law of "conscience," this Europe is
powerless to justify itself. More and more, she takes refuge in a hypocrisy that becomes more odious as her deception becomes less effective.

Europe is indefensible . . .

In itself militarily this is not serious.

What is serious is that Europe is morally and spiritually indefensible.

And today one finds that it is not only the European masses who
raise this accusation, but dozens and dozens of millions of men all over
the world who, from the depths of slavery, have raised themselves up as
her judges.

They, the colonialists, can kill in Indochina, torture in Madagascar,
imprison in black Africa, perform outrages in the Antilles. From now on,
the colonized know that they have an advantage over the colonizers.
They know that their temporary "masters" lie.

And that therefore their masters are weak.

Since today I must speak about colonization and civilization, let us
go directly to the principal lie from which all the others spring.

Reprinted in abridged form from *Discours sur le Colonialisme,*
Présence Africaine, Paris, 1966, pp. 7–13 and 19–27, by permission of the author and Présence Africaine. Translated from
the French by Irving L. Markovitz.

Colonization and civilization? In this matter the most common failure is to become, by acting in good faith, the dupe of a clever collective hypocrisy, to misrepresent the problem in order to better legitimize the odious solutions which it then proposes.

In other words, the most important thing is to see, think, understand, and respond clearly to the initial innocent question, what in principle is colonization? Let us be frank about what it is not: it is neither evangelism, nor philanthropic enterprise, nor a determination to push back the frontiers of ignorance, sickness, or tyranny, nor is it the enlargement of God nor the extension of law. Let us admit once and for all, without flinching from the consequences, that the decisive characteristic here is that of the adventurer and pirate, of the great spice merchants and shipowners, gold seekers and traders, appetite and force; and behind them, born in the shade, malignant, a form of civilization which at one moment in its history found itself obliged to extend the competition of its economic antagonists to the world level.

Continuing this analysis, I find that such hypocrisy is recent; that neither Cortez, discovering Mexico from the height of the great *Teocalli*, nor Pissarro before *Cuzco* (still less Marco Polo before Cambaluc), protested that they were the bearers of a superior order. They killed. They pillaged. They brought with them their helmets, spears, and lustful desires. The slavers came later. I place the major responsibility for all this on Christian pedantry for having dishonestly formulated the equation: Christianity equals civilization; paganism equals savagery. From this there could only follow the abominable colonist and racist consequences whose victims had to be the Indians, yellow-skinned races, and Negroes.

Having made this clear, I admit that placing different civilizations in contact with each other is good; that bringing together different worlds is excellent, that a civilization which only looks in upon itself whatever its particular genius, becomes enervated; that cultural exchanges are the lifeblood of civilization. The great opportunity for Europe was to have served as a crossroad. As the geometric crossroads of all ideas, the cradle of all philosophies, and the place of welcome for all beliefs, Europe has become the best redistributor of energy.

But then I must raise the following question: has colonization really acted as a force for contact? Or, if one prefers to put the question a bit differently, of all the ways of establishing contact, was this the best?

I answer *no*.

And I say that the distance from colonization to civilization is infinite. Out of all the colonial expeditions put together, out of all the colonial statutes drawn up, all the ministerial instructions sent out, it is impossible to find a single human value.

It is necessary, first of all, to study how colonization works to *decivilize* the colonizer, to *brutalize* him in the real sense of the word, degrading him and awakening in him buried instincts of lust, violence, racial hatred, moral equivocations. Then one must show how every time a head is cut off and an eye bashed in in Viet-Nam and this is accepted in France; a child is violated and this is accepted in France; someone in Madagascar is executed and it is accepted in France; something is added to that civilization which hangs heavily with its dead weight. A universal regression is brought about; a gangrene sets in; an infection begins which spreads throughout the system and—at the end of all these violated treaties, at the end of all the lies that are told, all the punitive expeditions tolerated, all the prisoners bound and "interrogated," all the patriots tortured; at the end of the encouragement of racial arrogance and a steady boastful swaggering—there is the slow but steady brutalization of the continent and a poison is instilled in the veins of Europe.

And then one fine day the bourgeoisie in their turn are awakened by a great shock: the gestapo has kept busy, the prisons are filled up, and the torturers go about their business, inventing, refining, and chatting about their techniques.

People are astonished; they're indignant. They say, "How curious this is! But, bah! It is like Naziism, it will pass." And they wait, and they hope, and they keep the truth to themselves—which is a barbaric thing to do; but the supreme barbarism, the one which tops them all, the one which sums up all the daily doses of barbarities—yes, it is Naziism, but it is more than Naziism—is that before becoming its victim, they have been its accomplices. They supported this Naziism before submitting to it; they absolved it; they winked at it; they legitimized it because before it had only been applied to non-European peoples. They cultivated this Naziism. They are responsible for it. They are responsible for the fact that it rises up and breaks through all the fissures of Western, Christian civilization drop by drop before engulfing all in its reddened waters.

Yes, it would have been worth the trouble to clinically study in detail the rise of Hitler and Hitlerism, and reveal to the very distinguished, very humanist, very Christian bourgeois of the twentieth century that he bore within himself a Hitler that he did not know; to show him that Hitler *inhabited* him, that Hitler was his demon, that if he vituperated Hitler, it was through a failure of logic, and that at bottom what he did not forgive in Hitler *was not the crime itself, the crime against man, it was not the humiliation of man in itself*, it was the crime against the white man, it was the humiliation of the white man. It was having applied to Europe colonialist procedures which until then had only been used on the Arabs of Algeria, coolies of India, and Negroes of Africa.

And this is the great reproach that I address to pseudohumanism:

For too long it has diminished the rights of man; it has had—it still has —a narrow, compartmentalized, unfair, and partial conception of the rights of man that was, all things taken into account, sordidly racist.

I have spoken a good deal about Hitler. His worth is that he permitted us to see and to understand that capitalist society in its present stage is incapable of establishing the rights of peoples because it is admittedly unable to establish any morality for individuals. . . . At the end of formal humanism and philosophic abnegation, there is Hitler. . . .

. . . . For my part, if I recall several details of those hideous butcheries [of colonialism] it is not because of any morose delight; it is because I think that those human heads, those collections of ears, those burned houses, those barbarian invasions, this smoking blood, those towns which disappeared under the hacking of the knife, cannot be gotten rid of so easily. They prove, I repeat, that colonization dehumanizes even the most civilized men. Colonial activity, the colonial enterprise, colonial conquest founded on scorn for the indigenous peoples and justified by this scorn inevitably tends to change those who undertook this venture. The colonizer who, in order to maintain a clear conscience, habituates himself to seeing the others as animals so as to treat them as animals objectively tends to transform himself into an animal. It is this reaction, this shock from the reaction of colonization, that is important to note. . . .

But let us speak of the colonized.

I see clearly what colonization has destroyed: the admirable Indian civilizations. Neither Deterding nor Royal Dutch nor Standard Oil will ever console me for the Aztecs nor for the Incas.

I see clearly those civilizations condemned to destruction, in which colonization has introduced the beginnings of ruin: Oceana, Nigeria, Nyasaland. I see less clearly what benefits colonialism has brought.

Security? Culture? Law? While waiting I look and I see that wherever the colonizers and colonized meet face to face there is force, brutality, cruelty, sadism, violence, and the hasty manufacture, in a parody of cultural training, several thousand subordinate officials, "boys," artisans, commercial employees, and interpreters who are necessary for the proper functioning of the colonial establishment.

I have spoken of contact.

Between colonizer and colonized there is only room for forced labor, intimidation, pressure, policing, taxes, theft, rape, forced farming, scorn, distrust, arrogance, roguery, and conceit towards the deranged élites and downtrodden masses.

There is no human contact, but only the relationship of domination and submission, which transform the colonizer into a pawn, a lieutenant, a convict, a guard, a whip, and the colonized into an instrument of production.

It is my turn to formulate an equation: colonization equals thingafication.

I hear a storm of protest. They speak to me of progress and "accomplishments," sickness conquered, higher standards of living.

I speak of societies emptied of themselves, of trampled cultures, undermined institutions, confiscated lands, of assassinated religions, annihilated artistic masterpieces, of extraordinary possibilities suppressed.

They throw up to me facts, statistics, the number of kilometers of roads, canals, and railways.

I speak of thousands of men sacrificed in the Congo ocean. I speak of those who at the time I am writing are in the process of digging out the port of Abidjan by hand. I speak of millions of men torn away from their gods, their land, their customs, their way of life, their livelihood, their dance, and their wisdom.

I speak of millions of men in whom fear, trembling, feelings of inferiority, despair, toadyism were knowingly inculcated and who were brought to their knees.

They have kept me fully informed about the tonnage of cotton or cocoa exported, the acres of olives or vines planted.

I speak of destroyed food crops, the beginnings of undernourishment, of agricultural development directed only toward the benefit of the metropole, of the seizure of produce and primary goods.

They boast about suppressed abuses.

I also speak of abuses, but in order to say that on top of the old very real abuses they have superimposed others that are very detestable. They speak to me of local tyrants who have been "straightened out," but I declare that in general they keep themselves in office very well with the new ones, and that a network of good services and complicity between the old and new tyrants has been established to the detriment of the people.

They speak to me of civilization; I speak of proletariatization and mystification.

For my part, I would systematically vindicate these para-European civilizations.

Every day that passes, every denial of justice, every police bludgeon, every workers' demonstration put down in blood, every scandal hushed up, every punitive expedition, every car of the secret service, every policeman and every soldier impresses us with the value of our old societies.

They were communitarian societies; never all for only a few.

They were not only *ante*-capitalist societies, as they say, but also *anti*-capitalist.

They were democratic societies, always.

They were cooperative societies, fraternal societies.

I would systematically vindicate those societies destroyed by imperialism.

They were fact—they had no pretense of being idea. They were, in spite of their faults, neither contemptuous nor contemptible. They were content with being. Neither the word *failure*, nor the word *avatar* made any sense to them. They kept hope intact. . . .

. . . Colonial Europe is treacherous in justifying after the fact its colonial activities by virtue of the apparent progress realized in some domains. . . . Nobody knows what stage of material development these societies would have reached without European intervention. The technical equipment and administrative reorganization, the Europeanization of Africa and Asia, were in no way necessarily tied—as the example of Japan proves—to the European *occupation*. The Europeanization of non-European continents could have come about other than under the boot of Europe. This Europeanization movement was already underway before colonization. Afterwards, in fact, it was even slowed down. In any case, this movement was perverted by the occupation of Europe.

For evidence, there is the fact that at present it is the inhabitants of Africa and Asia who are demanding schools, and it is colonial Europe who refuses them; it is the African who asks for ports and roads and it is colonial Europe who haggles; it is the colonized who wants to go forward and it is the colonizer who keeps him back.

Eduardo C.
Mondlane

RACE RELATIONS AND PORTUGUESE COLONIAL POLICY, WITH SPECIAL REFERENCE TO MOZAMBIQUE

Portuguese Claims and Actuality

The Portuguese have for many years tried to project a picture of themselves as a nation without racial prejudice; their government at home and overseas as never having tolerated any racial, ethnic, or religious bigotries or discriminations. According to Gilberto Freyre, a well-known Brazilian historian and leader of those who support this point of view, Portugal's Roman Catholic tradition, plus her long contact with world cultures and races, uniquely equipped her to cope with peoples of various racial, ethnic, and religious backgrounds without conflict. From this Gilberto Freyre goes on to propound a theory of lusotropicalism by which people of Lusitanian (Portuguese) background were preordained to lead the world towards racial harmony and to build a far-flung empire composed of peoples of various colors, religions, and speaking different languages.

A few years ago Dr. Antonio de Oliveira Salazar, Prime Minister of Portugal, stated: "These contacts have never involved the slightest idea of superiority or racial discrimination . . . I think I can say that the distinguishing feature of Portuguese Africa—notwithstanding the concerted efforts made in many quarters to attack it by word as well as by action—is the primacy which we have always attached and will continue to attach to the enhancement of the value and dignity of man without distinction of colour or creed in the light of the principles of the civilization we carried to the populations who were in every way distant to ourselves."[1] Likewise, the preambles of practically all of the frequent Portuguese ground-laws, decrees and statutes or amendments to these, affecting their overseas territories, make unctuous references to the "heterogeneous composition of the Portuguese people, their traditional community . . . the Christian ideal of brotherhood, which was always [sic] at the base of our overseas expansion, early defined our reaction to

1. "Salazar Says." *Portuguese Problems in Africa.* SNI, Lisbon, 1962, p. 6.

Reprinted from *Africa Today*, Vol. 15, No. 1 (February–March, 1968), pp. 13–18, by permission of the editors.

other societies and cultures, and stamped it, from the beginning, with a marked respect for the manners and customs of the peoples we encountered."[2]

Contrary to this idyllic picture is the actual situation in all the three colonies of Portugal in Africa—Angola, Mozambique and Guinea (Bissau)—whose clearly defined socioeconomic structures run along the racial, religious, and linguistic lines typical of all colonial situations. The Portuguese Government, suspecting that the facts of the situation in their African colonies may not conform to their favoured image, has assiduously blocked the efforts of social scientists who have tried to enter Mozambique, Angola, and Guinea (Bissau) with the declared intent of carrying out on-the-spot researches. Therefore, evidence of race relations in Portuguese colonies cannot as yet be expected to derive from objective studies by outside social scientists.

However, during the last fifteen years a number of determined British and American scholars have somehow managed to gather sufficient initial information to continue their studies of Portuguese colonial practices to the point where they could publish important monographs. These scholars are C. R. Boxer, Camoes Professor of Portuguese at the University of London, England; James Duffy, Professor of Romance Languages at Brandeis University, USA; and Marvin Harris, Professor of Anthropology at Columbia University, USA. The work of these scholars has helped not only to suggest the existence of a picture of race relations in the Portuguese colonies radically different from that presented by the Portuguese and their apologists, but also to stimulate a great deal of interest and activity among students of human behaviour in probing behind the facade of Portuguese lusotropicalism.

In the following few pages I shall try to combine my role as a student of human behavior with the advantage which I have as a native-born Mozambican, to present a picture of what I consider to be the true situation regarding race relations in Mozambique.

The Social Factors

There are three social factors which are the most important forces determining relations between individuals and groups in present-day Southern African society and on the basis of which all meaningful societal relations can be understood, namely *race* (as characterized mainly by a person's skin color and general physical characteristics), *politics*, and *economics*.

It is only after an objective analysis of the role played by these three

2. Decreto-Lei No. 43893, 6 Sept. 1961,
Boletim de Mozambique, LM, No. 36,
pp. 1098–9.

factors that we can determine the form and value of any relations between groups in any country in Mozambique, Angola, and, for that matter, Rhodesia and South Africa. In colonial Africa, including all of Africa before independence, the power relations between individuals and groups were, since the arrival of the first European settlers, determined first and foremost by the color of the skin of the individuals involved; secondly, by the amount of political power which they could wield, and lastly, by the material possessions which they had hoarded for themselves.

Anyone who tries to describe the relations between Europeans or people with predominant caucasoid racial characteristics and Africans or people with features tending towards negroid characteristics will soon find himself describing power and economic relations between them.

Therefore, in Mozambique, according to the *Junta de investigacao do Ultramar,* a Portuguese government agency, in its monograph *Promocao social em Mocambique,*[3] there are three distinct socioeconomic strata, distributed in a pyramidal manner, thus:

1. A minority population quantitatively—about 2.5 per cent of the total population. This group is composed of Europeans (caucasoids), Asians (Indians, Pakistanis, Chinese, etc.), the lighter-complexioned and better-educated mulattoes, and a very few Africans (including a very small number of comparatively well-educated Africans). In this group are a thoroughly Europeanized population, most of whom live in the urban areas or in the modern agricultural and mining areas. Most are in either the public service, the business trades, or in enterprises from which the State derives a greater proportion of its public revenues.

2. A numerical minority—3.5 per cent—composed of elements of various races, but above all Africans, tending to live in the peripheries of the most important cities. Practically all the Africans composing this population are of rural origin, still in the throes of detribalization, i.e., abandoning at least partially the cultural and social habits of their origin. Being wage-earners they represent an incipient proletariat.

3. The largest group—94 per cent— is composed of the Africans— we might as well say all of the African population. They are all peasants, living on a basically subsistence economy, supplemented from time to time by some wage work, mostly of a migratory nature. Among this group are a small number who are cash-earning peasant farmers. These are residents of the tribal regions, governed by tribal chiefs following traditional law.[4]

As can be seen, the Mozambican multiracial-multicultural population is distributed in about the same way as all populations living in a typi-

3. PSM, JIU, Iisbon 1964.
4. A. Lima de Carvalho, *Reflexoes para uma analise dimensional da estrutura de Mocambique,* from Mocambique, Insti- tuto Superior de Ciencias Sociais e Politicas Ultramarina, Universidade Tec- nica de Lisbon, 1964–65.

cally colonial situation in which there is a politically, economically, and therefore socially dominant group, usually a minority, who control the means of production and distribution and enjoy the fruits of the labor of the majority. All of Southern Africa, the Portuguese colonies, South Africa, and Rhodesia are in this kind of situation.

The Historical Process

The historical process which preceded this racial-socioeconomic structure follows the same lines as that of similar situations in Southern Africa. Its main features in the special case of Mozambique are as follows:

Early in the sixteenth century the Portuguese decided to build a maritime and commercial empire for the purpose of getting an upper hand in the flow of spices from the East. In carrying out this mission, the Portuguese kings discovered not only new continents and peoples but also new and probably more lucrative sources of wealth: the slaves of West Africa, the ivory and gold of East Africa, and the sugar, tobacco, and gold of the New World. Because the peoples of the countries in which these sources of wealth were found were not willing to hand them over to the Portuguese intruders, it became necessary to attack the natives and destroy their political machinery before the empire could be built.

In this connexion it might be interesting to note, following Professor Boxer, that "for centuries the most common official term for the Portuguese overseas possessions was *As Conquistas*," meaning "The Conquests," regardless of how they were acquired.[5]

From the first hours of their arrival in Mozambique in 1498, the Portuguese sought to establish themselves as a power over the various East African communities which they found. Since their main purpose in coming to East Africa was to find new sources of wealth and control its flow to Europe, it was necessary that they should identify and destroy the military or political power of whoever was in control before them. At that time the people of Mozambique were divided into the following three socioeconomic classes: the Arabs, who controlled most of the trade between the hinterland and the outside world; the Swahilis, who were the main traders between the continental Africans and the coastal and insular Arabs; and the Africans, who composed the majority of the population. First the Portuguese clashed with the Arabs. In 1508, a Portuguese official wrote to the king, from the island of Mozambique, advising him to use every means possible to do away with the "respect-

---

5. Boxer, C. R. *Race Relations in the Portuguese Colonial Empire, 1415–1825,* Clarendon Press, Oxford, 1963, p. 2.

able Moors" from East Africa, since they were dangerous competitors. The same official found the Swahilis acceptable and thought they could remain without damaging Portuguese interests, since "they are like animals, and satisfied with gaining a handful of maize, nor can they harm us, and they can be used for any kind of work and treated like slaves."[6]

After a number of years the Portuguese had managed to establish control over the East African coast from Malindi to Sofala, using every means then available to them, from being friendly to the African people to using force where peaceful means failed to achieve their purpose.

However, after the political and economic influence of the Arabs had been thoroughly eliminated, the Portuguese turned against the Swahilis, whom they had earlier considered harmless. They were now in a position to deal directly with the mainland Africans who brought the gold and ivory from the interior. But they did not succeed, for the Swahilis had been firmly established along the coast for several hundred years, had intermarried with the people from the hinterland, and were therefore far better integrated than the Portuguese.[7]

From time to time even the services of missionaries were harnessed to help pacify the native populations through conversion into the Christian religion; failing this, an excuse was always found to justify the use of force. General J. J. T. Botelho, an official historian for the Portuguese Government, tells of the sixteenth century military expedition which was sent to East Africa under the leadership of two famous Portuguese navigators, Pedro Alvares Cabral, the discoverer of Brazil, and Bartholomew Dias, the first European to round the southern cape of Africa, which he named Cape of Storms and later renamed the Cape of Good Hope. It is interesting to note the composition of the military expedition and its norm of procedure as given by the king. Aside from its two outstanding captains, the expedition was accompanied by a Father, who later became Bishop Henrique, six Franciscan friars, ten chaplains, and military forces. Although the expedition's main purpose was to conquer East Africa, the king's orders for its procedure included, *inter alia*, the following specification: that the regiment of Pedro Alvares Cabral had "to convert the idolatrous [sic] Moors to Catholicism, and if spiritual arms should not succeed, to utilize the material power of the sword."[8]

By the middle of the eighteenth century the control of East Africa by the Portuguese, especially of the central part of present-day Mozambique, was so definite, and the real purpose of the "conquest" of the area was so certain, that Alexander Hamilton, a British chronicler of the time, had this to say of the relations between the Africans and the Portuguese:

6. Quoted by Boxer, C. R., *op. cit.*, p. 43.
7. Boxer, *op. cit.*, p. 42.
8. Botelho, J. J. T., *Historia militar e politica dos Portugeses em Mocambique das descobertas a 1833;* Lisbon: Centro tipografico colonial, 1934, p. 51.

> They [the Africans] have large, strong bodies and limbs, and are very bold in war. They'll have commerce with none but the Portuguese, who keep a few priests along the sea coasts, that overawe the silly Natives and get their teeth [elephant tusks] and gold for trifles, and send what they get to Mocambique [Island].[9]

Lest someone distrust the opinion of a Briton such as Hamilton, being a potential competitor with the Portuguese for the same market, note what Joào Baptista de Moutaury, a Portuguese, had to say about the relations between the same people some seventy years later:

> In general, all the Kaffirs of Sena, who are either slaves of the settlers or else tributary vassals of the State, are docile and friendly to the Portuguese, whom they call Muzungos. They dislike anyone who is not a Portuguese, . . . This dislike derives from a superstitious fear that the Portuguese have spread among them, telling them that all the Mafutos [non-Portuguese white foreigners] eat the Negroes, and other absurd tales which they implicitly believe, and this is one of the chief reasons why they are so friendly to us, for they say that only the Muzungos are good and that all others are bad.[10]

In order to underline the political and economic value of the good relations which existed between the African and the Portuguese, Mountaury goes on to remark:

> It is to be hoped that this conviction will endure in the minds of the said Kaffirs, for in this way we will always be able to dominate them and to live undisturbed. They are most obedient and submissive to their masters and to all the Muzungos in general.[11]

The same Portuguese observer, after giving an example of the loyalty of the Africans in foiling an attempt of the Dutch to replace the Portuguese at Quelimane while the latter were under Spanish control, sounded a warning note, which may serve as another illustration of the master-servant relations then obtaining between the two racial groups, thus:

> On this occasion, the loyalty of the Kaffirs saved that State, because the port of Quelimane did not have then (nor has it now) any fortification whatsoever. Still, who can be certain that this friendship will last for ever, and that it will never change; *the more so, since these same Kaffirs are treated with excessive harshness by their masters?* May not this affection be changed into hatred, owing to the ill treatment they receive? May they do in future to the Muzungos what they formerly did to the Mafutos? This is worth thinking about, and it is not very sound that we should continue to rely solely on the good faith of these Kaffirs.[12]

9. Hamilton, A. *A New Account of the East Indies, 1727;* Foster, W., editor, London, 1930, Vol. I, pp. 16–17.

10. Boxer, C. R., *op. cit.*, p. 47.
11. *Ibid.*
12. Boxer, C. R., *op. cit.*, pp. 47–48.

MONDLANE: *Race Relations and Portuguese Colonial Policy,*
with Special Reference to Mozambique

During the years between the beginning of the eighteenth and the end of the nineteenth century the history of the relations between the Portuguese *Muzungos* and the Africans steadily evolved through the various stages of conquest and control, to the exploitation of everything that could be bought, grabbed by force, plundered, and sold, and reached its climax with the actual capture and selling of the vanquished Africans as slaves.

There are many monographs and texts on the slave trade during the last two centuries. In this connexion, the least that can be said for or against the Portuguese is that they were no better or worse than any other imperialist power of that time.[13]

From the beginning of this century to the present day, Portuguese policy in Africa has been marked by an attempt to soften the unpleasant implications of the master-slave relations which typify the relations between Europeans and Africans in all their colonies by emphasizing the use of such terms in their legal jargon as "contract labour" (*contratados*), or "voluntary labour" (*voluntàrios*), or by using the following terms: "the dignity of labour," "spiritual assimilation," "cultural evolution," and "black Portuguese citizens," etc., when trying to make their colonial policy palatable to the outside world. In fact the reality of the situation is, as Professor Duffy succinctly puts it, "pretty much the same today as as it has been for four hundred years: the indiscriminate use of the African for Portuguese profit."

Concerning this Duffy goes on to make the following meaningful comment:

> Had this vision of the African shown any marked change in these centuries, beyond the final abolition of slavery and the creation of an ambiguous legal language to define the African's status vis-à-vis the colonial administration, a discussion of slavery and contract labour would be only a historical exercise; but there has been no such change, and a study of this aspect of Angola and Mozambique should contribute to an understanding of present tendencies. Whether the African has been an export commodity, a domestic slave, a *liberto, contratado,* or *voluntario,* his fundamental relationship with the Portuguese has remained the same—that of a servant. When the African is supposed to emerge from his centuries-old apprenticeship and tutelage into the role of responsible citizen of Greater Portugal cannot be known, . . . but the idea of an Angola or Mozambique for the African seems to have about as much significance in Portugal's colonial plans as the notion of a United States for the Indian has in American deliberations.[14]

13. For the role of the Portuguese in the slave trade, see James Duffy, *Portuguese Africa,* Harvard University Press, 1961, and C. R. Boxer, *op. cit.*
14. Duffy, James, *op. cit.*, p. 131.

Legal Stipulations

The main features of the Portuguese legal manoeuvres to normalize relations between the two main racial groups in Mozambique included the promulgation of a series of laws instituting a judicial system known as the *indignato*. Under this system the bottom group in the pyramidal socio-economic structure described above, composing the overwhelming majority of the African people, was designated as *indigenas*, or natives. According to the *Estatuto indigena das provincias de Guine, Angola, and Mozambique*, 1954, "natives" (i.e., the members of the lowest stratum) are "persons of the Negro race or their descendants who were born or who habitually reside in the said Province and who do not yet possess the learning and the social and individual habits pre-supposed for the public and private law of Portuguese citizens."

On the basis of the above law, a person of the Negro race is an individual without citizenship and without civil rights. Also, all the persons falling under the category indicated above were subjected to a complex of administrative procedures and controls which virtually limited their freedom of movement. For example, while this law exisited, no "native" could attend Government-controlled schools, except those run by Catholic or Protestant missionaries, which were inferior in every respect; no "native" could seek employment anywhere without first obtaining a special permit from the administrator, who was always a European; no "native" could visit another country except South Africa and Rhodesia, and even in these two countries the purpose of the visit had to be to work under contract in the gold or coal mines of the Witwatersrand or in the tobacco farms of Rhodesia. In order to make these controls on the movements of "natives" effective, this law stipulated that all such persons should carry special "passes" wherever they were, including their own villages, and were prohibited from being seen in public places after certain hours of the evening. Native African economic activities were so restricted that in some cases they could not even slaughter their own cattle, sell them, or give them away without a special authorization from the Portuguese authorities. They could establish bank accounts, but could not withdraw their money without the permission of the local administrator, etc.

Relations between individual Africans and Europeans were regulated by the same rules as prevail in any master-slave society; e.g., it was obligatory for an African to stand up whenever a European appeared or passed by; Africans (including women) were obliged to give the fascist-Roman salute (raising one's right hand up to a 45-degree angle) whenever a car driven by a European passed by; whenever an African addressed a European he had to use the word *senhor* or *senhora*, while

the white man always said *rapaz* (boy) and *rapariga* (girl or maid);
whenever there were a limited number of seats it was the white man
who had to be seated first, regardless of the sexes involved. At public
stadia, cinemas, and theatres, African spectators were confined to special
sections and restricted to certain cinemas exhibiting specially censored
films.

In order to make certain that the African, as a labour force, could
be made available for the white man to use as cheaply as possible, the
Portuguese Government promulgated laws defining the areas of economic
activity which were open to Africans, in this way cutting off a large
proportion of the traditionally subsistence economic pursuits of the
Africans from the legally approved economic activites. Furthermore, millions of Africans, men, women, and often children were forced by local
Portuguese administrators, deriving authority from the same laws, to
cultivate large tracts of land and to plant cotton instead of their own
traditional subsistence crops, in order to enable some monopolistic con-
cessionary companies to realize unusually high profits.

Loss of African Political Power

In view of what has been said so far about the *indigenato system,*
one might conclude, as some students of Portuguese colonial policies
have, that it was these laws which produced the extremely unfair conditions of life which still prevail in Mozambique today. I do not share this
point of view. I believe, as I have tried to point out earlier in this paper,
that the real factors which make for the development of the racial-socioeconomic structure typifying the Portuguese colonial society today are,
first and foremost, the fact that the African people have lost their political power from the very beginning of their relations with the Portuguese.
In other words, Portuguese settlers are on the top of the pyramidal structure principally because their ancestors have wrested political power
from the ancestors of the African majority. The rest of the relationships
which developed followed as night follows day. Europeans came to this
part of the world not to "civilize" or "evangelize" or "make the African
Portuguese," as the Portuguese Government and its apologists would like
the world to believe. All the Portuguese settlers who, throughout the
centuries, have flocked to Africa, came to better themselves materially.
And in arriving here they discovered, if they did not know it before
leaving Europe, that they belong to the race that possesses the real power
in its hands, by dint of conquest made several centuries before them.

What are the symbols of the power of the white man in Mozambique? What does a European newcomer, who may not have left Europe

with racial prejudice towards the African, see when he first arrives in Mozambique? He sees the following facts which are advantageous to himself:

(a) that on arriving at any port all the administrative authorities with whom he has to deal are of his own race,

(b) that all the black people whom he sees are engaged in activities of a servile kind, working as stevedores, on the boats, as carriers and sweepers at the airport terminals, as porters, waiters, cooks, servants, cleaners in the hotel, or auxiliary police (not police officers!),

(c) that all commercial institutions are manned at all administrative levels by persons of his own race,

(d) if he happens to fall ill and has to go to a hospital he will discover that all the doctors are either Europeans or Asians, and occasionally Mulattoes; but not Africans. That the only Africans working in hospitals are auxiliary nurses, orderlies and ordinary servants,

(e) when he goes to the market he will find that all the nice stalls are manned by either Europeans or Asians, while the African traders are sitting on the ground, selling little mounds of the third or fourth grade of whatever is being sold by Europeans or Asians, and

(f) if he were an economist he might finally discover that no African owns any land on which the city stands, nor any buildings or businesses.

It would be an unusual person who would not sooner or later succumb to the temptation of identifying himself with the rest of the minority of Europeans who are enjoying the privileges deriving from this favorable situation.

Those Portuguese idealists who dream of the existence of a multiracial empire in which peoples of all races, cultures, religions, and what-not live happily in harmonious conviviality; who believe that the Portuguese administration and settlers so love their black subjects (*subditos*) that they are willing to allow them to share the political, economic, and social power which they possess are either fools or cynical liars.

New Interest in Situation

During the last fifteen years, or since the early 1950's, there has developed in Portugal a certain interest in the study of the true facts of the situation prevailing in the colonies, stimulated mostly by the evolution towards independence in the rest of Africa. The fact that Portugal is a member of the United Nations where the question of the status of non-self-governing peoples is constantly being studied and discussed, is slowly shaking some Portuguese people into raising some meaningful questions concerning the relations between their own fellow countrymen and the majority of the African people. The best example of this interest is found in some of the studies or analyses published during the last decade or so in the social science series of the *Instituto superior de ciencias sociais e political ultramarina* of the Technical University of Lisbon. (These series began with a compendium on Angola, 1963–64, followed by another on Mozambique, 1964–65, to be completed by one on Cabo Verde, Guine and Sao Tome, 1966–67.)

The reaction of those wielding political and economic power in Portugal, however, has not been too encouraging so far. Instead of reviewing the whole political structure upon which the socioeconomic pyramid is based, they tend to resort to reformist policies, reforms which are typically legal, that is, on paper only (for the English to see, as the traditional Portuguese saying goes). Either they were impossible to apply, or else the Portuguese had no intention of implementing them. Meanwhile the old traditional colonial practice goes on as before.

Since the beginning of this century the history of Portuguese legislation is full of case after case of laws aimed at stamping out practices which had been outlawed many times before but to no avail. Most of these relate to the regulation of labor relations affecting the majority of the African people. How can remedies which deal with the symptoms of a disease be expected to cure it? When there is a class system which clearly runs along racial-cultural lines, as is the case in Mozambique and in all Portuguese colonies, there are bound to be sharp conflicts between groups also following the same racial grooves. When finally the explosion takes place it will necessarily be mainly between the members of those communities which have the most extremely antagonistic and contradictory interests. In Mozambique today, the most contradictory interests are those of the settler class, which is a small (2.5 per cent section of the total population and those of the overwhelming majority of the African people).

It is on the basis of these incontrovertible facts that one must understand the development of the nationalism in Mozambique, Angola, and Guinea (Bissau). In summing up, the peoples of Mozambique, as those of the rest of Southern Africa, have at some point in their history lost political power to the Europeans. As a consequence they also lost their right to control their land (which represents the Africans' only means of eking out a living), and with it all, control of the natural resources, the means of production, and the right to buy and sell the fruits of their labor. As if all this were not bad enough, they lost even the freedom to sell their labor where it can earn them the best living. Thus, there was no alternative but for the Africans to occupy the lowest social position in the pyramidal scale.

The question of how to get out of the present situation has already been answered: *through changing the political machinery imposed by colonialism.*

Part II.   *THE STRUGGLE FOR*
INDEPENDENCE: THE TRIBE,
TRIBALISM, AND THE
CONDITIONS FOR SOCIAL
DEVELOPMENT

The tribe as an ongoing social structure capable of fulfilling the basic life needs of its members is disappearing in Africa. Tribalism, however, in the sense of ethnic identification, psychological commitment, historical membership, or set of shared values remains important everywhere. In many respects, like ethnic politics historically in the United States, tribal appeals and identifications are of the greatest importance in creating coalitions, swaying audiences, molding a nationalist movement, or affecting a political party. Insofar as African states are new nations still struggling with the processes of unity and arriving at a consensus on the basic nature of the political arena, insofar as the breakdown of traditional structures is not everywhere complete nor very far into the past, insofar as any great social transition brings with it tremendous strains, ethnic identifications will be particularly important and virulent. Tribalism today, however, particularly in the cities, is different than it was in the past.

W. W. Rostow has defined a traditional society as "one whose structure is developed within limited production functions based on pre-Newtonian science and technology and on pre-Newtonian attitudes towards the physical world."[1] By *Newtonian*, Rostow means the belief that the world is subject to a few knowable laws and hence systematically amenable to productive manipulation. This definition emphasizes the central fact about traditional society was that the amount and variety of goods that could be produced were severely limited, because the potentialities of modern science and technology were not available. The material condition of such societies and the way of life of their peoples remained continually the same. Their value systems reflected a long-range fatalism; the idea of progress (as in Greek civilization) did not exist; people believed that the future possibilities and standard of living of their children would be no better than their own.

Tribal systems, therefore, everywhere declined under the impact of colonialism, commercialism, and the new science. Subsistence farming became an insufficient mode of earning a livelihood at the same time that alternative occupations became available. Peasants could go —as they had in Europe a few centuries before—to the towns to find new ways of earning a living. They also began to produce new crops for the marketplace and began to treat everything—themselves and their land—as commodities.

New demands arose for services, occupations, and a standard of living that simply could not be met by the traditional systems. In some areas, Christianity, the preemption of the functions and duties of tribal authorities by the secular government, a growing centralization, and powerful bureaucracy added to the process of decline.

Traditional societies, however, varied enormously in size, structure, and complexity of organization, from the great centralized emirates of Northern Nigeria with coffers in the hundreds of thousands of dollars, to small groups of less than a few hundred based on kinship and without any separate political organization whatever. They also varied enormously in their ability to endure the colonial, technological, and commercial intrusions. Traditional elites sometimes

1. W. W. Rostow, *The Stages of Economic Growth*, Cambridge University Press, New York, 1960, p. 4.

The Struggle for Independence: The Tribe, Tribalism,
and the Conditions for Social Development

withered away as their ancient societies declined; others remained powerful as instruments of colonial rule backed by the force of foreign interests; still others succeeded in shifting the basis of their power by using their privileged status in tribal society to win new positions of influence. Formerly, their power in large measure rotated around their authority to allocate land. Today, these same people and their descendants as individuals rank high among the new intelligentsia, technocrats, university graduates, civil servants, businessmen, and, indeed, politicians.

Paula Brown presents some idea of the range and complexity of African traditional systems. Max Gluckman distinguishes between the meaning of tribalism in rural and urban environments. Jean Suret-Canale reveals the roots of disintegration of traditional legitimacy. Norman Miller shows how traditional leaders can survive as potent political forces even in the post-Independence era; and Elliott Skinner accounts in part for the continental wide variations in the durability of ancient rural systems by his presentation of the concept of uneven development. Finally, Gicha Mbee, an African farmer, in his own words describes the tensions in the bush between the young men and the elders.

Paula	**PATTERNS OF AUTHORITY IN**
Brown	**WEST AFRICA**

*T*he development of large centralized states in West
Africa has long been recognized. The complexity of organization of the
few well-known kingdoms, but not their differences in size and structure,
is constantly emphasized in the literature. The number and variety of
West African groups which have not developed states have, on the other
hand, frequently been underestimated. In a comparative review by Pro-
fessors Fortes and Evans-Pritchard[1] two types of political system, centralized and segmentary, have been described for Africa as a whole,
with examples of each in West Africa. A survey of West African societies
suggests, however, that finer distinctions are possible and that not all
these societies can be placed in one or another of these two categories.
In particular, this classification omits consideration of "stateless" societies
in which associations, rather than a segmentary lineage system, regulate
political relations; and it fails to distinguish different types of authority
and political structure in states.

In West Africa, as will be seen, authority is exercised by persons
holding positions in kinship groups, associations, and states, but the type
of authority, and thus the type of control effected, are variable. It is
therefore suggested that a classification of political systems can be approached through the combined study of the structure of groups in
which authority is held and the types of authority exercised by officials
as members of these groups. In addition to an analysis of the authority
exercised by persons holding certain positions in kinship groups, associations, and states, the total pattern of authority in societies having certain
combinations of these groups will be considered with reference to eight
West African societies: Ashanti, Dahomey, Ibo, Mende, Nupe, Tallensi,
Yakö, and Yoruba. Needless to say, the usefulness of the classification

1. *African Political Systems*, 1940.

Reprinted from *Africa*, Vol. 21, No. 4 (October 1951), pp.
261–278, by permission of the International African Institute
and the author.

and the relevance of the general conclusions to other societies and areas remain to be tested.

The analysis rests on a view of authority which has been previously used in social anthropology, and may be briefly summarized as follows: In every group, certain individuals hold authority, that is, they are able to obtain obedience to their commands. The content of the commands made by a particular person in authority may be narrowly limited by law or custom or may be allowed to vary over a wide range. A special limitation must be placed on "authority" as used here: it is only possible to deal with recognized prerogatives and acknowleged powers; illegitimate coercion and manipulation are excluded. Ability to obtain obedience rests upon the sanctions, direct or indirect, which the authority-holder can apply to his subordinates.

The present discussion is concerned only with such negative sanctions as are applied by persons in authority; it is not proposed to deal with conscience (a type of moral sanction) or with automatic supernatural sanctions. Sanctions may be broadly classified as moral, ritual, and legal, but within this framework several distinctions can be made. Public opinion is a moral sanction which may be expressed in mass action or verbalized by a person holding moral authority. A person with moral authority, then, is a spokesman for tradition and public opinion. A common set of values, and especially a high valuation set on the opinion of one's associates, are prerequisites for the effectiveness of moral sanctions.

Besides those ritual sanctions which are believed to follow automatically from an offence, others may be set in motion by excommunication (in West Africa, usually the refusal to sacrifice on a person's behalf) or by the curse of a ritual leader. But the effectiveness of such a ritual sanction rests on the ability of the ritual leader to convince the offender of his authority to invoke supernatural sanctions. A moral sanction is sometimes reinforced by an implicit threat of ritual sanctions; this sort of sanction can be called moral-ritual.

A legal sanction consists of the application or threat of force by an official body for infringement of rules. Banishment, deprivation of rights or property, and physical punishment are legal sanctions when applied by an official agent of the community acting in support of explicit rules of conduct. The effectiveness of a legal sanction depends on the agency of enforcement and on general willingness to accept the directions of the authority. There are borderline cases in which fines are collected from offenders without the threat of force; this could be called a moral-legal sanction. Approved vengeance is in some cases an accepted means of settling a personal dispute, and in such cases the avenger is supported by public opinion. This sanction could also be called moral-legal, as it involves force as well as public opinion.

The threefold classification of sanctions into moral, ritual, and legal, then, is useful only as a general guide. In addition to the hyphenated forms suggested above, it might be noted that ritual or legal sanctions are very commonly ultimate threats, while reparation follows normally from moral sanctions alone. We can classify persons according to whether they control moral, ritual, or legal sanctions, or some combination of these. Thus a person holding moral authority acts as a spokesman for tradition and public opinion. A ritual authority is an agent for super-natural forces; his pronouncements are believed to derive from super-naturally supported traditions. A legal authority is one empowered to apply force or to control the use of force in certain cases, e.g., if his orders in some spheres are not obeyed, or if certain rules are broken within his area of jurisdiction.

Before discussing the distribution of these types of authority among West African groups, some general statements about West African societies should be made. The peoples described here are primarily agri-cultural and rights over farm- and house-land were, and in most areas still are, transmitted within a lineage. Lineage property was nominally controlled by the oldest male member who acted as arbitrator in intra-lineage disputes and represented the lineage in its external relations.[2]

State organization is old in West Africa; it probably preceded both Islamic and European influences, but the impact of these foreign cultures further stimulated political centralization. Moslem influence took the form of missionary efforts and conquest by Islamicized peoples who introduced political as well as religious changes. For many centuries trans-Saharan trade provided the basis of commercial and political devel-opment in the Sudan.[3] European trade on the coast from the fifteenth century encouraged political centralization by making the capture of potential slaves and the control of certain goods (gold, arms, etc.) financially profitable and a source of power. This paper does not attempt to discuss the origins of West African political development, but is concerned rather with the analysis of the precolonial systems of authority in certain West African societies.

2. Although many, perhaps most, of the features described here hold today, no attempt is made to deal with administra-tion under colonial governments, and the systems described are those which, as far as is at present known, held at some period before colonial governments were established, and before modern constitu-tions were made. For uniformity of pre-sentation, the description is phrased in the past tense throughout.

3. Bovill, 1933; Greenberg, 1949.

Groups Based on Kinship

Among these West African societies, within the category of "kinship groups" we may distinguish the elementary family, the extended family (having as its nucleus a lineage segment), in many societies the lineage five to ten generations in depth, and, in some areas, the corporate clan.[4]

The elementary or polygynous family was a fundamental unit in West African as in most social systems. The education and discipline of children was a task performed mainly by parents. Parental authority was primarily moral, resting on the dependence, respect, and love that most children feel towards their parents. In West Africa, parental authority did not normally end when children, especially sons in patrilineal societies, reached adulthood. Often, parents made special demands for time and labor on adolescent and adult offspring, had the right to choose a spouse or prevent a marriage, and to grant or withhold land for farms and houses. Elementary families, and often individuals, had some economic independence—a personal farm-plot, craft-work, or trade—but economically, as well as in other ways, an elementary family was linked to other families of the extended family and to the lineage or clan. An elementary family resided in the dwelling area of the husband's lineage and formed only a semi-independent section of it. Ashanti family organization is a special case, for not all husbands and wives lived together.[5] Elementary family households in Ashanti often occupied a section of the husband's matrilineage dwelling area, while a woman with her children living apart from her husband resided in the woman's matrilineage dwelling area.[6]

Since the elementary family formed a section of the extended family, the authority of parents merged with the authority of the extended family head, who was senior by one or more generations to most members. Over such persons he often held parental authority as well as exercising the rights deriving from his position as extended family head. Only with respect to the male members of his own generation was there a conflict between the roles of parents and extended family head; his seniority here gave him nominal control, but in practice only greater weight in councils.

In the patrilineal West African societies considered here, the extended family consisted of the male members of a lineage three to five

---

4. There are striking similarities in the organization of kinship groups throughout West Africa, but a major contrast is found between the patrilineal societies and Ashanti, the only matrilineal society included in this survey. Yakö is classified as patrilineal in this section of the analysis, but it will be remembered that the Yakö have a dual descent system.
5. Fortes, 1950.
6. Some Dahomean households were also uxorilocal. *Cf.* Herskovits, 1937; Bohannan, 1949.

generations removed from the founding ancestor, the wives of these men, unmarried women, and often more distant cognatic or affinal relations or other dependent persons. Residence, and hence the composition of the extended family, among the Ashanti was variable, but a matrilineage segment was headed by the eldest male member. Where the extended family was a co-residential group, control was usually informal: there was mutual assistance in economic matters and disputes were settled by common consent or arbitration, with moral sanctions.

In the literature, "household" and "compound" are used for groups varying considerably in size and function; these terms will here be avoided, for the sake of discussing units similar in size and/or function, and of considering the authority held by the heads of such units. The basic unit of food production and consumption was often an elementary or polygynous family, but as the sons of this family married, they, with their wives and children, did not always establish independent economic units. Even at the death of their father, the set of brothers sometimes continued to share a dwelling and production unit. With wives, children, and other dependents, and continuing for another generation or two, such a unit (by now a lineage or lineage segment with dependents) could grow to include 100 people. However, the size of the economic unit varied with population density, land fragmentation, labor organization in the community, and the special labor requirements of staple crops. Except in large estates with many slaves, it probably rarely exceeded thirty people of all ages. Most women had personal land plots on which they grew vegetables for their own families, and children often had small plots of their own. Generally, in the rain-forest area, every married man had a separate plot of land which he cultivated with his wives, or a woman had her own farm. Each farmer was aided in the more arduous tasks by members of his lineage or other cooperative groups, and owed assistance to elders of his lineage. In Tallensi and Nupe, and in other grassland societies, extended family labor on a joint farm more commonly provided the staple cereal food, while personal plots were used for supplementary crops. But we do not find two types of household—elementary family and extended family; rather, we find a variety of rights and obligations among members of kinship groups with respect to labor and produce.

The situation regarding land rights was similar. In some communities, each adult male received one or more tracts of farmland either as a gift from his father (in Ashanti, from a matrilineal relative) or as an inheritance; in others the head of a lineage segment controlled and allocated plots of land each season. In either case, land holdings constituted rights of use only; the land could not be alienated without the consent of lineage members, and especially of lineage elders. The nonlineage members of an extended family did not normally inherit land but could, in time, acquire rights of permanent usufruct.

In many West African societies a lineage segment formed a cult group in the worship of the ancestors of the segment. The eldest male member of the group acted as ritual intermediary between living members and their ancestors, and could refuse to sacrifice on behalf of lineage members, thus exercising a ritual sanction. But this ritual sanction seems rarely to have been used; it acted, rather, as a final threat for continued misbehaviour. Any disputes occurring within the extended family were settled by the eldest male member, normally by arbitration. Small fines were often imposed in such settlements. In some of these West African societies, a constant offender might be dispossessed or expelled, and an Ashanti lineage segment head could pawn a member for debts owed by the lineage segment. While these implicit threats of legal or ritual sanctions may have been an incentive to speedy settlement of lineage disputes, in practice the moral authority of an extended family head, based on respect towards elders and the traditions of the wider society, was generally sufficient for the maintenance of order within the extended family.

The head of a lineage segment was a key figure for the members and their dependents in relations with other groups, and especially with other segments of a wider lineage, for he was the official spokesman of the lineage segment and represented their interests in external relations. Thus the extended family in patrilineal West African societies was unified by the head in two ways: members depended upon the head for land, economic assistance, and fair decisions in domestic disputes, and he represented the group in its relations with other groups.

A larger kinship group, the maximal lineage or localized clan (here distinguished only by the presence—in the lineage—or absence—in the clan—of specific genealogical ties between segments), was composed of a number of lineages or lineage segments. Wives, and often other dependents, retained, in principle, membership of the descent group of their birth, but, except in cases of disputes between their natal group and the one in which they resided, were, in practice, subject to the leaders of the group with which they lived. Offices in the lineage or clan were held by senior members of the descent group. Perhaps because of the size of the group, their moral authority seems to have been weaker or less effective than that of the lineage segment head. They often controlled ritual and limited legal sanctions, which they could apply to this larger group. In some cases, land was controlled by the head of a larger lineage or clan, but in fact he had authority to allocate (to kinsmen or strangers) only usufruct rights to land not used by individuals or extended families. Junior men commonly contributed labor, gifts of food, and other produce to lineage or clan heads. In some cases these offerings were used in sacrifices or were passed on to higher political officers as tribute.

Lineages and clans were often residentially compact, but offshoots of a descent group could establish bush hamlets when the main lineage settlement became overcrowded. However, unless a branch left the area altogether, it continued to be associated with the lineage or clan for some generations. Such demographic data as are available indicate that the maximal lineage or localized clan ranged in size from a minimum of six to twelve men (according to the genealogies recorded by Green[7] for the Ibo of Umueke) to a maximum of 150 adult males (in Yakö patri-clans[8]); while the Ibo figure is probably the lowest to be found in West Africa, 150 men may not be the upper limit of size in localized descent groups.

A cult of some kind, often ancestral, further emphasized lineage or clan unity. Among our cases only Nupe kinship groups (which were not more than two or three generations in depth and often included matrilineal or affinal relatives) lacked such a cult.[9] Among the other West African societies here discussed, the maximal lineage or clan head was a ritual leader. As such he commanded ritual sanctions in the right to refuse an errant member access to the deity, or to curse offenders, and he performed expiatory rites for the offences of members. Further-more, by virtue of his position, a lineage or clan head could speak with special authority on ritual matters.

Legal authority was commonly held by heads of West African line-ages and clans. In particular, they settled disputes between members, mainly by arbitration, and punished some offences committed by mem-bers. Small fines were usually imposed in such cases, but some lineage or clan heads had the further right to pawn, enslave, expel, or dispossess members. However, there are few recorded instances of the use of force against kinsmen; moral sanctions, backed by the threat of ritual or legal sanctions, seem generally to have brought submission. Furthermore, their moral authority rested on the support of lineage elders, whose consent was usually required for the application or threat of force.

The authority of the kin-group head was affected by the character of the larger political unit of which the group formed a part; for this poli-tical unit might limit the jurisdiction of kin-group heads or require them to use force against their subordinates who had committed offences. In-deed, the kinship group formed a basic political unit in many societies, and in states the kin-group head was confirmed in office by a chief. Thus

7. Green, 1941.
8. Forde, 1950a.
9. The absence of large kinship groups with legal and ritual functions is closely related to the presence of a strongly centralized state. Cf. Nadel, 1942, pp. 32–33.

in Ibo, Mende, Dahomey, Ashanti, and Nupe the kin-group head acted as his group's official representative to the community and was a member of the local council. The village chief in most of these communities was the head of a locally dominant or "senior" lineage. Among the Tallensi, the role of maximal lineage head was similar, but authority here was ritual rather than legal and there was no formal council. In Yakö, and in some Yoruba communities, the largest patrilineal groups were not specifically represented on local councils since ward government was organized on a nonkinship basis.

A few of these societies (Tallensi, Ashanti, Dahomey, and Yakö) had in addition larger nonlocalized clans. Among Tallensi clans (in the sense of clusters of ritually linked, often neighbouring, maximal lineages) friendly relations and the peaceful settlement of disputes were ritually required, and the leaders of the maximal lineages concerned arbitrated within such units. In Ashanti, all members of a given dispersed clan had obligations of friendship towards one another, but no ritual or political machinery for cooperation existed. The leaders of Dahomean dispersed clans performed rites for clan ancestors. In addition, the clan head arbitrated in clan disputes and could prevent marriage with clanswomen. Among the Yakö, matriclan priests exercised ritual authority over the members of their clans and, as a group, over all villagers.

To summarize, the leaders of corporate clans and lineages in West African societies were primarily concerned with the ritual and social well-being of members of their kin groups. Where kinship groups were the only units in which sanctions were regularly applied (e.g., Tallensi), the system was segmentary and gerontocratic, associated with moral and ritual rather than with legal sanctions. The leaders of kin groups often represented their kinsmen in community affairs; thus the segmentary system was subsumed in a community organization in which the kin groups formed units. Where a community council of lineage heads exercised legal sanctions, individual lineage heads sometimes acted as agents in applying them to their kinsmen. Those who failed in kinship obligations or committed offences against their kinsmen could be punished with moral-ritual, moral-legal, or, rarely, legal sanctions. But whatever sanctions they controlled, kin-group heads were never autocratic, since they depended upon the support of their kin groups, and especially of the elders, for effective administration.

Associations

An association may be defined as an organized and corporate group, membership in which does not follow automatically from birth or adoption into a kin or territorial unit. Associations with important authoritative functions are, in the main, permanent and have continuous organization. We are especially concerned here with those which exercise sanctions over groups extending *beyond* their own members; within these may be distinguished cult groups, controlling ritual sanctions, and secular associations, controlling legal sanctions, although many such associations control both. Conformity *within* an association was often accomplished only by moral sanctions. In contrast, associations with important functions of community control wielded externally effective ritual sanctions, associated with spirits believed to be powerful, or had recognized legal prerogatives; they did not rely predominantly upon moral sanctions.

Among those associations which exercised authority only over their own members, and where moral and legal sanctions prevailed, were savings clubs, widespread in West Africa and well described for Ibo, Dahomey, and Nupe, which might regulate behaviour among members in many spheres. Nonconformity to their rules as well as failure to make contributions were penalized by fines, sometimes by seizure of property, and continued infringements led to expulsion and the loss of subscriptions. In parts of Yorubaland, an association of the women who traded in a particular market managed their commercial affairs; its officers settled market quarrels, having in some cases the authority to exclude from the market women who refused to pay fines. Craft guilds in Dahomey worked cooperatively and fined members who broke the rules. In Yoruba, they set prices for the commodity and brought disputes before the town council. Nupe craft-guild heads arbitrated in disagreements between workers and represented the craftsmen at the king's court. In addition to organizing collective farm work in the village, Nupe age-sets were recreational and ritual groups; the leaders punished breaches of the rules by degradation (of rank), ostracism, and fines. Among the Ibo, age-sets fined their members for offences against outsiders as well as against members, and often brought culprits of their grade to the elders for trial. One or more age-sets sometimes acted as police for the elders and collected fines.

The Ibo village council is perhaps a borderline case of an association enforcing sanctions on the behaviour of nonmembers. It was not part of a state system, but neither was it simply a group of representatives of lineages, for it often included, in addition to the heads of lineages, the members of the senior age-set, the priests of important cults, wealthy and influential older men, and, in some areas, title-holders. This village council was not necessarily a permanent and fully corporate group. It may be characterized as an élite of influential older men, lacking formal organization but recognizing membership and providing the main organ of village government. While Meek's account[10] gives the village council legal powers—arrests, fines, property seizures, etc.—Green[11] describes cases in which fines were agreed to by the disputants but never paid, and no force was used by the elders or their agents. In Umueke, where the head of one lineage was a ritual leader for the village, although he commanded neither ritual nor legal sanctions, his ritual staff was used to swear veracity in trials, and false swearing was believed to result in ritual sanctions by the ancestors.

In southern Iboland, doctor-diviners were consulted as private practitioners in cases of illness, death, and misfortune, and had considerable influence over their clients. The doctor-diviners of a village group (a set of neighbouring and related villages) or even of a number of village groups could be asked as a body to judge a case. Whatever penalty they might set, it appears that the party found guilty feared the ritual sanctions they commanded. In some sections of the Awgu division,[12] members of a title society punished persons who offended them and settled local disputes, applying force if necessary. The members of title societies collected fines and tried serious cases within the village group in parts of Nsukka and other divisions as well. Ibo government, then, was limited to the village group (population *c.* 5,000) and was exercised mainly by a loosely constituted council whose personnel included kin-group heads, elders, other notables, and, in some places, members of title societies. In certain areas, members of title societies had special privileges, including the use of legal sanctions, while in many village groups only moral and implicit or threatened ritual sanctions could be applied to offenders.

Among the Yakö,[13] a multiplicity of associations exercised authoritative functions. Both ward (population 1,500-3,500) and village (population 11,000) associations, with fairly clearly defined realms of jurisdiction, were found in Yakö. The youths of a ward (comprising several patriclans) were organized into age-sets at four-yearly intervals. Younger age-sets were responsible for certain communal tasks, under the orders of the elders; men who refused to cooperate were fined by their own set or by the ward head. An organization of ward elders, actually including many middle-aged men, all priests, and men of distinction and at least moderate wealth, was headed by an elected official who, with the association's assistance, directed initiation and some other rites, and in addition intervened in serious intraward disputes. This group did not itself apply legal sanctions, but could request a warrior club, *Ebiabu,* composed of most men of the ward, to act as police. The association of ward elders thus directly controlled ritual sanctions; indirectly, it controlled legal sanctions by its authority to call upon *Ebiabu.* Another

10. Meek, 1937.   12. Meek, 1937.
11. Green, 1947.   13. Forde, 1939, 1950*b.*

ward association, *Nkpe*, could, at the request of the owner, place its symbol on property to guard against trespass and theft. A person who violated this protection was liable to be fined by *Nkpe* and the owner, on pain of the supernatural sanctions of the association's spirit; only *Nkpe* could perform expiatory rites to remove this supernatural danger. *Nkpe*, then, controlled ritual sanctions which followed if an offender refused to comply with its demands for payment; if the thief was not apprehended the ritual sanctions were believed to follow automatically.

Membership of Yakö village associations overlapped to a considerable extent that of various ward associations. *Okenka* was a ritual association which drew its members from among the more influential ward elders. A ward head could invoke its sanctions when he failed to keep order in his ward, and disputes involving persons or groups from two wards could be settled by *Okenka*. For its members, *Okenka* protected land and trees by placing the sign of its spirit cult upon them, and anyone who tampered with such property faced a heavy fine or the anger of the association's spirit.

The village council, which comprised all matriclan priests and other priests installed by them, formed the moral and ritual focus of the community; it intervened in serious disorders and matters involving supernatural dangers for the village and it heard civil disputes on appeal. The most serious ritual offences were taken before the village council of priests to be punished by fines and expiation, on pain of ritual sanctions. While the council ordered fines and expiation in civil cases, it applied only moral and ritual sanctions (excommunication from matriclan rites, etc.), since as priests its members could not use force. The council could, however, request the *Ikpungkara* society of the village to apply force against anyone who defied its authority. *Ikpungkara* was an association of rich and prominent men which, besides acting as an executive for the council of village priests, used sanctions in cases of infringement of its own protective symbols. Grievances concerning theft, nonpayment of debts, and farm boundaries could be taken to *Ikpungkara*, which would impose fines on a guilty party, backed by a threat of property seizure. Many Yakö associations were cult groups which relied for their authority upon the ritual sanction of their spirit and thereby exacted fines from those who disregarded their protective symbols. Civil disputes and infringements of minor rules and directives were handled mainly within the ward, but recalcitrant offenders could be taken to the village authorities.

Ibo and Yakö are the only West African societies in this sample where associations including village councils of an associational type, in combination, constituted the only governmental bodies beyond the kinship group. But associations exercised authority in certain realms among

The Struggle for Independence: The Tribe, Tribalism, and the Conditions for Social Development

many other West African peoples. Perhaps the most striking example is the Mende *Poro*.[14] All youths were initiated into the *Poro* and received training in masculine tasks and morals, but actual authority was limited to the senior members, who either inherited their posts or proceeded through the grades to reach the executive level. This primarily ritual association operated in conjunction with secular chiefship: its approval was essential to the election of a chief, and the chief was the *Poro*'s patron. In addition to the organization of initiation and other rituals, the *Poro* executive held a general moral authority over each community, buttressed by its powerful spirits and their ritual sanctions. Serious disputes between secular officials were tried in secret by the *Poro* executive, and recalcitrants were brought to heel by an armed band of masked *Poro* members. Thus they controlled ritual and legal sanctions. Other Mende associations held ritual authority over certain realms of conduct. *Sande*, a women's association parallel to the *Poro*, trained girls in feminine tasks and morals. It also punished offences against its rules, e.g., men having sexual relations with uninitiated girls. *Humoi* ritually guarded certain rules concerning sexual behavior, especially incest regulations. *Njayei*, another association, effected expiation, by initiation, for intrusion into its sacred bush or knowledge of its ritual secrets. Since all illness was believed to result from ritual infractions relating to the ancestors or the societies, an appeal to a society for expiation and cure was commonly prescribed by a diviner. Certain ailments were held to fall within the province of particular societies, and diagnosis was thus simplified.

In parts of Yorubaland, and especially in Abeokuta, the *Ogboni*, an association of prominent elders, had judicial functions. Local cases were taken to the *Ogboni* of the township (or ward) while intertownship cases were heard by the combined *Ogboni* of the townships concerned or by the entire *Ogboni* council of Abeokuta. Although force was not used by *Ogboni* members, the *Ode* society of hunters and scouts was at its disposal to seize the property of an uncooperative minor offender, and *Oro*, a ritual association, carried out executions ordered by *Ogboni*. The latter action required the approval of the *Alake*, ritual chief of Abeokuta, who, however, did not often refuse this, since both his election and his removal from office were in the hands of the *Ogboni*.[15] While the *Ogboni* and other associations were widespread in the Yoruba-speaking area, their functions were most clearly defined in Abeokuta.[16] In other places the legal jurisdiction of the *Ogboni* seems to have been

14. Little, 1948c, 1949; McCulloch, 1950.
15. The *Ogboni*'s jurisdiction was limited to certain matters of internal order. An association of trade chiefs handled cases arising in the market, and the war chiefs had authority to apply force in military matters.
16. Forde, 1951, and S. O. Biobaku, private communication.

limited to disputes between members or other prominent men. Bascom[17] describes *Ogboni* as a cult group having authority to bring disputants whose quarrels ended in bloodshed to the *Ogboni* house for trial; but its ritual sanctions, if any, are not reported. Other associations, especially *Egungun* and *Oro,* are said to have had powerful ritual sanctions and to have exercised force either on their own initiative—the execution of sorcerers is most commonly mentioned—or at the request of other bodies.

It should be noted that no associations were found in Ashanti,[18] and that the associations of Dahomey and Nupe did not use sanctions against nonmembers.[19] In these states the central government had a monopoly of the use of force and controlled state rituals; no important spheres of authority were left to independent bodies such as associations.

The associations of West Africa do not fall into any simple set of categories as regards the authority they exercised. Those which had command of ritual sanctions alone were cult groups attached to powerful spirits (Ibo doctor-diviners, a number of Yakö associations, and the minor Mende associations): their ritual sanctions were believed to operate automatically when the spirits' taboos were broken or their protective symbols ignored. Only members of the cult group could remove these ritual hazards, and in some cases members were thought to control powerful magic which could be used against those who defied their directives. These associations collected fines for certain offences and fees for their services in expiatory rites. The Yakö ward elders and village council, and, perhaps, the Yoruba *Ogboni* and the village council in Ibo communities, were associations of prominent men, who possessed moral and ritual authority without controlling powerful supernatural sanctions: while remaining aloof from violence they, in fact, controlled the use of force within the community, just as many secular rulers do. A few associations exercised only legal sanctions, without any connexion with supernatural forces. These included age-sets, mutual aid societies, and craft guilds, whose authority was limited to punishing the misconduct of their own members. Yakö *Ikpungkara* and *Ebiabu* used legal sanctions at the request of village or ward authorities, and *Ikpungkara* also applied force in dealing with cases brought to its court. Trade associations in some sections of Yorubaland enforced penalties in market quarrels and misdemeanours. Perhaps title societies could be included where, in Iboland, they constituted the village or village-group council and applied legal sanctions to offenders within the area.

A number of associations seem to have combined legal and ritual

17. Bascom, 1944.
18. The *Mmeranti* was composed of all adult men without political office and served as a town meeting to discuss

political issues.
19. Some Dahomean cult groups punished ritual offences against members, but had no further powers.

sanctions, and in these cases it is often difficult to tell which was primary. The authority of the Yoruba *Egungun* and *Oro* is most obscure. The Mende *Poro* officials were believed to control powerful supernatural forces, but not all punishment was left to the action of the gods or magic; rather, masked dancers were sent to compel obedience. Again, primarily ritual associations were not always content to allow an offender to suffer ritual sanctions alone, or to escape them by a sacrifice; they required a large payment for their services in removing supernatural dangers.

States

All of the West African states considered here (Mende, Ashanti, Dahomey, Nupe, and Yoruba) had certain features in common: administrative hierarchies whereby each lineage was responsible to a local governmental institution; some sort of district organization; a chief or king who maintained a considerable staff of agents and advisers; a system of courts of appeal leading up to the king and his council; and mythical and ritual support for political supremacy. These states varied in size from a few thousand people among the Mende to the Nupe and Dahomey kingdoms of several hundred thousand. Ashanti, and the Yoruba under Oyo, were at least as large as these, but they were loose confederacies composed of a number of federated smaller states. Offices in some states were hereditary within a lineage; others had mainly appointed officers, or a mixture of the two. The functions of individual officers were in some cases quite specialized, either within the central government or in respect of particular districts. West African states were based on, or held as an important end, expansion through military conquest; an army supported by taxation was used to defend and expand the state. The military force of commoners was led by state officials, provisioned from state funds, and armed by the state.

The leaders of West African states enjoyed economic privileges. This economic differentiation was related to the specialization of occupation, and especially to industries providing luxury goods which served as symbols of prestige. West African states also provided the rulers with goods by taxation, levies on trade, trade monopolies, death duties, compulsory labour, and rights over war captives. Slave labour maintained the rulers in Dahomey, Mende, and Nupe at a superior standard of living; the kings of Bono and Ashanti grew rich through the gold trade. The administrative staff was supported, at least in part, by a share in such income, either by gifts from the king or by retaining part of the tribute they collected. The ruling group, and especially the king, possessed prestige symbols in the form of horses, elaborate regalia, entourage, etc.

A Mende[20] state consisted of a capital town, one or more section towns which served as administrative centres for districts and, in these districts, other towns and villages. Each town had a council, composed of the heads of land-owning lineages, which dealt with local offences and complaints. The town chief was the senior member of the lineage which, according to tradition, founded or conquered the area. In addition to his judicial and executive functions, the town chief was the principal intermediary between his townsmen and the district chief and the paramount chief; he also collected taxes in the town and entertained strangers. Town chiefs and the heads of prominent lineages in a district were members of the council of the district capital, or section town. District chiefs were frequently members of the paramount chief's lineage, acted as his agents in the collection of taxes, and in turn sat on his council. Court cases not settled by town chiefs, and those arising between towns of the district, were judged by the district chief and his council which enforced fines and fees. A speaker, usually a member of an important lineage but chosen by the district chief for his ability, acted as the chief's deputy, receiving applications for court hearings and announcing decisions. In addition, he assumed the chief's functions during an interregnum and had an important voice in the selection of the chief's successor. The central officer of a Mende state was the paramount chief, always chosen from the lineage which traditionally founded the first settlement or conquered the area. His council, consisting of all the prominent men of the chiefdom, was a legislative and judicial body which used the army to enforce its decisions. Free labour service and slaves, as well as tribute, supported the chief. As long as the chief retained *Poro* support, his rule was secure, but he could be deposed by public opinion, at the command of *Poro* elders. As previously mentioned, the *Poro* elders had authority to hear in private disputes between prominent men and chiefs.

Mende chiefdoms appear to have been established by peaceful amalgamation of settlements in some cases, but more often by conquest and incorporation. Men who served as leading warriors gained land, slaves, and political position. Authority in Mende chiefdoms was held by the descendants of leading warriors, or, when expansion was peaceful, by descendants of the earliest settlers. The paramount ruling lineage was that of the first settler or warrior chief; district chiefs and town chiefs were descendants of the first chief's followers or members of a branch of the chief's lineage. *Poro* leaders and chiefs were linked by some

20. There were nearly seventy independent Mende chiefdoms in Sierra Leone.   *Cf.* Little, 1947; Fenton, 1948; McCulloch, 1950.

duplication of personnel and by the ritual support which the *Poro* provided for the legal acts of chiefs. Thus while a distinction existed between the legal authority of the chief and the moral and ritual authority of *Poro* leaders, successful social control depended on their close cooperation.

The three or four million people of Yorubaland[21] were never united in a single political unit, but at different periods and in several areas confederacies were formed under ritual or military leaders. In the absence of full modern studies and reliable accounts of eighteenth- and nineteenth-century Yoruba government, no comprehensive picture is possible, but some suggestions may be put forward concerning the political systems in Yoruba confederacies. Town organization varied with ties of dependency between the town and the capital of a confederacy, as well as with the secular or ritual position of the chief and councillors. Local administration was in the hands of a town council, which was variously composed of *Ogboni* executive, ward heads, lineage heads, and wealthy men; this council was presided over either by a ritual, hereditary *Oba* or, a rarer and later phenomenon, by an elected, secular *Bale*. In certain Yoruba areas political centralization was achieved under an hereditary ritual leader[22] and council; the central council adjudicated dispute cases and serious offences over a fairly large area, while in each town and village legal sanctions were applied by local leaders. Thus ritual and legal sanctions for serious offences or disputes between towns could be applied by a ritual chief, with the support of his council, over a large territorial unit. Mythical ties[23] gave weight to the authority of the *Oni* of Ife. The centralization under the *Alafin* of Oyo was perhaps more military, less ritual; the appointment of the *Alafin*'s relatives and councillors as overlords of the attached towns ensured the *Alafin*'s rule outside Oyo town. Nineteenth-century civil and Fulani wars brought into existence at Ibadan a strong political unit linking groups without previous ritual ties or strong hereditary leaders. A secular, elective, military state was established, the local agents of which exercised legal sanctions in carrying out the *Bale*'s orders. Abeokuta, in contrast, was ruled by a ritual chief, the *Alake*. Here there was a state council, *Ogboni*, with legal sanctions, a council of trade chiefs, and a military council which led in war. An open meeting of all adult males, led by these groups, was called to discuss major issues.

Whether the authority of a Yoruba chief was legal, ritual, or both, he headed a loose confederacy within which most administration was local, but major disputes or offences could be brought to his court. This

21. Johnson, 1921; Fadipe, 1940; Forde, 1951; Biobaku, private communication.
22. E.g., in Ijebu, the *Awujale;* in Ife, the *Oni.*

23. The claim that all Yoruba are descended from ancestors at Ife.

type of centralization was accompanied by some occupational specialization, urbanization, the appointment of agents of the central government in towns, compulsory military service, and the collection of
tribute.

In Ashanti[24] the head of the founding matrilineage was headman of
a village. He was assisted by a council of local matrilineage heads. Cases
between lineages or between members of two lineages could be taken to
the village headman by one or both of the parties swearing the oath of
the founding lineage. This insulted the headman's ancestors; they would
ritually punish the swearer unless his case was just. The village headman,
in consultation with his council, decided the case and stated the penalty
—in most cases a fine. If the party found guilty did not pay, he would
be ritually punished by the headman's ancestors. Intervillage cases and
appeals in village cases could be heard in the capital of a chiefdom or
state (*oman*) by the chief and his councillors. The chief's council consisted of the heads of matrilineages in the capital town; each acted as
intermediary between the chief and one or more of the outlying villages,
or a subdistrict. Cases were brought to the chief's court in the same way
as to the village headman's court: by swearing the oath of his lineage.
This court is vaguely said to have had jurisdiction over "important
cases" in the chiefdom. The Ashanti confederacy consisted of a number
of such chiefdoms, with Kumasi as the capital of the paramount chief.
The chief of Kumasi was the *Asantehene;* his councillors were the heads
of dominant lineages in Kumasi. As a chiefdom, Kumasi was administered
just like any other. But the *Asantehene* held the right to approve any
execution ordered by a lesser chief, that is, he alone could enforce
capital punishment. The councillors of the *Asantehene* were intermediaries between each chiefdom in the confederacy and the *Asantehene*
for ordinary affairs, but matters of war, interchiefdom disputes, and the
installation of a new *Asantehene* called for the full Ashanti council composed of the Kumasi councillors and chiefs of the several states. The
Asantehene and his council constituted the supreme legal authority in
Ashanti, having the power to call out a military force against rebel
chiefs. Furthermore, the *Asantehene* performed rituals vital to the well-
being of all Ashanti; his ancestors were the supreme ritual powers, who
punished offences defined as sins.

Dahomey[25] was more centralized and appears to have laid greater
stress on legal than on moral and ritual sanctions in maintaining the state
organization. While there seem to have been a number of districts, each
in charge of a chief, the king of Dahomey controlled most villages
directly. His personal agents were sent out to observe the actions of

24. Rattray, 1923, 1929; Manoukian, 1950;   25. Herskovits, 1937.
Busia, 1951.

district officials and village heads, whether these held hereditary offices or were themselves appointees. Such agents brought all important matters to the king's attention. The king extorted high taxes and required military service of all his people; all disputes not settled within a village, and all serious offences, were supposed to come to his court. It was believed that a culprit not apprehended by the secular authorities would be supernaturally punished, and some ritual surrounded the kingship; but the general impression is that the king's position was based mainly on the strong legal sanctions he commanded. He himself appointed all governmental officials and could dismiss them for disloyalty.

The Fulani Emirate of Bida[26] superseded the Nupe kingdom in the nineteenth century. The countryside was divided into (1) royal domains, administered by local officials responsible directly to the king; (2) fiefs which were smaller, also largely locally administered, but held by an official of the central government who collected tribute and might place his dependants on land there; and (3) lands outside Nupe proper from which tribute was exacted by members of the royal lineage. A Nupe village head had a clearly defined realm of legal jurisdiction, limited to minor cases in which he, in consultation with his council of village elders, could impose small fines or flogging. Serious cases were referred to the court of the *alkali*, a Moslem judicial officer, in the capital. Two kinds of offences, ritual offences and those limited to a kinship group (such as inheritance disputes and breaches of exogamy), were not handled by political officers but were punished by moral and/or ritual sanctions. The central government had increased its power by shifting legal jurisdiction from local officials to the Bida court. Titles of highest status were held by members of the Fulani royal nobility. Posts in the civil and military councils, and in the high ranks of Moslem judiciary and clergy, were all by appointment of the king, the royal nobility, and the state council. Each of these offices was associated with a fief.

The differences of legal and political structure among these states can perhaps best be understood by considering the ways in which the states were formed. Ashanti and the Mende and Yoruba states were confederacies, based on a group of previously independent smaller states. Dahomey appears to have incorporated previously uncentralized groups by expansion from a single military centre. When the Fulani took over Nupe, they took over a disintegrating state; Bida Emirate utilized some of the pre-Fulani political forms but further centralized the administration. Thus Ashanti, Yoruba, and Mende paramount chiefs reserved only a few legal powers, but they had the right to declare war and quell rebellion, civil disturbances, and attempted secession. Dahomey and Nupe

26. Nadel, 1935, 1942.

had greater legal centralization, although Nupe officials had somewhat specialized functions and considerable independence of action. Finally, the king of Dahomey was an autocratic ruler.

In all these West African states, the ruling group had economic privileges, and the use of legal sanctions was correlated with economic advantage. Where officials were hereditary or possessed special skills, they had some independent authority and income, but where, as in Dahomey, office depended on favoritism, the king controlled both authority and economic privilege.

Characteristically, in these states, authority was based on tradition; legislation was infrequent. Furthermore, the political system was supported by myth and ritual, either with sacred kingship (Ashanti, Dahomey, Yoruba), through its connection with a cult (Mende), or by a state religion (Nupe). Powerful ritual sanctions were available to the king. But in states, legal sanctions were applied to offences which were treated with moral or ritual sanctions in stateless societies, and the state's authority was guarded by legal sanctions. The population of a state seems to be too large and heterogeneous for effective overall control by moral and ritual sanctions.

West African Authority Systems

We seem to have, in West Africa, four general types of society: one, as in Tallensi, in which authority is exercised only in and through kinship groups; a second with authoritative associations and kinship groups (Ibo and Yakö); a third where authority is exercised by kinship groups, associations, and state organization (Mende and Yoruba); and the fourth which has state organization and subordinate kinship groups, while associations are absent or of minor political importance (Ashanti, Dahomey, Nupe).

In general, unilineal descent groups maintained order with moral and ritual sanctions, but a lineage head was often empowered to apply some legal or moral-legal sanctions. Descent-group heads were commonly thought to have a special relationship with the lineage or clan ancestors, and could exclude an errant lineage member from their ritual protection. Among the Tallensi ritual sanctions and social ostracism were the only mechanisms of social control beyond the lineage. Disputes between members of two clans or two ritual groups could be settled by the arbitration of the heads of the groups involved, but the heads could only threaten offenders with ritual sanctions. When arbitration failed or was not attempted, the disputing parties resorted to feud. Tribal ritual sanc-

tions forced a truce in Tallensi feuds during tribal ceremonies, but did
not end them.

Where a combination of kinship groups and associations was found,
as in Ibo and Yakö, disputes involving members of different kinship
groups could be settled by an authority empowered to exercise sanctions.
Umueke Ibo associations threatened ritual sanctions and acted with
public approval, but had no access to legal sanctions; associations in
some other parts of Iboland used legal as well as ritual sanctions. Some
Yakö associations had authority to apply legal sanctions, mainly at the
request of a ritually authoritative group, while others exacted by
threatening ritual sanctions. Associations in general relied less on the
moral sanction of public opinion than on the ritual or legal sanctions
which they controlled.

Mende and Yoruba combined state structure with active associations,
and had as their local base lineage groups. But they made quite different
use of these three types of groups in social control. The Mende had a
secular political structure consisting of a hierarchy of chiefs; these
offices were hereditary within particular lineages, so that the descent
groups had clearly defined positions in the political system. The activities
of Mende associations were, in the main, ritual, while chiefship was a
secular office employing legal sanctions. Yet the *Poro* could control the
actions of secular rulers. Yoruba paramount chiefs (except the *Bale* of
Ibadan) held ritual offices; legal sanctions were controlled by associations or by the state. However, the ritual chief's approval was required
before an offender could be executed or otherwise penalized by an
association. In both Mende and Yoruba, government was a combination
of chiefship and associations.

The activities of associations in Dahomey and Nupe were restricted,
as far as sanctions were concerned, to certain acts committed by their
own members. No associations are reported for Ashanti. Authority in
the Ashanti, Dahomey, and Nupe states was a monopoly of the state
organization. In Ashanti, the head of each lineage was placed in the
political hierarchy by the traditional position of that lineage in the
state. Nupe and Dahomey, on the other hand, were manned mainly by
appointed officers; only the kingship was hereditary. The king of
Dahomey controlled all offices personally, but in Nupe many positions
were prerogatives of members of the several branches of the royal
lineage. Under the Fulani, judicial powers in Nupe were in the hands
of a trained, specialist body, the Moslem *alkalai*.

Throughout West Africa, moral and ritual sanctions were an integral
part of the authority system. In the village everywhere moral sanctions
probably remained the most common control mechanism, and not even
the king of Dahomey could consistently defy the moral sentiments of

his subjects. In the state, legal sanctions were of increasing importance in maintaining authority, and the more highly organized states had elaborate legal systems; that is, offences were classified, and the punishments appropriate to them were defined and regularly applied by a particular body. Legal authority in all the states was supported by myth and ritual, and ritual sanctions were believed to punish some offences automatically.

In unilineal descent groups ritual sanctions supported moral authority in the control of members and dependants. Ritual associations might take physical measures to punish disapproved acts, but more generally effective was the belief that the association's spirit would punish offenders, either automatically or at the instance of association leaders.

West African societies seem, then, to have maintained authority in the local or kinship group with moral sanctions, variously supported by the threat of ritual or legal sanctions. Associations were an important organ of government in larger aggregates, where state organization was absent, and in the less centralized states. They exercised authority over the community by means of ritual or legal sanctions, or both. States were concerned with disputes in which moral sanctions had failed, and with regulations made by the state which moral authority was inadequate to maintain; in punishing these they applied legal sanctions, often combining them with the threat of ritual sanctions.

Bibliography

Bascom, William. 1942. "The Principle of Senority in the Social Structure of the Yoruba," *American Anthropologist*, xliv.

——1944. *The Sociological Role of the Yoruba Cult Group*. Memoir 63, American Anthropological Association.

Bohannan, L. 1949. "Dahomean Marriage: A Revaluation," *Africa*, xix.

Bovill, E. W. 1933. *Caravans of the Old Sahara*. London.

Busia, K. A. 1951. "The Position of the Chief in the Modern Political System of Ashanti." London.

Fadipe, N. A. 1940. "The Sociology of the Yoruba." Ph.D., Thesis, London University.

Fenton, J. S. 1948. *Outline of Native Law in Sierra Leone*. Freetown.

Forde, C. D. 1937. "Land and Labour in a Cross River Village," *Geographical Journal*, xc.

—— 1939a. "Government in Umor," *Africa*, xii.

—— 1939b. "Kinship in Umor," *American Anthropologist*, xli.

—— 1941. *Marriage and the Family Among the Yako in South-Eastern Nigeria*. London.

—— 1950a. "Double Descent among the Yakö," in *African Systems of Kinship and Marriage*, London.

—— 1950b. "Ward Organization among the Yakö," *Africa*, xx.

The Struggle for Independence: The Tribe, Tribalism,
and the Conditions for Social Development

—— 1951. *The Yoruba-speaking People of South-Western Nigeria.* London.

—— and Jones, G. I. 1950. *The Ibo and Ibibio-speaking Peoples of South-Eastern Nigeria.* London.

Fortes, M. 1936. "Food in the Domestic Economy of the Tallensi," *Africa,* ix.

—— 1940. "The Political System of the Tallensi of the Northern Territories of the Gold Coast," in *African Political Systems,* London.

—— 1945. *The Dynamics of Clanship among the Tallensi.* London.

—— 1948. "The Ashanti Social Survey," *Rhodes-Livingstone Journal,* vi.

—— 1949a. *The Web of Kinship among the Tallensi.* London.

—— 1949b. "Time and Social Structure," in *Social Structure.* London.

—— 1950. "Kinship and Marriage among the Ashanti," in *African Systems of Kinship and Marriage.* London.

Green, M. M. 1941. *Land Tenure in an Ibo Village.* London.

—— 1947. *Ibo Village Affairs.* London.

Greenberg, J. 1949. "The Negro Kingdoms of the Sudan," *Trans. New York Acad. Sci.* Series II, vol. ii.

Herskovits, M. 1937. *Dahomey.* New York.

Hofstra, S. 1937. "Personality and Differentiation in the Political Life of the Mende," *Africa,* x.

Johnson, S. 1921. *The History of the Yorubas.* London.

Le Hérissé, A. 1911. *L'ancien royaume du Dahomey.* Paris.

Little, K. L. 1947. "Mende Political Systems in Transition," *Africa,* xvii.

—— 1948a. "Land and Labour among the Mende," *African Affairs,* xlvii.

—— 1948b. "The Mende Farming Household," *The Sociological Revue,* xl.

—— 1948c. "The Poro Society as an Arbiter of Culture," *African Studies,* vii.

—— 1949. "The Role of the Secret Society in Cultural Specialization," *American Anthropologist,* li.

Manoukian, M. 1950. *The Akan and Ga-Adangme Peoples of the Gold Coast.* London.

McCulloch, M. 1950. *The Peoples of Sierra Leone Protectorate.* London.

Meek, C. K. 1934. "Ibo Law," in *Essays Presented to C. G. Seligman.* London.

—— 1937. *Law and Authority in a Nigerian Tribe.* London.

Nadel, S. F. 1935. "Nupe State and Community," *Africa,* viii.

—— 1940. "The Kede: A Riverain State in Northern Nigeria," in *African Political Systems.* London.

—— 1942. *A Black Byzantium.* London.

Rattray, R. S. 1923. *Ashanti.* Oxford.

—— 1927. *Religion and Art in Ashanti.* Oxford.

—— 1929. *Ashanti Law and Constitution.* Oxford.

Ward Price, H. L. 1933. *Land Tenure in the Yoruba Provinces.* Lagos.

Max Gluckman

TRIBALISM IN MODERN BRITISH CENTRAL AFRICA

During the last twenty years, fourteen members of the staff of the Rhodes-Livingstone Institute in Northern Rhodesia have studied both tribes and urban situations in British Central Africa. In this lecture I discuss some of the results of our researches. I am going to concentrate on describing how we see the persistence of tribalism into modern times, in spite of the industrial revolution which has produced such great social changes. Our main argument is that in the rural areas membership of a tribe involves participation in a working political system, and sharing domestic life with kinsfolk; and that this continued participation is based on present economic and social needs, and not merely on conservatism. On the other hand, tribalism in towns is a different phenomenon entirely. It is primarily a means of classifying the multitude of Africans of heterogeneous origin who live together in the towns, and this classification is the basis on which a number of new African groupings, such as burial and mutual help societies, are formed to meet the needs of urban life. In both rural and urban areas, these affiliations to fellow tribesmen have to be analysed as they operate alongside new forms of association, such as Christian sects, political pressure groups, and economic groups. These new groups are clearly more important in the towns than in the rural areas. Persisting loyalty to a tribe therefore operates for a man in two quite distinct situations, and to a large extent he can keep these spheres of activity separate.

The study of whether tribalism is dying out, or persisting and growing in strength, was obscured in early British studies by a fundamental fallacy in sociological analysis. It is easily understood that Government administrators and missionaries should think of an African miner in the new copper mines as being the same man as he who left his tribal

Reprinted from *Cahiers d'études africaines*, Vol. 1 (January 1960), pp. 55–70, by permission of the editors. This was taken from a lecture given at the Ecole pratique des hautes études, Sixth Section.

home a short time before. These men of affairs therefore considered that the African tribesmen who came to the towns were undergoing a process of "detribalization," in which they were changed; and change here meant being spoilt. Worse than this, in the towns, away from the control of their chiefs, they fell gullibly into the arms of agitators. Most British administrators, and many missionaries, considered that Africans who tried to form trade unions or political associations, and Europeans who tried to help them, were subversive, corrupting the simple and honest tribesmen. I myself found that this attitude had persisted among administrators in Northern Rhodesia as late as 1947. I remember an intelligent Labor Officer, in the Department responsible for the relations between European employers and African laborers, telling me that things would be better if the Northern Rhodesian European Mineworkers Union went out of existence, and the problems of European mineworkers were handled by the Labour Department. As I say, we can understand that many administrators should fail to read the lessons of the last two hundred years of history, which show that modern industrial towns have everywhere produced specific types of associations arising from the needs of urban life, and hence that we must expect these associations inevitably to develop in Africa. It is important to remember that the early British administrators came largely from upper-class and middle-class country backgrounds, and hence knew little about the problems of industrial society. In Africa, they lived and ruled in vast rural domains, and the traditions of a paternalistic government looking after simple tribesmen developed there. Later administrators continued to be drawn from the same groups, with, in addition, sons of professional people. I met no administrator who was acquainted at first hand with the problems of industrial life. All newly appointed administrators served their first years on rural stations, and thus were indoctrinated with the Government tradition that towns and mines were almost places of iniquity in an Arcadian tribalism, where the decent natives were exposed to luxurious temptation and seditious developments.

These doctrines were never, of course, explicitly formulated, but they ran like a thread through the approach of administrators to the problems of modern life, until the end of the War, and perhaps the advent of a Labor Government in Britain, brought some change.

It is more surprising to me that British and other anthropologists were to some extent influenced in a similar way, and I am not sure that all have yet escaped from these influences. Our anthropologists, like our administrators, were reared on the rural tradition of the tribes. For them, the tribe was the "zero point," the start from which people changed as they came under urban and other Western influences: hence the starting point of analyses was the original tribe and the original tribesman.[1] Correspondingly, when some anthropologists began to study Africans in the towns, they saw the problems to be studied as those arising from the adaptation of a tribesman to urban conditions, and formulated these in terms of a process of "detribalization," which had to be analysed and measured as the tribesman slowly changed. . . .

I have said that it is surprising that anthropologists should adopt this point of view, because the whole stress of our analyses lies on the difference between persons and the roles they occupy in the social structure. Furthermore, our theories stress the extent to which the social structure exerts pressure which controls the behavior of the occupants of roles. Hence it has always seemed to me that we must approach the study of African towns dominantly by regarding them as towns: in short, the fact that Africans now live, for longer or shorter periods, in towns, will influence their behavior far more than the fact that they come from tribal homes and cultures. An African townsman is a townsman, an African miner is a miner: he is only secondarily a tribesman. That is, I would anticipate that as soon as Africans assemble in towns and engage in industrial work they will begin to form social relationships appropriate to their new situation: they will try to combine to better their conditions in trade unions, and so forth. Of course, these Africans continue to be influenced by many factors arising outside the urban situation: the rapid growth of the towns and their own inexperience of towns, the constant movement of African laborers between tribe and town and between towns, and the tribal culture and life from which they come, as well as customary linkages and hostilities between different tribes. But even these tribal influences operate now in an urban milieu, and not in a rural milieu. Thus I stated in an early essay that "in a sense every African is detribalised as soon as he leaves his tribal area, even though he continues to be acted on by tribal influences. He lives in different kinds of groupings, earns his livelihood in a different way, comes under different authorities."[2] He walks on different ground, for roads and pavements may be paved; he draws his water from taps and his food from stores; etc. He is ruled now not by District Commissioner and chief, but by District Com-

---

1. See essays in L. P. Mair (ed.), "Methods of Study of Culture Contact in Africa," Memorandum XV of the International Institute of African Languages and Culture, 1932 (here only I. Schapera and M. Fortes took the point of view I shall advocate). The view I am criticising emerges clearly in B. Malinowski, The Dynamics of Culture Change (Yale University Press, 1946); cf. my critical essay, "An Analysis of the Sociological Theories of Bronislaw Malinowski," Rhodes-Livingstone Paper, No. 16, 1948.

2. M. Gluckman, Seven-Year Research Plan of the Rhodes-Livingstone Institute, Human Problems in British Central Africa, Rhodes-Livingstone Journal, No. 4, Dec. 1945.

missioner and municipal authority and location superintendent and European manager. In my own view, therefore, it seemed essential to start analyses of town life by saying that the moment an African crossed his tribal boundary, he was "detribalized," outside the tribe, though not outside the influence of tribe. Correspondingly, when a man returns from the towns into the political area of his tribe he is tribalized—de-urbanized—though not outside the influence of the town.

The first study of a British Central African town was by the late Dr. Godfrey Wilson, first Director of the Rhodes-Livingstone Institute, in the mining town of Broken Hill.[3] Wilson formulated some of his main problems in terms of the changes in behavior of African town-dwellers, according to the length of time they had resided in the town. His study is penetrating and important, but I consider it was still dominated by the tribal outlook I have been describing. My colleagues who followed Wilson in making studies of Rhodesian towns have approached these from the opposite point of view. That is, they have started their analyses on the assumption that they are dealing with town-dwellers, many of whom come from tribes and retain ties with these tribes. Here perhaps the most important books are Professor J. C. Mitchell's *The Kalela Dance,*[4] and Dr. A. L. Epstein's recent book on *Politics in an Urban African Community.*[5]

One main theme of Epstein's study is an analysis of how, during the growth of a copper-mining town, typical urban associations and industrial groupings ousted European attempts to work with authorities based on tribal affiliation. I summarise this history fairly briefly, and will then draw out some of the sociological implications which have been analysed by Mitchell and Epstein. When the copper mine at Luanshya was established in the early 1930's, Europeans provided the managerial and skilled working force: the heavy labor was performed by thousands of Africans from tribes spread over British, Belgian, and Portuguese territories. The mine, like many industrial enterprises in Europe's industrial revolution, had to provide both order and some social services for this heterogeneous population. Government's resources were not adequate for these tasks, and in any case both European and African mineworkers dwelt on the private property of the mine. The mine provided houses for Europeans and Africans, hospitals, recreational facilities, institutions to distribute food to the Africans. The Africans were housed in a vast compound under a Compound Manager (later called African Personnel Manager). He

3. An essay on the Economics of De-tribalisation in Northern Rhodesia, in 2 parts, *Rhodes-Livingstone Papers,* Nos. 5 and 6, 1941 and 1942.
4. *Rhodes-Livingstone Paper,* No. 27, 1956.

5. Manchester University Press for the Rhodes-Livingstone Institute, 1958. See also his publications on the work of African Urban Courts, cited in his bibliography.

was responsible for the housing and welfare of the Africans, for dealing with their working conditions and complaints, and for maintaining order among them and settling their quarrels. In this work he was aided by African clerks, mine police, etc. Faced with thousands of Africans of different tribes, the mine officials, reasonably enough, thought that it would be wise to deal with them through representatives of the tribes as groups. Therefore the Compound Manager instituted a system of Tribal Elders. They were given special houses and robes. His idea was that the mine management could communicate with its African laborers through the Elders while the Elders in turn would inform the management of the wishes and complaints of their tribesmen. In addition, the Elders would see to the welfare of newcomers to the mine until these were allocated houses or found friends, a most important duty in a system of migrant labor with men moving constantly from tribe to town and back again, and between town and town, and between jobs in each town. Finally, the Elders acted as judges in the small disputes that arose between men and their wives. The Elders together constituted a Council. The People themselves welcomed this institution. Meanwhile a similar system was established in the Municipal Location which had grown up in the town, distinct from the mine's compound.

Most of the Elders or Tribal Representatives, chosen by the Africans themselves, were fairly closely related to the royal families of the tribes concerned. The authority system of the tribe was projected into the urban, industrial sphere.

This system of administration worked fairly well until, in 1935, there were major disturbances throughout the area of the copper-mining towns (which is called the Copper Belt). These disturbances arose out of African demands for better pay and working conditions. A strike began in two other mines, and the Superintendent at Luanshya asked his Tribal Elders what would happen in Luanshya. They assured him that there would be no disturbances there. The Superintendent asked the Elders to go among the miners and calm them, but one of the Elders, a senior man, was driven away from a meeting and accused of being in league with the Europeans. A mob stormed the Compound Office, and the Elders had to seek sanctuary within it. Clearly they had neither influence nor power within the strike situation. Yet after the disturbances, the Elders resumed their previous role. By 1937 there was some forty accredited Elders on the mine, and Epstein says that "the system of Tribal Elders operated satisfactorily in the main, and was appreciated by the mass of the people" (p. 36).

I have time only to touch on Epstein's analysis of the background to this development. He stresses the tribal background of the Elders— their frequent affiliation with the families of chiefs, their acquaintance with tribal customs and values, their skill in adjudicating disputes, and so forth. Yet, in a way paradoxically, they came simultaneously to be associated with the European mine management. During the strike they were driven away as in league with the Europeans. Two important elements in their positions have therefore to be stressed. First, as tribal representatives, whose authority was based in the political system of the tribe, they had no connection with the situations in which African miners worked in the mine itself. Here the workers were organised in departments and gangs within which tribal affiliation was irrelevant; and it was in this situation that common interests had brought the miners to joint action in the strike. This was industrial action, and here tribal divisions and allegiances did not operate. So the Elders lacked all influence over the workers in this situation. But, secondly, in the administrative system the Elders had become representatives of the mine itself, in dealing with its workers, and hence when those workers came into conflict with the mine, they regarded the Elders as enemies. When the strike had ended, the Elders could resume their former role.

This position changed slowly until a second series of strikes broke out on the Copper Belt in 1940. There were disturbances, with shooting of miners, at Nkana mine, but none at Luanshya. At Mufulira mine a strike committee of seventeen men was set up to negotiate with the management. At all mines, the authority of the Elders was rejected, and the strike committee at Mufulira was the beginning of a new regime which was to oust tribal affiliation as a basis for handling industrial matters among African miners. For eventually after the War, the British Government (now a Labor Government) sent out trained unionists to help Africans form trade unions. The development of trade unionism was present among the Africans themselves, but it was now encouraged by Government policy. Eventually, the African Mineworkers Union emerged as a powerful, organized, industrial union throughout the mining towns of Northern Rhodesia, negotiating with the management. As its last step on the way to power, the Union insisted that the Tribal Elders system be abolished, for the trade union leaders saw the Elders as a threat to their own authority, and as a means which the mine might use to oppose them. A referendum was held among the miners: 85 per cent of the 35,000 miners voted, and of these 97 per cent voted for abolition of the Tribal Elder system. The trade union had finally ousted the formal organized power of tribal representatives from the industrial field, though later I will describe how tribal affiliation continued to influence trade union politics.

The story of developments which Epstein gives for the municipal compound is similar, but not so clear-cut. He suggests that the monolithic structure of the mine with its centralized power over the working, residential, etc. lives of the workers, provoked the response of a monolithic African trade union, also catering for many aspects of the miner's life, and unable to tolerate any rivals. On the other hand, the municipal compound is inhabited by the employees of many different employers in various trades, by domestic servants, by independent tradesmen, and so forth. Hence there has been less pressure to combined action by Africans in trade unions, and less possibility of their organising thus. Nevertheless in the municipal compound also, developments have been similar to those on the mine. The authority of Tribal Elders, outside of the settlement of small disputes, has been steadily ousted by bodies including better educated and more profitably employed Africans, who have less connection with families of chiefs and who are more permanently settled in the town. Secondly, wherever the Government has set up administrative councils or even courts to help it deal with the heterogenous African population, a spontaneous opposition has developed in the urban population itself. The two processes have worked together, for the Government's policy has been based on the use of tribal affiliations, while the educated Africans have been insisting that leaders in the towns must be acquainted with urban ways of life, and need not be guardians of tribal customs. But here the position is far more fluid than on the mine.

Epstein goes on to point out that the dominance of the trade union did not eliminate tribal allegiances within the industrial field. To some extent, they have ceased to be so significant in industrial matters where the Africans are opposed in their interests to the European mine officials and management. But in matters between Africans, tribal affiliation is important. Thus elections within the union for official posts in the union have to some extent been fought on tribal lines: other tribes complained that the leadership was dominated by the Bemba tribe. And, at the other end of the scale, Nyakyusa tribesmen from Southwest Tanganyika talked of forming a separate Nyakyusa trade union, though in practice they joined in a general strike. Epstein explains that the Nyakyusa are so far from home that during a strike they do not get support, as Northern Rhodesian tribes do, of food from their rural homes. In addition, they are mostly without their wives, so do not have women to cultivate gardens for them as additional support. But it is in the struggle for power in the leadership that tribal allegiances have most significance.

Nevertheless even here it is not straight tribal hostility and loyalty that are operating. During the early years of the mine, the posts open for educated Africans were largely taken by Nyasalanders, for the educational system in Nyasaland was earlier established and better than in Northern Rhodesia, and by Barotse, who were similarly advanced. The Nyasalanders had also early gained mining skill by going to work in Southern Rhodesian mines. Finally, Bemba, who are the nearest powerful

The Struggle for Independence: The Tribe, Tribalism, and the Conditions for Social Development

tribe, had filled many of the minor authoritative posts on the mine. Hence while many Africans see the struggle for leadership on the mine in tribal terms, this covers a struggle between groups of different skill. After the firm consolidation of the trade union's power, a dispute began with the mines and the European trade unions not only for better pay for Africans, but also for the opening of better paid posts demanding higher skill. Hence the issue emerged, whether the union was to press for a few highly paid openings for a few well-educated Africans, or for much better all-round opportunities for the mass of relatively unskilled laborers. Out of this struggle, a new and militant leadership, more representative of the laborers, won many union elections. The struggle reached its climax when the mine management opened new skills to Africans and put them on a monthly salary, instead of payment by ticket of work done. It also insisted that they join a new and separate union, formed by salaried Africans and led by a Barotse. The old union came out on strike against this move; and eventually the Government, holding that this was a political strike, arrested sixty-two trade union leaders and deported them to their tribal areas.

The significance for us of this strike is that it brought into the open the emergence within the African urban population of affiliations based on what we can call "class principles." In the most recent struggle for leadership of the union, and in the formation of the new union, we see that there has emerged among the Africans a division of interests in the industrial field. As soon as the trade union had consolidated its power against the potential rivalry of old tribal leaders, its members (like allies in other situations) split apart in pursuing independent interests. This, perhaps, we might also expect from the history of Europe.

The division on class lines has what Dr. Epstein calls a "pervasive" effect. It spreads into many institutions. For the ideal of a Europeanized and civilized way of life is the ideal which the Africans now follow. Professor Mitchell has examined the effect of this situation on the Kalela dance. His analysis is based on the interpretation of how the general social situation influences the structure and actions of a single dance team. The Kalela dance is a very popular dance on the Copper Belt. It is danced by teams of Africans who come from single tribes. During their dances they mock other tribes, by alleging, among many unpleasant habits, that they have loose, and even perverted, sexual lives. Thus on the surface the dance proclaims proudly the virtues of the team's own tribe, and derides other tribes. Yet the members of the derided tribes attend the performance and laugh as loudly as any at the salacious wit against themselves. Mitchell was struck by the fact that despite this surface of tribal competitiveness, the dancers had named their hierarchy of officials after the hierarchies of British military or civil dignity. Moreover, the dancers did not wear tribal dress: instead, they were dressed in smart and clean European clothes, and they had to maintain their tidiness and smartness throughout the dancing. This was insisted on, although the dancers themselves were mostly unskilled, and poorly educated, laborers. From this point of view he interprets the dance as reflecting the aspirations of all Africans after a European way of life, or civilization, and he shows from other data how the values implicit here form a prestige scale for all Africans. But, he argues, these unskilled laborers are not striving through the dance to participate in the European part of Central African society: this is cut off from them by the color bar. They are striving in the dance to associate themselves with the new African elite. Mitchell shows that in political activity, such as the African opposition to the establishment of the Central African Federation, Africans of all classes and tribes (except the Barotse who are protected by special treaty) united against the Europeans. Internally, they are differentiated on a class scale, which people are striving to ascend. This is one marked trend in the towns, and it seems clearly distinct from tribalism.

Yet the dancing team is a tribal team, deriding other tribes. Its actions have therefore also to be related to a persisting significance of tribal allegiances in the towns. Here Mitchell works out that tribalism in the town operates as a primary mode of classifying the heterogeneous masses of people whom a man meets into manageable categories. With his fellow tribesmen he can converse, and he shares their customs and way of life. In practice, Mitchell discovered that there was far less tribal intermarriage in the towns than is usually assumed, so that a man marries the sisters and daughters of his fellow tribesmen. More than this, by the use of social distance scales, Mitchell found that all the many tribes in the towns were grouped into several limited categories by other Africans, and that specific institutionalized modes of behavior had developed between various tribal categories. Thus he discovered that joking relationships between tribes in this region had developed in modern times, and were not, as previously thought, traditional. Mitchell thus stresses that tribes in towns form categories by which people group one another, and this categorization determined a lot of action in casual as well as intimate relationships. Both he and Epstein stress that in domestic situations, where as we have seen most marriages occur within tribes, tribal custom and practice are effective, though much modified by the demands of the urban situation.

In short, to understand the persistence of tribal links in the towns we have to assess their significance in relation to dominant forms of association, which are produced by the demands of the urban and industrial situation. The people live in towns, as workers, and they associate here in terms of common interests which override tribal divisions. But

The Struggle for Independence: The Tribe, Tribalism, and the Conditions for Social Development

tribal loyalties may influence the internal politics of these urban associations, and political struggles in these associations may, from historical accident, be cast in tribal terms. In leisure activities and in casual intercourse tribalism, in various categories, forms a basis for classifying people. Tribal allegiance and custom dominate in the sphere of domestic life, so far as the situation allows. And in many towns, though not in the Copper Belt, associations of mutual help, funeral societies, etc. are based on common tribal affiliation. But class relationships are becoming increasingly important and, in Epstein's words, pervade every situation. It is worth adding that Epstein found in a later study in a commercial town that former pupils of certain schools felt themselves to be linked together.[6]

Epstein concludes his study by stressing that in our studies of the new African towns we can find plenty of systematic regularities. These are obvious in that people live and go about their business within the towns in relative peace and absence of fear. Hence clearly there is some kind of working, integrated social system in these towns. But the social system must not be thought of as rigid, tight, or self-consistent. The social field of the towns consists of many semi-independent areas of life, in which people associate for specific purposes: to run a home and raise children, to be entertained with friends, to work and improve status, to achieve political objectives, etc. Different principles of social organisation may be effective in the various areas of relations. Hence a trade union can oust Tribal Elders, and with them tribal authority, from the town, without affecting tribalism as a category or even loyalty to a tribal chief in other situations. Let me stress, too, that this situation is not confined to Africans. Tribalism acts, though not as strongly, in British towns: for in these Scots and Welsh and Irish, French, Jews, Lebanese, Africans, have their own associations, and their domestic life is ruled by their own national custom. But all may unite in political parties and in trade unions or employers' federations. Tribalism in the Central African towns is, in sharper form, the tribalism of all towns.

These urban studies all emphasize that tribal associations in these towns do not dominate political life. Tribalism is not an organized set of political relations. Here modern urban tribalism differs radically from tribalism in the rural areas. In the rural areas, under British rule, each tribe is an organized political unit, with a complex internal structure. At its head, in Central Africa at least, there is usually a traditional chief, with a traditional council of elders, and a system of villages and other political units. For here it has been government policy to rule through the tribal organization. Government has thus lent its powerful support

6. Unpublished lectures on Ndola.

to the continued working of the African tribal political systems, as systems. We may also say that continuing, and in the sociological sense conservative, loyalty to chiefs has been important here. Moreover, since the new industrial and urban political associations develop in the towns, they only affect tribal allegiances indirectly. But we also consider that the tribal system in the rural areas serves new needs of tremendous importance to the modern African.

All Africans now want to earn money. They must have money to pay taxes, and they want it to pay for clothes and other European goods, and for schooling and other welfare services. A few of the Central African tribes have been able to earn this money by selling crops and fish; most of them migrate for longer or shorter periods to work in European enterprises, mainly in the towns. But they consider that they have little security in their industrial life. Housing as well as sentiment makes it difficult for them to rear children there; till recently, they could not own houses, which were tied to jobs, and this situation is only slightly changed; there is no provision for unemployment; sickness and accident compensation is very low; there is no provision for work by, or care of, the old, and there are few pensions, and those there are, are small. The insecurity of town employment is constantly brought home to them. All tribal areas have tales like the incident recorded by one of my colleagues, who, when working on the Zambezi River, one morning saw men appear on the other bank—the bank of another territory. One of the men shouted for a canoe, and they were brought across. It was a policeman, repatriating an old blind man. He had left the tribal home thirty years before and never communicated with his kin: now, old and disabled, he was brought back to it, to be supported by whosoever would accept responsibility or feel pity for him. And finally all Africans remember the Great Depression, when the mines closed and thousands of them returned to their tribal homes—as millions of Americans were absorbed back into eking a living on the land in the same crisis. Industrial and urban life offers little security to the vast majority of African labourers, and for this security they cling to their land in their tribal homes. They mostly want to return home, and look forward to it, but in addition this security of land is an ever-present need in the total field where they make their living.[7]

We must think here of these tribesmen who get their money by going out to work as earning their total living in two widely separated

7. The two works which stress this problem most for the region are W. Watson, *Tribal Cohesion in a Money Economy* (Manchester University Press for the Rhodes-Livingstone Institute), and M. Gluckman, Essays on Lozi Land and Royal Property, *Rhodes-Livingstone Paper*, No. 10, 1943.

areas. Basically they depend for security on the land, and many of them leave their wives and children to get their subsistence from the land. Here the old must live. Hence Watson says of the Mambwe on the border of Tanganyika and Northern Rhodesia that they raid the towns for money. If the tribesmen are to exploit their land and to raid the towns, they have to spread their economic activities very widely, and if they are to do this successfully, they need to cooperate with others. In short, there needs to be a group of kin, some of whom go out any one time to earn money, while others remain at home and cultivate the soil and care for cattle—as well as wives and children. Some tribes seem to achieve this organised deployment of men more successfully than others, for a complex of reasons which Dr. Watson has examined, but which I cannot set out here for lack of time. Other tribes are markedly unsuccessful. But all turn to the land for ultimate support.

Land here is not an individual item of land which a man owns for himself and by himself. For he secures his rights to land in two ways. First, as a citizen of the tribe he is entitled to some arable and building land, and to the use of public pasturage, fishing waters, and wild products. Secondly, in all tribes except those who shift their gardens widely and have an abundance of land, he gets rights to land from membership of a village and a group of kinsfolk. That is, a man's rights to land in the tribal home depend on his accepting membership of a tribe, with all its obligations. He holds land as a Barotse, and not a Lunda, and the tribe jealously safeguards these rights. You all know that under Bantu systems of land tenure, which we may summarise as prefeudal, the chief has to distribute land to his subjects, and he often does so through a complicated social hierarchy. I examined the development of land-holding in all the Central and Southern African tribes, and found that in no case, as land got scarcer and hence more valuable, had chiefs expropriated to themselves an unreasonable quantity of land. Instead, they had in various tribes, as pressure on land increased, steadily legislated to safeguard the fundamental right of every tribesman to some land. Thus the first step, taken, for example, among the Ngwaketse in Bechuanaland, was for the chief to take power to commandeer land allocated to a subject which he was not using, for distribution to the landless. Then the chief took power to take over for the landless people land which had lain fallow for a certain period: you will see that when this is done, the cycle of land degradation has begun. The final step is seen in Basutoland, where each family is restricted by law to two-and-a-half acres. People get around these laws by various devices, of course, but the trend of development in the view of both the leaders and the mass of the tribes is clear. Every man who is a member of the tribe has a right to live and support his family on the tribal land.

I am sure that honest fellow-feeling and sympathy and justice have contributed to this legislation. But in addition those who remain behind have an interest in the work of those who go away to the towns, for they bring home the money which the people require. In a way, those who stay at home hold the land as security for support in money from those who go out to work. And those who go out to work pass money to those who remain, in payment for this security. So that they get security by their continued allegiance to the tribe, for they hold land from the chief in return for loyalty and support. Hence they adhere to their chiefs; and as they adhere to the chiefs, they accept with the chiefs, for the rural areas, the organized system of tribal political relations. Very few tribesmen wish to overturn the tribal political system as such, though new interest groups, and new elites, in the tribes may struggle for power in tribal councils. With acceptance of the tribal political system goes acceptance of many customs and observances built into that system.

In tribes where land is worked in cooperating groups of kindred, or where kin organise their departures to towns as I have described before, security in holding of land also involves acceptance of kinship obligations, and with these of many other parts of the tribal culture. I cannot enter further into this part of our analysis, for my time is running out; nor have I time to deal with developments in tribes which earn money by fishing or selling crops.

We see, in short, that tribalism persists in the rural areas because of government support, and because the tie to tribal land is of the utmost importance to a man. With this tie goes acceptance of the tribal political system with its culture, and of its smaller constituent groups with their culture. In short, tribalism in the rural areas consists of participation in a highly organized system of social relations, based strongly on the chief's rights as trustee for his people over the tribal land. Dependence on land and the social relations arising from this dependence, give modern Africans many satisfactions they cannot find in urban life, and also security against the vicissitudes of industrial employment. Tribalism in the towns is not such an organized system of political and other social relations. In the towns, specific urban-type groupings and industrial associations develop, and have ousted the attempts of Europeans to transplant African tribal authority systems to deal with urban industrial problems. But tribal linkages and hostilities affect the struggles within these new forms of association, though sometimes they cloak struggles based on other principles. Tribal ties and attachments still dominate domestic life. And tribalism is a most important basis for grouping people into categories, which determine how a man treats

The Struggle for Independence: The Tribe, Tribalism,
and the Conditions for Social Development

those whom he meets casually. Some associations emerge in which fellow tribesmen band together to help one another. But class linkages are also beginning to pervade the life and the culture of the new towns. In all these respects, African towns differ only in degree from any town, anywhere in the world probably. In crisis, common interests arising from industrial and urban association seem steadily to overcome tribal ties and divisions.

To some extent, though developments in urban and in rural areas affect one another, as I have shown, the specific associations of each may exist independently. Tribal Elders were ousted from the mines by the trade union, yet the leaders in this move treated a visiting chief with respect—until he tried to intervene in an industrial dispute. The Africans' lives are partly dichotomized, and they live in separate compartments— like other men. But there is a mutual influence, which I have not time to examine.

What, then, becomes of "detribalisation," the problem I raised at the beginning of my lecture? Perhaps my intellectual opponents are right, as well as myself. The African is always tribalised, both in towns and in rural areas; but he is tribalised in two quite different ways. As we see it, in the rural area he lives and is controlled in every activity in an organized system of tribal relations; in the urban areas, tribal attachments work within a setting of urban associations. Hence the African in rural area and in town is two different men; for the social situation of tribal home and of urban employment determine his actions and associations, within the major politicoeconomic system covering both areas.

Postscript

I make three points which were raised in the discussion after my lecture:

1. Though I speak of the separation of the African's activities in town and tribal area, I do not consider that this is achieved without both social and mental conflict. Nevertheless, there is considerable resolution of this conflict through the separation of the spheres of activities.

2. The analysis made here is for Northern Rhodesia and Nyasaland, and developments elsewhere may well be different. Industrial and other urban associations have developed less successfully, e.g., in the Union of South Africa, where legislation obstructing these associations are severe. In British Central Africa, until recently, Parliament in Britain had considerable influence on policy. In the Union of South Africa it

appears that tribal affiliations in towns are more significant than in Rhodesia.

3. The whole situation of the chiefs is affected by the presence of both a superior colonial government and European settlers. Hence in the recent political crisis chiefs aligned themselves with urban leaders. The development of local self-government, not dominated by settlers, might here produce a radical difference, as in Ghana; for an indigenous government may be required to reduce the autonomy of tribes and hence the power of chiefs.

Jean
Suret-Canale

THE END OF CHIEFTAINCY IN
GUINEA

On December 31, 1957, there appeared in the official journal of French Guinea a decree signed by Keita Fodeba, Minister of Interior of the 1957 (*loi cadre*) government, suppressing the "so-called customary chieftaincy" over all the territory of Guinea. Nobody would deny that without the suppression of the chieftaincy the success of the "No" vote in Guinea at the time of the constitutional referendum of September 28, 1958, would not have been assured. Several weeks after the referendum, M. Jacques Rabemananjara (today a minister in the Madagascar government) wrote in the preface to the volume reporting on the Conference of District Officers held at Conakry, July 25 and 26, 1957:[1]

> . . . One of the bastions of the [colonial] regime, its heavy artillery used only in grave circumstances, is called African feudalism. There is a paradox in this: faithful to its traditional mission, France declared her intention to lead the peoples for whom it had responsibility to the freedom of self-administration and the ability to democratically manage their own affairs:[2] everywhere she professed to teach the cult of democracy, and yet she never ceased, ever since her original institution in Africa, despite the most eloquent constitutional preambles, to favor either openly or covertly the anachronistic, the most antidemocratic institution that one can imagine: the support, multiplication, and protection of the Galaoui[3] in miniature.

Mr. Rabemananjara continued, citing an African correspondent of the weekly *France-Observateur:* "Let us congratulate Sékou Touré who clearly foresaw the advantages in wiping out the chieftaincy. Liquidation

1. Guinée: prélude à l'indépendance, vol. 1, Report on the conference which made the colonial administration of Guinea confirm the decision to suppress the chieftaincy. *Presence Africaine*, Paris, 1958, foreword, p. 11.

2. Text borrowed from the preamble to the French Constitution of 1946.

3. The Pasha of Marrakech, [great feudal lord and] strong supporter of the French administration of the Moroccan protectorate.

Reprinted in abridged form from *The Journal of African History,* Vol. 7, no. 3 (1966), pp. 459–493, by permission of the publisher. Translated from the French by Irving L. Markovitz.

of feudalism permitted him to lead his own country to independence
on September 28.[4] And he concluded: "Nothing could be truer. Sékou
Touré would have shared the fate of Bakary Djibo[5] if he had not known
how to dismantle, and pulverize, the worm-eaten cadre of unpopular
and reactionary notables."[6]

The opinion of M. Rabemananjara is today almost universally shared:
whether one considers the abolition of the traditional chieftaincy and
the "No" vote of September 28 favorably [as in the case of this author]
or unfavorably, the connection between the two is generally accepted.
The circumstances and the significance of the abolition of the chieftaincy, however, are not always clearly understood. By attributing the
responsibility (and eventually the merit) of this development to Sékou
Touré and his comrades in the *Parti démocratique* of Guinea, one will
probably conclude by imagining that the regulatory measure was something isolated that simply resulted from a freely taken decision in 1957;
a further assumption would be that other leaders in other countries
could have had the same results if only they had been a bit more fore-
sighted. This view of the situation appears in the previously cited text
of M. Rabemananjara, when he writes: "His true merit [that of Sékou
Touré] was to have had an intuition about what were the most important tasks that had to be accomplished without delay. Was not the
loi cadre Defferre under the control of all African leaders? None of
them, except for Sékou Touré, knew how to use it or to transform it
into an effective instrument of government."[7]

Moreover, certain authors who consider themselves politically of
the left, but who no longer share the enthusiasm they felt during the
first years for the regime of Sékou Touré, have come to place the
democratic significance of this measure—if not its very reality—into
doubt. Thus, a collaborator of the review *Revolution*, who uses the
pseudonym "Africanus"[8] but who would not appear to have any direct
knowledge of Guinea, doubts that a simple regulatory measure would
have been able to abolish the chieftaincy and leaves one to understand

4. *France-Observateur*, No. 440, October 9, 1958, p. 23.
5. Leader of the Niger "*loi cadre*" government who called for a "No" vote but
was neutralized by the administration,
then deposed. Today he lives in exile.
(*Loi cadre government* refers to the
1956 enabling law that established the
institutional framework in the territories
for autonomy. In 1958, the De Gaulle
government sponsored a popular referendum in her black African territories
that asked if the people wished to continue their association with France and
that provided an option for independence. To vote "No" meant a complete
and immediate rupture with France.
Only Guinea took this course, and
France, in a great huff, left with everything she had. In 1960, the other territories of French West and Equatorial
Africa became independent on a friendly
and mutually acceptable basis.)
6. *Op. cit.*, p. 12.
7. *Ibid.*
8. *Revolution*, No. 3, 1963.

that, in fact, the disintegration probably has not really occurred at all. Another author, M. Ameillon, who apparently performed administrative functions in Guinea during 1957–1958, sees the suppression as the result of a legal battle or high-level decision made essentially because of political objectives: "It [the chieftaincy] constituted the single restriction to the total power of the Party."[9] It was also a restriction on the interests of big business, insofar as the existence of the customary work obligations could constitute an obstacle to the mobility of labor.[10]

We propose to show, on the basis of documents from the Guinea archives, that these diverse interpretations cannot be maintained. These documents show that the fall of the Guinea chieftaincy was the result of a deep-seated popular movement well before the years 1957–1958. Sékou Touré and the *Parti démocratique* of Guinea doubtlessly contributed to the development and orientation of this movement, but their intervention goes back to a time well before the *loi cadre*, and by 1957–1958 events had already been set into motion. The disintegration of the chieftaincy was an accomplished fact. Its legal suppression was only the final act of a social movement, and it is doubtful that Sékou Touré and his friends could have been in a position to maintain or revive the chieftaincy in 1957—even if they had wanted to.

On the other hand, we can ask if the leaders of the other territories would have been in a position, if they had wished, to suppress the chieftaincy in 1957–1958. Only an examination of the facts and the collection of evidence will enable us to come to a valid conclusion about this question.

Before going to the heart of the matter, it seems necessary to us to rapidly examine the nature of the social situation of the chieftaincy in French West Africa during the classic colonial period (before the Second World War) and particularly what it was like in French Guinea.

Chieftaincy in the French Colonial System[11]

It is traditional to contrast the French system of "direct administration" with the British system of "indirect administration." In fact, the differences between the two systems of administration are much less radical than the terminology that is used would allow one to suspect. Nowhere in Africa did French colonization really put a system of

9. B. Ameillon, *La Guinée, bilan d'une indépendance*, Paris, Maspero, 1964, p. 24.
10. An argument developed after a speech by Sékou Touré at the conference of the *commandants de cercle*.
11. On this question, see R. Cornévin, "Evolution des chefferies dans l'Afrique noire d'expression française," *Recueil Pénant*, Nos. 686–688, 1961; and J. Suret-Canale, *Afrique noire—L'ère coloniale*, Paris, Editions sociales, 1964, pp. 106, 406–413.

"direct administration" into effect. It had always had recourse to the intermediary of the chieftaincy. However, the French did not maintain the legal form of the protectorate in tropical Africa, which gave the principle of sovereignty to the traditional chiefs. Sovereignty was left totally in the hands of the protecting power. Legally, there was no authority other than the colonial authority.

A turning point was reached when the radicals won power at the beginning of the century. The Land Decree of October 23, 1904, ended the fiction of the protectorate in West Africa by annulling the recognized land rights of the local chiefs and wholly transferring them to the French state. The policy of "direct administration," which was the official doctrine from 1904 to 1914, tended to "suppress the great native authorities who were nearly always a barrier between us and our subjects."[12]

This policy was rigorously applied, particularly in Senegal and Guinea. It ended in the liquidation of the great indigenous authorities, including those led by men who had been faithful servants of the French cause, such as Alfa Yaya, "King of the Labe."

However, as a result of the lack of competent personnel, dependency on native intermediaries ended in the *de facto* support of the chieftaincy at the level of the village and district (the traditional political unit in the Malinke country, but more or less artificial elsewhere). In the eyes of the law, these chiefs, who more or less kept their ancient titles and powers, were only non-civil service agents of the colonial administration without any status, and hence without any rights, who were freely removable by the higher administration and subject to the same sanctions applicable to the other "native" subjects. Their essential role was to collect taxes (on which they were granted a rebate—their sole official income) and to furnish laborers for the diverse needs of the administration (porters and men for the construction and upkeep of roads, public buildings, etc.). They benefited by deducting money or work allotments for their own profit (under guise of rent or customary allowance). These exactions were tolerated and, if necessary, even imposed (recalcitrants could be administratively fined or imprisoned under the "Native Code" as being guilty of resistance to the authority's representatives), but since they had no legal basis, they could be used as evidence against a chief that the authorities wanted to get rid of.

No chief could manage without recourse to these methods. The rebates on taxes and the very meager salary which was added later, were not enough to provide a sufficient standard of living or meet his many obligations. The chief had to receive and shelter (royally) the district officer and other representatives of the administration and their retinue

12. Governor-General M. Ponty, *Afrique française*, No. 7, July, 1910.

when they were on tour; pay for a secretary, messengers, one or more representatives to the district headquarters. . . . He had to maintain a court of followers and henchmen, as much to establish his prestige as to affirm his authority by force if necessary.

> When one reproaches the chiefs for surrounding themselves with questionable characters, they, with some reason, answer: "Yes or no, do you wish that we collect taxes, that we provide forced labor and conscripts? We can't do this through sweetness and persuasion; if the people don't fear to be bound and beaten, they will laugh at us.[13]

The absence of a specific statute for the chieftaincy, coupled with its dependent position, contributed to degrade its prestige and moral authority. If the representatives of the traditional hierarchies showed themselves to be insufficiently docile, the colonizer did not hesitate to replace them with parvenus or foreigners who had their confidence— former soldiers or police, indeed even *boys* or cooks who had the favor of a governor. . . . When the war of 1914–1918 intensified and the subsequent reduction of European personnel quickened an appreciation for the importance of the role played by the chieftaincy, Van Vollenhoven reacted by proposing measures indispensable to the consolidation of the chieftaincy's authority: respect for the customary rules in the designation of chiefs, the granting of decorations, raising of pensions, condemnation of abuses in administration, etc. But he strongly maintained the principle that there was but one single source for all authority: "there are not two authorities in the district, the French authority and the native authority; there is only one. Only the District Officer orders; only he is responsible. The native chief is only an instrument, an auxiliary."[14]

As a result, then what was the social condition of the chieftaincy? Certainly, it constituted, as it did during the precolonial period, a privileged social class. Instead of exploiting the peasant masses for its own account, it was reduced to the role of instrument in this exploitation, with the right of collecting a few crumbs along the way. Its integration into the colonial system was accomplished in this manner, but the methods of exploitation remained the same.

This is not the place to debate the usefulness or inapplicability of the term *African feudalism*. We would like to simply note here that, if on the level of political structure the analogy between traditional African aristocracies and the medieval feudalism of Europe is often striking, a major difference separated them on the social and economic

13. Gilbert Vieillard, "Notes sur les Peulhs du Fouta-Djalon," *Bull. I.F.A.N.* No. 1, 1940, p. 129.

14. Circular of August 15, 1917, *Afrique française*, No. 12, December 1917, p. 270.

level. In Europe, feudal relations between vassals and subjects, and the consequent duties of the subjects (especially in matters of rent and dues), were the relationships between the holders of private rights. Individuals were bound to obligations either by virtue of their social status or through their capacity as private property owners (based on rents and land rights). The normal system to which land was submitted was that of private property (and the Church, principal beneficiary of gifts and bequests of land, contributed to its imposition). The relations of the African chief to his subjects applied much more to communities than to individuals. Private property in land was unknown; everywhere land remained collective and inalienable. The chief as heir or usurper of the traditional rights of the "chiefs of the land" could dispose of the land (within certain limits he could have it cultivated for his benefit by control over its usage), but in the precolonial period this right never took the form of a true right to property that would have included the possibility of definitively alienating the land. Rents or *corvées*—even if raised "by head"—were always owned by the village community and raised collectively through the intermediary of the village chiefs as heads of the patriarchal families.

The colonial establishment took over these useful forms of collection for its own use: the district and the village were taxed in money or men (for forced labor or conscription), which were furnished under the personal responsibility of the chief. Customary dues, which to a certain extent had assumed a character that was, if not personal, at least dynastic under the colonial regime took on a character that was much more purely functional. They were part of the offices of the chief. As long as an individual was invested with the chieftaincy, he could dispose of men and land. Within the limits established by usage (and if necessary a little beyond, if he had the means to impose his authority) he could dole out extensive fields and have them cultivated by obligatory labor. But when he was deposed he lost everything to his successor, including the right to assign fields set aside for the village lands, as well as the right to the "customary allowance" without which these fields could not be put to use. He only kept his family lands. In sum, the chieftaincy was not able to transform itself into a land-based aristocracy with hereditary rights. . . .

.   .   .   .

The Chieftaincy in Fouta-Djalon

An analysis in depth of the situation of the chieftaincy in Guinea would require a district-by-district study that we have not had the means to undertake. One can, however, propose a region-by-region overview without too great a risk of serious error. Undoubtedly, it is in the Fouta Djalon district that the position of the chieftaincy was the most firmly based. The chieftaincy here was in effect recruited from a dominant aristocracy whose economic and social positions were not seriously disturbed by colonization. The aristocracy of the "great Peuls" continued to live on the labor of its subjects: the Foulbé Bouroué (the people themselves translate this as "Foulas of the bush"), vassals or clients who were in charge of the herds; and "Matioubé, captives, farmers of Soussou or Diallonké origin who were enslaved and progressively assimilated. Until the Second World War, the situation of the captives (shamefully designated in the administrative reports as "servants") had not seriously changed.

In certain regions of the Soudan, massive emancipation had been effected as much to oblige the former masters to enter productive work as to ruin their political power.[15] In Fouta-Djalon, the necessity of such a measure was not felt from the economic point of view (the only important trade product there was rubber, the product of a type of collecting that was easily adapted to the traditional social framework). Emancipation would have been absolutely contraindicated from the political point of view: by and large the Peul aristocracy had accepted French trusteeship without any resistance, and it would have appeared logical for the colonial administration to base itself on them.[16]

Battles between aristocratic factions had facilitated the occupation of the Fouta by French troops in 1896. The Almamy Soriya Bokar Biro, defeated and killed at the battle of Porédaka, was unpopular even within his own party because of his severity and avarice. A number of his vassals, first among them the chief of the Diwal of Labé, Alfa Yaya, appealed ceaselessly for French intervention against him.[17]

The introduction of the (at first very incomplete) French occupation allowed certain allies, such as Alfa Yaya, to consolidate their position.[18] But this passing tolerance did not mean that the French administration had decided to allow the chiefs much latitude for long. The treaty of the protectorate established on February 6, 1897, with the Fouta (where the Almamy's Oumarou Bademba and Sori Eli replaced Bokar Biro) declared in Article 2: "France commits itself to respect the present constitution of Fouta-Djalon. This constitution will function under the authority of the Governor of Guinea [sic] and under the

15. Cf. Paul Marty, *La politique indigène du Gouverneur-général Ponty*, Paris, E. Leroux, 1915, p. 14.
16. Cf. M. Verdat, "Le Ouali de Goumba," *Etudes guinéenes*, No. 3, 1949, pp. 2–66.

17. Cf. "Lettre du lieutenant Le Brun," April 17, 1896, *Archives nationales du Mali*, Satadougou.
18. *Archives nationales du Mali*, Satadougou, Special report, Feb. 1, 1898.

direct control of a French official who will have the title of Resident of the Fouta-Djalon."

The authority of the Almamys and their rotation in power were maintained by Article 3 of the treaty. But Alfa Yaya was recognized as the " 'permanent chief' [the rule of alternating had been in effect for all chiefs up until then] of the Labé, Kadé, and Gabou. . . . He remained placed under the dependency of the reigning Almamy, but he could address himself directly to the affairs of his province to the Resident of the Fouta-Djalon."[19]

By Ordinance No. 1 of the Resident, approved by a plenary session of chiefs held at Timbo, July 13, 1897, the head tax was introduced at the rate of two francs a person, or ten francs per hut, "each hut being supposed to shelter a minimum of five people."[20] A decree of the government dated November 28, 1897, confirmed this decision while adding work "allowances." The Resident, M. Noirot, dissipated any ambiguities by stating: "The chief must concern himself with the tax and furnish labor for the public works, or if not, he will be broken like glass."[21] The length of the commitment given by the 1897 treaty did not last much more than a year. After the Almamy Eli Sori was assassinated by a brother of Bokar Biro, a proclamation of the Resident Noirot on December 16, 1898, named his son Baba Alimou the Almamy and limited his authority to three out of nine areas. . . . The other areas became independent, especially the area of Labé, where Alfa Yaya took the title of "King of the Labé."[22] "Divide to conquer was the only policy to follow in the Fouta-Djalon," concluded the official report on the situation in Guinea in 1898. . . .[23]

In the same period, when the Almamy Baba Alimou died at the beginning of 1906, his already reduced domain was divided between the representatives of the two families who, up until then, had always alternated in governing.[24] . . . The annual report of 1906 noted that it was one step more towards "the progressive suppression of the great chiefs and the parcelling out of their authority until the village becomes the only administrative entity."[25]

In 1909, Alfa Alimou, the personal enemy of Alfa Yaya and designated for this reason a chief of the province of Labé with a territory that was even more reduced than the former kingdom of Alfa Yaya,

19. *Archives nationales de Guinée*, I.E., 6.
20. *Ibid.*
21. André Arcin, *Histoire de la Guinée française*, Paris, Challamel, 1911, p. 529.
22. *Archives nationales de Guinée*, I.E. 6.
23. *Rapport d'ensemble sur la situation générale de la Guinée française en 1898*, p. 81.

24. We have described this affair in "La Guinée dans le system colonial," *Présence Africaine*, Vol. 29, Dec. 1959–Jan. 1960, pp. 16–18.
25. *Rapport d'ensemble sur la situation générale de la Guinée française en 1906*, Conakry, Imprimérie Ternaux, 1907.

was sentenced to three years in prison and dismissed: the chieftaincy of the province was suppressed. When in 1910, the administrative penalty against Alfa Yaya was concluded, the governor, M. Guy, did not allow him to get further than Conakry. There he was rearrested on February 11, 1911, and this time sent to Mauritania where he died the following year.

At the same time, steps were taken to liquidate a certain number of Marabouts, who the French feared would take over the influence of the traditional aristocracy. The Marabouts Karamoko Sankoun and Ba Gassama of Touba were arrested March 30, 1911. On the other hand, the attempt to arrest the Ouali of Goumba, planned for the same day, failed; the detachment in charge of the operation was annihilated. In reprisal, the region of Goumba was subjected to an array of repression; goods of the Peuls were confiscated and their slaves freed. The Ouali, who sought refuge in Sierra Leone, was extradited, condemned to death, and jailed at Fotoba, where he died in 1912 before the date fixed for his execution.[26]

Finally, in 1912, the administrator Thoreau-Lévaré, friend of Noirot and one of the French colonial officials who best knew the Fouta,[27] proceeded to a knowledgeable division of the traditional provinces to dismember the ancient historic units. The functions of the "Almamy," "a useless machinery, become irritating,"[28] were suppressed. The Almamys of the two branches were transferred from their ancient residences to places located on the railroad which had just been constructed . . . and were reduced to the duties of district chiefs.[29] After this, the situation was stabilized. Reduced to the subordinate functions of district chiefs, the ex-Almamys (who continued to bear this honorary title) received some distinctions and pensions that placed them above their colleagues.[30]

However, the political operations of 1910–1912 brought certain reverses of fortune. Thus, the family of the traditional chiefs of the region of Dalaba, compromised in the affair of the Ouali of Gomba, was removed in favor of an obscure village chief from the family of the Loudabé. Ba Tierno Oumar then succeeded in making a "great fief" out of the district of Dalaba which grew without stopping at the expense of neighboring districts. Among the Peuls, he was considered a *parvenu*, and some compared him to the Glaoui of Marrakech—a small personnage become a "great feudal lord" by grace of the French administration. Thanks to his connections, he knew how to get rid of district

26. Cf. M. Verdat, *op. cit.*, *Archives nationale de Guinée*, I.E. 7.
27. He is the author of a copious volume that served as a source for *Islam en Guinée*, bu Paul Marty.
28. "Gouvernement général de l'A.O.F.,"

Annual report of the meeting of 1912, Paris, Larose, 1915.
29. The regional archives of Mamou, Guinea, have a report by Thoreau-Lévaré, dated 1914, on these operations.
30. Local decree of December 21, 1934.

officials who were insufficiently understanding, and he lost no opportunity to reinforce his credit through demonstrations of loyalty.

Because of the absence of power based on social structures comparable to those of the Fouta, the authority of the chieftaincy was clearly weaker in the other regions. . . .

Guinea Chieftaincy during the "War Effort"

The Guinean chieftaincy hardly evolved at all between the two world wars; its function and methods remained the same, and its situation remained ambiguous: on the one hand, colonial doctrine emphasized the necessity of maintaining and reevaluating the institution in the name of respect for "tradition," . . . but, on the other hand, it did not fail to recall that authority belonged only to the colonizer and that the chief was only an instrument, liable at any moment to be dismissed if he was judged inept for his job. The local decree of December 21, 1934, for the first time fixed the chief's status and salary, without, however, clearing up the confusions. The chief remained an agent of the administration without being an official, tradition served here as a pretext for what was useful and economical. The Second World War then put the institution to a test from which it never recovered.

As in 1914–1918, the period of the war from 1939–1942 was marked by a considerable increase in the demands placed upon the population. However, there were differences: the defeat of 1940 diminished the burden of military recruitment to which the people had become accustomed. But from 1943 on, these charges were again added to economic requirements that were unprecedented. . . .

When Guinea, with the rest of French West Africa fell into the Allied camp, its situation did not improve. On the contrary, the meager provisions that the allies sent in were less for the purpose of improving living conditions than to help raise the output of the war effort (trucks and gas were sent in to help accelerate the collecting and exporting of local products).

Caught between the hammer and the forge, the chiefs had to satisfy these "insane demands" at the expense of those they were supposed to administer. They found the means on occasion to gouge even more out of their subjects than in the past. The rare shipments of goods designated for the bush—sugar and cloth especially—were divided under their supervision. They profited in this by serving themselves and their entourages first, and paying themselves for their services. What was left, with rare exceptions, passed on to the black market.

But it was not easy for them to satisfy the demands of their superiors.

The Struggle for Independence: The Tribe, Tribalism, and the Conditions for Social Development

More than ever, it was necessary to provide goods for export, especially those that the allied war machine needed. More than anything else, these were products that depended completely on the African peasantry for their output. Along the coast and in the forests, there was a demand for tons of palm nuts. Because of a lack of mechanical crushers, men, women, and children had to spend day after day breaking nuts, one by one between two stones. . . .

Immediately following the war, the journal of the RDA, *Le Réveil*, wrote:

> Down to the present time, the African chief was the servant of the district officer. Because he himself was only able to communicate with the D.O. through intermediaries, the chief also had to bow to the authority of its implacable whip. . . . The chief was the man with requisitions for chickens for the commandant, for laborers for the commandant, etc., etc. In a word, he was the inexorable attendant for the administration. He was graded according to his aptitude and his celerity in satisfying the innumerable administrative requirements. Ferociously oppressed, he in turn oppressed.[31]

Despite the rule exempting him from the penalties of the native code, the district chief remained at the mercy of the district officer. This applied even more rigidly in the case of the village chief who was personally responsible for a defaulting community. . . . There was scarely one who had not had a taste of prison at one time or other. . . . The cowardly or too compassionate chief risked the worst, while one who was pitiless was well noted and lived in ease. The war legislation gave such a chief the means: the offense of "opposition to the authority of the chiefs," normally punishable by a fine under the Native Code of one to five days, now received penalties of up to six months in prison.[32] The administrators were not unaware of this situation, but they accommodated themselves to it. In 1942, the deposed chief of the district of Sankaran, Lamine Kondé, was condemned to three years in prison (modified to six months) for being "against the French authority." Translated from administrative language, this meant that "for more than ten years, the population of the district displayed a marked lack of discipline for everything concerned with the execution of their services."[33] On the other hand, the administration had no reproaches for the chief of the Oulada district, Doussou Mori Nabé. It confided its appreciation to the confidential dossiers: "appointed in 1926, a sinister figure of perfect villainy. . . . Former trader, living from monstrous and criminal exactions, he created a veritable terror in his district."[34]

31. *Le Réveil* (Dakar), October 10, 1949.
32. R. Cornévin, "L'évolution des chefferies dans l'Afrique noire d'expression française," *Recuil pénant*, No. 687, 3rd quarter, 1961, p. 388.
33. Political report, 1942, *Archives de Kouroussa*.
34. *Ibid.*, Political report, 1945.

After the War

The end of the conflict, the opening of the first electoral contests, the disappointment of the elites and veterans confronted with the administration's determination to maintain the colonial regime, then the vote by the French Constituent Assembly for laws granting citizenship to the former subjects and abolishing forced labor, opened a crisis which in certain territories seriously disturbed the chieftaincy. This current also swept across Guinea, but did not leave any serious or long-lasting backwash.

For the first election—that of the first Constituent Assembly—the chiefs of the Fouta met at Pita on September 14, 1945, to invest a candidate of their choice, the teacher Yacine Diallo. The electoral body, confined to officials and notables, remained sufficiently restricted so that the chieftaincy's decision could prevail.[35] In 1946, when a second seat in the French National Assembly was accorded to Guinea, another teacher, Mamba Sano, was elected alongside Yacine Diallo. The latter entered the SFIO, while his colleague joined the ranks of the RDA.

The basis of politics was the "ethnic" association: *Association Gilbert Vieillard* (Peuls), *Union du mandé*, *Union forestière*, *Union insulaire* (for the island of Los), *Comité de la Basse Guinée*. These ethnic associations themselves were groupings of "associations d'originaires" from different districts who in Conakry played the role of self-help societies and acted as spokesmen for local interests.

Ethnic and personal rivalries played a much more important role than considerations of political orientation, insofar as these associations had the character of committees of notables much more than mass movements.[36] In spite of the abstention of Yacine Diallo (who was, however, a signer of the appeal for the Bamako meeting), representatives of the ethnic groups participated in the founding congress of the *Rassemblement démocratique africaine* at Bamako in October, 1946.

In the Malinké country, the return of the demobilized troopers provided several shocks. At the beginning of 1947, a former Koranic teacher, a member of the chiefly family of Kanka Lamine Kaba, aroused the veterans against the colonial regime. Immensely vain, demagogic and vague,[37] Lamine Kaba was rapidly bypassed by his own troops. Three to 5,000 veterans installed themselves in the district office of Kankan. After a period of extreme tension between that part of the town which was in the hands of the insurgents and that held by the French army sent

35. Political report, 1945, *Archives de Dalaba.*
36. Sékou Touré, *L'Action politique du Parti démocratique de Guinée*, I, Conakry 1958, pp. 7–12.

37. At the time, RDA denounced him as a provocateur . . . he died in 1960 a deputy to the Guinean National Assembly.

as reinforcements, the movement broke up by itself. Lamine Kaba was arrested and deported to Mauritania. It is interesting to note that in his speeches Lamine Kaba laid the blame on the chieftaincy. Before going on to Kankan his followers destroyed the houses of the district chiefs in several places.[38] But the administrative reports indicate that they directed themselves against particular persons, rather than the principle of the institution.

It was not until May, 1947, before the Guinean section of the RDA was created, following a tour of Gabriel d'Arboussier, its Secretary-General. D'Arboussier had interviews with the chiefs of the Fouta, especially Ba Thierno Oumar. He thought he had won their commitment, but the new section, which was a simple coordinating committee uniting the delegates of the ethnic groups, very rapidly fell apart, especially when the eviction of Communist ministers from the French government emphasized the antagonism between the administration—faithful to the colonial methods—and the RDA—affiliated on the parliamentary level with the French Communist Party.

The chieftaincy, after having appeared to accept the advance of the democratic tide, recoiled. "The Guinean section of the RDA burst apart, allowing a small minority of democrats to speak in its name and on the basis of its program."[39] Thus, the political report of 1947 mentioned the formation at Dakar of a branch "which grouped together fifteen Africans with a bureau of teachers or agricultural monitors and two notables" in difficulty with the chief of the district.[40] At the beginning of 1948, the RDA was "reduced to a few units" despite the entrance of Sékou Touré, who founded a local trade union. . . .

Apart from a few isolated cases, such as the territorial councilor Camara Kaman of Macenta and a small group of stalwarts at Conakry, the civil servants, who in 1947 constituted the principal clientele of the RDA, abandoned the struggle because of threats to their careers. Supported by the administration, the chieftaincy either took over the situation or kept it in hand. But its moral authority was henceforth profoundly impaired. In spite of turmoil and condemnations, the Guinean RDA, at the same time that it consolidated its urban positions through the unions, confronted the chieftaincy. In 1950, the mimeographed RDA journal, *Coup de Bambou*, took on the Kebali District Chief, Alfa Bakar Diallo. The notes of the administration indicate that "nominated [imposed] in 1933 . . . he gave proof of his brutality and ineptness from 1934–1935 in the collection of taxes, and after 1945 he perpetuated the

38. Personal communication of M. le Général Lansana Diané.
39. Sékou Touré, *op. cit.*, p. 10.
40. Political report, 1947, *Archives de Dalaba.*

methods of the war effort."[41] But the administrative reports indicate that it was in the company of the young chief, Thierno Ibrahima Ba[42] that Alfa Bakar came to Conakry to depose a complaint of defamation against the journal. The attacks of *Coup de Bambou* clashed against the united front of the chiefs.[43] The editor-in-chief of the journal was heavily censured. In 1952, "a complaint against El Hadj Alfa Bakar, district chief of Kebali, was brought by some villagers of Kebali to Conakry."[44] There was no follow-up. The official administration opinion was that the Fouta traditional chieftaincy remained intact—a superficial opinion which did not take into account either the moral discredit that the war effort had imposed upon the chieftaincy, nor the tension which resulted from increased demands at a time when the subject populations were no longer disposed even to bear the traditional requirements.

Of what did these "customary dues" consist? As applied elsewhere, they included work on the fields of the chief by the people of the district and the upkeep and repair of his houses. However, in the name of "custom," exactions were added in harvests and estates. These dues "were eminently variable, depending on the district, or even the subdistrict, because they were a function of the personality and the rapacity of the chief and his entourage."[45] The administrator who wrote the report from which we excerpted the above lines declared that the "batoulabé" (executive agents of the chieftaincy spread throughout the country at the time of the collection of taxes or gathering of harvests) constituted "the plague of the Fouta."

However, the new needs of the chiefs led them to multiply their extraordinary dues—for the construction of a house, the purchase of an American car, the financing of a pilgrimage to Mecca. These dues were no longer "legitimatized by the duties of assistance, protection, or hospitality, which justified them at their origin." We are informed about these exactions by a large dossier thick with complaints brought against the chiefs of the subdivision of Dalaba (complaints filed away without any follow-up). The chief of Kankalabé was reproached for collecting more than ten per cent of the harvest; collecting a tax "for the birthday meal of the chief" (ten francs per married man); and collecting another tax for his receptions (in kind and money). The money given for the payment of laborers at the time of the construction of the road from Dalaba to Konkouré was shared between the chief and his followers.[46]

A signed complaint dated August 15, 1953, against the chief of Dalaba

41. Dossiers of the chefs de canton, *Archives de Dalaba.*
42. He succeeded his father.
43. Trimester reports, 1950, *Archives de Dalaba.*
44. *Ibid.,* 1st trimester.
45. *Ibid.,* Report of the Commandant de cercle of Dalaba.
46. *Ibid.*

made public the following exactions: 50 francs per family for each holiday [probably each Muslim religious festival]; 15 francs per head at the time of the census; 25 francs per head for the 14th of July and the 11th of November; some presents when the chief went to Conakry; special contributions for the purchase of cars and houses. Other complaints concerned kidnapped women and confiscated beef. An anonymous complaint of April 1, 1954, indicated that for every death of a man or woman older than twenty-five, the required estate "tax" was 10,000 francs or two cattle. If the heirs could not or did not want to pay, the goods of the deceased were sold for the benefit of the chief. If the deceased was without children, the chief took the whole of his herd, and even emptied his store bins and left nothing for the surviving husband or wife. A tax on the death of children from the age of seven was required. If the money was not paid without delay, the cattle of the defaulters were seized, the defaulters were beaten, their clothing torn, and, as an example, they were left for two days attached to a tree without anything to eat.[47]

The pace of life and expenses of the chiefs became more and more disproportionate to the resources of their subjects. . . . One official observed:

> The chiefs, whose opulence contrasts a little too much with the misery of the majority of their subjects, still hold the population in their hands.
> But it will soon be incumbent upon them to reconsider either elements in their style of life or the means to keep them up, because part of the country is becoming more and more impoverished, and others of their subject are becoming increasingly recalcitrant in the payment of their customary duties.[48]

By this time, when the final crisis had already begun, the highest officials blindly refused to take these warnings into account. Until 1954, the political reports of the administrators declared that the political situation was satisfactory. Although the RDA of Guinea followed Houphouet-Boigny in his "turning" of 1951, the colonial administration continued to see it as the principal enemy, if not the agent, of international communism.[49]

In truth, the new positions of the RDA "at the summit," as far as the

47. Dossiers of the chefs-plaintes, *Archives de Dalaba.*
48. Trimester reports, 3rd, 1954, *Archives de Dalaba.*
49. An astonishing report of the BTLC (Service de renseignements du ministère de la France d' Outre-Mer), confidential communique under No. 710 APA/BTLC of September 13, 1950, explained that the new base of the "Cominform" in Africa is ". . . Liberia from where arms are sent to subversive Guinean forces by a series of roads . . . that the administrator of N'Zérékoré observed did not exist!" *Archives N'Zérékoré,* Confidentiel, Liberia, Note et réponse du 17 Octobre, 1950).

Parti démocratique of Guinea was concerned, stemmed essentially from tactical considerations: the desire not to break the unity of the movement; and the taking of a course of action based on the fact that the political situation in France had changed, removing the prospects of a government that had Communist participation. This rendered parliamentary affiliation with the Communists more irritating than advantageous. The fate of Africa in the final analysis would be decided in Africa itself and not in the National Assembly in Paris.

The leadership of the PDG, therefore, considered that from then on their major objective was to make their party into a party of the masses. General proclamations against colonialism and big business, and considerations of foreign policy, had no chance of mobilizing the masses for whom these issues did not represent anything concrete. Their objective, therefore, was to create and reinforce the trade-union movement on the basis of a struggle over bread-and-butter issues, especially the struggle against discrimination in salaries, social rights, etc. Then, after an organizational base was created in the towns (especially among the workers, civil servants, subalterns, and artisans), they could proceed to the conquest of the countryside. Militants from the urban centers infiltrated the villages to create RDA committees on the basis of minor local demands (schools, roads, etc.), and above all, on the issue of the struggle against the chieftaincy—simultaneously, the essential machinery and weak point of the colonial apparatus.

The 1951–1954 period was particularly hard. The shift of position at the RDA summit disoriented a good number of militants, without disrupting the repression that they met. The administration continued to persecute the RDA militants and systematically supported the opposition "administration" parties; it denounced the contradiction between "the promises of collaboration made at the summit and the incendiary speeches given in the villages."[50] The legislative election of 1951 celebrated the defeat of the RDA, which did not elect anyone. . . .[51] Trade-union authority was almost nonexistent: "The RDA branch was completely broken up following the departing of the majority of its members."[52] In 1953, [the administrator wrote]: "As in the preceding year, a reassuring year as far as the general spirit of the population. . . ."

The Offensive of the RDA

In 1953, the election of Sékou Touré as territorial councilor of Beyla, despite the intense opposition of the chieftaincy, was a sign of the

50. Political reports, 1955, *Archives de Kissidougou.*

51. Political reports, 1951, *Archives de Kouroussa.*

52. *Ibid.*, Political report, 1952.

beginning of a new evolution. The interim legislative elections of June 27, 1954, following the death of deputy Yacine Diallo, marked the turning point. Barry Diawandou, son of the Almamy of Dabala, was doubtlessly elected to the French National Assembly against Sékou Touré. But the RDA profited from the electoral campaign by establishing itself everywhere and, although beaten, successfully pursued its organizational work.

"The year 1954 has demonstrated, if there was need, that the atmosphere of this country can rapidly be altered because of the credulity of the population, provided that one caters a little to its hopes and appetites." The preceding year has been reassuring "despite the too-heavy burden that taxes constituted in proportion to the vassals' weak resources." The poor rice harvest of 1957 in certain districts forced the peasants to sell part of their cattle to pay the tax. The RDA subsection was reconstituted: the propagandizers of the RDA and Sékou Touré himself visited numerous villages, stimulating resurgence particularly in Amana against the district chief Karfa Keita. The action of the RDA was directed against the chieftaincy. The bureau of the subsection was almost exclusively composed of artisans (tailors, jewelers, shoemakers). In the village, success with the women and young people was especially clear. The *Union du Mandé*, sponsoring the candidacy of Barry Diawandou, on the other hand, was marked by a steadfast passivity.[53]

At Dalaba, fief of the terrible Ba Thierno Ibrahima, the situation evolved more slowly, but in the same direction. The *Association Gilbert Vieillard* was dormant.[54] The 1954 election gave a majority of the votes to Barry Diawandou, but his rival Barry Ibrahima, called Barry III, the local leader of the Socialist Party (in 1954 called the "DSG," *Démocratie socialist guinéene*), polarized hostility to the chieftaincy. The administrator, a personal friend of the chief of Dalaba district, but clear-sighted, sounded a cry of alarm at the beginning of 1955:

> They [the chiefs] doubtlessly wish that we continue to cover up all their abuses, their exactions, all their pillage, because unfortunately, this is the case with most of them.
> How many voluminous dossiers of these characteristic exactions have been buried in the district offices since the time of administrative justice? How many more or less suspect affairs have been treated with indulgence in the districts of the Fouta? One day, however, there must arrive a moment of truth for these chiefs who live opulently on the sordid misery of their subjects, who live undernourished on a handful of meal and a bowl of sour milk, ... In this area, the responsibility of the administrator—at all levels—is great and absolutely certain."[55]

53. Political report, 1954, *Archives de Kouroussa.*

54. Trimester reports, 2nd, 1953, *Archives de Dalaba.*

55. Report of January 9, 1955, on the state of the chieftaincy, *Archives de Dalaba.*

Opposition, however, still remained latent. "I believe that Dalaba is the only district in the territory not to have an RDA subsection," an administrator noted in 1955.[56] But one may consider that all over Guinea the year 1955 marked not only the acceptance of the RDA by the rural masses, but the massive conversion of the Guinean population on the political issues.

Evidence of this was produced by the legislative elections of January 2, 1956. For the first time, these elections were really based on universal suffrage. Besides, the administration, although hostile to the RDA, found itself troubled by the presence of the leader of the movement, Felix Houphouet-Boigny, in the [French] government. For the first time, the administration maintained a relative neutrality during the campaign. The striking victory of the RDA, which obtained two out of three seats for deputy, signaled the end of the chieftaincy. The district chiefs, who had not expected such a landslide, everywhere had sided with the opposition candidates. Their failure in their own districts demonstrated their political bankruptcy. In his political report for 1956, the District Officer for Kouroussa noted:

> . . . following the election of January 2, 1956, which marked the victory of the RDA, this party was established almost everywhere in the district, creating village committees, dividing up the district into sections, and increasingly becoming involved in the administrative life of the area.
>
> . . . .
>
> The two other parties represented in the *cercle* (BAG of Barry Diawandou and DSG) had practically no organization or authority.[57]

At Faranah, the District Officer noted that the RDA victory came about because of the many judicial complaints against the chiefs. The chiefs requested the support of the administration, but the administration stayed neutral: "Events will not often turn to the chiefs' advantage."[58] A violent demonstration, "started by the town scoundrel," broke out on March 28, 1956, against the District Chief of Kouranko, Layba Camara. Later, things calmed down a bit, but "the dismantling of the district chieftaincy was well advanced. In the absence of administrative support, the chiefs floundered, thus emphasizing the real decline of their authority. It was no longer *politique* to be committed to the support of a chieftaincy discredited by the customs of yesterday."[59]

A typical example [of the withdrawal of administrative support] concerns Layba Camara, finally condemned to hard labor for life, for murder. In 1944, the administrator noted in his behalf that he was "a

56. *Ibid.*, 2nd trimester, 1955.
57. Political report, 1956, *Archives de Kouroussa.*
58. Oral testimony of passage of service,

December 22, 1956, *Archives de Faranah,* D.
59. *Ibid.*

The Struggle for Independence: The Tribe, Tribalism,
and the Conditions for Social Development

very good chief . . . punctually satisfied all administrative demands (goods, labor, cattle)."[60] In 1956, it was another sound of the bell. . . . multiple complaints which constituted an enormous dossier were brought against him. The administrator [in charge] concluded:

> In the case of an adverse judgment, the fate of Layba would be sealed. Thus would disappear a chief, who, although having rendered excellent service through the fear he knew how to establish throughout the district for fifteen years, did not know how to adapt to new conditions. He is at present more embarrassing than useful.[61]

In many regions, the district chiefs (especially the most detested) fled to seek refuge in the capital. Thus, a note from the Macenta administrator, dated April 30, 1957, warned the Governor that the chief of Guizima, Foromo Gorovogui, was found at Macenta for two months and did not deem it necessary to explain himself. He suggested his dismissal.[62] Those who remained often had to confess their helplessness. . . .

In certain regions where authority in fact had passed into the hands of the RDA village committees, especially in the forest region, the district chiefs had to give an accounting: "After the 1956 elections, the masses rose up and made an inventory of the goods of the chiefs and their men and forced them to pay back what they had pillaged (in one case as much as 200,000 francs)."[63]

In the Fouta-Djallon, here are several testimonies on the situation: At Dabola, the district officer observed:

> At present, the political situation is characterized by the total pre-eminence of the R.D.A. over the district—much more because of hate of the Almamy and his family than because of political opinions.
> The customary tribunal practically no longer functioned. Liberations of slaves were very frequent.[64]

At Dalaba, the battle was more bitter. At the election of January 2, 1956, the majority of the district voted for Barry III (DSG candidate, "the personal and declared enemy of the district chief Ba Ibrahima). They voted DSG because they were against the chiefs.[65] . . . Then there occurred something unbelievable. . . . Thierno Ibrahima, hardest of the Fouta chiefs—but also the most intelligent—on the eve of the Territorial Assembly elections, publicly gave his support to the RDA (not without difficulty, for the Dalaba section of the RDA required a

60. *Ibid.,* report of March 26, 1944.
61. *Ibid.,* oral testimony of December 22, 1956.
62. *Archives de Macenta.*
63. Oral testimony of M. Mamady Sagno,

former Mayor of N'Zérékoré, 1959.
64. Report of passage of service, December 31, 1956, *Archives de Dalaba.*
65. Trimester reports, 1955–1956, *Archives de Dalaba.*

self-critical declaration on his part). He was presented as a candidate by the RDA. Everywhere in the district the RDA had a small but clear majority. The territorial elections of March 31, 1957, gave the RDA fifty-eight seats out of sixty. Thus the Council of Government of the *Loi Cadre* then and there became entirely RDA.

Conclusion

From January 2, 1956, the Guinean chieftaincy was doomed. In a circular dated April 14, 1956, the governor of Guinea hoped to once again "reguild the coat-of-arms of the chieftaincy through reform":

> [He recognized that the chieftaincy] was gravely compromised by the success of a party opposed to it and that it was no longer admissible that we maintain against wind and storm chiefs who no longer represent anything; their authority would not gain anything and ours would be diminished.
>
> We must confess our sins in many cases and recognize that because of administrative convenience we had for several years shut our lips to the behavior of chiefs who were our principal collaborators and rendered services to us.
>
> Let us recognize the part played by hypocrisy in the not-very-curious acceptance of them as means provided that the chief did his job.[66]

The considerable raise in the chiefs' salaries in 1956 did not resolve the problem. On the contrary, this raise made the chiefs appear as parasites who were in no way justified in receiving such salaries.[67] In vain, the district chiefs organized themselxes into *syndicats*, first on the Guinean level, then on the federal. The founding Congress of the *Union fédérale des syndicats de chefs coutumiers*, held at Dakar, March 27, 1956, under the presidency of Fily Dabo Sissoko, elected as its Secretary-General Mamady Kourouma, son of the district chief Kouroussa, former RDA Grand Councillor in 1947 (member of the Federal Assembly sitting at Dakar) and deserter to the Party. It was too late.

The elections of 1957 and the establishment of the government of the *loi cadre* rendered these chimerical hopes for restoration vain. It was no longer the men, but the institution itself which engendered general hostility—even in the Fouta-Djallon and perhaps there more than elsewhere, to the extent that the chieftaincy, however "traditional" it might have been, had there shown itself the most oppressive.

At the end of 1957, an administrative official touring Kebali and Kankalabé (whose chiefs had just been dismissed by the Minister of the

66. *Archives nationales de Guinée, no.* 26/CAB of April 14, 1956.   67. Cf. *Guinée: Prélude a l'indépendance*, p. 44.

interior) observed that "there exists in the country a spirit of hate and passion which ruthlessly desires the total destruction of everything from near and far that touches the customary chieftaincy of the districts. . . ."[68]

[Thus] . . . the decree of December 31, 1957, suppressing the traditional chieftaincy in Guinea, was not a simple administrative decision having no bearing on reality, but the legal consecration of a popular revolution. . . .

What has become of the district chiefs? An investigation done in half the regions of Guinea gives us an approximate idea. Those who had administrative jobs have taken other employment. . . . This was the case of the former chief of Dalaba, Theirno Ibrahima Ba, who became a regional governor. His was, however, an exceptional case. His joining the party at the last minute allowed him to keep his "concession" in Dalaba—not without contestations on the part of the villagers.

For the others, their dismissal was accompanied by the loss of labor, as well as land that had been appropriated or usurped at the expense of the village community. At Dalaba, where the Almamy had "suggested" to his subjects that they turn over to him lands which were among the richest in the district, the lands of the Tinkisso valley, monopolized by the District Chief and his people and often left uncultivated, were placed at the disposition of the population. At Beyla, the majority of the chiefs, deprived of their income and wives (most, except for a few of the elderly, rejoined their families), took their hoes and went into the fields like everybody else. A particularly hostile chief fled to the Ivory Coast; one from Damaro, nicknamed the "Red Devil of the Mountain," did not dare leave his house. At Kankan, it was the same: three-quarters worked in the fields, abandoned by their followers and the majority of their wives. One of them had a gasoline pump. At Faranah, there was some resistance: the chief of one district who wished to oppose an RDA demonstration was arrested following an attack on a market in November, 1957, by his men that resulted in thirty-three wounded and one dead. At the local elections of May 18, 1950, deposed chiefs tried to present a list. They received 50 votes (theirs and their families') against 20,000 for the RDA.

At Banya, the terrible Layba Camara became furious, and in an attempt to prevent RDA meetings in his village, on June 17, 1957, he attacked his adversaries with guns. Balance: one dead, dozens wounded. He was arrested and sentenced to hard labor for life. Two coffee plantations which belonged to two chiefs in the South were "nationalized," as was the house of Layba Camara, turned into a dispensary. Elsewhere "the chiefs did not have plantations and there was therefore nothing to be done. . . ."[69]

68. Trimester reports, memo of October 4, 1957. *Archives de Dalaba.*

On August 24, 1958, a delegation of the Territorial Assembly on tour was attacked by followers of the ex-chief of the district Ziana.[70] There were two deaths and numerous wounded, including the Secretary-General of the Macenta section. The population wished to nationalize the plantations and houses constructed by forced labor, but this measure was taken only in the districts of Ziana, Balizia, and Loo.

At N'Zérékoré, nationalization was put into effect in 1960 . . . but it was necessary to back-track because the population was divided, and some objected that since the chiefs had already been fined it was unjust to take their means of existence away from them. On the other hand, in the districts of Gueckédou and Kissidougou . . . the plantations and buildings were nationalized at the time of independence.

In Lower Guinea, where the introduction of private property was relatively old, some former chiefs kept their sometimes considerable plantations. In all events, when the former chiefs were able to keep their personal property intact, they were integrated into the bourgeoisie of planters and businessmen without constituting a separate social category.

For the Guineans of 1966, the chieftaincy appeared as an outmoded institution, perhaps even more than feudalism appeared to the French of 1797. In France at that time, there were partisans of the old regime who believed in the possibility of a reaction. In the Guinea of 1966, it was possible that some former chiefs dreamt with melancholy of the splendor of the past: I doubt that any of them, even in the secret of their consciences, could imagine its resurrection.

69. Oral testimony of the Secretary-General of the PDG of Faranah, 1959.

70. Oral testimony of the chief of Savané Moricandian District, 1959.

Norman N.
Miller[1]

THE POLITICAL SURVIVAL OF
TRADITIONAL LEADERSHIP

Viewed from the higher echelons of government in the new nations, the rural leader is an insignificant individual who goes about managing his local affairs and carrying out—with varying degrees of success—the policies and hopes of the government. Viewed from below, from the inner recesses of the village, the leader is a man of authority; a man who has used wealth, heredity, or personal magnetism to gain a position of influence. As seen by nation builders and development experts, the rural leader is tacitly pointed to as the key to success. It is he who can mobilize the people. It is through him that more energy will be expended, more muscles used, and more attitudes changed. Conversely, it is the leader's lack of initiative that will entrench the *status quo* and doom the modernization schemes before they begin.

An important group of these rural leaders comprises the former traditional authorities—chiefs, sub-chiefs, and headmen—who occupied bureaucratic positions within the indirect rule systems of colonial regimes. Although legally deposed by many independent African governments, such leaders continue to exercise substantial influence, particularly in the building of local institutions in the rural areas. Some have been able to move into party or administrative positions; others have been so strong that the local authorities have been forced to deal with them directly as spokesmen for their area. Other traditional rulers have no formal leadership position but, through manipulation of their past legitimacy, have continued to dictate local policies and shape major decisions. Whatever the basis, the political survival of traditional leaders

1. The author is indebted to the International Development Research Center (Carnegie) of Indiana University for field support in East Africa, 1964–6. The African Studies Center, Michigan State University, and the Inter-University Research Program in Institution Building (Ford) provided additional support during 1967–8.

Reprinted from the *Journal of Modern African Studies*, Vol. 6, No. 2, pp. 183–198 with the permission of the author and the publisher, Cambridge University Press.

is significant because they provide the vital linkage between the government and the people. They influence the success of specific modernization schemes by serving as translators, interpreters, and mediators of government goals. This form of leadership is basically syncretistic, a leadership pattern among chiefs and headmen which is a synthesis and reconciliation of the opposing forces of traditionalism and modernism.[2] The result is a form of leadership which is neither modern nor traditional but an incorporation of both. The process is one of accommodation and compromise. It is a reconciliation of demands from (1) the traditional, custom-bound elements of rural society, and (2) the modernizing bureaucratic groups made up of local administrators and political party leaders.

A key characteristic of syncretistic political behavior is constant change. The political system is one in which values and guidelines for action come from two competing subsystems—a fluid situation, which allows a great deal of personal jousting and bargaining on the part of the traditional leaders. The individual leader can respond to a peasant in one way on a given topic and answer a bureaucratic administrator on the same topic in another manner. This phenomenon promotes the speaking to two worlds in different tongues, a duality of response. For the villager, the situation is often in flux. New syncretistic guidelines, principles, and practices are mixed and are not fully understood. The leader himself is unpredictable; he will often vacillate between extremes of what is traditional and what is modern. Specific examples of syncretistic behavior include speeches which mix the names of national leaders and tribal heroes; the use of amulets, charms, and protective medicines to ensure victory in a difficult political test; the use of diviners, practitioners, and religious technicians to aid the leader in solving modern problems; the constant mixing of slogans that refer to heroic tribal myths alongside national modernizing propaganda; and the employment of vernacular proverbs to gain support for bureaucratic demands.

From the administration's point of view, such syncretistic leaders cause difficulty and delay. Each new project or procedure usually needs a new bureaucratic overture. Most syncretistic leaders view each innovation as something that must be reconciled with both traditional and modern values; there are no precedents and no procedures that can be easily repeated. The leader must weigh his position in the new situation

2. The term "syncretistic" is occasionally applied to prophets' movements and separatist church movements in the sense that they derive a part of their doctrines and ritual from traditional religion. It can also have broader meaning, as Hodg- kin points out, in the search for some form of synthesis between European culture and traditional values. See Thomas Hodgkin, *Nationalism in Colonial Africa* (London, 1956), pp. 99 and 171.

and mark his course carefully to gain the needed synthesis. A project can take on extreme political overtones for the entire rural area, and be negotiated *ad infinitum*. The delay often continues until the leader can find his footing among other rural influentials. Like politicians in any society, his continuing goal is to maximize his future bargaining potential and to safeguard his current leadership position.

Modern syncretistic leadership is based on the very real need of both peasants and government to have a rural intermediary. The fundamental issue at stake is *the application of coercive force*. Alien bureaucratic leaders, administrators, and even party officials have the ability and the authority to use coercive force in the rural areas. What they do not have is the necessary degree of consensus to obtain the needed cooperation on bureaucratic projects. Conversely, the traditional leaders still hold some authority and are accepted as legitimate in the eyes of the peasant. This is in spite of the fact that they lack the legal ability to use coercive force. The result is that each system of leaders needs the support of the other. The marriage between the two systems tends to produce forms of syncretistic leadership behavior, which may be distinguished as either *alliance* or *coercion*. A third distinction is made when syncretistic leadership breaks down and disappears, and a situation of *mutual hostility* exists.

Alliance. This form occurs when communication between the traditional leader and the modernizing agent (administrator or party official) is established, and the traditional leader translates the desires of the modernizing agent to the people. The main elements in the relationship are that (1) the traditional leader's authority has been bent to serve the ends of the modernizing agent, probably by some type of persuasion, (2) articulation to the people has been favorable and activating, and (3) the task, program, or campaign will be undertaken. The alliance situation closely resembles the relationship between chiefs and the colonial administration under indirect rule. Communications between the two groups tend to be good on specific issues, and cooperation is forthcoming. Consensus has been established on an *ad hoc* basis, and there is agreement on the bureaucratic norms to be used. The interest groups that exist in the rural areas tend to be sympathetic to cooperation between the two positions and support syncretistic behavior. Group allegiance remains unchanged and common interests are articulated by the reconciling leader.

Coercion. This form occurs when overt bureaucratic coercion is applied to the traditional leader and partial cooperation is gained. The traditional leader, however, goes only as far as he is forced to go in activating the people. From the administrator's point of view, plans and projects are delayed, barriers are encountered, and obstructionism and inaction are commonplace. Communication between the two groups is distorted through the various selective processes. Consensus is tenuous and there is often disagreement on the bureaucratic norms to be applied. Traditional interest groups are somewhat hostile to the modernizing pressures, and the syncretistic leader has difficulty holding support for the issues at stake. Group allegiance can shift rapidly, and there is no clear-cut common interest. Traditional leaders become increasingly wary of decrees and written words; they tend to demand the familiar face-to-face methods of doing business as a prerequisite to cooperation.

Mutual hostility. This situation occurs when the relationship between the two leadership groups has broken down and syncretistic leadership is nonexistent. Traditional leaders withdraw and attempt to avoid contact with bureaucratic agents. Entrenchment takes place and the *status quo* is idealized. Projects, plans, and campaigns flounder; as a result, incriminations and reprisals are aimed at the 'uncooperative' traditional leaders. Communications are ruptured. Little or no consensus exists, and there is blatant disagreement on norms and bureaucratic rules. In this situation, interest groups lack cohesion and members may shift allegiances rapidly. Government attempts at gaining public participation meet with failure and there tends to be an entrenchment of the leaders in each camp. Structures that do exist become binding, in that the bureaucratic leaders are increasingly formalistic, petty, impersonal, and critical of the "backward" traditional leadership. Both types of leaders are inclined to articulate their built-in biases. Attitudes and opinions bind the individual to the system of which he is a part. Modernization attempts are usually abortive.

The alliance and coercion forms of syncretistic leadership promote one or more forms of neo-traditionalism. Because traditional leaders are constantly reconciling traditional values, it is understandable that many of these values may be brought forward in slightly altered form and embraced as significant and important. This may be termed revivalism, in that the people's current beliefs need "to embody the moral prescriptions of the past and apply them to modern conditions."[3] This is not necessarily a resurgence of historic interest in the past, as has occurred in Ghana and Buganda, but a revival of past guidelines for application to modern behavior. Because most Africans are not very far from the land-based, practical problems of rural life, the solutions to contemporary problems could be expected to be land-based, and familiar in terms of past symbols and ritual. Syncretistic leadership exists because of this traditionalism and the ability of rural leaders to capitalize on traditional habits.

3. David Apter, *The Political Kingdom in Uganda* (Princeton, 1961), p. 27. Also see Apter's "The Role of Traditionalism in the Political Modernization of Ghana and Uganda," in *World Politics* (Princeton), XIII, October 1960, pp. 45–68.

In summary, the fundamental argument is this: Rural traditional authorities survive in modern times as local political leaders. They do so by serving as intermediaries between modernizing bureaucratic authorities and the custom-bound populace. When they fail to serve as intermediaries, a condition of mutual hostility between themselves and modernizing authorities develops, and there is a failure to reach bureaucratic goals. When some accord is reached, the situation is in essence syncretistic, that is, the traditional leader serves to balance the demands of the populace and the bureaucratic groups. Syncretism can take the form of alliance or coercion. Under either situation traditional leaders must capitalize on certain culture-bound factors that support traditionalism, and also specifically manipulate such things as local myth, ritual, symbol, and customary law. If this balance is maintained, a tendency toward neo-traditionalism can be expected. When neo-traditionalism persists, the modernizing bureaucratic authorities will attempt to check such tendencies as threats to bureaucratic goals. Conflict may be expected because the syncretistic leader tends to rely on the more traditional basis of influence, and in essence to tip the balance in favor of the customary values. This, in turn, causes modernizing agents to exert pressure on the syncretistic leader to realign with bureaucratic goals. The result is either a rebalance under alliance or coercion conditions, or a rupture in relations causing mutual hostility. This over-all thesis may best be illustrated and expanded upon by focusing on a particular nation and a specific ethnic group.

A Case for Analysis: The Nyamwezi of Tanzania

The political organization of an ethnic group such as the Nyamwezi includes, in the broadest sense, the traditional institutions by which law and order are maintained, the organization of authority in subsystems—the chiefdom, village, or family—and those institutions which safeguard the integrity of the political units.[4] As used here, the political organization is the widest effective social group which creates and maintains order, forces compliance with the norms of that social order, and socializes and maintains support for the authority figures who are in positions of leadership.[5] In a study of a non-western, multicentred, traditional

4. The writer is indebted to Mary Eaton Read Nicholson and Richard Simpson for helpful comment and criticism on this portion of the manuscript.
5. See discussion of the political organization of the related Sukuma people in J.

Gus Liebenow, "Responses to Planned Political Change in a Tanganyika Tribal Group," in *The American Political Science Review* (Menasha, Wisconsin), L, 2, 1956, pp. 442–61.

society, leadership and authority are functionally diffuse. Leaders perform political activities from a position which may be attained through a combination of religious, economic, and familial legitimacy. Kin relations and ritual activities take the place of the more specific functions in western societies associated with political office and binding contracts.

THE BACKGROUND: NYAMWEZI POLITICAL ORGANIZATION[6]

Three key factors characterize the Nyamwezi traditional political system. First, there has never been a paramount chief who has unified all the Nyamwezi. Each chiefdom was autonomous and, except for a few periods of consolidation, chiefs were always wary of attempts at unification. Political cohesion among the Nyamwezi does not lie in an over-all centralized political authority, but is based on similarity in customs, laws, language, and political and economic structures. Second, the political organization of each chiefdom has been a pyramidal hierarchy; below the chief are headmen with territorial jurisdiction, and below the headmen are subheadmen with village or neighborhood jurisdiction. Third, in the person of the chief was found the main decision-making authority affecting the individual peasant.

Basically, political life in each chiefdom centred around the chief, whose sources of authority were his magical-religious functions, his administrative position, his role as the military commander, and his position as supreme judge. Specifically, he was believed by his people to be the earthly representative of the founder of the chiefdom. He was thought to be able to influence the fate of the land and was generally believed to be able to enlist ancestral spirits to aid the community. Most chiefs were thought able to call on the ancestors to control the elements —to bring rain or to stop floods.[7] When functioning as judges, chiefs traditionally had the power of life and death.[8]

6. The Nyamwezi number some 363,252 (1957 census) and are the second largest of Tanzania's 120 ethnic groups. They mainly inhabit Tabora, Nzega, and Kahama districts in the central plateau region. Tabora district is the focus of the present study. The most important background literature includes Rev. Fr. Boesch, *Les Banyamwezi, peuple de l'Afrique orientale* (Münster, 1930), and R. G. Abrahams, *The Political Organization of Unyamwezi* (Cambridge, 1967).

7. Some of the ritualistic functions of the chief included magical preparation of seed, control of rain, village cleansing after twins were born, and control of

epidemics and calamities such as famine, rinderpest, hail, or man-eating lions. The responsibility of each chief was to find the cause of the problem and to initiate measures against it, usually with the aid of a diviner.

8. Within the memory of living elders, death sentences were given for treason, cattle theft by a stranger, adultery with a chief's wife, and occasionally for witchcraft. Murder, arson, and assault generally received less severe penalties. Execution in the Unyanyembe chiefdom, for example, was by mutilation and leaving the condemned to the hyena.

The Struggle for Independence: The Tribe, Tribalism, and the Conditions for Social Development

The specific sources of chiefly power may be briefly summarized: (1) the chief was the sole proprietor of land and controlled the allocation of such land to the cultivators; (2) in time of famine the chief controlled the dispensing of food from chiefdom granaries; and (3) his accumulated wealth from fees, fines, booty, tools, and unused property enabled him to purchase the loyalty of key subjects, including warriors.

Conversely, the traditional restrictions on a chief's power came from several sources: (1) subjects could demand a chief's removal if his supernatural powers were believed to have failed; (2) the delegation of chiefly authority for war, adjudication, religious ceremony, and ritual performance effectively reduced the over-all authority of a chief and often made him dependent on functionaries in the chiefdom; (3) the fear of ancestral vengeance in a vanquished area kept most chiefs from occupying conquered lands and expanding their territorial holdings; (4) the ability of families to "hive off" from an abusive chief and to join another chiefdom restricted a chief for fear of losing manpower and tribute; and (5) collective action by peasants to remove an abusive chief was possible as a last resort, and meant complete loss of property, wives, and livestock for the chief.

In the years of British colonial administration, 1915–61, the consolidation of many chiefdoms took place and chiefs were given local administrative and court responsibilities.[9] Politically, however, few chiefs gained influence outside their districts, and most were only involved with parochial events within their chiefdoms. Important administrative functions stayed primarily in the hands of the British district officer, and political participation and intra-district integration were not attained. In positive terms, however, some consensus was undoubtedly achieved, and a degree of inter-area cooperation reached. Certainly the underpinnings of the post-independence structure of local government were established—such as the district councils and village development committees—and some experience gained in governmental procedures and parliamentary rules.

In the final years of the British administration, when nationalistic forces began to gather strength (1945–61), the institution of chieftaincy came under the greatest stress. Throughout the country chiefs faced a classic dilemma: whether to support the demands of the Tanganyika African National Union (T.A.N.U.) that colonial rule be abolished, or to support the British administration in attempting to contain the nationalistic protest. Fear of losing their paid positions as government administrators kept most Nyamwezi chiefs from joining the party. In the late 1950's, however, as independence became more probable, a few

9. Tabora had 12 chiefdoms in 1961. The other Nyamwezi districts of Nzega and   Kahama had a total of 20 chiefdoms.

chiefs secretly joined the political movement and allowed their personal membership cards to be used to aid local recruitment.

Because the chiefs were generally apathetic in the nationalistic movement and because they represented the *status quo*, they were repeatedly accused by the party of being lackeys of the colonial government. This conflict between the traditional and party leaders is a significant legacy in Tanzania's attempt at economic and political modernization. In hundreds of individual cases T.A.N.U. officials so harassed traditional leaders that a major impasse was created between the two groups. Differences arose between peasants who supported chiefs and headmen and those, generally younger individuals, who supported the party leadership.

Chieftainship has remained particularly strong in the remote hinterland where urban influences have not penetrated. It is in the same remote areas that the party is attempting to gain the support of the people and to provide the interpretation and guidance originally gained from traditional leaders. As could be expected, the old disputes between chiefs and party leaders often militate against the party overtures. Party statements are no longer nationalistic protests designed to end colonialism, but are attempts to mobilize the people for modernization schemes. Often new goals are espoused by old T.A.N.U. personalities. For traditional leaders, this in itself is reason enough for noncooperation. The upshot is often a destructive whispering campaign against any modernization project backed by the party.

In essence, a major source of the chief's difficulties was the necessity of having government support and popular support at the same time. Simultaneously withstanding accusations from the party, maintaining popularity with the peasants, and being a government agent caused the institution of chieftaincy to rest on a tenuous balance.

THE MODERN SURVIVAL OF TRADITIONAL LEADERS

The long-established institution of chieftainship, around which so much of Tanzania's political history had evolved, was dramatically abolished by the independent African government on 1 January 1963.[10]

10. By the African Chiefs Ordinance (Repeal) Act of 1963 (Act no. 13 of 1963, effective on 1 January 1963). The Act states that the African Chiefs Ordinance, Cap. 331 of the Revised Laws, is repealed (section 1) but that if any Chief is an ex-officio member of a Council or Board he may continue to be a member if the Minister concerned concurs (section 2). Earlier, in 1957, the powers of the chiefs had been curtailed by the African Chiefs (Special Powers) Ordinance, which laid down that any chief whose chiefdom was in a district where a District Council was being formed remained the authority for the chiefdom, but "must not . . . encroach on the jurisdiction of the new district council in any way."

The Struggle for Independence: The Tribe, Tribalism,
and the Conditions for Social Development

Chiefs were legally dethroned, but their influence did not end. As the Government moved to fill the administrative void with civil servants, the chiefs and headmen moved to consolidate their remaining influence. Throughout the nation examples of chiefs retaining power in a local area and gaining some governmental recognition were common. In these cases the government reaction was to appoint the chief a local government official; and, where the situation demanded more administrative expertise, to appoint a deputy with the chief.

Traditional Leaders in Tabora District, 1963 and 1966[11]

	Chiefs	Headmen
Traditional leaders in power when chieftaincy was abolished, 1963	11	97
In governmental positions, 1966	2	88
Employed by political party or cooperative society, 1966	1	2
Detained by government for political activity, 1966	1	0
Under arrest for peculation, 1966	0	2
Deceased, 1966	1	2
Others: local councillor, retired farmer, other work, 1966	6	3

The village headmen who served under the chiefs in the colonial administration have also been able to remain in power as paid officials. These individuals are basically traditional leaders, in that they generally came from families who historically retained the headmanship. Many also had kinship links with the local chief. Others gained their position because they served some magical-religious functions or because they were acceptable to the people, to their chief, and to the British administration. In modern times headmen usually hold posts as village executive officers in the local government structure or serve as village representatives on district councils.

Specific evidence of the contemporary political survival of traditional chiefs and headmen may be seen in data concerning the Nyamwezi leaders of Tabora District (table above). The chiefs who gained some official position were those who had enjoyed widespread popular support in their chiefdoms and had also had strong ties with party and administrative leaders. The chiefs who survived politically were those who had attained the highest education and, significantly, the shortest tenure of office. Chiefs who were reduced to the status of local councillors or retired farmers had been in office the longest and were the more closely identified with colonial rule. Most had smaller chiefdoms and a more localized base of support, and thus faced a greater possibility that local

11. Source: author's research. A survey of other Tanzania districts, including Nzega, Mpanda, and Rungwe, indicates that 25–35 per cent of the chiefs were able to remain in governmental positions of power.

antagonisms weighed against them. Chiefs with longer tenure were also more conservative and more out of touch with changes in the nationalistic period. Undoubtedly they had few contacts with African party and government leaders, a fact that limited their opportunities when the new governing elite abolished chieftaincy in 1963.

Traditional headmen had an even greater political survival rate than did the chiefs, largely due to the headmen's appointment as village executive officers in the local government system. It is in this situation that an impasse for the administration has occurred. The headman deals directly with the people; it is through him that effective administration, adjudication, and modernization must come. He has continued to hold village administrative posts, although often uneducated and uninterested in the efficient administration which the government desires. To replace him with an "enlightened" headman is to remove the most acceptable leader and to incur the distrust and objection of the people. To leave him in his crucial position is to jeopardize the modernization goals of the central government. Although most central government officials recognize this problem, chiefs and headmen have not been eased out of power. The fundamental reason is that a number of complex attitudinal and environmental factors favor their retention.

ATTITUDINAL FACTORS IN TRADITIONAL SURVIVAL

Modern support for the institution of chieftaincy is so ingrained in the behavior of most rural cultivators that, in spite of legal changes, a chief's influence continues. Habit, fear of rapid change, and the nonacceptance of local government administrators who have replaced traditional authorities underlie local attitudes. Other reasons persist. The peasants' widespread insecurity about the future promotes the survival of traditional leaders; for example, a former chief may hold power because his followers are sure neither of what the future will bring nor that the old chief will not be reinstated. Administrative changes are rapid enough to keep most peasants confused. The knowledge that other chiefs are still in authoritative governmental positions promotes the idea that the old chiefs may eventually regain influence. Caution and the desire not to burn bridges allow an atmosphere of tolerance toward traditional leaders to exist.

If a chief's tenure reaches back through two generations, his position as a respected leader may be confused with his position as a former chief and a general aura of authority accorded him. For many conservative peasants the deposed traditional chief is the closest and most trusted leader. For others, the fear of an ex-chief on the basis of his magical-religious power is enough to sustain his authority. Moreover, since the

Government has legally withdrawn support from the chief, he can now define his relationship with peasants on a more intimate basis than before and join vehemently with them in criticism of the Government. Criticisms of the administration on the basis that it does not do enough for the people is a common bond among cultivators. Since the new African Government cost the chief his livelihood and official position, there is every reason for him to join the people in the criticism of Government.

Basic Nyamwezi attitudes toward authority are also important. First, there is no tradition of questioning an authority figure unless he has flagrantly abused his powers. A chief's or headman's early authority would carry over to the present because he was originally in power. Such an individual would be far more acceptable than the imposed authority who is alien to the village.

Secondly, attitudes towards generosity are important. Authority figures have always been expected to be generous and to look after the needy. Europeans seldom recognized this custom, often with the result that the peasant was confused and annoyed and the administration's goals frustrated. This was basically a failure to realize that, as authorities, Europeans were expected to be generous with their food, drink, transport, medicine, and the like. Modern African local government officials share the European attitudes and seldom fulfil the peasants' expectations of generous leaders. Consequently it is more natural for a peasant to support the familiar leader who at least pays lip service to the old custom. A similar belief that the chief will look after the people in time of calamity is not transferred to the local government authority. Such authority is too far removed from the individual, there usually cannot be a face-to-face request for help, and there is little assurance that the administration would help an individual even if it could.

Considering over-all village behavior, support for traditional leaders comes mainly from five village groups whose members rely on the chiefs and headmen as councillors, ritualists, confessors, or interpreters of modern events. These groups are: (1) the generally conservative elders over 50, (2) men between 15 and 50 who are uneducated, untravelled, and generally apolitical, (3) nearly all uneducated women over 30, (4) children under 15, and (5) the practising group of diviners, healers, medicine men, and soothsayers. Groups that tend not to support the traditional leaders are: (*a*) educated or semi-educated men between 15 and 50, (*b*) village dissidents, agitators, rebels, (*c*) enterprising or innovating local-level educators, administrators, politicians, and (*d*) the few semieducated women between 15 and 30.

THE USE OF SPECIFIC TECHNIQUES

In analysing how traditional leaders remain in power, however, a distinction should be made between the more general attitudes operating in Nyamwezi society and the specific customary practices which provide traditional leaders with a basis for political action. A further distinction may then be made concerning how leaders manipulate myth, ritual, symbols, customary law, and the like, for their own ends. First, the following customary practices persist and lend credence to the traditional system:

(*a*) *Use of political assassination.* The ultimate control of a Nyamwezi chief has been assassination by the royal family or headmen, usually by suffocation or poison. Occasional reports of headmen being assassinated occur today, and the deaths of two chiefs in the last ten years have led to trials and imprisonment under accusations of poisoning.

(*b*) *Use of traditional medical practices.* Various types of practitioners exist today to promote cures, dispense herbs and medicines, and in some areas to act as diviners and soothsayers. Some practitioners aid traditional leaders in ritualistic activity and help them gain success in specific undertakings. A traditional leader's dispensing of amulets, protective devices, and special medicines to ensure success in political undertakings is commonplace.

(*c*) *Continuance of dance groups.* Societies composed of specific groups (old men, young men, women, etc.) carry on the traditional dances, often for modern occasions such as celebrations marking independence day or the founding of the party. Vestiges of the past that tend to support traditional leaders are seen at such times when dancers clad in modern dress shout the names of honoured warriors of Nyamwezi history and refer to the heroic deeds of past chiefs.

(*d*) *Continuance of tribute.* Although the filling of chiefs' private granaries ceased officially in 1927, some chiefdom granaries continued to be kept as an administrative guard against famine: and small homages and gifts are still presented to traditional leaders in return for their favor.

(*e*) *Use of honorific greetings.* Honorific titles and the clapped-hand greeting to honour a chief are widely used.

(*f*) *Use of traditional elders' councils.* The newly constituted village development committees for most Nyamwezi villages are composed largely of elders who have previously served on the village councils. More progressive individuals such as the local teacher or dispenser are occasionally on the committees, but former chiefs and headmen often dominate such meetings.

The Struggle for Independence: The Tribe, Tribalism,
and the Conditions for Social Development

(g) *Use of traditional boundaries.* The boundaries of traditional chiefdoms are used today in delineating local government, court, and village development committee jurisdictions. Tax rolls are kept on the basis of chiefdom boundaries, and traditional headquarters are often used for modern offices. The result is a tendency for farmers to think of the new administrative units in terms of the old chiefdom, and to think of the new administrators in terms of chiefs and headmen.

A major reason why the above practices persist—and thus allow an environment which promotes traditional leadership—is that the chiefdom itself has remained the broadest political unit with which a rural African is directly concerned. The individual is first and foremost a member of a chiefdom whose geographical borders are known, whose leaders are dealt with on a personal basis, and whose authority system the farmer still understands most completely. Within the context of the chiefdom the traditional leader can use specific techniques to promote his own survival. Such techniques include the manipulation of ritual, the use of symbols, the reliance on a semi-judicial position in customary law, and the use of a position in a secret society.

Most ritualistic ceremonies carried out by chiefs and headmen in modern times are either those connected with the agricultural cycle or those employed to prevent disease and natural calamity. The ceremonies take the form of appeasing ancestral spirits, visiting the graves of former chiefs, protecting against witchcraft, controlling rainfall, ensuring fertility, and the like. For the more conservative elements of Nyamwezi rural society, these practices are important. The more educated chiefs and headmen who carry out limited ceremonies usually do so to appease their followers. Other chiefs use the ritual function for self-aggrandisement and as a basis of authority.

The importance of symbols and regalia lies in their actual possession. The physical holding of the regalia meant the holding of office. A modern transposition of these symbols has occurred; the possession now of the symbols of an administrative chief, such as records, files, books, pencils, and the like, has come to be equated with a position of authority. Most deposed chiefs and working headmen have these trappings of office and rely on them to give an official air. Other symbols of chieftaincy are still maintained by retainers and guardians of the chief's quarters. When worn by the chiefs and headmen, such regalia remind the peasants of the customary power of the office and, in fact, give modern authority to the traditional leader.

With reference to customary law, the traditional leader had a dual judicial role in the colonial period. He was the most important informal interpreter of customary law, and he had the full legal and administrative powers of a court magistrate. When chieftaincy was abolished in

1963, it became illegal for chiefs to hold court. In fact, however, many chiefs continued to act as unofficial judges in such matters as bride-wealth, marriage, divorce, guardianship, land tenure, and rights regarding property, claims, and wills. Headmen, moreover, continued to have the legal right to hear local disputes and are, in fact, semi-judicial. Under Nyamwezi customary law the headman is particularly prominent in the allocation of land and the settlement of land disputes. Other conflicts, such as those over cattle, bridewealth, or inheritance, usually reach the headman when a family or families find themselves dead-locked. If the headman fails to reconcile the problem, the village development committee is the next step.

For both chiefs and headmen, the adjudication of customary law has remained an important function, and a continuing basis of authority. The removal of a case to the primary court, with an alien magistrate who is not from the local area and who probably is not a Nyamwezi, represents either a serious breach in the processes by which internal conflicts are resolved in the community, or a case between individuals who fall under different headmen or chiefs. In terms of political survival, any traditional leader who holds a position as a judge and mediator is in a strong position to continue his authority.

Secret societies are also used to give a former chief a claim to author-ity. Those that exist today are basically voluntary, and operate for such reasons as the curing of sickness, divining, spirit possession, ancestor worship, totemism, rain-making and the hunting of specific animals. Although these societies have diminished in popularity and have not in recent years been overtly political, they do exist in most places. The significant point is that chiefs and headmen occupy the higher ranks of the organizations. Because the societies cut across village and chiefdom boundaries, the officers have a potentially wide scope for political activity. Contemporary evidence suggests that traditional leaders use their positions in secret societies to reach influential elderly audiences, or as one of several claims to legitimacy.

SYNCRETISM AND NEO-TRADITIONALISM

Syncretistic, reconciling behavior depends in part on the persistence of some form of neo-traditionalism—a revival of past values. Traditional leaders must selectively use the past to ensure their position in the deci-sions of the future. Periodically, old values must be re-embraced and new conditions must be interpreted in light of earlier values. A movement of this nature occurs within an ethnic group and is in response to the encroachment of unacceptable modernistic values.

Such a neo-traditional movement occurred among the Nyamwezi

between 1958 and 1964. The leaders of the movement, who were mainly chiefs, religious leaders, and trade-union officials, preached the long-term support of chiefly rule, the use of Swahili as the official language, and a re-emphasis on African dress and culture. Prior to independence in 1961 the movement was anti-administration, anti-European, and against the multi-racial local government ideas then under consideration. Following independence, the neo-traditional leaders continued to be against the African administration and against limiting chiefly powers. Criticism was also leveled at African government leaders because they were allegedly pro-Christian and discriminated against Muslims. The Government's reaction has been to negate the movements by emphasizing the modernizing, nation-building values that citizens should embrace and, in specific Nyamwezi areas, by forcing a few powerful chiefs to recant publicly.

Moderate neo-traditionalism, however, continues because the Government is not yet in a position to withdraw totally the powers of headmen and a few chiefs. The syncretistic leader is still the intermediary. Four main reasons exist for the persistence of these neo-traditionalists. First, to obtain literate, competent, and acceptable leadership at the village level requires higher pay and more rewards than the local government can afford. Secondly, to recruit competent village leaders entails persuading the individual that he should live in a remote village far from the more interesting urban areas. This constitutes a hardship that most educated leaders find difficult to accept.

Thirdly, potential rural leaders often do not come forward from within the local area because they fail to understand what the new positions entail, or because they fear responsibility. Such reluctance is based on not wishing to incur the jealousy of neighbors, not wanting to appear prosperous or grasping, and not wishing to supersede a more traditionally qualified person. Fourthly, the ostracism of unpopular local officials is common enough to be a major restraint on over-ambitious individuals. The social position of anyone who is ostracized is, in Nyamwezi terminology (*bubiti*), equated with a hyena-like condition—all that is anti-social, dirty, nocturnal, and scavenging. In summary, neo-traditionalism is condoned and inadvertently promoted by the Government simply because only traditional leaders can be found to fill the rural leadership vacuum.

Syncretism in political leadership is promoted by the persistence of traditional values and attitudes, and the counter-demands of the modernizing bureaucratic state. The necessary environment for syncretism is perpetuated by the specific culture-bound revival of customary values, and the manipulation by leaders of symbols, ritual, customary laws, and the like. The syncretistic phenomena will continue as long as traditional value systems are in conflict with intruding modernizing systems. Predictably, the traditional system will be changed by the implanting of new rural institutions, such as cells, cooperatives, parties, and administrative structures, which demand mass participation, which require new behavior patterns, and which establish new goals for rural peoples. The success of the rural institutions will depend on the extent to which rural people manipulate these structures merely to create new forms of old organizations. In some places this will happen; gradualism will hold sway, traditional leaders will refuse to be influenced by administrators, and the organizational goals will not be reached. In other areas, innovative local leaders will accommodate the new rural institutions and the government's goals will be attained.

In general, there is a paradoxical co-existence of action and inaction in the rural areas. The situation is one of constant stimulation, reaction, and reformation. It is an ongoing process of change set upon a seemingly static society. The irony is that the human and the bureaucratic systems are experiencing constant upheaval, and yet the ebb and flow of rural life seems to be that of a dull monotony, unaltered and unchanging.

Elliott P.
Skinner[1]

THE "PARADOX" OF RURAL LEADERSHIP: A COMMENT

*T*his admirable analysis of the role of traditional leaders among the Nyamwezi in Tanzania throws light on some of the most intriguing problems of government in contemporary Africa. Recent reports from African societies confirm Dr Miller's finding that the traditional rulers are not withering away, but on the contrary have survived and are helping their people to adapt to the modern state. This would not be surprising had not many of the revolutionary and non-revolutionary leaders of the modern African states shown such hostility to the traditional leaders. Many politicians felt that the chiefs were reactionary and should be eliminated so that the African states could modernize and develop. Other modern leaders favored retaining the chiefs while encouraging or coercing them to help modernize their societies. A few modern leaders felt that the chiefs should be honored as custodians of the cherished values of their respective societies. But even here the hope was that the chief would help in a dialectical process of change by providing a secure base from which the society could take off.

What happened in fact, however, was that the chiefs did not disappear and even when they were legally dethroned their influence remained. Moreover, village headmen had a higher survival rate than chiefs, and were better able to resist the loss of power. They, like many chiefs, were able to retain their power because of the "habit" of the local people, their "fear of rapid change," and their refusal to accept local government administrators who replaced traditional authorities.

Dr. Miller concludes his useful study of the Nyamwezi of Tanzania with a reference to the "paradoxical co-existence of action and inaction

1. The United States Ambassador to Upper Volta, who acted as discussant on Dr. Miller's paper when it was originally presented at the 1967 annual meeting of the (American) African Studies Association in New York.

Reprinted from the *Journal of Modern African Studies,* Vol. 6, No. 2, pp. 199–201 with the permission of the author and the publisher, Cambridge University Press.

in the rural areas." It is unfortunate that he leaves us with "paradox" and does not try to put the "irony" within a more understandable context. This is especially unfortunate since he had the answers at his finger-tips. The survival of the traditional leadership in African societies is not paradoxical, given the financial and technical inability of the modern African states to "implant new rural institutions," etc. Moreover, it is doubtful whether any new political leaders could successfully supplant older ones without the economic power and institutional apparatus with which to do so.

The manner in which the Mossi chiefs in Upper Volta held on to their power throughout the rigors of the colonial regime, but lost—and regained—it afterwards is a case in point. These men became in many instances the tools of the French administration and were made to recruit forced labor for the coastal plantations, recruit soldiers for the army, and pay all types of levies. The people did not like these exactions, but were powerless to curb the power of the chiefs, now backed by French arms, and could not escape the new forms of taxation which the chiefs adapted from the French patterns. But what really saved the chiefs was the fact that the French ruled from the capital and did not impose a parallel political organization in the rural areas. As far as the Mossi chiefs were concerned, the French were like locusts—they came periodically, drained the districts, but then left government to them. The Mossi chiefs only began to lose power over their subjects when the French abolished forced labor and other grievous forms of taxation, and began an "enlightened" rule. Now, instead of having one administrator for 60,000 people, they created many subdivisions and administrative posts in the rural areas and brought their administrators into direct contact with the people. The French introduced institutions to rule the people directly and gradually began to curb the power of the chiefs. However, here, as in many parts of Africa, the coming of independence was to stop this process and give rise to another.

The rulers of most of the newly independent African states attempted to Africanize their bureaucracies or to set up new ones, and to build new political institutions. Africans received ministerial posts, became district commissioners and *commandants de cercle*, and new party organizations were created to *encadrer* the rural populations. However, almost all the African leaders soon found out that they did not have the money, the technical skill, or the personnel to staff their bureaucracies, or to create new institutions. In almost every country, Europeans were retained or imported to do the technical work in the ministries, and very few party organizations in the new states got off the ground. The rural areas suffered more in comparison with the cities because in most cases there was no money and no staff for the new but now moribund institutions.

The Struggle for Independence: The Tribe, Tribalism, and the Conditions for Social Development

Indeed, in Tanzania Julius Nyerere felt it necessary for a time to give up his position as Prime Minister to work at party organization in the rural areas.

It was as much the inability of the new states to provide and employ modern institutions as it was the syncretising ability of the local chief that was responsible for the survival of the traditional leaders. As soon as the rural bureaucracy or party apparatus ceased to be effective, the chiefs resumed their traditional roles, or modified these to suit the times. In Mossi country the rural chiefs who in 1955–7 were apprehensive of the new political leaders of Upper Volta, took swift advantage of the decline of the single-party organization, and by 1964 had effectively resumed control over their people, especially the older ones. The result was not unlike that which Dr. Miller found among the Nyamwezi.

However, I do not consider the events in Upper Volta or in Tanzania either ironical or paradoxical. They were the direct result of uneven development or, if one wishes, of a transitional development stage in which there is a lack of congruence between the political ideology of the state and the existing political organization in the rural areas. There is no doubt in my mind that conditions in the rural areas of modern Africa will change. Chiefs may continue to provide leadership for rural Africans but only until the modern bureaucratic nation-state can afford to create and effectively use its own local institutions.

| Gicha | **LETTER FROM MBUGWE,** |
| Mbee | **TANZANIA** |

*I*n my earlier letters I wrote about some of the events in Mbugwe during 1960, 1961, and the year of Independence, 1962. First there was the episode of the bird that spoke like a human being. Secondly there was the woman who appeared to only a few people, and that I also explained. These things had never before appeared in the country of Mbugwe, and therefore they made people think deeply. Those who had seen for themselves believed; those who had not seen doubted what their friends said. The affair concerning the bird was believed by many, but the affair of the woman by only a few.

[Translator's Note: Gicha Mbee, the author of the following report, is a member of the Mbugwe tribe of northern Tanzania. I first met him, then a youth of about fifteen, in 1951 while doing an anthropological field study of the Mbugwe. I soon discovered that he was proficient at writing, although he had had only four years' schooling at the local mission school, and engaged him as an informant to write ethnographic texts. Since then he has corresponded with me and has continued to send me ethnographic material written in Swahili—about 700 pages altogether, including a detailed sketch of his childhood which I am at present translating for publication. In 1963 I suggested to him that he compose a narrative of recent events in Mbugwe, giving special attention to the local effects of [then] Tanganyika's independence. He sent the report in several installments, and this, translated from his Swahili, constitutes the article which follows.

The Mbugwe, with a population of about 8,000, are located in the Rift Valley at the southern end of Lake Manyara. They are a Bantu-speaking people but have non-Bantu neighbors—the Masai to the north and east, the Iraqw above the Rift Escarpment to the west, and the Gorowa to the south. In pre-European times the tribe was divided into six or seven sections, each ruled by a rainmaker-chief. A short account of this traditional political organization is given in an earlier paper of

Reprinted in abridged form from *Africa*, Vol. 34, No. 2 (April 1965), pp. 198–208, by permission of the publisher. Translated from Swahili and edited by Robert F. Gray.

mine.[1] In a recent paper[2] I discuss rainmaking and some of the other magical activities to which Gicha refers. Some features of the lineage and kinship systems are described in a third paper.[3] Under British colonial administration a paramount chief was appointed over the whole tribe, but his rule was never accepted as legitimate by all the people. It would appear from Gicha's report that there is a small but vigorous party of traditionalist elders who hope that national independence will bring about a return to the old system of tribal government supported by ritual and magical sanctions.

Gicha has seen very little of the world outside Mbugwe, and for some years has been farming his land as an ordinary tribesman, recording ethnographic texts only as a sideline. Thus he writes of tribal affairs from an entirely inside viewpoint, which is very unusual in contemporary writings on Africa.]

There has developed a difference in outlook between the youths of the tribe and the older men. The elders have great faith in these unusual things as omens of significance for the country. In the case of the talking bird, they believed that it explained the cause of the famine in Mbugwe. The elders look to the past for the explanation and solution of present problems. We younger men have no belief in ancient lore, and regard the past as a matter of history.

For example, the elders believe in the rainmakers. We have all been taught that in olden times if the rains were late in starting a group of notables went to the rainmaker to find out what the trouble was and why he delayed the rain. There they were told what was needed. Perhaps the country needed a certain kind of sacrifice, or something may have happened that annoyed the rainmaker. The elders accepted this advice and took appropriate action. They carried out any sacrifices that were directed, and took pains to remedy any action that was displeasing to the rainmaker. If he demanded tribute they did their best to collect it and satisfy him.

During the last three years the Mbugwe have been afflicted with famine, until the people began to harbour dark thoughts. As the day of Freedom approached, many were assailed by doubts. But when the day arrived all doubts were thrown aside and there was only rejoicing. I must say that everyone believed in Freedom; there was no one, young or old, who had not had it explained to him.

The trouble with Freedom in the country of Mbugwe is this: everyone understands Freedom to mean that we shall rule ourselves—this has been thoroughly explained—but the elders and the youths interpret self-

1. R. F. Gray, "The Mbugwe Tribe: Origin and Development," *Tanganyika Notes and Records*, no. 38 (1955), pp. 39–50.

2. R. F. Gray, 'Some Structural Aspects of Mbugwe Witchcraft,' in *Witchcraft and Sorcery in East Africa*, ed. by John Middleton and E. H. Winter (London: Routledge & Kegan Paul, 1963).

3. R. F. Gray, 'Positional Succession among the Wambugwe,' *Africa*, xxiii (1953), pp. 233–43.

rule in different ways, and this has caused misunderstanding and quarrelling. In the old days the Mbugwe elders ruled themselves and did as they wished without any outside coercion, and this was the case until the Germans imposed their rule upon us, and after them the British. Under the old system every district had its chief, called *msungati*. Altogether there were eleven districts and six chiefs. Some chiefs ruled over two districts, while one of the districts, Ubwa, had no chief at all—the people governed themselves directly.

After independence there were many meetings at which a representative of the TANU committee explained Freedom and what it would do for us. Every time he would tell us that we were now the rulers of our own country. But after each meeting the elders would grumble and say that conditions were much the same as under the British. If we are really ruling ourselves, they said, should not each district have its own *msungati* as in the days before foreign rule? If we are now free, why do we still pay taxes? If we are supposed to be independent, then surely every man should be allowed to do as he pleases, for example, hunt game without being required to get a licence. We younger men tried to explain the meaning of Freedom under modern conditions, but the elders would not listen to us.

In March 1963 the elders held a big meeting at which they discussed the need for returning to the traditional ways of protecting our shambas [cultivated fields]. They affirmed that their reason for rejoicing over Freedom was that now the old customs would replace modern innovations as taught in school. Elders from all over the country came to this meeting. Their first resolution was that native medicine men must thereafter be respected, especially those who practised shamba medicine. The second resolution was to follow the advice of medicine men concerning house medicine, that is, medicine prepared for the purpose of preventing sickness from appearing in the community. It was agreed that every person must obey the orders of the medicine men. A third resolution demanded the return to an old custom which in recent times has been neglected by the youths. In the old days, if two men fought and drew blood, they could not go home until the spilled blood had been cooled through the sacrifice of a goat. The people believed that human blood was harmful and could cause a sickness called *cari*. Therefore, when a fight resulted in spilled blood it was necessary that every individual involved should produce a goat to be sacrificed. Only then was it safe for them to go home. For a long time now this rule has been neglected, and I dare say only a few people still observe it. The elders were very firm about this matter at their meeting. They noted that there is a good deal of fighting among the youths with sticks and knives, and insisted that the old rule be strictly observed.

The Struggle for Independence: The Tribe, Tribalism,
and the Conditions for Social Development

The young men were startled to hear all these resolutions and dire warnings. They could see no sense in restoring the custom of making medicine to prevent communal sickness. When this medicine is used the people are first told to prepare their houses—to lay in firewood and water and to sweep out the house—for during the days of the treatment they are not allowed to do this. All housework must be done in advance. The medicine is prepared by some eminent medicine man. First he orders a goat to be brought to him by the elders, and then he slaughters the goat in a certain way. An elder is appointed from each ward to obtain a share of the medicine.

I have seen with my own eyes how this medicine is distributed and used. Each elder is given a small gourd of the medicine, which is made from the stomach contents of the goat—called *ofu* by the Mbugwe. The elders go to their own wards and stop at every house, applying the medicine to the door. The elder informs the house owner how long the medicine must be left—usually for three days, or as long as the medicine man orders—and during this time there must be no housework.

The young men do not like this custom, and have quarrelled with the elders about it. One point of contention is the method of obtaining the goat which is sacrificed both for anti-sickness medicine and for shamba medicine. Let us say this medicine is for shambas, then the goat must be black, and when a sacrifice is required the elders seize the first black goat they see. The owner of the sacrificial goat is paid back after the harvest. Every household is then taxed a gourd of grain or one shilling to pay for it.

In 1963 medicine of this kind was administered by the elders, and after the harvest they tried to tax the people to pay for the goat. But that year there was no harvest, for the crops had been destroyed by insects. The medicine had been completely ineffectual. Therefore the people had no grain and most of them refused to pay a shilling. The owner of the goat complained until the principal elders and the medicine man paid him themselves.

A meeting was called, and the elders accused the young men of spoiling the medicine. They decided that even with a bad harvest everyone must pay for the sacrificial goat. The reason for the bad harvest that year, so they said, was the delay in applying the shamba medicine. This should have been done before the ears of grain began to form. Had they gone to the medicine man in time there would surely have been a good crop. At this meeting the Agricultural Assistant was present, and he talked to the elders about modern agricultural practices. Old-fashioned medicine was no longer used, he said. Nowadays there is a reliable medicine for protecting crops against insects; this is called DDT. After listening to this the elders seemed dissatisfied and reproachful, making foolish remarks. The Agricultural Assistant was a Catholic and therefore the elders were suspicious of what he said. Some of the elders stated openly that it is the Catholics who are obstructing our traditional customs and destroying the country.

When shamba medicine, or *mpefo*, is applied in the old way, the people must refrain from hoeing for as long as the medicine man orders —usually three or four days. Earlier in 1963 the elders decided to make *mpefo*, and the order went out that there must be no cultivating for three days afterwards. The *mpefo* was prepared on Thursday, and it was forbidden to cultivate on Friday, Saturday, and Sunday. On Monday it was lawful to hoe again. This affair led to quarrelling between Catholics and Pagans, until there was danger of serious fighting. The Pagans were burning with anger. They accused the Catholics of trying to destroy the traditional Mbugwe life. When we prepare *mpefo*, they said, the Catholics go and hoe during the forbidden days while the medicine is spreading through the shambas.

The trouble arose because the Catholics refuse to participate in these pagan affairs. They do not believe in the *mpefo* of the pagan elders. Therefore, when the elders arranged for the shamba medicine and ordered the people not to cultivate, many of the Catholic youths, and also some Pagans, scorned this order and went on cultivating during those days. The Catholics said they intended to work every day except Sunday. When the elders found these people working on the *mpefo* days they held a big meeting to decide what to do about the Christians. There was a very large attendance at this meeting. The elders of the Church were told to attend, and the secretary and chairman of the TANU committee were also present.

The Mbugwe elders accused the Catholics before these committee officials. "Now that we are independent," one of them said, "we can do as we wish. Our first desire is to make our country pure so that it will again produce sufficient food. We have medicine men who are expert at treating the crops so that they will not be destroyed by pests. Furthermore, we wish to acknowledge our rainmaker and allow him to function as in the old days—to show our respect by helping him hoe his shamba, and to correct anything that annoys or irritates him. If we are truly free, then we have the right to do anything that is for the good of the country. But we are obstructed in our attempt to purify this country by the mission people, who refuse to participate in the *mpefo* ritual and who continue to hoe on the days when this is forbidden because it would spoil the medicine. Now we have decided there is only one thing to do: the mission people must live apart from us and their shambas must be separated from ours, for they do not wish to cooperate with us."

The Struggle for Independence: The Tribe, Tribalism,
and the Conditions for Social Development

This speech startled everyone. These elders were proposing that the country be divided so that the Pagans and Catholics would live apart from one another. One of the church elders spoke up and explained the meaning of this proposal. "You Pagans have a perfect right to use any medicine you wish," he said, "and to employ your own rainmaker. We Catholics have no right to hinder you in this. However, you have no right to apply your medicine to our shambas. We have the right to cultivate every day except on Sunday and certain obligatory rest days. If you wish to work on Sunday, no one can stop you. If I forbid you to work on Sunday, would you obey me? Of course not! Because Sunday is not your day of rest. The rule these days is for every person to follow his own religion and let others follow theirs. The thing that distressed us to hear was that Catholics should live apart from the others with their own shambas. If some of our children go to school and become baptized, are they to leave their parents' home and go to live in the country of the Catholics? Surely you don't mean that! Every one of us prays that the country will be healthy and prosperous, but to God, not to man. It is our desire that our children go to school and obtain modern learning, not belief in ancient medicine. You said that we now have Freedom. But was this Freedom obtained through medicine, or through learning and knowledge? Entirely through learning!"

When the church elder had finished his speech many of the young Catholics came up to shake his hand in approval. But the pagan elders were dissatisfied and continued to accuse the Catholics of various faults. One elder stood up and spoke in this vein. "We hear from time to time," he said, "that the mission people do not consult the divining stones, that they do not believe in native medicine, and are scornful of our traditional *mpefo*. But if one of these mission folk gets sick, or especially if his child is sick, you will see him after dark running to the diviner to consult the stones, and then sneaking back home so that he will not be seen by other Catholics. Everything the medicine man tells him to do he does, but secretly, so that no one knows about it. If told to sacrifice a goat to his ancestors he does so late at night. But is not the *mpefo* that we want to apply to our shambas the same kind of thing as consulting the diviner or sacrificing to the ancestors?"

He went on to say that if anyone denied this he could name several Catholics, present at the meeting, who came to his place at night to consult the stones. "Then how can you say that Catholics do not share our beliefs? Do we not all believe in divination by stones?"

This speech left the people astounded, especially the mission people. He had asked some serious questions, and each man had to search in his own heart for the answer. Everyone started talking and arguing. The Pagans tried then and there to force their resolution on the meeting.

The crowd became disorderly and open fighting would have broken out except for the presence of the officials. The Catholics would not agree that pagan medicine was acceptable to their religion, and they steadfastly refused to participate in any rites which were unlawful to them.

.   .   .   .

In the present year of 1963 there has been a determined movement, led by certain elders, for a return to the magical practices of the past. For a long time the Pagans had been blaming the Catholics for the crop failure in Mbugwe. In my opinion this was unreasonable, for truly we are all in the hands of God. Without the help of God, man can accomplish nothing. People pray to God in different ways, and this the Pagans failed to understand when they accused the Catholics. Taking everything into consideration, I can see only one solution to our trouble: every man must pray to God in his own way, or according to his own religion. Those who trust in the spirits of their ancestors must pray accordingly. If someone wishes to pray to the Devil, that should be his privilege.

Early in the year the elders decided again to follow the advice of the medicine man and treat the country with traditional medicine—*mpefo*. They all agreed to pay for the sacrificial goat. The reason why the elders turned to these ancient practices, as I explained above, was that with the coming of Independence to Tanganyika they thought they were now free to do as they wished. At this meeting there were elders from every ward of Mbugwe. The main topic for discussion was the prospects for rain during the coming year. It was decided to restore some old customs that had been neglected for a long time. Each elder promised to inform the people of his neighborhood of this decision, and to explain that everyone must receive the *mpefo* and do as the medicine man ordered. Moreover, every person in the country would be expected to contribute something towards the cost of the sacrificial goat that would be required.

Some of the elders at this meeting were very truculent and insisted that something be done to show the rainmaker that he was held in honour. A day was finally set for honouring the rainmaker. On that day the leading elders started their march to the rainmaker's place, accompanied by other men who had joined them. Altogether there were sixty or seventy men, each carrying a hoe on his shoulder. They marched to the rainmaker's shamba, singing and rejoicing as they went. Arriving at the shamba, they set to work with their hoes, and within half an hour they had finished cultivating it. The rainmaker himself was astonished to see this company of men come singing and then cultivate his shamba. Such a thing had not happened in Mbugwe for many, many years. When the shamba was finished these men bowed down before their rainmaker saying: "Now that we are independent we can go back to our old ways. We have cultivated your shamba, not for money or beer, but for rain. We pray that you give us your answer today."

For us younger men it was astonishing to see this archaic behaviour. At first we thought they were just pretending, but they seemed to believe in it wholeheartedly. The rainmaker gave them only an indirect answer. He assured them that if they hoed with confidence and energy there would be sufficient rain. He expressed great pleasure that they had remembered the old customs. The elders returned to their homes singing in the manner of joyful men.

On the eighth of May 1963 all the people of the country together with the elders held a big meeting to discuss the curse that afflicted Mbugwe. Many people had been angered at the first meeting by the speech of the pagan elder in which he proposed that the Catholics should live by themselves. Words of this kind could end in war. It was decided to inform the government officials of that affair, and when the Pagans heard of this they were frightened, for they knew that most of us had been very displeased with the blather of the pagan elder. We were saddened at the idea of one tribe being divided into two parts. That would certainly be the end of Mbugwe. It was a godless idea which greatly distressed the mission people. The Pagans evidently wished to stop the progress of Mbugwe and go backwards. The time had come to bring the question of the partition of Mbugwe to a head. Otherwise there would be disorder in the country. The matter was settled at this meeting of 8 May. The following resolution was approved: everyone may pray in his own way. Those who follow a religion may pray according to the rules of their religion. Those without a religion may pray however they wish.

.   .   .   .

Now let us return to the meeting of 8 May. The first matter to be dealt with concerned the religious division of the country. It was decided that there could be no separation. Every person—Pagan or Catholic—could pray in his own way, and seek the welfare of his home and shamba in whatever manner he wished.

The meeting then discussed the question of taxing the whole country to pay for the goat sacrificed in the pagan ritual. This idea was overwhelmingly rejected. Someone pointed out that this would be very profitable for the tax collector. The price of a goat is 14 or 15 shillings. If 300 people are taxed a shilling apiece the total would be 300 shillings for one goat. Is this not the same as stealing from the people? If people really want to sacrifice a goat in this way, the thing to do is to pay for the goat before it is killed. Those who wished to share in the sacrifice could divide the cost among themselves. This might come to only 5 or 10 cents apiece. In this way the Pagans could have their sacrifice and pay for it easily and justly, with no need to accuse the Catholics of spoiling the ritual. The speaker then turned to the TANU chairman and asked his opinion. The chairman gave his approval, and it was decided that thereafter the goat must be paid for in full before the sacrifice.

This decision led to the discussion of another controversial question, namely the demand by the Pagans that the entire tribe should participate fully in the traditional agricultural rites which were being restored. The point at issue was the three-day period during which field work is prohibited. The Catholics were quite willing to suspend work on Sunday, but refused to abstain on the other two days. It was for this reason that the Pagans accused the Catholics of spoiling the shamba medicine and ruining the country. Thus there was complete disagreement between these two parties.

The TANU chairman stood up and spoke. He said, "The new motto of our country is *Uhuru na Kazi*—'Freedom and Work.' You are free to use any medicine for your land that you wish, but you must also work hard. Can the elders not plan their ritual so that the medicine is distributed and spread through the fields in one day? The answer is that they can easily do this. To spend three days on the medicine is nothing but idleness, and the people of Tanganyika do not approve of idleness."

Two other resolutions were passed before the meeting ended. It was decided that the orders of the medicine man were not binding on those people who do not believe in him. As for the custom of helping the rainmaker by hoeing his shamba, it was ruled that this work should be purely voluntary, and that no one could be compelled to work against his will.

Most of the people were satisfied with the meeting and went home happy that these controversial matters had been settled, but the pagan elders were disgruntled about the decision restricting the shamba medicine to only one day. I myself got to wondering why they had insisted on the three-day work ban, and made a point of discussing this question with a number of elders. It seems that there is nothing intrinsically wrong with working on the medicine days, provided one hoes slowly and carefully. However, it is a very dangerous thing if any blood should drop on the land during these days, as often happens when people hoe in a hurry and cut themselves. It was to prevent this from happening that all work was prohibited on the days when the medicine was working.

Some of the Mbugwe elders assert that there is no other way of purifying the land and bringing back good crops except by returning

The Struggle for Independence: The Tribe, Tribalism, and the Conditions for Social Development

to the old traditional customs, especially the custom of rain *mpefo*. They believe that the rainmaker must be restored to a position of honour, as in the old days, and that his orders must again be obeyed by the people. We younger men do not believe in *mpefo*, and this annoys these elders.

As for me, I have learned all about rainmaking in olden times through talking with my grandfather and other old men of Idulu. I explained earlier that it was the custom to sacrifice a black goat. However, in very ancient times there was another custom. If the goat sacrifice failed to bring rain, the rainmaker would ask for a black bull, and if the drought continued he might demand the sacrifice of a human being. The man selected for the sacrifice had to have a black skin, as in the case of the goat, and be in good health. The rainmaker would cast a spell over the victim so that he was compelled to do whatever the rainmaker wished, and had no will of his own. The rainmaker's assistants called the victim at night, and he followed them silently, for he was unable to speak and did not know what he was doing. It was as if he were dreaming. The rainmaker would be waiting for them in the forest. At his command the victim was strangled so that the rain sacrifice might be enacted.

At one of the big meetings that I mentioned earlier a young man stood up and raised this question of human sacrifice. If we are to restore all the old customs relating to rainmaking, he said, would this not lead us, step by step, all the way back to human sacrifice? The elders assured us that this would not happen. However, we had heard them state that in order for the country to prosper the rainmaker must again be honoured, that we should all turn out to cultivate his shamba, and that his orders must be obeyed. If we agreed to all this, how could we be certain that the rainmaker might not some time order a human sacrifice to be carried out in secret? We regard the rainmaking rites as foolish and dangerous and shall oppose the return to old customs which in the end might oppress the hearts of the people; for the motto of our country is "Freedom and Work," not "Freedom and Magic."

The new government of our independent country has given the Mbugwe elders the opportunity of organizing their own tribunals for trying minor cases. These are mostly witchcraft cases, and the verdict is usually based on divination. The new officials found that these witchcraft cases took up too much time of the tribal court, meeting at the baraza, and often ended in disorder, so they have turned them over to the local elders to be dealt with outside the baraza. Recently I attended one of these tribunals and observed the proceedings in a case which involved witchcraft. Before going on to describe this case, let me say that I was shocked at the way in which some of these people dishonestly slandered one another.

A girl named Magdalena was married to a young man named John. They lived together for three months, and in the fourth month the girl became sick. She stayed on a few days with her husband, then asked permission to go home and be taken care of by her mother. The husband agreed to this, so she went to stay with her mother. Her husband came to visit her occasionally, bringing her money to pay for medicine. In two weeks she was well again, and her husband came to fetch her home.

When the girl and her mother saw the husband coming they waited for him in the doorway. When he arrived they at first greeted him politely and explained that the girl had completely recovered. He then told them that he wanted to bring his wife home with him. Upon hearing these words his mother-in-law turned and upbraided him savagely. "You have no right to take my daughter away again," she told him. "Your mother bewitched my child and almost killed her. Do you think I will now give you another chance to kill her? Certainly not! Leave this house immediately and never let me see you here again. Your marriage is finished."

The young man went directly to his parents and told them what had happened. His parents went with no delay to the baraza to accuse his mother-in-law of slander, and that woman was served with a summons to appear before a tribunal of elders at ten o'clock on Monday morning. The young husband testified first at the trial; he told how he had gone peacefully to get his wife and had been insulted and abused by his mother-in-law. When he finished, the girl's mother stood up and told about her daughter's sickness and that it was caused by witchcraft on the part of the husband's mother. She had discovered this through consulting a diviner. The husband's mother then requested the court to appoint a committee of elders to find out the truth of the matter by divination. The court agreed to this, but warned her that she would have to abide by the verdict of the tribunal. "If you are proved guilty by the divining stones before these elders," she was asked, "do you agree to remove your witchcraft spell from this girl?" The woman answered that if her guilt was confirmed by divination she would remove her spell here before all the people.

The tribunal then addressed the girl's mother: "If the woman you accuse of witchcraft is proved innocent, do you agree to pay all expenses —that is, the divination costs, the committee of inquiry, the court fee, and the penalty of a bull for false accusation?"

The woman responded, "I will have no choice but to pay."

The tribunal appointed four elders, all of different wards, and ordered that everyone come back early Wednesday morning for the divination. At the appointed time they all went to the house of a diviner, the committee of elders leading. The diviner consulted his stones and they indicated that the accused was innocent of witchcraft. They went to another diviner and again obtained a negative answer. They consulted a third diviner, and then a fourth, always with the same result—the woman was not a witch. The elders asked the accuser if she wished for further proof, but the woman said she had had enough. They asked her if she still believed her daughter's mother-in-law to be a witch, and now she said it was not true.

The divination was finished and everyone went home. When the tribunal met again both women were summoned. The sick girl's mother was informed of the fine she must pay. This included 40 shillings for the committee (10 shillings to each elder for one day's service), 10 shillings for the court fee, 12 shillings for the cost of divination (3 shillings to each diviner), and one bull to be paid as compensation to the innocent woman for falsely accusing her of witchcraft. The total fine came to 62 shillings in cash plus a bull. The woman now refused to pay the fine and began to make trouble, so the court ordered her to be put in jail. After three days she cooled off and paid her fine.

Under the new arrangements, troublesome cases of this kind are no longer tried at the baraza. The officials have left them to be settled at native tribunals meeting under a tree.

Part III   *THE STRUGGLE FOR INDEPENDENCE: THE DYNAMICS OF NATIONALISM*

Karl Deutsch has argued that the growth of a sense of nationhood is the result of improved communications, intensified social contact, the growth of perceived economic advantages that would spring from a new unity, and the successful establishment of a common system of coercion. In order to understand the development of nationalism, one must focus on these underlying conditions of economic and social change. A shift from subsistence agriculture to an exchange economy brought larger numbers of people into sustained contact with each other. Previous "ethnic" situations became "loosened," and populations became amenable to restructuring. The growth of towns created reservoirs of new skills, capital, and labor—new opportunities for self-advancement, as well as dangers and difficulties for all. "Communication grids," networks of transportation, migration, and information systems of all sorts, brought more and more people together. The old social, economic, and political structures withered, and people sought new patterns of behavior and evaluation.

More and more people became aware of their wants and conscious of how little was previously done to satisfy them. Expansion of what Deutsch calls the "politically relevant strata of the population"—i.e., all those who had to be taken into account in politics, who counted for something in political life, created a mounting pressure for the transformation of political practices and institutions to allow for their participation in politics. Moving to the cities, engaging in new occupations, challenging old habits, traditions, and ways of thinking created new needs. Housing, illness, old age, unemployment, education, and sharp fluctuations in the prices of commodities posed problems that could not be dealt with individually. This need for a wide range and large amounts of government services, combined with increasing numbers of the politically relevant, underlay the rise of modern mass nationalism. Recognition spread even in rural areas of the need for political organization on a scale wider than the local community or tribe. Benefits to the individual and community ranged from healthy water supplies, improved roads and marketing facilities, to a new sense of belonging and commitment.

By the end of the Second World War, a new African elite had also emerged. The original African elite consisted of interpreters, clerks, lower civil servants—those who acted as the bridge between the foreign establishment and the indigenous population. In reality, this first elite possessed only a poor education, yet they constituted a distinct class. Numerically weak, they could aspire to the same standard of living as the colonists and could hope to assume some of their power. Even when a small African bourgeoisie of lawyers, doctors, teachers, and administrators emerged, they continued for the most part to look to the Europeans as models. For these elite, politics was a part-time affair, and they did not cultivate a popular following.

After the war, growing numbers of highly educated Africans increasingly resented their subordinate rule. This new elite stimulated the growing numbers of the discontented, the new urban dwellers, those who faced the breakdown of the rural systems, and helped along the spreading mass awareness of the colonial situation. A new leadership found a new following. These full-time activists galvanized all voluntary associations into vehicles of nationalism, created political organizations that extended to the remotest village, and demanded immediate independence and *Self Government Now!*

James S. Coleman discusses in a continentwide study the multiple causes of a variety of different types of nationalism. George A. Shepperson places the development of African nationalism within the context of world events and foreign influences. Carl G. Rosberg, Jr., and John Nottingham reveal some of the special problems of the multiracial areas. Jean-Pierre N'Diaye, in his interviews, allows African students to express their personal feelings about independence and self-government.

James S.
Coleman

NATIONALISM IN
TROPICAL AFRICA

P ostwar uprisings and nationalist assertions in Tropical Africa—that part of the continent south of the Sahara and north of the Union—have directed increased attention towards the nature and implications of the awakening of the African to political consciousness. Among scholars this neglected area has long been the preserve of the scientific linguist or of the social anthropologist; only recently have American sociologists, economists, and political scientists developed an active interest in its problems.[1] As a consequence, apart from certain efforts by anthropologists to popularize their findings and insights we have been obliged to rely primarily upon the somewhat contradictory accounts of colonial governments seeking to explain imperial connections, or of African nationalists determined to achieve self-government and the good life of which national self-determination has become the symbol.[2] Thus, we have been placed in the uncomfortable position of having to formulate opinions and policy and to render judgments without sufficient knowledge, or, what could be worse, on the basis of evaluations provided by participants in the nationalist struggle. There is, therefore, a very real need for independent and objective research regarding the character and probable course of African nationalist development.

Adapted from a paper discussed at the Conference on Problems of Area Research in Contemporary Africa, held at Princeton University, October 14–16, 1953, sponsored jointly by the National Research Council and the Social Science Research Council under a grant from the Carnegie Corporation.

1. Two notable prewar exceptions were Professor Raymond Leslie Buell and Dr. Ralph J. Bunche.

2. As an excellent example of the application of the insights of anthropology to the problems of political development in this area, see William R. Bascom, "West and Central Africa," in *Most of the World*, ed. Ralph Linton (New York, 1949), pp. 331–405. For a historian's appraisal, see Vernon McKay, "Nationalism in British West Africa," *Foreign Policy Reports*, Vol. 24, pp. 2–11 (March 15, 1948).

Reprinted from *The American Political Science Review*, Vol. 48, No. 2 (June 1954), pp. 404–426, by permission of the author and publisher.

What Is African Nationalism?

Not the least burdensome of our tasks is the problem of correlating or distinguishing between the generally accepted political concepts elaborated with specific reference to developments in the Western World (i.e., state, nation, nationality, nationalism) and the conceptual tools developed by the Africanists. The latter have tended to feel that the traditional concepts and methods of the political scientist are unserviceable in the study of the political structure and life of preliterate societies.[3] Yet, notwithstanding the importance of the lineage, clan, or tribe; the role of the diviner, the chief, or the age-grade society; or the wide variations in the organization of power within such societies, the concept and the institution of the modern nation-state, towards the creation of which African nationalism tends to be directed, is distinctly Western in its form and content. It is as exotic to Africa as Professor Toynbee has suggested that it is to the rest of the non-European world.[4] Nevertheless, just as the Indian National Congress has largely created an Indian nation, so African nationalists are endeavoring to mould new nations in Africa (e.g., "Ghana," "Nigeria," and "Kamerun").

On the level of abstraction at which the political scientist is accustomed to roam, *nation* is not a loose catch-all term denoting a larger grouping of tribes (e.g., Zulus, Basutos, Mende, Buganda, or Hausa); rather it is a posttribal, postfeudal terminal *community* which has emerged from the shattering forces of disintegration that characterize modernity. This does not mean that the Hausa peoples of Northern Nigeria cannot become a nation, nor does it mean that the "national"

3. *African Political Systems*, eds. M. Fortes and E. E. Evans-Pritchard (New York, 1940), pp. 4 ff. Insofar as *traditional* concepts and methods are concerned, ethnocentrism has been freely confessed by political scientists in recent self-criticism. See David Easton, *The Political System* (New York, 1953), pp. 33 ff.; also Report of the Inter-University Summer Seminar on Comparative Politics, Social Science Research Council, this REVIEW, Vol. 47, pp. 641–57, at pp. 642–43 (Sept., 1953). Amongst the modernists in political science one finds the argument that the political scientist should not be rejected too readily since he has developed skills and acquired insights that might well shed new light on the political process and pattern of government of preliterate societies after the anthropologist has exhausted his resources. Another argument, rather different, is that such societies might profitably be regarded as microcosms in which the political scientist can discern with greater clarity the essentials of government that might be obscured in the more complex Western systems. A final argument might be found in the recent psychocultural studies, especially in terms of their implications for policy formulation. See Ithiel de Sola Pool, "Who Gets Power and Why," *World Politics*, Vol. 2, pp. 120–34 (Oct., 1949).
4. Arnold Toynbee, *The World and the West* (New York, 1953), pp. 71 ff. It is difficult to accept without qualification Professor Toynbee's argument that the "national state" was a "spontaneous native growth" in Europe. One could argue that the centrally-minded, nation-building elites of emergent Asia and Africa are but the present-day counterparts of the centralizing monarchs of early modern Europe.

consciousness of the ordinary Hausaman must reach the level of intensity of the average Frenchman before there is a nation. It does suggest, however, that there must be a much greater awareness of a closeness of contact with "national" compatriots as well as with the "national" government.[5] This closeness of contact on the horizontal and vertical levels has been a distinctly Western phenomenon, for the obvious reason that it is the result of modern technology.

Not only is a political scientist quite precise in his use of the concept "nation," but in poaching on the insights of the Africanists he also finds it difficult to place under the cover of "nationalism" all forms of past and present discontent and organizational development in Africa. Thus, it is believed useful at the outset to distinguish the following:

TRADITIONALIST MOVEMENTS

1. Spontaneous movements of resistance to the initial European occupation or postpacification revolts against the imposition of new institutions, or new forms of coercion, referred to herein as "primary resistance."

2. Nativistic, mahdistic, or messianic mass movements—usually of a magicoreligious character—which are psychological or emotional outlets for tensions produced by the confusions, frustrations, or socioeconomic inequalities of alien rule, referred to herein as "nativism."[6]

SYNCRETISTIC MOVEMENTS

1. Separatist religious groups, which have seceded and declared their independence from white European churches either because of the desire for religious independence or because the white clerics were intolerant regarding certain African customs; hereafter referred to as "religious separatism."[7]

5. Royal Institute of International Affairs, *Nationalism* (London, 1939), pp. 1–7; Karl W. Deutsch, *Nationalism and Social Communication* (New York, 1953), pp. 1–14.

6. Nativism is here used in its broad and universal sense, as defined by the late Professor Ralph Linton: "Any conscious, organized attempt on the part of a society's members to revive or perpetuate selected aspects of its culture." See his "Nativistic Movements," *American Anthropologist*, Vol. 45, pp. 230–40, at p. 230 (April–June, 1943). The concept thus includes traditionalist movements in either the European or non-European world. This point is stressed because of the understandable sensitivity of many educated Africans to the root word "native," which as a result of the colonial experience tends to carry with it the connotation of inferiority. See also A. LeGrip, "Aspects actuels de l'Islam en A.O.F.," *L'Afrique et l'Asie*, pp. 6–20 (No. 24, 1953); Katesa Schlosser, *Propheten in Africa* (Albert Limbach Verlag, 1949).

7. Daniel Thwaite, *The Seething African Pot* (London, 1926), pp. 1–70; George Shepperson, "Ethiopianism and African Nationalism," *Phylon*, Vol. 14, pp. 9–18 (1st Quarter, 1953); Hilda Kuper, "The

The Struggle for Independence: The Dynamics of Nationalism

2. Kinship associations, organized and led by the Western-educated and urbanized "sons abroad" for the purposes of preserving a sense of identity with the kinfolk in the bush and "brothers" in the impersonal urban center, as well as of providing vehicles for pumping modernity— including the ideas and sentiment of nationalism—into the rural areas.[8]

3. Tribal associations, organized and led by Western-educated elements—usually in collaboration with some traditionalists—who desire to resurrect, or to create for the first time, a tribal sentiment ("tribalism), for the purpose of establishing large-scale political units, the boundaries of which will be determined by tribal affiliation (i.e., those who accept the *assumption* of common blood and kinship) and the forms of government by a syncretism of tribal and Western institutions.[9]

MODERNIST MOVEMENTS

1. Economic-interest groups (labor unions, cooperative societies, professional and middle-class associations) organized and led by Western-educated elements for the purpose of advancing the material welfare and improving the socioeconomic status of the members of those groups.

2. Nationalist movements, organized and led by the Westernized elite which is activated by the Western ideas of democracy, progress, the welfare state, and national self-determination, and which aspires *either* (a) to create modern independent African nation-states possessing an internal state apparatus and external sovereignty and all of the trappings of a recognized member state of international society (e.g., Sudan, Gold Coast, Nigeria, and possibly Sierra Leone); *or* (b) to achieve absolute social and political equality and local autonomy within a broader Eur-African grouping (e.g., French and Portuguese Africa) or within what is manifestly a plural society (e.g., except for Uganda, the territories of British East and Central Africa).[10]

Swazi Reaction to Missions," *African Studies*, Vol. 5, pp. 177–88 (Sept., 1946), Jomo Kenyatta, *Facing Mount Kenya* (London, 1953), pp. 269–79.
8. James S. Coleman, "The Role of Tribal Associations in Nigeria," Proceedings of the Second Annual Conference of the West African Institute of Social and Economic Research, Ibadan, Nigeria, April, 1952. See also *East Africa and Rhodesia*, October 5, 1951, p. 106: "Nairobi is the happy hunting ground for the organizers of tribal associations, as there are to be found in the city representatives of practically every tribe in East and Central Africa." Also K. A. Busia, *Report on a Social Survey of Takoradi-Sekondi* (Accra, Government Printer, 1950).
9. Most advanced amongst the Yoruba, Ibo, Ibibio, Ewe, Buganda, and Kikuyu peoples.
10. The difference between the goal orientations of the two categories of movements is partly the result of the objectives of differing colonial policies (i.e., the British policy of self-government and differentiation versus the French, Portuguese, and, in a qualified sense, the Belgian policies of assimilation

3. Pan-African or transterritorial movements, organized and led by the Westernized elite, frequently in association with or under the stimulus of American Negroes or West Indians abroad, for the purposes of creating a global *racial* consciousness and unity, or of agitating for the advancement and welfare of members of the *African* race wherever they may be, or of devising plans for future nationalist activity in specific regions.[11]

Once these very arbitrary analytical distinctions are drawn it should be stressed that none of the categories can be treated in isolation. Each of the movements is in one way or another a response to the challenge of alien rule, or of the intrusion of the disintegrating forces—and consequently the insecurity—of modernity. The recent so-called nationalism in Central Africa has been a mixture of "primary resistance" by the chiefs and traditionalists of Northern Rhodesia and Nyasaland and the nationalist agitation of the Westernized elite. Until the project of Federation became an active issue, African movements in this area were confined principally to religious separatist groups, tribal associations, or, in the case of Northern Rhodesia, labor unions.[12] On the West Coast, where nationalism is far more advanced, traditionalist and syncretistic movements have not been and are not absent. In some instances, kinship associations and separatist religious groups have been the antecedents of nationalist organizations; in others they have provided the principal organizational bases of the latter (e.g., the National Council of Nigeria and the Cameroons was first inaugurated as a feder-

and identity) and in part the result of the presence or absence of a settled white population. Confronted with the overwhelming obstacles to the full realization of *African self-government*, African leaders in the second category tend towards the extreme either of accommodation (Union of South Africa) or of violence (Kenya). In the territories of the Central African Federation the leaders of the African Congress have tended not to define their ultimate objectives, preferring to act empirically. The strength and persistence of the autonomic drive is reflected, however, in their reported attraction to the original Gore-Brown partition plan adopted by the European Confederate party. See David Cole, "How Strong Is the African National Congress," *New Commonwealth*, Vol. 27, pp. 5–10, at p. 9 (Jan. 4, 1954).

11. For a variety of reasons these move-

ments have thus far apparently accomplished little more than to dramatize their existence at infrequent *ad hoc* conferences. Until recently the initiative tended to be taken by Americans or West Indians of African descent (e.g., Marcus Garvey, W. E. B. DuBois, and George Padmore), although in the early 1920's there was a National Congress of British West Africa organized by the late Casely Hayford of the Gold Coast. Also, M. Blaise Diagne, a Senegalese, was President of the first Pan-African Congress in Paris in 1919. For recent pan-African nationalist activity in British West Africa see *West Africa*, Dec. 12, 1953, p. 1165; and for British Central Africa see Cole, *op. cit.*, p. 9.

12. See Ian Cunnison, "The Watchtower Assembly in Central Africa," *International Review of Missions*, Vol. 40, pp. 456–69 (Oct., 1951).

ation mainly of kinship associations, and the African National Congress of the Rhodesias and Nyasaland was the product of fusion of several African welfare societies). In certain cases unrest or protest of a nativistic flavor has been instigated by nationalists for their modernist ends; in others nationalists have claimed such uncoordinated uprisings, as well as purely economic protest movements, to be manifestations of "nationalism," when in reality the participants were unaware of such implications.

One of the interesting differences between prewar and postwar nationalism on the West Coast of Africa is that in the former period nationalism tended to be—as Lord Lugard insisted—the esoteric pastime of the tiny educated minorities of Lagos, Accra, Freetown, and Dakar; whereas in the latter period these minorities—greatly expanded and dispersed in new urban centers throughout the interior—have made positive efforts to popularize and energize the nationalist crusade in two ways.[13] The first has been to preach education, welfare, progress, and the ideal of self-government among the masses, largely through the nationalist press, independent African schools, and kinship and tribal associations. The aim here has been, in the words of one of their leading prophets, Dr. Nnamdi Azikiwe of Nigeria, to bring about "mental emancipation" from a servile colonial mentality.[14] The second method has been to tap all existing nativistic and religious tensions and economic grievances among the tradition-bound masses, as well as the grievances and aspirations of the urbanized clerks and artisans, and channel the energies thus unleashed into support of the nationalist drive. The technique here has been (1) to make nationalism, and in particular its objective of self-government, an integrating symbol in which even the most disparate goals could find identification, and (2) to politicize— one would like to say nationalize—all existing thought and associations. Until recently, many observers—including colonial administrators— tended to live in the prewar climate of opinion and therefore underestimate the power which had thus been harnessed to the nationalist machine.

In the case of the Mau Mau [a terrorist movement instrumental in the achievement of independence. See article by Rosberg and Nottingham below.] in Kenya we are confronted with a complex mixture of nationalism, with a strong traditional bias on the part of the Westernized leaders, and nativism, manipulated by the leaders, on the part of the masses. Both have been generated to an especially high level of intensity as a consequence of the acute and largely unassuaged sense of frustration on the part of the Westernized elite, growing out of the very bleak outlook arising from the almost total absence,

13. Sir F. D. Lugard, *The Dual Mandate in British Tropical Africa* (London, 1923), pp. 83 ff.

14. *Renascent Africa* (Lagos, 1937).

until recently, of meaningful career and prestige opportunities within either the old or the new systems, and of the masses, resulting from the land shortage and the overcrowding on the reservations. The presence of a sizeable Asian "third force," which virtually monopolizes the middle-class sector, and which has been and is politically conscious, provides a new variable of no little significance in the total situation. The fact that the pattern of organization and the strategy and tactics of the Mau Mau revolt indicate a higher level of sophistication than sheer nativism would imply suggests that our analytical categories need further refinement or qualification.

A particularly striking feature of African nationalism has been the literary and cultural revival which has attended it. A renewed appreciation of and interest in "African" culture has been manifested, in most instances by the most sophisticated and acculturated Africans (e.g., Mazi Mbono Ojike's *My Africa*, Dr. J. B. Danquah's studies of the Akan peoples of the Gold Coast, Jomo Kenyatta's *Facing Mount Kenya*, Fily-Dabo Sissoko's *Les noirs et la culture*, Léopold Sédar Senghor's *Anthologie de la nouvelle poésie nègre et malgache*, the French African journal *Présence africaine* edited by M. Alioune Diop, and the writings of Antoine Munongo in the Belgian Congolese journal *Jeune Afrique*).[15] In some cases this cultural renaissance has had a purely tribal emphasis; in others it has taken a "neo-African" form, such as the African dress of Dr. Nnamdi Azikiwe, nationalist leader in Nigeria. It has usually been accompanied by a quest for an African history which would in general reflect glory and dignity upon the African race and in particular instill self-confidence in the Western-educated African sensitive to the prejudiced charge that he has no history or culture. In short, there has emerged a new pride in being African. In French areas, the accent until recently has been upon French culture and literature, but there are increasing signs of a shift to African themes amongst the French African literati. The important point is that African nationalism has this cultural content, which renders more difficult any effort to separate rigidly the cultural nationalism of the urban politician from the nativism of the bush peasant.

15. See Rosey E. Pool, "African Renaissance," *Phylon*, Vol. 14, pp. 5–8 (First Quarter, 1953); Albert Maurice, "Union Africaine des Arts et des Lettres," *African Affairs*, Vol. 50, pp. 233–41 (July, 1951); Alioune Diop, "Niam n'goura," *Présence Africaine* (Nov.–Dec., 1947), pp. 1–3. The cultural revival is the product of four forces: (1) reflection and introspection on the part of educated Africans, frequently those confronted with the stimulating contrasts of a foreign environment while abroad; (2) the American Negro renaissance which commenced in the 1920's; (3) encouragement and sponsorship of European governments and unofficial organizations such as the International African Institute; and (4) support of missionary societies such as the United Society for Christian Literature in the United Kingdom.

Yet the differences are important to the student of African national-ism. Primary resistance and nativism tend to be negative and spontaneous revolts or assertions of the unacculturated masses against the disruptive and disorganizing stranger-invader. They are a reflection of a persistent desire of the masses to preserve or recreate the old by protesting against the new. Syncretism is different in that it contains an element of ration-ality—an urge to recapture those aspects of the old which are compatible with the new, which it recognizes as inevitable and in some respects desirable. Whereas all forms of protest are politically consequential—at least to colonial administrators—only nationalism is primarily polit-ical in that it is irrevocably committed to a positive and radical alter-ation of the power structure. In brief, nationalism is the terminal form of colonial protest.

Another reason for distinguishing between the various categories of assertion, which are basically differences in goal orientation, is not only to provide some basis for judging the nature of the popular support of a nationalist movement during its buildup, but also to have some means of predicting the stability and viability of the political order established by the nationalists once they achieve self-government. The governments of Pakistan, Burma, India, and Indonesia have each been plagued by internal tensions arising from what are fundamentally South Asian variants of traditionalism and tribalism. If a colonial nationalist movement comes to power atop a wave of mass protest which is pri-marily or even in part nativistic in character, this would have a direct bearing upon the capacity of the Westernized leaders of that movement, not only to maintain political unity and stability but also to carry out what is at the core of most of their programs—rapid modernization by a centralized bureaucratic machine. Any thorough study of the anatomy of a nationalist movement, therefore, must seek to determine the linkages and compatibilities between the goal orientations of the several forces from which that movement derives its élan and strength.

Factors Contributing to the Rise of Nationalism

It is far easier to define and describe nationalism than it is to general-ize about the factors which have contributed to its manifestation. Put most briefly, it is the end product of the profound and complex trans-formation which has occurred in Africa since the European intrusion. It is a commonplace that the imposition of Western technology, socio-political institutions, and ideology upon African societies has been violently disruptive of the old familistic order in that they have created new values and symbols, new techniques for the acquisition of wealth, status, and prestige, and new groups for which the old system had no place. The crucial point here is not that nationalism as a matter of fact happened to appear at a certain point in time after the "Western impact," but rather that the transformation the latter brought about has been an indispensable precondition for the rise of nationalism. Nationalism, as distinguished from primary resistance or nativism, requires considerable gestation. A few of the constituent elements have been:

ECONOMIC[16]

1. *Change from a subsistence to a money economy*. This change, consciously encouraged by colonial governments and European enterprise in order to increase the export of primary products, introduced the cash nexus and economic individualism, altered the patterns of land tenure and capital accumulation, and, in general, widened the area of both individual prosperity and insecurity.

2. *Growth of a wage-labor force*. This development has resulted in the proletarianization of substantial numbers of Africans, which has weakened communal or lineage responsibility and rendered those concerned vulnerable to economic exploitation and grievances.

3. *Rise of a new middle class. Laissez-faire* economics and African enterprise, coupled with opportunities for university and professional education, have been factors contributing to the growth of a middle class. This class is most advanced in Senegal, the Gold Coast, and Southern Nigeria, where it has developed despite successive displacement or frustration by the intrusion of Levantines and the monopolistic practices of European firms.

SOCIOLOGICAL[17]

1. *Urbanization*. The concentration of relatively large numbers of Africans in urban centers to meet the labor demands of European enterprise has loosened kinship ties, accelerated social communication between "detribalized" ethnic groups, and, in general contributed to "national" integration.

16. L. P. Mair, "The Growth of Economic Individualism in African Society," *Journal of the Royal African Society,* Vol. 33, pp. 261–73 (July, 1934); Allan McPhee, *The Economic Revolution in British West Africa* (London, 1926); G. Wilson, *An Essay on the Economics of Detribalization in Northern Rhodesia,* Part I (Rhodes-Livingstone Institute, 1941). Cf. Karl Polanyi, *Origins of Our Time* (London, 1946); P. C. Lloyd, "New Economic Classes in Western Nigeria," *African Affairs,* Vol. 52, pp. 327–34 (Oct., 1953).

17. J. D. Rheinallt Jones, "The Effects of Urbanization in South and Central Africa," *African Affairs,* Vol. 52, pp. 37–44 (Jan., 1953).

2. *Social mobility*. The European-imposed pax coupled with the development of communications and transport has provided the framework for travel, the growth of an internal exchange economy, and sociopolitical reintegration.

3. *Western education*. This has provided certain of the inhabitants of a given territory with a common lingua franca; with the knowledge and tools to acquire status and prestige and to fulfill aspirations within the new social structure; and with some of the ideas and values by which alien rule and colonialism could be attacked. It has been through Western education that the African has encountered the scientific method and the idea of progress with their activistic implications, namely, an awareness of alternatives and the conviction that man can creatively master and shape his own destiny.

RELIGIOUS AND PSYCHOLOGICAL[18]

1. *Christian evangelization*. The conscious Europeanization pursued by Christian missionary societies has been a frontal assault upon traditional religious systems and moral sanctions. Moreover, the Christian doctrine of equality and human brotherhood challenged the ethical assumptions of imperialism.

2. *Neglect or frustration of Western-educated elements*. Susceptibility to psychological grievance is most acute among the more acculturated Africans. Social and economic discrimination and the stigma of inferiority and backwardness have precipitated a passionate quest for equality and modernity, and latterly self-government. Rankling memories of crude, arrogant, or insulting treatment by a European have frequently been the major wellspring of racial bitterness and uncompromising nationalism.

POLITICAL

1. *Eclipse of traditional authorities*. Notwithstanding the British policy of indirect rule, the European superstructure and forces of modernity have tended to weaken the traditional powers of indigenous authorities and thereby to render less meaningful precolonial sociopolitical units as objects of loyalty and attachment. There has been what Professor Daryll Forde calls a "status reversal"; that is, as a result of the acquisition by youth of Western education and a command over Western techniques in all fields, there has been ". . . an increasing trans-

18. William Bascom, "African Culture and the Missionary," *Civilisations*, Vol. 3, pp. 491–501 (No. 4, 1953).

fer of command over wealth and authority to younger and socially more independent men at the expense of traditional heads. . . ."[19]

2. *Forging of new "national" symbols.* The "territorialization" of Africa by the European powers has been a step in the creation of new nations, not only through the erection of boundaries within which the intensity of social communication and economic interchange has become greater than across territorial borders, but also a consequence of the imposition of a common administrative superstructure, a common legal system, and in some instances common political institutions which have become symbols of territorial individuality.[20]

These are a few of the principal factors in the European presence which have contributed to the rise of nationalism. As any casual observer of African developments is aware, however, there have been and are marked areal differences in the overt manifestation of nationalism. Such striking contrasts as the militant Convention People's party of the Gold Coast, the conservative Northern People's Congress of Nigeria, the pro-French orientation of the African editors of *Présence africaine,* the cautious African editors of *La voix du Congolais,* and the terroristic Mau Mau of Kenya are cases in point.

There are a number of explanations for these areal variations. One relates to the degree of acculturation in an area. This is a reflection of the duration and intensity of contact with European influences. The contrast between the advanced nationalism of the British West Coast and of Senegal and the nascent nationalism of British and French Central Africa is partly explicable on this basis.

A second explanation lies in the absence or presence of alien settlers. On this score the settler-free British West Coast is unique when contrasted to the rest of Africa. The possibility of a total fulfillment of nationalist objectives (i.e., *African* self-government) has been a powerful psychological factor which partly explains the confident and buoyant expectancy of West Coast nationalists. On the other hand, as previously noted, the tendencies toward accommodation or terrorism in the white-settler areas is a reflection of the absence of such moderating expectancy.

Certain African groups exposed to the same forces of acculturation and the same provocation have demonstrated radically different reactions. The Kikuyu versus the Masai peoples of Kenya, the Ibo versus the Hausa peoples of Nigeria, and the Creole and Mende of Sierra Leone are cases in point. It is suggested that the dynamism, militancy, and

19. Daryll Forde, "The Conditions of Social Development in West Africa," *Civilisations,* Vol. 3, pp. 471–85 (No. 4, 1953).
20. See R. J. Harrison Church, *Modern Colonization* (London, 1951), pp. 104 ff.; Robert Montagne, "The 'Modern State' in Africa and Asia," *The Cambridge Journal,* Vol. 5, pp. 583–602 (July, 1952).

The Struggle for Independence: The Dynamics of Nationalism

nationalist élan of the Ibo peoples of Nigeria are rooted partly in certain indigenous Ibo culture traits (general absence of chiefs, smallness in scale and the democratic character of indigenous political organization, emphasis upon achieved status, and individualism). Much of the same might be said for the Kikuyu peoples of Kenya.

Differing colonial policies constitute another cause of these areal differences. Nationalism is predominantly a phenomenon of British Africa, and to a lesser extent of French Africa. Apart from the influence of the foregoing historical, sociological, and cultural variables, this fact, in the case of British Africa, is explained by certain unique features of British colonial policy.

It was inevitable that Britain, one of the most liberal colonial powers in Africa, should have reaped the strongest national reaction. A few of the principal features of British policy which have stimulated nationalism deserve mention:

1. *Self-government as the goal of policy.* Unlike the French and Portuguese who embrace their African territories as indivisible units of the motherland, or the Belgians who until recently have been disinclined to specify the ultimate goals of policy, the British have remained indiscriminately loyal to the Durham formula.[21] In West Africa, this has enthroned the African nationalists; in Central and East Africa, the white settlers.

2. *Emphasis upon territorial individuality.* More than any other colonial power, the British have provided the institutional and conceptual framework for the emergence of nations. Decentralization of power, budgetary autonomy, the institution of territorial legislative councils and other "national" symbols—all have facilitated the conceptualization of a "nation."[22]

21. Regarding Belgian policy, see Pierre Wigny, "Methods of Government in the Belgian Congo," *African Affairs*, Vol. 50, pp. 310–17 (Oct., 1951). Wigny remarks (p. 311) that " . . . Belgians are reluctant to define their colonial policy. They are proud of their first realisations, and sure of their intentions." Since this was written, there have been some very dramatic changes in Belgian policy, especially regarding the educated elite, the potential nationalists. The great debate in Belgian colonial circles on "le statut des Congolais civilisés" was terminated by four decrees of May 17, 1952, according to which educated Congolese are assimilated to Europeans in civil law. Regarding Portuguese policy, see Marcelo Caetano, *Colonizing Traditions, Principles and Methods of the Portuguese* (Lisbon, 1951). The keynote of the policy is the "spiritual assimilation" of the Africans to a "Portuguese nation dwelling in European, African, Asiatic and Indonesian Provinces." The African *Civilisado* is thus a citizen of Portugal.

22. Partly in response to nationalist pressures, the French government has recently initiated certain measures of financial devolution to French West Africa. See G. Gayet, "Autonomies financières française," *Civilisations*, Vol. 3, pp. 343–47 (No. 3, 1953). These measures may enhance the powers of the territorial assemblies to the point that the latter might ultimately become the foci for territorial nationalisms.

3. *Policy on missionaries and education.* The comparative freedom granted missionaries and the *laissez-faire* attitude toward education, and particularly postprimary education, has distinguished and continues to distinguish British policy sharply from non-British Africa.

4. *Neglect, frustration, and antagonism of educated elite.* Not only have more British Africans been exposed to higher education, but the British government until recently remained relatively indifferent to the claims and aspirations of this class, which forms the core of the nationalist movements.

5. *Freedom of nationalist activity.* The *comparative* freedom of activity (speech, association, press, and travel abroad) which British Africans have enjoyed—within clearly defined limits and varying according to the presence of white settlers—has been of decisive importance. It is doubtful whether such militant nationalists as Wallace-Johnson of Sierra Leone, Prime Minister Kwame Nkrumah of the Gold Coast, Dr. Nnamdi Azikiwe of Nigeria, Jomo Kenyatta of Kenya, and Dauti Yamba of the Central African Federation, could have found the same continuous freedom of movement and activity in Belgian, Portuguese, and French Africa as has been their lot in British Africa.[23]

All of this suggests that African nationalism is not merely a peasant revolt. In fact, as already noted, nationalism where it is most advanced has been sparked and led by the so-called detribalized, Western-educated, middle-class intellectuals and professional Africans; by those who in terms of improved status and material standards of living have benefited most from colonialism; in short, by those who have come closest to the Western World but have been denied entry on full terms of equality. From this comparatively affluent—but psychologically aggrieved—group have come the organizers of tribal associations, labor unions, cooperative groups, farmers' organizations, and—more recently—nationalist movements. They are the Africans whom British policy has done most to create and least to satiate.[24]

23. The stringent police measures adopted recently in Kenya and Nyasaland, the special press laws which have long been in effect in British East and Central Africa, and the obstacles to nationalist activity which have existed in the Muslim areas of Northern Nigeria do not necessarily invalidate this *comparative* historical generalization.

24. The thesis here is that there are at least four ingredients in the psychology of colonial nationalism, and that British policy in Africa has come closest towards inculcating or providing them: (a) an awareness of the existence or possibility of alternatives to the status quo, a state of mind produced by Western education and particularly by study and travel abroad; (b) an intense desire to change the status quo; (c) a system within which the major alternative to the status quo—self-government—has the status of legitimacy; and (d) an area of relative freedom in which that legitimate alternative may be pursued.

The Struggle for Independence: The Dynamics of Nationalism

This brief and selective treatment of a few of the factors which have contributed to the African nationalist awakening suggests certain avenues which might be profitably explored and more fully developed by subsequent research. Specifically, what is the relationship between the nature and intensity of nationalism and the degree of urbanization, the degree of commercialization of agriculture, and the size and geographical distribution of the wage-labor force and salariat? In short, what is the causal connection between "detribalization" and nationalism? Certain aspects of such an inquiry could be subjected to statistical analysis, but the results could only be suggestive, and in some instances might be positively deceptive. In the case of urbanization, for example, the highly urbanized and acculturated Yoruba peoples of Nigeria for nearly a decade lagged far behind the Ibo peoples in nationalist vigor and élan. Ibadan, the largest urban center in tropical Africa, has been until recently one of the most politically inert towns of Nigeria. Again, in terms of the proletarianization of labor and urbanization resulting from European industrialism and commercial activity, the Belgian Congo is one of the most advanced territories, but one in which nationalism is least in evidence.[25] Freetown, Sierra Leone, one of the oldest nontraditional urban centers, became a haven of respectability and conservatism, being eclipsed by the less-developed Protectorate in the push towards nationalist objectives. Urbanization has been an important ingredient in the nationalist awakening, but it has been a certain type of urban development—mainly the impersonal and heterogeneous "new towns"—which has occurred in conjunction with other equally decisive factors.

In the case of the relationship between the degree of commercialization of land and labor and the degree of nationalism, the figures set forth for the Gold Coast in Table 1 suggest either a casual connection or a parallel development. Yet in turning to similar figures for other territories —especially the Belgian Congo and Nigeria—it is clear that the relationship between commercialization and nationalism, important though it may be, must be considered and interpreted in the light of other variables.

Again, the fact that the nationalist movements have been organized and led by intellectuals and the so-called middle class suggests a relationship between nationalism and the number of Africans with higher education, the size of per capita income, the degree of the individualization of land tenure, the size of middle-class and professional groups (i.e., independent traders, produce middlemen, farmers employing labor, druggists, lorry owners, lawyers, doctors, etc.), and the degree of vertical mobility within the emergent socioeconomic structure. In any event,

25. The Belgian policy of stabilization of labor in the urban centers of the Congo, in which 83 per cent of the men have their families with them, is one of the several factors which may help to explain this.

Table 1—Commercialization and Nationalism in Certain African Territories

Territory	Percentage of Cultivated Land Used by Africans for Commercial Production (1947–1950)[a]	African Wage Earners as Percentage of Total African Population (1950)[b]	Degree of Overt Nationalism
Gold Coast	75%	9.0%	Advanced
Belgian Congo	42	7.6	None
Nigeria	41	1.2	Advanced
Uganda	33	3.9	Nascent
Kenya	7	7.6	Nascent

[a] E. A. Keukjian, "Commercializing Influence of the Development of Exports on Indigenous Agricultural Economics in Tropical Africa," unpub. diss. (Harvard Univ., June, 1953); United Nations, Economic and Social Council (15th session). World Economic Situation. Aspects of Economic Development in Africa. New York, Document E/2377, March 20, 1953.

[b] United Nations, Department of Economic Affairs. Review of Economic Conditions in Africa (Supplement to World Economic Report, 1949–50). New York, Document E/1910/Add.1 Rev.1-ST/ECA/9/Add.1, April, 1951, p. 76.

the insights of an economist are indispensable for a complete anatomy of African nationalism.

The Christian missionaries have been blamed frequently for their ruthless assault upon native religious systems and the thoroughgoing Europeanization, conscious or implicit, in their evangelization. This has suggested the formula: missionaries = detribalization = nationalism. Yet the postwar figures shown in Table 2 do not bear out this assumption.[26] Missionaries have been important catalytic agents in the transformation of African societies, but the causal connection between their activities and nationalist assertion cannot be established by mere quantitative analysis. The figures in Table 2 hint at a possible causal relationship between preponderant Protestant evangelization and advanced nationalism (viz. Gold Coast and Nigeria) and preponderant Catholic evangelization and the absence of nationalism (viz., Portuguese Angola and the Belgian

Table 2—Christianity and Nationalism in Certain African Territories

Territory	Percentage of Christians to Total Population	Percentage of Protestants to All Christians	Percentage of Catholics to All Christians	Degree of Overt Nationalism
Belgian Congo	37%	29%	71%	None
Nyasaland	26	49	51	Nascent
Gold Coast	15	58	42	Advanced
Angola	15	22	78	None
Kenya	10	51	49	Nascent
Nigeria	5	67	33	Advanced

26. World Christian Handbook (London, 1949).

Congo). Yet this connection must be examined in the light of other relevant factors, such as the degree of control and direction extended to missionary societies by colonial governments; the freedom allowed such societies to establish schools—particularly secondary schools—and to determine the curriculum; the tolerance accorded antiwhite or anti-colonial sects (e.g., the Jehovah's Witnesses are permitted in most of British Africa but proscribed in non-British Africa); the latitude allowed African sects of a syncretistic, revivalistic, or puritanical character; the extent to which evangelical bodies have *Africanized* their church organization, the priesthood, and the propagation of the gospel; and, finally, the strength of Islam.

The corrosive influence of Western education has been a significant ingredient in the rise of nationalism. Yet the Belgian Congo claims a higher percentage of literacy than any other colonial territory in Africa.[27] In order to establish a relationship we must move beyond the superficial analysis of literacy statistics and ask the following questions:

1. *The nature of the curriculum.* Has it been and is it literary and based upon the model of a European grammar school, or is it practical and designed to train the student to be a good farmer, artisan, or clerk in European employ, and incidentally to limit his sophistication and contact with unsettling ideas? Is instruction conducted in the vernacular or in a European language?

2. *Opportunities for postprimary education.* Are secondary schools (particularly those operated by missionary societies or by enterprising and nationalist-minded Africans such as Eyo Ita in Nigeria or Jomo Kenyatta in Kenya) allowed to mushroom into existence, or are they carefully planned and rigidly controlled by the colonial government as to both number and curriculum? What are the opportunities for study in universities abroad? What is the latitude granted students to determine their own careers? Here we touch upon a crucial factor—in 1945, Free-town, Sierra Leone, and Lagos, Nigeria, each had more Western-type secondary schools than all of the non-British territories in Africa combined. In 1952 over 4,000 Africans from British territories were studying in universities and technical schools abroad and nearly 1,000 in territorial universities in Africa, whereas only a handful had such opportunity or inclination in Belgian and Portuguese Africa. This is in part a reflection of the existence of a larger African middle-class in British Africa, but it is also the result of the unique British attitude regarding the relationship between higher education and emergent African leadership. French

27. United Nations, *Non-Self-Governing Territories.* Vol. III: *Special Study on Education.* New York, Document ST/TRI/SER.A./5/Add. 2, January, 1951.

policy and practice, despite differing assumptions, most closely approximate those of the British.[28]

3. *Openings of careers for the talented.* The stability of any political or social order is determined by this factor. Is there any planned relationship between the output of the schools and opportunities for satisfying employment or careers? In French and Belgian Africa, colonial governments have maintained a stringent control over the supply-demand situation as between *postprimary* schools and the requirements of government and the developing economy. In British Africa there are hundreds of thousands of unemployed or underemployed "Standard VI" boys clustered in the coastal towns and urban centers of the interior.

The most potent instrument used in the propagation of nationalist ideas and racial consciousness has been the *African-owned* nationalist press. In Nigeria alone nearly 100 newspapers or periodicals have been published by Africans since the British intrusion, of which 12 dailies and 14 weeklies—all African owned—are currently in circulation. The crucial role performed in the nationalist awakening by African journalistic enterprise on the British West Coast is well known.[29] Until the publication of *Afrique Noire* (organ of the *Rassemblement démocratique africaine* of French West Africa) there was nothing in non-British Africa which even closely approximated this development. And even this journal is no match for the pungent criticism and racial consciousness one finds in the pages of Dr. Nnamdi Azikiwe's *West African Pilot* in Nigeria.[30] Needless to say, the nationalist press is one of our major sources of data regarding nationalist motivation, objectives, and organization. It is not the number of newspapers published which is significant, but rather the volume of circulation and areal distribution, the news and editorial con-

28. By decree of April 16, 1950, the *Institut des hautes études* was established at Dakar; and on January 1, 1952, there were 1,640 scholarship holders in continental France, of whom 572 were pursuing higher education. *Civilisations,* Vol. 3, pp. 575–83 (No. 4, 1953). On British educational policy in tropical Africa see *African Education* (Oxford: The Nuffield Foundation and the Colonial Office, 1953). The Belgians within the past few years have dramatically reoriented their policy regarding higher education for the Congolese. Since 1952 Congo students have been admitted to the Albert I College at Leopoldville; the first Negro University of the Congo is scheduled for opening in 1954; and recently the Belgian press has drawn attention to the admission to Louvain University of a Negro student from the Congo. *Civilisations,*

Vol. 3, pp. 599–602 (No. 4, 1953).
29. Compare with the number of African-owned and edited dailies and weeklies (combined totals) in the following territories of British Africa: Gold Coast (17), Uganda (8), Sierra Leone (7), Gambia (3); French West Africa (10); and none, insofar as is known, in Belgian, Portuguese, or Spanish Africa; or in Kenya, the territories of the Central African Federation, or in the Union of South Africa.
30. On the other hand, there appears to be no newspaper in British West Africa comparable with the European-owned and edited journal of French West Africa entitled *Les Echos de l'A.O.F.,* which "week after week passionately attacks the administration. . . ." See Thomas Hodgkin, "The Metropolitan Axis," *West Africa,* January 9, 1954, at p. 6.

tent and the nature of the appeal, the types of readers, the existence of competitive papers sponsored by colonial governments, the financial stability of the paper, and other factors which would reflect its impact and influence upon the ideas, aspirations, and activities of those literate groups predisposed towards nationalism.

These are but a few of the more important factors in the rise of nationalism which require evaluation and weighting before the student of comparative colonial nationalism can go beyond the mere description of the history and anatomy of a particular nationalist movement. There is great danger in doing a disservice to scholarly research in Africa if one generalizes on the basis of observations made and data assembled in one territory. As has been suggested, there are certain general predisposing and precipitating causes of modern nationalism which are applicable to the whole continent; yet once these are mentioned, it is necessary to examine each area of nationalist activity for that special combination of factors which explains the origin, strength, and orientation of its nationalist movement.

Factors Conditioning Nationalist Development

Normally, a colonial nationalist movement directs its efforts towards the attainment of two main objectives: (1) the achievement of self-government, and (2) the creation of a cultural or political sense of nationality and unity within the boundaries of the area of the nation to be. Nationalists are obliged to adopt the second objective because imperial powers either did not or could not establish political boundaries which embraced only one self-conscious cultural unit; and certainly those powers made no conscious effort to build nations. The nationalist dilemma is that in most cases pursuit of the primary goal (self-government) lessens the likelihood of achieving the secondary goal (cultural and political unity). Put another way, the drive behind African nationalism in many instances is not the consciousness of belonging to a distinct politico-cultural unit which is seeking to protect or assert itself, but rather it is the movement of racially-conscious modernists seeking to create new political and cultural nationalities out of the heterogeneous peoples living within the artificial boundaries imposed by the European master. Their task is not only to conduct a successful political revolution and capture power, but also the painful job of national political integration. And as Professor Crane Brinton has shown, the lessons of history are that nation-building is the product of both consent and coercion, and usually the latter.[31] It is the colonial power, of course, which has had a monopoly over the means of coercion.

31. Crane Brinton, *From Many One* (Cambridge, Mass., 1948).

The major factor conditioning the development of a particular nationalist movement, therefore, is the degree of internal politicocultural unity, tolerance, or compatibility amongst the peoples of the area moving into its national era. Disunities can exist in a given territory for a variety of reasons:

1. Traditional precolonial hostilities and cultural incompatibilities such as exist between the Kikuyu and Masai peoples of Kenya, or the Ibo and the Tiv peoples of Nigeria. In some instances these have been exacerbated as a result of imperial policies; in others as a consequence of the mere fact of lumping them together and endeavoring to impose territorial uniformity.

2. Tensions between groups resulting from unevenness in development, acculturation, and the acquisition of modernity. These can be the product of original cultural differences (i.e., the variations between groups in their receptivity and adaptability to modernity—e.g., the Ibo and Hausa); historical circumstances (i.e., differences in the duration and intensity of the European impact—e.g., the Creoles of Freetown vs. the Mende peoples of the Protectorate of Sierra Leone); or of constitutional reforms pointing towards African self-government. One could argue that Ibo-Yoruba hostility in Nigeria is the product of all three factors. Just as the advance towards independence precipitated a cleavage between Muslims and Hindus in India, so has the development of nationalism and the move towards self-government in Africa brought to light a multitude of disunities. Fear of domination by the more advanced and acculturated groups—European or African—is one obvious explanation.

3. Tensions between the Westernized elite—the nationalists—and the traditionalists and the masses. This nationalist disability has tended to be exaggerated in the past, usually by imperial spokesmen endeavoring to repudiate the nationalists or to isolate them from the traditionalists. The intensity of the cleavage varies widely according to circumstances. In several areas such as the Protectorate of Sierra Leone, the Northern Territories of the Gold Coast, Western and Northern Nigeria amongst the Kikuyu in Kenya, and in Northern Rhodesia and Nyasaland the educated nationalists and some leading traditionalists have cooperated in varying degrees.

4. Differences within the ranks of the Westernized elite. These disagreements—and one is struck by their persistence, strength, and virulence—may arise from several causes, including normal competition for power and prestige or honest differences over aims, timing, or methods to be employed in the nationalist drive. Such differences as separate Messrs. Fily-Dabo Sissoko and Mamadou Konaté in the French Sudan; Lamine Gueye and Léopold Senghor in Senegal; Felix Houphouet-Boigny and Kouame Binzème in the Ivory Coast; Prime Minister Kwame Nkrumah and Dr. J. B. Danquah in the Gold Coast; the Sardauna of Sokoto, Oba-

femi Awolowo, and Dr. Nnamdi Azikiwe in Nigeria; Eliud Mathu and Jomo Kenyatta in Kenya; and Harry Nkumbula and Godwin Lewanika in Central Africa, have very materially affected the course and strength of nationalism in the territories concerned.

These nationalist disabilities are the product of a complex mixture of hard historical and cultural facts, of changes introduced and differentials created by the Western intrusion, as well as of the provocations of the nationalist drive itself. The success of any nationalist movement will in a large measure depend upon the extent to which these internal tensions are softened or dissipated. The latter will depend, in turn, upon the degree of repressive opposition, or unwitting or intentional cooperation, of colonial governments; upon the development of panterritorial political associations, the membership of which is rooted in all ethnic groups and in which there is free vertical mobility into the "upper crust" which that membership constitutes; upon the emergence of panterritorial economic-interest groups (e.g., middle-class associations or labor organizations); and upon many other sociological processes (out-group marriages, commonsality, etc.) which Professor Karl W. Deutsch has suggested are essential building blocks of any new national community.[32]

It would be naive and unhistorical to argue that a large measure of politicocultural integration is required—as distinguished from being desirable—in order for a nationalist movement to succeed in wresting self-government from an imperial power. Most successful colonial nationalist movements have been organized and led by small minorities which have been able either to gain the support of the masses or to capitalize upon their inertia and apathy. It would be unrealistic, however, to contemplate the success of a movement which did not have at least a minimum of unity or tolerance within the "upper crust," even though it be of the sort displayed by the unstable truces negotiated from time to time between the Sardauna of Sokoto, Mr. Obafemi Awolowo, and Dr. Nnamdi Azikiwe, the regional leaders in Nigeria.

Some of these forces contributing toward integration are measurable and provide rough indices upon which the research scholar can base predictions of the development of a particular nationalist movement. In an interesting new theory regarding the growth of nations, Professor Deutsch has suggested certain criteria which might be profitably employed in seeking to determine the prospects of success of a nationalist movement in its nation-building endeavors.[33] His central thesis is that cases of successful political integration in history show a number of patterns which seem to recur. As he puts it, a nation "is the result of the transformation

32. "The Growth of Nations," *World Politics*, Vol. 5, pp. 168–96 (Jan., 1953).
33. *Ibid*. See also Deutsch's *Nationalism*

and Social Communication (cited in note 5), pp. 81 ff.

of people, or of several ethnic elements, in the process of social mobilization." The prospects of success are indicated by the completeness of that transformation and the intensity of social mobilization around the symbols of the new national community. A nation is not only a subjective affirmation of will of zealous nationalists; it is also the product of the operation of powerful objective forces, several of which have been mentioned.

Thus far it has been assumed that the leaders of nationalist movements in Africa will seek to build new national communities out of the diverse human materials located within the artificial boundaries of the existing colonial territories. This was precisely what happened in Latin America (Spanish imperial provinces), in the Middle East (European and Turkish regions), and in Southeast Asia (Dutch Indonesia, Burma, and in a qualified way, British India). In the case of British Africa, where nationalism is most advanced, this same tendency for nationalism to follow boundaries established by the imperial power rather than those coincident with precolonial and sociopolitical groups is in evidence (e.g., Gold Coast and Nigeria). On the other hand, in many areas the situation is still relatively fluid. Togoland nationalism has been predominantly an Ewe affair, and the Ewes are a transterritorial group stretching from the Gold Coast to Dahomey. Separatist sentiment in Northern Nigeria is an example, *par excellence*, of incomplete social mobilization. This, when coupled with growing Yoruba and Ibo self-consciousness, suggests that earlier pan-Nigerian nationalism may be eclipsed and Nigeria may ultimately become three or more states. Until the recent decision to give the Southern Cameroons greater autonomy within the emergent Federation of Nigeria, Cameroonian nationalists were wavering between remaining an integral part of the Eastern Region of Nigeria, or seceding and joining with the nationalists in the French Cameroons in an endeavor to create a Kamerun nation based upon the artificial boundaries of the short-lived German Kamerun.[34] In Kenya, Mau Mau and all earlier protonationalist movements have been predominantly Kikuyu endeavors, even though the name Kenya has been employed. In Tanganyika, the Chagga Cooperative movement may be the basis for a Chagga separatism; and in Uganda, it is questionable whether pan-Uganda integrative forces can erase the "national" separatism implicit in the Buganda Kingdom. Again, in Central Africa, will the territorial separatism symbolized by the Northern Rhodesian and Nyasaland National Congresses be eclipsed by the common sentiment and institutions growing out of the new Federation?

In the case of French Africa, dissimilarities in colonial policy (i.e., assimilation and direct rule) have tended to produce a somewhat different situation. Yet since the reforms of 1946, as a result of which each of the

34. *West Africa*, January 30, 1954, p. 87.

The Struggle for Independence: The Dynamics of Nationalism

territories of the two federations of French West Africa and French Equatorial Africa received their own representative assemblies, territorial nationalist movements have tended to eclipse the pan-French African *Rassemblement démocratique africain* in much the same fashion as Nigerian, Gold Coastian, and Sierra Leonian nationalist movements have replaced the earlier National Congress of British West Africa. Thus one finds the *Parti républicain de Dahomey, Parti progressiste sudanaise, Union démocratique du Tchad*, and similar organizations in each of the territories. The future "national" orientation of nationalist forces in French Africa would seem to depend upon the extent to which pan-Federation forces and institutions, such as the *Grand conseils*, or the assimilationist forces of the French Union, such as the metropolitan parties and labor movements projected overseas, operate to retard the growth of territorial symbols and sentiment. One thing, however, seems certain: French Africa—because of the French policy of assimilation and direct rule—is less likely to encounter such movements as the *Egbe Omo Oduduwa* of the Nigerian Yorubas, the Kikuyu Central Association in Kenya, and the *Bataka* movement of Uganda.

In general, it would seem that where nationalism manifests itself in considerable strength it is evidence that disintegration of the old and social mobilization around the symbols of the new order have occurred on a scale sufficient to weaken or destroy attachments and loyalties of the nationalists to precolonial sociopolitical units, either because they have been crushed and are beyond memory or because they are unattractive or manifestly unsuitable as "nations" in a modern world of nation-states. The European presence has done much towards the creation of new nations, the "national" sentiment of the nationalists being a reflection of this.

A few of the many factors which might be observed and evaluated in order to determine the probable success, as well as the territorial implications, of an African nationalist movement or nation-building endeavor are as follows:[35] (1) the degree of internal social mobility, economic interchange and interdependence, intermarriage and commonsality, and the intensity and level of social communication among the ethnic groups comprising a given territory; (2) the location of population clusters and "core areas," as well as of "subnational" regions of more intense economic interchange or of cultural focus; (3) the powers and functions of "subnational" political institutions (i.e., regional, tribal, etc.), and the degree of *meaningful* participation in them by the Western-educated elements; (4) the rate at which "national" institutions and activities are capable of

---

35. For several of the concepts used here the author is indebted to the works of Professor Karl W. Deutsch, previously cited. See especially his *Nationalism and Social Communication*, pp. 15–45.

attracting and absorbing new social strata from all ethnic groups into the "national" life (e.g., the ethnic composition of the central administrative and technical services); (5) the centrality and nationalness of educational institutions, particularly the professional schools and universities; (6) the degree of panterritorial circulation of nationalist newspapers and literature and the extent to which these play up "national" events and personalities; (7) the differentials in the material development, per capita income and wealth, the acquisition of modern skills and knowledge, and the concentration and capacity for accumulation of capital amongst the different subnational areas and ethnic groups;[36] (8) the ethnic makeup of the Western-educated categories and particularly of the active membership of nationalist or protonationalist groups; (9) the development and extent of usage of a transtribal panterritorial language, be it English, French, Portuguese, Swahili, or Hausa; (10) the compatibility of the "detribalized" basic personality types produced by the indigenous cultures; (11) the extent to which the territory concerned embraces total cultural groups, or, put another way, the degree to which artificial colonial boundaries have bifurcated ethnic groups whose division may be the source of later irredentism; and (12) the rapport between the Western-educated nationalist elements and the traditionalists, including the existence of nativistic tensions or economic grievances which the nationalists could manipulate or exploit in their mobilization of mass support.

Results obtained from inquiries along these lines would go far to explain the present orientation of a nationalist movement, as well as possible future trends. And yet an emphatic note of caution should be sounded: objective forces of integration and disintegration are powerful determinants in the nation-building process, but so also are subjective factors.[37] By all laws of geography and economics Northern Ireland should belong to Eire, and East Pakistan to the Republic of India; but they do not. By the same laws, the Gambia should belong to Senegal, French Guinea to Sierra Leone and Liberia. Mozambique to the Central African Federation, and so forth; and yet present trends suggest that such will not be the case. The principal forces currently operating to shape Africa's emergent nations are either tribalism or a nationalism following artificial imperial boundaries; and, with few exceptions, neither

36. It could be argued, for example, that apart from historical and cultural factors, the difference in the per capita income of the three regions of Nigeria (£26 for the Western Region, £16 for the Northern Region, and £23 for the Eastern Region) is of no little significance in the recent and current drive for greater regional autonomy. See A. R. Prest and I. G. Stewart, *The National Income of Ni-* *geria*, abridged ed. (Lagos: Government Printer, 1954), pp. 14–16.

37. Given suitable conditions, including a politically favored milieu and the proper techniques, there would seem to be no reason why subjective factors such as loyalties, attitudes, and attachments to national or "subnational" symbols, could not to some extent be measured.

of these is directed towards the creation of political units which the geographer or economist would classify as ideal. In this respect, of course, Africa is not unique.

The foregoing raises the crucial question of whether it is possible for the peoples of Africa—in their own interest—to avoid the balkanization implicit in the full application of the national principle to their continent. So long as the rest of the world is organized according to that principle, and so long as the national idea universally embodies aspirations which cannot be satisfied by other forms of human organization, the answer would seem to be in the negative. The quest for racial equality and acceptance is as important an ingredient in the African revolt as is the desire to determine one's own destiny. Rightly or wrongly, self-government within the confines of the sovereign nation-state has become the supreme symbol of the equality of peoples. The only possible alternative would be broader Eur-African political groupings or self-governing plural societies in which emergent African leaders could play what they would feel to be an equal role. In the light of the persistence of national self-determination as a symbol, and particularly in view of the growing strength and contagion of African nationalism, the future of such multiracial experiments will depend in a large measure upon the rapidity with which European governments and leaders provide for such a role.

Special Problems of Research into African Nationalism

There is perhaps no other type of research venture capable of evoking stronger feeling than an inquiry into colonial nationalism. The word "nationalism" in a colonial milieu has tended to be treated as the equivalent of sedition, or even treason. And this for good reason: by definition colonial nationalists are seeking to bring about a radical alteration in the power structure; namely, to evict the imperial power and to enthrone themselves. From the moment it makes its presence known, therefore, a nationalist movement is, in effect, engaged in a civil war with the colonial administration, the constitutionality of its methods varying according to the liberality of the colonial regime and the moderation of the nationalist leaders.

As regards colonial officialdom, an American undertaking a study of African nationalism is handicapped by the fact that in a large measure the African nationalist awakening is the product of American influences. Since the turn of the century, American Negro religious sects have contributed so little to religious secessionism, particularly in South and West Africa. The Garveyism of the early 1920's had an influence among sophisticated Africans which has tended to be overlooked or minimized. Since 1919 a growing number of American Negro intellectuals have taken an increasingly militant stand on African colonialism. Anti-imperialist sentiment in the United States, especially during the Second World War, was the source of considerable inspiration and delight to budding African nationalists, as well as the cause of no little acrimony between wartime allies. The Atlantic Charter, the Four Freedoms, and public statements by Mr. Willkie and President Roosevelt have bulked large in postwar African nationalist literature. The most important American contribution, however, has been the impact of our culture upon African students who have studied in America. Many of the important pioneers in the African awakening were profoundly affected by their American experience. Of this group the late Dr. J. E. K. Aggrey and Prime Minister Kwame Nkrumah from the Gold Coast, and Professor Eyo Ita and Dr. Nnamdi Azikiwe from Nigeria are the most prominent and best known. During the Second World War the number of African students in America was less than 25; since 1945 it has increased to over 500. With few exceptions these students have been and are strong nationalists, many of them having become leaders upon their return to Africa. In the eyes of colonial officialdom, therefore, an American inquiry into nationalism tends to raise certain doubts.

There has been a tendency in the past for American visitors making quick tours of Africa to rely mainly upon the white colonial administration for an appraisal of nationalist sentiment and activity. This is unfortunate in many respects. In the first place, it is most likely that any information bearing on nationalism is locked up in classified files. Secondly, most colonial administrators have tended to be antinationalists, even though many in British West Africa have adapted themselves to working with nationalists towards a mutually agreed goal of effective self-government. Their evaluation of nationalism is bound to be colored by their preconceptions and vested interests or by their honest fears regarding the welfare of the bush peasant, for whom they tend to have a preference and a strong paternal affection. Thirdly, circumstances have tended to place them too close to events or too far removed from the people. Their growing preoccupation with headquarters administration and development schemes, the social impediments—created frequently by the presence of white wives and families—to effective and continuous contact with the masses, and the almost total lack of rapport or confidence between nationalists and administrators, have given the latter many blind spots. Their past miscalculations of nationalist strength and trends tend to confirm this. In short, instead of being used as informants, a role they are not anxious to perform, they should be objects of study. Their fears, their adjustments, and their efforts to suppress, retard, manipulate, or encourage nationalism are all relevant in a complete study of the many interacting factors present in a nationalist situation.

Unlike the field anthropologist, who consciously seeks to work among the traditionalists, the student of political nationalism is concerned mainly with the attitudes, activities, and status of the nationalist-minded Western-educated elite. Here one is in a world very different from that of officialdom or the traditionalists. It is a world of great idealism, crusading zeal, and high resolve, as well as one of suspicion, hypersensitivity, and exaggeration. It has its careerists and opportunists, and its chronic nonconformists; but it also has its emergent statesmen, its enterprising industrialists, and its distinguished scholars. Only here can one get a partial glimpse into the depth of nationalist feeling, the sources of inspiration and ideas, and the key elements in nationalist motivation. Yet there are distinct limitations to the interview technique, not the least important of which is the possession of a white skin. Moreover, a colonial nationalist movement must have its arcana as well as its propaganda.

In the quest for knowledge regarding African nationalism, the most fruitful as well as unprovocative avenues to explore are those already indicated in earlier sections. African nationalism is something more than the activities of a few disgruntled journalists and frustrated intellectuals to whom Lord Lugard referred in his *Dual Mandate*. It is the inevitable end product of the impact of Western imperialism and modernity upon African societies; it is also the inevitable assertion by the Africans of their desire to shape their own destiny. Imperial systems are disintegrating, new nation-states are emerging, and new forms of political organization transcending the national state are under experiment. These political aspects of African nationalism, however, are but the surface symptoms of a great ferment about which we know very little. The study and analysis of the many complex factors in this unfolding drama provide not only a stimulating challenge to the social sciences, but also a compelling invitation to greater interdisciplinary cooperation.

George A.
Shepperson

EXTERNAL FACTORS IN THE DEVELOPMENT OF AFRICAN NATIONALISM, WITH PARTICULAR REFERENCE TO BRITISH CENTRAL AFRICA

Political relations may change a name," wrote David Clement Scott, in *A Cyclopaedic Dictionary of the Mang'anja Language Spoken in British Central Africa* (Edinburgh, 1892, p. 140).

At a time when nationalism is marching across Africa with giant strides, the relevance of the concept to African conditions has been questioned, and various substitutes, such as "Africanism,"[1] "African consciousness,"[2] "tribalism," and "racialism,"[3] have been suggested. Those, however, who are critical of the term "nationalism" in the new Africa are often unaware that it has frequently been called misleading in a European context as well, and has had to be assisted in this by a battery of supplementary adjectives. Miss Hannah Arendt, for example, who finds "racialism" as pronounced a characteristic of the European history scene as the critics of the term "nationalism" proclaim it to be in Africa, is compelled to invent for her study of European history the expression "tribal nationalism."[4]

Indeed, that Africa is obliged to express its most pressing political problem in these vague European terms indicates the importance of external factors in the growth of African "nationalism."[5] In one sense, of course, all nationalism is the product of a reaction against external forces. But in Africa, whose partition and introduction to the apparatus of the modern state came at a time when Europe was throwing up chaotically those processes for which the terms "nationalism," "imperialism," "racial-

This paper was given as a public lecture and also discussed in a private session at the Leverhulme History Conference at the University College of Rhodesia and Nyasaland. Southern Rhodesia, September, 1960, to which acknowledgment is made for permission to publish it.
1. Lord Hailey, *An African Survey* (London, 1956), p. 251.
2. *East Africa and Rhodesia* (London, February 18, 1960), p. 590.
3. *New York Times*, February 22, 1960: letter, "Africa's Loyalties."
4. *The Burden of Our Times* (London, 1951), pp. 227 ff.
5. Cf. *United States Foreign Policy. A Study prepared at the request of the Senate Committee on Foreign Relations*, October 23, 1959 (Washington, 1959: 46905), pp. 22, 53.

Reprinted from *Phylon*, Vol. 22, No. 3 (Fall 1961), pp. 207–225, by permission of the editors.

ism," and "socialism" are inadequate but necessary labels, external factors have a peculiar force. It would be possible, certainly, to group them all in one great bracket of externality: the forcible imposition of the European-style state system. Yet by breaking this down into a number of elements, the special features of African nationalism, as well as those which it shares with Europe, may be more readily appreciated. Six external factors have struck me as particularly important. I am sure that they could be expressed differently and that others could be added. Nevertheless, I shall state them in the manner I have found most useful in my own studies, add a few examples from outside my special field of African interest, and then go on to illustrate these factors with particular reference to that field, Nyasaland [now Malawi], or, as I shall sometimes call it, by the old name, British Central Africa, because that brings to mind the fluidity and artificiality of its frontiers.

The first of these factors is, quite simply, the character of the culture of the occupying power, a factor which seems to be proving remarkably persistent—especially in the divisive forces of the French and English languages. A minor, amusing example comes from McGregor Ross's 1927 book on Kenya, in which, paying tribute to the *pax britannica* and its improvement of communications, he associated the British national passion, sport, and the development of African nationalism:

> Football teams now travel hundreds of miles by train and steamer to play the teams of other tribes. In 1922 a Kikuyu firebrand [Harry Thuku] . . . was addressing enthusiastic meetings, 5,000 strong, in Kavirondo—where some few years earlier he would have been swiftly clubbed. Our Administration officers are welding tribes into a *nation.* . . .[6]

A second external factor is the agency in the growth of African nationalism of a person, originally alien to the particular society, who comes into it from outside, identifies himself enthusiastically with it and then *plus écossais que les écossais* [more Scotch than the Scots], as it were, plays a leading role in the development of its consciousness. The outstanding example is, undoubtedly, Edward Blyden, that remarkable West Indian whose writings and speeches did so much to lay the theoretical foundations for the concepts of "African personality" and *négritude*. What Blyden's work began was completed by another West Indian, George Padmore.

The third external factor, which seems to me to be of great importance, is a period of residence overseas. Almost all of the modern African political leaders have spent some formative part of their lives in Europe or America: an alien environment has strengthened their feeling

6. W. McGregor Ross, *Kenya From Within* (London, 1927), p. 184.

181

SHEPPERSON: *External Factors in the Development of African*
Nationalism, with Particular Reference to British Central Africa

of national consciousness which, before they went overseas, had sometimes been the prey of local and ethnic differences.[7] An interesting early
example is Orishatukeh Faduma,[8] who was baptized in Sierra Leone as
William Davis; adopted a Yoruba name in 1887 at a time when the
"Africanizing" influence of Edward Blyden was growing; went to America; associated with a wide range of Negro American movements to which
he contributed several influential papers[9] and which increased his African consciousness; and returned to Africa late in 1914 as a leader of a
"back-to-Africa" movement of colored Americans. He was read by early
Nigerian nationalists. This is clear from the use of Faduma's denunciation
of Europe in a 1918 pamphlet by Patriarch J. G. Campbell, leader of the
separatist "West African Episcopal Church": "The two gods of Europe
are the idolatry of Domination and money before which great nations
bow and crush weaker ones in the name of religion."[10]

African political movements, however, can be influenced by periods
of residence by Africans not necessarily overseas but in other states in
Africa. This is a fourth external factor worth examining. Labor migration is an obvious example. But there are the movements of individuals
from state to state which should not be overlooked. What, for example,
would the South African political scene of the 1920's have been like
without Nyasa migrant Clements Kadalie and his Industrial and Commercial Workers Union of Africa, the famous ICU? And what was the
role in the growth of nationalism in West Africa during the First World
War of the Ivory Coast "prophet movement" led by William Wade
Harris from Liberia? Certainly, Casely Hayford of the Gold Coast saw
in this wandering preacher, thrice imprisoned, a political figure of some
importance.[11]

This First World War character draws attention to a fifth factor of
enormous significance in the rise of African nationalism: the impact of
two world wars. One must not, however, exaggerate the significance
of the 1939–1945 war,[12] the real importance of which was to accelerate

7. An important work in the study of
this type of external influence is James
S. Coleman, *Nigeria: Background to
Nationalism* (Los Angeles, 1958), pp.
243–48, etc.
8. I am indebted to Mr. Christopher Fyfe
for a number of details about Faduma.
9. "Africa or the Dark Continent," *Afri-
can Methodist Episcopal Church Review*
(Philadelphia, 1892), pp. 1–8; "Religious
Beliefs of the Yoruba People in West
Africa" and "Success and Drawbacks of
Missionary Work in West Africa by an
Eye-Witness," *Africa and the American
Negro*, ed. J. W. E. Bowen (Atlanta),

pp. 31–36 and 125–36; *The Defects of the
Negro Church* (Washington, 1904).
10. *Some Thoughts on Abeokuta during
the Reign of His Highness King Ghadebo
the Alake 1898–1918* (Lagos, 1918), p. 1.
11. Casely Hayford, *William Waddy
Harris. The West African Reformer*
(London, 1915). See also Raymond Leslie
Buell, *The Native Problem in Africa*
(New York, 1928), II, 66–68; W. J. Platt,
*An African Prophet. The Ivory Coast
Movement* (London, 1934).
12. *Cf.* Colin Leys, "Nationalism in Africa," *The Listener* (London, June 2,
1960), p. 967; also June 10, 1960, p. 1063.

dramatically a trend which went back to 1885 when Bismarck said at the West African Conference of Berlin that "The evils of war would assume a specially fatal character if the natives were led to take sides in disputes between the civilized powers."[13] The coming of the 1939 war did not hit Africans with the same force as the 1914 war which brought about a "deep and fundamental" change "in the relations of the African people with the great unknown world which suddenly fell upon them and insisted that they must become a part of it, however unwilling and without understanding they might be."[14]

In one sense, of course, this war and its 1939 successor are special instances of my third and fourth external factors. Certainly, it was the Africans who served with European forces, in Africa and overseas, who may be assumed to have felt the influence of these two wars the most. One must remember here the effect of the 1914–1918 war on French African nationalism through the recruitment of black troops for service with the French armies in Europe, the role of the Senegalese politician, Blaise Diagne, in the recruiting drive and the part which he played in the post-war Pan-African Conference in Paris.

But these two great external events affected also those Africans who stayed at home, not only by their economic consequences and through the new ideas which were brought back by returning soldiers but also through the feelings about those who did not come home. Mr. F. D. Corfield notes appropriately the effect of service in the 1914 war on the widening of Kikuyu political horizons and claims that wilful misuse of postwar gratuities embittered many Kikuyu ex-servicemen, who "refused to accept the fact that their mistakes had been of their own making," against the government.[15] He does not, however, mention the loss of Kikuyu and other African lives in the carrier corps. For this, one must turn to Sir Philip Mitchell's testimony:

> A large number died on service, a larger number than that service justified, for, though there were exceptions, the feeding and care of the porters and protection against excessive loads were seldom of an adequate standard.[16]

This became a grievance of the Kikuyu and other African people and passed into their political folklore.

Yet perhaps the most serious outcome of the First World War was its deflation of the white man's prestige. "It cannot be pretended," wrote Mr. F. S. Joelson mordantly in 1920, "that it will ever be as high as it

---

13. *Protocols and General Act of the West African Conference* (London: C.4361, Africa No. 4, 1885), p. 301.
14. Sir Philip Mitchell, *African Afterthoughts* (London, 1954), pp. 49–50.

15. *Historical Survey of the Origins and Growth of Mau Mau* (London: Cmnd. 1030), pp. 17, 23.
16. Mitchell, *op. cit.*, pp. 48–49.

183

SHEPPERSON: *External Factors in the Development of African*
Nationalism, with Particular Reference to British Central Africa

was before the war taught blacks to butcher the ruling whites."[17] This was the main legacy of the 1914 war to emerging African nationalism, out of which the 1939 war made a dramatically increased but by no means new kind of political capital.

A sixth external factor is what may be termed foreign ideological influences. I am not here thinking of Christianity, not only because it has as long a history in Africa as in Europe but mainly because I feel that Christian influences should be construed initially in terms of the culture pattern of the first European country which introduced them to particular African regions: that is, in terms of my first external factor. The foreign ideological influences I am thinking of are those which have entered Africa relatively independently of this culture. Here one must include the nationalist movements, both in Europe and its empires, especially Indian and Irish nationalism. Marxism is a relative latecomer and its onslaught on Africa had to wait until after the Second World War. Before this, the attention of official Marxism in the colonial sphere was largely focused on Asia.[18]

A specially interesting foreign influence has been the role of American Negroes in the emergence of African nationalism.[19] As President Nkrumah put it at the end of the first All-African Peoples Conference at Accra in 1958:

> Many of them have made a contribution to the cause of African freedom. Names which spring immediately to mind are those of Marcus Garvey and W. E. B. DuBois. Long before many of us were even conscious of our own degradation, these men fought for African national and racial equality.

It may be worth noting here that, although the Conference at which these words were spoken endorsed "pan-Africanism," paid a special tribute to its founder, the Negro American, Dr. W. E. B. DuBois, and saw itself in the line of descent from the five Pan-African Congresses in Europe and America from 1919 to 1945, it did not style itself "pan-African" but called itself an All-African People's Conference. Was the change fortuitous? Certainly, it served to mark a new epoch in which such conferences were to be in Africa and under the direct control of African peoples. The prefix "pan" calls to mind the European and American "pan" movements of the late nineteenth and early twentieth centuries. The first, premature Pan-African Conference in London

---

17. *The Tanganyika Territory* (London, 1920), pp. 255–56.
18. David T. Cattell, "Communism and the African Negro," *Problems of Communism* (Washington, 1959), VIII, No. 5, 35–47.

19. See, in general, George Shepperson, "Notes on Negro American Influences on the Emergence of African Nationalism," *The Journal of African History* (London, 1960), I, No. 2, 299–312.

in 1900 clearly took over this prefix from the pan-Slav, pan-German, pan-Islamic and pan-American complex of its time. In 1892, DuBois went to the University of Berlin for two years[20] for postgraduate work and travelled in eastern and central Europe at a moment when all these "pan" movements—and the rise of antisemitism in Germany—were in rapid growth. The young DuBois thus saw the continent at a time when the kaleidoscope of racialism and nationalism, out of which emerged the Europe of the First World War, which he was to see again when he went to Paris in 1919 to organize the Pan-African Conference, was being shaken so fiercely.[21] Out of these European experiences came some of the ideas and attitudes which the father of pan-Africanism handed on to the movement, irregular, halting and often confused, but still a movement, that led to the 1958 Conference in Accra.

The relevance of these six external factors for the growth of African nationalism may be seen more clearly by referring them now to British Central Africa.

The predominant European culture in Nyasaland until very recent times has been Scottish: in fact, the histories of Scotland and Nyasaland pursue remarkably parallel courses. Both are poor; but both have distinctive educational traditions which have reinforced the conviction of their many migrants that they are worth better jobs than their homeland can offer them. From such conditions, there has sprung up in both countries a very definite radicalism, at home and abroad. Both have created an interesting mixture of calculation and impulsiveness in their inhabitants:[22] the nation which produced the careful Robert Laws and the impulsive Leander Starr Jameson has its counterparts in the shrewd but heady two generations of Nyasaland African politicians since John Chilembwe returned from America in 1900. Yet, at the same time, both have produced many loyalists through their heavy contributions for small countries to imperial military forces. The old-soldier patriot has been as notable a feature of Nyasaland as of Scotland. In both, the abrupt entrance into a larger state (Scotland in 1707, Nyasaland in 1953) has stimulated nationalist feeling.

How much of these common features is due to genuine parallels and how much to imposed patterns may be seen better by examining a little more closely the culture which the Scottish pioneers brought to British Central Africa.

It is, of course, a notoriously difficult task to describe Scottish culture which many would say, with a considerable degree of justification, is

20. Francis E. Broderick, *W. E. B. Du-Bois* (Stanford, 1959), pp. 26–27.
21. W. E. B. DuBois, *Dusk of Dawn* (New York, 1940), p. 47.
22. See George Shepperson, "David Livingstone the Scot," *Scottish Historical Review* (Edinburgh, October, 1960), CXXVIII, 113–21, which has some documentation which will be found useful for the Scottish section of this paper.

185

SHEPPERSON: *External Factors in the Development of African Nationalism, with Particular Reference to British Central Africa*

in no way homogeneous. Indeed the Scots' pioneering of British Central Africa and their spirited opposition to the possibility of its passing to Portugal in the late 1880's may be envisaged, from one angle, as the attempt by a group of peoples who had all the aspirations of a nation but little of the structure and substance of one to make a final fling at nationhood by acquiring at last the Caledonian colony which had been denied them since the failure of the seventeenth-century Darien venture. Yet I believe that there is such a culture and that it shows itself never more clearly than overseas.

One of the essential elements of this, which the Scots imposed upon Nyasaland, was a stern but serviceable concept of democracy in church and school. In spite of its authoritarianism and paternalism, it was none the less democratic in aspiration. Thus, when the Blantyre missionaries wrote in their journal in 1895 that " 'Africa for the Africans' has been our policy from the first, and we believe that God has given this country into our hands that we may train its people to develop its marvellous resources for themselves," they were voicing a genuine aspiration, part of which was realized when the control of the Blantyre and Livingstonia Synods of the Church of Central Africa Presbyterian passed into African hands in the late 1950's.

The rigorously rational and practical Scottish education, in school, technical college, and university, with its predominant appeal to the "lad o' pairts," however humble his origin, was one of the glories of nineteenth-century Scotland. It was this tradition, admittedly restricted by financial resources, which the Livingstonia and Blantyre missionaries took to Nyasaland. Before the 1914–1918 war, at least, they provided a thorough training in the three R's and practical handwork for many Nyasas which gave them "a high reputation beyond their own country for loyalty, for intelligence and industry."[23] This reputation, which ensured them a job, acted as an additional incentive to that labor migration from the Protectorate which has played such an important role in its development.

One feature of the missionary regime, in church and school, which deserves examination is its characteristic Scottish discipline and the emphasis which it placed on a proper course of training, with no short-cuts, before baptism and graduation. Revolt against this was one element in the growth of independent African churches in Nyasaland.[24] And then,

23. Frank Debenham, *Nyasaland* (London, 1955), p. 175. An example of the Livingstonia standard of education is to be seen in the letters from Clements Kadalie to Walter Citrine. A. Creech Jones and Winifred Holtby in the Winifred Holtby Papers, File 11/50, Central Library, Kingston upon Hull, England.

24. E.g., George Shepperson and Thomas Price, *Independent African* (Edinburgh, 1958), p. 158, to which reference may be made, through the index, for documentation of most of the following points unless otherwise stated.

in 1915, there was the case of the youthful African pupil-teacher, small in stature, at the Livingstonia examination for entrance to the teacher's training center who, because he had to sit at the back of a crowded hall, was forced to stand up to see the questions on the blackboard. The Scottish missionary in charge, with the full rigor of traditional examination invigilation, "misconstrued the action and debarred the boy from further participation in the examination."[25] His career being apparently nipped in the bud, three weeks later he left home and did not return until July 9, 1958. His name was Hastings Kamuzu Banda [today President of Malawi].

That spirit of independency in church affairs which has been a pronounced feature of Nyasaland African politics clearly has fundamentally local causes. Nevertheless, it parallels the frequent splits in Scottish church life, with their markedly political characteristics, which did not pass unnoticed by Africans or Europeans in Nyasaland.

Most of the early missionaries had been born at the time of a new wave of national consciousness in Scotland. Some of them were radical in politics. This is apparent from the many sardonic comments on civilization by David Clement Scott in his remarkable 1892 Mang'anja dictionary. Scott's was one of the first missionary voices to be raised against the British South Africa Company and what, in early 1890's, appeared to be its attempts to incorporate Nyasaland into its domains. Indeed, the Blantyre missionary magazine often discussed what it called the "Cape colonization" of Nyasaland and the "Rhodesian ring closing in on our little colony."[26] From this time onwards, groups of Scottish missionaries kept alive in Nyasaland a suspicion of Rhodesian intentions. This was shown during the First World War, when they speculated on the political future of Nyasaland, whose anomalous position was only too clear to them. Identifying Southern Rhodesian with South African Native policy, they suggested that the imperial government should compensate the British South Africa Company for its interests in Northern Rhodesia and then amalgamate it with Nyasaland.[27] These discussions, with other criticisms of government policy, appeared in the local mission journals that many Africans read.[28]

Another missionary contribution to Nyasaland African political consciousness, in the spirit of the characteristically Scottish amateur scholar and linguist of the nineteenth century, was work on local languages

25. Cullen Young and Hastings Banda, Our African Way of Life (London, 1946), pp. 26–28.
26. George Shepperson, "The Literature of British Central Africa," Rhodes-Livingstone Institute Journal (Manchester, June, 1958), XXIII, 22.

27. Life and Work in Nyasaland (Blantyre, Nyasaland, July–September, 1916), pp. 2–5.
28. E.g., "The Native Hut-Tax—A New Departure," The Aurora (Livingstonia, April, 1902). VI, No. 1, 64–66.

187

SHEPPERSON: *External Factors in the Development of African Nationalism, with Particular Reference to British Central Africa*

and history. The Scottish missionaries laid a basis for the use of Nyanja as a lingua franca that could become a linguistic unifying medium for the emergence of a nationalism. Furthermore, as Cullen Young's Malawi researches[29] indicate, they stimulated Nyasaland Africans to search their past for the elements from which a myth of origins and an indigenous name for their own state could be created.

Not to see, therefore, that the predominant European influence in Nyasaland is Scottish is to miss much of the point of the rise of African nationalism in British Central Africa. Yet, once having gained a Scottish perspective, to make this too uniform is to oversimplify. One must note the special influences of Highlanders, Islanders and Lowlanders—but this is too big a subject to explore at this stage.

My second external factor in the growth of African nationalism, the precipitative agency of a person originally alien to a particular society, is well exemplified in Nyasaland by two examples, African and European. The African example is Charles Domingo. As his Portuguese-sounding name indicates, he came into Nyasaland from Mozambique. In 1912, Domingo could speak of the struggle for "jewels of independence among we the Nyasas." This seems to be the first full-fledged and unadulterated statement of African nationalism in Nyasaland. There are, of course, no Nyasas as such, and Domingo was extracting from "Nyasaland," the new name for British Central Africa which had been in existence only five years, an expression to cover all the British Central African tribes. It is possible that he was, again, the first Nyasaland African nationalist to do this. But if Domingo had spent the whole of his life in Nyasaland, would he have been so ready to do it?

When the missionary, John Rebmann, made his notes from Central African slaves in Zanzibar in the 1850's for the first dictionary of a Nyasaland African language, he provided evidence that the various tribes around what is now called Lake Nyasa had been grouped together by the coastal Swahili as "Waniassa" or "of Nyasa."[30] Thus, when Domingo used the term "Nyasas" with assurance for all the Africans from Nyasaland, it is just possible that his coming from the coast had something to do with it. It seems very likely that the concept "Nyasaland" originated with the coastal Swahili of the slave trade and was then adopted independently by the British during the Scramble for Africa: it has, therefore, a double foreign significance and it does not seem unreasonable that Africans should seek a substitute term with more indigenous roots.

29. T. Cullen Young, *Notes on the History of the Tumbuka-Kamanga Peoples* (London, 1932), pp. 15–26, etc.; Young and Banda, *op. cit.*, pp. 9–10; S. Y. Ntara, ed. Cullen Young, *Headman's Enterprise* (London, 1949), pp. 14–15; etc.

30. Rebmann, *Dictionary of the Kiniassa Language* (Basle, 1877), pp. iv–v.

The Struggle for Independence: The Dynamics of Nationalism

The European example is Joseph Booth, who had a pronounced influence on all of the African politicians of Nyasaland before 1915. If his influence was nowhere so profound on the emergence of African nationalism as it was in Nyasaland, he made some little mark on the South and East African political scene before the First World War. I suspect also that he may have had more influence on Majola Agbebi,[31] Ekiti pioneer of politically oriented independent African churches in Nigeria, than at first sight can seem possible.

The third external factor, the importance of a period of residence overseas in the strengthening of national consciousness, seems to have particular relevance for Nyasaland. A long journey always appears to have had some special significance for the peoples of the Nyasa regions, even before the coming of the Europeans. As Scott noted in his 1892 Mang'anja dictionary, "A journey to a great distance may so impress a person's life that he comes back with a name taken from the limits of his travel."[32] Perhaps because of the unsettling influence of the Arab slave trade, Ngoni incursions from the south and forays from Portuguese territories in the east, the peoples of these regions have always been great travellers. A freed slave, a Yao, from the country "between Lake Nyasa and the coast" was taken by the British Consul at Zanzibar to England in 1862 and educated there. He seems to have been the first of his people to go to Europe.[33] But he never went back to his homeland and there is no way of judging what effect this trip may have had on his political consciousness. Similarly, little can be discovered of the political effects of the journey to Britain in 1897 by the two Africans from the Blantyre Mission, the first of many whom the Church of Scotland was to introduce to the world overseas. It is known, however, that they noticed sharply the different treatment meted out to natives in Nyasaland and South Africa, where they broke their journey. Similarly, the Yao and Tonga soldiers who went with the King's African Rifles contingent to London in 1902 for Edward VII's coronation have left no record of their impressions. Nevertheless, there is evidence to suggest that, even before the First World War, overseas service by British Central African soldiers—the historic core of the KAR—had political effects

31. Circumstantial evidence in Booth papers on loan to the author. For collection of references on Agbebi, see Shepperson, "Notes on Negro American Influences," *op. cit.*, footnotes 72–74.

32. Scott, *op. cit.*, p. 140.

33. George Shepperson, "The Military History of British Central Africa," *Rhodes-Livingstone Institute Journal* (Manchester, December, 1959), XXVI, 29. Another mysterious account of a wandering Nyasa turns up in Atlanta, Georgia, in *The Foundation* (II, 2, February, 1912, p. 8) published for the Stewart Missionary Foundation for Africa at the Negro Gammon Theological Seminary. It describes a Yao who went to Europe and returned to found his own church. This does not seem a garbled account of John Chilembwe and it is difficult to see to whom it refers.

189

SHEPPERSON: External Factors in the Development of African
Nationalism, with Particular Reference to British Central Africa

in Nyasaland. This does not appear to have helped much in smoothing out tribal differences—for one thing, the main recruited tribes were grouped into separate companies—but it is possible that service so far away from home, in, for example, the Gold Coast in the 1900 Ashanti campaigns, may have broken down tribal differences to some degree. The main effect of this kind of service was to provide material for protest by emerging nationalist politicians, such as John Chilembwe, who spoke out against the use of Nyasaland troops in these campaigns.

It was men of this kind whom a period overseas affected most. In particular, it was experience in the United States which precipitated or increased their sense of national identity. Here, of course, John Chilembwe's two or three years in America between 1897 and 1900 is of considerable importance to Nyasaland nationalism. He plunged into much the same kind of militant Negro American society as influenced Faduma. But, whereas Faduma's Africanist feeling was only increased by his American experiences, they largely created Chilembwe's. Before he went to America, he had been content to call himself "Ajawa" or "Yao"; on his return, he began to discard his tribalism and to appeal to a wider, protonational group drawn from different Central African tribes. While some of these early nationalist ideas undoubtedly came from the Negro circles in which he moved in America, they probably have a much simpler origin: the sheer distance factor, that thousands of miles from home, in a totally alien environment, Chilembwe started to feel that he had much more in common with the various tribes around Lake Nyasa than he had with the people of America, white or colored.

My fourth external factor, the influence on African political ideas of a period of residence not necessarily overseas but in another state in Africa, may also have a special significance for British Central Africa. Africans from Nyasaland who have travelled to other parts of Africa may be divided into two groups: those who have never gone home again and those who have.

The first group includes, of course, almost all the slaves. The Nyanja word for "freedom" comes out of the Arab slave trade.[34] Descendants of Nyasa slaves are scattered all over East Africa. Other East Africans of Nyasa descent are the offspring of Africans from Nyasaland who, when the Arab trade had been stamped out, sought work along the accustomed lines of the old slave routes. Whether of slave origin or not, many of these Nyasa emigrants are aware of their origins. I have been told that one important member of the Afro-Shirazi Party is proud of his Kota-Kota ancestry. The rapid developments in African political activity in

34. Shepperson, "Literature of B.C.A.,"
ibid., p. 23, and Oxford Magazine (1960),
LXXVIII, No. 16, 242. Cf. also Ndaban-
ingi Sithole, African Nationalism (Cape
Town, 1959), pp. 75-76.

Nyasaland have given East Africans of British Central African descent[35] with kindred political ideas an additional reason for pride in their Nyasa ancestry. Indeed, another Nyasaland parallel with Scotland may be that, one day, emigrants and their children will form societies of patriots in exile and, just as the Scottish societies usually call themselves "Caledonian," thereby employing an old name—though many North Britons forget that it is still a foreign name—their Nyasa equivalents will hark back to "Malawi."

Labor migration from Nyasaland into the Rhodesias and South Africa has produced a sort of political cross-fertilization. An example of this is the African National Church of the northern part of the Protectorate, which was founded by Africans who had worked in the Union and with Kadalie's ICU.[36] Other Nyasas in South Africa have played a role in the development of the South African Native National Congress. One of these was Peter Nyambo who was for some time the chairman of the Cape Town branch of the African National Congress.[37]

Participation of Nyasas in this South African movement, which was founded in 1912, is interesting in its own right. But more intriguing from a British Central African point of view is what effect this may have had upon the growth of the idea of a Nyasaland African Congress. It is usually reported that the Nyasaland African Congress began in 1943.[38] In terms of the modern body in Nyasaland, this is no doubt true. But there were enough Nyasas in South Africa in 1912 to notice the formation of the South African Native National Congress and to create, on however slender and informal a scale, a parallel organization for themselves.[39] An African source for 1932 from the Union reports that the Reverend Juma Richardson Albert Ankhoma, a Lakeside Tonga who went to Johannesburg in 1909 and became in 1912 a minister of the Apostolic Faith Church, was in 1918 the chairman of the "Nyasaland National Congress."[40] It is clear from the use of this expression in 1932 that some sort of Nyasaland National or African Congress was in existence well before 1943. Indeed, it seems to me most probable that this movement, like modern Irish nationalism, which was strongly influenced by Irish in the United States, began outside their homeland amongst Nyasa immigrants to South Africa and then moved into Nyasaland,

35. Cf. the case of Tom Mbotela who had a Nyasa father: Cmnd 1030, *op. cit.*, p. 55, etc.
36. Monica Wilson, *Communal Rituals of the Nyakyusa* (Oxford, 1959), p. 171.
37. T. D. Mweli Skota (ed.), *The African Yearly Register* (Johannesburg, 1932), p. 231; see also Shepperson and

Price, *op. cit.*, pp. 203–9, etc.
38. E.g., Guy Clutton-Brock, *Dawn in Nyasaland* (London, 1959), p. 52; quoting Lord Hailey, p. 186; Leys, *op. cit.*, p. 967.
39. Shepperson and Price, *op. cit.*, pp. 184, 414.
40. T. D. Mweli Skota, *op. cit.*, p. 130.

SHEPPERSON: *External Factors in the Development of African
Nationalism, with Particular Reference to British Central Africa*

perhaps with new leaders, when conditions there warranted and permitted it.

Certainly, Nyasas had been going to and from South Africa for long
enough to make this possible. South African political conditions began
to influence Nyasas at least from 1896 when Booth took Gordon Mathaka
to South Africa and he was turned against the white man by embittered
Zulu.

A dramatic illustration of the way in which a period of residence outside the homeland has influenced the development of Nyasaland nationalism is the effect on the people at home of those who have never
returned, the *machona*, the lost ones, not only to the mines but on military service,[41] of which the loss of two Nyasa companies in the battle
at Gumburu in Somaliland in 1903 was a notable early example. But it
was in service in the First and Second World Wars that this was felt
most. It is to this fifth external factor, in a British Central African context, that reference must now be made.

The impact of the Gumburu battle shows that the incidence and influence of military service began to be felt in Nyasaland well before
the First World War. Yet it was this war which has passed most notice-
ably into modern political folklore. As elsewhere in Africa, its first most
noticeable effect in Nyasaland was to lower the white man's prestige.
Sir Hector Duff, Chief Secretary to the Nyasaland government for
part of the war, who saw active service himself, provided a document
in an article which he wrote after the war about the African's part in
it which illustrates the beginning of this process. It was a letter to his
wife from a corporal in a Nyasa battalion, written only a few weeks
after the war had begun and after one of the first Nyasaland actions
against the Germans:

> I may as well tell you that I killed one white German myself. A bad thing
> that; but now I am afraid because I did it, and I cannot sleep because I
> killed that white man. I have killed many black men and was not afraid,
> but now I am very much afraid because I shot that white man and he is
> dead.[42]

But, said Duff, at the end of the war, Africans were boasting about the
number of white men they had killed.

Yet what sank most deeply into Nyasa consciousness was not so much
the number of European casualties as the death rate amongst the African servicemen. As in other parts of East and Central Africa, it was the
fatalities amongst the carriers, the *tenga-tenga*, that were most noticed.

41. On Nyasa military service in general,
see Shepperson, "Military History."
42. Sir Hector Duff, "White Men's Wars
in Black Men's Countries," *The National
Review* (London, September, 1924–February, 1925), LXXXIV, 905.

Often underfed, overloaded, and overworked, more died than was necessary. By contrast, the British South Africa Company's regulations of the conditions of service for carriers from the Rhodesias ensured a better fate for these,[43] and so the burden of casualties amongst porters on military service from British Central Africa fell on Nyasaland. The effect of the war, furthermore, was felt more heavily in Nyasaland because it had, from its foundation, supplied the King's African Rifles with its core of soldiers and because its territories had a strategic significance for the fight against Von Lettow-Vorbeck's armies.

Many of the present generation of Nyasaland African politicians are sons or relatives of men who fought or carried in the First World War. Many bitter memories were passed on to them. And would it be altogether fanciful to suggest that the modern political rallying cry, "Kwaca," which is too often construed simply as "Freedom," has a military significance? Originally it was the cry used, before as well as during the war, to wake porters up at dawn and to stop them on the march. It meant "up with your burdens, off with your loads."[44] It is thus a term which may well have some militant associations for the sons of the *tenga-tenga*, in whose ears it was an all too familiar cry during the 1914–1918 war. It might also be seen as an older word for "firing a gun,"[45] the old-style flintlock of the slave days. Thus, "kwaca" is a word with complicated associations for Nyasaland, from the times of the slave trade, through the First World War, down to the modern age of political slogans.

In these indirect ways, the First World War reached out into modern Nyasaland nationalism. There is also a very real sense in which part of that nationalism may be said to have begun directly during the war with John Chilembwe's abortive movements against the Europeans in 1915. His manifesto, written in the early months of the war, was critical of African participation in it, and sounds a clear and unadulterated nationalist note as Chilembwe speaks "in behalf of his countrymen" and uses, with a fierce pride, the name "Nyasaland."

There can be little doubt that the Second World War accelerated the nationalist tendency in Nyasaland. One element here, as in the 1914–1918 war but to a much greater extent, was the lowering of the European's prestige. The main factor in this was probably not so much the spectacle of the whites fighting each other as the increasing recognition of the fact that all Europeans did not enjoy a privileged position. Service in the Southeast Asian theater of war introduced Central African askari to large numbers of British private soldiers who, if they had greater privileges and pay than Africans, possessed little akin to the

---

43. Mitchell, *op. cit.*, p. 49.
44. Scott, *op. cit.*, p. 254.

45. *Ibid.*, p. 253.

193

SHEPPERSON: *External Factors in the Development of African Nationalism, with Particular Reference to British Central Africa*

privileged status of the white workers in South and Central Africa with whom many Nyasas had labored in peace time. This observation could have been strengthened by criticisms of the Europeans in their colonies by the Indian nationalist movement and Japanese propaganda, and perhaps even by contact with English-speaking West African soldiers who came from countries with more mature nationalist movements.

Powerful though this tendency may have been in stimulating Nyasa nationalism, I think that it acted in a negative rather than a positive fashion: it may have made selected groups of Africans critical of, and sometimes hostile to, the Europeans but, by itself, it could not fill the gap which loss of confidence in the European created. This could be counteracted, to some extent, by the growth of the idea of "Nyasaland" in a territorial and cultural sense. Askari were grouped into specifically "Nyasaland" battalions. This practice, of course, goes back to the beginnings of the King's African Rifles; but tribes were grouped into separate companies. The Second World War, with its insatiable demand for soldiers, accelerated the tendency which started after the 1914–1918 war to break down tribal segregation.[46] The "Nyasaland" battalions, therefore, of the Second World War were, by and large, intertribal. This tendency was strengthened when some of the battalions and allied services made the long journey overseas to the Southeast Asian theater and nostalgia for home became identified with the distinguishing mark of "Nyasaland." If primary loyalties were usually to village and district, for many they were increasingly supplemented by an affection for that *dzikho la Nyasaland* which featured in so many askari songs and in whose name they were obliged to answer, anyway, whenever they were asked by strangers, white, black, and brown, where they came from. Many began to experience for the first time the full emotional force of territorial nationalism. It may have been, for several, nostalgic and sentimental rather than political; but it created a mould which would endure and into which politics could be poured when the right mixture was ready after the war. It was in this way, it seems to me, rather than through the lowering of white prestige or the introduction of radical political ideas from abroad, important though these factors may have been, that the Second World War, which took so many Nyasas so far from home, influenced the emergence of modern Nyasaland nationalism. Furthermore, in an age of mechanized transport, there was no necessity for a *tenga-tenga* problem. Battle casualties there certainly were; but, with the absence of the *tenga-tenga* situation and the fighting close to Nyasaland itself, it would appear that the Second World War, for Nyasa-

46. E.g., H. Moyse-Bartlett, *The King's   African Rifles* (Aldershot, 1956), p. 459.

land as a whole, was not the traumatic experience that the First had been. It was the sheer distance factor acting on important groups which mattered most, I think: Nyasaland, so far away . . . *Dzikho la Nyasaland* . . . *kutali kwabasi.* . . .

It was during the Second World War in the Southeast Asian theater that some Nyasas met for the first time a people of whom they had heard many rumors from their childhood onwards: American Negroes serving in the United States forces. The image and influence of the American Negro in Nyasaland is, in the main, responsible for my introducing a sixth external factor: foreign ideological influences. If today, like other parts of Africa, Nyasaland is subject to a variety of foreign influences from Marxism to moral rearmament, I would suggest that, with the overriding exception of more orthodox Christianity, up to the mid-1920's, the leading foreign ideological influences came from America. One ingredient was the Watch Tower doctrine and organization, either in the pure American form, the "Watch Tower *wa* Brooklyn," or in African adaptations. Unless evidence can be produced to the contrary, however, I do not believe that, in Nyasaland itself, this offered much of a threat to law and order after the failure of the Kamwana Watch Tower movement of 1907–1908 and the imprisonment or execution of the small number of Watch Tower preachers who followed Chilembwe in 1915, although, from time to time, Watch Tower groups have been stirred by the general unrest affecting the country, as, for example, when about one hundred and forty Jehovah's Witnesses are reported to have marched on the Lilongwe *boma* in 1953.[47] What appears to have happened is that convinced Watch Tower adherents of the Africanist variety from Nyasaland moved into the neighboring Central African territories. A fascinating historical study could be made of emigrant Nyasa participation in the complicated and often highly political Watch Tower movements in Northern Rhodesia.[48]

Watch Tower in British Central Africa,[49] for all its ultimate Africanist developments, was an ideology which came originally from white Americans. But colored Americans have also been influential on African nationalism in these regions. Before the 1920's, five Africans from Nyasaland went to the United States and were soon plunged into a Negro-

---

47. *East Africa and Rhodesia* (London, November 12, 1953), p. 298.
48. Ian Cunnison, *The Luapula Peoples of Northern Rhodesia* (Manchester, 1960), pp. 204–8, provides a good brief introduction. There appears to be reasonable documentary material in the Central African Archives.

49. See George Shepperson, "Nyasaland and the Millennium" in 1961 supplement of papers presented to the Conference on Religious Movements of a Millennial Character, Chicago, 1960, *Comparative Studies in Society and History* (Chicago, 1961).

195

SHEPPERSON: External Factors in the Development of African
Nationalism, with Particular Reference to British Central Africa

American milieu; in the same period, seven American Negroes came to Nyasaland as missionaries. Out of the relations between these five Africans and seven American Negroes, woven into a complicated network of interactions between America, Britain, and Central Africa, various Negro American influences entered Nyasaland: a reinforcement of critical feelings towards the white man; something of the philosophy and political techniques of Negro America; confirmation of the idea that one of the first spheres in which colored peoples could gain independence of white control was through separatist churches. These influences were exercised mainly on two levels: first, through the leaders of African discontents, in whose minds they may be said to have been conceptualized with a reasonable degree of definiteness; and second, at a lower, more popular level, where they took the form of vague but none the less disturbing rumors. After the return of Chilembwe from America at the turn of the century, the picture which the Arab slavers had implanted in many Nyasa minds of America as the land from which no black man could ever return alive began to turn into its opposite: a picture of America, if not as a sort of paradise for black men, certainly as a place where Negroes had wealth and power. A fantasy that emerged from this, particularly after the death of John Chilembwe in 1915 and his burial out in the bush in an unrecorded place which led many Africans to believe that he was not dead but had escaped to America, was the belief that, one day, American Negroes would invade the Protectorate and overthrow the rule of the whites.

One element which contributed to this Nyasa myth of the liberatory Negro was the movement which flourished under the leadership of the Jamaican Negro, Marcus Garvey, from his arrival in America in 1916 until his deportation in 1927, the Universal Negro Improvement Association and African Communities League. Garvey's movement had provided, for the first time, an organization clearly headed by the slogan, "Africa for the Africans," and dedicated to the proposition of taking American Negroes back to Africa. There was some connection between the aftermath of the Chilembwe movement and Garveyism, difficult though it may be to trace this accurately. A much more obvious source for the dissemination of Garveyism in Nyasaland, however, was the migratory labor cycle, especially those sections of it which reached down into South Africa. The same Africans who were attracted to the ICU newspaper, *The Worker's Herald*, edited by Clements Kadalie, the Nyasa emigrant, were also drawn to Garvey's organ, *The Negro World*. It would be wrong to suggest that there was necessarily any personal connection between Garvey in Harlem and Kadalie in Cape Town. It is true that Kadalie, like Garvey, often saw himself in the role of a dark Moses, "the legendary 'Black Man from the North' who was ordained to save the black people of the South from their white oppressors,"[50] and that Garvey's organ often reported Kadalie's activities.[51] But what connection there was between the two movements was more likely to have been through ICU members making individual contacts with Garveyites in Cape Town and elsewhere in South Africa, sometimes very transient contacts in the form of visiting Negro seamen. That something of this complicated ideological tangle penetrated into Nyasaland is clear from the case of the African from Chilembwe's old district, Chiradzulu, who was sentenced to three years' hard labor in September, 1926, for importing into the Protectorate two copies of *The Worker's Herald* and six of *The Negro World*, one issue of which contained an article entitled "Stirring up the Natives."[52]

This brief and necessarily selective study of external influences on African nationalism has concentrated on its emergence, mainly in the period before the Second World War. After 1945, external influences gained a new importance; and, in a recent article, Miss Margery Perham has listed some of them.[53] One might add to or argue about her list. But it is clear that, even in the period of independence, the new nation states of Africa will be subjected to a variety of outside influences, practical and theoretical.

It seems that the tendency of all new nations is to seek a breathing space of isolation or semi-isolation in order to consolidate the newly captured positions against the counterattacks of disruptive forces from inside or out. But the days are over when new nations could shield themselves completely behind vast natural barriers of land and water, as the infant American Republic tried to do—although the isolation of the young United States with its dependence on the British Navy, capital, and culture was never absolute. Yet America, before the mechanized age, did achieve a partial isolation which allowed her to build a nation from disparate elements. In an age of nuclear energy, this privilege must be denied to the new African states.

It is likely, however, that they will follow American experience in one way: historical introversion, a kind of turning in upon themselves to find elements in their national heritages which are of indigenous, not foreign, origin. From a historian's point of view, the excesses of this natural tendency are easy to deplore: nationalist history, from whatever part of the world it comes, can readily acquire a tendentious character

50. Vera Brittain, *Testament of Friendship* (London, 1940), p. 237. I am grateful to Senator W. G. Ballinger for confirming this story.

51. Check of file of *The Negro World* in Schomburg Collection of Negro Literature and History, New York Public Library.

52. *Nyasaland Times*, September 24, 1926, p. 3.

53. Margery Perham, "The Psychology of African Nationalism," *Optima* (Johannesburg, 1960), X. No. 1, 31-33.

197

SHEPPERSON: External Factors in the Development of African
Nationalism, with Particular Reference to British Central Africa

which, in the long run, may darken rather than illuminate the path of the people it seeks to help. Its real danger is the slick production of emotive generalizations. But where it serves to provide an incentive to ransack the obscure and scattered sources in which lie the details of African history, although it may color them with over-roseate hues, the nationalist drive towards history may perform a valuable service: the roseate hues will ultimately wash off but the detail discovered will remain.

Furthermore, in African historiography, when it gets beyond what European historians still have to call the Middle Ages, an overintroverted attitude is not too easy to maintain, if only because external influences, from Europe and America, are woven deeply into its texture. It could be that the self-evidence of many of these will ultimately save the African nations from the worst dangers of historical introversion.

But white historians who maintain that African "nationalism" is something very different from their own can only assist this dangerous process. As Miss Perham has rightly pointed out, "The difference between these older nations and those coming into being in middle Africa lies in the time factor."[54] Yet she is not altogether reconciled to the use of the term "nationalism" for them. "We must use the word," she says, "for convenience if not with exactitude."[55] With this generalization I would agree—except that I would say that it is also applicable to Europe. Indeed, it may be that, as the historian puzzles over the nature of the new political forces at work across Africa, he may find basic clues to the understanding of that vague and explosive process called "nationalism" in Europe. As the striking title of Sir Lewis Namier's essay on the 1848 era in Europe, *The Revolution of the Intellectuals*, should remind one, European nationalism can be like African nationalism in which, it has been said, "leaders have arisen to create a movement rather than that a movement has thrown up a leader."[56]

One task in which historians inside and outside Africa who are interested in the study of the emergence and development of African nationalism should cooperate without delay is in the finding, before they are irretrievably lost or destroyed, of the scattered materials of the lives of the pioneers of African nationalism. Detailed and imaginative study of these leaders would undoubtedly illuminate a series of processes which, without it, are condemned to remain in the limbo of jejune generalization. One thinks immediately of some of the major gaps here: biographies or biographical studies of such leaders as Edward Blyden, Herbert Macaulay, Casely Hayford, Blaise Diagne, Clements Kadalie, and even of men as recently deceased as Bankole Bright and George

54. *Ibid.,* p. 28.
55. *Ibid.*
56. *Ibid.,* p. 29.

Padmore. But such studies must not concentrate only on major figures: it is the minor figures, the Orishatukeh Faduma's and the Majola Agbebi's, whose lives must also be traced. Sometimes it will be the very minor figures to whom attention must be given. I am thinking here of such a person as Bandele Omonoyi of Ife who published in Edinburgh in 1907 three articles criticizing British rule in West Africa[57] and, in 1908, *A Defence of the Ethiopian Movement*.[58] He matriculated in 1906-7 and 1907-8 in the Faculty of Medicine at Edinburgh University, wrote down his nationality as "Yoruba," though his writings show that he had a West African and, indeed, a Pan-African perspective, and thereafter, apparently, disappears from the picture. There are scores of very minor characters of this sort whose brief but, cumulatively, impressive contributions to the theory and practice of emerging African nationalism must be dug out of ephemeral sources scattered around the world.

Both the foothills as well as the major peaks of African nationalism must be explored. When this has been done—perhaps as it is being done —a gigantic natural feature may be revealed whose bedrock is not restricted to the "Dark Continent" but forms part of a great stratum that has been pushing itself, over a very long period, above the surface in many continents, amongst which Europe occupies an interesting but by no means unique position and Africa is distinguished mainly by the speed of its thrust and the volcanic nature of its eruptions. And, to maintain the geological metaphor, he who would trace the lines of these forces in Africa must not sit back watching the official seismograph of public record office and Establishment family papers, important though these may be for the demonstration of the eruptions when they have finally burst forth; but he must trace the seams and the strata and the fissures, often when cracks are barely revealed at the surface, in many out-of-the-way places. Above all, he must not wait for the mountain to come to him: he must go to the mountain.

57. *The Edinburgh Magazine*, VII, January 19 and 26 and February 2, 1907, pp. 1435, 1453 and 1476 (this page number is wrongly printed as 1452) respectively.

58. This book states on p. vii that Omoniyi had also written a work called *Socialism Examined*. I have never managed to find this.

Jean-Pierre N'Diaye

AFRICAN STUDENTS AND THE IDEOLOGY OF INDEPENDENCE

After a long period of struggle and intense political participation, the African student now feels himself responsible for the building of his nation, which has finally gained recognition of its independence and sovereignty. From this stems his intensified vigilance over all the political problems of Africa and the Third World.

It is not enough, however, to build upon independence. It is more necessary to reaffirm this independence in numerous areas where it is still threatened from within. It is necessary to defend and increase our independence at all levels. . . .

Bandung 1955 [the first important meeting of the new leaders of Asia and Africa after the war, which was held at Bandung, Indonesia, and which solidly expressed a new-found determination for independence and self-development—ed.] was the first major landmark along the journey of the anticolonialist struggle, a rejoinder to the Berlin Congress of 1885 where the European powers divided the Black Continent among themselves. But does the spirit of Bandung still preside over the political actions of all the African states? Is the conception of independence as revolutionary, dynamic, and neutral between the two blocs always upheld? We must search for these answers by examining in depth the Afro-Asian countries, the policies of their leaders, and various recent developments.

The answer to all these questions constitutes the *ideology of independence* of African students in France. . . .

What meaning does Independence have for you?

Since all the students interviewed in this study come from African countries that have already achieved independence, we thought that it would be particularly interesting to ask them what significance they attached to this independence. . . .

Reprinted in abridged form from *Enquête sur les étudiants noirs en France,* Editions réaliteés africaines, Paris, 1962, pp. 162–174, by permission of the author. Translated from the French by Irving L. Markovitz.

199

Their responses can be divided into two levels:

1. The static level. Some students responded to the question in terms of what independence was in law or in fact (whether independence had been acquired or not). We have labeled this designation a legal definition.

2. The dynamic level. Other students answered by expressing themselves in terms of what independence involved . . . in future commitments. . . .

1. The "Static" Level

.   .   .   .

Independence, very simply, is life itself. (Gabon—Colonial Affairs)

Independence is life, liberty, the right of each man to preserve his being as well as his interests; it is the expression of economic and political development, the fulfillment of a nation; the free expression of its being, of its feelings, of the ideal to become a better state. (Upper Volta—Science, Physics, and Chemistry)

It is a right—all countries today must have their independence. Colonization is another form of slavery, of oppression. Independence condemns colonialism by free self-determination and the act of direct self-administration without the necessity of going through a foreign administrator. The independence of peoples is a corollary of the right of each man to his liberty. (Law and Dramatic Arts)

A symbol for the whole world that all peoples or countries are self-determining on the basis of their own characteristics and values. . . . (Central African Republic—Engineering)

It is, above all, recognized and recovered dignity.

Independence retrieves us from a semislave condition to raise us to a true human condition. (Cameroons—Letters)

It is the possibility of being able to expand individually and collectively. It is the indispensable framework for all progress. (Senegal—Science)

That which is to be gained immediately is dignity. All the rest will follow. (Ivory Coast—Engineering)

The end of exploitation by the foreigner. . . . The end of paternalism, of the feelings of incapacity. (Central African Republic—Statistics)

The recovery of national dignity. Economic expansion. Suppression of all social injustice. (Guinea—Mathematics)

The dignity of African man and the acquisition of a modern African personality. The possibility of developing economically without seeing the results pass you by, right under your own nose. (Political Economy)

The end of alienation. The affirmation of the African personality. The beginning of a lot of efforts whose fruits will remain in the country. (Ivory Coast—Diplomacy)

A step towards the reevaluation of African civilization. (Technology)

To render to the African the value and dignity that one accords to man. (Cameroons—Law)

And, more than this great word dignity, Independence is quite simply the right to live, or the awakening to life, to the condition of man:

It is night which has given way to day, to the sun. It is the day when all the individuals who form a people discover themselves "men" with the duty, the responsibility to advance in all domains. (Ivory Coast—Medicine)

To be one's self collectively and nationally, that is, to be a free man among free men in a free population integrated into a free nation which counts its destiny and battles for the progress of man among the men of the same nation. (Senegal—Architecture)

Good, because I am proud to be a free man. (Guinea—Technology)

I love independence because I am free and we are all now free to do and to learn that which we wish to—no more to be subordinated to the European. (Ivory Coast—Technology)

Joy to rediscover my country free, to construct its future according to its vocation with the help of all friendly peoples. (Mauritania)

Liberation from the colonial grip is finally the right to govern oneself, and the end of a whole era of negation.

For me, independence means the end of the regime of subordination, the reconquest of human dignity, long scuttled by the colonizer. Peace inside and outside. Legal independence goes hand in hand with our economy; previously our economy was in effect only a function of that of the colonizer and served him only as an accessory. Our homeland then ought to have an economic independence, that is, a balanced national economy. But, above all, independence means the reinforcement and preservation of new liberties [in protection] against neocolonialism. (Ivory Coast—Grande Ecole)

It means the concrete power to determine [the country's] destiny in all respects. (Guinea—Economics)

The seizure of the destiny of a country by the inhabitants themselves. (Congo—Law)

To free oneself from the grip of Europe or other nations. To consolidate the vibrant forces of the country—first, for their defense from the outside and, second, to build the economy, administration, and culture from the inside. (Mali—Physics)

It means first throwing off the tutelage of the whites, then rethinking and reevaluating African problems and the African himself, from whom the white has obliterated all originality. (Dahomey—Technology)

Liberty to wish to live, liberty to wish to die, liberty to make mistakes as well as to undertake great efforts. (Cameroons—Mathematics)

While these later responses translate the significance of independence almost to a personal level, the majority [of students] place the right to live at the level of the community, the people:

All people have a right to life, to work and its fruits. All people reject paternalism to direct their own destiny and develop their personality. (Cameroons—Grande Ecole)

Independence permits a people to rediscover its dignity, work for its interests, develop its personality . . . and bring something new into the world. (Mali—Economics)

The liberty for a people to chose the way by which it can find fulfillment. Also, it is rarely a people who chooses its way, but rather a group of men supplied with authority who incarnate the people. (Guinea—Science)

To be oneself for an individual or a people is to be self-affirming by becoming conscious of one's responsibility. Independence is thus perceived as the awakening of a new self-awareness [*prise de conscience*]:

The self-awakening of the personality and the evolution of the idea of responsibility. (Cameroons—Mathematics, Physics)

Becoming suddenly conscious of oneself, then the beginning of a great labor. (Ivory Coast—English)

The liberty and responsibility of us Africans from now on to speak of our own particular problems, to carry on a dialogue with all countries, as one equal to another, to have the people progress through the exploitation of our riches. (Niger—Engineering)

To be independent is to resolve *all* our problems by ourselves. (Accounting)

.   .   .   .

For me, Independence means to shift for oneself all alone—being responsible. "Independence" is the same as saying, "You wish to speak like every man? Very well, speak, we will listen to you." Independence for me means pride in making myself heard, and from this comes the responsibility and care to do my best before all who look on me. (Guinea—Diplomacy)

2. *The "Dynamic" Level*

The resolutely *engagée* orientation of the concept of "self-awakening" introduces us to the category of responses which perceives Independence on a dynamic, constructive level. We note this still more clearly in the following quotes, where independence is always linked with "self-awakening":

A sense of responsibility and a consciousness of being for oneself, by oneself. (Upper Volta—Economics)

One must be aware of all the responsibilities that weigh upon us and, from this awareness, know how to sacrifice. (Ivory Coast—Technician)

Liberation and work, in the form of self-discipline. (Ivory Coast—Biology)

The development of self-consciousness requires the *will to work:*

To work hard in liberty for the profit of my country. (Gabon—Medicine)

Independence constitutes an increase of work. To prepare for it, it is necessary that the will of all be joined in order to educate, instruct, and cultivate all the masses. To do this it is also necessary to banish racism. (Cameroons—Economics)

.   .   .   .

The willingness to work, necessary to maintain Independence, is expressed in the construction of one's country:

.   .   .   .

To develop the standard of living of the masses. To nationalize all economic resources of major importance. To unite with brother countries on the march towards unity. (Mali—Technology)

To make up for backwardness accumulated since colonization in order to be at the same level as the other nations. The social backwardness is the most important. (Dahomey—Secretary)

Independence is simple: build, always build. (Guinea—Technology)

To create an industry for the transformation of agricultural products within the country. To develop teaching. To restore African history (Benin, etc. . . . .). To establish a successful internal market and hasten the economic unity of the African states. (Dahomey—Sciences)

The possibility to constitute a nation which will from now on exploit its resources for its own benefit. The possibility of destroying such curses as illiteracy and hunger, in order to establish an economy for the national interest of the people. Afterwards to hold out our hand to our friends. (Senegal—Social Science)

To raise the standard of living, the social level, and the patriotic conscience of the people. To destroy such scourges as the lack of hygiene and illiteracy. (Togo—Secondary School)

.   .   .   .

First, to teach the people how to read. To establish a centralized economy that is able to raise the standard of living of the people. . . . (Cameroons—Medicine)

To rid the man of the people of all his alienations—first cultural, then spiritual and economic; and to establish, beginning with man, a more human society. (Upper Volta—Law)

Cultural development means the battle against ignorance and illiteracy, as well as the education of the people and the battle against certain inadequacies caused by economic underdevelopment:

> To battle against the inadequacies of man: sickness, laziness, vice, which go hand in hand with illiteracy. It is a question of promoting a new man—and, of course, battling for socialism. (Mauritania—Medicine)

Note that the *development of man* very often goes hand in hand with the *inauguration of socialism:*

> To free oneself from the grasp of the colonizers and others. . . . To install a socialist regime and to allow a people to humanly raise itself towards all the possibilities that stem from the nature of man. (Senegal—Agriculture)
> Within the framework of a socialist state, to develop man at the material, spiritual, and cultural levels. To collaborate with all other states and work for world peace. (Togo—Letters)

.   .   .   .

> Independence is total. It promotes a socialist economy for the well-being of Africa. (Mali—Economics)
> Let all the resources be under the direction of the state and the political system of socialism. (Dahomey—Mathematics)

The sense of justice and respect for democracy:

> To inaugurate social justice and a democratic government in which all tendencies will be represented. (Cameroons—Medicine)
> Social justice and the suppression of the bourgeoisie, black as well as white. (Ivory Coast—Agriculture)

.   .   .   .

> For me, independence has no other meaning than to permit the raising of the standard of living and an adequate social justice. (Ivory Coast—Law)

But development, the installation of a social regime, and the respect for democratic laws would be deprived of their content if the first duty dictated by Independence was not to *revalue man* [to instill a concept of his own worth] . . . :

> This would permit a people to build its own personality, faith, future, destiny, to be at last responsible and free: to be free men. (Senegal—Commerce)
> First duty: to reestablish the dignity of the black man. Then to allow

a harmonious development of our economic resources and the complete fulfillment of African values. (Upper Volta—Mathematics)

To rediscover the personality that will characterize us as a people about to bring its contribution to the world. To render to the child and to the woman the part which they desire in the new community. (Togo—Midwife)

But . . . this promotion of man is indissolubly linked to a concern for Africa, and the African renaissance. . . .

Independence is the same as the promotion of Africa by Africans who up until now have been transplanted and their personality humiliated. (Guinea—Mathematics)

To choose a properly African way. To choose our friends and trade with other nations solely to the extent that they respect our sovereignty and our interests. (Ivory Coast—Law)

.   .   .   .

Its real content is the worth of a nation, with all the advantages and obligations that this involves for all citizens. . . . For us, the content of Independence is especially the birth of Africa and, therefore, of the men who can then be true Africans. (Ivory Coast—Grande Ecole)

.   .   .   .

To retrace all the frontiers established previously by the colonizers. [To encourage] the unity of our states, and to nationalize all the resources of the private sector. (Mali—Law)

To extend one's hand to all African countries. To help those who are still colonized. To have a program of African unity. To battle for social justice. (Ivory Coast—Law)

To unify the African states. To teach one or two African languages as national languages. . . . (Guinea—Letters)

.   .   .   .

To create national unity and African unity and to proceed step by step towards socialism by allying with other brother countries. (Cameroon—Agriculture)

Unity of the superficial regions created by the colonizer; the institution of a strong state that will centralize all in a socialist direction. (Cameroon—Grande Ecole)

The following responses emphasize strongly that independence by itself is nothing if it is not followed by a program, because independence must be safeguarded:

Independence does not reside in the fact of governing oneself, of sending ambassadors to all countries, but in the everyday actions of preserving this independence by battling against the economic tutelage of the great powers. (Ivory Coast)

To safeguard this Independence by economically extricating colonialism from our continent. (Cameroon—Technology)

It is the necessary framework for the realization of great things in Africa—to realize Africa itself. It is a beginning and not an end. (Mali—Science)

The beginning of a new era—the postcolonial. (Senegal—Political Science)

. . . There were, however, some rare students for whom the word *independence* meant nothing:

The present Independence has the same meaning for me as dupery—for it has yet to provide anything for the citizens of the countries. (Gabon)

No meaning, if after independence a bourgeois class can be created that will exploit the laboring masses. This is the situation which is happening now in Africa. (Upper Volta—Agriculture)

Nothing. For everything is still to be done. (Senegal—Science)

Carl G.
Rosberg Jr.
and
John
Nottingham

THE MYTH OF MAU MAU: NATIONALISM IN KENYA

T his study of African social and political responses to alien rule in Kenya has essentially been an exploration into variant aspects of colonial nationalism. Though the patterns of social mobilization and political organization reflected many distinct features, the objectives and ideology of Kenya colonial nationalism were broadly similar to African nationalist movements elsewhere. To elaborate this argument, it is necessary first to discuss some of the diverse usages of the term *nationalism* in the context of colonial Africa.

Nationalism was initially a European concept which occurred in a given historical context and led to the emergence of political systems that have been referred to as "nation-states." It has been argued that nationalism as an analytical concept relates to certain *objective* criteria, such as a common historical experience, language, and culture, as well as clearly articulated ideologies and myths. Since the criteria suggested by Western experience have seldom been applicable to the African environment, there have been some who have rejected the concept—notably Lord Hailey, who spoke of "Africanism."[1] Most observers, however, have employed the concept of nationalism in describing African protest in the colonial context, though they have differed in the need for rigor and precision of definition. Thus Thomas Hodgkin has considered every social movement of protest against alien rule as nationalism.[2] In criticism of this all-embracing definition, it has been argued that to include all social protest as a part of nationalism obscures the concept's political meaning, for nationalism must be predicated on at least the aspiration of a future self-governing nation.

Though significant differences have existed in respect to the rigor of

1. Lord Hailey, *An African Survey*. Revised 1956. (London, 1957) pp. 251–54.
2. Thomas Hodgkin, *Nationalism in Colonial Africa*, p. 23. Here Hodgkin refers to James S. Coleman's pioneering paper, "Nationalism in Tropical Africa" 1954), in which he argued that the term nationalism should be limited essentially to

Reprinted from *The Myth of Mau Mau: Nationalism in Kenya*, Frederick A. Praeger, Inc., and the Hoover Institution, New York, 1966, pp. 348–354, by permission of the publishers and authors.

definition, these differences have not essentially encumbered analysis, for all were concerned with describing a somewhat similar colonial situation of alien domination and African assertion—to employ Professor Emerson's exceedingly useful term.[3] Indeed, most analysts have come to similar conclusions, for they were employing the concept of nationalism not so much as a conceptual tool but as a means of describing common processes of political and social mobilization and the search for power and dignity by Africans within a highly structured colonial framework. This monolithic situation, in which African leaders were concerned with a limited number of political functions and choices associated with the acquisition of power and the definition of the new nation, has facilitated the making of propositions by reference to readily comparative situations.

The analysis of this book, as well as much of the literature on nationalism in other parts of colonial Africa, points to two major perspectives in the evaluation of preindependence African politics: ideology and organization. The development of the ideology of African nationalism during the colonial period may be seen as taking place along a continuum whose opposite poles (in value terms) were acceptance of a subordinate role with the deference values fostered by the colonial system, and total rejection of subordinate status and the assertion of a distinct African personality. The first expression of political demands in the colonial context was, essentially, a demand for assimilation. In insisting upon equality before the law, African elites spoke the language of civil liberties in the search for human dignity. In demanding personal and civil liberties, social protest movements paid little attention to the problem of territorial political control and directed their demands to the local agents of the metropolitan powers. The crucial turning point in colonial nationalism was the rejection by the protest movements or political parties of the legitimacy of the colonial system. At this point there occurred a marked shift from a limited civil-liberties ideology to demands for the acquisition of political power and ultimately for a monopoly of coercive powers—a shift in which the values of civil liberties became instrumental rather than consummatory.[4]

The general ideological problem of African leaders was to apply

political movements whose objective is self-government or independence of a recognized African nation or potential. See also James S. Coleman, *Nigeria: Background to Nationalism* (Berkeley and Los Angeles, 1958), p. 425, and Martin Kilson, "The Analysis of African Nationalism," *World Politics*, April, 1958.

3. Rupert Emerson, *From Empire to Nation: The Rise to Self-Assertion of Asian and African Peoples* (Cambridge, 1960).

4. See David E. Apter, *The Political Kingdom in Uganda* (Princeton, 1961), pp. 85–91, for this use of the consummatory-instrumental distinction.

western liberal nationalism—ideas of social justice and self-determination—to their local conditions and to define membership in terms of a
new political community and territory. In Kenya, African leaders had not
only to confront a European political and cultural elitism demanding
conformity to the rituals of deference, but as European racialism gave
way to multiracialism, they had the additional ideological problem of
combatting a doctrine which appeared both liberal and to some extent
nationalist. The language of multiracialism—of racial equality, of "partnership," of equal rights of all civilized men, of the Protestant ethic—
was superficially similar to that of African nationalism. In opposing the
multiracial ideology as it came into prominence in the 1950's, African
leaders were prone to lay themselves open to charges of tribalism or
racialism. "Multiracialists" demanded that all liberals of whatever race
work together under white leadership to create the economic and social
conditions of a nonracial society. But African leaders emphasized social
and personal discriminatory treatment that coexisted with this manifest
ideology; a solution to their problems, they urged, required not individual
representation but political power. This different emphasis was vital and,
in laying such stress on it, African political leaders were frequently
castigated as racialists.

Though African nationalism in colonial Kenya shared many common
ideological perspectives with other nationalist movements, Kenya protest
movements failed to become vehicles for territorial integration. Not only
was meaningful political organization primarily limited to the Kikuyu in
the pre-Emergency period, but also some tribal groups were little concerned with the ideology of colonial nationalism. Given this essentially
organizational or building-block approach to the study of preindependent
African politics, did what occurred in central Kenya—culminating in
violence in the early 1950's—constitute nationalism?

It is a central assumption of this study that such an organizational
approach can only provide a partial answer to this question. To understand more fully both the meaning and impact of African politics
in this crucial period, we must combine both the objective indices of
nationalist organizational development with the subjective intentions of
the actors involved.

African nationalist organizations have had infrequent success in pro-
jecting their ideological aspirations toward the objective of a united territorial political community. In certain parts of West Africa and in Tanganyika in East Africa, the search for political power and the building
of party organization for national integration tended to be congruent.
An array of factors associated with the character of social mobilization,
ethnicity, and the presence of permissive colonial authorities amenable
to radical political change fostered the simultaneous pursuit of both. In

many parts of Africa, the characteristics of a successful "acquisition" movement have been quite different from those fostering an "integrational" movement. Indeed, the organizational forms and techniques employed to advance what may be called the "acquisition" function of colonial nationalism have in a number of situations militated against the solutions of the "integration" problem. For the main task of nationalism in a "colonial situation" of alien rule has been the acquisition of political power and authority in the colonial state; to this, all other tasks have been secondary, including the development of organizations capable of fostering territorial integration.

Uneven patterns of African social mobilization have been a common variable in obstructing the integrative function of nationalism in colonial Africa.[5] In Kenya the differential rate in social mobilization among the diverse cultural sectors of African population was very marked and was crucial in restricting the development of transtribal political organization. Though significant segments of the subordinated African population possessed a community of grievances, the rapid social mobilization of the Kikuyu in response to the colonial experience meant that the quality and intensity of their demands on the settler-oriented colonial system were immeasurably greater than that of the less mobilized groups.

White settlement rapidly created a crisis for Kikuyu traditional culture, limiting many of the evolutionary adjustments to the new colonial system that other tribal groups were able to make. The quantity of Kikuyu land alienated for white settlement, as contrasted to the Masai, was relatively small. But we have seen that in ecological and social terms the Kikuyu could least afford to lose land. Moreover, their social system, which was closely linked to pioneer land settlement, now found barriers placed on its expansion. As the population expanded and internal conflict deepened, the cry for the return of the "stolen land" emerged as the salient political issue for the Kikuyu masses. But this issue was of slight appeal to such groups as the Luo or the Luhya, which had been little affected by the pattern of European land settlement.

Though their traditional value made the Kikuyu very receptive to the acquisitive and achievement-oriented values of the new white power elite, there was little opportunity for mobility for thousands who sought to enter the market economy. At nearly every point in the European-dominated hierarchy, barriers appeared to advancement and to positions of prestige and status. Lack of technical skill, education, and capital were factors inhibiting mobility within the colonial society, but politically more significant was the character of the white-settler-oriented economy, which essentially restricted the role of the African to that of

5. Karl Deutsch, *Nationalism and Social Communication* (New York, 1953).

a low-wage earner. Deeply enmeshed in a colonial state characterized by segregation, racial discrimination, and separate development, and bitterly frustrated by their marginal economic, social, and political roles, Kikuyu leaders relentlessly attacked the racial barriers to upward mobility.

While in the immediate postwar years KAU [Kenya Africa Union] strove to achieve a countrywide organizational structure representing the interests of all the Africans in Kenya, the Kikuyu areas of central Kenya not only provided the hard core of leadership, but also the vast bulk of protest against colonial rule. As the Kikuyu demands for change intensified, the willingness and capacity of the colonial-settler elite for reform seemed to diminish. Increasingly, in the early postwar period, the administration, the settlers, and the missionaries had drawn together to the extent that, in most Kikuyu eyes, they were regarded as part of a single, permanent, and integrated racial coalition.

The inability of KAU to obtain any significant redress of economic, social, and political grievances led to the adoption of new organizational means to achieve the cohesion and unity required for militant and prolonged resistance. In the politicized environment of central Kenya, the oath was a simple weapon. It emphasized rural and traditional characteristics in Kikuyu culture, and served as well to bind together militant urban and rural protest. However, as we have argued, it is part of the myth of Mau Mau to fail to distinguish between the form and meaning of the oath. Preoccupation with the ritual and traditional aspects of the oathing procedure obscured the deeper significance of the oaths as an organizational weapon in a context of mass mobilization.

Although oathing strengthened the Kikuyu organizational ability to challenge the colonial state, it nonetheless had the additional effect of limiting the institutional spread of the national movement to non-Kikuyu groups. This dilemma was not unrecognized by the Kikuyu leadership, for they envisaged the creation of other tribal oaths which would serve to mobilize and commit non-Kikuyu people to their style of militant nationalism. Lack of sufficient time and the administration's success in compartmentalizing and controlling African political activity were two important factors that prevented this from occurring in any extensive manner. Thus, the pattern of nationalism as it unfolded stemmed from a rationally conceived strategy in search of political power within a context of structural conditions which severely inhibited the growth of a countrywide national organizational movement.

In contrast to the nationalism of the pre-Emergency period, that of the late 1950's possessed several distinct advantages in its assertion for political power. Foremost among these was a colonial situation far more amenable to rapid change owing to a competitive international situation and shifts in British policy as well as to the existence of a greater number of educated African leaders drawn from an array of tribal groups. Nonetheless, only in part was this new nationalism able to advance national or territorial integration. Organizationally, nationalism remained fragmented and dominated by tribal parochialism—a condition encouraged by administrative policy. Though the goal of African independence was achieved and the immediate crisis of stability was overcome by a consolidation of power and Africanization of the institutions of state management, the complex problems and issues of national integration will long endure.

Part IV

THE CONSOLIDATION OF POWER: THE DEFINITION OF THE POLITICAL ARENA

"Decolonization," Fanon argued, "is always a violent phenomenon." The minimum demand of the colonized is to create a *tabula rasa*, in order to change the social structure from the bottom up. Nothing less will suffice for the creation of a man free of complexes and a society with truly autonomous political institutions designed for his own purposes. If not all African leaders have sustained these objectives, upon the attainment of independence all are faced with the necessity of reconsolidating their power and defining the basic nature and objectives of their government.

Most of the new governments, upon independence, opted for systems of African democracy and socialism, with the emphasis on the word *African*. African leaders insisted that democracy did not necessarily mean a two- or multiparty system, with an organized opposition and periodic formal elections. Julius Nyerere has elsewhere argued that, for the Greeks, democracy simply meant government by equals who discussed issues until they reached agreement. Although this procedure may be too awkward in conducting a modern state, Nyerere maintains that the main point is that some sort of *organized* opposition group is neither theoretically nor historically necessary, nor practically desirable. In newly independent states, governments must above all maintain unity—which is the prerequisite of all freedoms—in the face of those who would destroy it. Opposition for the sake of opposition, many African leaders have argued, is a luxury that cannot be tolerated. To find genuine alternatives and mature, responsible opposition is, at least for the moment, rare. Hence, the nature of the political arena is of necessity different in Africa.

Sékou Touré in the selection printed here argues that Africa did have an experience with Western democratic institutions under colonial tutelage and found that "parliamentary life was nothing more than a sum of disordered activities tending to satisfy selfish ambitions and interests." In an African version of the "iron law of oligarchy," Touré warns that the universal tendency of organization leaders, including elected officials, to be primarily concerned with the advancement of their own interests, even at the expense of the needs of their constituents and the perversion of democratic processes, is compounded by the importation of a foreign bourgeois regime. The only truly democratic government is one that has the support of all the people because it works for their advancement in practice, through the achievement of common, well-defined objectives.

On the other hand, although he fully appreciates the antiopposition stance of the new governments, David Apter argues in his article that African leaders, on their own terms, for their own purposes, will find a classically organized opposition invaluable because of the varied and useful functions served, ranging from the representation of interests to the provision of information otherwise impossible to obtain.

Socialism, government leaders have also argued, must be African above all. They have not freed themselves from Western colonialism to succumb to Soviet or any other kind of domination. To begin with, given the fact that socialism as a doctrine originated in Western Europe and is an analysis of its highly industrialized societies, and furthermore requires a high level of productivity for its fulfillment, it is paradoxical that historically socialism's greatest successes have been in underdeveloped countries. Those who explain Marxism as a reaction against industrialization argue that the appeal of socialism derives from a feeling of the cold emptiness of the Machine Age, accompanied by the exaltation of science and technology, and Marxism's promise to use one to overcome the other. For those bewildered by the breakdown of traditional societies, Marxism offered an explanation that made sense of how new forces of production organized by new social forces caused exploitation and alienation. Capitalism, Marx argued, contained within itself not only the seeds of its undoing, but also the promise of a better society. Science and technology would yield a productivity of such tremendous abundance when freed of social and political restraints that men would be liberated from the necessity to labor and thus freed from the machine for all except a minimal amount of time. Man could then, for the first time, be truly free and hence capable of forming a wholly new type of nonexploitative society.

In new nations recently under colonial hegemony, where the gulf between social groups is immense, where an American-style middle class does not exist, class conflict and exploitation are real experiences for millions and the Marxist conception of a ruling class is experienced as personal reality.

Two questions remain, however: (1) In an underdeveloped country with limited resources, dependent on foreign aid, short of technology and capital, what, *in practice,* can socialism mean? and (2) Given the conditions of underdevelopment, might not African *capitalism* be a more practical way of achieving economic development? The Arusha Declaration of Tanzania's governing political party formulated by President Nyerere and adopted on February 5, 1967, is one attempt to state a practical policy of socialism and economic development. Beginning on February 6, Tanzania's government moved to implement this policy by nationalizing foreign-owned commercial banks, certain import-export firms, and insurance companies, as well as by assuming a controlling interest in selected large industries and agricultural estates. Today, a great deal of debate still centers on how effective this policy will be. Debate, however, also occurs over the program of the apparently booming, capitalistic Ivory Coast and the nature of capitalism there. Samir Amin challenges some of the current interpretations, even as he explains the meaning of capitalism in a non-Western structure.

In the process of the consolidation of power, socialism and democracy both have fallen victim to one military *coup* after another. The hard realities of practical politics would, in any event, have raised questions as to the meaning of ideology and the difficulties of unity. Fred Greene categorizes various types of military intervention and provides valuable insight into the widespread existence of this phenomenon. Colin Legum, and Irving L. Markovitz each focus upon a different country and major problem area to highlight some of the further difficulties in the consolidation of power and the creation of the political arena. Colin Legum reveals how the tragedy of the Biafra-Nigerian conflict is related to the pressures of modernization, rather than "primitive tribalism." Markovitz analyzes the overthrow of Nkrumah as the result of a series of conflicts evolving through a succession of distinct stages in Ghana's political evolution. Relating the nature of major social forces to political development and government policy, this final case study suggests the continuing significance of ideology and indicates that a fundamental question is not only one of stability and unity, but stability and unity for whom?

Sékou

Touré

AFRICAN DEMOCRACY AND
THE WESTERN
PARLIAMENTARY SYSTEM

*I*mmediately after World War II, as a result of the profound changes in the balance of forces, both on the international and African plane, the people of Guinea were legally admitted to active political life. From 1945, they sent representatives to a Territorial Assembly and to a Federal Assembly seated in Dakar, as well as deputies, senators, and French Union Councillors to the French Assemblies in Paris.

Elections took place after electioneering campaigns in which the political parties, which were linked to ethnic groups and lacked any national commitment, competed for the clientele of male and female electors, not on any rational, democratic platform, but on the plane of pure demagogy, calling upon religious, regionalistic, or racialist feelings. Thus, at the outset, *parliamentary life was nothing more than a sum of disordered activities tending to satisfy selfish ambitions and interests.*

Throughout that period, from 1945 to the end of 1955, Guinean representatives in the various Assemblies had almost no direct contact with the people, except for the sterile agitation periodically stirred up by electioneering campaigns. Those elected behaved like feudal rulers, profiting both from the naivete, lack of consciousness, and disorganization of the people and from colonial bribes. Scandalously, the parliamentary system snared political power for the benefit of the elected officials, whose behavior was marked by corruption, irresponsibility, and unpardonable indifference to the harsh living conditions of the people and the future of their country.

These anti-democratic, anti-popular trends of parliamentary life were the direct consequence of the importation into our countries of the bourgeois regime and of French political customs aggravated by the direct intervention of the colonial administration in the choice and nomination of candidates. These practices precluded close contacts between the people and their representatives. . . .

This selection has been excerpted from Sekou Touré, *Guinean Revolution and Social Progress*, Société Órientale de Publicité, Cairo, H.D. pp. 331–353. Reproduction authorized.

The Democratic Party of Guinea was to put a final end to these practices which prejudiced the political and moral evolution of the people and prevented the establishment of sound foundations for our nation. *Instead of electoral mystification and methods which resulted in imposing unpopular representatives, the P.D.G. established the rule of free and judicious choice by the people of their representatives in law-making bodies at all levels....*

.   .   .   .

Contrary to the corrupt methods brought into honor by the former ethnic groupings—Union du Manding, Comité de la Basse-Guinée, Union Forestière, Amicale Gilbert Vieillard in the Foutah-Djalon, Union des Insulaires, Union des Toucouleurs, Foyer des Métis, etc.—the P.D.G. worked out a program for nation-wide economic, social, and cultural advancement, which became the platform of its candidates in all constituencies, without any reference to petty interests or subjective considerations.

Thus, as the P.D.G. became the dominant party on the Guinean political scene, people began to choose their representatives by consciously mobilizing themselves in the rank and file of a national party, which focused their activities on the implementation of one program, aimed at happiness for one and all, wide democratic progress, effective, emancipation of our society, and full development of the human person.

The national leadership of the P.D.G. resorted to appropriate methods to liquidate the difficulties of regionalism and individualism, for example in municipal elections, by nominating candidate-mayors who were not directly related, ethnically or otherwise, to the people they would administer. The same method was used for the nomination of General Councillors and the election of people's representatives to the Territorial Assembly. The latter—who, after our independence, became our "députes"—were asked, after each Assembly session, to report on party activities in areas other than their own. For example, a Conakry representative was sent out on a mission to the Foutah or Upper Guinea, while representatives from those areas were sent out to the Forest or Lower Guinea. By such practices, electors were soon won over to the unitary approach of the P.D.G., as they became aware that P.D.G. cadres were committed to the nation as a whole.

As another effect of the political approach to all activities, individual and collective, *the elected were placed under the direct and permanent control of the people, and totally engaged in the struggle conducted by the party.*

Instead of deceiving the people with misleading promises, P.D.G. officers established militant relations with their electors, and committed themselves wholly to the correct performance of their political mandate. The P.D.G. eliminated the harmful consequences of the parliamentary system, and established a democratic, popular, fundamentally revolutionary regime. . . . The negative features of the bourgeois parliamentary system—antagonism between law-making and executive bodies, indifference, and lack of contacts between the people and law-making bodies— have forever been banned from Guinea's institutional life. . . .

The success of the Revolution depends on the sum of positive achievements of the Regions, the everyday behavior of civil servants towards local people, the clearsightedness, competence, and dedication of the responsible cadres of regional services, companies, and enterprises. This is why it is important that responsible officials should discharge efficiently their vast responsibilities over primary and secondary administrative entities and satisfy the local population.

The National Political Bureau and the government have to go ahead with two processes, to consolidate the foundations of our Nation:

1. Political and administrative decentralization, involving a wide distribution of responsibilities from the base to the top;

2. Concentration of the powers of orientation, legislation, and planning the nation's development.

A sound understanding of the dialectic contradiction between either process should prevail, so that national authorities will not stifle the life of regional units, and the regions will not become parochial.

If decentralization is conducted with a view to national unity, the activities of central and local bodies will supplement and fulfill each other.

Between the national party leadership and the government on the one hand, and the citizens or primary militants on the other hand, there are transmission belts which should work smoothly, under constant supervision. In this context, we have to stigmatize the isolationist trend of some regional executives who are exclusively concerned with the solution of local problems.

In democratic centralism lies a dialectic contradiction which, when it is overlooked, leads to dictatorship if the rules of its orderly functioning are flouted at the top, or to anarchy, incoherence, and scattering of efforts if its spirit is violated at the base.

In a democratic state, all things hold together and supplement each other. If the complementary nature of responsibilities assumed at different levels of government is ignored, if conflicts arise between base and summit, one is running counter to the revolution, jeopardizing the nation's build-up and ultimately hampering the development of the individual administrative regions. This is why far-reaching decentralization entails, of necessity, a permanent supervision of all activities.

He who abhors control, or brands as a trouble-maker the citizen who denounces what he finds at odds with the political line of the party, shows that he is alien to the preoccupations of the people. He who is indignant at the cancellation of an arbitrary or unlawful act by a superior authority shows a tendency to "authoritarianism" or a false sense of self-respect; he wants to take advantage of his functions, instead of placing them loyally in the service of the nation's overriding interest.

Although our theories are excellent, and although our principles for the operation and management of our services and enterprises are in keeping with the requirements of the rapid development of this country, we have to admit that, in practice, *it frequently happens that these ideas remain a dead letter because they fail to give rise to the vigorous action that their correct implementation demands,* or again because agents who deliberately transgress them seem to be covered by the indifference, or sometimes even the complicity, of senior officials.

For the revolution to make rapid headway, the sense of responsibility must dominate all the deeds of every Guinean, and supervision at all levels, in all sectors, must become its permanent, effective manifestation. In the exercise of responsibility, checking is never superfluous; indifference, on the contrary, is a sign of inability or inadmissible resignation.

The government, which assumes the highest responsibilities in the practical implementation of decisions reached by the party, must be at all times and in all its activities a living example of patriotic consciousness and revolutionary commitment. Perfect unity and coherence must distinguish its action. The duties vested in it by the party do not admit of the internal contradictions generated by irresponsibility and unconsciousness. On the contrary, it is the duty of the government to encourage, advise, enlighten—in a word, to untiringly educate civil servants in particular and the people in general.

But this social aspect of government action must go along with firmness, when it appears that firmness is needed to impose justice and secure the primacy of the interests of the masses over interests of individuals or groups of individuals. Then it has to punish with exemplary severity all the mistakes, misconduct, negative behavior, and counter-revolutionary attitudes, to call a halt to bribery and to ban, once and for all, any passivity, lack of professional conscienciousness, carelessness, inadmissible wastefulness, and misappropriations . . .

If the government, the National Assembly, and the heads of administrative divisions ceased to embody, in each of their members, the values and virtues which bestow stainless prestige and exemplary moral force upon their authority, it is the state which would be weakened and brought into disrepute.

In a popular and democratic regime, the responsibility of public servants is not limited to their respective departments; on the contrary, they should feel responsible at all times for all the services, all the regions, all the villages of the country.

Not only should public bodies be inspected and their management checked; the findings should, furthermore, give rise either to the delivery of a certificate of orderly conduct, or to heavy punishment of those who deliberately infringe upon the rules prescribed for the management of public funds—men who sabotage the economic reconstruction of the country and thus hold back the political and social advance of our people are enemies of the nation.

We have repeatedly said that *a state's political independence is not real unless it is founded upon economic independence.* Men guilty of stealing or misappropriating public funds and properties should be regarded as the most dangerous enemies of the Guinean Revolution and, accordingly, be brought before the Revolutionary Tribunal, which will inflict hard penalties on them and, moreover, pronounce immediate confiscation of their belongings, either to the benefit of the nation or of the region, depending upon whom the fraud was perpetrated against.

You all remember that cattle theft once plagued the life of our villages, owing to the vigor and firmness with which the struggle was conducted against cattle thieves, we were able to check that plague. Today, everyone expects the party and its government to take similar steps so that the unscrupulousness of some civil servants should give way to honesty, patriotism, and dignity. Then *the morality crisis observed in some elements, prompted by cupidity and even by the will to prejudice the nation, will yield to vigilance and conscientiousness.*

A morality crisis always reveals a lack of confidence in the regime, i.e. in the nation's prospects for sound development. *A militant or a cadre who is sincerely committed to the revolution has no other ambitions than those which will be satisfied by the victory of his party and the success of his state in safeguarding, expanding, and consolidating the gains of the revolution.*

We denounce people who cannot afford to buy a car or to build a house, and who resort to dishonest practices to live in affluence, prompted by their desire to show off. The revolutionary struggle must tend to impart a moral quality and social usefulness on all activities—notably economic activities. The correct implementation of our policy of economic planning, the establishment and consolidation of fair social interrelations within our community, the primacy of general interests over selfish, individual interests, and the acceleration of our social progress demand that we should intensify the revolutionary struggle against this crisis of morality engendered by people who lack any patriotic conscientiousness and sense of progress. . . .

The civil servant who is appointed head of a service or manager of an enterprise knows the privileges that his colonialist predecessor enjoyed under the defunct regime: free housing, car, holidays in Europe, etc. . . . Sometimes, he longs for that regime, because such privileges are now abolished. This senior official wants to "command" and "be obeyed," not to lead efficiently the collective action of the workers of his department.

As for the bad political cadre, he yearns for the time of the *chefferie*, which dealt arbitrarily with the goods and persons of the population under its authority. After angry words and menaces, he "settles accounts" with his adversaries, and tries to subdue and humiliate them.

Using the authority of the party or the power of the state against guiltless people is a crime, but using the power of the state against the party and vice-versa is a double crime.

Since the party is the people's most efficient tool to master and steer its destiny, he who endangers its development prejudices the overriding interests of the people. Since the state is also—in all countries of the world—an instrument of direction and administration, he who disparages or paralyzes the state prejudices the interests of the nation.

In any country, the nature of the state, characterized by its structures, is inseparable from the political regime established by the country's ruling forces.

Need we recall that, for promoting the progress that our people want, the democratic and popular regime irreversibly adopted by the Guinean Revolution commands two great media: Party and State, both of them instruments of a popular, democratic, and human dictatorship. If we want to safeguard the gains of our revolution, no conflict is permissible between state and party bodies.

No individual may substitute himself for the people and confiscate its sovereignty. The deputy, the minister, the chairman of a party section's steering committee, the governor of a region are all, servants of the people.

Anarchy makes for conflicts, which in turn result in more anarchy. On the contrary, order and discipline make for harmony and balance. Militants and cadres of the P.D.G., the trade-unions, the cooperatives, as well as agents and heads of state services must support the revolution in resolutely combatting irrational behavior and demobilization.

The first phase of our party's action consisted in awakening the mass of the people of Guinea to the necessity for a single anti-colonial movement, and enrolling them in conscious action for the achievement of a concrete program, making no reference to a man's ethnic group, race, religion, or social origin. Since that time, the regime of national democracy that we have established finds expression in a single national program, a collective sense of our responsibilities—which are no longer at the nation's level, a development which has resulted in the establishment of new militant and brotherly relations—and a perfect unity in the action of our working masses, alive to their overriding common interests. This political unity is, objectively, the Nation's strongest foundation. Today we may proudly affirm that we have no longer a nation of the Fulani, a nation of the Malinké, a nation of the Soussou, a nation of the Guerzé, etc. . . . Now all the members of these ethnic groups belong to one and the same geographical, economic, political, and human entity: the Republic of Guinea.

The second phase of the P.D.G.'s action was marked by the common struggle of our people against foreign domination and colonial rule, for the nation's political liberation.

After the proclamation of independence and the creation of a sovereign state, we entered upon a third phase: that of the Revolution, i.e. of continuous democratic progress. This is the most difficult phase, because a people striving for continuous progress has no right to stop on the way, nor to remain indifferent to any of the problems which condition its future. Thus, a party which wants to promote continuous progress has to found all activities of the people on a rational, dynamic basis, and to coordinate these activities with a view to liquidating all the contradictions which emerge within the society. . . .

Political parties which stand for social classes espouse integrally and exclusively the cause of the class from which they emanate and whose fractional interests they defend against wind and tide, against the interests of other classes. This clear, absolute delineation of the interests they have to defend makes it easy for class parties—whether they represent the working class or the capitalist class—to conduct their militant action.

As for our regime, it is *a popular, democratic, and progressive regime, animated by a national democratic party. In the rank and file of this party, all citizens of the Republic of Guinea, male and female, work for the achievement of common, well-defined objectives.*

This regime of "national democracy" may be a short-lived one which after some time will give way to a class regime, or it may as well insure its permanence by ever further consolidating its groundwork and controlling the behavior of all individuals—i.e., the conformity of their behavior to the political line defined by the people in keeping with their rightful interests and aspirations.

We should never forget that the P.D.G. incorporates in its rank and file:

1. On the one hand, progressive elements with a high level of revolutionary consciousness, animated by an ardent will for qualitative transformations in our social system, who wish to liquidate all conflicts and contradictions, all forms of exploitation and oppression, and all arbitrary differentiations—i.e., differentiations not founded on standards of ability or output;

2. On the other hand, men imbued with feudal mental habits, who talk of democracy but would give it a real content in keeping with their own concepts of inequality, i.e. of the superiority of some persons over others in view of their race, caste, or kin.

Some officials remain imbued with a superiority complex towards the workers, farmers, and illiterates in general; they are inclined to exert dishonest pressures upon the citizens in order to maintain the privileges of a few. Greedy merchants applaud our mottoes of economic sanitation, but refuse to implement in practice the resolutions adopted by the party, or ignore the laws and regulations of our state, or even systematically by-pass or trespass these laws.

In a word, the P.D.G. brings together a variety of opinions and attitudes equal to the variety in the conditions of its members, linked to antagonistic interests which can be transcended only by the realistic, unremitting action that the party conducts and will conduct until all causes for clashes of interests or social differentiations are eradicated.

Thus we should not ignore the fact that, notwithstanding the general agreement on a common program adopted by the mass of the people enrolled in the rank and file of our party, notwithstanding the identical aspirations and unanimous will of the various social layers of which our people is composed, the life of this people is marked by the existence of contradictory elements that tend to social dissociation, contrary to the sense that we attach to our will for progress and social balance.

This is why the Sixth P.D.G. Congress should unequivocally affirm that unity is not an end in itself, for the sake of unity, but is essentially a means to accelerate the revolution while safeguarding individual liberties and the inviolable rights of the human being. . . .

A solid groundwork for democratic and social progress will not be secured by merely adding contradictory interests together, or by compromises between the unjustified interests of feudalism and imperialism and the rightful interests of the working classes and exploited masses. The groundwork for democratic and social progress will be secured by our courageous choice of methods and practices likely to achieve the systematic liquidation of all sources of arbitrary differentiations within the community, and by our action for social justice, to develop a society in which there will be no mutually antagonistic classes.

David E. Apter

SOME REFLECTIONS ON THE ROLE OF A POLITICAL OPPOSITION IN NEW NATIONS

The Role of a Political Opposition

The role of a political opposition has proved ambiguous in most newly independent nations. New governments rarely see the necessity for a regular opposition party nor do they always accept the idea of opposition as a normal feature of government. There are many reasons why this is so. Most new nations have come into being after a prolonged period of struggle with colonial authorities which has caused nationalist leaders to monopolize loyalties. Also, opposition groups having themselves been associated with nationalism at some stage of their existence, often have an antigovernment reflex common to those whose political actions have been aimed at changing the fundamental character of a country rather than accepting well established rules of political life and working within them. Indeed, many opposition leaders in new nations regard the new government much as they did their colonial predecessors, i.e., as basically illegitimate.

Considering such factors as these, we shall seek to show that an opposition in new nations needs a more limited and specialized role in order to safeguard its position and gain widespread acceptance. A great deal of discretion and responsibility is required on the part of those in the community whose views differ substantially from the government's. The key features of this role will be the subject of this paper.

In order to understand why an opposition needs to find a limited but indispensable role, we must recognize the special difficulties facing political leaders after independence. New nations are plagued with almost the entire range of political problems known to man. They are beset by an accumulation of immediate and often mundane tasks such as building up adequate medical, health, educational, transport, and other services, as well as improvement of housing, food supplies and other basic necessities

Reprinted from *Comparative Studies in Sociology and History*, Vol. 4, No. 2 (January 1962), pp. 154–160, by permission of the author and the editors. A version of this paper was read at a seminar held by the Congress of Cultural Freedom, Ibadan, Nigeria, March 1958.

beyond the subsistence level. To state this more sharply, in most of these countries per capita caloric intake remains far below that considered necessary for ordinary labor. Vivid in the minds of many political leaders are memories of the days when, not so long ago, they slept on the verandah and suffered from want of food and shelter. Some political leaders rose from poverty and obscurity to power in a short time. Politics is their only profession. For them to go out of office is, in effect, to become unemployed.

Concern with the role of a political opposition thus appears to many such political leaders as an academic exercise, divorced from the realities of life, or at best suitable for wealthy countries where political life is less stern and the future more secure.

We shall seek to show that this evaluation of political opposition is short-sighted, even though understandable. In the day-to-day bread-and-butter politics of a nation, an opposition can help to determine the success or failure of a government wrestling with its problems. A political opposition is neither a luxury nor a danger. If it performs its functions well, an opposition can be of crucial service both to the government of the day, and to the people of a new nation.

In the West the idea of opposition is not often questioned. It is assumed to facilitate representation and channel diverse demands into constructive paths. This view is by no means common elsewhere. The western view of democracy as the open competition of political parties catering to diverse public needs and thereby transforming demands into policy, is not wholly accepted in most new nations. Since theirs is rather a perspective of struggle, political leaders do not regard struggle as at an end when independence is achieved. Instead they ask the public to work for the "higher" phase. This might be liberation of a continent from colonialism, as is the aim of Ghana, or integration of a single nation out of several autonomous states, as is desired in the Middle East and in parts of former French West Africa.[1] In addition most new nations are anxious to industrialize. Whatever the obstacles, industrialization is attractive to political leaders. The urge is great to catch up with the West and modernize economic and social institutions. Whether cast in the role of crusader, or anxious to produce economic growth, political leaders easily accept the view that a political opposition is troublesome and dispensable, restricting the pace of development, at least in the early years following self-government.

Hence, when we look at many nations which attained independence since the war, the outlook for the opposition appears bleak. In Burma charges of party corruption and selfishness led to the army taking over government. It was the army rather than politicians who swept the

1. Such as the Sahel-Benin Entente.

squatters from the cities and distributed food to the hungry. In its zeal and efficiency, the army made the politicians look like foolish men, more proficient at scrutinizing monastic texts than dealing with the problems of the day. Facing similar problems, Indonesia is riddled with factionalism. Political party conflict can be found in every organized sector of life; in the army, the trade unions, the civil service and even in clan and village organizations. The country is so divided by party conflict that even "guided democracy" is impossible to achieve. If anything, opposition there is all-pervasive. Even the government is a coalition of oppositions.[2]

In the Sudan, the independence of the nation was challenged by political groups retaining strong ties with Egypt. The army took over in part to safeguard newly won autonomy. Even in Ghana, where the opposition has certainly not been extinguished, the entire executive committee of the Accra branch of the opposition United Party was put under preventive detention.

Fear that opposition will produce factionalism, corruption, and separatism is pervasive in new nations. The opposition is often blamed for producing a situation which in fact is inherent in the postindependence period of a nation. When the cement of nationalism is weakened a new basis for social solidarity must be found. Independence is an act of parliament or a stroke of the pen. Then the real difficulties begin. There is far more to self-government than a simple administrative transfer of power. Power is left to the nationalists like gold dumped in the streets, and many are bruised in the hectic scramble to gather it up again to place it in the strong box of the nation where it can be used for public good.

New governments have a tendency to set impossible goals for themselves. To accomplish many of the objectives which they attempt to achieve, "human obstacles" have to be overcome. Some of these obstacles derive from the traditional conservatism of people who are loath to change familiar ways. But nationalist political leaders, fresh from their victory against the colonial powers, want to show the world what they can produce with freedom. They desperately desire to breathe a new vitality into their corner of the world. Hence no new nation is without its dramatic and expensive development plan. Set for five years or ten, emphasizing industry, or agriculture, or mining, each new nation seeks to fulfill the grand plan which will produce net growth, steady economic savings, high levels of investment, and material benefits for all.

Impatient of the men in the villages who push the soil with out-

2. See Herbert Feith, *The Wilopo Cabinet, 1952–1953; a Turning Point in Post-* *Revolutionary Indonesia* (= Ithaca: Modern Indonesia Project, 1958), pp. 165–193.

moded implements and cling to rural ways, the new emphasis is upon discipline, education, and innovation. Unity is the demand of the hour— and cooperation. Join the party and the nation can be free and prosperous. A house divided cannot stand.

About such matters there is no "wrong" or "right" view. At the moment of independence the need for unity is great. It is easy for responsible leaders in government to take the view that an opposition simply magnifies grievance and exploits differences. Those who won independence know that it was not granted because of the kindness of colonial officials. Fought for by those willing to risk and dare, power has been captured by the nationalists, and having won it they intend to hold it by almost any means. The result is known. Rare indeed is the responsible opposition which can prosper in such a political climate.

Typical Patterns in New Nations

New nations tend to have either a great many parties, or a single dominant party with the opposition purely nominal. The Sudan was an example of the first, with the two main parties divided over the issue of closer union with Egypt. Government was a shaky coalition between large and small parties. India and Ghana are examples of the second. They possess a large mass "Congress-type" party which grew out of the nationalist movement, while competing parties remain small and relatively helpless.

In the first instance, competition between the parties characteristically weakened the unity of the state. Indeed few examples of a successful postindependence multiparty system can be found among the new nations except Israel and Nigeria. [This article was written well before the military coups-d'état in 1966; see below.] Others show a growing public dislike of party government. There develops a characteristic desire for a strong man who will be powerful and pure, leading the nation to harmony and achievement.[3] Hence it becomes possible for a single well-organized group to be popularly preferred to several political parties. This is particularly so when bitter rivalry between parties divides the public. The greater the rivalry, the more people with passionate political attachments wish for an end of party conflict; but they are less willing to accept the dominance of any party other than their own. Hence they may look to an outside force (army, civil service) to save them from themselves. Excessive fear of tyranny thus produces oligarchy.

3. See E. Shils, "The Concentration and   Vol. XI, No. 1 (Oct. 1958).
Dispersion of Charisma," *World Politics,*

Where there is a dominant party of the congress type and a nominal opposition, factionalism and intraparty intrigue become the prevailing political style. Politics then is similar to that in a bureaucracy, where each party official builds up his own support inside the party and seeks to outmaneuver the others.

To avoid this, mass party leaders attempt to impose discipline under the guise of fraternalism. Effectively organized, the single mass-party system can become the weapon of change and discipline in a society. For example, political leaders in Ghana were struck with the Liberian system where the True Whig Party has prevailed for many generations. Conflict occurs within the ranks, but the party presents a united front to outsiders. Hence conflict and difference do not appear to challenge the unity of the party. Loyalty to the party becomes loyalty to the state.[4]

Political leaders in single mass party nations often discover that political opposition has not disappeared but is latent and underground. If, in order to prevent this, government tries to control information, public opinion (or expression of it), voluntary associations like trade unions, etc., democracy itself becomes hopeless. Often using the phrases of democratic socialism to mask a power position, government becomes the "organizational weapon" and seeks to eliminate all groups which might challenge its power. To oppose then becomes identified as an act of treason. In such circumstances, opposition must, of course, go underground. When the government becomes alive to its presence, it declares that the opposition is engaged in treason, sabotage, and other acts against the state.

The Functions of an Opposition

The problems which we have discussed are not only of concern to the leaders of governments in new nations. They are also problems for the opposition. Both need to discover issues which are popular but which will not so divide the public as to generate mutual contempt between citizens. The opposition must oppose but not obstruct. Both must nourish and preserve society by helping to transform private demands into acceptable public policy. To enlarge on this theme is is necessary to discuss the functions of an opposition in more specific terms.

4. This view is shared by other observers. For example, Pye indicates that "the fact that the ruling party in most non-western countries identifies itself with an effort to bring about total change in the so-ciety makes it difficult to limit the sphere of political controversy." See Lucian W. Pye, "The Non-Western Political Process," *The Journal of Politics,* XX (1958), p. 473.

INTEREST REPRESENTATION

The opposition has an important task in representing *interests* which have been overlooked by the majority party. Otherwise groups in the population whose interests have not been effectively represented, can become discontented. One feature of democratic government is that while it cannot appease all interests simultaneously, it will not, for long, continue to give advantage to one group over another. The long-run prospect of equal treatment for all thus kindles an interest in government on the part of the public, and creates a faith that government will deal, sooner or later, with the problems that plague them. Increasingly the public takes an interest in its government.

Still another factor enters here. Let us make a distinction between values and interests. Values are the basic beliefs and attachments held by the public. Interests are the immediate desires which they wish to satisfy. A belief in freedom or equality is a value. A demand for assistance to cocoa farmers, or for an irrigation system, or for a local council is an interest. Interests and values are, of course, related, and the ensemble of interests is one means of judging values. However, value conflict is a different matter from that of interest conflict. The latter is competition between groups for getting their demands met. If, for example, a government is to engage in development planning, interest groups will try to indicate types of development of immediate concern and benefit to them. They may ask for a scheme to be sited at points most beneficial to them. Value conflict, on the other hand, involves fundamental beliefs about what is right and wrong. *Value conflict challenges the foundations of society as a moral order, because at the value level, such conflict cannot be reconciled except by victory in a power struggle.*[5]

The task of an opposition, then, is to express interests as the basis for the perpetuation of the values to which it adheres, rather than to oppose government on value grounds. It can do this by advocating the interests of those who feel themselves aggrieved, and by suggesting alternative policies to the government. If, for example, it is proposed to create a semi-industrial area by the use of forced savings, planned allocations of the labor force, and the commitment of resources which might otherwise be available for other schemes, opposition might arise from the population affected by the program. Ancestral land might be violated for example, or control over land hitherto vested in a particular group might be upset. Pursuing the original plan at the expense of the wishes of the local people might engender value conflict. Government, taking as its

5. See Bertrand de Jouvenel, *Sovereignty*, trans. J. F. Huntington (Chicago, 1957), pp. 265–266.

primary value the need to produce material benefit and equality for all people, might assume that the original plan is of critical importance in achieving this. If in its zeal it rides impatiently over the interests of the local population, the opposition might well charge that individual rights are being trampled underfoot, and that liberty is impaired. There develops value conflict. Value conflict produces rupture in social behavior between people who become scandalized at one another's behavior, impairing, often irreparably, the relations between them. Government can easily leap to a position of repairing the damage by eliminating the aggrieved group in the interests of harmony and progress.

Hence, the opposition has a fundamental role to play here. It needs to act as a mediator, formulating and representing diverse interests in such a way that tact and compromise become the style of political life, rather than strife and persecution. The reconciliation of interests is one important means to this end.

PROVISION OF INFORMATION

Another important function of an opposition is to provide otherwise unavailable *information* to government about public reaction to a particular official policy. In this respect, the opposition keeps the government informed about the consequences of official policy.

This function is particularly important in those nations dominated by a single mass party. The assumption here is this: Where the leadership in control of government is aggressive, impatient, and progress-minded, the government soon begins to lack information, because the party itself becomes identified with the state. People will not care to make known their opposition to government leaders or the local followers of the dominant party because the risks might be too great. For example, a farmer who wants a loan for developing his farm might well understand that an agricultural loans board is dominated by people from the majority party who would be less likely to give favorable judgment on his application if they knew he belonged to an opposition. The same is true for families with children seeking scholarships from the government, or jobs and sinecures. The majority party controls all the patronage and all the avenues of opportunity. Political cynicism begins to spread and the public becomes adept at producing "spontaneous support" for the leaders even if in their hearts they despise them. This is a kind of political corruption which is far more harmful than such characteristic forms of corruption as misappropriation of funds, because society is then based on delusion and deception.

Indeed, if dissatisfaction remains hidden, only to break forward in sporadic but bloody intervals, the government sits on a powder keg. Its own party gets information pleasing to the ears of government officials. The true state of affairs remains uncertain, and political leaders therefore seek to control the entire organized life of the community. To reduce the consequences of ignorance when they are denied information, government leaders use coercion. By this means they seek to avoid blame for mistakes, and so remain invulnerable at the polls.

An opposition which indicates important centers of controversy and dissatisfaction is thus performing a valuable task. If people can freely ventilate their grievances by allowing the opposition to voice them, government is thereby provided with a knowledge of sensitive changes in public opinion and can modify its policies accordingly. This helps to make political goals more realistic, and avoids that kind of political ignorance which produces coercion. Just as the fluctuations in the glass of a barometer indicate information about the weather, so the rise and fall of support to an opposition indicates to government the effectiveness of its policies.

EXERCISING CRITICISM AND PROVISION OF ALTERNATIVES

The opposition has the responsibility of providing *criticism* and posing useful alternatives to government policies. This function, properly performed, helps government to set goals best qualified to produce public satisfaction. On matters of budget, welfare, and other major concerns, criticism keeps the government responsive to the public and aware of weaknesses in its program. This is a classic function of an opposition and does not require extended discussion here.

The three functions, representation of interests, provision of information, and constructive criticism, are the main contributions of an opposition. We shall see how these three functions relate to representative government.

Opposition and Democracy

An opposition capable of performing the functions we have listed is instrumental in preserving the structure and spirit of representative government if these functions operate within three important spheres. The first involves the *values of democracy* itself, the second refers to *conciliar or parliamentary control over the executive,* and the third *involves effective representation.*

Our conception of democracy is of a political system committed to democratic values, conciliar control, and representation, especially through universal adult suffrage.

All democratic systems possessing these characteristics are, in the actual practice of government, operated by a party system. Competing parties can make each of these spheres active and meaningful, or they can dull them and make them inoperative. Hence, in this sense, democracy depends upon the performances of political parties.

Israel, with a responsible multiparty system, has been operating effectively in all these spheres. Ghana, for a time threatened with conflict over values, especially those pertaining to individual rights, seems now to be most effective in the first and third spheres, with conciliar control rather ambiguous. There was a time in 1957 when twenty-seven members of the backbench of the Convention Peoples Party, the government party, threatened to bolt to the other side. Government took strong action to bolster up temporarily fading fortunes and has emerged triumphant. At the moment conciliar control would appear to be weak. Other nations as well show a mixed picture. In few can it be said that democracy is flourishing—but there is no doubt that democratic values are the dominant mode of politics. Even in Pakistan or the Sudan, there remains a strong commitment to democratic values even if, for the moment, conciliar control is in abeyance. Indeed in both those countries there remains a strong possibility that the political parties, having been chastened by the unexpected intervention of the military, will be restored to life when the army considers the moment propitious.

Political parties play the key role in the way these three spheres of democracy can work.

The Preservation of Values

Political values are a reflection of preferences and beliefs and therefore underlie the formal or constitutional appearances of government. Political values must be shared and accepted by the people who need to be willing to support them. Confusion over political values can destroy the consensual basis for a viable nation.

To breathe life into representative institutions requires genuine commitment to democratic values. These provide the rationale for this relatively complex political form. No system can survive on purely instrumental grounds. Values become the basis for emotional feeling about the society itself. Values are the symbolic expression of political right or wrong.

What are the values with which we are particularly concerned? Those most characteristic of democracy are the product of four hundred years of struggle in the West. First there was struggle against religious orthodoxy. Orthodoxy was identified as a form of repression and dogma. *Liberty* was viewed as freedom of thought. Next, the idea of liberty was extended to include *individualism*, and the political rights of men. This took the form of struggle against automatic monarchs. *Political equality* subsequently led to demands for economic equality with an emphasis on opportunity, fair shares for all, and public education. Through socialist criticism along these lines, and through nineteenth-century notions of progress, democracy thus acquired an economic dimension distinct from private property. Today we have the notion "psychic inequality," a consequence of social inequality, and there are efforts to obliterate those characteristics of a social order which breed feelings of inferiority and shame.

Although it took the West centuries to identify and realize these values, new nations strive to achieve them simultaneously. Modern nationalism is a demand for their realization. The problem is, however, that effort to achieve one can controvert the others. A paradox emerges. Overwhelming emphasis upon any one set of the values which are characteristic of democracy leads to a denial of others. The historical experience of the West was largely a process of realizing, *in turn*, each of the values we have identified. To achieve them all simultaneously is immeasurably more difficult.

Ghana, for example, emphasizes expansion of opportunity. Political leaders wish to emancipate people from ignorance and to utilize their talents. By this means they seek to restore respect to Africans and give people of color in all nations, including South Africa and the United States, courage to fight discrimination. Ghana also wishes to demonstrate through her own achievements after independence that the colonial powers cannot presume to judge the welfare of others and decide when a country is ready for independence. Ghanaians know that the best way to achieve these objectives is by demonstrating progress in Ghana. There is concentration on economic growth while attacking tribalism, separatism, and rural backwardness. Conflict has been produced between those anxious to achieve "progress" and those whose ways are more set in favor of custom and tradition and who, if they are not bewildered, become antagonistic to government policy. Values are challenged because liberty and freedom have become practical questions of liberty and freedom for whom. These are no longer regarded as inalienable rights. From a government point of view the question is whether or not a part of the population is free to jeopardize the development of the country as a whole. The opposition charges that the majority cannot be allowed to ignore the minority on such issues. Each side challenges the legitimacy of the other's acts. Value conflict, hitherto incipient, can easily become open and manifest.

However, if we consider the case of Ghana further, it turns out that in practice, most of the conflicts over value are directly derivative from inadequate reconciliation of interests. Rarely has it been the case that what the people want, and what the government seeks to accomplish are as far apart as it appears. In performing its function, i.e., indicating to government what the interests of disaffected groups might be, pointing out the most crucial demands, communicating to government the depth of feeling and emotion involved, and proposing some compromise suitable for both groups, value conflict can be avoided through actions of the opposition.

This is not simply a matter of niceties. If there is value conflict government endangers its own success. Nothing is more desperate for progress-minded political leaders than to find that the public becomes not an asset, a pool of talent, and a reservoir of strength, but a weight to be shifted from one shoulder to the next, finally crushing those who are attempting to march forward with the burden.

Local support, and the transformation of interest conflict into satisfactory cooperation thus is possible if the opposition represents, communicates, and criticizes government policy. The public begins to share the burden of government. Otherwise plans worked out in Accra or Lagos or Cairo or Delhi have a way of being just enough out of perspective that they have unanticipated consequences which jeopardize their success and perplex leaders. No plans are perfect.[6]

It can be argued that all this requires considerable nobility from political party leaders. Opposition leaders commonly complain in new countries that the opposition can scarcely perform its functions if its very existence is being threatened. Indeed, many of the differences which arise between government and opposition bear little relationship to problems of national progress. Quite the contrary, it is often the case that the government and the opposition shared much the same objectives in the past, i.e., national liberation and independence, and continue to support much the same aims. Often what is involved is personal conflict between men who share an intimate social environment. They know all about one another. The vulnerability of each is exposed, and exploited. It is by no means rare that when one side becomes politically dominant, the leader who is personally an anathema to members of the opposition taunts them and goads them with displays of power. In such instances the surge of resentment and bitterness which comes over the opposition leads it into acts which play directly into the hands of government.

6. See the discussion on planning by W. Arthur Lewis, "On Assessing a Development Plan," *The Economic Bulletin, the* *Journal of the Economic Society of Ghana,* June–July 1959.

Engaged in that kind of struggle, each side preempts the "public interest" as their party interest.

The problem is especially acute where the opposition is a combination of brilliant and educated men joined with embittered renegades from the dominant party and with a sprinkling of confused traditionalists. Characteristically, oppositions in new countries are a blend of traditionalists, renegades, and sophisticates. They fail to discipline themselves, perform erratically and inconsistently (although at times brilliantly), and do not give the government assurance that they can be relied on for responsible action.

Where the mass party is overwhelmingly preponderant numerically, the opposition is not only small in numbers, but often composed of an elite antagonistic to popular and diverse membership of a mass party. Quite often a form of "class" conflict is built into the relationship between government and opposition in which the latter is alienated by being deprived of a share in power. Meanwhile the former may have leaders who take pleasure in humiliating the self-titled aristocrats who represent all that the mass parties dislike.

If an opposition party is to survive in such a situation, it requires unusual discipline and self-control. Normally, however, such oppositions are incapacitated by their membership. Rarely can they resist personalizing the issues and maligning the motives of government leaders.[7]

A delicate tread is thus required, the more so because mass political organizations are themselves riddled with factionalism and easily threatened. The more powerful the mass party, the more intense will become intraparty intrigue and fighting. It is here that the mechanism of conciliar government becomes so important because among other things, a legislature and an election system help to transform conflict between parties by putting them in a forum in which the performance is open to the public. The public makes the ultimate decisions about which side is preferred. If government and opposition carry their conflicts outside of the parliament and into all the other institutions of the country, public and private, a struggle for pure power soon emerges. Power then inheres in the dominant party, rather than in the institutions of government, to be won and lost, in turn, through the normal vagaries of electoral fortune. And if the power of the state inheres in the dominant party, then value conflict is profound and violence and coercion lurk on all political paths.

7. The question has been raised whether or not an opposition could survive at all. The assumption here is that such opposition members have the choice of nominal opposition or oblivion. The benefits of opposition are preferable to oblivion. Hence recruits to the opposition can be found, especially where they do have an impact on government policy.

Conciliar Control over the Executive

The most burdensome problem for an opposition is to respect the legitimacy of government, when that government is dominated by a party which the opposition finds abhorrent. When the distinction between government and party breaks down, then representative government is at end, because embedded in the idea of democratic government is the concept that the party is a conveyer of the people's will through the institutions of government, but is not the repository of state power.[8] Here lies one of the fundamental differences between democratic and autocratic political belief. In the former, there is a respect for the limitations of office, a belief that such office is temporary for any occupant.

The opposition has an important responsibility for preserving these ideas through its action in parliament. It needs also to perform its functions in ways helpful to government, and by doing so to facilitate the system of political representation.

An opposition has to strike that difficult balance between being an enemy and a contender for the government. If it poses a threat to a majority party such that it serves as a potential center of gravity, pulling members away from the majority party to the extent of destroying it, the opposition may be viewed as an enemy. We indicated that factionalism characterizes the mass party in power. The opposition can sometimes attract enough factions to split the dominant party. This is undesirable, because it encourages mass party leaders (especially those trained in doctrine which assumes the party is "everything") to void such threats through punitive action. Majority party leaders may be propelled toward coercion under the guise of populism and discipline. And, since the mechanism of coercion is an application of state power, i.e., police or courts, the institutions of government are brought into contempt. Neither the government nor opposition parties can long have faith in their own government under such circumstances.

On the other hand, the opposition has to pose enough of an electoral threat to the dominant party so that both develop party discipline. Although we do not have space to discuss it adequately, an underlying feature of representative government is the coherence and discipline by which parties are organized so that they can represent the public, decide policy, and put it into practice.

Party discipline is important not only for representative purposes, but it is crucial also in the sphere of conciliar control over the executive. The opposition which finds the difficult point of balance between threats to the government party and ensuring party discipline will be

8. See D. E. Apter and R. A. Lystad, "Bureaucracy, Party, and Democracy," *Transition in Africa*, ed. by Carter and Brown (Boston, 1958), pp. 42–43.

respected and be able to carry out its functions in a parliamentary setting. The opposition can do this by (1) convincing the government back-bench of the correctness of opposition views on particular policy so that backbenchers bring pressure on their own party leaders; and (2) in rare circumstances, it can threaten the life of the government by a potential antigovernment coalition with disgruntled government back-benchers joining with the opposition to force a general election.

Parliamentary party discipline, however, has other effects. It pro-motes an atmosphere of constraint and propriety in the legislature so that reasonable discussion can prevail, despite moments when tempers become inflamed. Such a climate is necessary if the functions of an oppo-sition are to be achieved. In such a climate issues can be more easily decided on the basis of general merit. Alternative policies can be more clearly phrased and made more comprehensible to the people themselves. In this way parliament itself can become more meaningful to the public, which expects so much from a new government and its leaders.

It takes a delicate combination of forces to produce a climate of respect for the institutions of government and a situation where issues can be made more clear, so that a concept of the public interest grad-ually can become identified.

If such a pattern begins to take root, a whole series of subtle con-straints upon the arbitrary power of the executive can be exercised, even when there is a preponderant government majority in parliament. In-stead of "cabinet dictatorship," responsible government can develop. And instead of multiparty factionalism arising (as is often the case where parties are evenly divided) the government has assurance of a strong enough majority to carry through its program.

Party discipline then gives rise to coherence. Coherence allows policy alternatives to be posed in clearer fashion. Alternatives can provide government with knowledge of the best policies to carry out, and indicate necessary modification, and in the forum of parliament ministers can be made more responsive to legislators. In this fashion, the opposi-tion can preserve the second sphere of representative government, i.e., conciliar control. At the same time, it can reflect, more adequately, those interests of which the government may not be cognizant, and help to prevent unforeseen political difficulties.

Representation

Representation, the third sphere of democratic government, is as important as the other two. Political party competition, i.e., the struggle between the party in power and the opposition, is the life blood of democracy. Indeed one observer argues that "the democratic method is that institutional arrangement for arriving at political decisions in which individuals acquire the power to decide by means of a competitive struggle for the people's vote."[9]

By electoral means leaders are selected, a mandate for a program provided, and the public participates in the process of government. It is in competing for elections that the three functions of an opposition are carried out at the public level. They must seek out interests which they think are popular and which reflect public feeling. They need to communicate this to the public by arranging their program and ideas in a package which shows the public at a glance what the contents are. Finally, the opposition attempts to sharpen the responsibilities of the electorate by criticizing the program and policies of the government and pointing out weaknesses and failures.

Hence, the representative aspect of government, underwritten by electoral competition, requires an opposition which is allowed to perform freely. Under these conditions generalized factionalism in the country becomes crystallized into main groups. And one of the practical rules of politics which works out in normally functioning democracies is that *when there is open party competition and free elections, both parties, government and opposition, seek the support of the large middle spectrum of voters,* i.e., those who comprise the bulk of the voting population. Hence, gradually, both parties draw closer together in their ideology and their programs to the point where relatively minor differences become the issues on which elections are fought. This is the experience of every successful parliamentary system.[10]

Nor is it difficult to see why this is the case. If we take the simplest possible case, a government with a "radical" program and an opposition with a "conservative" program, we find that in real terms most people in the country conform to neither one extreme nor the other, but fall somewhere in the middle. That is, they are in favor of some "radical" policies and some "conservative" ones. On the other hand, the extremists on either end of the political spectrum have no hope of winning elections themselves.

The important electoral factor is the middle group, and in making coherent appeals to them, neither the government nor the opposition can have an extreme program. Hence the importance of free party competition—*it does not divide where all political parties are responsible,*

9. See J. A. Schumpeter, *Capitalism, Socialism and Democracy* (New York, 1942), p. 269.
10. There are, of course, exceptions. Where the middle spectrum does not show an identity of interest or is very small, political parties exacerbate differences. The Third and Fourth French Republics are good examples of what can happen.

APTER: Some Reflections on the Role of a Political
Opposition in New Nations

but instead exerts a constant pull on the parties drawing them together.
It neutralizes the extremists.[11] Thus party competition is basically not
divisive, as is commonly thought, but most often unifying instead.

The forms of disunity which characterize governments in new nations
are thus often premature. Equally, an opposition which fears and mis-
trusts the government of the day helps to magnify the fears of a majority party leadership that the opposition, in its efforts to achieve power,
is out to destroy all. In those first years of self-government both sides
need to recognize how absolutely necessary each is to the other.

Conclusion

We have indicated the challenge to opposition which has appeared
in almost every new nation. Opposition, we have tried to show, is
essential if the problems of governing new nations are not to engulf
those in public office and impel them to coercive solutions. In representing interests, providing information, criticism, and alternative policies
to government, the opposition can aid government in the three critical
spheres of a democratic system, namely, preservation of a belief and
acceptance of democratic values, helping to control the acts of the
executive by conciliar control and advice, and giving coherence and
meaning to the representative system.

In addition, by serving as a rallying ground and focal point for
grievance, a responsible opposition can transform potential disenchant-
ment with government into positive channels, preventing apathy and
avoiding cynicism about democracy.

New nations need more than bargaining power to gain the respect
of the world. They need to demonstrate positive achievement. A responsible opposition can help win the struggle for unity, freedom, social
betterment, and racial equality.

11. Where government is composed of
the extremists these generalizations are
of course inoperable. Rarely is it the case
in new nations that extremists do in fact
run the government.

| Fred | **TOWARD UNDERSTANDING** |
| Greene | **MILITARY COUPS** |

T

The Military Seize Power

he rash of military takeovers in Africa in recent months has again focused attention on the role of the armed forces in underdeveloped countries. Latin America experienced a wave of military takeovers in the 1940's, saw a recession of military rule after 1955, and experienced a resurgence of the problem after 1960. In the Middle East, the question has been in the forefront in many Arab states since the failure of the Arab League to win the Arab-Israeli war in 1948–1949. To the east, many of the Asian states have gone through military *coups* or *coup* scares since 1958. Africa has now joined the other major areas of the nonindustrialized world in which the military have become a force to be reckoned with.

Two major difficulties confront efforts to analyze these events according to a meaningful pattern. The first is that the great number of states in which the military must be taken into account must stagger the imagination and strain the capacity of even the boldest analyst. What features these countries possess in common seem to be more than balanced by dissimilarities in their cultural traditions, political experience, international relations, dominant social concepts, the influence of ideology, and—not the least—in the role of force in the society in question. Moreover, we still have but a rudimentary grasp of what is involved in political development and modernization. The task is so sweeping that both governments and scholars are still devising explanations for what is, or even should be, going on. Though research and analysis are beginning to show results, we continue to lack the experience for mature judgments.

It is wise to recognize our limitations, but this should not deter us from attempts at systematic analysis. With each effort a stepping stone for the next, we may yet arrive at a full understanding of the problem. Among those who have struggled valiantly in this field is William Gutteridge, whose *Military Institutions and Power in the New States*

Reprinted from *Africa Report,* Vol. 11, No. 2 (February 1966), pp. 10–14, by permission of the editors.

(New York, Praeger, 1965) is an expansion of an earlier study. Though he is critical of attempts to generalize about so vast a topic, of which *coups* are but a part, he nonetheless recognizes the need to do so. Gutteridge concentrates on new states, while seeking meaningful lessons from Latin America, Ethiopia, and other long-established polities. His thoughtful analysis uses the old British Empire as a general focal point, and it is salutory for Americans, as they consider their country's impact abroad, to view key aspects of the military question from this different perspective.

Even when confined to the newer states, the topic may appear too broad for systematic research. Taking but one crucial aspect, what can we learn about the problem of *coups* in underdeveloped lands? Given the instability in many of these countries, a military takeover can be viewed as a step in the arduous search for order and progress, but at the same time it may be a setback in the process of maturation. What makes for *coups*, for a "lowering of the threshold" to the critical point at which the military move in? What is the effect of increased military professionalization? Can we generalize about the cumulative effects of *coups* in terms of gains for Communist ideology, organizational penetration, and revolutionary activity? For further research and evaluation, I would like to suggest related topics in the form of propositions to be tested or questions to be answered.

1. *The military is a "heavy institution" in underdeveloped lands.* We recognize that military threats to civilian rule can arise in developed states in every continent. Among the newer countries, however, they dramatize the weakness of administrative systems, the uncertainty of political cultures, the ambiguities of national loyalty, and the lack of confidence in a government's capacity to execute its self-appointed tasks. In this porous civilian-political order, the military have a capacity to act with authority and force. As the army modernizes, a dangerous "competence gap" grows between it and the rest of the community. The influx of technical training and ideas from industrialized countries underlines this point and widens the gap.

Development of the military services thus arouses suspicions among the civilian elite groups, who may seek to keep the armed forces on a leash even at some cost to their military efficiency. But weak states often face real external security problems. Failure to defend national interests in a security matter deemed vital—for instance, of Egypt against Israel, Ethiopia against Somalia, or Algeria against Morocco—may induce the frustrated armed forces to act against the regime.

2. *The apolitical tradition is an unsteady guide.* The apolitical military traditions of the West are of only marginal assistance as a code to keep the armed forces out of politics in other regions of the world. When the military do stay out, they tend to remain on the sidelines as aloof judges

of the political leadership. In this role they often measure civilian performance against an abstract standard that lies beyond the government's reach. Military officers the world over hold "politicians" in low esteem, but they have more opportunity and more incentive to act on this view in underdeveloped lands. In some instances, a political leader anxious to cement his authoritarian control, or simply his role as commander-in-chief of the armed forces, may look with grave suspicion on an apolitical army. If such a ruler fails to justify his regime ideologically, or undermines an existing constitutional order through "civilian channels," the loyalty of the armed forces may be irreparably strained.

3. *Coups have many motives, but major policy issues are growing in importance.* Military takeovers used to reflect a resurgence of conservatism, or the maintenance of a status quo through a palace revolt. Though Latin America provided such examples after 1960, this era is fading. Uprisings are still sparked by administrative matters such as the status of expatriate military advisers, demobilization procedures, pay scales, and the manner of recruitment, but with increasing frequency the cause of unrest is a particular policy in domestic or foreign affairs. In some instances a regime is unable to resolve a policy crisis, thus tempting the military to intervene to break a political deadlock.

Coups are often triggered by such immediate considerations, but of rising significance are the longer-range political motives that now lie behind them. Belief that the existing system is a failure, a desire to weed out corruption and inefficiency, an urge to make nation-building efforts more effective, adherence to an ideology (however vague it may seem by civilian intellectual standards), an urge to reorient foreign policy—all have played key roles in recent takeovers. A systematic study of *coups* in relation to these and the less sophisticated causal factors over the past two decades would illuminate the general nature of the military in underdeveloped lands.

4. *Military leaders in power are surprisingly vulnerable.* It is quite difficult for new military regimes to consolidate their power. They fall into three categories: failures, successes, and a third type that voluntarily yields power to civilians, in whole or in part. Classification of military regimes into these broad categories, and an analysis of why events turned as they did, would shed much light on our problem. In those states in which the military have successfully retained power, the armed forces encounter the major difficulty of isolation from the political community. Again, the cause and dynamics of this phenomenon require further study.

With the passing of time, the new leaders find that they must to a certain extent "politicize" themselves. In so doing, they often alienate the professional military corps, their original base of power, without winning over important civilian segments of the population. How can the new leaders maintain support in one or both camps? Why do some lean toward revivals of democracy, while others hold power with varying degrees of repression?

5. *What elements of political strength enable governments to avert or call a halt to coups?* Both democratic and authoritarian regimes of various types have had mixed records in averting *coups.* A strongly dominant party along Indian or Mexican lines, or a meaningfully competitive party system, helps to sustain many nonauthoritarian lands. Among the one-party states, Guinea and Mali suggest the value of a strong party in settings that many would consider authoritarian. Equally, a form of government that enjoys political legitimacy gives a regime strength to ride out unavoidable periods of stress. Devoted efforts to resolve the country's problems, a coherent and generally acceptable ideology, the absence of a belief that a right-to-power rests with groups outside the regime, and the personalities of individual leaders, all help in the quest for legitimacy.

6. *Professionalism plays an ambivalent role.* The relationship between the level of military professionalization and political activism has been difficult to define. Added technical competence means new skills that should bring the military closer to the civilian-industrial sector of a society. One might suppose that the elite of the armed forces could thus be more easily accommodated in the economy and society, its sense of apartness reduced, and its inclination to political action dulled. Yet this is only part of the picture, for how is the armed force to blend into an economy that is too underdeveloped to use its skills effectively? Even in Argentina, a rather highly developed state, the military services actually became more active politically as they acquired more skill in their profession.

The other side of the argument holds that a less professional officer corps, as in Mexico, may show greater respect for the civilian order. In Mexico, officers combine the military profession with careers in politics or commerce, and do not seek to oust the established government. But we must also recall the years of grim experience and intense political effort required to end the dominant role of the army after the Mexican Revolution.

In the Middle East, personalism and lack of professionalism contributed greatly to political instability in Syria, whereas in Egypt, the more professional officer corps that seized power in 1952 has refrained from attempting further *coups* against the Nasser regime. In many African states, however, even a modest degree of professionalism can lead the armed forces to believe that they alone can save the nation from political strife and economic stagnation. Even so small and weak an army as the CAR's [Army of the Republic of the Congo] with 450 men possessing only a few modern skills, may be a dominant element in the extremely brittle states that have appeared in the wake of the old colonial empires.

7. *Dilution of the military's security role involves risks.* Armed forces that become involved in community projects and other kinds of civic action programs may help the country to overcome poverty and perhaps at the same time bring themselves closer to the people. However, much depends on how this is done, for deep involvement by an army in such nonmilitary matters can also lead to corruption and inefficiency. Foreign advisers who stress the importance of the military's role in nation-building may inadvertently be encouraging the army to judge its record—and its hopes—against that of a lackluster regime. Conversely, such programs may draw important resources away from the nation's security position in the face of possible threats, and thereby encourage the armed forces to take matters into their own hands.

Efforts to balance the power of the regular armed forces with other official and semiofficial security elements—for example, the police and constabulary, or paramilitary party militias and "young pioneer" brigades —frequently generate difficulties. When the army feels itself slighted and under political pressure, as in Honduras, it will take violent action against a rival force such as a militia in the course of seizing power. A delicate balancing act is required to keep the regular forces, constabularies, and party militias in constructive security roles, as in Venezuela, rather than in positions of rivalry that lead to instability, as in Bolivia.

8. *Recruitment and stationing of forces present serious problems for internal stability.* Imperial and traditionalist states relied in the past on minority ethnic, tribal, or regional groups to furnish the bulk of their military manpower. This practice created difficult problems of transition in the shift toward modernization. Even today, serious splits may arise when hard-pressed regimes recruit special units along such parochial lines. Countries that are subject to regional or ethnic tensions face a major strain in devising proper means of recruitment, balanced units, and an equitable distribution of forces. The role of Ibo officers in Nigeria following the army uprising of January, 1966, is likely to be clouded by the resistance of northerners to "protection" by national forces from another section of the country.

9. *Ideological considerations rise in importance as the officer recruitment base broadens.* In past centuries, aristocracies such as Bourbon France and Imperial Germany recruited officers from the middle class on their own ideological terms, and could absorb them without undue stress. In our century, governments must seek their military personnel in wider milieus. During the 1930's, Japanese officers from peasant communities did not accept all of the values of the army's aristocratic founders; in fact, many became economic and political radicals. Changes

in recruitment in many major states in the underdeveloped world, from Brazil to Egypt, have profoundly affected the political behavior of their armies. Studies of the correlation between changed recruitment bases and political activism among the military (including new politicomilitary ideologies as well as the incidence of *coup* attempts) would be most helpful.

Though many takeover attempts today involve radical motivations in political and economic policy, their leaders may nevertheless favor only limited change in social and religious affairs. Radical younger officers may be dissatisfied with senior military figures who wish to preserve so much of the old order, or who aim at an eventual return to civilian rule. Conflicts between generations, social groups, and ideologies may thus readily arise within the dominant military establishment.

10. *Weakness in the international arena is a major source of instability.* The armed forces of underdeveloped states may appear very strong in domestic politics, but their capacity for action in international affairs remains limited. Despite their recognition of a common enemy in their midst, efforts to establish meaningful regional commands have foundered in Africa and the Middle East, from a lack of power as well as from national rivalries.

Foreign military aid complicates the scene. Though at times it is essential for national security and is widely desired for prestige, it can disproportionately strengthen the military arm and give it the wherewithal to seize power. The point is clearly illustrated by events in Algiers, Baghdad, and Djakarta in which military establishments sustained by heavy Soviet assistance moved against regimes supported by Moscow. On the other hand, foreign aid may have sustained conservative regimes in Africa and the Middle East by strengthening the economy and armed forces of lands whose rulers depend upon a modicum of economic progress and the loyalty of their soldiers to remain in power. The net effect of foreign assistance is very mixed and requires further analysis.

Many other issues exist in the international field alone, for example the use of military aid for security against a neighbor, or to further an ambitious foreign policy. The approach followed here is open to the criticism that our data are derived from individual states, and that the points discussed in the above categories are relevant only in national contexts. It is true that Mexico's ideological tradition, strong party, civilian-oriented army, cautious foreign policy, and moderate economic development program are all of a piece, and are separable for analytical purposes only at some risk. Yet it is only by undertaking cross-national and intercontinental comparative studies—by grouping our knowledge in meaningful categories, and seeking (but not forcing) significant patterns—that we can progress in the difficult study of political development, or its more "manageable" aspects such as the role of the military.

Colin
Legum

THE TRAGEDY IN NIGERIA

F or fear of promoting an even greater tragedy, the Nigerians have been sheltered from knowing the full magnitude of the disaster that has overtaken the Ibos in the Northern Region. The danger is that truth will not be believed, and so no proper lessons learnt, once the horror is over.

While the Hausas in each town and village in the North know what happened in their own localities, only the Ibos know the whole terrible story from the 600,000 or so refugees who have fled to the safety of the Eastern Region—hacked, slashed, mangled, stripped naked, and robbed of all their possessions; the orphans, the widows, the traumatized. . . .

The total casualties are unknown. The number of injured who have arrived in the East runs into thousands. After a fortnight, the scenes in the Eastern Region continued to be reminiscent of the ingathering of exiles into Israel after the end of the last war. The parallel is not fanciful.

There is not the least doubt the Hausas of the North decided to rid their region forever of the Ibos. They sanctioned enough thuggery to start a panic among the Ibos: the full impact was checked by the authorities to enable the exodus of the survivors to proceed, if not without serious hazard, at least with some chance of escape. But no one was safe until he had finally crossed the frontier.

There were reportedly over 2,000,000 Ibos in the North, but it is still impossible to determine how many have left. The refugee escape routes were still crowded in mid-October with desperate people trying to make their way out. One man, his head battered and his leg broken in two places, is reported to have stood for five days up to his neck in water, coming out only at night before he made his getaway. "I was smelling rotten," he said.

Since the beginning of the century, Ibos have been leaving home in large numbers because there is not enough land or opportunity in Ibo-

Reprinted in abridged form by permission of The Observer (London), Oct. 16, 1960.

land. Like the Jews, the Indians, and the Chinese, they have made their home where they have made their living. They diligently converted their wages into property and trading stock and education for their children. Compelled by Moslem Northern society to live beyond the pale, they built their own flourishing strangers' towns with schools, churches, hotels, and stores. Here their clan unions flourished.

They looked down upon their Hausa hosts as unenterprising, lazy, backward, and feudal. They were arrogantly self-conscious of their superiority and they showed it. They became the wealthiest community in the North. They also became the leaders of progressive politics aimed at destroying the feudal North. Their aim was to build a modern nationalist movement linked with the radical southern parties. These objectives laid them open to the accusation that they sought to take over the North and to dominate the whole country.

Although there were other stranger-communities—such as the Yorubas who have not been touched by the massacres, which do not appear to have any element of religious intolerance—the Ibos numbered over 80 per cent of the incomers. Like all petty traders the world over, they exploited their customers and ignored their resentment. The hatred that grew up around them was dismissed as jealousy fanned by the Northern emirs. They were the sharpest, shrewdest, most successful, and most pushful element in a slow-moving society. When self-government came to the Northern Region in 1956, the Hausas excluded the Ibos from their civil service, but the Ibos remained indispensable as technicians and skilled workers in the federal service. With government jobs closed to them, they concentrated more in the money-making private sector.

The local propaganda against the Ibos has for years been of a virulent nature. A particularly notorious pamphlet published in 1964 elections caricatured them in very much the same way as Julius Streicher caricatured the Jews in *Der Stürmer*. Last year I visited the North and was disturbed by the intensity of anti-Ibo feeling. While the peasants complained of exploitation, the educated Northerners spoke of the Ibos as vermin, criminals, money-grabbers, and subhumans without genuine culture. "Their god is money," they said.

The Coup Intensifies Distrust

Last January [1966] witnessed the first military *coup* which brought General Ironsi, an Ibo, to power. It destroyed the old political system and killed the North's leading politicians, as well as a number of southerners. But no Ibo leader died. Although the *coup* was master-minded by Ibos, their ardent supporters included Yorubas and Hausas.

The Northerners, however, saw the *coup* as part of an imagined Ibo strategy to dominate the country. Nor were they reassured by the arrest and killing of most of the young Ibo officers who had originated the *coup*. They saw it all as part of a devilishly cunning Ibo plot. They had been particularly incensed by Ibo rejoicing in the North over the killing of the Sardauna of Sokoto, the North's Premier.

Quietly, the Northerners planned their vengeance. In May, when General Ironsi decreed the unification of the civil service—with the full agreement of the Northern military leaders—several thousand were killed. There is no doubt that it was carefully planned. The Ibos packed their families off to the east, but their panic was stopped by the Eastern Region's military commander-governor Colonel Ojukwu who urged the Ibos to remain in the North and to work for a United Nigeria. He now admits it was a terrible mistake.

Then in July, the Northerners brought off their counter-*coup*, killing General Ironsi and putting a Northerner, Colonel Gowon—not a Moslem —in his place. In so doing they introduced a significant new factor into the situation—the Tivs, who want their own state and who are now an important military factor. But this is another story.

The second *coup* had sparked off a second massacre of Ibos in the North. Still they stayed. Finally, and without any immediate pretext, a third massacre started at the end of September, leading to the holocaust. Now the Ibos have finally given up and returned home. They have lost confidence in a federated Nigeria and have no illusions left about the chances of welding Nigerians into a single nation. They feel themselves to be a nation wrought out of their own sufferings.

What Causes Mass Killings?

What is to be learned about the nature of mass killings from these events in Nigeria? To dismiss them simply as acts of political vengeance or as another example of "African savagery" is Monday Club mumbo-jumbo. In the last two decades, the Asians have shown far greater savagery than the Africans, and in the decade before that the Europeans in Germany surpassed all.

The fact is that under certain conditions all peoples are capable of brutal massacres. It is important to try to establish, if possible, under what circumstances most killings become likely. One is struck by the obvious parallels between the Armenians in the Ottoman Empire, the Jews in Europe, the Chinese in Indonesia (and, tomorrow, it may be the Indians in East Africa), and the fate of the Ibos.

In each case, one finds a highly gifted people living in an alien society as traders, entrepreneurs, and skilled craftsmen. Either by choice or by force of circumstance they remain separate from their hosts. They invest in education and in promoting their family interests. They are energetic and ambitious—characteristics in sharp contrast from those of their hosts, who usually have been slow to take to modern ways, are easy-going and traditionalist-minded. The ambition and success of the incomers often makes them arrogant or at least leads them to affect patronizing attitudes toward their hosts. In several of these cases, they are identified with progressive politics and what is sometimes felt by the hosts to be alien influences.

These conditions alone do not produce mass killings. Two essential factors seem to be needed to release the capacity for mass killing. The first is that the host community should feel itself to be threatened by alien domination either economically, politically, or culturally. The second is that the host society should be in a state of great tension, malaise, or confusion. In other words, the host community must itself be caught up in a paroxysm of change. In such conditions, political leaders can exploit actual or imaginary grievances against the alien minority. The danger signal is when there is official sanction for talking about a minority group in nonhuman terms. This process seems essential to provide some kind of justification for dealing with other human beings as one would treat dangerous animals—exterminate them.

These ideas are obviously tentative and exploratory. There is a great need to explore the phenomena of mass killing if we are ever to get beyond superficial explanations of such terrible misfortunes as those which have overtaken the Ibo nation.

Irving
Leonard
Markovitz

GHANA WITHOUT NKRUMAH:
THE WINTER OF DISCONTENT

Some observers have been surprised by the apparent unanimity of support in Ghana for the little-known army officers who led the *coup d'état* against President Kwame Nkrumah on February 24. Their astonishment paralleled the embarrassment of the Chinese chief of protocol who had to seat the deposed leader at a state banquet in Peking even as the Ghanaian Embassy was removing Nkrumah's portrait from a sidewalk display case in the Chinese capital. In Accra itself, members of Nkrumah's personal guard regiment mounted an armed resistance to the takeover, but it was all over in a few hours. The old regime died quickly, and with it the nine-year rule of West Africa's original and seemingly best-established nationalist leader.

From an overseas viewpoint, it has been hard to reconcile the *coup* with the fact that a consensus on government and policy had seemed to emerge in Ghana out of the struggle between originally antagonistic interests. Unlike many other African countries, including several that have recently experienced military takeovers, Ghana seemed to have passed successfully through its time of troubles. Some regimes are unstable because important elements are neither represented in them nor decisively suppressed; but in Ghana, in one way or another every major social group had apparently reached an understanding with the regime. Politics was not the monopoly of an elite coalition of middle-class intellectuals and a traditional hierarchy that excluded the peasants, skilled laborers, and businessmen. There was considerable unrest and dissatisfaction, several assassination attempts against Nkrumah, and constant rumors of *coups*, yet the government had made conciliatory gestures toward its opponents both within and outside its ranks, and showed every sign of having attained a durable balance of interests.

Perhaps the kindest verdict on Nkrumah in the Western press was that he tried too hard and was in too much of a hurry. He was called a

Reprinted from *Africa Report*, Vol. 11, No. 4 (April 1966), pp. 10–15, by permission of the editor.

"clown" in the London *Observer*, and "Stalin-like" in the *New York Herald Tribune; The New York Times* made his 1961 proclamation of compulsory education appear to have been a totalitarian act. Yet, to interpret Nkrumah as a ruthless totalitarian leader—a kind of sub-Saharan Hitler—is to misunderstand both the sources and the loss of his power.

Seeds of Change

Ghana was neither a terrorized nor a poverty-stricken country. In traveling overland to Accra from francophone Africa, for example, two things were striking: the visible wealth of Ghana, and the visible breadth of its distribution. The number of cars, the condition of residential areas, roads, restaurants, shops, markets, office buildings, and department stores —and the widespread use of these facilities by Africans, not just the European commercial and technical elites—produced the image of a far from destitute country. Beneath the surface there were chronic periodic shortages of many imported goods, including basic foodstuffs, and mounting inflation.

Civil liberties were in a chaotic condition marked by the dismissal of judges and the retrial of cases which resulted in verdicts unfavorable to Nkrumah. The abuses of preventive detention and the outlawing of opposition parties were notorious. To assert, however, that the mass of the people lived in terror would be quite wrong. The commonly accepted estimate of the number of Nkrumah's political prisoners is 1,100, and reports of individual beatings by prison guards may well be believed. On the other hand, credible evidence of systematic torture has yet to be produced, and though the old regime sentenced several people to death for participating in one of the assassination plots, no one in Ghana appears to have been executed for a political crime.

In these circumstances, a mass revolt against tyranny or impoverishment was unlikely, and to suggest that the Army intervened only when the government had begun to lose control of the "forces of discontent" explains little. Every African country harbors similar discontents arising from unemployment, low wages and economic and social disparities.

The Army is said to have chafed at Nkrumah's nonmilitary decision to ask the USSR to train and equip one part of its forces, and Britain and the Commonwealth the other part. Another irritant was Nkrumah's proposal to create a "People's Militia" that would be separate from the Army, and hence a potential threat to the Army's authority and its share of the annual budget. Colonel E. K. Kotoka, commander of the second army brigade at Kumasi and leader of the *coup*, announced on the day of the takeover that the Army was motivated by Ghana's serious economic and political situation. It was unthinkable, he said on Radio Accra, that Ghana's economy had developed in the last three years at a rate of only three per cent per annum, given its vast potentialities. He accused Nkrumah of running Ghana as his personal property and bringing the country to the "brink of bankruptcy." He promised a sweeping revision of economic, financial, and political affairs that would include a constitutional referendum on a new system of government based on the separation of powers, and a reversal of Ghana's mounting economic dependence on the Communist world.

The military regime quickly announced that it would redirect trade toward the West, make no new barter agreements, curtail Communist aid, reverse Nkrumah's long march toward "scientific socialism," outlaw the ruling Convention People's Party (CPP) and all other political activities, and eventually return Ghana to civilian rule. The Soviet, East German, and Chinese technicians were asked to leave. At the Army's request, senior civil servants took charge of all ministries and the provincial administrations, and eight of them issued a statement in support of the new regime.

Taming the Opposition

The Army's seizure of power was the climax of a long sequence of changes in Ghana's society and governmental system. Ghana has undergone a very rapid evolution in which the Convention People's Party, which brought the country to independence in 1957, continued to govern in the postindependence period, while successfully overcoming opposition from distinctly different sources. Before Ghana became self-governing, the issues were the pace of advance to independence, and who would control the government at this critical transition point; deep conflicts arose over the purpose and nature of every significant governmental institution.

As far back as 1954, the particularistic National Liberation Movement in Ashanti and the cocoa growers had found common cause in opposing the growing influence of the "coastal modernizers." The Ashanti-cocoa grower nucleus attracted other interest groups, among them the Togoland Congress and the Northern People's Party. The British-sponsored constitutional instrument drafted just prior to independence in 1957 sought to accommodate these forces in a semifederal system, but the postindependence government did not wait long to adopt a hard line toward them. It repealed the constitutional provisions that encouraged regionalism, passed legislation against regional and tribal political parties, and compelled the opposition forces to recombine in a national organization which in fact incorporated regionalism under a different name.

After 1957, the only opposition group with a significant mass follow-ing was the United Party, a coalition of disparate ethnic and religious interests joined principally by their resistance to the unifying policies of the CPP. This original anti-Nkrumah group was founded with the blessing of the Asantehene, traditional leader of the Ashanti, soon after the passage in 1954 of legislation reducing the government price for cocoa and thus increasing the amount of money available for government development schemes. The names of the five groups that composed the United Party are indicative of the interests involved: the National Libera-tion Movement (itself a coalition of anti-CPP interests), the Northern People's Party, the Moslem Association Party, the Togoland Congress Party, and the Ga Shifimo Kpee. The old middle-class intellectuals—the doctors and lawyers who had advised the colonial administration and were the first moderate reformers—were also opposed to the CPP's pol-icies of socialization, and still resentful of having been pushed aside by the more vigorous young nationalists. Combined, these forces were a powerful movement for the redress of individual grievances, and the strong traditional loyalties attaching to the Asantehene, plus the organ-izational and theoretical ability of the intellectuals, enabled the party to attract a mass following.

None of the groups embraced in the United Party thought primarily in terms of national unity or orderly economic development based on a mass mobilization of the people. The cocoa farmers were unwilling to postpone immediate consumption for enforced savings; at most, they held that funds not paid directly to them should be invested in their local area, and not spread thinly over the country to be used to the ad-vantage of "foreigners." Tribal leaders, who at one time were willing to hand over the government to freely elected representatives and admit that they had no place in party politics, were encouraged by their al-liance with the cocoa farmers to revive their aspirations to a share of power. The opposition platform advocated a complex system of federa-tion in which regional governments were to assume most of the powers of the central government. Traditional leaders were not only to head each region, but were also to dominate the cabinet and the upper house of a bicameral parliament. Most significantly, these officials would not be elected, but would rule by virtue of their ancient positions; only the lower house was to be chosen by universal suffrage. Revenue for the federal government was to be derived from limited sources, and a broad-based tax prohibited.

Nothing could have been more irritating to the CPP. Federation would strengthen tribalism and virtually stifle economic development, and Nkrumah accordingly considered the United Party's proposals a funda-mental challenge to the system of government. Western standards of secular government, he believed, could not accommodate the divisive loyalties commanded by "uneducated and parochial-minded" tribal leaders. Loyalty to the Asantehene meant focusing on the past and Ashanti, instead of looking to the future and the nation. Chieftaincy might be exalted as a monument to Ghana's proud African heritage, but it could not be allowed to play an active role in contemporary politics.

At stake were opposing philosophies of government. In view of the latter-day cynicism of the Nkrumah regime, it may well be difficult to recall the moral fervor of the time. Followers of the CPP were convinced that they were fighting not for selfish interests, but for the creation of a national society. Because they could not agree on basic ends, the antagonists sought victory through intense conflict rather than compromise; and because the CPP saw the traditional interests (which would grow fat on cocoa surpluses while others went hungry) as a national menace, it believed that harsh repression was morally justified and socially necessary.

Among the first people thrown into jail under the Preventive Detention Law were wealthy Ashanti cocoa farmers, antigovernment intellectuals, and tribal leaders who wished to subordinate the disciplines of economic development to the interests of a weak federation based on an indirect electoral system that would favor the traditionalists. This original opposition challenged the authority of the government, and the structure and policy of the state itself.

To cope with an opposition that threatened the unity of the state and widespread public disorder that included assassinations and bombings, the government resorted to a series of repressive measures, deportations, arrests, censorship, and overt intimidation. For the most part, these acts were directed at limited political objectives, and in the circumstances some of the measures were obviously needed. Moreover, for an understanding of the recent *coup d'état*, it is important to note that the government's actions were not altogether arbitrary, but were sanctioned by law. Each of the legal measures was approved by a popularly elected parliament and was accepted by the elements in the governing groups, as well as by many of the bureaucrats and technicians. Increasingly, however, the government enacted capricious and arbitrary laws marking a sharp departure from the standards of rationality established by the British Colonial Service, and from the standards of the revolution itself.

At the same time, the government was installing the machinery of coercion. It obtained an increasing number of antiriot vehicles and other quasimilitary hardware, enlarged the police force, established a reserve army, and organized a secret service. Again, given the circumstances, these measures seemed not unreasonable. The net result, however, was the strengthening of an institution—the Army—that proved lethal to the regime that nurtured it. This history differentiates the Army of Ghana from the armed forces of most other African states, and provides the context for the *coup d'état*.

As the clash of political objectives drove the CPP to greater militancy against the United Party, the opposition in turn was compelled to reassess and eventually modify its position. It dropped the issue of federation and began for the first time to place a high value on parliamentary institutions within a unified Ghana as a forum for the expression of its demands. Chiefs abandoned their interference in secular life. Economic development was universally accepted as the major objective of all social groups. Where once Nkrumah stood almost alone in arguing that "progress could be measured by the number of children in school, the quality of their education, the availability of water and electricity, and the control of sickness," these goals became the aspiration of the whole society. Long before the end of the regime, large numbers of traditional notables had joined the CPP, taken their seats in many councils, and proved themselves flexible enough to become influential and persuasive spokesmen. The drawing of new boundaries to the political arena was perhaps Nkrumah's major accomplishment.

Cracks in the Consensus

In September, 1961, hundreds of workers went on strike, and a qualitatively different kind of opposition began to arise in the ranks of organized labor. Originating among the harbor and railway workers in Takoradi, the walkouts spread to the industrial and commercial workers in Sekondi and Kumasi. Municipal transport employees in Accra soon joined the movement, and workers staged brief sympathy strikes throughout western Ghana. The walkouts were essentially a protest against government austerity measures that reduced the average worker's buying power by raising the cost of basic imports dramatically, almost overnight. Clothing and shoes rose by a third, and food prices soared as transportation costs increased. To forestall inflation, the government tightened existing controls on wages, and imposed a compulsory savings scheme by which 5 per cent was deducted from all wages and salaries in excess of £120 a year, and invested in interest-bearing development bonds.

The strikers ignored back-to-work appeals from their union leaders as well as from the government, which came under heavy fire not only from the formal opposition but also from loyal CPP supporters who ordinarily looked to Nkrumah for leadership. The strike thus marked the beginning of a different type of opposition from within the government's own ranks. It touched the heart of its mass support in the coastal cities, where the strikers had earlier endorsed the government and its policies by large majorities. This new opposition sought some compromises and modifications of the program for reaching the goals they had already agreed on, though they did not challenge the goals themselves.

When the government imprisoned the leaders of the strike, thus adding a new category of prisoners held under the Preventive Detention laws, the CPP appeared to be on the threshold of a period of violence and terror in which the government turned against its own mass base and suppressed the very people who had brought it to power. In an earlier day this possibility would have been academic, for the government did not command sufficient instruments of repression to dismember the old, semifeudal opposition by force. By 1961, however, the coercive apparatus of the state had increased enormously in strength, and there was a wing within the ruling party that urged its use.

A showdown was avoided as the government retreated from the system of compulsory savings, and a return to normality seemed to follow. Behind the façade, however, the strikers had revealed not only a growing discontent with the government's austerity measures (which had indeed been anticipated), but also the extent to which the trade union leaders were acting as tools for the CPP and the state.

Meanwhile, the influence of the CPP's militant wing was shown in attempts to intensify the ideological indoctrination of the people and the key elites. Several new doctrinaire journals were established; the Kwame Nkrumah Ideological Institute was opened at Winneba, and an effort was made to reorient the university along ideological lines. Soviet, Chinese, and East German technicians began to arrive in increasing numbers; trade with the Eastern bloc was increased, sometimes under disadvantageous conditions; attacks against United States policies became increasingly vituperative, and the ideological theme shifted from an emphasis on the uniqueness of the African personality to the universal applicability of scientific socialism. Most important of all, economic decisions apparently came to be made primarily on the basis of ideological factors rather than economic calculations. The expenditure of millions on a convention hall or an Olympic sports center, and the decisions to continue losing money on an airline or unprofitable factories, or in disadvantageous barter deals with the USSR, were justified in terms of a certain political calculus. These apparently self-defeating choices can be viewed as highly rational in the perspective of men who believed strongly in building African unity and scientific socialism in a short time.

Granting that millions were spent on prestige projects, the key question remains unanswered: what percentage of the government's total expenditure did these projects represent? The assertion that Nkrumah brought Ghana to the verge of bankruptcy does not take into sufficient account the catastrophic drop in the price of cocoa on the world market, and ignores long-range, highly productive projects, such as the Volta development scheme, which are coming to fruition years ahead of schedule, but which had until now been a drain on the economy. It turns a blind eye to what Ghana got for its money: an extended life expectancy from fundamental improvements in medical services, nutrition, and hygiene; a huge educational system serving a larger percentage of school age children than in any other Black African country; the creation of thousands of jobs; and an economy at the threshold of self-sustaining development.

Nkrumah and the militants of the CPP would argue that these accomplishments were achieved not despite, but because of, political persuasion and manipulation and an ideology to guide the selection of objectives and strategies. To them, independence from the British, unity within the state, and financing for the Volta project were equally *political* objects. They believed that without a sound "ideological" and "political" foundation, Ghana could not hope to prosper.

Alienation of Peasants and Bureaucrats

It is well known that the ideological militancy of the regime was accompanied by corruption. The effects of corruption were felt deep in the bush, where the farmers accepted Nkrumah's overthrow for reasons far removed from the policy questions that seem to have motivated the military. People in the bush know whether a regime is corrupt. The farmer is rightly suspicious, for there is always some doubt as to the social consequences of any innovation. After he has spent six to nine months hoeing, sowing, weeding, and harvesting a crop of maize, cocoa, cotton, or peanuts, what must he feel—a man who has never been to town—as he holds for the first time a few banknotes in his hand and watches the truck with his stuffed sacks trundle down the road—to where?

Ultimately, corruption in an underdeveloped country operates to milk the farmer. The salaries of functionaries and politicians, who are the best organized interests in the society, tend to be downwardly inflexible, but farmers, to the extent that they are engaged in a market economy, have a minimum of economic resources and organizational skills, and are highly vulnerable to economic exploitation. Corruption poisons the atmosphere; the government loses authority as enclaves of power are established in urban areas where a small, Westernized elite holds a monopoly of influence. In such a situation, the farmers always oppose the regime—or, more precisely, they are increasingly separated from it. To avoid unnecessarily alienating the peasantry is one of the principal reasons that Communist regimes are notorious for their puritanism.

Whether corruption is equivalent to waste depends on the type of social system in which it occurs, for it may serve functionally to keep certain elites and classes satisfied. If assuaging such interests is a necessary consideration, then corruption may be the least painful (because it is the most indirect) method of achieving stability. From the perspective of economic development, however, corruption perpetuates stagnation by curtailing capital, and robs the government of its political persuasiveness and moral authority. The technical knowledge necessary for the introduction of scientific agriculture is a monopoly of the educated government intelligentsia. To educate the peasant involves convincing the peasant to listen and to do a great many things that seem unnatural and threatening. Leadership of this kind is possible only when there is moral authority, not simply force, and this is true no matter how knowledgeable the technician.

As corruption was alienating the farmers in Ghana, it was also arousing resentment among the civil servants and technicians who worked with the farmers in the back country. Their task of inducing the farmers to accept modern agricultural techniques became increasingly difficult in proportion to the government's loss of credibility among the rural masses. The alienation of both groups in turn affected what the French call *encadrement*—that is, the reorganization of the populace into a social structure that makes the resources of the community available for economic development. *Encadrement* was not only the next logical step following the government's defeat of semifeudal rural interests; it was also essential if unfulfilled material ambitions—the so-called revolution of rising expectations—were to be satisfied in the country at large.

The unsolved problem of restructuring the rural society was a basic issue underlying Nkrumah's ouster. On the one hand, the government could choose among a variety of ideological solutions ranging through Chinese communalization to Moshavism or *laissez-faire* capitalism. On the other hand, the problem could be viewed simply as a technical exercise in maximizing output. Militants within the ruling party, the press, radio, youth organizations, and trade unions pressed for an ideological solution. Opposing them were the "technocrats," who included members of the higher civil service.

Two things distinguished the technocrats from the nucleus of civil servants carried over from preindependence days. First, their large numbers: the government acquired thousands of employees as it Africanized the administrative structure, extended its services from the large cities to millions of people in the bush, and undertook sweeping programs of welfare and economic development, instead of confining itself (as did the colonial administration) to the household tasks of maintaining peace, order, and a system of justice.

A second distinction is their awareness of membership in a technocratic elite. From the apolitical British tradition, in which neutrality is a source of pride and effectiveness is conceived as a concomitant of non-involvement, the newcomers to Ghana's bureaucracy slowly developed an awareness of a collective interest distinct from the interests of the politicians, who, in the British tradition, were entitled to make policy. By their style of dress, patterns of speech, education, training, vocabulary—and by the images in their heads, their attitudes toward economic development, political goals, and methods of governing—the administrative elite can be distinguished from the political elite. They found Nkrumah's personality cult objectionable, and the servile flattery bestowed on him in many quarters demoralizing, because it clashed with the tastes and traditions of the civil servant.

This is not to say that the technocratic elite, a bulwark of the new military government, is democratic. The men most deeply concerned with economic development have a manipulative attitude toward the rural groups with whom they work. They make no hortatory appeals to the crowd—a major distinction between the technocrats and the ousted politicians. Their approach is that of the social worker to his culturally and educationally deprived brethren. They appeal to the villagers' "home-town spirit" and "reason" with them until they accept previously decided projects, then reward the village with a ceremony attended by the local notables and honored by greetings from national officials. In going about their work, the civil servants make little effort to identify with the villagers; rather, they attempt to persuade the villagers that they, as technicians, can be of use by virtue of their unique knowledge and skills. Nor, in Nkrumah's day, did they make an effort to identify themselves to the people as party members. They often cooperated with the party, particularly in local community development projects, and some indeed were card-carrying members of the CPP. But when they joined the party, they did so because membership was useful to their careers, not out of political conviction.

These functionaries are little interested in ideology or indoctrination. They brush aside questions on socialism or the African personality, preferring to discuss their programs in terms of specific goals and rational techniques to meet them. They judge their accomplishments objectively and honestly, and readily admit mistakes. In sum, their efforts are directed toward the creation of a social system based on rational calculations demanding predictability and regularity in the conduct of affairs. By their attitudes, training, and objectives, they consider themselves a class apart from the politicians as well as from the people—a purposeful class that knows how to get a job done, if left alone to do it. Perhaps their biggest complaint was that Nkrumah's government did not always consider their work important enough. Their budget requests were often cut, their resources limited, and their advice rejected; worst of all, the government made decisions on the basis of criteria they could not accept, on the counsel of ideologies they could not tolerate.

New Dangers for the Future

Ghana's real problem on the eve of the *coup* was deeper than the threat of bankruptcy, for national productivity was still increasing as the economy began to unlock its potential. A more basic issue was the system of decision-making legitimated by Nkrumah, for which he was held personally responsible by the bureaucratic elites. Nkrumah saw himself in the historically appointed task of "sweeping away the fetters on production," eliminating "feudal elements" and "neocolonialism," so that the "productive forces of society could be liberated." Ironically, the new technicians, though they use a different vocabulary, see themselves as performing the identical tasks, freeing the economy from the waste and inefficiency spawned by wayward ideologists and corrupt politicians. In their eyes, Nkrumah had become the chief fetter on the forces of production.

In many respects, the army and police are also bureaucracies, their officers sharing many of the attitudes and concerns of the civil service. Unlike politicians, neither the army officers nor the bureaucrats include the art of persuasion in their usual kit of tools. To govern, however, it is not enough to be "modern-minded" and incorruptible. The value of the politician lies in his ability to manipulate opposing factions, and thus mitigate conflict through compromise. In the absence of the politician's special skill, Ghana's military government may turn ineluctably to the use of authoritarian measures, a tendency that would be reinforced by the paternalistic attitudes of the technocrats.

The regime's general prohibition of political activity and membership in the Convention People's Party raises the fundamental issue: how to avoid a gulf between the government and the governed that would compel the regime to use increasing force to remain in power. The CPP was a mass party with tens of thousands of members. For the Army to reform the party is one thing, but to eliminate it altogether is to burn the bridges between the citizens and the state. Moreover, the National Liberation Council is heir to the economic frustrations and unfulfilled popular aspirations of the previous regime. The experiences of military governments in the Sudan, Burma, and several Latin American countries suggest that neither the army nor the bureaucracy can move far forward fulfilling popular aspirations in Ghana without some form of mass support. Since the regime cannot maintain itself in power indefinitely without a social base, to whom will it turn?

Other recent moves cast additional light on the political complexion of the new regime. Communist aid technicians have been ousted from the country; trade patterns with the East are being revised; the end of "disastrous" scientific socialism has been proclaimed; the regime has jailed several militant intellectuals; the Asantehene and traditional chiefs have declared their allegiance; and the very name of the National Liberation Council recalls the name of a former conservative opposition group, the National Liberation Movement. By themselves these actions are not conclusive evidence of the nature of the regime. One could reasonably assume, for example, that any of these moves could have occurred without demolishing the original framework of government established by Nkrumah and the CPP.

They assume a different aspect when viewed in context of the regime's announcement on February 26 that the new constitution of Ghana is to establish a government based on the separation of powers. The proposal of a system in which "sovereign powers of the state are judiciously shared among . . . the legislature, the executive, and the judiciary" was of course inspired by the constitution of the United States; but Ghana resembles neither the U.S. today nor the thirteen original states of 1787. In the revolutionary American colonies, the separation of powers was designed not only to ensure personal freedoms, but also to establish a "negative" government without a social program and endowed only with limited authority. The system was intended to inhibit the formation of a tyrannous majority by deliberately pitting faction against faction; it recognized the existence of antagonistic interests, and institutionalized them in the government itself.

A formal separation of governmental powers in Ghana would not necessarily mean that the government will be unable to assert authority in the hinterland. Nevertheless, to weaken the powers of the central government in a country where the countervailant forces are hostile to the state is to engage in an experiment that could imperil national unity and slow the pace of economic development. A revival or institutionalization of regional, tribal, and class interests would alter the evolution of Ghanaian society, and jeopardize the continued existence of either democracy or stability. If that prospect came to pass, who would then mourn the passing of the "clown"?

Postscript

Since the overthrow of Nkrumah in February, 1966, the National Liberation Movement has introduced fundamental changes in the fields of agriculture and industrial policy, as well as foreign affairs and political organization. In their search for a social base, Ghana's ruling technocrats in large measure have aligned themselves with the members of the liberal professions and commercial elite to produce one of Africa's outstanding examples of "technocracy-capitalism."[1] The commercial bourgeoisie, whose predominance skyrocketed with expanding Africanized industrial and economic development, have prospered even more greatly under the new regime.

On March 2, 1966, General Ankrah, in a keynote speech on Ghana's economic situation, stated that private enterprise was to constitute the most important sector of the economy in terms of personnel and output. Active state participation was to be limited to certain basic and key projects. No private enterprise would be forced to accept governmental participation. The cooperative movement's activities would be purely economic instead of having further political or social objectives. The NLM abolished rent tax, as well as income tax paid by cocoa farmers on income from the sale of cocoa. They also raised the exemption limits on taxable income.

During 1967 and 1968, continued efforts were made to consolidate and stabilize the economy, while on the political front criticisms of the military government mounted and demands for civilian rule intensified.

On March 31, General A. A. Afrifa stipulated four conditions for a return to representative government: (1) the people must be reeducated as to their political rights; (2) they must become accustomed to their newly won freedom and understand the qualities of leadership; (3) the image of Nkrumah's Convention People's Party must finally be destroyed; (4) the National Liberation Council must be assured that the country is on the way to economic recovery and the administration has been cleansed of the faults that led to the *coup*.

On January 29, 1968, the NLC published the draft constitution recommended by the commission headed by Chief Justice Edward Akufo-Addo. The constitution provided for a President with limited executive powers; a Prime Minister as head of government; a council of state to aid and counsel the President, composed of officials and prominent citizens; a cabinet subject to approval by the legislature, a unicameral legislature of 140 members to be elected by universal adult suffrage; and a powerful independent judiciary. The Constitutional Assembly which would ratify the proposed constitution was to consist of a majority of nonelected members: ten appointed by the NLC, forty-nine by local councils; ninety-one by a variety of organizations, including houses of chiefs and trade unions. Following the adoption of

1. *Cf.* Irving L. Markovitz, "Ghana Ten Years after Independence: the Development of Technocracy-Capitalism," *Africa Today*, 14, no. 3 (1967) 6–12.

the Constitution, parliamentary elections leading to the institution of a civilian government would be organized and the ban on political parties lifted.

Nevertheless, almost three years after the new regime had come into power, serious questions remained not only as to Ghana's political future, but her economic development as well. The answer to the question of who was to rule and who would benefit from economic growth had, however, become somewhat clearer. By the end of 1969 political parties were again legally maneuvering for positions of prominence in the forth-coming elections.

P.P.S. In elections held during August, 1969, The Progress Party of Kofi A. Busia, former leader of the organized opposition to Nkrumah, won 101 seats in an assembly of 140. The N.L.C. then designated Dr. Busia as the first Premier of the Second Republic. Although the N.L.C. was scheduled to dissolve itself upon the convening of Ghana's National Assembly, a three-man Presidential Commission (instead of a President, as originally planned) will continue to hold important reserve powers. Brigadier Afrifa, the last N.L.C. chairman, Police Chief J. W. K. Harlley, and Major General A. K. Ocran, Chief of the Defense Staff, composed the Commission.

Julius K.
Nyerere

THE ARUSHA DECLARATION AND TANU'S[1] POLICY OF SOCIALISM AND SELF-RELIANCE

Part Two: The Policy of Socialism

(A) ABSENCE OF EXPLOITATION

A truly socialist State is one in which all people are workers and in which neither capitalism nor feudalism exists. It does not have two classes of people: a lower class consisting of people who work for their living, and an upper class consisting of those who live on other people's labour. In a true Socialist State no person exploits another, but everybody who is able to work does so and gets a fair income for his labour, and incomes do not differ substantially.

In a true Socialist State it is only the following categories of people who can live on other people's labour: children, the aged, cripples, and those for whom the State at any one time cannot provide with employment.

Tanzania is a nation of peasants and workers, but it is not yet a socialist society. It still contains elements of feudalism and capitalism— with their temptations. These feudalistic and capitalistic features of our society could spread and entrench themselves.

(B) THE MAJOR MEANS OF PRODUCTION AND EXCHANGE ARE UNDER THE CONTROL OF THE PEASANTS AND WORKERS

To build and maintain socialism it is essential that all the major means of production and exchange in the nation are controlled and owned by the peasants through the machinery of their Government and their co-operatives. Further, it is essential that the ruling Party should be a Party of peasants and workers.

The major means of production and exchange are such things as: land; forests; minerals; water; oil and electricity; news media; communications; banks, insurance, import and export trade, wholesale trade; iron

1. Tanzania African National Union (TANU) is the single government political party. This statement was adopted as government policy at an official party meeting in Arusha, Tanzania in January 1967.

Reprinted and excerpted with permission of the Office of the President of Tanzania.

and steel, machine-tool, arms, motor-car, cement, fertilizer, and textile industries; and any big factory on which a large section of the people depend for their living, or which provides essential components of other industries; large plantations, and especially those which provide raw materials essential to important industries.

Some of the instruments of production and exchange which have been listed here are already owned or controlled by the people's Government of Tanzania.

(c) THE EXISTENCE OF DEMOCRACY

A state is not socialist simply because its means of production and exchange are controlled or owned by the government, either wholly or in large part. For a country to be socialist, it is essential that its government is chosen and led by the peasants and workers themselves. If the minority governments of Rhodesia or South Africa controlled or owned the entire economies of these respective countries, the result would be a strengthening of oppression, not the building of socialism. True socialism cannot exist without democracy also existing in the society.

(d) SOCIALISM IS A BELIEF

Socialism is a way of life, and a socialist society cannot simply come into existence. A socialist society can only be built by those who believe in, and who themselves practise, the principles of socialism. A committed member of TANU will be a socialist, and his fellow socialists—that is, his fellow believers in this political and economic system—are all those in Africa or elsewhere in the world who fight for the rights of peasants and workers. The first duty of a TANU member, and especially of a TANU leader, is to accept these socialist principles, and to live his own life in accordance with them. In particular, a genuine TANU leader will not live off the sweat of another man, nor commit any feudalistic or capitalistic actions.

The successful implementation of socialist objectives depends very much upon the leaders, because socialism is a belief in a particular system of living, and it is difficult for leaders to promote its growth if they do not themselves accept it.

We Are at War:

TANU is involved in a war against poverty and oppression in our country; this struggle is aimed at moving the people of Tanzania (and the people of Africa as a whole) from a state of poverty to a state of prosperity.

We have been oppressed a great deal, we have been exploited a great deal and we have been disregarded a great deal. It is our weakness that has led to our being oppressed, exploited and disregarded. We now intend to bring about a revolution which will ensure that we are never again victims of these things.

A Poor Man Does Not Use Money as a Weapon:

But it is obvious that in the past we have chosen the wrong weapon for our struggle, because we chose money as our weapon. We are trying to overcome our economic weakness by using the weapons of the economically strong—weapons which in fact we do not possess. By our thoughts, words, and actions it appears as if we have come to the conclusion that without money we cannot bring about the revolution we are aiming at. It is as if we have said, "Money is the basis of development. Without money there can be no development."

. . . .

In brief, our Five-Year Development Plan aims at more food, more education, and better health; but the weapon we have put emphasis upon is money. It is as if we said: "In the next five years we want to have more food, more education, and better health, and in order to achieve these things we shall spend £250,000,000." We think and speak as if the most important thing to depend upon is *money* and anything else we intend to use in our struggle is of minor importance. . . .

. . . .

When it is said that Government has no money, what does this mean? It means that the people of Tanzania have insufficient money. The people pay taxes out of the very little wealth they have; it is from these taxes that the Government meets its recurrent and development expenditure. When we call on the Government to spend more money on development projects, we are asking the Government to use more money. And if the Government does not have any more, the only way it can do this is to increase its revenue through extra taxation.

. . . .

What of External Aid?

One way we employ to try to escape the need for increased taxation for development purposes is to put emphasis on money coming from outside Tanzania. . . .

.   .   .   .

Our Government and our leaders and other people keep on thinking about ways of getting money from outside. And when we get the money, or even the promise of it, our newspapers, our radio, and our leaders announce the news so that everybody may know that salvation has been obtained or is on the way. When we get a gift we make an announcement; when we get a loan or a new industry we make an announcement. In the same way, when we are given the promise of a gift, a loan or a new industry, we make an announcement of this promise. Even when we have merely started discussions with a foreign Government or institution for a gift, a loan, or a new industry, we make an announcement—even though we do not know the outcome of the discussions. Why do we do all this? Because we want people to know that we have started discussions which will bring prosperity.

Do Not Let Us Depend upon Money for Development

It is stupid to rely on money as the major instrument of development when we know only too well that our country is poor. It is equally stupid, indeed it is even more stupid, for us to imagine that we shall rid ourselves of our poverty through foreign financial assistance rather than our own financial resources. It is stupid for two reasons.

Firstly, we shall not get the money. It is true that there are countries which can, and which would like to help us. But there is no country in the world which is prepared to give us gifts or loans, or establish industries, to the extent that we would be able to achieve all our development targets. There are many needy countries in the world. And even if all the prosperous nations were willing to help the needy countries, the assistance would still not suffice. But prosperous nations are not willing to give all they could. Even in these prosperous nations, the rich do not willingly give money to the Government to relieve want.

Money can only be extracted from the rich through taxation. Even then tax revenue is not enough. However heavily we taxed the citizens of Tanzania and aliens living here, the resulting revenue would not be enough to meet the costs of our development programme. Neither is there any Government in the world which can tax the prosperous or rich nations in order to help the poor nations. Even if there was such a government, the revenue would not be enough to do all that is needed. But in fact there is no world Government. Such money as the rich nations offer to poor nations is given voluntarily, either through their goodness or for their own benefit. For all these reasons it is impossible for us to get enough money for development from overseas.

Gifts and Loans Will Endanger Our Independence

Secondly, even if it were possible for us to get enough money for our needs from external sources, is this what we really want? Independence means self-reliance. Independence cannot be real if a Nation depends upon gifts and loans from another for its development. Even if there was a Nation or Nations, prepared to give us all the money we need for our development, it would be improper for us to accept such assistance without asking ourselves how this would affect our independence and our very survival as a nation. Gifts which start off or stimulate our own efforts are useful gifts. But gifts which weaken our own efforts should not be accepted without asking ourselves a number of questions.

The same applies to loans. It is true that loans are better than "free" gifts. A loan is intended to increase our efforts or make those efforts more fruitful. One condition of a loan is that you show how you are going to repay it. This means you have to show that you intend to use the loan profitably and will therefore be able to repay it.

But even loans have their limitations. You have to give consideration to the ability to repay. When we borrow money from other countries it is the Tanzanian who pays it back. And as we have already stated, Tanzanians are poor people. To burden the people with big loans, the repayment of which will be beyond their means, is not to help them but to make them suffer. It is even worse when the loans they are asked to repay have not benefited the majority of the people but have only benefited a small minority.

How about the enterprises of foreign investors? It is true we need these enterprises. We have even passed an Act of Parliament protecting foreign investments in this country. Our aim is to make foreign investors feel that Tanzania is a good place in which to invest because investments would be safe and profitable, and the profits can be taken out of the country without difficulty. We expect to get money through this method. But we cannot get enough. And even if we were able to convince foreign investors and foreign firms to undertake all the projects and programmes of economic development that we need, is that what we actually want to happen?

Had we been able to attract investors from America and Europe to come and start all the industries and all the projects of economic development that we need in this country, could we have done so without questioning ourselves? Would we have agreed to leave the economy of our country in the hands of foreigners who would take the profits back to their countries? Supposing they did not insist on taking their profits away, but decided to reinvest them in Tanzania. Would we accept this situation without asking ourselves what disadvantages it would have for our Nation? How can we build the Socialism we are talking about under such circumstances?

How can we depend upon gifts, loans, and investments from foreign countries and foreign companies without endangering our independence? The English people have a proverb which says: "He who pays the piper calls the tune." How can we depend upon foreign Governments and Companies for the major part of our development without giving to those Governments and countries a great part of our freedom to act as we please? The truth is that we cannot.

Let us therefore always remember the following. We have made a mistake to choose money, something which we do not have, to be our major instrument of development. We are mistaken when we imagine that we shall get money from foreign countries, firstly, because to say the truth we cannot get enough money for our development and, secondly, because even if we could get it such complete dependence on outside help would have endangered our independence and the other policies of our country.

We Have Put Too Much Emphasis On Industries

Because of our emphasis on money, we have made another big mistake. We have put too much emphasis in industries. . . . It is a mistake because we do not have the means to establish many modern industries in our country. We do not have either the necessary finances or the technical know-how. It is not enough to say that we shall borrow the finances and the technicians from other countries to come and start the industries. The answer to this is the same one we gave earlier, that we cannot get enough money and borrow enough technicians to start all the industries we need. And even if we could get the necessary assistance, dependence on it could interfere with our policy on Socialism. The policy of inviting a chain of capitalists to come and establish industries in our country might succeed in giving us all the industries we need, but it would also succeed in preventing the establishment of Socialism unless we believe that without first building capitalism, we cannot build Socialism.

Let Us Be Concerned about the Peasant Farmer

Our emphasis on money and industries has made us concentrate on urban development. We recognize that we do not have enough money to bring the kind of development to each village which would benefit everybody. We also know that we cannot establish an industry in each village and through this means effect a rise in the real incomes of the people. For these reasons we spend most of our money in the urban areas and our industries are established in the towns.

.   .   .   .

This fact should always be borne in mind, for there are various forms of exploitation. We must not forget that people who live in towns can possibly become the exploiters of those who live in the rural areas. All big hospitals are in towns and they benefit only a small section of the people of Tanzania. Yet if we have built them with loans from outside Tanzania, it is the overseas sale of the peasants' produce which provides the foreign exchange for repayment. Those who do not get the benefit of the hospitals thus carry the major responsibility for paying for them. Tarmac roads, too, are mostly found in towns and are of especial value to the motor-car owners. Yet if we have built those roads with loans, it is again the farmer who produces the goods which will pay for them. What is more, the foreign exchange with which the car was bought also came from the sale of the farmer's produce. Again, electric lights, water pipes, hotels, and other aspects of modern development are mostly found in towns. Most of them have been built with loans, and most of them do not benefit the farmer directly, although they will be paid for by the foreign exchange earned by the sale of his produce. We should always bear this in mind.

.   .   .   .

The People and Agriculture

The development of a country is brought about by people, not by money, and the wealth it represents is the result and not the basis of development. The four prerequisites of development are different:

they are (i) People; (ii) Land; (iii) Good Policies; (iv) Good Leader-ship. Our country has more than ten million people and its area is more than 362,000 square miles.

Agriculture Is the Basis of Development

A great part of Tanzania's land is fertile and gets sufficient rains. Our country can produce various crops for home consumption and for export.

We can produce food crops (which can be exported if we produce in large quantities) such as maize, rice, wheat, beans, groundnuts, etc. And we can produce such cash crops as sisal, cotton, coffee, tobacco, pyrethrum, tea, etc. Our land is also good for grazing cattle, goats, sheep, and for raising chickens, etc.; we can get plenty of fish from our rivers, lakes, and from the sea. All of our farmers are in areas which can produce two or three or even more of the food and cash crops enumer-ated above, and each farmer could increase his production so as to get more food or more money. And because the main aim of development is to get more food, and more money for our other needs, our purpose must be to increase production of these agricultural crops. This is in fact the only road through which we can develop our country—in other words, only by increasing our production of these things can we get more food and more money for every Tanzanian.

The Conditions of Development

(A) HARD WORK

Everybody wants development; but not everybody understands and accepts the basic requirements for development. The biggest require-ment is hard work. Let us go to the villages and talk to our people and see whether or not it is possible for them to work harder.

In towns, for example, the average paid worker works seven-and-a-half or eight hours a day for six or six-and-a-half days a week. This is about 45 hours a week, excluding two or three weeks' leave every year. This means that an urban worker works for 45 hours a week in 48 to 50 weeks a year.

For a country like ours these are really quite short working hours. In other countries, even those which are more developed than we are, people work for more than 45 hours a week. It is not normal for a young country to start with such a short working week. The normal thing is to begin with long working hours and decrease them as the country becomes more and more prosperous. By starting with such short working hours and asking for even shorter hours, we are in fact imitating the more developed countries. And we shall regret this imitation. Nevertheless, wage-earners do work for 45 hours per week and their annual vacation does not exceed four weeks.

It would be appropriate to ask our farmers, especially the men, how many hours a week and how many weeks a year they work. Many do not even work for half as many hours as the wage-earner does. The truth is that in the villages the women work very hard. At times they work for 12 or 14 hours a day. They even work on Sundays and public holidays. Women who live in the villages work harder than anybody else in Tanzania. But the men who live in villages (and some of the women in towns) are on leave for half of their life. The energies of the millions of men in the villages and thousands of women in the towns which are at present wasted in gossip, dancing, and drinking, are a great treasure which could contribute more towards the development of our country than anything we could get from rich nations.

We would be doing something very beneficial to our country if we went to the villages and told our people that they hold this treasure and that it is up to them to use it for their own benefit and the benefit of our whole Nation.

(B) INTELLIGENCE

The second condition of development is the use of *intelligence*. Unintelligent hard work would not bring the same good results as the two combined. Using a big hoe instead of a small one; using a plough pulled by oxen instead of an ordinary hoe; the use of fertilizers; the use of insecticides; knowing the right crop for a particular season or soil; choosing good seeds for planting; knowing the right time for planting, weeding, etc.; all these things show the use of knowledge and intelligence. And all of them combine with hard work to produce more and better results.

.   .   .   .

None of this means that from now on we will not need money or that we will not start industries or embark upon development projects which require money. Furthermore, we are not saying that we will not accept, or even that we shall not look for, money from other countries for our development. This is *not* what we are saying. We will continue to use money; and each year we will use more money for the various development projects than we used the previous year because this will be one of the signs of our development.

What we are saying, however, is that from now on we shall know what is the foundation and what is the fruit of development. Between *money* and *people* it is obvious that the people and their *hard work* are the foundation of development, and money is one of the fruits of that hard work.

From now on we shall stand upright and walk forward on our feet rather than look at this problem upside down. Industries will come and money will come but their foundation is *the people* and their *hard work*, especially in *agriculture*. This is the meaning of self-reliance.

. . . .

Part Four. TANU Membership

Since the founding of the Party greater emphasis has been put on having as large a membership as possible. This was justified during the struggle for independence. Now, however, the National Executive Committee feels that the time has come for emphasis to shift away from mere size of membership on to the quality of the membership. Greater consideration must be given to a member's commitment to the beliefs and objectives of the Party, and its policy of Socialism.

The Membership Clause in the TANU Constitution must be closely observed. Where it is thought unlikely that an applicant really accepts the beliefs, aims and objects of the Party, he should be denied membership. Above all, it should always be remembered that TANU is a Party of Peasants and Workers.

Part Five. The Arusha Resolution

Therefore, the National Executive Committee, meeting in the Community Centre at Arusha from 26/1/67 to 29/1/67, resolves:

A. THE LEADERSHIP

1. Every TANU and Government leader must be either a Peasant or a Worker, and should in no way be associated with the practices of Capitalism or Feudalism.

2. No TANU or Government leader should hold shares in any Company.

3. No TANU or Government leader should hold Directorships in any privately-owned enterprises.

4. No TANU or Government leader should receive two or more salaries.

5. No TANU or Government leader should own houses which he rents to others.

6. For the purposes of this Resolution the term "leader" should comprise the following: Members of the TANU National Executive Committee; Ministers, Members of Parliament, Senior Officials of Organizations affiliated to TANU, Senior Officials of Para-Statal Organizations, all those appointed or elected under any clause of the TANU Constitution, Councilors, and Civil Servants in high and middle cadres. (In this context "leader" means a man, or a man and his wife; a woman, or a woman and her husband).

B. THE GOVERNMENT AND OTHER INSTITUTIONS

1. Congratulates the Government for the steps it has taken so far in the implementation of the policy of Socialism.

2. Calls upon the Government to take further steps in the implementation of our policy of Socialism as described in Part Two of this document without waiting for a Presidential Commission on Socialism.

3. Calls upon the Government to put emphasis, when preparing its development plans, on the ability of this country to implement the plans rather than depending on foreign loans and grants as has been done in the current Five-Year Development Plan. The National Executive Committee also resolves that the Plan should be amended so as to make it fit in with the policy of self-reliance.

4. Calls upon the Government to take action designed to ensure that the incomes of workers in the private sector are not very different from the incomes of workers in the public sector.

5. Calls upon the Government to put great emphasis on actions which will raise the standard of living of the peasants, and the rural community.

6. Calls upon NUTA (National Union of Tanzania) the Co-operatives, TAPA (Tanzania African Parents Association), UWT (Union of Tanzania Women), TYL (Tanzanian Youth League), and other Government institutions to take steps to implement the policy of Socialism and Self-reliance.

C. MEMBERSHIP

Members should be thoroughly taught Party ideology so that they may understand it, and they should always be reminded of the importance of living up to its principles.

Samir
Amin

CAPITALISM AND DEVELOPMENT
IN THE IVORY COAST

T he years 1958–1960 were those of independence for
the majority of the former French and English territories of the [African]
continent. A certain number of newly created African states at that time
chose "the socialist path to development," an apparently radical socialism; others chose the more moderate path of "African socialism"; still
others proclaimed their attachment to the free initiative of capital, even
if it was foreign. Almost all hastened to create planning organizations,
and almost all the plans that were produced established ambitious objectives for these new nations. Ten years later, the first balance sheet appeared meager for all of them: stagnation or even a relapse of production, as well as difficulties in public financing and foreign payments
precipitated by the extravagant development of administrative expenses,
ended in the final analysis by actually increasing foreign dependency.
The sociopolitical meaning of independence everywhere appeared to be
the same in spite of ideological divergences which, in any case, diminished
little by little. In every country there was a rapid rise of new indigenous
classes, including a new privileged class consisting almost entirely of administrative officials whose power and property depended on foreign aid,
and who gave no proof of economic dynamism; there was also disaffection of the masses, and political instability caused in great part by the
battle of "clans" [factions] within the new classes and by outside interference. . . .

Doubtlessly in proportion to the illusions of the first years of independence, there was a disaffection of European opinion: some people
began to talk about an Africa which was "off to a false start," and an
Africa which could not "take off." Others, in contrast, complacently
justified their optimism, by taking a very deterministic perspective of
history, although they wondered at the development of a local "elite."

Reprinted in abridged form from Le développement du capi-
talisme en cote d'Ivoire, Les éditions du minuit, Paris, 1967,
pp. 265–81, by permission of the publisher. Translated from
the French by Irving L. Markovitz.

277

Are there no exceptions in Africa? The Ivory Coast would seem to be the most brilliant. Nobody who is interested in the future of the continent has the right to ignore this experience, even if he is of socialist conviction and, because of this conviction, the capitalist path of development appears regrettable to him.

In several respects, the growth of the Ivory Coast economy in the course of the fifteen years from 1950–1965 has been remarkable, and not only because of its rate of growth—around 9 per cent per year over this whole period. At least three other positive aspects of this growth should be noted.

First, the pace of growth, which began in 1950 with the opening of the Vridi Canal and the creation of a deep-water port at Abidjan, accelerated from 7 to 8 per cent during the ten-year 1950–1960 period, to 11 to 12 per cent during the five years from 1960–1965. The latter rate, calculated by us, is far greater than the one of 6.5 per cent furnished by the official authorities.

This gain of momentum after independence was accompanied by a relatively harmonious sectoral distribution of growth: agriculture, 7 per cent, including 3 per cent for food crops, 9 per cent to 10 per cent for agricultural exports, and nearly 20 per cent for the development of lumber; 11 per cent for other sectors, including 13 per cent to 14 per cent for industry, artisans, and building, 10 per cent for transportation, commerce, and services, and 12 per cent to 13 per cent for public administration. One result has been that agriculture was reduced from more than half of the gross internal product in 1950 to almost a third in 1965, while industry rose from 9 per cent to 17 per cent; transport, commerce, and services from 34 per cent to 40 per cent, and administration from 6 per cent to 9 per cent. Two particular positive facts should be added to these general conclusions: the speed-up in the growth of a modern processing industry rose from 15 per cent a year for the first ten years to 25 per cent for each of the last five years; and there was a slow-down in the growth of administrative expenses beginning from 1961 to 1962 to no more than 5 to 6 per cent per year.

Secondly, structures for the financing of growth evolved in a favorable way. . . .

. . . .

Parallel to these developments, thanks to the evolution of income and public expenditures, a growing surplus of capital could be spent on equipment. Although the fiscal charges were progressively raised from 15 per cent of the internal output around 1950, to 20 per cent at the end of the period, current administrative expenses did not go above 16 per cent of the output in 1965, against 12 per cent in 1950. If, at one time between

1956 and 1961, one would have thought that the Ivory Coast, like most African countries, was on its way towards an overrapid and disordered increase of public expenses (in 1961, these expenses represented 21 per cent of the gross product), the country subsequently reacted to this temptation and returned to the relative austerity of the colonial period previous to the *loi cadre*. The result was the progressive reduction of the foreign share of financing: from 50 per cent around 1950, to 25 per cent around 1965.

Third, in spite of its rapid growth, the Ivory Coast's economy during the 1956–1965 period did not have any balance of payments difficulties.

This strategy of development was in effect based upon a priority given to exportable primary crops. In fifteen years, exports multiplied 4.4 times, against only 3.5 for internal produce. Although the imports that were induced by a development of this type increased parallel to exports, i.e., more quickly than internal domestic production, the surplus of the commercial balance necessarily increased in both relative and absolute terms. Under these conditions, the Ivory Coast was able, without any difficulty, to withstand the transfer abroad of profits and foreign savings which grew along with production, even though the share of foreign private and public capital diminished.

On balance, there is nothing miraculous about all these mechanisms of rapid growth. In the history of the colonial period one finds numerous examples that are analogous even in their details: e.g., Senegal at the time of the great expansion of peanut cultivation and the establishment of light industry in Cape Verde; Ghana, Southwest Nigeria, and the Congo, with the expansion of plantation economies (completed in the Congo at the time of the Belgian colonization by the opening up of the mineral riches of Katanga). The only difference between these colonial developments and that of the Ivory Coast resides in the fact that the former cases, which are older, were elaborated over longer periods of time, while the Ivory Coast found itself in 1950 still in the state of a colonial "reserve" whose development had not yet begun. There then resulted a pace of growth in the Ivory Coast that was still more rapid than elsewhere.

Except for this difference of time and pace, the experience of the Ivory Coast belongs to a known category. Moreover, she encounters the same limitations, whose three major aspects will be recalled here.

First, it will probably be impossible to continue to advance in the area of agricultural development without radical changes in policy. The fundamental reason for this is that an expensive plantation economy (whose results have been too easily obtained without direct investments in agriculture, but only in the transportation infrastructure), thanks to the introduction of a foreign-salaried work force, has fashioned a regressive social structure. However, a geographical extension of this type of economy will still undoubtedly be possible for some time to come through the opening up of the Western region of the country—if conditions permit finding an external market for this additional production.

Let us add several important observations to these conclusions. . . .

. . . . Ultimately the progress of the Ivory Coast agriculture has not allowed the country to acquire self-sufficiency in food production, hence she has become one of the large importers of foodstuffs, with these imports having increased at an only slightly slower pace than that of the gross internal product.

Secondly, in the area of industrial development it will undoubtedly be equally impossible to continue to advance without radically changing direction. Actually, only after the disintegration of AOF (The Federation of French West Africa) could a group of light industries be started in the Ivory Coast because they took the place of Senegalese industries in the market. Nevertheless, for some time to come some possibilities in this direction will remain because the retardation of the Ivory Coast in this area has not yet been completely overcome.

Third, the means of financing used for the growth of the economy has seriously mortgaged the future. The domination of foreign capital is exercised in an absolute manner over the entire economy of the country. Its remuneration at very high rates indicates the external dependence of this growth. Like the other territories during the colonial period, the Ivory Coast is rapidly passing from the stage of the establishment of industries characterized by a major dependence on foreign capital, to the stage of exploitation of these industries, characterized not only by the return flow of profits, but of the original capital as well.

One will perhaps say that this rapid opening up of a territory by foreign capital is better than nothing; the experience of neighbors who refused this possibility with no other result than stagnation would appear as evidence in favor of the Ivory Coast option. Some African leaders will go so far as to admit that political independence in Africa has preceded its capacity to develop economically other than by depending on foreign capital whose domination will prevail for still some time. Certainly, the positive historical role of this stage would not appear debatable. One often has a tendency to forget the positive aspects of colonization. The Ivory Coast experience comes as a reminder that the possibilities of foreign capitalism are not yet exhausted.

But it is important to know that these possibilities are limited and do not depend on African governments but on objective economic laws. Nigeria displayed the best will toward foreign capital: because she was already well advanced in the colonial style of development, the southern region of the country experienced stagnation in the same way as Ghana, whose ideological options were different. Therefore, only through an analysis of the mechanism blocking this type of growth, based on the study of the practical experience of others as well as on theory, can one begin to have a critical appreciation of the Ivory Coast experience.

In the *Perspectives décennales*[1] which applied to the period 1960–1970 and included projections for as far as 1975, as well as in recent public declarations of certain Ivory Coast leaders, one finds indisputable proof that, at least as far as the technicians in charge of the drafting of the plan and a certain number of leaders of the national economy are concerned, they are conscious of this danger. These fears have already given birth to several concrete measures, such as the law on the public domain, designed to end the chaotic pillage of the forest wealth. But we have the feeling that this consciousness is still limited. . . .

The possibilities of a continuous and rapid growth in the exportation of tropical products are limited. First, on the production side, there is a ceiling which is not far from being reached without an intensification of methods, except in the west of the country. Secondly, on the side of international demand prospects are mediocre. The solution evidently would be to intensify and diversify.

But if the *Perspectives* declare that in the area of coffee and cocoa, their objective is less the increase of production than an increase in the rate of return, to our knowledge it remains mute regarding the only effective way this can be done—we mean the modification of the social system in the countryside in a way which would oblige the developers to invest their capital through the workings of the economic system itself; for example, through the institution of a land tax. In the case of diversification, *Perspectives* sees the essential effort dependent on other tropical export crops, especially palm oil and rubber, crops for which there is a foreseeable deterioration in the long-run terms of exchange. In our opinion, true diversification must first focus on food crops, where the primary objective ought to be to completely feed the towns of the Ivory Coast, and secondly to furnish some industries with supplementary primary material within the framework of creating complementary West African arrangements. *Perspectives* on this point is so discreet one has the impression that they only raise pious hopes that are hardly believable.

It is the same with industrialization. Light industries for the direct substitution of imports are not very developed, and their possibilities of

1. Editor's note: *Perspectives décennales*, a document drawn up on the eve of the Ivory Coast's independence in 1960, under the direction of former Finance and Economic Minister R. Saller, set forth the basic orientations of the Ivor- ian economy. Certain observations of Samir Amin have been taken into account in later modifications of the original proposals of the *Perspectives* (see *Jeune Afrique*, October 1, 1967, p. 26).

expansion are limited . . . by the growth of revenue. The next stage should consist of starting basic industries. At the beginning of this stage the rates of growth must be much higher than the rates of income or consumption. But the beginning of such industries obviously makes sense only within the framework of great economic spaces. Although these truths are well known, *Perspectives* hesitates to confront this problem head on and remains silent on the fundamental problem of the voluntary creation of complementary industries which must be submitted to a common decision-making and planning center, probably because this requirement is considered to be outside the possibilities of the present political structures. The result is that *Perspectives* for the years to come does not propose any important industry outside the classic framework of light industries for the substitution of imports and the increase of the value of primary exports. This is the case in respect to mechanical industries, the transformation of metals and steel, chemicals, etc. . . . . When the possibilities of examining slightly more ambitious projects is timidly envisaged, they do not raise the fundamental issue of whether foreign capital would be willing to commit itself in this direction, taking into account the reduced returns of this type of industry.

Evidently, contradictions have resulted from these gaps in *Perspectives*, which are reflected in the projections for financing and the balance of payments. If the type of growth of the last fifteen years is projected into the future the result would doubtlessly be first a slowdown in the growth of exports; secondly, the continuation of the rate of growth of imports at a high level; and thirdly, the relative increase in the proportion of the rate of profits and savings exported.

The first of these consequences is clearly recognized by *Perspectives*, which indicates a declining rate in the growth of exports in its projections.[2]

The second, on the other hand, does not appear to have been sufficiently taken into consideration. Light consumer industries do not have as favorable an effect on the commercial balance as it is often believed. Because of the large-scale expenditures of revenue entailed, which, under the conditions of underdevelopment, are mainly on imported manufactured products, these industries have a negative stimulating effect—so much more so because the elasticity for the demand of these types of products is growing. Moreover, because of a lack of basic industries, intermediary products must to a great extent be imported: the assembly industries (bicycles, automobiles, electrical appliances, diverse machinery, etc.) and those of small plastics—industries envisaged with great favor in this type of development strategy—constitute the best example of

2. 5.9 percent per year for the 1970–1975 period, against 7 percent for the five years preceding.

this negative backsliding effect on the commercial balance. The experiment of the fifteen-year period, 1950–1965, shows that it was similar in the Ivory Coast. Imports increased more quickly than the gross internal product, going from 19 per cent in 1950 to 24 per cent in 1965. . . .

.   .   .   .

The third characteristic—the growing relative importance in the transference of profits and savings abroad—also does not seem to have been sufficiently taken into account according to the projections of *Perspectives*, which do not include detailed developments on financing in general and financial flows in particular.

What lessons, then, can be drawn from the experience of the past fifteen years? We have established that, from 1950 to 1965, revenue from the European sector—gross revenue from the developments of the great foreign enterprises, the gains of individual entrepreneurs, and the salaries of non-Africans—has represented a constant and very high proportion of the nonagricultural income—about 50 per cent. As the share of non-agricultural activities in the gross product has increased on the one hand, the proportion of gross profits of the large foreign enterprises—destined by their nature to be re-exported—rose from 7 per cent of the gross internal product in 1950 to 15 per cent in 1965. Evidently, this is nothing more than the inevitable consequence of growth dominated by foreign capital, and there is nothing particularly characteristic about the Ivory Coast in this respect. There is no reason why the same strategy would not involve the same consequences in the future.

.   .   .   .

. . . The type of growth that the Ivory Coast has experienced since 1950, therefore, does not automatically result in an economic "take-off," but in an increased external dependency and the blocking of growth. This is why *Perspectives*, which optimistically foresees that all the conditions for the take-off of the Ivory Coast will be met by 1970, appears to us to be debatable. Certainly by 1970 the level of achieved savings would be theoretically sufficient to assure an internally generated, self-sufficient growth. But a great part of these savings are fundamentally destined to be exported, and no financial technique for the mobilization of savings would permit breaking this objective law. It is not possible for us to figure out here the magnitude of foreseeable deficits if the present type of growth continues.

We will admit that these problems have not escaped the notice of the technologists, but contend that awareness of these problems can only slowly infiltrate into the milieu of the leaders of the political economy, that *Perspectives*, like all analyses that hope to have a decisional impact, is the expression of one stage in the progressive ripening of problems, and that in these respects it is the result of compromise and contradictions.

The fact remains that even a clear understanding of the nature of these factors does not lead to a solution of their difficulties. There is the problem of knowing if the social structures established during the course of a certain type of development, like that which the Ivory Coast has known since 1950, are not going to be obstacles to the change of strategy.

The Ivory Coast during the last fifteen years has been the theater of considerable social upheavals, both in the countryside, with the development of a class of rich planters, and in the towns, where the population comprised 7 per cent of the total population of the country in 1950 rising to 17 per cent in 1965.

On the national level, the proportions of the indigenous and immigrant populations have been upset in the rural plantation zones as much as in the cities. Although the natural population increase from 1950 to 1965 was at the rate of 2.2 per cent per year, the immigration of workers from the North added another 1.6 per cent. The foreign African population at the end of this fifteen-year period constituted about a quarter of the total population, 35 to 40 per cent of the active male work force, half of those of the urban areas, more than 60 per cent in urban zones outside of the public works, and half to two thirds of the work force in the rural plantation areas.

Evidently the extensive commercialization of the rural economy in the plantation zones and—to a lesser degree—in some small areas of the north, and the rapid urbanization and foreign immigration with the increased populations that this implies have deeply modified social relations and behavior of every type. Changes in the size and composition of rural communities and changes in their food habits . . . are only symptoms of those events whose repercussions are found on many other levels, including religion and family organization. This is not the place to analyze social change in all its aspects, but only from the perspective of development. What is involved is answering the following fundamental question: How have relations between the different classes and social layers evolved during the course of the last fifteen years of development in the Ivory Coast? More precisely, since the regime has opted for a capitalist way of development, is an Ivory Coast bourgeoisie in the process of being created? Will it eventually be able to take over from foreign capital?

Let us recall, in terms of the Ivory Coast countryside, the principal results of our analysis. First, although the share of European agricultural production rose from 9 per cent of agricultural and lumber production in 1950 to 23 per cent in 1965, the share of agricultural production proper—that is, with lumber production excluded—remained constant. . . .

Secondly, economic and social change have not as yet touched the whole of the Ivory Coast countryside, although the isolated and stagnant traditional zones today include no more than a third of the rural population, compared with 60 per cent in 1950. Economic and social changes have been less important in the Northern cereal zones, which include 8 to 9 per cent of the rural population, and whose monetary income per head went from 1,400 francs CFA ($5.60) in 1950 to 5,200 CFA ($20.80) in 1965 (in 1965 constant values). The southern plantation zones have developed considerably. Ordinary plantations that included 23 per cent of the rural population in 1950—with a per capita income of 11,700 francs CFA ($46.80) in 1965—encompassed 49 per cent in 1965, with an income of 15,300 francs CFA ($61.20) per head; the privileged zones, which involve 8 to 10 per cent of the rural population, have seen their per capita income rise from 19,400 francs CFA ($77.60) in 1965 values, to 26,000 francs ($104).

In the plantation zones, important social differentiations have appeared. In 1965, about 20,000 rich planters cultivated nearly one fourth of the land, employed two thirds of the salaried labor, and benefited from an average annual income of 400,000 francs CFA ($1,600). This allowed them an important surplus for prestige consumption destined to reinforce their social control and for the financing of urban investments (housing, taxis and trucks, etc.). However, this rural bourgeoisie is not a progressive one because—and this is one of the most alarming conclusions of the Ivory Coast experience—the economic mechanisms, up till now, did not oblige it to invest.

In 1950, this rural bourgeoisie was still embryonic and numbered only a few hundred families. The reason for this was because, until 1950, the system of forced labor had reserved the manual worker—half salaried, half slave—almost exclusively to the French planters.

The response found by the *Rassemblement démocratique africaine* (started and taken over from its origin in 1946 by the traditional chief, doctor, and planter, M. Felix Houphouet-Boigny) and the violence of the battles of the masses that it directed, especially in 1950 (motivating the resurrection of the colony of Upper Volta by the colonial authorities who desired to isolate the Ivory Coast's "communist" contagion), are explained by the conjunction of the bourgeois leadership of the movement and the support of the African masses. The planters knew that "freedom of work" would allow them to develop plantation economies for their own profit, and they also had the enthusiastic support of the peasant masses because they had been victims of forced labor. It is noteworthy that this bourgeois substratum gave the peasant movement a power that it had never known in countries where either semifeudal or communitarian modes of production dominated (as in the loop of the Niger, peanut-growing Senegal, etc.). Here there is food for thought concerning the nature of nationalist movements and their connection with the demands of the rural bourgeoisie that is of considerable importance in formulating a political theory of the Third World.

If rural development was for the benefit of a bourgeoisie of planters, this class nevertheless came directly out of the traditional chieftaincy. The latter class granted themselves rights over the land which, little by little, established a sort of private appropriation of the land for their own benefit. Confusion about the position of the traditional chief invested with social authority and the modern planter perhaps explains certain aspects of the social changes: the limits to the degradation of the traditional communities (whose dependents, although reduced to the status of semi-employees, were not deprived of all rights as were the foreign employees); the relatively tenacious survival of the traditional animist religion, etc.

In the urban economy, the changes were less important because urban society was somewhat more extended than transformed. In effect, the distribution of social income showed a remarkable stability, although the total volume increased strongly. The three fundamental characteristics of the social structure are as follows:

First, the share of foreign income on the whole remained almost stable—about 50 per cent of the gross nonagricultural product. The growing domination of foreign capital is shown by the growing share of big business, which rose from 28 to 40 per cent of nonagricultural foreign income. It was manifested as well by the importance of European salaries, which continued to represent about 40 per cent of the total amount of salaries paid by the productive economy (against 60 per cent in 1950). Non-Africans still occupy all key posts and alone assure the operation of the technical structures; they also have administrative and economic responsibility over the economy.

Secondly, the great mass of African incomes were either dependent incomes (salaries, especially of African workers employed by European enterprises) or the gains of small entrepreneurs too small to permit a progressive accumulation. Correspondingly, the revenues of African capitalist enterprises were almost negligible—almost nonexistent in 1965 as in 1950.

Thirdly, salaries paid by public offices not only occupied a very important place in the total of African incomes, but one that is still increasing. These salaries represented 20 per cent of the mass of African income, and 42 per cent of salaries in 1950; they represented 28 per cent and 48 per cent, respectively, in 1965.

We are now, then, in a position to reply to the question that we posed: In what way have social classes developed during the last fifteen years?

Ivory Coast society, like African societies everywhere, contrary to the frequent denials of some political leaders and compliant sociologists, was divided into different classes. These classes were differentiated by their roles in the economy, their standard of living, and their social behavior. In the countryside the essential factor of the last fifteen years is the appearance of a class of rich planters—about 20,000—and, correspondingly, a proletariat of agricultural workers. In the towns one can distinguish three distinct categories of classes and social strata: (1) the mass of people that includes more than 90 per cent of the population and is composed of a good third of workers, another good third of artisans and small merchants, and a slim third of subordinate employees of business and administration; (2) the middle layers, few in number, composed mainly of middle-rank civil servants and secondarily of comfortable shopkeepers; and (3) a bourgeoisie, whose members are still extremely small (less than 2,000 heads of family) whose income is too mediocre to permit a true accumulation; members of this group are composed mainly of high officials and "partners" associated with foreign businesses, and they are only accessorily true entrepreneurs. . . .

This structure of a dependent society is evidently regressive. First, because the planters were not obliged by the functioning of the economic mechanism to invest. Secondly, because the opportunities that foreign capital left the rich urban classes were so constricted. Finally, because the elites of the country are almost entirely administrative and paraadministrative, and do not include any more businessmen than elsewhere in black Africa. If one can speak, therefore, of the development of capitalism in the Ivory Coast, one cannot likewise speak of the development of an Ivory Coast capitalism. Ivory Coast society does not have its own autonomy: it is not included in the European society that dominates it; if the proletariat is African, the true bourgeoisie is absent, domiciled in the Europe that furnishes capital and cadres. In the course of the past fifteen years, this dependent and contradictory society has little by little taken form; it has been marked by the appearance and growth of a modern proletariat and local strata who, although rich, hardly merit the title of bourgeoisie in the sense that the bourgeoisie were, above all, entrepreneurs in the economic domain. These strata, whose prosperity is linked to the State and to foreign capital, find a profitable use for their surplus revenues in land and apartment-building speculation and the exploitation of certain services. They do not play any role in the development of the country.

Political stability and the popularity of the regime (a regime that does not permit the superficial journalist nor the complacent sociologist to see behind the façade of national unity to where there exists a structure composed of classes and different social strata) doubtlessly stems from the great prosperity that accompanied the remarkable development of foreign capitalism in the Ivory Coast. Up until now, everybody has gained something in this development. In the countryside, the traditional chiefs who became planters were enriched, as were the workers who immigrated from the North and who left very poor and stagnant traditional societies. In the towns, unemployment remains limited in comparison with what it already is in the large cities of older African countries. But problems exist that could cause further grave discontentment—especially if prosperity should cease. First, there are antagonisms between the immigrant peoples of the North and the indigenous peoples of the South, with the former becoming conscious of the importance of their role and demanding access to public offices, major roles in the economy, better salaries on the plantations, and even access to the ownership of land. Then there are the antagonisms between the young African generation leaving their schools and the Europeans—the former bound to be more and more sensitive to demands for Africanization. History will tell whether the embryonic African bourgeoisie will know how to overcome these contradictions of Ivory Coast society (especially by assimilating the Northern immigrants), or whether it will allow these antagonisms to become worse and degenerate into unmanageable conflicts.

The experience of the Ivory Coast's evolution during the last fifteen years is rich in lessons. It might be summed up with a single expression, "growth without development"—that is, growth engendered and kept up from the outside, without the construction of socioeconomic structures that would enable automatic passage to a still further stage, that of a self-centered and self-maintained new dynamism.

Part V

PROCESSES OF ENCADREMENT:
BUREAUCRATIC DEVELOPMENT
AND ECONOMIC GROWTH

*I*ndependence does not automatically create a new, higher standard of living. In order to maintain the allegiances of their people, leaders of the new states must develop; they must produce concrete results. They have no choice in this decision, for otherwise the people will throw them out and seek new leaders. Appetites and desires previously stimulated must now be satisfied. Legitimate aspirations long denied must now be fulfilled. Yet the difficulties of achieving economic development are enormous. Poverty breeds its own vicious cycle. Low levels of real income make possible only low levels of investment, and both are cause and consequence of the low level of demand for goods and services, which in turn causes a low rate of investment, a capital deficiency, and hence reinforces the low levels of real income. Nearly all African countries are, moreover, dependent on a small number of primary products with precarious export prospects, falling demand, wildly fluctuating prices, and a market in developed countries which, because of a superior technology, can find substitutes and add far greater value through scientific improvements. Although in most areas, pressures upon land have not become overwhelming, African countries face mounting increases in population. New natural resources are uncovered every day, but without capital and know-how they remain unexploited. An untrained and unskilled labor force complements large segments of the population unaccustomed to commodity and investment arrangements. African economies remain foreign-trade oriented and influenced. Colonial regimes scarcely developed internal markets; overseas interests remained, in most instances, as mere enclaves—especially in extractive industries which hardly affected internal development.

Until the mid-1950's, Europeans governed Africa from Europe and in Africa. They trained few Africans in government or advanced administration. Upon the achievement of independence, dependence on technical experts grew larger, not smaller. Inadequate numbers of trained Africans made it necessary that substantial numbers of expatriates stay on to keep the economic and government machinery going. Later, independence meant the assumption of new responsibilities ranging from the creation of new armies, foreign affairs ministries, and diplomatic representation, toward a greater effort at economic development. A central problem became the Africanization of the civil service, its rapid expansion, and the socialization as well as training of the new technicians. Creation of a coordinated development machinery constituted an enormous undertaking. African leaders also considered motivating the new civil service to a commitment to national objectives—of the greatest importance.

Tom Mboya admitted that the "decade of development," the sixties, which was to have ushered in a new era of prosperity, became a decade of discouragement, but he felt that if the proper measures were taken there was still hope, Surendra J. Patel, in a startling comparison of the historical rate of development of the West and underdeveloped areas today, dramatically and daringly argues that African societies will achieve relatively high standards of living in a relatively short period of time. R. Cranford Pratt reveals some of the practical domestic and foreign difficulties of creating a realistic plan and getting development moving. A special French study group of agronomists and technicians centered at the University of Aix presents a most revealing analysis of the motivations of those "middle-level" civil servants who are the links between the peasants and policy-makers, and who have been called the motors of development.

Compagnie
d'Etudes
Industrielles et
d'Aménagement
du Territoire
(Society of
Industrial
Studies and
Territorial
Management)

THE MEANING OF DEVELOPMENT
IN SENEGAL

Changes in behavior and an improvement in the attitudes of the population that favor the prospects of development do not require simply superficial action or organization of social and economic structures. The most important necessity is a re-ranking in prestige scales of the professions in Senegal and, in certain cases, perhaps a modification of the values held by the various ethnic and social groups.

To obtain these changes, it is first necessary that the concept of "development" have a real meaning, and one that is right for the Senegalese.

Secondly, there must exist means for the propagation of new ideas and methods of organization, education, and information, arranged so that they reach the masses of the population and create a revolution in depth.

Finally, it would be advantageous if dynamic groups existed within the country that could provide the ferment for this revolution.

Reprinted in abridged form from "Propositions pour améliorer les facteurs humains," in *Rapport général sur les perspectives de développement du Sénégal*, Vol. 2, 2nd ed., Dakar, 1960, pp. 1–6, by permission. Translated from the French by Irving L. Markovitz.

The Meaning of Development

Among the major negative elements affecting attitudes and behavior relating to development is the fact that "development" itself has no significance for the majority of Senegalese . . . because of the following difficulties:

1. The ascendency of the environment over the individual, with the family parasitism involved, and the constriction of individual abilities, particularly in the area of economic initiative;

2. The priority almost all the social groups invest in the search for security, with the consequence that the attitude of the people towards the administration becomes marked by passivity and docile expectations of personal gain.

The disappearance of a feeling of individual responsibility and sense of responsibility at the level of the basic community unit unfortunately are replaced by a search for all kinds of false security that lead to indebtedness, parasitism, etc.

3. An unfavorable attitude towards technical progress and better ways of doing things; attitudes of fatalism and discouragement. Persuaded that he is exploited and subject to the dictates of nature, rural man is convinced that his fate cannot be improved, an attitude that is not negative but passive. [Traditional man] remains convinced that "progress" does not concern him.

Under these circumstances, the tasks of the state would appear to be as follows: (1) to promote a certain climate of feeling, a certain type of *ambience;* (2) to put the necessary structures into place; (3) to provide the proper education. Together, these aims will enable the individual alone and with his fellows . . . to march towards progress.

The passage from a passive situation of nondevelopment to a dynamic orientation will certainly be favored by the establishment of new social or economic structures. But one must guard against thinking that the renewal of these structures by themselves necessarily means the passage to an active phase. Development is written in actions. The individuals who will succeed are those who decide to become more competent, or richer, or more useful; the nation itself will progress through the accumulated results of these individual accomplishments.

Four outstanding ideas that should be at the heart of the educational programs and initiatives undertaken by the political and educational officials for the development of Senegal are (1) the idea of progress; (2) the idea of responsibility; (3) the idea of a dynamic community; and (4) the idea of the nation. If these key ideas are taken up by all the great corporate groups that make up the nation (the political party, the administration, the different religious groups, etc.), it is possible that they will provide the myths necessary for development.

The Myth of Progress

In traditional society, a type of society that one can describe as "static," the idea of progress rarely exists. The whole educational apparatus of this society has as its objective teaching the young that their economic and social role in the village is to imitate everything their elders did and in the same manner.

From the perspective of what is necessary for development and a dynamic society, a new role for individuals must be learned. The ideas of change and progress must come to be considered as great values, while feelings of helplessness, satisfaction with the status quo, and fatalism are abolished. The greatest difficulty is demonstrating to the people that progress is possible; that the advantages to be gained are worth the efforts involved in making the changes necessary to rise out of ignorance.

At the individual level, each person must learn how to improve himself every day of his life. These self-improvements must not only be in terms of cultural attainments, but in terms of technical qualifications as well.

At the community level, the situation should be avoided where the betterment of individuals becomes too distinct from the improvement of the community. To accomplish this objective, all training or education given to individuals within the society ought to rebound to the benefit of all. The desire for progress should be passed along from the level of the individual to that of the entire society.

The Sense of Responsibility

In principle, the basis of every action or educational effort should be that *each individual and every group satisfy their own needs by themselves;* they should try to achieve most of the objectives they desire through their own resources. The state should provide aid only in the form of educational and technical advice and neither seek to constrain nor do itself what individuals or the people do by themselves on their own initiative.

It is therefore important that the actions taken by the state with these groups be fulfilling and not constraining, and that they favor the development of a sense of initiative. . . . The state should only assume a secondary role, and then only to perform actions of general import that are beyond the capacity of the group; these should be acts in the form of investments, services, or credit introduced after the effective participation of the population toward their own development is already underway.

The Community

Every person must develop his potentiality to the maximum in order to better fulfill his role in the society in which he lives. . . . Each person must realize that by himself he cannot change the situation and behavior of the group.

.   .   .   .

Belonging to the Nation

Every action and every project must be oriented towards the well-being and fulfillment of all.

This perspective justifies the planning and priority given to the satisfaction of the needs of the community before those of the individual, even though the possibility of the fulfillment of the person is respected. . . .

From this perspective, one can also justify sacrifices in the standard of living shared by all. Unless the rate of increase in the standard of living remains low, development will be impossible, a factor that should not only be accepted, but understood by the people if the nation as a whole is to develop a sense of progress.

Finally, a widespread feeling that the common good should have priority will help eliminate the vices of clannishness and nepotism.

All this can only be done if the nation becomes a living reality and really has the same meaning for all citizens.

What is the situation at present in regard to the two major groups of the nation, the peasants and the civil servants?

For the peasants. Too often [the peasant's] country scarcely extends beyond the limits of his village or immediate region. "Senegal" for an inhabitant of the Casamance is the world of the people from the North who are almost more foreign to them than their brothers and neighbors from Guinea; in spite of their ethnic and cultural community, the men of Fouladou and those of Fouta-Toro know practically nothing of each other.

For the civil servants. It is not unusual to confuse Nation and Administration, if not theoretically, at least at the level of personal behavior. This confusion is evidence of an especially negative influence and unfortunately persistent viewpoint that came from the former colonial administration which formed the majority of the present-day civil servants. For a European civil servant under colonialism, Senegal was merely a branch of his own nation, France; his mission as civil servant and even his conception of the role of the administration were confused by the ambition to extend the cultural and economic influence of his country. And he was only secondarily in the service of the development of the territory itself, in terms of its own needs and resources.

Even if this kind of development succeeded within its own terms, such success could only be a surface type of phenomenon: the administration worked in only one direction—from the summit to the base. Administration came from headquarters and was not truly democratic. The administration worked for the colonial regime and functioned in practical terms primarily for itself.

There is no question of saying that the present Senegalese civil servant is without consciousness of the reality of the nation, but it is necessary to see clearly that, in general, he continues to think and act as though the administration were an end in itself . . . too rare are the civil servants who consider the administration as a service of the nation, and who do not limit the "nation" to the confines of the civil service. Too many civil servants separate the nation in their minds and actions into two parts; the nation that belongs to them, the administration; and the nation that is the other, the masses. They give to these two parts a very unequal importance. The civil servant is more concerned with the place he holds in the administration than with the role that he must play in the progress of the nation, i.e., in the progress of raising the standard of living and culture of all. He does not feel that the nation will build itself up through the mutual efforts of [those at] the base and summit.

A discovery of the true meaning of what constitutes a nation has yet to be made by the majority of citizens who are still ignorant and who do not feel themselves concerned by the national reality.

This self-realization is a condition that is indispensable for development. . . .

Tom
Mboya

AN ESCAPE FROM STAGNATION

*T*he first six years of the Development Decade have passed. It has been a period of disappointment bordering on failure whether measured in terms of UN targets, expectations in developing countries, or possibilities as indicated by the wealth of the advanced countries. Over that period the average person in the wealthy countries improved his income by approximately $220 to $1,800 per annum, while per capita income in the very poor nations advanced by perhaps $7 to $90 per annum. Admittedly the $7 could have been less, and it is therefore a measure of both slight accomplishment and major defeat. If progress continues at this rate, we will be able in retrospect to rename the Development Decade the Dollar-a-Year Decade. That, to me, is an apt description of utter failure.

Where is the flow of official capital that was to approach 1 per cent of the gross national product of the advanced countries? Where are the softer loans and the longer maturities? Where are the reduced trade barriers, the effective commodity agreements, and the improved terms of trade? Where is the assault on ignorance and the development of natural resources? These objectives remain visions of intellectuals and promises of politicians. The harsh reality is that too little has been done. Indeed, if we base our future outlook on the present state of affairs our pessimism is fully warranted. We are in danger that the bright promise of the Development Decade, already tarnished, may yet dissolve completely in the dull reality of abject and prolonged poverty.

Net Flow is Dropping

The net flow of long-term capital from the rich world to the poor is not increasing. The Organization for Economic Cooperation and

Reprinted in abridged form from *Africa Report*, Vol. 12, No. 3 (March 1967), pp. 14–39, by permission of the editors.

Development (OECD) has estimated that in 1961 the net flow (including the cost of technical assistance) of official and private capital was $9.2 billion, that it dropped to $8.3 billion in 1963, but rose in 1965 to $10.0 billion. The flow of official capital, which reflects better the policies of governments, has scarcely changed over this period, moving only from $6.1 billion to $6.4 billion, and commitments in 1965 were actually $1.6 billion less than in 1964. None of these figures has been adjusted for price changes. It is probable that the 1965 flow would not in fact buy more investment goods than the 1961 flow. During this same period the terms of trade have deteriorated, populations have grown, and the terms of loans have hardened, all of which have reduced the value to developing countries of the 1965 flow as compared with the 1961 flow. The flows are disappointing also in terms of the target of 1 per cent of gross national product in the advanced countries. In this respect, the net official flow has fallen from 0.60 per cent in 1961 to 0.49 per cent in 1965.

But the full picture is even worse than this. The figures reported by the OECD are net of repayments of principal and the repatriation of capital, but no account has been taken of other reverse flows of capital, such as investments in industrial countries by residents of developing countries, and interest and dividend payments.

The outlook when these factors are taken into account has been stated very clearly by President George Woods of the World Bank:

> These [reverse] payments are continuing to rise at an accelerating rate, and in a little more than 15 years, in the present form, would offset the inflow completely. In short, to go on doing what the capital-exporting countries are now doing will, in the not too long run, amount to doing nothing at all.

Let's face it—the developing countries are in great danger of not developing at all. Hampered by bare subsistence-level incomes, domestic capital can scarcely be accumulated, even with the strictest of taxation measures, at a rate sufficient to maintain per capita incomes in the face of growing populations.

The prospect that foreign capital may dry up occurs at a time when the wealthy nations are achieving unprecedented rates of growth. Indeed, it is not unlikely that per capita income for the whole of the rich world may double over the next thirty years from $1,800 to $3,600 per annum. Even astounding success in the very poor countries could not narrow this gap. Increasing incomes by ten times from $90 to $900 would still mean that thirty years hence, the gap would be $2,700 as compared with $1,710 today. But to be threatened with no growth at all is intolerable.

The shrinkage of foreign capital is already having a number of undesirable side effects. First, spheres of influence, from which all newly independent nations want to escape, are instead continuing and indeed in many cases becoming more clearly defined. Declining aid means that bilateral sources are becoming more and more selective in determining which countries should be privileged to receive it. After all, a "friends-first" policy is not illogical so long as the bulk of aid is bilateral in nature. The obvious pressure on the developing nations to choose or suffer is regrettable but real. Second, the developing nations themselves—finding their joint efforts to increase total aid unavailing—are being reduced to scrambling, competitively and ignominiously, for the limited funds that are available. When Country A gets a soft loan from the International Development Association, everyone knows that there is less for the rest. Finally, declining funds means that all aid negotiations and preliminary red tape are prolonged—perhaps simply to keep corps of experts busy, possibly to make the shortage of funds less apparent.

The growing complexity of aid negotiations, some of which are more than the developing countries can cope with, is also contributing to an apparent ambivalence toward foreign capital among developing countries. The stark reality of the need for foreign capital is opposed by the irritation of bargaining for it, the frustration of growing numbers of refusals, and the increasing external supervision which at times borders on interference in domestic affairs. The ambivalence is therefore, and to an increasing extent, the mere reflection of the scarcity of foreign capital and the onerous terms on which it can be obtained.

This dire outlook is further hardened when one notes the growing hostility to foreign aid in the advanced countries. When aid is not received with the "appropriate" degree of humility and gratitude, that fact is noted in political forums everywhere. The priority accorded aid is reduced, and it frequently is given the status of a sacrificial lamb—something to be given up whenever other problems arise. Thus aid, much of which must be a long-term commitment to be effective, is curtailed as a means of alleviating short-term balance of payments problems even though these problems are largely the result of dealings among the developed nations themselves. Aid may be cut if recessions threaten, wars escalate, or political parties change power. Thus aid becomes unstable and useless as a basis for planning; its effectiveness is considerably reduced. The growing hostility toward aid also reinforces the attitude that aid should be tied—tied to direct imports even though at higher-than-world-market prices, to quality standards even though they make no sense in a poor country, to glamour projects even though these are of marginal value to development, and to political support even though the support is not genuine.

The Wheels Must Be Unlocked

The status of aid today holds no promise for the future. Optimistically, it means gently rising per capita incomes to achieve for the very poor countries perhaps $200 per annum by the end of the century; it means rising debts and perennial balance of payments problems; it means continually falling terms of trade and continued barriers to the sale of industrial products; it means no escape from the abyss of primary production.

This future cannot be regarded with complacency anywhere in the world. It is a future that is unacceptable, unstable, and unrealistic. But that future will not be changed unless the urgency of change today is recognized and the wheels of motion unlocked. It is no longer enough to exaggerate our meager accomplishments and to disregard the enormous problems that remain unsolved. We have a choice which is really not a choice at all—we can wait for the debacle, we can sit idly by while our hopes and aspirations turn into despair; or we can recognize the signs and initiate a constructive and cooperative program for the development of the poor countries of the world to the mutual benefit of both the rich and the poor. The generation ahead will be decisive: we either solve the problem, or set the stage for worldwide turmoil and catastrophe.

In one sense we seek a worldwide revolution in values and priorities; in a financial sense, however, we need only a minor change. To achieve either, the problem of uneven development throughout the world must be seen as a world problem and not as a case of charity to the poor. Both the urgency and the enormity of the problem must be appreciated and the spending priorities in developed nations readjusted accordingly. Today the world is spending well over $150 billion per annum on the actual or potential destruction of lives and property as compared with the capital transfer from rich to poor countries of about $10 billion per year.

The distortion in world values can be found in the budgets of nearly all advanced countries. The recently announced U.S. budget is an example. Of a total budget of $169 billion, over $73 billion is earmarked for defense, of which nearly $22 billion is allocated to Vietnam. By comparison, only $3.1 billion is set aside for foreign aid, and of this figure over one-half billion is for military aid. The cold war and ideological differences account for the bulk of the world's defense spending. These are issues which reduce development capital and at the same time put pressure on developing countries to take sides.

We in the developing nations are not interested in a blind commitment to one side or the other. The problem of development transcends such issues. Most of the developing nations in Africa have made their approach clear: a mixed economy with room for both public and private investment, but with government policy a deciding factor in promoting growth and ensuring an equitable distribution of income. The ideological debate is essentially irrelevant. In any event, a concern with it should not disguise the fact that the growing breach today is the gap between the rich and the poor nations. Solve that problem and we can all play intellectual games together.

The distortion of values that leads the developed world to spend over $150 billion a year on defense is to be deplored, but it is not likely to be quickly or drastically changed. What a dream world to imagine that sum being transferred annually as development capital to the developing nations! The poor nations need a massive infusion of capital to put them on the road to rapid growth, but a "massive infusion" to them is a pittance to the advanced countries. Another $10 billion per year would be a huge increase that would double the present net flow—yet is is only 6 per cent of the world's defense expenditure and a bare 0.8 per cent of the gross national product of the wealthy nations.

If the urgent needs of the developing nations are to be met, the advanced countries must themselves accept a different image of foreign aid and see capital flows to developing countries in true perspective. "Aid" has the unfortunate connotation of a gift whose donor receives nothing in return except perhaps the Biblical satisfaction of being a "good Samaritan." A good share of aid is not a gift, however, and much of that which is labelled "Grants and Grant-like Contributions" by the OECD is not for development purposes, but is intended for military aid. The term also covers subscription capital furnished to multilateral organizations, sales for recipients' currencies, and loans repayable in recipients' currencies.

To a considerable extent, therefore, aid is falsely identified, and information is not available to correct the illusions involved. Of the $6.3 billion of net official aid in 1965, at least $1.0 billion and perhaps as much as $1.7 billion was for military aid. About $0.8 billion was sales for recipients' currencies, mostly for famine relief, and over $1.0 billion was for technical assistance. Assuming the remainder was intended for development capital, approximately $3.0 billion of the $6.3 billion was for that purpose. Of this amount, $2.0 billion was in the form of loans net of repayment, and $0.5 billion was grants and subscriptions to multilateral organizations, most of which, incidentally, is passed on to developing countries in the form of loans.

· · · · · · · · ·

Finally, technical assistance and development capital, even if financed by grants, are not devoid of benefits to the richer countries which supply them. The bulk of development capital is immediately used to buy investment goods produced by the richer nations and thus create incomes and employment in those countries. And much of the income created in the developing nations increases the demand for consumer goods imported from abroad. Indeed, much of the potential growth of the richer nations is conditioned on a rapidly growing external demand. That condition can be created at very little cost in the developing areas of the world in which over two-thirds of the world's population now lives. A small investment today will pay handsome returns in the future. . . .

.   .   .   .

We need, as my friend, Mr. Traoré of Chad, has suggested, a Marshall Plan for Africa—a massive infusion of manpower and capital. [See "A New Marshall Plan?" *Africa Report*, December 1966, p. 42.] Admittedly the situation of Africa today differs in many respects from that of Europe after World War II, but the imaginative concept and vigorous approach are readily adaptable. The Marshall Plan involved a capital movement twenty years ago of nearly $14 billion from only one country over a three-year period, 80 per cent of it in outright grants. Since then, the gross national product in the rich nations has doubled and all of them are capable of assisting Africa, perhaps none more than the European countries which benefited so directly and greatly from the original Marshall Plan, and which also were the colonizers of Africa. It is for us in Africa to identify our problems, to prepare a comprehensive, coordinated, and integrated program suited to the specific needs of Africa, and to interest the advanced nations in the implementation of that program.

There are today in Africa thirty-nine independent countries, as compared to four prior to 1950—South Africa, the United Arab Republic, Liberia, and Ethiopia—and ten prior to 1960. In the Development Decade itself, therefore, twenty-nine African nations have emerged from colonial rule to political independence, and the struggle to eliminate colonial and fascist domination of our people is not yet over.

The belated achievement of independence by so many African states is the major reason that a massive development program is so essential today. It also explains why development needs in Africa differ in so many ways from requirements in other developing parts of the world. These differences mean that a development program in Africa must be specifically designed to solve our problems. Indeed, many of the global policies and institutional arrangements that now govern the distribution of development capital were created before Africa threw off the yoke of colonialism, and in many ways they are better suited to the needs of the older developing nations. New policies and institutions may be needed to achieve more rapid development in Africa.

The problems of achieving independence and building national unity and political stability have occupied some of our best minds, so that only now can we concentrate on our economic problems. We have had to reorganize and in some cases to create government and tax structures suitable to independence, to find equitable means of accommodating minority groups, to overcome the fears and pessimism of domestic and foreign investors, and to prevent flights of our precious capital.

I would not suggest that all of these problems are finally solved, but I do feel that the time has come when we must coordinate our efforts in a major pursuit of economic development. Africa contains 20 per cent of the world's land area and 9 per cent of the world's population, but it has been estimated that 80 per cent of our potential natural resources and 90 per cent of our potential human resources have yet to be realized. Our people, fresh with independence, are eager to advance. We must use that eagerness for development if it is not to degenerate into disappointment and despair.

I propose, therefore, that we in Africa should take the lead in planning and coordinating a program for the economic development of our continent. This program will require a massive inflow of capital over perhaps thirty years and an equally massive inflow of technical assistance personnel over ten to fifteen years. It will also require—and this is not a simple task—the close cooperation and full support of all independent developing African nations.

Such a program should include the following four critical aspects: (1) the construction of a continental infrastructure; (2) the collection and analysis of economic information; (3) the expansion of food production, storage and marketing; (4) the development of human resources. I have not mentioned industrialization explicitly in this list, but you will see as I go on that several of these points are directly related to industrialization.

As the colonial powers withdrew from the continent, they left behind a substantial infrastructure built up with extensive investments in those facilities needed to make the colonial system effective and profitable. As African countries have gained independence, further large investments have been made in extending and modernizing that infrastructure.

· · · · · · · · ·

But the infrastructure inherited from the colonial powers was designed mainly to facilitate trade between the colony and the metropolitan country. The principal aim was to maintain "spheres of influence" and to link the "possessions" as effectively as possible with the home economies. Thus the railways ran from the interior to the coast; roads were built to serve the railways; posts and telecommunications also served primarily the need for communication between colony and homeland. The infrastructure effectively tied Africa to Europe, but the African territories could scarcely communicate or trade with each other. There were practically no transverse roads and railways linking the African countries with each other. Even today it is virtually impossible to travel from Addis Ababa to Nairobi except by sea or air; goods cannot be transported by railway across the continent, and telephone calls between many African countries must still be routed through London or Paris.

. . . .

An effective continental infrastructure is also a necessary means for promoting the export of industrial, mineral, and agricultural products. Many areas of the continent still do not have economical methods of transport to the coast or the electric power to develop natural resources. A wealth of opportunities therefore awaits the development of infrastructure. Indeed, that development is a principal method by which private foreign capital can be attracted to Africa in large amounts as an important and growing supplement to official development capital. . . .

. . . .

Development plans already prepared by African countries show how much can be done in a positive way on the basis of very limited data. But every development plan emphasizes the need for more information if better and more effective plans are to be formulated and if the implementation of plans is to proceed on schedule. Sources of assistance frequently seek information which is not readily available; potential investors inquire about opportunities about which we ourselves know very little; and data for evaluating our progress are sketchy and often become available too late to be fully useful. Substantially better basic information is not only needed for national planning, but also for the planning of our continental infrastructure.

It is well known that the resources potential of Africa is huge and greatly underutilized, but it is equally true that much of our potential wealth is unknown or inaccurately assessed. We therefore need to mount an intensive and thorough survey of our natural resources. Indeed, such a study must proceed concurrently with the planning of our continental infrastructure, for the most economical location of transport and power facilities can only be determined in conjunction with our production and marketing potential.

. . . .

As I have pointed out, an improved continental infrastructure will open up many opportunities for industrial development, but we must also ensure that these opportunities are widely known and understood. In many advanced countries, the identification and evaluation of industrial opportunities is readily performed by the private sector in the competitive race for profit. In many African countries the initial approach to this problem was also to assume that private enterprise could be left to itself to accomplish this task. Experience now suggests, however, that reliance on private enterprise alone to discover industrial opportunities will not yield the rapid industrialization necessary to make a noticeable impact on poverty and underdevelopment.

In the first place, the very scarcity of indigenous entrepreneurs means that the people with the most intimate knowledge of African resources and aspirations are unable to recognize, appreciate, or take advantage of the abundant opportunities in the industrial field. In the second place, many of the industrialists and financiers outside Africa have not yet acquired a first-hand knowledge of Africa, and must therefore spend substantially more time and money to investigate the feasibility of a project in Africa than would be necessary in the familiar surroundings of their home country. In the African context therefore, it has become absolutely necessary to increase our investment of time and money in surveying and evaluating industrial opportunities as a service to potential foreign and domestic investors.

· · · · · · · · ·

The third aspect of the program to fill the information vacuum is the intensification of our research activities. There is a wide range of problems to be solved in Africa, and only concerted, well-organized research will yield the solutions we seek. Three problem areas in particular merit special attention: nutrition and food production, education and training, and the social and economic problems of development.

· · · · · · · ·

The methods now employed to develop our human resources are both archaic and unsuited to our needs. Rote learning and examination passing, frequently in irrelevant subjects, have become almost an end in themselves. Research on the learning process, the identification of aptitudes, teaching methods, and curricula should enable us to educate many more people more suitably and faster for the same money. The waste in education is apparent in the advanced countries too, but they can afford waste. We can't. Research on formal means of human learning and development and on the acquisition of traits such as integrity, imagination, and initiative, is also needed if we are to make full use of our human resources.

Finally, we need extensive interdisciplinary research on the social and economic problems associated with development. How can we best adapt modern technologies to our needs? Can we find solutions to our growing unemployment problem? Are the fiscal policies and tax measures we have borrowed from advanced countries, which have abundant capital, a shortage of labor, and no subsistence sector, appropriate for us? Can we distribute incomes so that our food production is accessible to all our people? Should each country aim at self-sufficiency in food, or are there advantages to be gained from specialization and exchange? How can traditions antagonistic to development be modified? What is the impact of rapid change on the moral and cultural values of our people? Equally important questions could be added to this list—but where is the research effort needed to answer any of them?

I suggest that in Africa we need at least one large-scale research institute to deal with each of these three sets of problems. . . . The research we need must be done here, not in Paris or London, and not at Yale or Harvard. We have contributed, not always willingly, a number of our well-educated people whom we could ill afford to lose to bolster professional ranks in the advanced countries. The institutes I propose may help to reverse this flow.

.   .   .   .

A Food Program Related to Needs

.   .   .   .

The most critical and immediate problem is the storage and preservation of food. In particular, we need in Africa capital for the construction of storage facilities and finance for the crops to be stored. Continuing famine conditions in many parts of the world and the rapid depletion of surplus food stocks in the United States could signal a major catastrophe for mankind. . . .

I suggest, therefore, that the United Nations make advance commitments to purchase essential stocks of basic foods at negotiated prices from those African nations which may be able to grow surpluses. The UN should also construct essential storage facilities in these countries. Both the storage facilities and the grains stored would remain the property of the UN, and the food could be drawn upon and shipped by the UN whenever and wherever the need arises. It is no longer sufficient for one or a few nations to assume the responsibility for supplying and otherwise arranging to meet the needs of famine areas. It is a world problem requiring a coordinated solution. The UN is an appropriate organization; Africa can contribute and benefit by participating. I am aware that proposals of this kind have been a subject of discussion for many, many years. Now is the time for action.

.   .   .   .

To economize in the handling and marketing of food products, I suggest that much of the processing of food that now takes place in advanced countries should be transferred to the developing countries where the basic crops are grown. It makes sense to transport food as cheaply as possible and to process it quickly if waste and spoilage can be reduced by so doing. The canning of various foods before shipment is an obvious example. It would also be more economic to make instant coffee and tea where the products are grown. The production of powdered milk and other dehydrated foods must also be encouraged in developing countries. What is needed here is not capital and technical assistance—private investors will supply these readily enough. We need the elimination of those trade barriers in advanced nations that prevent these kinds of economies from being realized and at the same time make the development task so much harder.

Development of Human Resources

Perhaps the most rewarding and fundamental task confronting us is the development of human resources. While it must be given the highest priority today for economic reasons, the benefits of success will extend well beyond material welfare alone. We are faced with a gigantic shortage of high- and middle-level manpower and a general illiteracy problem that hamper labor efficiency and effective agricultural extension work. While 97 per cent of the people fifteen years of age and over in many advanced countries are literate, probably less than 20 per cent in that age group can read and write in Africa. Literacy rates are considerably higher in most other developing countries, being, for example, about 85 per cent in Argentina, 70 per cent in Thailand, 60 per cent in Mexico and Burma, and 50 per cent in Brazil. Our vast shortages of trained manpower are also not typical of the rest of the developing world. India today even has a problem finding employment for its university graduates. The problem in Africa is a very different one, demanding special attention on a vast scale.

Our shortage of high- and middle-level manpower requires a large and rapid expansion of secondary school and university facilities. We do not, however, want monuments for universities; we want practical centers for effective study and learning. We cannot afford luxurious accommodations or exotic subjects and must ensure that our facilities are fully employed throughout a lengthy academic year. We cannot afford the low student-teacher ratios or the elite pattern of education typical of some of the advanced countries.

. . . . In particular, we must have curriculum materials prepared for African needs, including specialist training courses and prevocational work, as well as history, geography, and social institutions courses. . . .

Adult illiteracy is not simply a social and cultural problem. It must be stamped out in order to promote national unity and to lay a basis for an efficient labor force in both rural and urban areas. To be effective, however, adult literacy efforts must have a purpose that is meaningful not only to the nation but to each participating adult. Too frequently in the past, literacy has been taught for its own sake and quickly forgotten when meaningful follow-up materials were not available.

We need, then, strong educational programs in all three of these areas—manpower, primary level, and adult literacy. The molding of our nations and the development of our continent cannot be wholly successful until all of our people can participate effectively in both the effort and the benefits.

Policies and Procedures

The program I have sketched will be expensive in both development capital and technical assistance. The earliest and most pressing need will be for technical assistance on a significantly greater scale than in the past. There is first of all the need to plan and design the infrastructure program, which will be an enormous task if carried out properly. The preparation and coordination of projects in the other program will also demand more expert and professional manpower than we in Africa can supply.

There is no question in my mind that all of us in recent years have greatly underestimated the time and manpower required for project preparation. This is partly because the red tape and mass of detail involved has increased, often unnecessarily; partly because we are relatively new in this development business; finally, because the African situation is not a simple replica of situations in other developing areas, and experience in those areas by people and institutions has not been readily transferable to Africa. The project formulation bottleneck, which has now reached serious proportions, must be broken.

. . . .

But the bulk of this proposed Development Program for Africa must be financed on a more liberal basis than we can obtain in the commercial capital markets. We must therefore seek a substantial expansion in the flow of official development capital and, indeed, considerable liberalization of the terms on which it is now being received. Official bilateral loans in 1965 averaged 22.2 years in length at 3.6 per cent interest. But investments in information, education, continental infrastructure, and even basic agricultural services are not likely to begin paying off soon enough to be financed safely on such terms. On the other hand, basic investment of the kind I have outlined will ultimately pay off for centuries. These investments are absolutely necessary to our development, but we need capital for them on terms that make sense.

The external development capital for the program I have sketched should be largely in the form of grants or, alternatively, 99-year loans at low interest rates with a 20-year moratorium on both principal and interest. The external capital should be channeled through the African Development Bank. It should be raised through an international consortium of advanced nations in the form of special subscriptions in order to avoid jeopardy to existing aid programs. Clearly an appropriate balance must be maintained among continental, subregional, and national projects. The crash program I am proposing is not a substitute for what we are already doing; it is an important and necessary addition.

I know that questions will be raised about the realism of my proposals, and more particularly about the likelihood that the African countries can secure among themselves the substantial degree of economic cooperation necessary to initiate the program and see it through to fruition. I have confidence that we in Africa can do our part. The needs of our various countries are uneven. Some have ample foreign exchange; others are short of it. Some have small surpluses of high-level manpower; most have serious shortages. Some have arid lands; others tropical rain forest. Some are land-locked; others are little more than coastal strips. Some have emphasized industrial development; others have concentrated on agricultural diversification. It follows that the various programs of the development strategy for Africa will affect our several countries differently. It is, however, clearly to our common benefit to build a continental infrastructure, to assemble basic information to educate our people, and to contribute what we can to the world's food supply.

Our differences are also a source of strength. They are a means by which we can help each other. Those countries in a position to do so can assist others with their manpower needs. Neighboring countries can pool their resources to ensure more even development. They can also share markets so that large-scale enterprises have a reasonable chance of success. Foreign exchange problems, too, can be alleviated through mutual effort. Much more can be done to harmonize development plans and thus ensure a coordinated approach to common problems. The success of the program I have outlined rests squarely on the degree of economic cooperation we in Africa can achieve.

.   .   .   .

Our development is at stake. Nothing less than a major effort, both within Africa and by our friends overseas, can produce the progress we seek and make our continent a mature contributor to the world economy. What is more, it is only through the process I have suggested that we can achieve real continental economic cooperation and create what may be termed an "African economy." Otherwise a few of our countries may develop while the others stagnate.

Above all, I fear that our dependence on the countries outside Africa will never come to an end. We shall continue to be manipulated and expected to respond to economic demands and pressures from outside. Africa will remain in danger of economic domination by "spheres of influence" projected by the developed nations.

The initiative and the decision to cooperate must come from Africa itself. In this spirit, I invite my colleagues to consider most critically but positively all that I have said here today.

Surendra J. Patel   ECONOMIC TRANSITION IN AFRICA

Africa is a vast continent. It embraces nearly one fourth of the land surface of the earth. The last decade has witnessed a profound transformation of its political landscape. Thirty-four countries have attained their independence. The rest of the continent will soon be governed by its people. The broad sweep of the surge towards independence has belied those predictions of only a decade ago that the political transition to independence in Africa would take a long time. This has already come about. But the continent yet remains mostly ill-fed, ill-clad, ill-housed, and illiterate. The popular pressure to overcome the age-old afflictions of mankind—poverty, disease, and lack of knowledge—is mounting. The new African governments are beginning their first faltering steps towards the economic transition from poverty to relative affluence.

How long will this economic transformation take? Will it be endless centuries, as some seem to suggest, or can it be attained relatively rapidly? What will be its main stages? Obviously there can be no precise answers to these questions. The gaps in our economic knowledge of the continent are many. But even a preliminary attempt at answering these questions has its value, not as a precise indicator of things to come, but merely as a general frame of reference outlining future development. This article represents such a modest attempt.

The main features of the African economic landscape are fairly well known. But some of them need repetition since they are often over-

The author is a member of the secretariat of the United Nations Economic Commission for Africa, Addis Ababa. This is a revised version of a paper read at the Dag Hammarskjöld Seminar in Addis Ababa, March–April 1964. The author here expresses his own personal views, which should not be taken as those of ECA.

Reprinted from The Journal of Modern African Studies, Vol. 2, No. 1 (1964), pp. 329–349, by permission of the Cambridge University Press.

looked. The continental land mass of Africa is as yet poorly explored. It is slowly yielding to the patient work of the surveyors, prospectors, cartographers, and geologists. But even the very inadequate surveys of its natural resources suggest a vast potential.

Let us begin with land. The area of arable land (under trees and crops) amounts to some 223 million hectares, or more than twice that of Latin America or China. It is nearly one and a half times as large as that of India, although the population in Africa is only half of India's. Compared with the industrial countries of Europe, the area of land under cultivation per person is three times as high, and the units of livestock per person twice as high; the pastures and meadows available to each head of cattle to graze are seven times as high. Climatically, the continent is ideally suited to growing all kinds of crops—both for human consumption and for industrial raw materials. It produces all the roots and tubers, the major cereals, most fruits and vegetables, beverages, tobacco, sugar cane, fibres, and oil-seeds. Even at the present low level of agricultural productivity, it grows 5 per cent of the world's output of cereals, half the cassava, and a quarter of the sweet potatoes and yams.

The scope for grazing cattle on its vast and nearly evergreen pastures is wide indeed. The oceans around it, its lakes and rivers, provide unlimited opportunities for fishing. Its forest resources, accounting for one sixth of the world's total, are rich.

The continent already produces nearly one seventh of the world's mineral output. The Sahara, for so long a death-trap for intrepid travellers, is turning out to be, through the patient labor of many prospectors, a rich reservoir of petroleum, the prime mover of the world's machines. The desert is dry of water, but rich in oil.

The continent's energy potential—principally coal in the south, hydropower in the center, and oil and gas in the north—is almost unlimited. Its mighty rivers account for 40 per cent of the world potential of hydroelectric power. Its total output in 1960 was the equivalent of 80 million tons of coal. By 1970 this is expected to increase nearly threefold, giving 0.8 tons (coal equivalent) per inhabitant.

The natural resource endowment of the continent is thus immensely rich. But its exploitation for the benefit of the people has so far remained limited owing to the very slow adoption of modern techniques of production, and that too in only a few sectors. Consequently, the share of the continent in world output is only 2 per cent, although it accounts for 8 per cent of world population. The net value of its annual output amounts to about $25 billion[1]—that is, half that of the United Kingdom, and almost equal to that of Italy. Its per capita income is about $100 per year, or one twelfth of that in the industrial countries. But this figure of

1. Billion is here used throughout in the   American sense of one thousand million.

average per capita income is misleading, since approximately one fourth of total income is received by a tiny minority of non-Africans.

Economic Changes over the Last Century

An understanding of the main lines of economic development over the last century would facilitate the assessment of African prospects. What was the world economic landscape midway in the nineteenth century like? By then, mankind had left behind some 6,000 years of settled existence. The new Stone Age, the Bronze Age, and the Iron Age each formed a 2,000-year-long step on the ladder of humanity's history. By the middle of the nineteenth century the world was about to take a step forward from the Iron Age—to the Machine Age.

In the areas north of the Mediterranean, there was a great ferment. Old ideas were being questioned. New experiments were being tried. Established systems of thought, explanations, and ways of doing things were crumbling. By 1850 many inventions had been made. But their adoption was restricted mainly to Great Britain, and even there mostly on a small scale, except in the textile industry.

The horse and carriage were still the major means of communication. Ocean-going steamers, churning the water with a screw at the back, were yet to appear. Stephenson's Rocket, the first real steam locomotive, had had its first successful run only in 1826. The Machine Age was just beginning. The early steam engine was a huge, clumsy affair, its numbers counted in a few thousands. The internal combustion engine, the electric motor, and the generator were still a quarter of a century away. The muscles of men and animals provided 94 per cent of the energy available to men in 1850. The age of enlightenment had begun, but not spread widely. Over one half of the population in Western Europe still could not decipher the magic of the written word.

The world was still in the last days of the Iron Age. The art of producing steel, the metal needed for all the moving parts of machines and engines, had hardly left the handicraft stage. The Bessemer converter was invented in 1856, and the Martin-Siemens process perfected during 1864 to 1867. Even then, the world output of steel as late as 1870 was only 700,000 tons, or less than one fifth of India's in 1961.

At the midpoint of the last century, Western Europe presented an image far different from what its citizens are now familiar with. It was almost a twin brother, perhaps a slightly older one, of the poor countries now. More than half of its population was engaged in agriculture. The land-man ratio, the yields per hectare of land, the share of industries in total output, the population in urban centers of over 100,000 inhabitants, the literacy ratio—in all these Western Europe in 1850 resembled the preindustrial countries now. The peoples of Western Europe simply did not have at that time the means to be much better off than the poor countries today. The familiar has so often been taken by so many to have been the eternal, or at least of an extremely long duration.

It is now possible to derive estimates going back 100 years or so of the average per capita income at present-day prices in the "industrial" countries. In 1850 this was about $150, or only $30 higher than the average per capita income in the poor countries now, and $50 higher than theirs in 1850.[2] But the "industrial" countries were in temperate climates, requiring higher caloric intake, warmer clothing and covering, air-tight houses, and some form of internal heating. The real difference between the rich and the poor countries only 100 years ago could not, therefore, have been very large.

Thus, even as late as 1850, the world economic landscape was pretty flat. The differences between countries in the levels of per capita income were relatively minor. But during the 100 years that followed, the economic face of Europe was to be unrecognizably altered (see Table 1). The population nearly trebled, but output increased over twenty times. The faint thud of the "population explosion" was drowned in the thunder of the "economic explosion". Per capita output increased more than seven times. Agricultural output rose four to five times, and industrial output about fortyfold.[3]

This profound economic transformation concentrated great power in the hands of the industrial countries. It was to be a powerful instrument for maintaining, establishing, or extending political control over the rest of the world. Throughout this period the poor countries remained just as poor. There was some development, but its benefits did not accrue to the people. Population increased roughly in line with output, so that per capita income stagnated—a little up here and there, and a little down elsewhere, but no recognizable change.

As a result of the rapid economic advance in one area and the relative stagnation in the other, the economic landscape of the world had altered significantly by 1960. The per capita income in the industrial countries

2. Based on a weighted average and straight-line extrapolation of the data in Simon Kuznets, *Six Lectures on Economic Growth* (Glencoe, 1959), p. 27.
3. Detailed aspects of economic changes over the last century are discussed in the following studies of mine: "Rates of Industrial Growth in the Last Century, 1860 to 1958," in *Economic Development and Cultural Change* (Chicago), IX, 3, April 1961; "The Economic Distance between Nations: its origin, measurement and outlook," in *The Economic Journal* (London), LXXIV, March 1964; "Main Features of Economic Growth over the Last Century," in the *Indian Economic Journal* (Bombay), March 1964; "What Holds up Agriculture?," in the *Economic Weekly* (Bombay), XV, February 1964.

Processes of Encadrement: Bureaucratic Development and Economic Growth

Table 1—Estimated Changes in World Distribution of Population and Output, 1850–1960[a]

Item	INDUSTRIAL COUNTRIES[d]		PREINDUSTRIAL COUNTRIES		WORLD TOTAL	
	1850	1960	1850	1960	1850	1960
Amounts in figures:						
Population (millions)[b]	300	850	870	2,150	1,170	3,000
Output ($ billions)	45	930	85	260	130	1,190
Per capita output ($)	150	1,100	100	120	110	400
Percentage shares:						
In population	26	28	74	72	100	100
In output	36	78	65	22	100	100
Annual compound percentage growth rate:	1850–1960		1850–1960		1850–1960	
Population	1.0		0.9		0.9	
Total output	2.8		1.0		2.0	
Per capita output	1.8		0.1		1.2	

[a] Owing to the severe statistical limitations, the figures for population and output are to be treated as broad orders of magnitude, rather than precise statistical measurements; they are rounded to the nearest 5 or 10.

[b] Population estimates for 1850 are based on W. S. and E. S. Woytinsky, World Population and Production (New York, 1953), and for 1960 on UN documents.

[c] Output estimates are explained more fully in my article, "The Economic Distance between Nations"; they are calculated at constant (1960) prices.

[d] "Industrial countries" means those that had become industrialized by 1960, i.e., the following: Austria, Australia, Belgium, Canada, Denmark, Finland, France, Western Germany, Ireland, Israel, Italy, Luxembourg, the Netherlands, New Zealand, Norway, Sweden, UK, USA, USSR, and all of Eastern Europe.

(including Eastern Europe and the USSR) had risen to a level nine times as high as in the poor countries. In the long race for the conquest of poverty, the industrial countries had in the last century by far out-distanced the preindustrial ones. The economic distance between the two areas had widened.

The world distribution of income changed profoundly in the process. In 1850 the countries now industrialised contributed nearly one fourth of the world population and one third of its output. By 1960 their share in the world population had increased slightly; but they produced nearly 80 per cent of world output. As a result the international inequality of income became much sharper than the inequality of income within the underdeveloped countries. And this is a relatively recent phenomenon. It is only against this background that the rapidly rising pressures for a more rational distribution of world income can be appreciated properly.

Economic growth in the industrial countries since 1850 has thus been impressive indeed. But there are two features of this growth which have considerable significance for outlining future prospects for the developing countries. The first is that the growth rates were relatively modest by recent standards. The annual growth rates over the century for the industrial countries combined as a group were 1.0 per cent for population, 2.8 per cent for overall income, and 1.8 per cent for per capita real income. Total income expanded only a little under three times as fast as population. But the continuation of this difference for over a century raised per capita output not by three times, but by more than seven times.

If the same relationship between growth rates were to continue for another century, the level of per capita output in, say, A.D. 2050 would be almost 50 times higher than in 1850. In appreciating the dynamics of growth, the relationship between divergent growth rates is thus extremely significant when cumulated over a long period of time. The small initial difference is magnified manifold when compounded over a long period.[4] This is why the past century produced an economic explosion which was so much more powerful than the much-talked-about population explosion. But it is a pity that the demographers have proved more skilled, or perhaps more noisy, propagandists than the economists.

Index Numbers of Per Capita Output (Year 1 = 1.00)

Years	ANNUAL GROWTH RATES									
	1%	2%	3%	4%	5%	6%	7%	8%	9%	10%
20	1.22	1.49	1.81	2.19	2.65	3.21	3.87	4.66	5.60	6.73
50	1.64	2.69	4.38	7.11	11.5	18.4	29.4	46.9	74.4	117
100	2.70	7.24	19.2	50.5	132	339	868	2,200	5,529	13,700

Source: Frederick C. Kent, *Compound Interest and Annuity Tables* (New York, 1956), Table 1; calculated to only one decimal place after the index rises over 10, and to the nearest whole number when it goes beyond 100.

The second main feature of the economic growth indicated in Table 1 is that there was a progressive rise in the overall and also the per capita growth rates for each of the new entrants in the field of economic development. Table 1 relates to the combined group of all industrial countries, in both the west and the east. But the average growth rate for the whole group is not of much use in assessing the pace of change for individual countries, which obviously began their economic development at different times and under different circumstances. An analysis of growth rates for individual countries brings out an important trend.

As industrialization spread from Great Britain to other countries, there was a marked tendency towards a progressive rise in the total and also the per capita rate of annual growth. The tools of the economic archaeologist are still too crude to ascertain with precision the exact dates of the beginning of industrialization in a country. But the chrono-

4. The explosive power of cumulation at compound rates may be seen from the table below, which summarizes the results of growth at annual rates of from 1 to 10 per cent for periods of 20, 50, and 100 years.

logical sequence for the groupings listed below may be widely accepted.[5] The annual per capita economic growth rate tended to rise as follows:

1.2 to 1.4 per cent for the United Kingdom and France;

1.6 to 1.8 per cent for Germany, Denmark, Switzerland, the United States, and Canada;

2.1 to 2.8 per cent for Norway, Sweden, and Japan;

4 per cent or higher, depending upon the estimator, for the Soviet Union under the period of planning, but excluding the civil war and World War II years; and

5 to as high as 9 per cent during the last dozen years for a number of countries both in the west and the east; for instance, Japan, Italy, Germany, Israel, the Congo (Leopoldville), Rhodesia, the Soviet Union, and all other centrally planned economies. This list is obviously incomplete.

The progressive rise in the rate of growth of per capita output and the even greater rise in overall output (since population growth has quickened) represent a fairly clear tendency. When this fact is combined with the staggering force of growth at compound rates over a long period, there is a powerful operational tool for the most rapid economic transformation in the poor countries. Some people do not see this clearly, but that is not unusual. In their quest for the complex they often overlook the obvious and the simple.

The century-long experience of economic growth may be briefly summarized thus: the economic differences between countries in the middle of the nineteenth century were rather small. In terms of economic dynamics, or economic mechanics, the dimensions of time and pace (to rephrase slightly the expressions "time" and "space" in physics) for their evolution were: a modest annual growth rate of 1.8 per cent in per capita output maintained for a little over a century in the industrial countries against a near stagnation in the preindustrial ones; and a progressive rise in this rate as industrialization spread from the original centers to the periphery. These elements form the bedrock of our outline of economic prospects for the developing countries in Africa and elsewhere.

Africa in the World Economy

The prospects of economic growth in Africa can hardly be outlined without obtaining a working idea of the economic distance between

5. See my article, "Main Features of Economic Growth over the Last Century."

Africa and the industrial countries. How is this distance to be measured? So far it has been usually measured by the conventional yardstick of per capita income—this handy expression in easily remembered numerals of a country's economic well-being. During the last decade, such estimates for nearly every country have been prepared by economists and statisticians. Politicians, planners, and the people in general have seized upon this mystic entity. It has been used as an infallible indicator for measuring progress, diagnosing ills, and prescribing remedies. Such use has been subjected to critical evaluation in recent years.

The annual per capita income is about $100 in Africa. The average for the industrial countries (excluding Eastern Europe and the USSR) as a group is $1,200, or twelve times higher than in Africa. But such a comparison is misleading since it tries to compare incomparables—areas with different price structures. The main reason for the distortion arises from the difficulties of assigning any meaningfully comparable prices to agricultural products, particularly in the subsistence sector, and to services.

In a recent study prepared for the OEEC, it was brought out that if the per capita income of Italy were to be compared with that of the United States, it needs to be raised by about 80 per cent.[6] Rough estimates of per capita income for many underdeveloped countries suggest that they should be increased two to four times upwards for comparison with those of the industrial countries.

Statistics are not available to carry out a similar exercise for Africa. But the illustrative data in Table 2 are meant to give an approximate impression of the present position. The per capita output for each sector is derived by dividing the output in that sector by *total* population, and *not* by the population employed in that sector alone. The aim of this exercise is to measure not the level of productivity, but the quantity of goods made available by that sector for each inhabitant. Changes brought about by external trade are excluded.

What do the comparisons in Table 2 suggest? In the industrial countries the per capita agricultural output is only twice as high as that in Africa, valued at US relative prices. The agricultural distance between these two areas is much narrower than is commonly imagined. This distance could be covered if an annual per capita growth rate of 1.5 to 2 per cent were maintained for some forty to fifty years. Thus, the distance that now separates agricultural scarcity in Africa from surplus in industrial countries is neither very large nor very difficult to cover.

The gap in the industrial field is very wide—output being thirty-two

6. Milton Gilbert and Irving B. Kravis, *Comparative National Products and Price Levels* (Paris, 1955), p. 165.

Processes of Encadrement: Bureaucratic Development and Economic Growth

Table 2—The Economic Distance Between Africa and the Industrial Countries, 1960[a]

Per capita Net Output[b]

Output by Industrial Origin	AFRICA		Indus-trial Countries ($)	Ratio Between Africa and In-dustrial Countries	REQUIREMENTS FOR AFRICA TO REACH 1960 LEVEL OF INDUSTRIAL COUNTRIES	
	At Domestic Prices ($)	At US Relative Prices[c] ($)			Annual Percent-age Rate of Growth	No. of Years
Agriculture	45	60	120	2.0	1.5 to 2.0	40 to 50
Industry	15	15	480	32.0	7.0 to 9.0	40 to 50
Total commodity output	60	75	600	8.0	5.0	40 to 50
Other sectors (services)	40	?	600	?	?	?
Total output	100	?	1,200	?	?	?

[a] Sources: based on national statistics for industrial countries (defined as in Table 1); and U.N. Economic Commission for Africa, *Industrial Growth in Africa* (New York, 1963), ch. 1. The figures based on domestic product at factor cost are very crude and have therefore been rounded to the nearest 5 or 10.

[b] Value of output in each sector related to the whole population, and *not* to the number of persons engaged in that particular sector.

[c] The data in this column are not based on detailed price relatives of all the items in national accounts, but are the product of a rough and ready calculation, with an arbitrary adjustment for agriculture.

times as high in the industrial countries. This appears formidable, but it could be overcome in only forty to fifty years if industrial output per capita were raised annually at a rate of 7 to 9 per cent (that is, a growth rate of about 9 to 11 per cent for total industrial output). This is a high rate, but many countries have attained it in recent years.

The total per capita output of industry and agriculture in the industrial countries, measured on this basis, is some eight times higher than in Africa. The real economic distance between Africa and industrial countries is thus not so high as indicated by the usual comparison of per capita incomes from all sources. If the per capita output were raised eight times in Africa, it could supply the average inhabitant of the continent with the same quantity of goods which is now available to an average citizen in the industrial countries.

What are the economic dynamics in terms of time and pace for such a transition? It would require a per capita growth rate of 5 per cent main-tained for forty to fifty years, or only an adult's lifetime. The growth rate is neither forbiddingly high, nor the period unbearably long. There is thus little basis for the pessimist's pathetic patience to postpone the possible—the very rapid elimination of want and poverty.

The Economic Transition in Africa

Most of the discussion on economic development has so often remained either perched on an inaccessible plateau of philosophical speculation, or lost in a web of mathematical models where complexity deceptively appears as completeness. In either case, the personal predilections of the participants predetermine the assumptions. Geography, climate, temperature, laziness, aptitude, culture—all these form the basis of the assumptions which are often not even expressed. Viewed from these Olympian heights of philosophy or econometric elegance, the problems of the poor countries appear indeed formidable, often insoluble, except over a span of many centuries.

The ideas expressed in this article are fairly simple. But then, as Keynes emphasised in the Preface to his *General Theory:* "The difficulty lies, not in the new ideas, but in escaping from the old ones, which ramify, for those brought up as most of us have been, into every corner of our minds."

As suggested above, the engine of economic expansion has moved since 1850 at a modest pace. The economist was not in the driver's seat. But the engine moved on, often despite dire predictions by the most learned members of the profession. Continuous creeping for over 100 years even at this slow pace has brought massive economic expansion in the industrial countries—a sevenfold or eightfold rise in per capita incomes. The measurable dimensions of the economic transition were (1) time: a little over 100 years; and (2) pace: 1.8 per cent per capita per year. Any country which moved at this pace for this period could accomplish approximately the same transition. And the more rapid the pace, the shorter the period. These are the operational dimensions for the economic transition. The discussion on development could then be brought down to the level of economic dynamics, of economic mechanics —indicating the requirements to attain a set of given objectives in about the same manner as a bridge-builder prepares a list of materials needed for building the bridge.

The period in which the African countries may accomplish the transition depends on the speed of their progress. The treasure house of world technology is now almost bursting at its seams. As Veblen so persistently stressed, the pace of economic growth now need not be cramped by the speed of new technological advance, as was the case in the industrial countries. There is so much that these countries can easily adopt and assimilate from the accumulated technological knowledge. Rising pressures for a more equitable distribution of international income and for competitive coexistence between rival political powers can be expected to lead to an increase in the flow of international assistance, particularly if some progress were to be made towards disarmament. Public pressure for accelerating the tempo of economic growth is acting as the most powerful solvent of the rigidities of an outmoded social set-up. Planning commissions and agencies are being set up. Economists are being called upon to help in the process. Their presence now, in contrast to their absence earlier, ought to make some difference in the growth rate.

Moreover, the nineteenth-century growth rate appeared very rapid to the inhabitants of Western Europe, as it indeed was much higher than ever before. But since World War II, many countries have experienced much higher growth rates. To plan for rapid progress now is no longer like venturing in uncharted waters without a rudder and a compass.

These considerations have found their reflection in development plans in the African countries. Most countries have adopted planning as an instrument of national policy aimed at accelerating the pace of economic and social transition. Twenty-two countries, accounting for around 80 per cent of the national income of Africa, have already formulated development plans, with growth rates for total output varying from 4 to 8 per cent per year. The average growth rate for industrial countries over the last century (2.8 per cent) was thus below the lowest targets in Africa.

The lower African growth targets are usually found in countries where the new plans are attempting to overcome long-term stagnation and prepare the basis for faster growth in the next plan. These are usually the countries where the level of investment has been lower, exports are increasing more slowly, natural resource endowment is perhaps less, and where the planning leadership is still groping for a development strategy and outlook. On the other hand, the planned growth rate is high in the countries with some development in the past, a reasonable level of investment and a strong export sector, often combined with a dynamic and popular political leadership, and with far-sighted planning commissions.

Since planning is an even more recent experience than political independence, it is to be expected that the plan performance will often fall short of expectations. But the wide acceptance of forward-looking goals is now acting as a catalyst in the process of overcoming the obstacles —almost in the same manner as the goal of political independence swept aside the obstacles in its path.

It is therefore the higher growth rates which are used as the basis of the projected outline of Africa's future economic transition, which is set out in Table 3. It needs to be emphasised that the figures suggested represent only a first order of approximation. Their main purpose is to

Table 3—An Outline of Economic Prospects in Africa, 1960, 1968, 2000[a]

Sector of Origin	NET PRODUCT ($ BILLION AT 1960 PRICES)			NET PRODUCT (PERCENTAGE OF TOTAL)			ANNUAL PERCENTAGE RATE OF GROWTH	
	1960	1980	2000	1960	1980	2000	1960–1980	1980–2000
Agriculture	11	30	75	45	30	20	5	4
Industry:								
mining	1 }	11	100	6	11	25	11	12
heavy mfg.	0.4 }							
light mfg.	1.6 }	19	65	9	19	15	11	6
small scale	1 }							
total	4	30	165	15	30	40	11	9
Total commodity output	15	60	240	60	60	60	7	7
Other sectors	10	40	160	40	40	40	7	7
Total product	25	100	400	100	100	100	7	7

[a] Estimates should be treated as broad orders of magnitude only.

indicate the broad contours of what is generally possible, and not to measure with precision each step as it is taken in each country. The estimates outline the possible changes in total and sectoral output by the years 1980 and 2000 for the continent as a whole.

Some of the main features of this outline of prospects may now be summarized. In the first place, the total output of goods and services could increase, at constant (1960) prices, from $25 billion to $100 billion in 1980 and to $400 billion by the end of the century. This would mean that it would double every decade, and quadruple every twenty years, giving a total in A.D. 2000 as high as sixteen times the initial level in 1960. This may appear at first sight an incredibly high expansion. But the growth rate required to bring it about is only 7 per cent per year. The mysterious power of growth at compound rates speeds economic development as the westerlies did many a sailing ship.

Table 3 also indicates the structural changes which might accompany these increases. The growth rates for each of the sectors are rough approximations. Their effect would be to bring about a structural transformation similar to that which took place in the course of past economic development. The essential features in this process are (a) the output of the noncommodity (service) sector shows no clear or marked upward or downward trend in relation to total output; (b) the ratios between agricultural and industrial output are almost completely reversed—the share of agriculture falling from two thirds or more in commodity output at the beginning, to one third or less towards the end, and that of industry rising correspondingly; and (c) a somewhat similar transformation occurs in the structure of industrial output, light industry falling from two thirds or more of total industrial output to one third or less, and heavy industry rising correspondingly.

What will be the effects of such changes on per capita income? Population will also continue to increase during this period. Its growth rate may be as high as 2.2 per cent per year up to 1980 and thereafter may well begin to decline. The present total of some 250 million people would on these assumptions rise to about 385 million in 1980 and 570 million by the end of the century. As a result of the growth of population at a little over 2 per cent, and output at about 7 per cent, the per capita income at 1960 prices would be approximately $250–260 by 1980 and $700 by 2000. Only one more decade of similar expansion would then be needed to raise it to $1,200, or the average level now current in the industrial countries.

It may be suggested that the assumed rate of growth for population (about 2 per cent for the forty years) is low. This may in reality turn out to be somewhat higher, say 2.5 per cent per year. It is unlikely to be higher than that, because the decline in the birth rate associated with the transition to higher incomes should begin to make itself felt towards the end of the period. Moreover, there is a certain ceiling to birth rates and a floor to death rates. As a result, the population growth rate—in sharp contrast to the economic growth rate—can move only within a fairly narrow range, say from zero to an approximate maximum of 3 per cent. The higher rate, by its nature, can be only a transient phenomenon; it cannot continue indefinitely in the absence of economic growth. In any case, even if a somewhat higher growth rate of population is assumed, it would influence the final level of per capita income only marginally.

Resources Needed for the Transition

At this point, we must pause to reflect upon the question that must be uppermost in the minds of many. This all sounds very good, may even be called exciting indeed. But is it realistic? Can it be done?

The economist can only attempt to answer this question by making an inventory of the resources that would be needed to complete the transition. For convenience, these may be itemized under three broad headings: (1) natural, (2) technical, and (3) economic. Some of the main considerations involved in assessing them are discussed below.

1. *Natural resources.* Attention was drawn in the first section to the immense richness of natural resource endowment in this continent.

Moreover, resources are not to looked upon as an unchanging, given stock of materials allocated by nature. They are always changing in line with the development of man's capacity to master what he has. Millions of tons of coal buried in the bowels of the earth meant little until Watt could enclose the mighty power of steam in a cylinder with a shaft that moved the wheels of a cumbersome contraption, now known as the steam engine. The black liquid that oozed out of earth's cracks was used only as an ointment until means were found to explode its power inside the chamber of an internal combustion engine. The turbulent water of a mountain torrent or a mighty river simply flowed away until it was harnessed behind the blades of a turbine to produce the magic electric current. And so on.

Moreover, what is not to be found on or under the soil of a country need not be treated as unavailable. If so, the cotton textile industry would have never developed in Europe; nor would the iron and steel and the engineering industries in Italy, Japan, and many other places. Trade and commerce between individuals and nations have provided a means of equalizing surpluses and scarcities.

2. *Technical skills.* Even the most fabulous endowment of natural resources would be lying untouched if it could not be transformed into desirable products through the combination of various skills. Africa has only recently entered, almost burst, into contact with the modern world. During its period of dependence little attention was paid to training its people in modern techniques. But the unquenchable thirst for education, for enlightenment, made thousands of families send their children to faraway places and lands to master the modern "magic."

Many inhabitants of Africa have now begun to control the complex processes of the industrial age as mechanics, skilled workers, administrators, teachers, doctors, or pilots of jet planes. Past generations' competence or qualifications, or their absence, have little to do with the new generation's ability to acquire and master an entirely different level of skills and knowledge. That is why an illiterate peasant's son may turn out to be a genius, whereas a Nobel prize winner's progeny may struggle with their studies.

Literacy, secondary education, and technical and higher university education are rapidly spreading in Africa. There are many gaps and weaknesses. Many modifications are needed in what is being taught. But according to the Addis Ababa Plan for education in Africa and estimates for North Africa, over a million students may be receiving higher education by 1980. The total may well jump to four or five million by the end of the century—or higher than the actual number now in the United States, Western Europe, or the Soviet Union. The spreading of the age of enlightenment is now more rapid than population growth or even economic expansion.

Everybody talks about the pressing need for technical education. But it is not easy to give any precise answers as to how many persons trained in various technical fields are in fact needed in order to raise the level of economic activity from one stage to another in a given period of time. The men with all types of training and skills—lower, medium, and higher—needed to carry out the economic and social transition in Africa cannot be assumed to be forthcoming automatically. Their supply forms the most strategic factor. It cannot be assured without planning in a long perspective the training of people with those types of skills that are most needed.

3. *Economic resources.* It is legitimate to ask, Do the African countries have the capital resources to carry out such objectives? After all, is there not a shortage of capital? There is little doubt that such transition will be no more than a paper project if economic resources are not mobilized both at home and from abroad to improve agriculture, construct plants and factories, create an adequate transport network, build schools, hospitals, and other ancillary facilities that go with an advanced standard of living.

Before making a total of such resources, it may be worthwhile to look a little more closely into what is really meant by capital, or economic resources. In the first place, there is the machinery and all types of equipment. Then the buildings and other construction needed to house, transport, and operate them, which in turn require bricks, lime, wood, cement, steel, etc. It is the availability of all these goods, and mostly in the right combinations, which may be called the capital resources. Since these diverse items cannot be added up into a total, each of them is given a money expression. But behind this sum of money needed for investment, there are actually various commodities in the same manner as the cost figure of building a bridge really symbolizes so many materials. It is the ability of a bridge builder or a planner to assemble these items in a given combination that determines his capacity to build a bridge or carry out a plan.

What would be the total of the capital expenditure needed for carrying out the main objectives of rapid economic transition in Africa? Some estimates are given in Table 4. They are based on assuming certain incremental (gross) capital-output ratios (ICOR's) for various sectors.[7] The ICOR's assumed are 1.5:1 in agriculture, 2.5:1 in industry, and 4:1 in the other sectors. The ICOR is only an analytical tool, useful

7. The ICOR may be defined as the ratio of a given increment in capital resources to the resulting increment in annual output. Increments in capital are here measured in terms of gross capital formation.

enough to form estimates in advance but not firm enough to provide precision. Moreover, conditions in countries differ and so would the estimated ICOR's. The assumed ICOR's approximate to the experience of various developing countries showing an annual growth rate of about 7 per cent.

These ratios are applied to the estimated increases in output during 1960 to 1980, and 1980 to 2000. The capital requirements thus derived come to some $215 billion (at 1960 prices) for the former period, and $890 billion for the latter.

Table 4—Estimated Capital Requirements for Africa's Economic Transition, 1960–2000[a]

Sector of Origin	Increment in Output		TOTAL GROSS CAPITAL FORMATION REQUIRED FOR THE PERIOD	
	1960–1980	1980–2000	1960–1980	1980–2000
	$ Billion at 1960 Prices			
Agriculture	19	45	30	70
Industry	26	135	65	340
Other sectors	30	120	120	480
Total	75	300	215	890

[a] Source and methods: Based on Table 3; estimates of capital derived by assuming incremental capital output ratio (ICOR) to be 1.5:1 in agriculture, 2.5:1 in total industry, and 4:1 for the other sectors. The derived overall ICOR for both the periods would thus be a little under 3:1.

The sums involved are indeed large. They cannot be financed out of the present level of income in Africa. But they are spread over twenty years and are to be drawn from the income level which because of them is also rising. Thus for instance the average investment for each year during 1960 to 1980 would be $10.7 billion. This is nearly three times the present estimate of annual gross capital formation in Africa ($3.5 billion).[8] When the present capital formation is raised on a straight-line basis a little faster than income in the first period, the level of capital formation in the end-year (1980) required to supply a total of $215 billion would come to about $20 billion, or around one fifth of annual income in 1980. The level of investment would thus rise from 14 per cent in 1960 to about 20 per cent in 1980. This can hardly be considered an unmanageable level of effort.

Similar calculations for the second period suggest that capital formation would have to rise from $20 billion in 1980 to some $80 billion in 2000, or about one fifth of output both in 1980 and in 2000, implying that no additional efforts would have to be made to raise the level of investment.

These may be considered ambitious targets, but can hardly be dis-

8. Estimate based on development plans,   where available, and national statistics.

missed as unmanageable. Such a large effort becomes feasible when it is considered as a part of a dynamic process in which investment, output, and consumption all increase, though of course at varying rates. The ICOR's used here may be altered to suit other assumptions. That would produce a different set of estimates, but it is unlikely to alter the substance of the line of development presented here.

The provision of such a large amount of capital resources is conceivable only in a dynamic context. Current discussion on economic development is usually dominated by a static or a very short-term view. Investment has been regarded as a deduction from income, which it will be very difficult to raise since per capita incomes in the poor countries are so low. The other, and more positive, role of investment as an instrument of raising income is sometimes lost sight of. Investment merely appears as a cost, as a burden, as bearing an inverse correlation with consumption.

Only in a long-term view does investment assume its real role as the major factor in raising output. Hence its correlation with consumption becomes direct rather than inverse. The greater the investment, the higher the output, and the larger the consumption. If investment was only a costly monument to national grandeur and did not contribute directly to increasing the level of output, it would be impossible to raise it from $3.5 billion in 1960 to $20 billion per year in 1980. But since it also raises output in the process (from $25 to $100 billion in this case) it would appear feasible. In this sense, it is growth which finances growth.

From the figures given above, it is possible to calculate the required incremental savings/output ratio (ISOR), or the proportion of the *additional* income that would have to be ploughed back into investment to obtain these results. For the period 1960 to 1980, the ISOR would be 0.2; that is, about one fifth of the additional income in each year must be devoted to investment if the objectives given here are to be realized. This would not happen automatically. New policies are required to attain it. But an ISOR of 0.2 is not so high, since it permits as much as 80 per cent of additional income to be devoted to consumption. Moreover, an ISOR of 0.2 implies that all the investment is domestically financed, that there is no net external assistance.

The considerations discussed above relate only to the domestic side of the economies. But most of these countries are at present dependent on imports for all their capital equipment. Consequently, even if they were to succeed in raising the level of investment as indicated above, they would be faced with serious difficulties on the external account if their foreign purchasing power did not rise in line with their needs. At present, Africa imports $1.4 billion worth of capital equipment annually. This is about 40 per cent of current gross capital formation.

Assuming that this percentage remains unchanged for the first period and rises to 50 per cent by the year 2000, the machinery and equipment content of the investment level proposed here would come to $8 billion for 1980 and $40 billion for 2000. How much of this will be imported depends on the foreign exchange available and on the expansion of domestic output. In view of the difficulties which most exporters of primary products are facing in raising their exports, it is fairly reasonable to suggest that export proceeds alone will not rise as fast as import requirement.

There would then be an impasse. Even if the governments succeeded in raising domestic savings to the extent suggested here, they would be unable to import the necessary machinery and equipment and hence to carry out their investment programs. The position would be similar to that of the bridge builder who has a bagful of money but cannot get the cement, stones, and steel he needs. Slowly rising ability to import combined with a rapidly rising requirement for machinery and equipment: these contrary movements would lead any development plan to certain failure, unless far-sighted policies were pursued from the beginning to surmount them.

The solution could be sought along two lines to be followed simultaneously. One would be to obtain foreign assistance on as large a scale as possible; and the other would be to use the available resources of total foreign exchange in such a fashion that the stranglehold of slowly rising foreign earnings is eventually broken—that is, by developing in cooperation with other African countries the machinery and equipment industries. The total market for it, as indicated above, would be quite large.

The requirements of foreign assistance need careful study. But assuming that net foreign aid may form for the period as a whole the same share of gross capital formation as now, the total assistance needed for 1960 to 1980 would be about $40 to 50 billion. If it rises as capital formation increases in Africa, it might grow from about $1 billion in 1960 to between $3 and $4 billion in 1980.[9] This may be regarded as a large sum. But with progress towards disarmament, and the establish-

9. Such foreign aid need not be regarded just as charity. Africa has also contributed heavily to the development of the industrial countries. For instance, the estimated value of the slaves in the United States on the eve of the Civil War was a little higher than the total capital investment in the modern sectors —manufacturing, mining, transport, and communications. A rough estimate of what the Europeans have received from Africa since the turn of the century may be about $100 to $150 billion in 1960 prices—one third of which may be assumed to have been consumed in Africa, one third invested in Africa, and the remaining one third sent outside the continent. Africa's pressing demand for external aid now may therefore be interpreted as a reverse lend-lease rather than charity.

ment of some kind of a system of international taxation in order to assure a more equitable distribution of world income and a more rapid development of the poor countries, it is well within the realm of possibility.

Africa by the End of the Century

It was only just over three quarters of a century ago that the political map of Africa was redrawn by a handful of rival powers at a small conference table in Berlin. Part of the continent, deep in the lap of the forest and the desert, was as yet untouched by the outside explorers. For a long time the successive acquisitions of mankind's restless technical advance had bypassed most of the continent. The deserts, the forest, the tsetse fly, the forbidding cataracts, and the swamps in the rivers—all these had stood in the way. The wheel, the sail, the rudder, the compass, the scripts, paper, printing, counting, astronomy, alchemy—few of these ever crossed to most of the continent beyond the deserts. And then, all of a sudden, the walls came crumbling down. That was a little more than just half a century ago.

In the fifties, there was another outburst. The political walls that a few powers had built fell down. Now the continent, almost completely independent, gazes to its future. The revolution of rising expectations is sweeping it as anywhere else. The age of Africa's awakening has begun.

Many scholars have puzzled over knotty questions which yet remain unravelled: Why this isolation? Why this slow pace of development? These questions may be answered, or may never be—just as the where, why, how of the origin of the universe still remains shrouded in a fascinating mystery. But man has gained an immense insight into the way the universe operates. The future movements of most of the objects in it are now known with a considerable degree of precision. It is this type of search, the search for solutions to operational questions, which has animated many of those who now have to chart the course of this continent's economic journey through what remains of the century. In the meantime, the final questions, fascinating though they are, will have to wait.

The aim is to raise the current low level of economic well-being in the continent to that in the industrial countries—and this to be attained in half a century, or an adult's lifetime. Many of those in their late thirties could still be alive to witness it.

An annual growth rate of about 7 per cent for total output; a sevenfold increase in the output of agriculture, fortyfold in industry, sixteenfold in the total of goods and services, and about twenty-fivefold in university enrollment by 2000; a rise in real per capita income from $100 in 1960 to $260 by 1980 and to $700 by 2000, when it will be equal to the average in industrial countries in the early 1950's; capital formation of some $215 billion between 1960 and 1980, and $900 billion between 1980 and 2000; external aid of about $40 to $50 billion between 1960 and 1980. These in short are the main pillars of the economic transition in Africa outlined here. Can they be attained?

The assumption of this article is that they are feasible, but only with a great deal of effort. Naturally, there will be many difficulties, but the burdens and the costs of growth are better by far to bear than those of stagnation. This is a goal for which every African can be justly proud to work, with sacrifice and enthusiasm.

There is no religious sanctity about these estimates. Questioning would only help to improve them. If they open up a discussion in which the participants point out the inaccuracies and help improve them, their original purpose will be more than served.

A children's story may be to the point here. It concerns a Mr. Can and a Mr. Cannot. Both are terribly bright and well-meaning. They are nervous minds, always exploring problems. Mr. Cannot spends his sleepless nights adding another important reason why it cannot be done to a long list of other reasons already discovered by his fertile brain. And the list keeps on growing long in direct functional relationship to his brilliance. Mr. Can proceeds quite differently. His restless mind goes on adding the reasons why it can be done. And when he thinks he has added enough, he goes and does it. Real problems can of course never be solved by stories. But this one is not entirely without relevance to what may happen in the poor countries in the years to come.

R. Cranford
Pratt

THE ADMINISTRATION OF ECONOMIC PLANNING IN A NEWLY INDEPENDENT STATE: THE TANZANIAN EXPERIENCE, 1963–1966

*T*he literature which is available on the implementation of development plans is markedly less abundant than that on problems involved in the formulation of these plans.[1] What literature there is suggests a widespread despondency about the actual operational significance of many of the economic plans that have been so laboriously devised for an increasingly large number of developing countries. Three quite different types of factors explain the frequent failure of governments in developing countries to make the implementation of their development plans a central policy preoccupation. In some countries the development plan itself has caused this; some have been too ambitious or have been based on unrealistic premises or have involved serious internal inconsistencies. In other countries there was not the will among the political leaders to accept the discipline in their decision-making which development planning would involve. Finally, weaknesses in the machinery of government and inadequacies in its procedures have been further major factors undermining any vigorous endeavor to implement development planning.

The Tanzanian experience is of particular interest. Development planning in Tanganyika[2] during the first eighteen months of the five-

1. This is the judgement also of Dr. Aryeh Altir in his paper "Government Organization for Development," in M. Kriesburg (ed.), *Public Administration in Developing Countries* (Washington, 1965). Dr. Albert Waterston's important *Development Planning—Lessons of Experience* (Baltimore, 1965), however, goes a long way to fill this gap.
2. Although the United Republic of Tanzania was created before the publica-

tion of the Five-Year Plan the Plan does not include Zanzibar in its coverage, and to this day the economic policies and programs of Zanzibar have remained outside the purview of the planners. Throughout this paper the planning that is referred to is that done by the government of the United Republic of Tanzania for its mainland component, Tanganyika.

Reprinted in abridged form from *The Journal of Commonwealth Political Studies*, Vol. 5, No. 1 (March 1967), pp. 38–59, by permission of the author, the editors, and the publishers, Leicester University Press.

year period covered by the Development Plan has not been a great success. Yet there have been in Tanganyika a number of factors which ought to have helped to ensure that the implementation of the Development Plan remained a central preoccupation of the government. The Tanganyika Five-Year Plan is an able and highly professional document[3] which has already deservedly attracted favorable professional comment.[4] The Plan is far more than a forward projection of public capital expenditures plus an intelligent surmise of the developments that are likely in the private sector. It is a comprehensive and integrated economic plan in which all sectors of the economy are assigned individual and mutually consistent targets. So far as was feasible the planners also sought to make explicit the economic, financial, educational, and general policy implications of the Plan, and these form an integral part of it. Moreover, the Plan is presented as the first, detailed portion of an overall longer-range plan which establishes basic targets to be reached by 1980. Despite its technical detail and professional competence, the Plan identifies its central objectives in terms at once comprehensible to the general public and also perhaps capable of enlisting widespread commitment to the achievement of the Plan.[5]

The political climate was and is favorable in many ways to a vigorous national effort to achieve the objectives of the Plan. President Nyerere and the Tanganyika African National Union (TANU) have sought, since the achievement of independence, to make the "war against poverty, ignorance, and disease" as compelling an objective as *"Uhuru Na Umoja"* (Freedom and Unity) was before independence. There is also a continuing concern to maintain the integrity and honesty of public life[6] and to achieve genuine and meaningful popular participation in the governmental process.[7]

3. *The Tanganyika Five-Year Plan for Social and Economic Development, July 1964–June 1969* (Dar es Salaam, 1964).
4. See, for example, R. Green, "Four African Development Plans," 3 *Journal of Modern African Studies* (1965), P. Clark, *Development Planning in East Africa* (Nairobi, 1965), W. J. Keegan, "Tanganyika's Five-Year Development Plan: Sober Realism or Buoyant Optimism?" in T. J. Farer (ed.), *Financing African Development* (Cambridge, Mass., 1965), and H. E. Smith, "Economic Development and Planning in Tanzania," in H. E. Smith (ed.), *Readings on Economic Development and Administration in Tanzania* (Nairobi, 1966).
5. The main objectives of the Plan are: "By 1980 (i) to raise our per capita in-

come from the present £19.6 to £45; (ii) to be fully self-sufficient in trained manpower requirement; (iii) to raise the expectation of life from the present 35–40 years, to an expectation of 50 years." *Five-Year Plan*, viii.
6. See, for example, the recent establishment of a Public Commission of Inquiry, an Ombudsman-like Commission, whose chairman is the eminent and highly respected Chief Mangenya.
7. This was most dramatically reaffirmed by the elections held in October, 1965, under a new constitution based on the recommendations of a Presidential Commission. See *Report of the Presidential Commission on the Establishment of a Democratic One-Party State* (Dar es Salaam, 1965) and *An Act to Declare the*

There has also been a sustained political endeavor to propagate political values which will be compatible with the democratic socialist state which it is one of the aims of TANU to promote.[8] TANU and President Nyerere have thus succeeded in maintaining an ideological momentum without succumbing to that rigid and xenophobic version of African socialism which in one or two African states has become a serious barrier to economic development.[9] Finally, Tanzania has no grandiose ambitions beyond its borders and its leaders do not hold an inflated view of the possible international role which either they or their country might be able to play. There has therefore not been a serious and unnecessary diversion of resources to nonproductive expenditures.

Many development plans are prepared in a political vacuum leaving their policy implications to be discovered by others. Many fail to consider whether administrative reorganization might be necessary before the plans could be effectively implemented. These criticisms cannot be made of the Tanganyika Plan. A real effort was made during the production of the Plan to articulate its major policy implications and to present proposals for an administrative reorganization which would facilitate its implementation. Nevertheless despite these favorable circumstances, it had become clear within a year of the Plan's publication that the government had not succeeded in making the accomplishment of the Plan central to its operations; nor was it ensuring that the implications of new proposals were adequately assessed within its decision-making procedures. It is this breakdown in development planning, despite so many favorable omens, which needs to be explained.[10]

Development planning is a continuous process. The production of a plan marks the conclusion of an important phase in this process; it is not, however, its culmination nor its final objective. The objective is a decision-making process in which those government decisions which bear upon the economic development of the country are taken with

Interim Constitution of Tanzania, No. 43 of 1965. This election is examined in detail in W. Tordoff, "The General Election in Tanzania," 4 *Journal of Commonwealth Political Studies* (1966), 47–64.

8. See, for example, President Nyerere's Pamphlets *Ujaama, Basis for African Socialism* (Dar es Salaam, 1962) and *Principles and Development* (Dar es Salaam, 1966), and the Presidential statement of the "National Ethic" which is reproduced in the *Report . . . of a Democratic One-Party State*, 3–4.

9. See, for example, E. Berg, "Socialism and Economic Development in Tropical Africa," 78 *Quarterly Journal of Economics* (1964).

10. Much of the material on which the rest of this article is based was secured in interviews with Ministers and senior civil servants in Dar es Salaam. These discussions took place on the understanding that the information derived from them would not be directly and personally attributed to the individuals interviewed. Throughout these discussions ministers and senior civil servants displayed a most admirable concern to learn of the experience of other developing countries and to share their own experience with them.

reference to an integrated and comprehensive plan and according to an agreed and internally consistent set of national priorities. In this process the plan, of course, plays a crucial role. But few countries have been able, for long after the production of their plan, to regard the plan itself as a final guide. Discovered inadequacies within it and changing circumstances normally require an early and continued modification of any plan if it is to remain a central guide to policy. The truth of this proposition was very quickly established in Tanzania. Four important groups of factors each contributed to the Plan's becoming quickly out of date, irrelevant, or erroneous on a number of points of central importance.

First, the Plan had its own inadequacies. Insufficient account had been taken of the time which would be needed to prepare feasibility reports on projects for which foreign aid was being sought, to negotiate for this aid, and then, when the negotiations were finally successful, actually to initiate projects. At the very least, therefore, important adjustments would be necessary in the timing of a large number of projects for which foreign finance was being sought.

The planners were also unjustifiably optimistic about the amount of foreign aid that Tanzania would be able to attract. The Plan assumed that no less than 80 per cent of the capital development expenditures of government would be financed by foreign aid, whereas no amount of wise negotiations and good fortune would have secured such a high percentage for the Tanzanian Government. Many capital items within the Plan were most unlikely to interest overseas governments. Few would undertake many projects which did not involve a reasonably high proportion of imports from the country concerned. Most foreign countries were also unlikely to support projects which by their unglamorous nature or too sensitive character were judged inappropriate for foreign aid. The Plan therefore needed to be revised to take account of the fact that local sources of capital would have to provide a higher proportion of total capital government investment than had been envisaged.

A final weakness of the Plan is that it avoids discussion of two basic policy matters. There is no discussion of the need for a wages policy which would keep building and other costs under control and avoid the development of too drastic a gap between the income of the still tiny urban working class and that of the vast majority of Tanganyikans working in the countryside. The Plan also avoids any definition of the areas of economic activity in which private capital would be welcomed and encouraged. The implications of the Plan on both these issues are obvious: it implies a stable wage policy which will ensure that urban workers are justly treated but do not receive continuously rising wages at the expense of the advancement of the countryside; and it wants private investors to feel that they would be welcome to play a full role in important sectors of the economy. As long as government policy is not itself clear and explicit on issues as controversial as these, however, they cannot be regarded as having been settled by the production of the Plan. In both these cases the Plan might need to be recast, or at least its details would need to be retested, when finally the Government either announced definite proposals or permitted the evolution of definite policies by a failure on its own part to define objectives.

In addition to these features of the Plan, there were factors external to it arising from the circumstances in which Tanzania found itself in the period from July 1964 to December 1965, which were far more significant in rendering invalid important projects and targets within the Plan. Although 1964 was a reasonably good year for agricultural production, 1965 was disastrous; drought conditions greatly reducing the output of several important crops, particularly maize and rice. The fall in the world prices of sisal, cotton, and coffee in 1965 more than offset increased output in Tanganyika, and rural incomes therefore fell slightly. This fall in the world prices of several of Tanzania's most important exports also had a major impact upon government revenues, for export taxes, based on a sliding scale related to prices, were an important source of public revenue. The planners had assumed, for example, a higher export price for sisal than was in fact realized and consequently government revenue from sisal taxes, estimated in the Plan at £2,100,000 for 1964–1965, fell to approximately £800,000 in that year and disappeared altogether in the following year when the price of sisal fell further.

The planners had also been unduly optimistic over the extent to which foreign governments would be willing to channel their economic aid to Tanzania into projects selected by the government. Initially the government had hoped that the Director of Planning would be able to preallocate development projects in the Plan between the various possible external sources of assistance. It quickly became apparent, however, that donors wished to play a more active role in the selection of projects within the Plan which they might finance and, more than that, they advocated other projects not included in the Plan. These extra projects could not be regarded as additional to the assistance which these foreign governments might be willing to give towards the implementation of the Plan itself and inevitably cut into the amount of foreign aid which might otherwise have been available for the support of projects within the Plan. Furthermore, in the pursuit of these new projects resources were allocated and foreign exchange used up which were not therefore available for alternative projects which had been judged important enough to be included in the Plan. An example of this is the powerful short-wave radio transmission station which is the first large item financed from the first Chinese loan of £10,000,000, although it does not appear in the Plan but was proposed by the Chinese negotiators.

There is a final factor of great importance which caused the Plan quickly to appear unrealistic and overoptimistic. The planners recognized that many more highly trained men and women would be needed in the Civil Service if the Plan's objectives were to be achieved. There were not and are not enough Tanzanians to fill these posts, nor indeed are all the vacancies within the present establishment which may occur during the five-year period likely to be filled. The planners fully recognized the manpower implications of their proposals, estimating that, during the five-year period, after taking full account of the increasing supply of African graduates, 444 new expatriates exclusive of teachers and nurses would need to be recruited to fill high-level posts in the public service. Nothing like this number of expatriates have been recruited.[11] On the contrary, in 1965 there was a net loss of 187 noncitizens in the staff, administrative, and professional grades of the Civil Service.[12]

This has inevitably affected the ability of the government to accomplish the targets which it had accepted under the Plan. Project after project has been held up because of the shortage of high-level manpower even though finance was available. Moreover, the tardiness with which the new feasibility studies are prepared and the doubts of prospective donors about the ability of the government to carry out new major projects have affected the supply of new aid. This shortage of skilled personnel, more than the lack of either foreign aid or foreign exchange, has been the most important single reason why the rate of development has been slower than envisaged in the Five-Year Plan.[13]

For all these reasons it was inevitable that the Five-Year Plan would need early revision if its implementation was to remain a central preoccupation of government policy. If the scarce resources of manpower and finance were to be allocated to uses which reflect national priorities, the Five-Year Plan needed to be supplemented by either an annual plan or a continuous forward development budget. The very difficulties which Tanzania had encountered underline the value of a continuous planning effort to ensure that scarce resources are used to the best possible advantage.

This continuous effort did not take place. Instead, when the Plan

11. The shortage of teachers and nurses was expected to be greater than the overall shortage in all the other professional and administrative posts. See *Five-Year Plan*, Chapter 6.
12. *Localization of the Civil Service* (Establishment circular letter No. 21 of 1965, 18.11.65).
13. In 1964–1965 the National Income at constant prices rose by 4.5 per cent and in 1965–1966 by under 2 per cent. These compare with the target set in the Plan of 6.7 per cent.

proved unrealistic and impossible to achieve, the government not only in effect abandoned the Plan but also very nearly abandoned the whole planning process. It began to give up the effort to coordinate the activities of government and the private sector or to focus the efforts of each on to the achievement of an integrated set of targets which reflect national priorities and would be most likely to promote development.

It had not been intended that this should happen. The government had been determined to make the implementation of the Plan central to its activities and to the activities of the Party. The Plan was launched with a major publicity campaign and, simultaneously with its publication, there was a major reorganization of the machinery of government to help ensure that the Plan would be implemented. . . .

.   .   .   .

A wide variety of administrative and political factors contributed to this dramatic failure of development planning in Tanzania. Firstly, . . .

.   .   .   .

A draft plan was presented to the Economic Development Commission in January, 1964. By this time sharp disagreement on a number of important points had developed between the Ministry of Development Planning and several other ministries. The Ministry and the Treasury clashed over the rate of economic expansion likely to be achieved, the Ministry wishing to base the Plan on a growth rate of 6.7 per cent at constant prices, the Treasury arguing that this was unrealistically high. The Treasury also took very strong exception to the inclusion in the draft plan of proposals relating to the future tax structure and to the possibility of major structural changes in the operation of the East African Common Market, for these were matters which had always been primarily the Treasury's responsibility.

A long and acrimonious debate on educational policy also developed between the Ministry of Development Planning and the Ministry of Education. The Planners sought to establish that significant economies could be made in the operation of primary and secondary schools and that the capital and recurrent requirements of the Ministry of Education therefore need not be nearly as high as the figures proposed by the Ministry of Education. They disagreed also on the rate of expansion to be encouraged in the field of primary education, the planners wishing to limit expansion more severely than did the Ministry of Education.

There was, finally, an important disagreement between the Ministry of Development Planning on the one hand and the Ministry of Agriculture and the Treasury on the other over rural development policies. The Ministry of Development Planning had taken up the distinction first made in relation to Tanganyika by the World Bank Report of 1959 which distinguished between the transformation approach and the improvement approach to rural development.[14] The transformation approach referred to those policies which sought dramatically to change the whole pattern of life in the countryside by a major effort to plan the coordinated cultivation of agricultural holdings and to gather the farmers into villages where resources could be more easily provided for them. The improvement approach, in contrast, stressed those policies, such as agricultural extension work, which seek to increase agricultural productivity without involving a major effort to transform the social and cultural life of the rural areas. The Directorate argued strongly that the government's main efforts in agricultural development should be a vigorous pursuit of the transformation approach; the Ministry of Agriculture, supported by the Treasury, was very sceptical of this and felt that economic progress would be much surer and that investments in agriculture would be much more likely to show early returns if the older improvement methods continued to receive the main emphasis.

Disagreements such as these were no doubt inevitable but they did illustrate the tendency of the Ministry of Development Planning to press its views strongly on a number of important matters which lay within the professional competence of other Ministries and were within their constitutional responsibilities.

By January, 1964, when these issues reached the Economic Development Commission, positions had been firmly taken. The Ministries, by and large, felt themselves beleaguered and seriously intruded upon by the Ministry of Development Planning. Nevertheless the Economic Development Commission, under President Nyerere's chairmanship, did at least take most of the necessary difficult decisions at this meeting, and the Directorate of Planning was able then to prepare the final draft of the Plan in time, but only just in time, for presentation to the May, 1964, session of the National Assembly.

Several Ministries failed entirely to cooperate with the Ministry of Development Planning in the preparation of the Plan, submitting estimates of neither recurrent nor capital needs to the Directorate. In consequence the Ministry of Development Planning had in the end no alternative but to insert into the Plan figures of its own devising for these Ministries. It appears that these figures were not then questioned at the Economic Development Commission and were thus included in the Plan with the formal approval of the Committee and the acquiescence of the Ministers directly concerned.

To go through the process of consultation, however, does not neces-

14. *The Economic Development of* cially 101–41.
Tanganyika (Baltimore, 1961). See espe-

sarily generate a consensus. In this instance, to meet its deadline and possibly also to ensure that a coordinated Plan was produced at all, the Directorate had so to press the pace that the Plan could not be regarded as the expression of a widely negotiated common view. Rather the reverse. The suspicions which had been built up during the months of controversy when the Plan was being prepared left a heritage of hostility and a mood of noncooperation which were important obstacles to the effective implementation of the Plan.

The second administrative factor which contributed to the failure to implement the Plan and to introduce effective planning procedures was the lack of any well organized and systematic reporting to the Directorate on the progress being made, project by project, in each of the Ministries. Although the Ministries' suspicion of the Directorate helps to explain the inadequacies of the reporting procedure, there were other important contributing factors. Many Ministries have still to recognize the full implications of the Government's commitment to plan the country's economic development. While older procedures, which gave, for example, the Treasury and the Comptroller and Auditor-General significant supervisory powers over the Ministries, were established and unquestioned, the new controls implicit in economic planning were neither fully understood nor fully accepted. In consequence many Ministries failed to accept the need to supply the Directorate of Planning with the flow of information which was essential if the Directorate was to fulfil its responsibilities.

A further reason for the frequent failure of the Ministries to supply information to the Directorate has been the extreme scarcity of senior administrators and professionally qualified staff. As a result very few Ministries have established planning units and the responsibility for coordinating the planning of projects within each Ministry, and for relating these projects to the overall planning being done by the Directorate, was added to the responsibilities of senior officials already far too hard pressed. As a result copies of letters appealing for this information, sometimes plaintive and sometimes aggressive, appear frequently in the Directorate's files. The information has not, however, been forthcoming and the Directorate has never had the information which it needs to do its job effectively.

The shortage of senior staff in the Directorate of Planning must be counted as a third separate administrative factor contributing to the failure to implement the Plan. Six senior economists were the senior staff of the Directorate during the fifteen-month period preceding the publication of the Plan. All six were expatriates and had been provided under one form or another of technical assistance. . . . As is so often the case, the expatriate experts were on short two-year contracts and this international and highly able team began to disperse within a few months of the publication of the Plan. . . .

.   .   .   .

The . . . final administrative weakness in the follow-up of the Plan was the failure initially to present the Plan in a form intelligible to the middle and lower ranks of the Party and the administration, and to the local authorities. In consequence it was extremely difficult for the enthusiastic local official to know how best to organize local effort for the achievement of the Plan. Too often the initial momentum and mobilization of opinion that occurred as a result of the Plan's publication and the publicity it then received was dissipated because at the local level it provided no immediate and specific targets. The original intention of the planners had been to construct a Plan very much on the basis of projects submitted by the individual Ministries and on the basis of local development objectives submitted by local development committees. In theory the Plan should have represented a consensus among both Ministry and regional officials on what was feasible in the five-year period. Had it represented such a consensus it would have provided a clear guide to everyone of their obligations if the Plan was to be implemented. In fact, however, the initiative which the Directorate had to take in building up the Plan, the heavy dependence on foreign aid which meant that there was no guarantee at all that many items in the Plan could in fact be proceeded with, and the poor quality of whatever plans were produced by local development committees meant that the Five-Year Plan did not provide a guide to action at the local level. What was needed was a centrally prepared set of local targets, each consistent with the Plan itself and with what could be discovered of the specific potential of each locality, so that local officials of both the state and the Party would have an effective guide in their efforts to mobilize the mass of the people for development activity.

Instead of this, an initial effort was made by the depleted Directorate to achieve "a generally consistent accounting framework" within each region and elaborate instructions were sent to each Regional Commissioner to assist him to prepare a Five-Year Plan for his region. This was a much more ambitious objective and required a skill with figures and an ability to follow economic arguments which few Regional Commissioners and still fewer Area Commissioners were likely to have. It was also an exercise which, even if successfully completed, would have very little administrative significance, for authority and responsibility for much that would be in such a regional plan were bound to lie with central government Ministries. It was only later that more straightforward regional targets were prepared by the Directorate.

These administrative factors would have been sufficient to cause major failures in the implementation of the Plan. They need not, however, carry the full responsibility. There were also political factors of the greatest importance. Firstly, however much Ministers affirmed a belief in socialism and an attachment to the Five-Year Plan, many in fact were not willing to concede a high priority to that disciplined review of all new policies and projects which is essential to economic planning. This can be explained partly in terms of their ambitions for themselves and for their Ministries; partly it may also be explained in terms of a shallowness in their commitment to planning and to socialism. A further aspect of any full explanation of this Ministerial ambivalence over planning is the style of politics which had developed in the earlier days of the nationalist movement and which gave to some of its leaders a personal authority and an autonomy in their actions which proved very hard to combine with the disciplined procedures of development planning. Thus, for example, several months after the publication of the Plan, the Minister for External Affairs, Mr. Oscar Kambona, was able with little difficulty to secure Government agreement to a significant increase in the number of Tanzanian embassies overseas and to a raiding of other Ministries to staff them. He was able also to secure presidential acceptance of these policies without reference to the procedures which had just been introduced to ensure that all new proposals would be carefully assessed to identify their impact upon the implementation of the Plan. There were also decisions in the latter half of 1964 involving wage and salary increases for the police and a very significant increase in the size of the armed forces which were taken outside the planning procedures that had only recently been established.

These decisions and the manner in which they were taken gave evidence of the continued existence of a nexus of relationships between the President and his Ministers which predated the formal relationships of government and which continued to have their own political logic which could not easily be denied. These undefined and unofficial relationships and the informal decision-making processes which they involved affected the operation of the Cabinet as well as the working of the new planning procedures. Rules existed from shortly after the achievement of independence which established the obvious procedure essential to a smooth operation of the Cabinet system. For example, all Ministerial decisions which have major political implications or which significantly impinge upon the responsibilities of another Ministry should first be referred to the Cabinet, and any policy matter which has financial implications should be referred to the Treasury prior to submission to the Cabinet, and the Treasury's comments thereon should be attached to that submission. Yet in fact decisions of wide political importance and of significant inter-

Ministerial implications have continued to be taken entirely outside the Cabinet and without conformity with these procedures. These have not been unconstitutional, for under the Constitution the Cabinet plays only an advisory role to the President. What has happened is that the President has found it either desirable or necessary to continue to take important decisions on the basis of informal consultations with some of his colleagues and entirely outside the formal machinery that he had established.

.   .   .   .

Reference must also be made, however, to much more general political factors and influences if the full complexity of the forces affecting development planning in Tanzania are to be understood. The first of these relates to a basic characteristic of TANU and to the pattern of national politics which has evolved from that; the second relates to the series of major political crises with which Tanzania had to cope in 1964 and 1965.

Tanganyika is a one-party state in which the dominance of the nationalist party, TANU, preceded the achievement of independence rather than being created by a postindependence assertion of government power on its behalf. In 1961 TANU was a national movement of nearly universal popularity in Tanganyika. In a state newly independent and with very few other important social forces working to create a national identity, the unifying character of TANU was understandably very highly valued. As a consequence of this, and no doubt also of the camaraderie and *esprit de corps* derived from early association together in the nationalist movement, a dominant characteristic of Tanganyikan politics since independence has been that of political accommodation. Whatever the disagreements between senior party members, the major political effort has almost always been to hold the contending Ministers within the movement rather than to drive one or several of them from office and into open opposition. It is no doubt arguable whether such "politics of accommodation" are preferable in developing countries to an alternative pattern within which more coherence and unity of government is achieved by shedding those who, though remaining in the party, are in fact hostile to the main direction of its policies.[15] It is hard to deny, however, that such accommodation has been an important characteristic of politics in Tanzania. The Cabinet includes several Ministers, in particular Mr. Babu, who are professed Marxists with a Peking orientation. It also includes a majority who are little interested in the internecine controversies of international communism and for whom Marxism appears to have little appeal. Equally significantly, the Cabinet also in-

15. The relevance of the Tanganyikan approach to countries whose national unity is so precarious that they might not be able to contain a sustained conflict between two major parties in deep conflict is, however, worth noting.

cludes Ministers whose style of politics, whose predilection for emotional anti-Western statements, whose susceptibility to racist African appeals, and whose inability to interest themselves in and cope with the detailed administrative work of a Ministry are in marked contrast to the honest commitment to nonalignment, the passionate belief in racial equality, and the serious preoccupation with development which mark the values of President Nyerere. Yet somehow all have been contained, and contained with comparative success, in a single Cabinet.[16] A political achievement of this magnitude must have its costs. Two are relevant to this article. The first is a tendency to avoid issues which might deeply divide senior Ministers. The second is a determination to handle any crisis which has divisive implications slowly and with great caution.[17]

These characteristics in the political life of Tanzania and the continuing high value which is attached to the maintenance of the unity of the national movement inevitably blunts the determined pursuit of many major policies. There will always be a tendency to shy away from the hard decisions which will offend an important section of the party or will seriously alienate an important leader within it. The effect of this upon development has been extensive. Thus the discussions of a national wage policy and of a national investment policy were not pressed to a conclusion. Neither, when it touched upon politically sensitive points, was discussion on the assurances by which the Government would best encourage private investment.

The politics of accommodation also lessened the ability of the government to respond critically to actions or proposals from some senior Ministers, even if they were likely to have adverse economic consequences. One can note in this context that Mr. Kambona's allegation in September, 1964, that the United States was secretly planning the overthrow of President Nyerere's government, although it rested on clumsy forgeries and was clearly damaging to Tanzania's relations with one of her major supporters, did not lead to an immediate rebuke or even to a categorical public denial of the allegations by the President. This particular crisis may have been a factor contributing to the later demotion of

16. In the last five years only four senior Ministers have been dropped, one when charges of corruption led to a court case (which was, however, unsuccessful), a second primarily as the result of a long-standing battle with Mr. Kambona, a third who clearly could not cope with a Ministry, and a fourth who was defeated in the October 1965 election. All now hold other prominent high offices.

17. The characteristic which I am here calling the politics of accommodation (a phrase for which I am indebted to Dr. Carol Fisher) can reasonably be cited as an important reason why the United Republic of Tanzania, formed in March 1964 when Tanganyika and Zanzibar united, has been able to sustain itself despite the extraordinary degree of autonomy which Zanzibar, because of its separate military establishment and its quite different political orientation, has been able to insist upon. The union has also, however, increased the strains involved in the exercise of the politics of accommodation and has raised its costs.

Mr. Kambona but, given the higher commitment to the maintenance of a harmonious national movement, the demotion of Mr. Kambona from the Ministry of External Affairs had to be handled with consummate skill (as it was) if his cooperation within the movement was to be retained.

In any country, then, in which a high priority is attached to the containment within the national movement of a very wide range of political opinions, compromise and concessions will lessen the single-minded pursuit of economic development. When such a policy of accommodation coincides with a period of extreme political crisis, the risk is that the maintenance of the unity of the party may be such an all-absorbing endeavour that the maintenance of development planning will be lost sight of altogether. The truth of this proposition was forcefully illustrated in Tanzania between January 1964 and October 1965. 1964 began with the revolution in Zanzibar which brought to power on that island the Afro-Shirazi Party which had historic ties with TANU but within which there was an important group of Moscow- and Peking-oriented Marxists. The revolution in Zanzibar was followed shortly by an army mutiny in Tanganyika which can be explained primarily by conditions in the army but which nevertheless severely upset the country's political life and required British intervention to suppress it. Union with Zanzibar, dramatic and exhilarating as it was, introduced an unsettling element into Tanganyikan politics, for the Zanzibar Revolutionary Council has to this day blocked almost all attempts to make union a reality. As the Zanzibar regime has its own battalions, one Chinese-trained and one Russian-trained, which are only nominally integrated into the Tanzanian army, President Nyerere has no means save his political skills with which to make the union a reality. In this situation each fresh indication of Zanzibar's determination to maintain her extraordinary autonomy has an unsettling impact on mainland politics and on the Cabinet's *esprit de corps*.

During 1964 there developed an increasingly sharp controversy first with Uganda and then with Kenya about the possibility of an East African Federation. When it became clear that such a Federation was unlikely Tanzania pressed for reforms in the economic relations of the three countries, which she claimed were in consequence essential. The need in this situation simultaneously to assert Tanzanian rights and to avoid a chauvinistic policy of autarky created further internal political strains. Finally, during the latter half of 1964 and throughout the first months of 1965 Tanzanian relations with each of the three major Western powers, Britain, the United States, and Germany, so far the chief sources of foreign aid, deteriorated in turn. In each case the crisis was dramatic and the damage to relations severe. Not only was the loss of foreign assistance which resulted from these foreign policy crises itself serious but inevitably also they entailed a reappraisal of the meaning which Tanzania attaches to its policy of nonalignment.

It is small wonder that, in the face of this series of major political difficulties, President Nyerere had little time or energy to devote to the processes of development planning. Not until late 1965, when a measure of comparative tranquillity had been restored to the political scene, was there any major effort to focus the Government's attention on economic development and to revise the political and administrative arrangements for development planning.

The Tanzanian experience supports a number of propositions relating to the administration of economic planning in newly independent states:

1. Economic planning, if it is to be effective, must be viewed as a continuing process in which the production of a plan marks an important stage in the process but is not its main purpose. The uncertainties are so many that no plan can remain the final word for many months. Unless there is an annual plan, a continuous process of revision of the plan, or some other means of bringing up to date a Five-Year Plan, it will very quickly be so out of date as to be irrelevant to policy making.

2. There must be political machinery which will ensure that new policy proposals are assessed in relation to the Plan and in terms of its basic economic priorities. There are bound to be decisions taken in defiance of these priorities, for every government will have other pressing matters to which it must attach high priority. There will also be pressure from individual ministries for the acceptance of proposals outside the Plan. But economic planning can hardly be said to occur if decisions such as these are taken without their economic costs being identified, their impact on the implementation of the Plan assessed, and other ministers being able to reaffirm the case for a primary emphasis on development.

3. There are certain administrative requirements for development planning—an adequate flow of information from the spending ministries, planning units in the major ministries, an adequate and professionally competent staff in the planning unit, for instance. Major administrative weaknesses in other ministries will decrease the rate of development but do not preclude effective planning. Indeed, they may make it all the more important. But such weaknesses must be anticipated by the planners and their plans must take account of them if the Plan is not to be hopelessly and discouragingly overoptimistic.

4. The Tanzanian experience underlines the argument that the planning unit must not be drawn into operational responsibilities. The planners should be responsible for the draft plan, for a continuing review of its adequacy, and for reporting fully to a political authority on progress

PRATT: *The Administration of Economic Planning in a Newly
Independent State: The Tanzanian Experience, 1963–1966*

being made, sector by sector and ministry by ministry, in its implementation. But they are not omnicompetent. The correction of inadequacies they uncover must lie within the ministry or ministries whose performance has disappointed; and if ministry officials are reluctant or obstructive demands insisting on such corrections must come from a political source of unquestioned authority.

5. The Tanzanian experience is relevant also to the debate on where the planning authority is best located in government. It provides an excellent example of the weaknesses of any system which expects a minister of no greater standing than his colleagues to exercise planning responsibilities over other ministries. It suggests, however, that it is not enough, in reaction to this fact, merely to locate the planning unit in the Office of the President. The period during which the Directorate was in the President's Office, but was in fact the direct responsibility of the Ministers of State, showed that this arrangement was little better than having the Directorate as a separate ministry. Only if the head of state, or possibly a vice-president of unquestioned political authority, is directly and intimately concerned with planning will the necessary discipline be imposed to ensure that priorities are respected and targets vigorously pursued.

6. The literature on economic planning in developing areas stresses that many plans have been undermined or ignored because of a lack of sufficient political commitment to planning. The Tanzanian experience illustrates the importance of the political factor. It also suggests, however, that what is involved is more than just the commitment of the political leaders. Political harmony has been maintained in Tanzania through an exercise in political accommodation which is an obstacle to the single-minded pursuit of development planning. Moreover, Tanzania has illustrated the fact that in periods of political crisis other political preoccupations may be so demanding that neither the machinery of government nor the political leaders will have the additional capacity to effect the major innovations or to take the further difficult decisions which effective economic planning is likely to entail.

Part VI   THE POLITICS OF RACE

*T*o the general pattern of political evolution in black Africa, there is one area that constitutes a vast exception, Southern Africa: Mozambique, Angola, Southern Rhodesia, and, above all, the Republic of South Africa. Of South Africa, the question most frequently asked is, When will the explosion take place? Revolution is expected momentarily, and—if oppression and injustice be sufficient cause—for good reason. Political repression and economic exploitation are nowhere more visibly blatant. Race differences, compounded by class differences, creates an insurmountable obstacle to any effort on the part of the European dynasty to erect a façade of legitimacy. The lower classes, the vast majority of black and colored, cannot identify with the existing system. As authority diminishes, South African society as now constituted relies increasingly on naked force. A growing consciousness of their deprived status stirs the black population.

In theory, apartheid claims to be far more than a policy of segregation. Official doctrine argues that every race has a special genius that must be encouraged to develop along its own lines. Separation of the races, then, for the purposes of this theory, ultimately benefits all individuals, according to the apologists for apartheid. Insofar as the European races are technologically and scientifically productive, these talents will continue to result in higher education and social services per capita than in any African country, for blacks as well as whites. Indeed, having the most advanced industrial economy in all of Africa, the Republic can and will trade and provide technical assistance to other black-controlled nations. Finally, according to this theory, Africans will assume final political autonomy in their own self-controlled enclaves, the so-called Bantustans for Bantus.

In practice, apartheid would require a price white society is unable and unwilling to pay: complete economic disintegration. Without black labor, the mines, factories, shops, and even homes cannot operate. White minorities have buttressed their entrenched economic position by political legislation going back even before the Franchise Acts of 1936 that took non-Europeans off common voting rolls. The ruling Nationalist Party has piled atrocity upon atrocity. The Suppression of Communism Act, first passed in 1950 then amended to broaden its power, defined *communism* to include any protest against racial regulations. Native Laws Amendment Acts of 1952 and 1957 prohibited Africans from attending white churches, schools, clubs, hospitals. The Industrial Conciliation Act of 1954 declared strikes by Africans illegal. Past laws regulate every aspect of a person's movements from country to city, from home to work, from night to day. By the Bantu Education Act of 1957, the state determines who will be the professionals and who the manual workers. Group Areas Acts of 1950, 1952, and 1956 locate housing and business in areas by race. By the Mixed Marriages Act of 1949 and Immorality Amendments Act of 1950, even some of the oldest African families have had a son or cousin suddenly declared to be racially black.

These legal foundations of apartheid have constantly been expanded and interpreted by additional decrees and judgments. Mary Benson's testimony to Congress clearly reveals the accumulated repressive effect of these measures. Today, to even mention the name of one held to be an enemy of the government is sufficient cause for punishment. Stanley Trapido analyzes the economic stake of the Afrikaner in maintaining political control, demonstrating that his very social existence requires positions of government command. Together, these two articles demonstrate both the coercive mechanisms and the intensity with which the Boers are willing to use them to maintain their continued hegemony. If Africans have not yet revolted, small wonder. Yet, if it is true that men rise up not because of despair, but out of hope, then surely the winds of change are blowing even in the southernmost part of Africa today.

Giovanni Arrighi in the third article of this section provides the essential background to the unilateral action of Southern Rhodesia's ruling white minority in arbitrarily declaring their country's independence from Great Britain. Because this action precluded the possibility of majority government, black Africans vehemently expressed their opposition and violent conflict on both the domestic and international plane at one moment appeared as a most definite possibility. Arrighi analyzes and relates the economic base of the Rhodesian social system to recent political events and attitudes.

| Mary | **POLITICAL LIFE IN** |
| Benson | **SOUTH AFRICA TODAY** |

.　　.　　.　　.　　.　　.　　.　　.　　.

Personal testimony

I feel an extreme sense of urgency in testifying to you. In South Africa the major forces that have struggled for freedom and a sane society have been crushed for the time being. The state, with its massive armaments and wealth, is supreme. Others who have testified to you have warned of the dangers not only for South Africa but for the world at large. The time to confront the South African government is now. In five to ten years' time it will be more powerful, more tyrannical. It gave me hope in South Africa to read that Ambassador Goldberg had said: "We have reached a junction in history when we must act." I trust you and your committee can help influence the policy beyond words that are becoming cliches to imaginative action.

Today I feel intensely the difficulty of expressing all I have been a witness to in South Africa in the past sixteen months because it is still so close. And I feel an overwhelming sense of responsibility toward those friends, or people whose experience I know something of, who are silenced and cannot speak for themselves because they are in jail, or under severe banning restrictions, or banished, or are denied passports.

Another factor is how strange I feel, partly due to the unexpected and profound psychological effects of house arrest and bannings, and of the risks constantly run in South Africa if one is to be at all true to one's self; but largely I feel strange because living there, for anyone involved in opposing the evils of white supremacy, is like being in the frontline of a battle, and when one withdraws, the outside world seems unreal. Even now, in the freedom of Washington, I dream of the security police, and of my fears. Yet what I personally experienced is mild compared to what thousands and thousands there are suffering—besides, I

Reprinted in abridged form from testimony before the Subcommittee on Africa, Committee on Foreign Affairs, United States House of Representatives, in *United States-South African Relations,* May 24, 1966, Government Printing Office, Washington, D.C., 1966, pp. 464–477, with permission of Mary Benson.

knew that so long as I wasn't actually imprisoned, I could, with a British passport, leave the country.

How can I bring it all to life for you? How to convey the shattering deterioration between the time I was last there, in 1962, and when I returned in December, 1964? In that time the government had succeeded in blasting a chasm between white and black. There has been a scattering, as after a bombardment. Quite apart from the fact that most of my black friends were in prison or in exile, and their wives restricted, the laws, the enforced physical separation of whites and blacks, and sheer mistrust, have shriveled the possibility of contact. And again, as I shall try to show, there was a further deterioration just in the time I was there, between the end of 1964 and April, 1966. Of course, investors would see only the short-term expansion in trade, the rise in profits.

I notice your press handout mentions my friendship with Nelson Mandela. Actually it was not through him, but the Anglican Bishop of Johannesburg, that I became secretary of the Treason Trials Defense Fund in South Africa in 1957. When I returned to South Africa in May, 1961, Mandela had organized a nationwide stay-at-home, yet one more nonviolent protest from Africans. The State retaliated by ruthlessly suppressing the protest with all the forces it could command.

I met Mandela underground at the time and he told me, with bitter regret, that after fifty years of disciplined nonviolence the Africans had been driven to the conclusion that the increasingly organized violence of the state could only be answered by counterviolence. Thereafter, sabotage broke out, mainly against installations, but resulting in a handful of deaths. The saboteurs hoped thereby to impress on white South Africa and Western investors the gravity of the nonwhite people's affliction and the urgency of their anger. But as you know, within three years they were routed, most of the leaders were imprisoned for life, a number being executed. Meanwhile, young white intellectuals had also turned in despairing frustration to sabotage, one even to a terrorist act, while other Africans resorted to anarchistic rioting and murder in several incidents in the Cape.

.   .   .   .

I'm sure Mandela, now with about 1,000 other men imprisoned in Robben Island's maximum security jail, would be glad to know I have come before you, but as he is, like almost all nonwhite political prisoners, graded category D, he can have only one letter, and one half-hour visit every six months.

I wish I could imbue you with a feeling of what it is like in South Africa today. How on the surface there is law and order, stability, as the government and British and American investors like to point out; how on the surface there is white complacency and black apathy; and we know little of what goes on below except that now and then something breaks surface, as happened last October.

There was a trainload of African workers—as always monstrously overpacked for they, not being voters, can be pushed and shoved around like that, and the train crashed, killing scores—in all ninety-one; whereupon enraged survivors turned on the first white man they saw, who in fact was coming to their aid, and battered him to death. No, for the most part we can only guess what goes on below the surface.

South Africa then, is a "stable" country, but at what cost. The leaders of the Afrikaner people, those once notable fighters for freedom, have not the courage, the generosity, nor the common sense to extend freedom to others. Instead, as a rare and splendid Afrikaner, the Reverend Beyers Naude, has pointed out, there are more and more parallels to Nazi ideology in Afrikaner nationalism; not only in the methods used to "preserve" the white race and "Christian Western civilization" but in the fear which is "freezing South Africans into silence and acquiescence."

When you come to think of it, the Afrikaner extremists and the sinister Broederbond who rule South Africa, most of them admirers of Hitler, in all the world find avowed support for their policies only from Portugal, from the Rhodesian rebels, and from a handful of societies like the Ku Klux Klan, the John Birchers, and the League of Empire Loyalists.

But of course there is the other kind of support; support that is tangible however much apartheid may be verbally castigated, and despite the denial of arms to the present government; support that comes from many English-speaking white South Africans and from British and American investors, not to mention the implicit support of the policies of some Western governments, including Britain and America. Such is the power of gold.

You have had first-rate testimonies from several people. All I can contribute is a few examples of what has become the South African way of life, as I saw it, in 1965 and 1966. In essence, what is being done to people there is this, which is their only life on this earth:

In Johannesburg, recently, there were at night regular police raids on domestic servants' quarters. All who were not actually employed at each house were arrested: husbands, boyfriends, wives, children, etc. In one raid, for example, 800 police "netted" 800 men, women, and teenagers. The raids were followed by mass trials, not in courts but in the cells, with four magistrates, in one instance, trying 1,000 people in three and one-half hours. A police officer was reported to say:

> We have to have these raids. We've caught five or six housebreakers among the petty offenders. . . .

In 1962, near Cape Town, I visited a young African woman and her four children, who were being forcibly driven 500 miles from her husband and from the *pondokkie*—the small shack—(in the sandflats "reserved" for nonwhites) which she had cherished into a safe, neat home. This still goes on—she is but one of thousands; and in April last year in the Black Sash Advice Office near Cape Town, I again listened to pathetic appeals from Africans facing the enforced break-up of their families.

Simply to satisfy an apartheid edict, Indians continue to be torn from homes and businesses in towns they have helped to prosper and are stuck miles outside in underdeveloped country. Other edicts, toward the end of the year, killed off District 6, the traditional home of colored people in Cape Town; they, like Africans, will be confined to bleak sandflats. And through the year, the Immorality Act took its toll with reputations, lives destroyed. All these laws and edicts are idiotic.

Idiotic—for South Africa, prosperous, spacious, could easily provide opportunities and security for all its racial groups were it not for the life-denying ideology of its rulers. And food they could provide too. Yet, when I passed through the Ciskei, one of those African areas where many live on the borderline of starvation, an African clergyman to whom I gave a lift, from being stolidly taciturn, suddenly burst into a passionate description of how children in his village on some days of each week went without food. Government aid is begrudging, and offers from voluntary societies are frequently rejected by the authorities who like to pretend there is no starvation.

Perilous, then, is the sickness of South Africa. For white supremacy does not simply breed cruelty, it brings with it intellectual decline and moral decadence, not only in the small Afrikaner tribe which seeks self-preservation through tyranny, but among the English-speaking whites mainly preoccupied with profit and pleasure. What a waste it was when young liberal intellectuals felt constrained to attempt ill-conceived sabotage. In court many of them spoke of the futility of their acts.

But if present policies are regarded as abominable, think of what lies ahead. Mr. Balthazar Vorster, the Minister of Justice, who was detained in the 1939–1945 war for his subversive, pro-Hitler activities, has been given and will continue to grasp more and more power. Education of Afrikaner youth, Afrikaner newspapers, the state-dominated broadcasting system, combine to isolate, to indoctrinate.

A number of the elite of Afrikaner youth at the University of Pretoria —among them perhaps future Cabinet Ministers—expressed their contempt for Opposition United Party speakers at the election in March by throwing chairs and violently preventing meetings from taking place. Is this surprising when their leaders regard "liberalism" and "humanism" as dirty words? One of the few Afrikaners to maintain the best in their forebears, independent, brave and generous, the Reverend Beyers Naude, set up the Christian Institute—dedicated to a loving God. He is constantly harassed by fellow Afrikaners in authority.

I should mention one seeming aberration on the part of the state that confuses people abroad: the fact that a few fearless people can express perpetual criticism of government policies without being silenced. Well, of course, Alan Paton's passport was withdrawn, as was that of Laurence Gandar, whose editorials in the *Rand Daily Mail* are a source of inspiration to many South Africans, black and white. One factor is that it's convenient for the government to present an apparently free press to the world and, besides, these men are internationally distinguished, which still has meaning for a government that spends a fortune in trying to whitewash its image, as Dr. McKay revealed.

Inevitably justice was long ago subverted by the spate of unjust laws. While I was there, a number of cases drew fierce comment from the few English-language newspapers still putting up a fight. To mention only one case: four young white men were convicted of raping an African woman after three of them had assaulted her escort. Three were sentenced to six strokes of a light cane and the fourth to six strokes with an adult cane, and a year's imprisonment suspended for three years. In an editorial Laurence Gandar remarked: "Just imagine it: a half an hour's sharp pain and a week or so of discomfort for one of the most serious and revolting crimes in the book. From the court proceedings it is quite clear that this was a particularly vicious and brutal episode. The men had been drinking that evening but according to the evidence of a white girl at whose home they had been for a time, they were not very drunk. They had left saying it was a good night to chase 'kaffirs.' After passing sentence the judge recommended these men should make use of their free time by joining a club." As the editor pointed out, had the rapists been black and the raped woman white, they would surely have been sentenced to death.

But the area where justice is most blatantly being subverted by the whole process of the administration of the laws is the Eastern Cape where important American automobile and other factories flourish.

It was in this area that Africans first felt the glow and excitement of new ideas and of education brought by missionaries from the 1830's on. In those days Africans there even had the vote. Outstanding African intellectuals and leaders emerged, and the area became the center of militant African activity.

Now the security police are intent on purging the area, particularly Port Elizabeth's African townships, of the last drop of political consciousness. But the purge goes further, it is aimed at the very heart of this society, at the qualities of independence, self-respect, and mutual trust, without which human beings become corruptible.

During the past two and one-half years, about 1,000 men and women have been arrested there, and in innumerable trials most have been charged with membership in the unlawful African National Congress or, in fewer cases, in the Pan-Africanist Congress. None of these cases is concerned with acts of violence, which would go before the supreme court, but increasingly the state produces evidence of talk of violence.

The local press had barely reported these trials and I was the first overseas correspondent to do so. It is painful to try to tell you about it all—what I witnessed was peculiarly sinister and odious. The accused, usually simple men and women, are held for between five and nineteen months, awaiting trial. If they crack under interrogation, which may include assaults and sometimes physical or mental torture, and agree to give the necessary evidence, they become state witnesses. Those who somehow hold out become the accused.

The Johannesburg *Star* has spoken of "the practice of arresting in haste and collecting evidence at leisure." Frequently the charges relate to actions allegedly committed three or four years ago, making it almost impossible to prove an alibi, yet state witnesses unable to recollect recent events, can give precise "evidence" about 1961, which, however nonsensical, they recite with an air of pride.

I found one state witness had already given evidence against sixty people, another learned his evidence off by heart, one had the history of a man in the pay of the police. They would vehemently deny torture or pressure of any kind. They had come to court to tell "the truth" and —in a startlingly repetitive manner—they would volunteer: "I was not forced to make a statement."

Increasingly their corroboration of small details of what happened in 1961 or 1962 stretched one's credulity. It was like hearing parrots come to court.

Virtually all the trials are held in camera, in villages remote from Port Elizabeth, on the grounds that state witnesses fear intimidation or reprisals, with resulting difficulty in finding defense counsel and in the press being able to attend, so that a dreadful pall of anonymity settles over them.

But where injustice is most apparent, though blessed by the law, is in the framing of the charges, for these have been broken down under multiple counts: membership in an unlawful organization, furthering its aims, collecting funds for it, attending meetings, allowing premises to be used for its meetings, distributing leaflets, the maximum sentence on each count being three years with, in some cases, each meeting, each leaflet, treated as a separate count.

The severity of sentences can be imagined: whereas in Johannesburg admitted rank-and-file members of the Communist Party—who collected subscriptions, distributed leaflets, painted slogans, and attended more than twenty cell meetings—were sentenced to two years, in the Eastern Cape ANC, and PAC members have been sentenced to up to ten years for a lesser series of activities.

The charges are framed under the Suppression of Communism Act which, as I'm sure you know, covers any particularly effective and active opponent of the government and has been used far more widely against African nationalists and white liberals than against the small group of Marxists.

One man, Tommy Charlieman, a trades unionist aged about sixty, after being imprisoned in four different jails for a total of nineteen months, was released in December, 1964, without any charge being laid. In January, 1965, he wrote to the Minister of Justice claiming damages for loss of health and wages. He was then rearrested, and charged with ANC membership and other counts emerging from a meeting in November, 1962. He was found guilty and sentenced to eight years. On appeal his sentence was reduced, I believe, by three years.

I attended several days of the trial of Nursing Sister Mpendu and followed the case subsequently. She, a middle-aged woman, had been trying to get a passport to study pediatrics in Britain when she was arrested in March, 1964. She was held, in prison—apart from a brief couple of weeks when bail was allowed—for sixteen months, awaiting trial. When defense counsel questioned the security police sergeant in charge of her case about this period, he replied it was "perhaps not too long." He added: "There were others who were more important, who had waited longer." Yet bail had been withdrawn from her fifteen months before and the state prosecutor had given as a reason that she was the "most dangerous" of the sixty-one prisoners awaiting trial before the court at the time.

Fifteen months in prison, a "most dangerous" woman, and when it came to her trial she was charged with a different set of facts from those for which she was arrested. The prosecutor declared her case centered on the "disposal of a motor van."

It was alleged that her man had been given the van by the ANC, and, after his arrest, she had taken over its sale. She denied the charges. State witnesses said she told them the sale was to raise money for the ANC, and would be used—according to one or another of them—for ammunition, explosives, firearms, petrol bombs, machineguns, rifles, revolvers.

For long days Sister Mpendu was made to sit on a backless bench while the case toiled on. The small courtroom was under a hair-dressing salon, next to a polo ground and a railway siding in a rich orange-growing area. The court had constantly to be adjourned because of the din of shunting trains. Eventually the magistrate, describing her as an evasive, hesitant witness, found her guilty on four counts: ANC membership, raising funds, having an ANC meeting in her house, and stamping a receipt with an ANC sign. All that talk of violence and not a single bit of evidence in relation to violence.

Allowing for the eighteen months she had by this time been in custody, he sentenced her to a further two and one-half years—in all, then, four years.

Men already fined or imprisoned for an offense are recharged years later for the same offense. Thus the employees of a bus company in Port Elizabeth were fined about $22 each in 1961 for having gone on strike, which is illegal for Africans. Three-and-a-half years later a score or more have been rearrested. It was then alleged that the strike had been organized by the African National Congress and, after more than a year awaiting trial in prison, they have now been sentenced to four, or four-and-a-half years' imprisonment.

Some found "not guilty" have been promptly rearrested. And now a new refinement has been thought up by the state: instead of releasing those who are completing their sentences, it is charging them again with violations of the same law. So far 160 or more have been named for this repeated incarceration. Imagine the feelings of the family of the prisoner —just as they are preparing to welcome him or her back. The first case, Dixon Fuyani, after serving two years before he left prison was sentenced to seven more. The second, Benson Ndimba, after two-and-a-half, to four and a half more.

I wish there were time to read you parts of my notes of the evidence and cross-examination in some of these trials. Perhaps I could tell you briefly about one other case I observed, in which a young white woman was found guilty of attending an ANC meeting in 1961.

The court sentenced her to four years' imprisonment, "with a prayer in its heart." On appeal the Supreme Court set aside the conviction. As the *Rand Daily Mail* commented:

> . . . This was a case in which the state relied heavily on the testimony of accomplices—who gave their evidence in the presence of the security branch. It was a case in which the defense claimed that one state witness had changed his story after spending an overnight adjournment with a member of the security branch; that another had learned his evidence off by heart; and that yet another had been in the pay of the security branch.
> Whatever the truth of these claims may have been, the fact is that the judge president of the Eastern Cape has now rejected the state evidence of five accomplices and declared that it was quite inconceivable that Miss Neame was ever a member of the ANC—as they had all sworn she was. . . .

(Incidentally, the judge did not ask why state witnesses should choose to lie about a white woman unknown to them.)

Much as I've taken of your time to tell you about the Eastern Cape trials, I am aware of how inadequately I've conveyed the reality of what is going on. The hopelessness that often deadens the atmosphere in the courts, the anguish of the families, their struggle against hunger, for even when a welfare committee is allowed to function it can afford less than $7 a month for each family. To provide school fees, clothes, and books has been virtually impossible.

"Law and order" has been maintained. The security police are in control. And they are there to stay.

Virtually all defense in the hundreds of political trials and in the appeals (a number of which have been at least successful in reducing sentences) has been paid for by the Defense and Aid Fund, of which Alan Paton was a leading member. I wish you could have seen the dedicated work of its organizers, battling selflessly against all the obstacles the state and security police could contrive, in order to see that people had some defense.

Over the years, hundreds of men and women have been saved from imprisonment or have had sentences lessened, through the efforts of D&A. It was clear the security police were enraged by its activities. Over many months last year police pressure intensified as one after another of the fund's workers were banned from its activities and placed under grim personal restrictions. Then two months ago the Minister of Justice outlawed the entire fund. The penalties for furthering its aims are one to twelve years' imprisonment, as in the ANC and PAC cases. When I came away, political accused were having to defend themselves.

.   .   .   .

This picture is dark. But I was in a court one day when the defense brought on a witness, Terrance Makwabe, straight from Robben Island prison where he was serving a two-and-a-half-year sentence. He was a slight, modest-voiced man who looked much younger than his forty-five years. The prosecutor rose to remind him that the effect of his giving evidence might well lay him open to renewed prosecution and a further sentence. He agreed. "Why then," asked the prosecutor, "was he giving evidence?"

"Andi soyiki," Makwabe replied. The interpreter translated: "He says 'I am no longer afraid.' "

It was a marvelous moment.

The weapon of "banning" has been part of the South African way of life since 1953. It is a penalty unique in the history of criminal law. No charge to answer, no trial, no effective appeal, nor can you protest as it is illegal for anyone to publish your remarks. Suddenly one day police arrive on the doorstep and, in my case, they handed me eight pages of bans beginning "Whereas I Balthazar Johannes Vorster, the Minister of Justice, am satisfied that you engage in activities which are furthering or are calculated to further the achievement of any of the objects of communism, I hereby in terms of subsection . . . prohibit you," and then it goes on—which I was supposed to study and absorb while they stood over me. The bans are under the Suppression of Communism Act and have been used to punish and silence Liberals far more than Marxists, and have been used in a deliberate policy of attrition to crush nonwhite trades unions.

There are about twenty-five different bans, with the Minister constantly thinking up new ramifications. For instance, in my case he almost doubled the previous number of restrictions on writing so that it became impossible to write anything at all for publication and even difficult to write letters. The novel I was working on had to be stopped. Alan Paton expressed his view to me: "This is to my mind unpardonable, not so much because it may take away your living but because it denies you the right to use gifts that are given you—that to me is one of the things that is within the province of God, not of the state."

About 520 people are at present "banned." Almost all are restricted for a five-year period in which they cannot ever leave one town, or one African township, or even one small suburb. Among new restrictions are those that forbid people to go into specified buildings. This increasingly deprives people of jobs. An African factory worker, for example, is banned from any factories. Mrs. Helen Joseph, the English-born social worker who was among the accused in the treason trial and who has done so much for the banished men and women in South Africa, after being house-arrested and under considerable bans for a number of years, recently had an extension of these bans which prevents her entering a building in which there is a trade union. She works for a medical aid society in the same building as a trade union. At the time when I left I heard that she, a woman in her late fifties, was trying to teach herself touch-typing in the hope of getting a secretarial job. Mr. Congress Mbata, banned just after I was, a research officer for the Institute of Race Relations, under the ban can no longer go into that office. On his behalf, a deputation of distinguished men, including two former judges, tried to see the Minister of Justice, but were curtly rejected. One colored writer, among the handful placed under twenty-four-hour-a-day house arrest, is also banned from writing and has to rely upon his wife keeping the family going.

I found painful the restriction on having any visitors. And, of course, even partial house arrest at nights, weekends, and holidays destroys one's social life. At Easter, for instance, I was confined throughout. For the first time in my life, I really felt my spinsterhood. But harshest of all, after the ban on writing, was that on social gatherings. Nowadays this is being interpreted in law as a banned person and one other. Tea, lunch, even conversing, are dangerous unless the gathering occurs casually or fortuitously. I sometimes went to town and walked the streets hoping to bump into friends. I wrote to the magistrate, to whom one can apply for exemptions, explaining that as a spinster with few relations, I would like permission to have occasional meals with my sister and brother-in-law. This was refused. On occasions when I made a discreet date with somebody to meet in a coffee bar, I did so with a lawyer's warning ringing in my ears, that it was all right for me to decide to take the calculated risk, but if I were arrested the person I was meeting might be called as a state witness against me; no one wants to be a state witness, and to refuse to be one could lead up to a year in prison.

I found the psychological effects disconcerting. The police had no sooner left than I felt a distinct drop in self-respect at the realization that I was obeying a series of bans from Vorster. I was tempted to disregard them and go on living in the ordinary way. But the thought of the penalty of between one and ten years for breaking most of the bans deterred me. Then came paranoia; not only from the thought of probable security police surveillance, but almost immediately it was as if one had the plague, and, from getting several phone calls a day, I felt excited if three or four people phoned me a week.

All this just arbitrarily slammed on one by the Minister of Justice because he can't find one guilty of any offense, even under the fantastic network of laws he already has at his disposal. About forty-five people have been partially house-arrested, and about twelve imprisoned in their own homes under total house arrest. Once a week I had to report to a police station and sign the parole book, but some, Helen Joseph for instance, have to report daily to the police station; the penalty for failing to do so is up to ten years' imprisonment. Professor Julius Lewin, of the University of Witwatersrand, has spoken of the grim uncertainty about the extent of these bans in the lives of every banned person. No lawyer can advise the client with any assurance whether attending this or that type of gathering or entertainment is safe. For instance, in the courts, snooker has proved all right on appeal, but bridge or tennis involving four persons has resulted in a sentence. A banned girl who climbed a mountain with two others and had a picnic on top was sentenced to two months, suspended.

A man who sat in the kitchen while a party took place and spoke to one person at a time, coming into the kitchen, was sentenced to a year, suspended. These suspended sentences hang over the person's head. In effect, what is meant—because I found every other day I was breaking one or the other of the bans—was that the police only had to watch consistently for a time to collect some bit of evidence.

Cruelest are the bans and house arrest orders that are immediately served on men and women who had been charged, tried, and sentenced to terms of imprisonment and, upon serving those sentences, have returned to their homes and families, only to be put under the severest possible restrictions—520 people banned, 520 lives broken up, and how many more hundreds or thousands intimidated from action as a result.

Almost the only protests recently have come from a handful of English-language newspapers, from Mrs. Helen Suzman, the Progressive MP, from the Black Sash, the Liberals, and one or two others. It was not till the Minister banned a student leader, Ian Robertson, who was to have been the host to Senator Kennedy in a week or two's time, that protests really became significant. There have been student marches and large protest meetings of citizens. In Johannesburg a few days ago, more than 1,500 people unanimously resolved to call on the Minister to charge or release those who are banned and restricted without a trial. As Uyskrige, the Afrikaans writer and poet, remarked: "What extraordinary habits we are acquiring. It seems to have become an old South African custom to accuse a man, or a woman for that matter, of something extremely serious, clap him in jail or ban him or silence him by other means, and afford him no trial, give him not the least chance to defend himself."

Far more atrocious are the physical and spiritual deserts and abysmal poverty to which African men and women, particularly those who have resisted the government's tyranny in tribal areas, are banished, some for many years on end. A report on thirty or more so condemned only reached the South African public after the New York *Times* had carried it.

The Security Police and Imprisonment Without a Trial

Above all, what came as a sickening shock to me on my return was to witness the corruption induced by widespread intimidation—*terrorism* would not be too strong a word for it—from the security police and their increasingly sophisticated interrogators. As a result South Africa is now riddled with informers. Sometimes, as you have been told, strong men have been broken by torture, three were driven to suicide under the 90-days law. That vile law was withdrawn in January, 1965, only to be replaced in September by a law precisely twice as terrible, the 180-days law. The first man so held tried to commit suicide. Since then about forty more men and women have been thus kept in solitary confinement for up to six months, without a charge, while they are interrogated with the object of inducing them to become state witnesses. The security police have developed a brilliant aptitude for psychological torture—through nonstop interrogation while the prisoner is held in isolation or through forcing prisoners to stay awake or remain standing for days on end. Most of those released are silent but one woman, Mrs. Violet Weinberg, after three months' imprisonment, told the court she had made a statement to the police only after relays of security men had questioned her continuously for three days. She was kept awake and standing, she said, with the physical effect of alarmingly swollen legs—her ankles hanging over her shoes—and her eyelids swollen till her eyes were slits. As a result of this and the intense psychological pressure, she had made a statement, but this she refused to repeat in court, choosing further imprisonment rather than to become a traitor. (Of course, there are those who simply out of self-interest turn traitor and give evidence against their friends.)

Inside South Africa legal experts have drawn attention to the failure of a number of judges to reject evidence given by such detainees, evidence which should be treated with the greatest suspicion. And a leading Progressive, Mr. Hamilton Russell, has referred to "the mountain of authentic evidence from experts that solitary confinement amounts to mental torture which is sometimes more serious than physical torture."

In Britain, three MP's of the different political parties said there was little doubt that numbers of state witnesses have been brainwashed in solitary confinement to give whatever evidence the police required of them. But a handful have superbly held out as Mrs. Weinberg did, preferring to serve terms of imprisonment rather than lose their souls.

In the trial of Abram Fischer, the Afrikaner descended from the President of the Orange River Colony, who became a Communist in the 1930's and who has had a distinguished legal career in South Africa, and a young woman, Mrs. Lesley Schermbrucker, a 180-day detainee, refused to give evidence for the state against Fischer. In an article Nadine Gordimer, the novelist, describes the moment:

> She turned to the magistrate . . . and said, "I've decided that not at this stage or any other stage will I give evidence. And I'm prepared to face the consequences."

When warned that she could be sentenced to a year's imprisonment if she maintained her refusal, she again said no. Miss Gordimer writes:

> She was sentenced to 300 days and she went down in the well of the court in the peculiar, awkward silence produced in onlookers by the spectacle of courage.

While on the subject of Fischer, who was sentenced to life imprisonment for conspiring to commit sabotage, along with Mandela and others who two years previously were thus sentenced in the Rivonia trial, may I quote from the *Manchester Guardian* in November, 1964, where I said, "Today, when the norm among white South Africans is to be fearful, apathetic, and mean, Fischer's country should be proud of the extremism with which this man gives himself. And when Afrikaner Nationalists have become rigid conformists, they should honor this 'son of our soil' (as a magistrate called him) who has kept the spark of rebellion against repression alive."

From studying the history of South Africa for the books that I have written about the African struggle for freedom there, and from personal experience in the days of the treason trials in 1957 when I first got over my bitter prejudice against Communists by knowing some of them as individuals, I have felt with ever greater regret the failure of Christians, in particular, to identify ourselves with that struggle. If only, instead of being terrified of being tarred with the same brush as Communists, or instead of competing in a negative manner, we could seek to transform our own too-inadequate record. I was glad that a member of the Society of Friends made a similar point to you. It is ironic that it is to a handful of white Communists who befriended Africans over decades that we owe to a large extent the refusal of so many African leaders to turn racist.

Protagonists of the South African system may reject the picture I have given as mainly of political "agitators." What then of the government's vaunted Bantustan, the Transkei, or of Zululand, to mention only two tribal places, what of the moderate men who lead the oppositions there? The government's favorite weapon against them has been to block passports to such fine men as Knowledge Guzana, leader of the opposition multiracial party in the Transkei, and Gatsha Buthelezi, a senior Zulu chief, both of whom had been looking forward to taking up State Department invitations to travel in the United States. This is just one more proof of the farce of the government's claim that these areas are heading for freedom and self-government.

And what more ludicrous a showing up of the government's color policy and the convenience of its prejudice than the case of the Japanese who have been made honorary whites—because they buy pig-iron—while Chinese and Indians and colored South Africans continue to be harshly discriminated against?

But having said all this, having given first-hand impressions of what

Mr. Nielsen called "the most flagrant and clearcut case in the world today of oppressed colored people by white people as a matter of official policy," I haven't given you the extra dimension provided by the few who continue to struggle on, not only bravely confronting the evil, but at times even creating. It would be indiscreet to say more for fear this little also would be destroyed. But I wish I could communicate to you the wonder of knowing these people. Even in the time I was there, the ranks thinned significantly—some were forced into exile because bans prevented their making a living, others were taken into 180 days or were cut off from normal life by bans. While I was amongst those few remaining, there was the constant refreshment of their company, inspiring and delightful. When one looks around the world—so much of it in a mess—and then thinks of these few of all races and beliefs, one feels inspired to carry on, to believe that perhaps a better future can be won.

I wonder if you realize that many in South Africa feel your country is their greatest hope. Perhaps if you thought of them as constituents you could imagine their anxious expectation? It is not only because the United States is the most powerful country. It is not only that they have given up expecting anything from Britain, with its billion pounds bound up in South Africa. It is that you have a very particular history and that you here are striving—with whatever stumbling and prevarication—to cope with a history of racial oppression and the resulting disasters. Your experience can help them, action on their behalf can help you.

Britain and America are deeply, irrevocably involved in South Africa —through investment and profits gained. Some of your firms have their fingers deep in the pie of Eastern Cape industry, and, as you now know, in the Eastern Cape terrible things are being done. Britain and America are involved because Dr. Verwoerd vaunts himself as a bulwark of Western Christian civilization and, in the lineup so far, has in fact been treated as such, and they are involved through Christian and educational connections.

South Africa is a microcosm of our world: in its races, its religions, its political beliefs, in its perilous division into "haves" and "have-nots." If no constructive way out of the deadly impasse is found and found soon, how can our world hope to survive?

Stanley
Trapido

POLITICAL INSTITUTIONS AND AFRIKANER SOCIAL STRUCTURES IN THE REPUBLIC OF SOUTH AFRICA

*T*he long-term Afrikaner drive for power has been strongly influenced by the demographic structure of the South African electorate. Within the framework of the primary political system, secondary structures make deviations from the demographic patterns extremely difficult. The purpose of this paper is to trace the relations between the population cleavage and the composition of basic social institutions, and their bearing on the distribution of political power; and to raise the question of the viability of the resulting system.

Let us start with demography. Power in South Africa resides in the two white linguistic groups—the Afrikaans-speaking descendants of mainly Dutch settlers and the English-speaking descendants of mainly British settlers—and parliamentary party affiliations have come to be determined almost entirely by linguistic and cultural ties; that is, by the structure of the society. The demographic composition of the electorate[1] (Table 1)—three voters speak Afrikaans to every two who speak English—has tended to influence the direction that the political system has taken. Because Afrikaners were always a majority of the electorate there were, amongst their political leaders, some who saw that if those who spoke the

1. In 1936, for every 100 English-speaking persons over the age of 20 there were 115.5 speaking Afrikaans. In the age group 7 to 20 there were 180.2 Afrikaans-speaking persons for every 100 English-speaking. The figures are even more significant for the group under 7 years of age. For every 100 found in the English language group 215 were found in the Afrikaans group. In these figures we can account for the growth of the Nationalist party's vote. See C. G. W. Schuman, *Die Ekonomiese Posisie van die Afrikaner* (Nasionale Pers) 1940. There are indications of a more recent decline in the birthrate of Afrikaners. A preliminary report of a survey made by a commission of inquiry undertaken by the Dutch Reformed Churches in Pretoria showed that in a sample of 1,551 families the average number of children was 2.37. The families from which the parents came had 6.19 children per family, a decrease of 62 per cent in one generation. *Natal Mercury*, 1 December 1959.

Reprinted, with an original postscript, from *The American Political Science Review*, Vol. 57, No. 1 (March 1963), pp. 75–87 by permission of the author and publisher.

Table 1—Home Language of South African Whites, by Age Groups, 1936

Age Group	AFRIKAANS-SPEAKING		ENGLISH-SPEAKING		AFRIKAANS AND ENGLISH	
	No.	%	No.	%	No.	%
Under 7 years	195,266	65.4	90,783	30.4	7,249	2.4
7 to 20 years	343,005	61.8	187,948	33.9	13,907	2.5
21 years and older	585,499	50.6	504,340	43.8	29,175	2.5
All Whites	1,120,770	55.9	783,071	39.1	50,411	2.5

Afrikaans language voted, not as workers, or farmers, or protectionists but as Afrikaners, then political power would be theirs. General Louis Botha, inverting von Clausewitz, had declared after the Boer War: "the battle which was won and lost in the fields of war must be fought again upon the political platform."[2] The history of party politics in South Africa is little more than an account of the various attempts, and the ultimate success, of Afrikaner leaders to attain this objective.

No attempt will be made here to give an account of that story. Rather in the pages that follow we shall try to show that—given the primary drive of electoral demography—Afrikaner economic, religious, and educational structures have tended to bolster, reinforce, and even add momentum to the drive for Afrikaner political power.

Afrikaners have always occupied a limited number of roles in the economy, and this has made comparatively easy the political leaders' task of creating homogeneity within the language group. The roles themselves, however, have tended to necessitate the holding of political power for their protection and advancement. The English language group with its far greater diversity of economic roles could, in the thirties and fifties, lose political power and still prosper. Presumably it might continue to prosper if that power was transferred to nonwhite groups. Not so for the Afrikaner. He had first to gain, and then to maintain, political power or be submerged as an economic group.

The homogeneity in the economic structure is reproduced in religious and educational institutions. The socialisation and recruiting processes now ensure that the Afrikaans language group and the Nationalist party's electorate coincide. Afrikaner political leaders, because of their awareness of the political function of church and school, long ago set out to control them as necessary adjuncts in the struggle for power. The integration of these institutions within the framework of the Nationalist Party's *Weltanschauung* provides the political structure with an extremely rigid cementation.

2. J. A. Coetzee, *Politieke Groepering in die Wording van die Afrikanernasie* (Johannesburg, 1941), p. 323, citing *Pretoria News*, 5 July 1905.

1

From the earliest beginnings of his separate identity the Afrikaner was a pastoralist or hunter—often a frontiersman—trading with the faraway towns, or the pedlar who wandered up and down the Cape Colony and beyond.[3] The Dutch-*cum*-Afrikaans word *Boer*—which means farmer—was interchangeable with *Afrikaner* in the nineteenth century. From the third quarter of the nineteenth century, however, the needs of the recently begun mining industry encouraged the improvement of commodity production and led to the greater concentration of agrarian units. This South African version of the enclosure movement led inevitably to displacement and the creation of a class of landless Afrikaners. At the same time the system of inheritance in operation in the nineteenth century and derived from Roman-Dutch law led to an uneconomic subdivision of farms and a consequent addition of those forced to seek work away from the land. This ". . . irrational subdivision and the primitive, wasteful, and unsystematic farming as of old harmed both the land and its owners. . . . For many families such an inheritance became a sure road to pauperdom."[4] By far the greater majority of these people, who came to be known as poor whites, were Afrikaans-speaking.[5] From their ranks were drawn the recruits for the urban white working class. Until quite recently the vast majority of Afrikaners have been either farmers[6] or members of a dispossessed working class. In South Africa, as we shall attempt to show, the occupants of these areas of the economy depend on the control of political power. Given a *laissez-faire* social order, groups playing other roles in the economy would—either because of their skills or their capi-

3. S. D. Neumark, *Economic Influences on the South African Frontier 1692–1836* (Stanford University Press, 1957), gives an excellent study of the frontier economy which dispels the idea that the frontiersman was a subsistence agriculturalist. Of the frontier I. D. MacCrone has written that "it is not merely a place or a population, but a process. While it certainly retains its geographical and demographic overtones, its main significance lies in what it does to a people who are subject to its influence over a number of generations." *Journal of Race Relations*, Vol. 28, No. 3 (July–September 1961). For a full treatment of this proposition see his *Race Attitudes in South Africa. Historical, Experimental and Psychological Studies* (Witwaters-rand University Press, 1957), pp. 328 ff.

4. C. W. de Kiewiet, *A History of South Africa, Social and Economic* (Oxford University Press, 1950), p. 191.

5. R. W. Wilcocks, "The Poor White Problem in South Africa. Part II, Psychological Report," *Report of the Carnegie Commission* (Stellenbosch, 1932), p. 1.

6. The 1936 census reported 87.5 per cent of white farmers to be Afrikaans-speaking. U.G. 11–42, *Sixth Census, 5th May, 1936*, Vol. VII, *Occupations*. Similarly, the 1946 census showed 85.54 per cent or 143,022 out of 167,198 whites employed in agriculture, to be Afrikaans-speaking. U.G. 41–54 *Population Census, 7th May, 1946*, Vol. V. *Occupations and Industries*, p. 42 (male) and p. 54 (female).

tal—be able to cope with the free play of market forces.[7] This is not the case for the majority of white agriculturalists and workers.

South Africa is poorly endowed as an agricultural country[8] and farmers have had a great deal at stake in controlling the state. The state has provided them with laws and law-enforcing agencies that have reduced to a minimum the mobility and bargaining power of the non-white labor they employ, and as a consequence, reduced the wages they would otherwise have had to pay. At the same time the state has constantly subsidized and protected South Africa's white farmers.

As early as 1908 [writes de Kiewet] the Transvaal Director of Agriculture declared that during the past twenty years more money had been spent per head on South Africa's farming population than any other country in the world. Much of the resources which were transferred to the rural industry was a waste of capital and not investment for the future.

The same writer has also noted that between 1910 and 1936 the State spent £112,000,000 from revenue and loan funds for agriculture.[9] There has been no abatement in this subsidization. The amount provided for agricultural subsidies for 1960–61 was £17,090,000, and the estimated expenditure on subsidies for the year ending March 31, 1962, is £15,818,500.[10] In addition very large sums were provided by the Land and Agriculture Bank. In 1959 the Bank provided loans worth £31,533,-244, whilst the amount for 1960 was £17, 463,896. All in all the Bank is owed £60,255,008 in long-term loans by individual farmers and £10,-616,270 also in long-term loans by cooperatives. In addition cooperatives owe £68,955,774 in short-term loans. The use to which the loans have been put is revealing (see Table 2).

Thus only 7.4 per cent in 1959 and 6 per cent in 1960 were employed in making fixed improvements, purchasing stock and equipment and for running expenses, whereas 67.4 per cent in 1959 and 49.5 per cent in

7. These skills or capital have been acquired in a color-bar society. The proposition, however, is made on the basis of the society as given.

8. "Agriculture in South Africa is poor and precarious. Much of it is beyond the reach of modern science and technical progress. The expenditure and effort required to overcome many of its handicaps are too great to be profitable. Indeed South Africa is not an agricultural country. It has no natural advantages which by the help of science and organization could win for its agricultural prod-

ucts a truly commanding position in the markets of the world. Of its pastoral products wool alone was able to compete successfully in the open market. Without subsidy and under conditions of free competition much of the land could not be economically cultivated." De Kiewet, op. cit., p. 259.

9. Ibid., p. 260.

10. UG 1 and 30—1961. Agricultural Economics and Marketing. Vote 46, p. 275. Estimates of the expenditure to be defrayed from revenue account during the year ending 31 March, 1962.

Table 2—Purpose of Land and Agriculture Bank Loans[a]

Purpose	1959	1960
Purchase of land	£ 7,954,222	£ 7,779,416
	25.2%	44.5%
Redemption of bonds	£15,125,637	£ 5,478,746
	48%	31.4%
Consolidation of debts	£ 6,118,179	£ 3,165,203
	19.4%	18.1%
Fixed improvements	£ 577,420	£ 310,978
	1.9%	1.8%
Stock and equipment	£ 1,622,396	£ 709,052
	5.1%	4.1%
Running expenses	£ 135,390	£ 20,501
	0.4%	0.1%
Total	£31,533,244	£17,463,896

[a] See G.P.S. 1029998, *Annual Report of the Board of the Land and Agriculture Bank of South Africa 1960*, Table II, p. 9, Table III, p. 10 and Statement of Liabilities and Assets, for loan figures in this table and in the text.

1960 went into the redemption of bonds and the consolidation of debts. At the same time 25 per cent in 1959 and 44.5 per cent in 1960 was set down for the purchase of land which would presumably soon provide additional sources for subsidy.[11]

The political rigidity of the agricultural community is not difficult to comprehend. Nor must we forget that every white agricultural community in Africa, so long as it held power, restricted representation to its own ethnic group. Where they have now extended representation, they acknowledge a decline in their power. English language communities in Natal, Southern Rhodesia, and Kenya have shown closer ideological affinity with Afrikaner farming communities than with urban members of their own language group.

11. The size of this assistance to the white agricultural community of no more than 400,000 persons can be gauged by comparing it with the recommendations of the Tomlinson Commission which urged the spending of £104 million in the next ten years to provide for the economic development of the reserves. Of this sum £55 million was to be interest-bearing and recoverable. The commission said that £9 million would be required for the first year of their program. The Minister of Native Affairs did not accept the Commission's recommendations and claimed that at most £36.6 million would be required over a twelve-year period, an average expenditure of £3 million. The population of the reserves in the 1951 census was 3,633,000.

TRAPIDO: *Political Institutions and Afrikaner Social Structures*
in the Republic of South Africa

II

The role of the white workers in South Africa was determined, at the crucial stage of industrial relations there by members of the English language group. The Afrikaans working class was, at the turn of the century, both small and disorganized. The first major battles between employers and labor in South Africa were between the mainly English-speaking white mine workers and the mining companies.

Table 3—Members of Dutch Churches as Per Cent of White Population, 1904–1936[a]

Town Area		CENSUS YEAR		
	1904	1921	1926	1936
Johannesburg and surrounding areas	13.7	19.0	20.7	23.8
Cape Town and surrounding areas	11.5	16.7	18.4	22.7
Pretoria and surrounding areas	30.0	40.8	43.1	4?.5
Durban and surrounding areas	0.4	3.8	5.3	8.5
Port Elizabeth	4.0	17.7	22.2	30.0
Kimberley	11.5	18.8	20.3	29.4
East London	4.7	13.5	15.0	16.8
Pietermaritzburg	1.8	7.8	9.6	15.5
Bloemfontein	—	44.0	45.9	56.9
Municipal of Germiston	18.5	33.3	38.4	44.2
Boksberg	18.0	32.4	34.6	40.4
Benoni	—	23.1	23.5	30.3
Brakpan	—	39.1	35.2	45.5
Springs	15.3	22.6	28.9	35.0
Roodepoort	27.8	29.9	31.2	36.8
Krugersdorp	32.0	39.2	55.3	51.9
Total	—	19.4	21.0	25.7

[a] Source: S. D. Pauw, *Die Beroepsarbeid van die Afrikaner in die stad.* (Stellenbosch, 1946), p. 127.

The latter sought to increase their nonwhite labor force and had they succeeded there would have been an increase of economic equality but by means of depressing white workers' living standards. Given the structure of the society it was inevitable that white workers should want a share in political power in order to maintain their relatively higher standard of living. With political power white workers have established statutory rights to a vast range of skilled and unskilled occupations.

<u>Virtually every trade or craft is closed to Africans. Increasingly fewer remain open to coloreds and Asians.</u>[12]

At the beginning of the twentieth century Afrikaners were almost entirely a rural people. By the third decade they were well on their way to becoming an urbanised one. This becomes apparent when we examine Tables 3 and 4.

Table 4—Birthplace of Persons Residing in Pretoria, 1936[a]

| | PERCENTAGE OF EACH AGE GROUP | | | | | |
Birth Place	0–4 Yrs.	5–14 Yrs.	19–34 Yrs.	35–39 Yrs.	60+ Yrs.	Total
Pretoria	77.6%	44.8%	19.0%	7.2%	2.5%	34.8%
Other towns	5.5	5.1	6.1	5.1	3.8	5.4
Transvaal rural areas	14.8	44.3	59.2	56.0	44.6	45.2
OFS rural areas	0.7	1.3	6.8	10.3	16.8	5.1
Cape rural areas	0.1	2.9	7.7	19.2	29.8	7.9
Natal rural areas	0.9	0.8	0.4	1.4	0.4	0.8
Outside	0.4	0.8	0.8	0.8	2.1	0.8
No. of persons in sample	904	1,422	1,497	787	238	4,848

[a] Source: S. D. Pauw, Die Beroepsarbeid van die Afrikaner in die stad. (Stellenbosch, 1946), p. 129.

The vast majority of urban Afrikaners have been found in low income groups. Sheila Patterson contrasts the incomes of the English- and Afrikaans-speaking populations in Johannesburg in 1952.[13] Only 1.5 per cent of Johannesburg's Afrikaans-speaking population had an income of £1,000 or more as opposed to 10 per cent of the English-language group. Only 10 per cent of Afrikaners but 16 per cent of the English-speaking group earn between £600 and £1000. At the same time 51 per cent of Afrikaners but only 40 per cent of the English-speaking population had incomes of less than £600 whilst 37 per cent of the Afrikaans group and 34 per cent of the English group were nonearners. Presumably a very

12. The Mines and Works Act (No. 27 of 1956), originally passed in 1911, prohibits Africans from doing skilled work in the mines. The Native Building Workers Act (No. 27 of 1951) prohibits African building workers from working in "white" areas. The Industrial Conciliation Act (No. 28 of 1956), as amended in 1959, reserves specified types of work for persons of a defined racial category. Determinations reserving work for whites have included: all skilled work in the clothing industry; the driving of motor transport vehicles in the Durban municipal cleansing undertaking, and fifteen categories of work in the Durban steel engineering and metallurgical industry; passenger-lift attendants and workers in the domestic appliances industry.

In addition, although the Apprenticeship Act (No. 37 of 1944) does not exclude Africans from apprenticeships, established practice in all trades prevents their being registered under the Act. The Industrial Conciliation Act and the Native Labour (Settlement of Disputes) Act (No. 48 of 1953) place obstacles in the way of African Trade Unions and specifically exclude them from the States collective bargaining arrangements.

13. The Last Trek (London, Routledge and Kegan Paul, 1957), p. 163.

large proportion of English-speaking nonearners were dependents who did not need to add to the family income. Afrikaans-speaking nonearners were more likely to need to supplement the family incomes but were insufficiently skilled to obtain employment in industry and commerce and unwilling to compete with Africans as low paid and unskilled laborers. Latterly, what Afrikaners have considered the indignity and insecurity of competition have been removed as a result of Job Reservation.

A similar pattern was revealed in Durban (Natal) in 1951 where the English language group had a mean income of £571.75 and a per capita income of £298.93 as compared with the Afrikaans group that had a mean income of £410.78 and a per capita income of £185.04.[14] In addition, increased mechanization has meant that the majority of urbanized Afrikaners are semiskilled or unskilled workers who have acquired their ability to perform production line tasks in a fraction of the time required to produce a journeyman. Until very recently the vast majority of skilled occupations, as would be expected from the income distributions, were filled by persons from the English-language group. This is strikingly illustrated from the 1946 census figures, in a breakdown by language group of persons employed in transport and communications (Table 5).

Table 5—Transport Employees, by Language Groups, 1946[a]

	English Home Language	Afrikaans Home Language
Rail	25,795	54,552
Road	5,253	9,607
Air	1,132	175

[a] Source: UG 41–54. *Population Census, 7 May, 1946.* Vol. V, *Occupations and Industries of the European, Asiatic, Coloured and Native Population,* p. 78.

Afrikaans-speaking persons form the overwhelming majority of employees in rail and road transport where the majority of tasks performed are either unskilled or semiskilled. Of the 16,109 whites employed as laborers by the railways, 14,837 were Afrikaans-speaking. But whilst two thirds of the white workers employed by the railways were Afrikaans-speaking, 33 out of 44 heads of departments were at that time English-speaking.[15] Similarly in the industrial professions (see Table 6) the vast majority were drawn from the English-language group.

14. L. Kuper, H. Watts and R. Davies, *Durban. A Study of Racial Ecology* (London, Jonathan Cape, 1958), Table XXII, p. 89.

15. UG 41–54. *Population Census, 7 May, 1946.* Vol. V, *Occupations and Industries of the Europeans, Asiatic, Coloured and Native Population,* pp. 48, 50.

Table 6—Industrial Professions, by Language Groups, 1946[a]

Profession	English Home Language	Afrikaans Home Language
Electrical engineering	1,277	156
Mechanical engineering	990	93
Mining engineering	630	34
Structural engineering	35	5
Civil engineering	1,701	189
Industrial chemists	1,097	272

[a] Source: UG 41–54. Population Census, 7 May, 1946. Vol. V, Occupations and Industries of the European, Asiatic, Coloured and Native Population, p. 52.

The Afrikaans workers, largely unskilled or semiskilled, surrounded as they are by a nonwhite population with a depressed standard of living, have been, and are, in an even more vulnerable position than their English-speaking predecessors. For them economic security can only be obtained if they are able to participate in political decision-making. Whilst more and more Afrikaners have entered the professions, and the imbalance between the two white groups has been redressed to some extent, the pattern of political behavior of the various nationalist Afrikaner parties was established during the period when the Afrikaners' economic roles were restricted to those of urban workers or farmers. This pattern has now gathered a momentum of its own and is difficult for the new class to defy because the majority of Afrikaners are still workers who depend on the state for the maintenance of their relatively advantageous standard of living. The Afrikaner professional classes show little evidence of wishing to defy the pattern for, although they no longer require the state's protection, political office, which in most cases they held, is dependent on maintaining the support of the Afrikaner working class.

Another area now occupied almost exclusively by members of the Afrikaans language group comprises the lower grades of the civil service. By 1936 59 per cent of whites employed in public administration were drawn from the Afrikaans language group.[16] Initially this *Afrikanerisation* of the civil service was largely determined by considerations of patronage but with time the question of power has become paramount. The pattern that has emerged suggests that it is the policy of the Afrikaner party to take control of all the key positions of state. But whatever the reasons that have led to the domination of the civil service by members of the Afrikaans language group, what is important for our argument is the fact

16. UG 11–42, *Sixth Census . . . 1936, op. cit.,* p. 13.

that the Nationalist Party has thereby created a large body of men and women with a vested interest in an Afrikaner party remaining in power. To share power with an English-speaking party would be to share patronage, particularly in the upper and middle grades of the administration. To allow a nonwhite political victory would be to end the statutory recognition of the color bar and lead to the dismantling of the enormous bureaucracy dependent on it.

In the last two decades a considerable effort has been made to gain an Afrikaner foothold in the commercial, industrial, and mining activities of the country. In 1939 an *Ekonomiese Volkskongres* brought together many prominent members of the Afrikaner community. These included Drs. Verwoerd, Donges, Van Rhijn, and Diederichs who were to enter the cabinet when the Nationalist Party came to power in 1948. Various Afrikaner organizations were employed to ensure that Afrikaners kept their savings "in the Afrikaner stream."[17] Members of the Afrikaans-speaking group were induced to insure only with Afrikaner-owned insurance companies, to build their homes with the aid of Afrikaner-owned building societies, and to bank with Afrikaner-owned banks. Dr. Diederichs, who was to become the Nationalist Minister of Economic Development, told the 1939 *Ekonomiese Volkskongres:* "As regards the relationship between business and sentiment, it has been our standpoint that business could not be based purely on sentiment, but that an Afrikaner business could in no way exist without sentiment."[18] In short, the entrepreneurs' economic activities coincided with the need for Afrikaner political unity.

These activities have contributed to remarkable economic progress by the Afrikaner group, and the rate of their development has been far in excess of the economy as a whole. Thus the turnover of business undertakings owned by Afrikaners increased from 5 per cent to 11 per cent of the national total in the ten-year period 1939–1949. In that decade the number of Afrikaner industrial undertakings rose from 2,428 to 9,585 whilst the turnover of these undertakings increased from £6 million to £44 million. Similarly the turnover of commercial undertakings increased from £38 million to £204 million. By 1949 Afrikaner entrepreneurs were estimated to be in control of 6 per cent of the country's industry and 25 to 30 per cent of its commerce. In this same period 1939–1949, the number of Afrikaner directors and manufacturers increased almost threefold, and business managers and traders slightly more than twofold. Nevertheless Afrikaner economic endeavors do not yet begin to compare with those of the English language group. In 1939

17. *Liberation*, September 1957, H. Lawson, pp. 11–23. 18. *Natal Mercury*, April 1959.

Afrikaners formed 3 per cent of the directors, 8 per cent of the business managers, and 4 per cent of the traders among the white urban population. Despite rapid strides these proportions had only increased by 1949 to 5, 15, and 10 per cent of the respective categories.[19] In February, 1959, Hermanus Martins, the Nationalist member for Wakkerstroom, told the House of Assembly that "The Afrikaner as far as mining is concerned, owns only 1 per cent of capital; in the industrial field only 12 per cent; and in the commercial field only 25 per cent." He claimed that Afrikaner capital controlled only £18 million of the £218 million invested in the wholesale trade.[20] On the other hand Dr. M. S. Louw [a leading Afrikaner financier], is quoted as having estimated the Afrikaners' share of commercial enterprises at an even lower figure. "It is a fact" he is reported to have said, "that 60 per cent of South Africa's white population controls only from 15 to 25 per cent at the outside of a certain sector of the economy." Of this 15 to 25 per cent share of commerce at least 80 per cent is located in the rural areas and this, as has been pointed out, means that "the Afrikaners' participation in commerce consists of a large number of small enterprises, not several big ones."[21]

Afrikaners have, as Dr. H. J. Simons has pointed out in a seminal essay, "shown an acute awareness of their relatively weak position in the economy and look to the state to provide opportunities that are not readily available under a system of free competition."[22] Economic structure fosters the political structure.

Whilst the state and Afrikaner private enterprise have been major employers—Dr. Louw has said of the *Ekonomiese Volkskongres* that it had as its "real aim . . . to strengthen already existing businesses and to *found and build up new Afrikaner undertakings which would give employment to Afrikaner boys and girls*"[23]—they could not provide positions for the entire language group. Hundreds of thousands of Afrikaner workers were forced to find employment in a commercial, industrial, financial and mining environment that has always been dominated by non-Afrikaners. Since the Afrikaans-speaking workers are comparative newcomers to an industrial society they had to be provided with new economic and political institutions. The potential of the Afrikaans working class has long intrigued political leaders. During the first election campaign of the new South African state in 1910 Louis Botha had already formed a rival workers' association to the English-speaking

19. D. P. Goosen, ed., *Triomf van Nasionalisme. Die Sakewereld-'n halfeeu opkoms en groei*, Johannesburg, 1953, pp. 715-718; S. Pauw, *op. cit.*, pp. 235-236.
20. *House of Assembly Debates*, February 5, 1959, Col. 458.
21. *Forum*, July 1961, Stanley Uys, p. 12.

22. H. J. Simons, "*Social Structures and Power in South Africa.*" Unpublished paper presented to the Africa Seminar, University of Cape Town. 8 pages (1960), p. 7.
23. Sheila Patterson, *op. cit.*, p. 168 (my emphasis).

Labour party.[24] It was only in the 1930's, however, that a systematic attempt was made to bring the Afrikaans-speaking working class within the framework of Afrikaner institutions. At the first *Ekonomiese Volkskongres* in 1939, it was reported that of the 118 trade union organizations 100 had non-Afrikaner secretaries though their membership might often be as much as 80 per cent Afrikaner.[25] And of those trade union leaders who were Afrikaans-speaking, it appears that few were *nationalgesind* (nationally oriented). A systematic and well-organized attempt was made to undermine the trade union movement for fear that the Afrikaans workers might be drawn away from the Nationalist Party. It has been said of that Party's electoral victory in 1948 that the white (Afrikaner) workers "brought the Nationalist Party to the position it occupies today and [they] will keep it in that position in future."[26]

Despite this claim, however, the Nationalist Party continued to feel uneasy about the position of the Afrikaner workers in the trade union movement. The chairman of the Redingsdaad Bond declared in his report in 1952:

> The Afrikaner worker is today forced to subject himself to the existing trade unions so that approximately half of the Afrikaner nation is today ensnared in the powerful machinery of the trade unions . . . an enormous task awaits to rescue the Afrikaner nation from the claws of this unnational power.[27]

Similarly Dr. Donges, a former leader of the Nationalist Party in the Cape Province, stated: "The foreign influences must be removed from our trade unions . . . and they [the unions] must take their place four square on a national basis," and it was "the task of the Redingsdaad Bond to keep the Afrikaner worker in the midst of foreign elements in his Church, language and volks environment."[28] From this latter statement to the exhortation to Afrikaners "to fight Communism, and help our

24. *Progressive Monthly*, Vol. 3, No. 5 (October 1909) noted: "The recently formed 'Labour' organization entitled 'Arbeid Adelt' held a meeting at the Lombardy Hotel on 14th September. . . . The society is supposed to be a labour organization formed for the benefit of the unskilled workers, but it is regarded in many quarters as a political move, designed for the purpose of alienating the Dutch-speaking workers from the Labour Party, which has plainly intimated that it will not support the Het Volk, as it did at the last election." The *Round Table*, Vol. 6 (1915–16),

p. 356, notes of the Nationalist Party fighting its first election that it "promulgated a domestic programme designed to attract labour support. . . ."
25. Sheila Patterson, *op. cit.*, p. 154.
26. Ray Alexander and H. J. Simons, *Job Reservation and the Trade Unions* (Cape Town, 1959), p. 8, quoting Cabinet Minister B. J. Vorster, *House of Assembly Debates*, February 6, 1956, Col. 1047.
27. Sheila Patterson, *op. cit.*, p. 168.
28. Gwendolen Carter, *Politics of Inequality*, p. 259, quoting Dr. T. E. Donges, "Die Toekomsrol van die R.D.B. in ons Ekonomiese Lewe," 4 pp.

own factory workers in their fight against it"[29] is no very long jump. The Suppression of Communism Act, one of the first major legislative actions taken by the Nationalist Government on their coming to office, was directed, to begin with, as much at the leadership of white non-Nationalist (many of whom were Afrikaans-speaking) non-Communist trade unionists as at nonwhite and allegedly Communist-influenced organizations. It was not specifically aimed at Communists. The function of the Act was to remove non-Nationalists from the leadership of the predominantly Afrikaans-speaking working class. B. J. Schoeman, who was to become Minister of Labour in the Nationalist Government, had long threatened that the trade union movement would be shorn of its powers and what "powers the union will have left will be in the hands of the volk, for all foreigners, *kaffirboeties*, Communists, and parasites will be removed."[30]

A striking example of the use of the Suppression of Communism Act is the case of E. S. (Solly) Sachs who was, in 1952, removed from his position as secretary of the Garment Workers Union. He had been expelled from the Communist Party in 1932, and had in addition a Supreme Court judgment that he was not a Communist. Nevertheless he was deemed to be a Communist by the Minister of Justice and compelled to withdraw from the activities of the union. It would seem that the major reason for his incurring the Nationalist Party's wrath was the influence he exercised over Afrikaner workers.[31]

29. *Ibid.*, p. 247, quoting *Die Johannesburge Skakelkomite Sekretariale Verslag*, November 1951–October 1952, 24 pp.
30. E. S. Sachs, *Rebels Daughters* (London, McGibbon and Key, 1957), p. 146.
31. Sachs notes, *ibid.*, pp. 138–139, that in 1938 at the time of the Voortrekker centenary celebrations his union decided to form a "Kappie Kommando" of women, dressed in the traditional Afrikaner costumes, who were to take part in celebrations. Sachs received the following letter from a D. B. H. Grobbelaar: "I enclose herewith a specimen copy of a pamphlet published by me, in which I point out the mockery of our national traditions your participation in the Centenary Celebrations will mean. The same applies to Johanna Cornelius and your other Communistic accomplices. The Afrikaner nation is busy uniting—to mobilise its forces against you and your sort. The thousands of Afrikaner daughters whom you have in your clutches will settle with you and, with them, the whole Boer nation, who are finding themselves in the Voortrekker year. Our people do not want anything to do with Communism and the Jews—the high priests thereof—least of all. The day when we Afrikaners begin to settle with you Jews, you will find out that Germany is a Jewish paradise compared with what South Africa will be! The garment workers will very soon be able to handle their Jewish bosses and do not need your so-called 'help.' We Afrikaners acknowledge no 'classes' as you and your satellites are trying to introduce—therefore, we do not want the garment workers as a 'class' to participate in the celebrations, but all together with us as Boers—the factory girl with the professor's wife. You and Johanna Cornelius, who all day organise and address kaffirs—will you dare to bring them also along to the celebrations? They are your fellow workers and 'Comrades.' "
Sachs invited Grobbelaar to share the platform at a meeting of the union and move a motion of no-confidence in his leadership. This Grobbelaar did, and

At the present time most Afrikaans-speaking workers find themselves in unions that are led by *nationalgesindes;* and Afrikaner political power has brought this about. At the same time the organization of Afrikaner workers in what are to all intents and purposes Afrikaner unions is a considerable aid to the maintenance of political power.[32]

III

The structure of the Dutch Reformed (Calvinist) Churches also contributes considerably to the homogeneity of the Afrikaner group and helps to reinforce the political structure. Most Afrikaners belong to one of three Reformed Churches,[33] the largest of which is the Gefedereerde Nederduitse Gereformeerde Kerk (NGK), comprising five autonomous synods, one in each of the provinces and in South West Africa. The other two Afrikaner churches are the Nederduits Hervormde Kerk (NHK) and the Gereformeerde Kerk van Afrika. These divisions are now historically rather than theologically determined, for they all subscribe to the same confessional standards, viz., the Belgic confession, the Heidelberg catechism and the Canons of Dordrecht. They do not represent the same theological diversification that is to be found in the English-language churches in South Africa.

It is a commonplace of South African politics that ministers of the various Afrikaner churches associate themselves with the Nationalist Party. The English-language press is constantly reporting, with some

Sachs claims that at a meeting of over 2,000 persons his opponent could get only thirteen votes.

32. The influence of the English-speaking labour movement should not be overestimated. E. S. Sachs writing in *Forward*, 15 July 1938, noted that "The masses of Afrikaner people, in spite of their ever-increasing poverty, were neither attracted to the Labour Movement nor did they seek entry. They looked upon Trade Unions and the Labour Party as foreign organisations, and the workers' organizations looked upon the Afrikaner people with an air of disdain. . . . Gradually masses of Afrikaner workers entered the mines, railways and factories. But the Labour Movement, although it did modify its policy somewhat towards the Afrikaner workers, and opened the doors of the Trade Unions to them has so far failed almost entirely to try to appreciate fully the development, tradi-

tion, sentiments and aspirations of the masses of Afrikaners. . . . The non-Afrikaners failed to realize that the vast masses of Afrikaners may enjoy full rights abstractly, but in concrete practice they feel as an oppressed nation . . . as a people which suffered cultural, economic and political oppression. People of a ruling race, including even class conscious workers, usually fail to understand the feelings of a conquered nation, of an oppressed people. Let us admit frankly that the Labour Movement in South Africa has failed to give a lead on the national question, failed to orientate itself to the masses of Afrikaner people especially those who live on the land."

33. *Union Statistics for Fifty Years*, A. 26, 1951 Census, 1,402,703 persons were members of the Afrikaans Calvinist Churches; 1,502,791 Whites cited Afrikaans as their home language.

chagrin, that a Nationalist candidate has been nominated or seconded by clergymen, or that clergymen have prayed for the success of Nationalist causes, or offered thanks for their victories.[34] As leader of the United Party, General Hertzog had complained in 1938 of the fact that he could ". . . no longer be oblivious to the fact that there are unfortunately pre-dikants—persons who are paid by their congregations to cultivate the finest and deepest feelings of love and esteem towards one another—who are entangling themselves in party politics."[35] On the other hand there is no record of his having dissociated himself from the political activities of the Afrikaans ministry during the period that he was leader of the Nationalist Party. The relationship between the churches and the Party is clearly understood by the politicians. In the midst of a controversy in which a small group of Afrikaans clergymen critized the Nationalist Government's apartheid policy, *Die Transvaaler*, official organ of the Party in the Transvaal, commented on the heated debate then taking place and the interest that non-Afrikaners were showing in the exchanges. In a leading article it referred to a "resurgence of hope and expectations in the ranks of the enemies of the Afrikaner people" who saw in the "schism and division in the Church" the conditions which could rob the Afrikaner of his strength.

"In such circumstances," *Die Transvaaler* noted, "it is fitting that every Afrikaner should reflect about the situation. This applies to the ordinary members of the Church as well as the Ministry.

"If a struggle should eventuate it can have but one result. It is the Afrikaans Church which will lose and with the Church the Afrikaans people will also lose."[36]

To underline the significance of these arguments, the Prime Minister, Dr. Verwoerd, took the unusual step in a Western society of entering what was primarily a theological debate. In a New Year broadcast to the country Dr. Verwoerd declared:

> I do not intend to discuss recent announcements on colour policy by individual churchmen. It is, however, necessary to correct the wholly wrong impression, created by antagonists of the policy of separate develop-ment that certain Afrikaans Churches have thereby declared their stand-point.

34. *Rand Daily Mail*, 11 September 1959, reported that the Nationalist candidate for Vereeniging, P. J. du Pisonie, had been either nominated or seconded by ministers of the Gereformeerde Kerk, the Nederduitse Gereformeerde Kerk and the Hervormde Kerk. *Natal Mercury*, 24 September 1960, reported that an Afrikaans clergyman had opened a republican referendum meeting with a prayer. *Sunday Times*, 18 October 1959, reported that a prayer of thanks was offered by Reverend S. J. T. Boshoff of Linden outside the polling booth when the election result for North West Rand was announced.

35. Sheila Patterson, *op. cit.*, p. 197.

36. *Die Transvaaler*, 29 December 1960.

The churches have in fact not yet spoken.

Through their synods, at which the members as well as the whole clergy will be represented, the voices of the Churches have still to be heard.[37]

A number of factors might account for the political position adopted by the Afrikaner churches. Their acceptance of the doctrine of predestination and the attendant concept of an elect chosen by God for a special destiny has often been considered a significant determinant. Whilst the elitist political theory of Calvinism may well be a source of support for the Afrikaner group it is not sufficient as an explanation of their political rigidity. Calvinist doctrines have not always given rise to Geneva-type political systems. An examination of the structure of Church government may help us to understand better the role of the Afrikaans churches in the South African political structure.

Church government in the Afrikaans Reformed Churches is popularly based and evolves from the grassroots. The original settlers cast themselves as members of an elite, albeit an open elite. Christians of whatever ethnic origins were accepted into their ranks. The expanding frontier and the importation of slaves gave rise to a series of barriers that finally made Christianity "a jealously guarded group privilege. By virtue of his religion he [the Afrikaner frontiersman] justified his right to dominate the heathen by whom he was surrounded."[38] The nineteenth-century evangelic enthusiasm that marked English-language churches by-passed their Afrikaner counterparts. When Afrikaners did enter upon missionary work, late in the nineteenth century, the South African Republic had established the creed of no equality in "Church and State." Although the NGK has nonwhite members these are confined to mission congregations, and unlike white communicants they do not participate, even to a limited extent, in Church government. The popular basis, therefore, for the white congregations is of considerable importance.

Each congregation has its own elected council of deacons and elders and these councils are responsible for calling their ministers. Congregations are gathered together in rings for local management and the rings in turn combine to form the synod. Laymen join the clergy on both the synod and the ring. A moderator whose office is elective presides over

37. *Natal Daily News*, 3 January 1961.
38. MacCrone, *op. cit.*, p. 127. He reports, *ibid.*, p. 129, a conversation between Dr. Vander Kemp, the famous missionary, and some Khoi Khoin people (Hottentots). A Koi Khoin called Courage asked Vander Kemp if it were not true that God had created them as well as the Christians, and the beasts of the field; "for you know (said he) that the Dutch farmers teach us that He never created us, nor taketh any notice of us!"

the synod. Since congregations call their ministers a selective process operates to ensure that political and social, as well as religious, nonconformity does not appear. Almost all ministers in the Afrikaans churches are South African born and trained. The Afrikaner clergy mirror positions taken up in other sectors of society; but this is to say no more than that the leader of a group is more closely bound to the group's image of itself than any of his followers. The leader, more than anyone else, may not deviate from the norm. . . . Afrikaner clergymen find that social or political nonconformity can lead to their rejection by their congregations and their withdrawal from the ministry.[39] So the Church structure reinforces the Afrikaner political system.

IV

The school teacher's status in the Afrikaner community is traditionally second only to that of the minister of religion. For this reason his

---

39. The Johannesburg *Star*, 27 April 1960, reports that the Reverend Nell, an NGK minister to the Paardekraal Monument (Krugersdorp) community, told his congregants, shortly after the Sharpville and Langa shootings and the mass arrests that followed, "that bullets and imprisonment could not solve the Native problem." A Church council meeting was held shortly after this, newspapers reporting that members of his congregation had taken exception to his sermon. Almost immediately afterwards Mr. Nell resigned for "personal" reasons.

The Johannesburg *Sunday Times*, 30 April 1961, reported that the Reverend A. J. Don had resigned from his congregation and left South Africa for Holland because of his inability to express his opposition to the government's apartheid policy.

The *Natal Mercury*, 8 August 1961, reported that the Reverend Redlinghuis of the NHK resigned from the ministry because, "As a servant of God I am compelled to preach the Gospel in all its consequences. I can no longer do that in my Church."

The Johannesburg *Star*, 16 March 1961, reported that the Synod of the Nederduitse Hervormde Kerk bitterly attacked two of its members who published essays in Vertragde Aksie (Delayed Ac-

tion), a critical symposium on the theological justifications of government policy. Members of the Synod called for their dismissal. The Synod rejected the request by the dissidents for a commission of enquiry to investigate the scriptural validity of the prohibition of non-white membership of the Church. The Synod declared their support for government policy, asking only that it be expedited. The dissidents, the Synod asserted, had started an "agitation" at a critical time for the Church and the Nation when both had their backs to the wall and both were fighting for self-preservation. The deviants were requested to submit to Church law and constitution and were given seven days to "think it over." If they still disagreed they would be asked to resign. A new clause was inserted into the Church constitution which prohibits ministers from publicly criticizing Church policy.

The Johannesburg *Star*, 7 January 1961, had earlier reported that a meeting of 700 people in the Brits Town Hall addressed by ministers of the NGK and the NHK unanimously passed a resolution deploring the publication of Vertragde Aksie and assured "the writers (of Vertragde Aksie) that as long as they retain the views they have expressed they will not be welcome to Brits."

selection is based on much the same criteria, and the *dominee* and the *meester* have always worked together in close cooperation. Leo Marquard has suggested that the system of school committees allows Afrikaner ministers of religion to play an important part in the appointment of teachers and that these appointments are generally made "on religious and denominational grounds."[40] It has been reported that an Orange Free State school inspector declared at a secret conference of the Afrikaner Broederbond[41] that

> The Afrikaans teachers will show the Afrikanerdom what a power they possess in their Teachers' Associations to build up the country's youth for the future republic. I know of no more potent instrument. They handle the children for five or more hours each day for five days in each week, while this contact continues unbroken in hostels and boarding schools for long periods. A nation is born by having its youth impregnated at school in the traditions, customs, ways and ultimate destiny of its people.[42]

This has ensured that almost all children within the Afrikaans-language group have been educated by those in sympathy with the Nationalist Party and intent on transmitting their own values. Educational ordinances in the Transvaal and the Orange Free State have now accounted for those who sought to send their children to English-medium schools. Since 1951, in those provinces the law has insisted that children receive their education in their home language.[43] The ideology that has guided the education of Afrikaans-speaking children is the widely accepted and authoritatively sponsored Christian National Education, where *Christian* is defined as "the creeds of the three Dutch Reformed Churches,"[44] and *National* as "love for everything that is our own with special reference to our country, our language, our history and our culture." The task of the history teacher, according to CNE, is to show that God "willed separate nations and peoples, and has given to each separate nation and people its special calling and task and talent."[45] This conscious socializa-

---

40. *The Peoples and Policies of South Africa* (Oxford University Press, 1960), p. 184.
41. The Broederbond appears to be a coordinating body, linking the activities of the *nationalgesindes* in political, economic, and cultural organizations. See Carter, *op. cit.*, pp. 250–256. General Hertzog in his famous attack on the Broederbond declared that one third of its members were school teachers. "There are few towns or villages in the country where the Broederbond has not already established cells of five to six members, with at least two teachers belonging to

each and whose duty it is to spread Broederbond propaganda." *Cape Argus,* 7 November 1938.
42. The Black Sash, *Education for Isolation.* Vol. 4, No. 5 (September 1960), p. 9, J. Malherbe, "Separation in Schools."
43. This is determined by Education Department officials. Parents sending their children to private (paying) schools may choose the language of instruction.
44. *Christelike-Nasionale Onderwys Belied Federasie van Afrikaanse Kultuur Vereninginge* (1949), Article I.
45. *Ibid.,* Article VI.

tion process has been so thorough that it is unlikely that the new generation of Afrikaners will question the role that the Nationalist Party has created for itself. As Dr. Albert Hertzog has declared: "Mother tongue education is the foundation of Nationalism. So long as there is mother tongue education, so long will there be Nationalism."[46]

Those who find their way to the universities will find similarly structured institutions. Most academics at Afrikaans-speaking universities are South-African born and few have studied abroad. Of these many were students at German universities in the 1920's and 1930's and were not unaffected by the National Socialist doctrines that they came in contact with.[47] One of the four Afrikaans-speaking universities, Potchefstroom University for Christian Higher Education, restricts its choice of academic staff to Protestants. For the most part teachers and research workers in the humanities and the social sciences at the Afrikaans universities have sympathized with the aspirations of the Nationalist Party and have provided the Party with much of its ideology.

The relationship between educational and political structures is most readily seen in Afrikaner student organizations. These were involved from their very beginnings in campaigns conducted to gain recognition for the Afrikaans language and an *Afrikaanse Studentebond* was established in 1916 having as its aims:

> (a) The scientific development of its members in accordance with the traditional character of the Afrikaans people;
>
> (b) The maintenance and furtherance of the Hollands-Afrikaans language, literature, arts and history.[48]

However, in 1924 when a National Union of South African Students was established, all the Afrikaans-speaking universities became affiliated. These were Grey University College (University of the Orange Free State), Potchefstroom University College (Potchefstroom University for Christian Higher Education), Pretoria University, and Stellenbosch University. These affiliations continued until 1933 when the students of Grey University College decided to break away from NUSAS. In giving reasons for this decision the President of the Students' Representative Council re-referred to an "imperialistic spirit" in NUSAS and to the fact that

46. *Natal Daily News*, 19 September 1959.
47. Scholars searching for the roots of African and Asian nationalism have noted that many colonial nationalist leaders were influenced by Socialist ideas that were current during their stay at British, . . . American universities in the period between the two world wars. A similar study of Afrikaner nationalist leaders could profitably examine the influence upon them of German romanticism.
48. N. Rubin, *History of the Relations between NUSAS, the Afrikaanse Studentebond and the Afrikaans University Centres*, p. 2.

A great deal of its membership consists of English members whose main object is to couple South Africa closer to Great Britain as 'home' and for whom South Africa must be maintained as a subdivision of the British Empire. This spirit differs from year to year according to the strength of the section mentioned in the control of the organization. From the nature of NUSAS organisation as an administrative body, there is nothing to prevent them gaining the upper hand. Therefore we say that NUSAS is un-Afrikaans.[49]

At the same time Grey University College accused NUSAS of negrophilism, giving as an example of this

the negative Native policy which was followed at the recent sitting of NUSAS Council. The admission to NUSAS of native students of Fort Hare was simply shelved by saying that the time was not yet ripe for this (a negative proposition which rests on a positive, hidden basis), and that it was not practical or constitutional at the moment. Thus by tactical means NUSAS avoids giving any lead through policy in order to achieve its ideal and its attitude to the native question. As soon as the admission of native students becomes practical and constitutional, something which NUSAS in the nature of things can easily bring about, as the Witwatersrand students suggested—what then? . . .[50]

This particular argument is revealing for it highlights the differences between Afrikaner nationalist attitudes and those held by the English-language group. The accusation was hardly justified for as it has been pointed out, the decision to refuse admission to Fort Hare was taken on specious and discriminatory grounds and was determined by the desire on the part of English-speaking students to maintain contact with the Afrikaans universities. Nevertheless there is a considerable difference between the pragmatic English-speaking groups and their doctrinaire Afrikaner counterparts. Whilst the former sought to bar African students on technical and practical grounds, the latter rejected altogether the principle of giving nonwhite students admission to their association. This distinction is of considerable importance and illustrates the structural rigidity of the Afrikaner group.

The students of Pretoria and Potchefstroom followed Grey College and disaffiliated from NUSAS in August and September 1933.[51] In October, 1933, the *Afrikaanse Nationale Studentebond* was formed. Significantly this coincided with the refusal of Dr. Malan to participate in the coalition government of Generals Hertzog and Smuts. The coincidence goes even further. On the day that the *Afrikaanse Nationale Studentebond* was formed, Dr. Malan addressed the convening conference on "Nationalism as an outlook on life."[52] In fact Afrikaner student

49. *Ibid.*, p. 3.
50. *Ibid.*, pp. 5, 7.
51. *Ibid.*, p. 3.
52. *Ibid.*, p. 10.

organizations appear to have exactly mirrored positions adopted in the political system by the *Nasionalegesindes*. During World War II when Afrikaner political organizations formulated exclusive and chauvinistic programs the *Afrikaanse Nasionale Studentebond* followed suit. At this time (1940–1943) the political leadership of the *Nasionalegesindes* was the object of a contest between the *Hereenigde Nasionale Volks* Party (Nationalist Party), the *Ossewa Brandwag* (a paramilitary mass fascist-like organization) and the *Nuwe Oord* (a National Socialist but elitist "study circle").[53] The latter two organizations stated explicitly that an Axis victory would pave the way to their coming to power. The ANSB unwisely associated itself with the *Ossewa Brandwag* and appointed J. F. van Rensberg, Commandant General of the OB, as their own leader. An allied victory, together with the astute outflanking tactics of the Nationalist Party, spelled the end of the *Ossewa Brandwag's* aspirations and dissolution of the ANSB. The formation of a new body, the *Afrikaanse Studente Bond*, coincided with the final crushing defeat of the *Ossewa Brandwag* by the Nationalist Party and the absorption of its members. The ASB has since 1948 closely followed the Nationalist government's policy and declined requests for cooperation from the English-speaking National Union of South African Students.

The influences.

V

We have traced how the economic, religious and educational institutions of the Afrikaner people add a rigidity to the South African political system that inhibits political concessions to the English-language white group, let alone the nonwhite groups. Yet any and every political system, if it is to survive, has to solve the problems of widening its political frontiers to groups that clamor for inclusion within its boundaries. . . . The dilemma of the South African political system is that whilst it is in dire need of reforming itself, it is structurally incapable of doing so. The consequence of such structural rigidity must be the growth of revolutionary movements. The fact that the Afrikaner government of South Africa has reconstructed both the police force and the armed services, because of the possibility of internal uprisings, means that they have consciously chosen periodic upheavals in preference to the widening of the boundaries of participation. It remains to be seen how long such a political system can survive.

53. For an excellent study of this period see Michael Roberts and A. E. G. Trollip, *The South African Opposition 1939–* *1945: an essay on contemporary history* (London, 1947, Longmans, Green and Co.).

Postscript

Since this article was written in 1961, there have been a number of major changes in the South African environment which, it has been widely suggested, have given Afrikaner politicians far greater flexibility than they previously possessed. It would require more than a postscript to examine this claim, but a brief attempt can be made to assess its validity. In 1960, after police opened fire at Sharpville and Langa on Africans demonstrating against discriminatory legislation, there was a sharp drop of confidence in the regime on the part of South African industrialists and the international financial community. The Chamber of Mines, the Federated Chamber of Industries, the South African Association of Chambers of Commerce, all advised the Government to reconsider its policies. The then Chairman of the General Mining and Financial Corporation summed up the general feeling, stating, "When the policies of the politicians threaten the basic economy of the country, . . . the leaders of industry have not only a right but also a duty to express their opinion and continue to do so until some change of policy is apparent."[1] But, as we have seen, Afrikaners were hardly represented in these circles, and their Government and party did not heed this advice, and kept a tight control on the political system. The effectiveness of this control was seen when a campaign of sabotage against Government property was begun by an off-shoot of the African National Congress, an organization which had been declared illegal in 1960. Successful operations by the security police against the African National Congress and its rival, the illegal Pan African Congress, broke the networks of both organizations. Gradually confidence was restored and an economic boom—probably delayed by the post-Sharpville reaction—began, which greatly accelerated the growth of the gross national product. Fortuitously, the Sharpville crisis created increased opportunities for the Afrikaner entrepreneurial class. First, foreign uncertainty led to a brief lack of confidence in mining shares, and an Afrikaner group was able to obtain its first significant foothold in the mining industry when the Federale Mynbou gained a controlling interest in the General Mining Corporation, one of the seven major mining houses. Secondly, capital was shored up in South Africa by exchange regulations, introduced during an outflow of capital after Sharpville, and these were maintained after the crisis had passed. The holders of this capital began to look for profitable sources of investment within the country. These investors could no longer afford to take little or no account of Afrikaner entrepreneurs and many of the new financial ventures included Afrikaners among their leading share-

1. *Cape Argos,* June 21, 1960.

Situation is settled.

holders. It was not simply that Afrikaner enterprises had increased in scale, but because they were better able than South African English-speaking and foreign investors to obtain government goodwill for new financial activities. A thriving economy, with Afrikaner financiers playing an increasing part, the defeat of African nationalists in South Africa, the weakness of the new states of tropical Africa which at an earlier stage were thought to be a threat to South Africa, all contributed to a growing confidence among White South Africans in general and Afrikaners in particular.

The fear that the surrounding British protectorates would provide succor for guerillas when they became independent was seen to be groundless, for apart from the protectorates' military vulnerability, their economic dependence has made them unwilling to assist forces hostile to the South African regime. Moreover, the more prosperous these states grow the more dependent they are likely to become upon the South African economy. A more sophisticated view of coping with a potential threat from these states has evolved, and this coincides with South Africa's new role as a capital generating economy. By investing in African states, an attempt has been made to enmesh these states in the South African economy. This policy has proved successful with South Africa's immediate neighbours, Botswana, Lestho, and Swaziland, and also in Malawi.

The South African government has not limited its activities beyond its borders to encouraging economic diplomacy. It has provided counter-insurgency forces to aid the Rhodesian government's illegal attempts to prevent the infiltration of guerillas and similar units that have operated in the Portuguese colonies of Mozambique and Angola. These outward-looking policies have led to criticisms from important sections of the Nationalist party. The economic policy is looked upon with suspicion because it requires relationships of equality, at managerial and diplomatic levels, with foreign Africans, and it is argued that these relationships must not be seen in isolation. What is sanctioned at one level can in time undermine the doctrine of racial separation at other levels. The critics of the new policy have been called the Verkramptes (the rigid ones) by their flexible opponents, the self-styled Verligtes (Enlightened ones). The conflict between the two groups has led to a break in Nationalist solidarity, although the departure from the cabinet of Dr. Albert Hertzog suggests a victory for the Verligtes. But this may be a premature verdict. The leadership of the Nationalist party is not threatened for the time being, even if it has shown its vulnerability by using the security police to uncover the source of disaffection within the party. The Verkramptes have tried to show that the Verligtes' policy is dictated by the increasing unity of interests between Afrikaner entrepreneurs and their English-speaking counterparts, and that this must be at the expense of the largely working-class Afrikaner population. Moreover, they point to the official policy of the party, which is now attempting, with some success, to recruit English-speaking South Africans into its ranks. The Verkramptes fear that a dilution of Nationalist views of race policy may take place, not because English members will encourage greater liberalism but because their presence will result in an even more pragmatic attitude to industrial policy. This is seen as a threat to the status of sections of the Afrikaner working class and, less realistically, to their material security.

Thus far the dominant group of Afrikaner leaders has had no difficulty in coping with their opponents within the Nationalist party. But there remains one area of policy, separate development, which may make the task of the Verligtes more difficult, particularly in the form it is taking in the Transkei. In 1958 the Nationalist Government yielded to international pressures to demonstrate a moral case for apartheid, which until then had been synonymous with white supremacy, and announced that the African reserves would be turned into potentially self-governing and independent regions. The Transkei was given a form of internal self-government with a legislature, and although the majority of the seats were occupied by government-supported chiefs, just over a third of the seats were elected by universal adult suffrage. In the first election in 1963 the pro-government party won only 15 of the 45 elected seats but was able to gain a majority with the support of the chiefs. The second election in 1968 led to a popular victory for the pro-government party as a result of the familiar band-wagoning process that comes with patronage. But this patronage is of a very limited kind. The Transkei, with its 16,500 square miles, has 1,500,000 African peasants engaged almost entirely in subsistence agriculture. Ironically, while the government is willing to permit investment of white-owned capital in independent African states, it is not willing to permit this in the Transkei for fear that it would increase the ties between the territory and the rest of South Africa, and diminish even further the barely visible dividing line between black and white areas—a division that forms a key part of the ideology of apartheid. There would, presumably, be less objection from Afrikaner intellectuals to state investment, because this could be made in the form of grants or non-recurring loans. Whatever form investment takes it must be introduced, for otherwise the Prime Minister of the Transkei, Paramount Chief Martzima, is likely to find himself under pressure from his own supporters to claim the independence that semi-official, but not government, agencies have claimed would be the long term result of separate development. All these variables create problems for the stability and unity of Afrikanerdom.

Unless state investment takes place in the Transkei, Afrikaner intellectuals, clergymen, editors, and academics are likely to become restive. *Dagbreek*, a leading Afrikaner newspaper, has been quoted as saying of the need for apartheid in its Transkeian form to succeed, "a whole philosophy and way of life is now at stake, and with it the foundation of Afrikaner nationalism. . . . It is this—or integration." But if the intellectuals, who have been closely associated with the Verligtes, do begin to question the feasibility of separate development and to concede that the alternative is inevitable, then there will be widespread working class demands for their repression and it will be the Verkramptes who will probably benefit. Alternatively, any attempt to use public funds on a large scale, which might satisfy the pro-apartheid intellectuals who feel that economic development in the Transkei is essential, will also be met by Verkrampte denunciations which will have popular support. Similarly, an attempt to grant independence to the Transkei would probably also provide the Verkramptes with popular support among working class Afrikaners.

It is not suggested that Afrikaners will turn and rend themselves, but it is possible that the present leaders could be outflanked by the Verkramptes, or a successor group, and if this were to happen, the authoritarian system which they have moulded for others would be used against them. It is more likely that Nationalist leaders will continue to create the impression of greater flexibility without translating this into any tangible change in policy. In spite of popular debate among white South Africans the system still appears as rigid as ever.

| Giovanni | **THE POLITICAL ECONOMY** |
| Arrighi | **OF RHODESIA** |

*T*he most important single element determining the nature of economic and political development in Southern Rhodesia was the British South Africa Company's overestimation at the end of the nineteenth century of its mineral resources and the persistence of this overestimation for roughly fifteen years. The reasons behind such a misconception can be partly detected in the political interruptions which characterized the early period of colonization (Jameson Raid, Matabele and Mashona rebellions, Boer War). The costs incurred in the meantime increased the stake of the company in the country and led to additional heavy development investment, particularly in railways. The overvaluation became apparent when, eventually, the Rhodesian gold fields failed to yield deposits comparable to those of South Africa. For example, even in 1910 against a profit of close to £7 million from the eleven leading Johannesburg gold mines, the ten leading Rhodesian mines yielded a profit of only £614,000. Large-scale workings were uneconomic because the deposits were scattered and the ore itself often of a low quality.

The desire to recover the original heavy outlays induced the Chartered Company to foster the formation of a white rural bourgeoisie which, by developing the country, would raise the value of its assets in the area—viz. the railway system, the mine claims, and especially land.

Settlement gathered momentum after 1902 when small workings of mine claims on a royalty basis were extended. "The influx of peoples, European and African, to the mining camps brought about a derivative demand for other products. Between 1901 and 1911 the European population doubled from 11,000 to over 23,000. Farmers began to settle and to feed the growing population and commercial undertakings became

Reprinted from *Studies on the Left*, Vol 30, Sept./Oct. 1966, pp. 35–65, by permission of the author and the editors.

established in the growing towns of Salisbury and Bulawayo."[1] Thus a cumulative process was started leading to a class structure which crystallized during the Depression of the 1930's.

THE WHITE RURAL BOURGEOISIE

Within this class structure the white rural bourgeoisie was the foundation of the capitalist sector of the economy. This bourgeoisie consisted largely of both owner-workers of small and medium-sized mines and farmers who were economically committed to the development of the country. This *national* character of the white rural bourgeoisie, even at that time, distinguished Southern Rhodesia from practically all other African colonial territories north of the Limpopo and South of the Sahara, where exploitation of resources was carried out by large-scale *international* capitalism. In these other territories, where exploitation was based on large-scale mining or plantation or monopoly trade, capitalist interests in the economy were not permanent but lasted until, for example, deposits were exhausted or the raw material was substituted in the industrial process overseas or some more economic source of supply was found.

In interwar Rhodesia about a third of the Europeans gainfully occupied belonged to the rural bourgeoisie, but to assess the full strength of this class, it is important to take into account the would-be agriculturalists. In fact "even the civil servant, business and professional man, miner or railway employee looked forward to retiring to a plot of land."[2] International capitalism was represented mainly by the British South Africa Company which, apart from its control over the railways, the bulk of gold production and coal mining, also owned land in part exploited for productive purposes (maize, cattle, citrus, etc.). In accordance with its interest in encouraging the growth of the white rural bourgeoisie, it also experimented with new crops.

Large estates had been given to companies and syndicates for certain interests acquired by the British South Africa Company.[3] Other big companies were already dominating asbestos and chrome mining.[4] Control over tobacco production was exercised indirectly through monopsonistic practices by the United Tobacco Company which, in Huggins' view, "was aiming at becoming the country's sole tobacco buyer, and managed to draw the best experts out of the government service." A third class consisted of craftsmen engaged in manufacturing, whose activity was totally dependent on the rural bourgeoisie and big inter-

1. *Report of the Urban African Commission.* Salisbury 1958.
2. R. Gray: *The Two Nations.* London, 1960. p. 13.
3. M. Yudelman: *Africans on the Land.* London, 1964, p. 141.
4. W. J. Barber: *The Economy of British Central Africa.* London, 1961, pp. 119–22, and L. H. Gann and M. Gelfand: *Huggins of Rhodesia.* London, 1964, p. 175.

national capital, mainly the British South Africa Company. It was typically a petty bourgeoisie and, indeed, the Colony's official Year Book of 1932 does not even mention the manufacturing industry.

Much more significant was the class of white wage-workers formed by artisans, semiskilled workers, foremen, clerical workers, administrative employees, etc. Demand for their labor was concentrated in mining, transport (mainly railways), and service activities (civil service especially). It is important to notice that, unlike South Africa, or Algeria, their settlement was a *consequence of*, and did not precede, capitalist development in the country. Therefore they had to be attracted by the offer of high wages, and with their skills they brought union-organizing abilities. This phasing of white settlement and capitalist development is at the root of the absence of "poor-white-ism" in Southern Rhodesia. This class of white wage-worker, together with the white petty bourgeoisie, i.e., handicraftsmen, shopkeepers, and small employers in agriculture and mining, already in the prewar period constituted the bulk of the European population in Southern Rhodesia.

The Africans were still essentially a class of self-employed rural cultivators. The African wage workers, the African middle class, and petty bourgeoisie[5] were merely appendages of the peasantry rather than independent classes. Land was not a saleable commodity, but each adult had rights to its use. The system of cultivation involved a form of land rotation whereby it was used until its fertility was diminished and then abandoned and left to recover until fertility was restored. Within the peasantry some division and hence specialization of labor could be observed.[6] The role of men was to regulate the community's relationship with animals (tending cattle and hunting) and to provide development works such as bush clearance and building huts. The women's role, on the other hand, consisted of routine tasks: sowing, weeding, threshing, fetching water, preparing food, and making beer. Communal ties were very strong,[7] and when the peasant left to seek wage employment he left his family behind and kept close links (through a flow of goods,

5. Middle-class and bourgeoisie (or capitalist class) are distinguished by the fact that the former consists of white-collar employees or self-employed professional men whereas the latter is formed by employers of labor for the purpose of profit. The members of the petty bourgeoisie are characterized by the fact that though employers of labor they themselves provide part of the manual labor.
6. M. Yudelman, *op. cit.*, p. 12–13, 132–133. Barber, *op. cit.*, p. 46.
7. *Report of the Mangwende Reserve Commission of Enquiry*, Salisbury 1961, pp. 18, 37.

cash, or occasional labor) with the peasantry to which he belonged
and meant to return, even after several years of absence. At the same
time the size and number of holdings under cultivation within the rural
areas contracted and expanded as the wage-laborers left or returned to
their wards. Thus, given this security in land tenure, we cannot, strictly
speaking, refer to the African wage-workers of the 1930's as a
proletariat.[8]

On the other hand the African middle class and rural (petty)
bourgeoisie were numerically economically insignificant. For example,
by 1930, i.e., before the Land Apportionment Act was introduced,
Africans had managed to acquire only 45,000 acres in the open market
while Europeans had purchased about 31,000,000 acres.[9] The reasons for
the failure of these classes to emerge are a consequence of the class structure itself and therefore they will be dealt with at a later stage.

To sum up, we can discern five main classes in prewar Rhodesia.
There were (1) the white rural bourgeoisie operating in mining and
agriculture, national in character; (2) large-scale international capitalism
controlling transport (railways) and power (coal) and engaged in primary production and speculation in land; (3) the white wage-workers
whose entrance into the economy followed and did not precede the
capitalist development of the country; (4) the white petty bourgeoisie
operating in all sectors of the economy but especially trade; (5) the
African peasantry and wage-earners.

Political Implications of Pre-World War II Economic Base

The key to understanding the outcome of the struggle for political
power in the period under discussion is the different degree of class
consciousness—that is, the awareness of their own interests, displayed
by the various classes. While the classes within the European section of
the population were characterized by a remarkable degree of class consciousness, particularly in periods of economic depression, the Africans
were not. In a scattered peasantry whose economic conditions had not

8. By *proletariat* is here understood the
class of modern wage-laborers who,
having no means of production of their
own, are reduced to selling their labor
power in order to live. This definition is,
however, too broad and must be qualified
to exclude the middle class. Such a distinction is unnecessary, and indeed impossible, at a high level of abstraction
when labor is defined as a homogeneous quantity, i.e., as abstract labor. In
the present analysis, however, this would
be an oversimplification preventing a
correct assessment of the class structure.
The proletariat will therefore include
only manual and semiskilled labor. The
distinction has its rationale in the fact
that the middle class sells its labor in a
seller's market, or at any rate in conditions less unfavorable to the seller than
is the case for the proletariat.

9. Gann and Gelfand, *op. cit.*, p. 79.

yet notably worsened and which still used the traditional mode of production based on kinship relations rather than impersonal market relations, class loyalty could not possibly substitute tribal loyalty. "In
Mashonaland . . . the small and broken tribes, scattered and restricted
to their separate and distant reserves, were prevented from developing
any cohesion or a wider outlook, while in Matabeleland the only rallying
point of national feeling—the family of Lobengula—was becoming . . .
more a family and sentimental affair than a national aspiration."[10] At
the same time the wage-workers still belonged to the peasantry and
furthermore their incessant movements "from job to job, from location
to kraal, from the Protectorates to the Union" prevented them from
"developing, as a community, any corporate independence, initiative and
self-respect."[11] It is true that protest movements were already appearing
in the 1920's, but either they were concerned with the status of the
negligible nucleus of educated Africans or they were vague and ill-
directed and disappeared as soon as they were faced by official repression.
In consequence, the African masses were politically inert, passive, and
hence virtually powerless. The only signs of a class struggle were therefore to be seen within the European section of the population. The rather
mild character of such a struggle can be ascribed precisely to the political
inertia and passiveness of the large majority of the population which
created the possibility of a deal between the different interests of the
white classes.

WHITE COALITION

The class structure sketched above obviously could lead to a coalition
of all white classes national in character (i.e., rural bourgeoisie, wage-
workers, and petty bourgeoisie, whose interests were compatible, if not
identical) in opposition to international capitalism, the conflict being
mainly focused on the issues of overhead capital expansion and monopsonistic practices. This is, in fact, what happened. Two stages of political
evolution can be discerned. At first the community of interests of the
Chartered Company and the rural bourgeoisie materialized in an ambitious program of investment and in legislation aimed at obtaining
labor from the indigenous population. The latter included (*a*) the ex-
propriation of land while encouraging the dispossessed peasantry to
remain where they were as tenants, their rent being commuted for
labor; (*b*) a hut tax which virtually compelled the adult African males
to spend between one and three months a year in wage-employment,
and (*c*) a Pass Law intended to direct labor where it was wanted.[12]
Labor could have been expanded in three ways: (*a*) through a system

10. Gray: *op. cit.*, p. 159.
11. Gray: *op. cit.*, p. 269.

12. C. Leys: *European Politics in Southern Rhodesia,* Oxford 1959, p. 10.

of forced labor; (*b*) by lowering the opportunity cost of the peasantry, i.e., by progressively reducing its overall productivity; and (*c*) by means of the proletarianization of the peasants. Alternative (*c*), however, runs against the other interest in limiting competition from Africans, since the proletarianization of the peasantry would bring about the emergence of a black agrarian bourgeoisie bound to compete on the markets of produce and of factors of production. Probably more important is the consideration that, by preserving the traditional system of land tenure, wages could be kept lower in the long run, since part of the real cost of the means for the subsistence of the migrant workers' families would be borne by the peasantry. In fact, forced labor was the solution relied upon at this stage.

With World War I the economic power of the national bourgeoisie and white wage-workers *vis-à-vis* international capitalism had grown stronger. Hostilities and their aftermath had produced a widespread shortage of skilled white labor and of world supplies of raw materials. This relative strength lasted throughout the 1920's, and by the time the Depression of the 1930's had set in, the coalition of the white national classes had managed to obtain a good share of political power. A decisive step toward greater national control was the achievement of responsible government as opposed to amalgamation with the Union of South Africa. This latter course was, according to Gann and Gelfand, favoured by international capitalism because of the reliability of Smuts as an upholder of Imperial interests.

RESPONSIBLE GOVERNMENT

Responsible government merely meant a greater share of power for the national white classes and by no means their undisputed rule. Economic dependence on foreign capital forced the settlers' government to adopt middle-of-the-road policies, compromising between the interests of the national bourgeoisie and white workers on the one hand and of international capitalism on the other. The result was that these conflicts fell into the background and that greater national control over legislative power found expression in an institutional framework strongly biased in favor of the interests of white national classes, which would regulate future class relations. This is reflected in the legislation passed before World War II (especially in the 1930's when the Depression stiffened the class consciousness of the white classes) to regulate the supply of labor, the reservation of produce markets, government expenditure, monopsonistic practices, and the expansion of overhead capital.

Though the railway system and coal supply remained under the control of the British South Africa Company, the government took important steps in other spheres to provide basic facilities for the economic development of the country in line with the class interests of the national bourgeoisie and white workers. Government intervention increased remarkably and moved in two directions; expansion of overhead capital and strengthening of the bargaining power of the national bourgeoisie on the raw materials market. Public works, especially in road building, were carried out on a large scale; several state enterprises were founded in the 1930's and early 1940's, including the Electricity Supply Commission power stations, the Rhodesian Iron and Steel Commission foundries and mills, and the Cotton Industry Board mills. Raw materials processing plants (e.g., a roasting plant for processing low-grade ores and the establishment of a Sugar Industry Board) and marketing organizations were also set up. A side effect of these developments was a reduced economic dependence on international monopolistic interests. More direct steps were however taken to strengthen the bargaining power of the white farmers *vis-à-vis* the United Tobacco Company. The Tobacco Marketing Act (1936), by limiting competition among growers, attempted to replace the monopsonistic market with a kind of bilateral monopoly. Whether the attempt was successful is a different matter. It is interesting that in 1943, seven years after the implementation of the act, the Southern Rhodesian Finance Minister still maintained that the price of leaf was controlled by powerful interests outside the Colony.[13]

THE LAND APPORTIONMENT ACT

More significant was the legislation passed to ensure an expanding supply of labor and to divide the economy into noncompeting racial groups. This was achieved by a series of legislative measures and finally by the Land Apportionment Act. This Act put a definite limit to the land available for African permanent settlement and in consequence made necessary the transformation of the traditional system of cultivation from shifting to continuous cultivation. The change was also encouraged by the government which "centralized" the African rural areas, i.e., divided them up into permanent arable and permanent grazing land. Given the techniques employed by the peasantry and the type of soil allocated to them, this move from shifting to continuous cultivation produced progressive soil erosion[14] and thus decreasing productivity of African land. However, since the criteria employed for allocating land to Africans was an average acreage per family rather than income off that acreage, the progressive decreases in the productivity of land were tantamount to a progressive decrease in the overall

13. Gann and Gelfand, *op. cit.,* pp. 175–76.
14. For the effects of continuous cultivation over African argiculture, see K. Brown: *Land in Southern Rhodesia,* London 1959, pp. 6–10. Also *Second Report of the Select Committee on Resettlement of Natives.*

productivity of the peasantry. Thus a built-in trend of decreasing peasant productivity was established, which would ensure an expanding supply of labor. Apart from these long-term implications, the Land Apportionment Act provided the European farmers with a pool of labor straight away. This was achieved by allowing a European farmer to enter into an agreement "whereupon a native or his family shall be permitted to occupy a portion of such land under condition that he supply labor to such owner or occupier." Similarly the hut tax guaranteed a steady flow of labor from the tribal areas. Furthermore, as time went by and contacts with the money economy increased, new needs were felt (especially for education and clothes) altering the means of subsistence.[15] In consequence the demand for cash was itself growing and, given the limitations on the production of cash crops, a further element was at work to expand labor supply.

The distribution of the total African labour supply between the different capitalist sectors, on the other hand, was not left to the law of supply and demand but was also legislated for, mainly through the Native Registration Act (1936). This Act tightened up the Pass Law and effectively contributed to the maintenance of a wage structure whereby the white farmers constantly paid unskilled labor lower wage rates than other employers.[16]

The second implication of land apportionment was to be the division of the economy into noncompeting racial groups. Racial competition could potentially take place between (a) white agrarian bourgeoisie and African peasantry; (b) white and black bourgeoisie in both the produce and the labor markets; (c) white and black petty bourgeoisie in retail trade; and (d) white and black wage-workers in the skilled labor market. In restricting competition in these markets the Land Apportionment Act drew the general lines whereas more specialized legislation tightened the restrictions in the individual spheres.

REDUCTION OF AFRICAN COMPETITIVENESS

The competitiveness of the peasantry on the produce markets was restricted in a number of ways. In the first place the Africans were confined to the poorer land resources of the country. Secondly, the conversion of part of the peasantry into tenant-laborers inevitably reduced the marketable surplus. Thirdly, the same effect resulted from the decreasing productivity of African agriculture. Fourthly, the clear

15. It is therefore assumed that a historical and social element (besides a physical element) enters into the determination of what is socially accepted as subsistence income and consumption. For a discussion of the meaning of 'Subsistence' see

Maurice Dobb: Wages, Cambridge, 1959.
16. Recruitment of labour outside Southern Rhodesia was certainly one of the major factors in determining both the rise and distribution among sectors of the total African labour force.

separation of land between Africans and Europeans made it possible to direct capital expenditure in roads, dams, etc., so as to widen the differential in overall productivity of European and African agriculture. These were indirect checks on African competition. At the same time more direct steps were taken in order to discourage African sales through discriminatory price policy (e.g., Maize Control Act of 1931).

Competition from an African rural bourgeoisie was potentially much more dangerous. Its emergence was accordingly prevented or at least contained within well-defined limits. This was achieved by preserving the traditional system, whereby land was not a saleable commodity in the African areas. Native Purchase Areas, where Africans could hold land in individual right, were set aside, but the African rural bourgeoisie was nevertheless bound to remain negligible. For land in the Native Purchase Areas was to be allocated by the government, and thus the formation and growth of the African bourgeoisie could be indirectly controlled by the very class which feared its competition. However, the total land to be allocated constituted only 8 per cent of the total land areas of the country, and it was generally located even farther away from markets, railway lines, and main roads than that of the traditional peasantry. Furthermore, though land once allocated was owned individually, there were many limitations to its transferability, such as maximum size of holdings and sales to Europeans. Among other things this meant that the extension of credit (which could possibly come only from European sources) to African farmers was hampered, and therefore a constant lack of finance was bound to hold back their development. In other words, quite apart from direct discriminatory practices in granting credit, the preservation of the traditional system of land tenure prevented the consolidation of land-holdings so that administrative difficulties made credit extension to Africans impracticable.

Interracial competition was also prevented in trading activities since the Land Apportionment Act, by prohibiting African ownership or lease of premises in the European areas (which included all towns and cities), banished African traders to the poorest markets, implicitly preventing their growth. Furthermore under the Native Registration Act of 1936 mentioned above, even hawkers were restricted to the African locations: only sales of curios, baskets, and similar articles were allowed in the towns whereas sale of such goods as chicken, eggs, butter, etc. was prohibited.[17]

WHITE WAGE-WORKERS' CONSOLIDATION

The greater political power achieved by the white wage-workers, through their coalition with the national bourgeoisie, also found expres-

17. Gray, *op. cit.,* p. 154.

sion in a number of acts and policies which aimed at improving their social economic conditions and at perpetuating the scarcity of skills on which their bargaining and political strength was based. Under the Industrial Conciliation Act (1934) and its Amendment of 1937, machinery was set up for settling disputes in practically all industries employing white labor. Agreements between employers and employees in the Industrial Councils were to become legally binding in the industry concerned. The Act explicitly excluded African workers from its definition of employee, but, all the same, wage rates and conditions of employment negotiated by the Industrial Councils were applicable to skilled white and black workers alike. In practice this meant that Africans were debarred from climbing the industrial ladder since no white employer would have employed an African if, for the same wage, he could obtain a European. Even more significant was the provision which empowered the Industrial Councils to regulate the conditions of apprenticeship. This provision created a situation strikingly similar to that governing competition between the white and black agrarian bourgeoisies. In other words, here, too, remarkable power was given to a white class (wage-workers) to control the rise of African competition. Thus the white workers came to control the scarcity of their own skills. This scarcity was also guaranteed by the government immigration policy which was, especially in the 1930's, highly selective and against any large-scale immigration of whites.

This body of legislation and policies was well summed up in the prevailing ideology of the period: the doctrine of "parallel development" or of the "two-pyramids policy" according to which interracial competition ought to be prevented. Having shown how the economic base has produced a certain superstructure we now turn to deal with the effects of the superstructure on the economic base.

War and Postwar Economic Development

The desire for industrialization and the progressive decrease of the peasant's productivity, implicit in the institutional framework produced by the class structure of the 1930's, were inconsistent with each other. For a necessary condition of industrialization was an expanding internal demand, whereas the deterioration of peasant productive capacity inevitably led to the opposite—an internal demand which, if not stagnant, grew at a negligible rate. In fact a growing population combined with constant per capita income in the subsistence sector simply means greater subsistence output rather than expanding aggregate demand for capitalist production. Thus, notwithstanding increased government intervention to foster economic growth, the system lacked an *internal* force sufficient to start development. The result was stagnation, and in fact in the 1930's, after nearly two decades of self-government, the country still had a typically colonial economy with no industrial sector apart from the railway workshop and small firms engaged in wholly subsidiary activities.

There was a second inherent contradiction in the institutional framework. The preservation of the traditional African system of land tenure was meant to prevent the emergence of a proletariat which, nonetheless, was an inevitable consequence of the decreasing productivity of the peasants combined with labor migration.

Once the process of deterioration of African agriculture had started, it became cumulative since the lowered and continuously decreasing opportunity cost of the peasantry in the traditional sector was bound to force an ever-growing number of men into wage employment. This was true, even though the average per capita income in the traditional sector remained constant, for two reasons: (1) the "effort-price" of that constant income increased, by extension of the acreage under cultivation; (2) a constant average conceals important variations from area to area. Furthermore the process was accelerated by the fact that cattle was the most important of the few forms of investment open to Africans, so that the population explosion was accompanied by remarkable increases in the cattle population which worsened pressure on the land.

Thus in the long run the savings of the wage-workers would not correspond, in the traditional sector, to an increased productivity of the peasantry that would make the production of a surplus above subsistence possible. Therefore when the limits of land available had been reached, the attempt by wage laborers to realize their "savings" would be frustrated, their security would be lost and a proletariat arise.

The upshot of this was that the institutional framework established in the 1930's, while it could not lead endogenously to economic growth, was unable to prevent the formation of a proletariat.

WORLD WAR II

The lack of internal demand represented a brake on industrialization and development, and the progressive decrease of overall peasant productivity increasingly worsened this obstacle. World War II was the external stimulant which more than offset the hindrance and started economic growth in Southern Rhodesia after the stagnation of the 1930's. Goods previously imported became practically unavailable, thus creating a demand for local industries; chrome and asbestos assumed strategic importance; world shortage of agricultural produce provided a rapidly growing outlet for farmers' output. More specifically an air training scheme was implemented in the country, in association with the British government, whereby Southern Rhodesia had to supply air stations, quarters, land, and buildings. "The air training scheme proved a major economic boom. Farmers and industrial firms suddenly found an almost insatiable market, and Guest[18] calculated that imperial expenditure on the scheme alone almost equalled the indirect benefit which the country derived from its entire gold-mining industry."[19] This explosion in demand could have led *merely* to inflation as it did in many other underdeveloped countries. Instead, it was under these circumstances that the *national* character of the white bourgeoisie and white workers which controlled the government became important. Contrary to what happened in the economies of the "enclave" type, controlled by *international* capitalism with no interest in the development of the country, the government in Southern Rhodesia could intervene both through direct anti-inflationary controls and by setting up actual iron and steel production and cotton spinning plants which made the growth of secondary industry possible. Though the shortage of manpower and especially of capital goods prevented the capitalist sector of the economy from taking full advantage of the high war demand, it was during this time that overhead capital was developed and resources were being accumulated which could finance future developments.[20]

By the end of the war the limitations on the expansion of the internal market (the institutional framework) had not been removed, and therefore a slump would have ensued were it not for new external stimulants. The world shortage of raw materials which followed the war was accompanied by a dollar shortage. Asbestos and chrome were both dollar-savers and demand for them increased considerably. More important still was the role played by tobacco production which, since the war, was greatly stimulated by the limitation of dollar expenditure by the United Kingdom: the amount of tobacco produced tripled between 1945 and 1958, its value rising fourfold. This remarkable increase in production was accomplished through an increase in the same period in the number of producers from just over 1,000 to 2,669[21] and was the main factor behind the high rate of immigration in the postwar years.[22] The influx of Europeans in turn created demand for goods and services, particularly housing, and the number of Africans in wage employment rose from 254,000 in 1936 and 377,000 in 1946 to more than 600,000 in 1956, thus keeping up internal demand for manufactured and agricultural products. These effects induced by the increased demand for tobacco and other raw mate-

18. Guest was the Head of Department of Air, set up in 1940.
19. Gann and Gelfand, *op. cit.,* p. 153.
20. C. H. Thompson and H. W. Woodruff: *Economic Development in Rhodesia and Nyasaland*, London, 1954, p. 20.

21. Barber, *op. cit.,* p. 131.
22. The yearly average of European net immigration, which was less than 800 between 1921 and 1946, shot up to more than 7,000 in 1946-56.

rials account for the permanence of a sustained rate of growth between the end of the war and the late 1940's. By then an additional external stimulant came into operation: the outflow of capital from the Union of South Africa and the United Kingdom.[23] In the Union the *national* bourgeoisie and white workers had seized power in 1948, and *international* capitalism, scared by the possibilities of nationalization of means of production in the interests of the new ruling classes, reacted by looking for alternative outlets for its investment. In fact, "the City . . . from about 1947, was increasingly inclined to channel money directly into Rhodesia instead of routing funds via Johannesburg"[24] and "considerable sums formerly earmarked for investment in the Union have been placed in Southern Rhodesia . . . to escape extremist Nationalist policies, or . . . hedging against the possibility of later migration under conditions where capital movements might prove more difficult."[25] Southern Rhodesia, with its developed overhead capital, growing industries, and European immigration could provide the alternative outlet for international capitalist investment. Thus, foreign investment in Southern Rhodesia, which amounted to £13.5 million in 1947, was more than double that amount in 1949 and reached £50.7 million by 1951.[26]

The overall results of this remarkable war and postwar economic development of Rhodesia can be gauged by the fact that the net domestic product at current prices had risen more than ninefold from £27.4 million in 1939 to £251.1 million in 1961, and that fixed capital formation in the period 1946–1961 was at a yearly average of more than £50 million.[27] However, even more significant changes occurred in the class structure of the economy, which we must now discuss.

Changes in the Economic Base since World War II

From 1901 to 1950 the productivity of the peasantry had been constantly declining so that the "effort price" of maintaining a constant subsistence income had been continuously growing. This helps to explain why the volume of African employment continued to expand between 1930 and 1945 notwithstanding the fact that real wages steadily declined, as shown, for example, by Barber. The formation of a proletariat, implicit in this trend, was accelerated by the active implementation of the

23. For the reasons for, and characteristics of, the outflow of capital from the United Kingdom see M. Barrat Brown: *After Imperialism*, London, 1963, chs. 7–8.
24. Gann and Gelfand, *op. cit.*, p. 212.
25. L. Tow. *The Manufacturing Economy of Southern Rhodesia* (mimeo-

graphed), Washington, 1960.
26. Thompson and Woodruff, *op. cit.*, p. 173.
27. Central Statistics Office; *Report on the Results of the National Income and Balance of Payments, of Northern Rhodesia, 1954–63*, Salisbury 1964. Also Thompson and Woodruff, *op. cit.*, p. 173.

Land Apportionment Act. This was started as soon as the squatting of the African peasantry on unalienated land encroached upon European cultivation, but especially when more land had to be provided for the postwar white settlement and tobacco cultivation. In 1948 close to 300,-000 Africans were either residing on European land or were occupying land within the areas marked for European use, and in the postwar years 85,000 African families were shifted in organized expulsions.[28] This settlement was accompanied by large de-stocking programs which curtailed the main form of investment open to Africans.

Declining real wages, deterioration of peasant productivity, restriction of land available for African use, curtailment of African investment—all these combined to make the wage-workers realize not only that their living conditions were constantly worsening but also that their savings were illusory and so was their "old age insurance." Frustration and insecurity ensued and with them the consciousness of being wage-workers for good—that is, of forming a proletariat. "I have grown up under the white people . . . My wish is that . . . we get *better treatment in the way of wages*. Today I am getting older and I have nothing. *I have not saved anything*. I might die and not know how my children are going to manage" [italics added, G.A.].[29] With this new consciousness came a wave of strikes and political activities on a completely new scale.[30] The emergence of a proletariat did not mean that the solidarity between wage-workers and peasants was diminishing. On the contrary, the interests of the two classes largely overlapped, for the decreasing productivity of the peasantry was at the root of the impoverishment of both classes. Unrest spread from the towns to the rural areas where grievances over de-stocking and the organized expulsions provided a ready demand for political leadership.[31] This solidarity of interests stemmed also from the fact that the transformation into proletarians was gradual and did not involve *all* wage-workers. In fact when in the early 1950's the government, now pursuing a policy of labor stabilization, tried to implement the Land Husbandry Act, the class consciousness of both peasants and proletarians gathered momentum.[32]

EMERGENCE OF A MANUFACTURING CAPITALIST CLASS

A second major change in the class structure was the emergence of a manufacturing as opposed to a rural capitalist class. The contribution to national income of manufacturing rose from 9 per cent in the late

28. Second Report, *op. cit.*, pp. 13, 51.
29. Evidence to the Howman Committee (1943).
30. Gray, *op. cit.*, pp. 283–90.
31. J. Van Velsen: 'Trends in African Nationalism in Southern Rhodesia.' *Kroniek van Afrika*. Universitaire Pers

Leiden, June 1964, pp. 146–7.
32. A leader of the African Nationalist movement, G. Nyandoro, is reported to have said that the Act had become "the best recruiter the African Nationalists ever had."

1930's to about 15 per cent in the early 1950's to over 18 per cent in the early 1960's. Even more important was the fact that the growth was matched by the concentration of production as the industry passed from the small family-shop stage to the large scale, mechanized, corporate-owned factory. The proportion of firms whose gross output exceeded £50,000 was more than a third in 1957 but accounted for less than 8 per cent in 1938 and "while the typical industrial unit is growing in size, there is also a growing concentration of industrial output in the largest units, as experienced by the fact that 85 firms with gross outputs of £250,000 and over, comprising only 9 per cent of the total number, accounted for 67.8 per cent of the gross values of manufacturing output in the territory."[33]

The labor requirements, both qualitative and quantitative, of this sector came to differ sharply not only from those of prewar manufacturing but also of mining and agriculture. With mass production and mechanical aids, complex jobs could be divided into simple operations. Hence new possibilities of substituting relatively unskilled labor for artisans arose. On the other hand, with greater capitalization of production, specialization and hence stability of labor became relatively more important than large supplies of cheap migrant labor. Demand for non-manual labor increased more rapidly than demand for manual labor.

OUTLETS FOR PRODUCTION

In order to gauge the interests of the manufacturing class, the outlets for its production must also be considered. As we should expect, the bulk of manufacturing has been concentrated in heavy construction materials, processing of local food production, and low-quality consumer goods. Production of heavy construction materials was stimulated by large expenditure in overhead capital and housing. Production of low-quality consumer goods has increasingly come to depend on the *growth of the purchasing power of the African peasants and wage-workers*. Its development can be explained by import substitution, European immigration, and the increases in African wage employment, but its long-run prospects are being hampered mainly by the institutional framework which had led to a continuous decrease in the peasantry's productivity. Processing of local farm production was stimulated by the expansion of the European market brought about by postwar immigration and import substitutions. The stabilization of the European population since 1960 (the natural increase has hardly offset net emigration) and especially the low-income elasticity of demand for food has been seriously limiting expansion in this field. African food consumption, on the other hand, "is dominated by the cheapest foodstuffs: mealie meal, low quality meat, dried and fresh fish,

33. Tow, *op. cit.*, p. 17.

bread and sugar, account for roughly 80 per cent of the food outlays of African families."[34] Hence, for this sector, too, the *growth of the purchasing power of the Africans* and their rapid proletarianization, and especially urbanization, became a condition for expansion.

Though the emergence of a proletariat and of manufacturing capitalism represent the major changes in the prewar class structure, important changes *within* mining and agrarian capitalism have also occurred. Three main changes can be observed: the relative decline and increased concentration of the mining industry; the economic strengthening of the agrarian bourgeoisie; the shift of emphasis from the internal to the external market for agricultural produce.

The contribution to national income of mining declined from over 25 per cent in 1938 to about 10 per cent in the early 1950's and about 5 per cent in the early 1960's. This general trend conceals significant internal variations. Gold output has decreased, mainly "because of the static dollar price of gold in relation to rising cost of production,"[35] while production of asbestos, chrome, and coal have shown a steady rise since the war. The fact that mining of these three minerals has been dominated by four large firms by itself accounts for the increased concentration of mining in general. Furthermore in gold production the "small workers" were eliminated by rising mining costs so that the total number of gold workings dropped from over 1,750 in 1935 to 700 in 1947 and 300 in 1956. This greater concentration was accompanied by the employment of more modern techniques and greater capitalization which reduced the dependence of the industry on a growing supply of labor.

Opposite trends appeared in European agriculture where the total value of output (at current prices) in 1958 was tenfold that of 1937. As mentioned earlier, war-time production and increased export of tobacco was the decisive factor behind this spectacular increase. Tobacco has become since the late 1940's Southern Rhodesia's most important single export commodity and therefore the major foreign exchange earner. Since the growth of the tobacco industry was accomplished through an influx of new producers, the number of firms increased.

The other significant change has been the shift from maize to tobacco as the main crop. Two important implications of this change must be made explicit. In the first place the emphasis was shifted from internal to external market, *thus reducing the agrarian bourgeoisie's dependence on, and interest in, the industrialization of the country*. In the second place, mechanization has been held back by the fact that tobacco-growing demands more labor-intensive methods than maize, so that agrarian capitalism remained on the whole more dependent on unskilled labor than mining and manufacturing.

34. Barker, *op. cit.*, p. 171. 154.
35. Thompson and Woodruff, *op. cit.*, p.

INTERNATIONAL CAPITALISM

Significant changes have also occurred in the relationships between national and international capitalism in Rhodesia. Before World War II the main foreign interests were centred around the appreciation of land values, the mineral rights, and the railway. The mineral rights were bought by the government in 1933, and the railway line in 1949. On the other hand, in the postwar period the interests of international capitalism came to involve practically every sector of the Rhodesian economy, non-agricultural industries in particular.

Within foreign capital, three main interests may be singled out: (1) interests connected with the Anglo American Corporation (AAC); (2) interests in primary production of large-scale foreign companies other than Anglo-American; and (3) interests of manufacturing firms.

1. The interests connected with AAC are centred around four "giant" corporations (Tanganyika Concessions, De Beers, British South Africa Company, and AAC itself) which are united by interlocking holdings and directorships.[36] The wealth and power of the group is based on the exploitation of the mineral riches of South Africa, the Zambian Copper Belt, and Katanga. Its interests in Rhodesia are subordinated to those of these other areas. It is probably right to assume that Anglo-American depends neither on British nor South African capitalism but is rather an "independent super-state," an economic empire centred in Southern and Central Africa (this is the reason for dealing with the group separately). Apart from the group's control over the extremely important coal supplies of the country, the Rhodesian economy has offered, particularly since the late 1940's, an outlet for investing the profits reaped in Zambia and to a certain extent (and for certain periods) in South Africa. In Rhodesia the group dominates coal and iron pyrites mining, ferrochrome and cement industries, and together with RST controls iron and steel production (formerly a government-controlled enterprise) and the Argus Group which has practically the monopoly of the Rhodesian daily press.[37] Other major investments include citrus and sugar estates, forests, clay products, financial houses, etc.

2. The other giant companies engaged in primary production in Southern Rhodesia are not locally based (i.e., on Southern Africa as a whole) and therefore their interests in the economy are less diversified and their profits generally flow overseas in a greater proportion. The Rhodesian (now Roan) Selection Trust (RST) is controlled by the American Metal Climax Company and has no significant mining interests in Southern Rhodesia. The Trust operates in the Copper Belt and its participation with AAC in certain sectors of the economy is subsidiary.

36. *The Economists*, Oct. 7th 1966, p. 55. Also J. Ziegler: *La Contre-Révolution en Afrique.* Paris, 1963.

37. Tow, *op. cit.*, p. 124. Ziegler, *op. cit.*, p. 34. Also O. Guitand: *Les Rhodésies et le Nyasaland.* Paris, 1964, p. 60.

Production of asbestos is dominated by the British company, Turner & Newall, which controls approximately 90 per cent of the territory's output, and also dominates the asbestos cement product industry.[38] Other examples of big foreign interests in primary production are Lonrho (gold mining, cattle, and ownership of the oil pipeline) and Forestal Land, Timber and Railways Company, one of the world's largest producers of tanning extracts, which through the subsidiary Rhodesian Wattle Company owns nearly all of the wattle acreage.[39] When account is taken of the monopsonistic practices in the purchase of tobacco, the general picture which emerges is one of a highly concentrated and to a great extent foreign-controlled primary production sector.

3. The situation in manufacturing is similar. Well over one third of the fifty largest British manufacturers have direct[40] interests (subsidiaries and not merely sales organization) in Rhodesia. As a result the presence of "giant corporations" can be observed in practically every sector of the Rhodesian manufacturing industry, with a relatively greater concentration of British capital in the first stages of production and South African capital at the other stages (including distribution).[41]

The overall control of foreign interests over the Rhodesian economy can to a certain extent be gauged by examining the results of a questionnaire sent to companies operating in the Federation in 1960. The results from Southern Rhodesia (which covered over 65 per cent of the total profits earned in the country) show that two thirds of the total recorded net operating profits accrued to companies not domestically controlled.[42]

THE NEW "CENTRE OF GRAVITY"

Meanwhile, economic development shifted the "centre of gravity" within the *white* community from the petty bourgeoisie to the wage-worker. The concentration of ownership over mining and manufacturing resulted in the elimination of the craftsmen and "small workers" which was only partially compensated for by the increased number of shop-keepers.[43] On the other hand, wages and general welfare of the white wage-workers have improved considerably since the 1930's. This class has become one of the better-paid working-classes of the world with average annual earnings well above £1,000 in the late 1950's. The main factor behind the trend has been the high rate of development and capital accumulation maintained in Rhodesia during the war and postwar

38. Tow, *op. cit.,* p. 50.
39. *The Rhodesia Herald,* July 8th, 1964.
40. The proportion of those who have direct *and* indirect interests (through South African subsidiaries) is certainly greater, but not easily ascertainable.

41. These are the conclusions I have tentatively reached from an examination of published material.
42. Report of *op. cit.,* Table 4.
43. For the pattern of the European employment in 1951 see (16, p. 81–82).

period, which kept the economy in a perennial state of over-full employment in the nonmanual and skilled-manual occupations. The result of this
state of over-full employment was the strong bargaining power of white
workers, which put them in a position not only to obtain economic concessions, but also to resist any infringement, let alone the repeal, of the
legislation passed in the 1930's. The entrance of Africans into skilled occupations was consequently hampered, and the growth of an African
petty bourgeoisie was prevented both by the institutional framework of
the 1930's and by the increasing concentration of production in mining
and industry, which was thus ill-suited to bring about the rise of an African artisan class. In agriculture, on the other hand, though the decreasing
importance of maize production reduced the resistance of European
farmers to African sales in the home market, the African petty bourgeoisie of the Native Purchase Areas was blocked from taking advantage
of the boom in export crops.[44] Furthermore their numerical increase was
held back by the government, the pretext being the lack of surveyors.[45]

CLASS INTERESTS

Given these changes in the class structure, what interests can be attributed to each class?

In the first place, there occurred the growth of an African proletariat
and a greater political consciousness in the African population at large.
This had many consequences. The pressure for higher wages, better
working conditions, and greater investment in industrial training and
African education increased; the opposition to an institutional framework,
which meant a decreasing productivity of the peasantry, grew stronger;
the loss of security of land tenure was resisted, etc.

Secondly, this phase saw the rise of manufacturing capitalism (induced
by a series of exogenous "shocks"), the growth of which was hampered
by the decreasing productivity of the African peasantry.

Mass production and the high capital intensity of operations in this
new sector meant a dwindling demand for unskilled migrant labor and
a growing interest in a more stable labor force. The substitution of the
traditional system of cultivation by African agrarian capitalism which
would bring about both greater productivity of African agriculture and
stabilization of the labor force thus suited the interests of manufacturing capitalism. *Greater competition* between African and European agriculture would inevitably follow such a substitution. The greater degree
of capital intensity also meant that high-level man-power has become
important in the cost structure of manufacturing; hence an interest in
fostering *competition* between European and African skilled and non-

44. Barber, *op. cit.*, p. 27.   45. Brown, *op. cit.*, p. 23–24

manual labor, i.e., an interest in a growing African middle class and consequent weakening of the white workers' bargaining position. At the same time the manufacturing sector of the economy was still dependent on the market of the white Rhodesians. In other words, manufacturing capitalism required for its expansion the relative worsening of living conditions of the very classes on which it still heavily depended.

Thirdly, the white agrarian bourgeoisie, having shifted from maize to tobacco production, had lost interest in industrialization and continued to require large supplies of cheap unskilled migrant labor. This further emphasizes the conflict of interests between white manufacturing and white agrarian capitalism.

Fourthly, there was a greater diversification and penetration of international capitalism in Southern Rhodesia. The interest of the giant foreign manufacturing companies overlap with those of manufacturing capitalism in general, but some important differences distinguished them from the interests of the corresponding national capitalist class. The big foreign companies engaged in primary production were even less interested in the country's industrialization than the agrarian national bourgeoisie. These big companies are specialized on a world scale in the exploitation of certain raw materials, so that what matters for their expansion is the growth of world demand for their products, and this growth does not in any way depend on local development. Since they employ or can easily adopt more modern techniques and greater mechanization their expansion is less dependent on migrant labour than in the case of national agrarian capitalists. The interests of AAC and related companies, given their "unique" position, lie somewhere between those of the other two categories of international capitalism, namely manufacturers and primary producers.

Lastly, there are some features which characterize foreign capitalists in general (whatever the nature of their activities) vis-à-vis the national bourgeoisie. Other things being equal, given their financial power, greater capital intensity, and scale of operations, they are much less vulnerable to local competition. Secondly, their size and concentration give them a stronger bargaining position at government level. Thirdly, their common and all-pervading interest is to prevent "nationalist" policies which might tamper with their local operations, irrespective of whether these policies are in favor of a national bourgeoisie, or a racial minority, or the majority of the population.

In conclusion, we can say that there is a certain coincidence of class interests between African middle class and African bourgeoisie on the one side and manufacturing capitalism on the other. But much more evident is the community of interests of the white agrarian (and petty) bourgeoisie and white wage-workers, focused on preventing racial competition. On the other hand the interests of foreign capitalism engaged in primary production were drawn nearer to those of the manufacturing class by the emergence of the African proletariat and its external manifestations, which acquired a broader political significance from the rise of African nationalism throughout the continent.

Political Implications of the Changes in the Economic Base

The changes in the superstructure resulting from the altered class structure were epitomized by the shift from the ideology of the "two pyramids" or separate development, to one of "racial partnership"; i.e., from noncompeting racial groups to the "color-blind" law of supply and demand. Competition was to concern mainly the African middle-class and bourgeoisie, since peasantry and proletariat were too weak to be able to compete with anybody but among themselves. The African middle class and bourgeoisie, as we have seen, had interests coincident with those of manufacturing capitalism and therefore their rise was to be fostered as industrialization proceeded.

As early as 1948, at the time of the African strikes and the emergence of the African proletariat, Huggins was led to think that "we shall never do much with these people until we have established a native middle class."[46] Later, in 1952, "*under the pressure of industrialization* . . . [he] quite deliberately thought of power in terms of social class, and aimed at a working alliance between the European ruling strata and the more prosperous Africans, bus owners and master farmers, building contractors and senior employees. . . ."[47] We can trace two complementary interests underlying these passages: the need of an African middle class and bourgeoisie as a *requirement* for industrialization and as an "insurance against the mass of Africans." As a matter of fact, the constant factor noticeable in government policies during the 1950's was the creation of an African middle class and bourgeoisie by inducing more interracial competition.

The institutional framework established in the 1930's no longer reflected the underlying class interests, and in consequence a series of reforms were attempted by the government.

GOVERNMENT REFORMS

Since the early 1950's, under Huggins but especially Todd[48] and later Whitehead, there was a reversal of policies, whereby all restrictions on

46. Gray, *op. cit.,* p. 314.
47. Gann and Gelfand, *op. cit.,* pp. 224–25. Italics added.
48. It is significant that Todd obtained the premiership with the support of the 'Action Group' formed by business and professional men.

competition were increasingly questioned. In 1954 a bill was introduced by the government to give recognition to African Trade Unions; the bill was referred to a Select Committee which after two years recommended an amendment to the Industrial Conciliation Act so as to include Africans in the definition of employee. Since the recommendation did not discriminate between the voting power of Europeans and Africans and sought to make all unions "vertical" (i.e., a single union covering a whole industry), African-controlled unionism could become a possibility.[49]

In African education the "whole emphasis had changed from the slow, steady uplift of the villages . . . to the rapid creation and training of an *elite*."[50] The number of teachers and pupils increased, between 1956 and 1959 by about 10 per cent each year; between 1954 and 1960 the number of pupils doubled, and multiracial university education was introduced.

Similarly, reforms were attempted in order to increase competition between Europeans and African agriculture. In the 1950's expenditure on African agriculture increased remarkably. "In the nine years from 1941 to 1949 inclusive, expenditure on agriculture development is estimated to have been close to £2.5 million. In the following nine-year period, 1950–58 inclusive, the level of expenditure increased very rapidly, totalling £18.8 million, a sixfold increase over the preceding nine years."[51] Between 1948 and 1958 the first serious effort was made to introduce purely cash crops such as cotton and Turkish tobacco.[52] Though a differential between the prices paid to Europeans and Africans remained, the lower prices were now paid in order to accumulate funds for the improvement of African agriculture. In 1961 a Select Committee recommended some purchase of European land for African use and the establishment of small unreserved areas where farmers of both races could buy land; and finally, at the congress of the United Federal Party, in October, 1962, Whitehead pledged himself to repeal the Land Apportionment Act in case of electoral victory for his party.

These attempts to accelerate the promotion of an African middle class and bourgeoisie were matched by reforms of the electoral system to enfranchise these classes. This enfranchisement had a double purpose; in the first place it aimed at compensating the loss of votes by the white classes whose interests were bound to be encroached upon by the very emergence of the African middle class and bourgeoisie.[53] Secondly it aimed at preventing the latter from becoming "agitators" by siding with the peasantry and the proletariat.[54]

It remains to examine the political implications of the formation of the African proletariat. The problem here was the stabilization of the pro-

49. Leys, *op. cit.*, pp. 116–18.
50. Gray, *op. cit.*, p. 207.
51. Yudelman, *op. cit.*, p. 159.

52. Yudelman, *op. cit.*, p. 240.
53. Leys, *op. cit.*, pp. 225–29.
54. Leys, *op. cit.*, p. 246.

letariat, because the high rate of turnover associated with migratory labor retarded specialization within the manufacturing sector. This stabilization, which as early as 1943 was deemed necessary by "several industrialists,"[55] had an urban and a rural aspect. In fact it implied the severing of the ties linking peasantry and proletariat, something which, in turn, had two implications. In the first place a rise in the minimum wages in urban areas and mining locations would become necessary in order to put the workers in a position to support, even at bare subsistence, their families in the towns. However, such a policy ran against the interests of the white agrarian bourgeoisie; in 1943 a senior official of the Native Affairs Department warned the Howman Committee, inquiring into the matter, that if a minimum wage was introduced in the towns "you are bound to have repercussions amongst the farming community and today the farming community rules this country, so that flattens out the minimum wage straight away."[56]

The second implication of urban stabilization was that the traditional system of land tenure in the rural areas ought to be abandoned in order to remove the right of free access to land for urban Africans. Here, too, the interests of manufacturing and white agrarian bourgeoisies conflicted. The interests of the former were voiced in the Legislative Assembly by Todd (at the time a government back-bencher): "We do not want native peasants. We want the bulk of them working in the mines and farms and in the European areas and we could absorb them and their families . . ." If 100,000 families moved from the rural areas, "we can begin to cope with what is left . . . and give each family 150 or 200 acres on a 99-year lease."[57] In other words, it was necessary to substitute an African agrarian bourgeoisie and proletariat for the peasantry but the change was bound to bring about greater competition for the European farmers and therefore conflicted with their class interests. The Land Husbandry Act (1951) represents a compromise between these conflicting interests. A money value was attached to farming rights which were granted to all individuals who were cultivators at the time. The rights expired on the individual's death and their transferability was limited. Thus the privilege of free access to land for urban Africans was removed, but at the same time the growth of an African agrarian bourgeoisie was prevented.

FAILURE OF CAPITALIST REFORMS

This wave of "capitalist reforms" failed conspicuously. The amendment of the Industrial Conciliation Act, recommended by the Select Committee, was not accepted, and the bill which was finally enacted was much less "revolutionary"; neither were the recommendations of the 1961

55. Gray, op. cit., p. 227.   57. Gray, op. cit., p. 299.
56. Gray, op. cit., p. 228.

Select Committee on Land Apportionment accepted. Though progress was made in African education it fell short of expectations and, particularly, of what was being done for Europeans. In agriculture more competition between Europeans and Africans had been introduced, but this was done in the less profitable markets.[58] Similarly, though government expenditure in African agriculture had grown, a dual standard was still applied to the two racial communities.

The ruling United Federal Party (UFP) lost the December 1962 election and the Land Apportionment Act was therefore never repealed. This electoral defeat of the UFP was itself the consequence of another, possibly the major, failure of the reformist program. This was the failure to achieve the aims pursued with the enfranchisement of the African middle class and petty bourgeoisie.

At the roots of this total failure, there were a number of inconsistencies inherent in the reforms themselves. First and foremost there was the fact that the new policies encroached upon the interests of those very classes on which manufacturing capitalism and its political counterpart still heavily relied, both economically and politically. As a consequence government actions were continuously hampered by its dependence on the ruling party's rank and file and on the electorate. Such a dependence explains the abortive nature of the reforms which, in turn, accounts for the failure to encourage the growth of a sizeable African middle class and bourgeoisie. The ensuing frustration induced these classes, condemned to remain a negligible economic force, to side with the peasantry and the proletariat whose grievances were also fostered by the contradictory policies of the 1950's.

A compromise between the conflicting interests of the white classes (of manufacturing and agrarian capitalism in particular) was attempted, as in the 1930's, at the expense of the Africans. The main example of this compromise is certainly the Land Husbandry Act. Labor stabilization was pursued through the stabilization of the peasantry, but, to guarantee the interests of the white farmers and workers, no urban counterpart of the policy (such as guaranteeing the subsistence of the *family* of the workers in the towns) was envisaged. The "deal" which might have been possible in the 1930's was bound, in the 1950's, to set up strong reactions on the part of the Africans whose political consciousness had greatly increased. In fact the reaction was such as to make the government discontinue the implementation of the Act. On the other hand, the resistance to the implementation of the Act strengthened the African nationalist movement which was joined by the African bourgeoisie and middle class frustrated in their growth.[59]

58. As mentioned earlier, African producers were almost completely prevented from taking advantage of the boom in tobacco exports.

59. For the political polarization of the 1950's in Southern Rhodesia, see Van Velsen, *op. cit.*, pp. 143–54.

These developments within African ranks brought about firm acts of suppression on the part of the government, and, at the same time, brought even closer the interests of manufacturing and international capitalism in accelerating the formation of an African middle class and bourgeoisie. When this "acceleration" was attempted in the early 1960's, the result was a polarization of white workers, agrarian and petty bourgeoisie, around the reactionary Rhodesian Front Party which obtained power with the elections of December, 1962.

Recent Political Developments

We have seen that in the 1930's a class structure which had its centre of gravity in a *national* agrarian bourgeoisie found expression in an institutional framework which meant (*a*) the division of the economy into largely noncompeting racial groups, (*b*) a continuously decreasing productivity of the African peasantry, and (*c*) governmental intervention to foster economic development through industrialization. The framework was internally inconsistent since a stagnant home demand for manufactures could not foster industrialization. It was also "unstable" because of the formation of a proletariat which would alter the class structure.

World War II, the postwar shortage of dollars and the increasing demand for raw materials, the outflow of capital from the United Kingdom and South Africa, and the creation of the Federation continuously increased external demand. This tendency which could have led merely to inflation was instead exploited by the government to foster economic growth. Development accelerated the rise of the African proletariat, altered the pattern of foreign investment in the country and, above all, brought about the emergence of manufacturing capitalism which became the new "centre of gravity" of the class structure. These changes resulted in strong pressures to remove the institutional framework of the 1930's. Greater interracial competition, stabilization of the proletariat, and creation of an African middle class constituted the new ideology. A wave of reforms ensued. But these reforms failed because they set up "centrifugal reactions" which culminated in the seizure of power by the white workers, the *national* agrarian capitalists, and petty bourgeoisie, who all rallied around the Rhodesian Front. These developments of the 1950's and early 1960's in Rhodesia were strikingly similar to what happened south of the Limpopo, roughly a decade earlier.

Today there are three fundamental political questions to be asked: (1) Is a neo-colonial solution possible in Rhodesia? (2) How can the seemingly absurd attempt of seizing independence unilaterally be explained? (3) Whither Rhodesia?

But before we turn to answer these questions, we need to adopt some interpretation of the behavior of the UK government *in colonial situations in general and in the Rhodesian situation in particular*. It seems a good working hypothesis to trace the rationale of its behavior in the interest of *large-scale international capitalism* (or British capitalism whenever a conflict of interests arise). If this assumption is accepted, the granting of independence to African territories can be explained as a strategy to retain economic power (i.e., to guarantee the interests of foreign capital) by concessions, in the political sphere, to the indigenous middle classes. This is the so-called "neocolonial" policy, the failures and successes of which need not be examined here. The creation of conditions favorable to the formation of an indigenous middle class has undoubtedly been one of the most general characteristics of the preindependence periods in colonial countries. In the Rhodesian context, as we have illustrated in previous sections, the affinity of the interests of the African middle class and those of large-scale capitalism can explain the series of reforms attempted during the Federal period, a corollary of which was the development of the African middle class itself. This affinity of interests, however, is not absolute. If the advantages to be derived from the development of an African middle class are offset by the reactions of other classes, then the interest of large-scale capitalism in such development fades away and a policy of "the second best" will probably emerge. The meaning of this will emerge in our discussion of prospects for a "neocolonial" solution to the Rhodesian problem.

1. PROSPECTS FOR A NEOCOLONIAL SOLUTION IN RHODESIA

In other African countries the development of an indigenous middle class was and is relatively easy, either because no class with an interest in resisting its emergence existed, or because those classes that had such interest had no sufficient political and/or economic power to organize themselves successfully and because the economic and political role to be played by the nascent class was to varying extents unsophisticated. In Rhodesia this was and is problematic. Here there is a vicious circle stemming from the cause-effect relationship between control of political power by the white settler and insignificance of the African middle class. The former induces the latter which in turn prevents the growth of a nationalist movement suitable for a solution of the "neocolonialist" type. Hence large-scale capitalism (and the British government) are in a weak position vis-à-vis the white workers and petty bourgeoisie who are thus enabled to consolidate their power position in the political as well as economic sphere. The circle is closed.

This vicious circle explains the fading away of the reformist attitude of large-scale capitalism and the British government in the three years between the end of 1962 and the end of 1965. During this period a series of political setbacks (advent to power of the RF at the end of 1962, Field's resignation in April 1964, Welensky's electoral defeat in October 1964, Referendum on independence in November 1964, General Election of May 1965) marked the retreat of the upholders of reforms and the consolidation in power of the Rhodesian Front and the classes it represents. The advent to power of the Rhodesian Front can be interpreted as an attempt to halt the wave of reforms of the Federal period and, in particular, the process of constitutional advancement which was a necessary condition for such reforms. After a period of transition (ended in April 1964 when Smith became Prime Minister) the long drawn-out *threat* of UDI and the tightening of the repressive machinery against the African nationalist movement proved to be most effective in reversing the political evolution from reforms to reaction. There was a return of the ideology and policies of the pre-Federal period. By means of mass arrests and restrictions the government was able to wipe the leadership of the African nationalist movement from the political scene. The relative ease with which the Rhodesian Front government succeeded in disrupting (at least temporarily) the organization of the nationalist movement cannot be explained, as is often done, especially by leaders of other African countries and in "liberal" circles, in terms of some inherent shortcoming of the Rhodesian African leadership as compared with the leadership of other African movements. A far more realistic explanation can be provided by the observation that the organization of the movement had, in the late 1950's and early 1960's, been shaped on the same pattern as that generally adopted in other African nationalist movements. This pattern showed a general bias in favor of securing power either by constitutional means (participation in elections, agitation and propaganda, lobbying and pressure group activities, etc.) or, if unconstitutional means were adopted, by nonviolent action (refusal to pay taxes, strikes, etc.). This type of strategy and related party structure and organization have undoubtedly proved successful in most African countries where, as suggested above, the socioeconomic formation (i.e., economic base and superstructure) was such that the groups controlling political power were willing and able to transfer it to the African middle class. In these countries the granting of independence was as much, if not more, the outcome of external circumstances as it was the result of the independence struggle waged by the nationalist movements. We have seen, on the other hand, that the classes controlling power in Rhodesia have altogether different class interests. The prevention of the growth of an African middle class and of a "neocolonialist" solution is the very objective of their rule. *It was the inadequacy of the African nationalist party as an underground revolutionary movement suitable to cope with this kind of superstructure that contributed to its repression.* The Rhodesian Front government in the year preceding UDI set up an effective repressive machinery, and thereby hampered considerably the functioning of the African nationalist party as a nonviolent movement. The significance of this achievement is that *it deprived the British government and the reformist groups of an alternative to the settlers' rule* and, what is even more important, *it hampered the growth of an African threat* which might have counter-balanced the UDI threat that accompanied the repression of the African nationalist movement.

UDI obviously expresses, in the ideological sphere, the interests of the classes represented by the ruling party. These interests were threatened by a possible political alliance of large-scale foreign capitalism and of the African middle class and petty bourgeoisie. UDI was brandished as the only way to eliminate the possibility of such an alliance. It was, there-fore, directed as much against large-scale capitalism as against the Afri-cans. The populist undertones of the UDI campaign were very noticeable. The effect of the UDI threat was to force the British government to realize that in *Rhodesia,* as opposed to the normal colonial territory, it had no viable substitute solution for settlers' rule. UDI, in other words, was a threat to bring the issue of "settlers' government versus neo-colonialist solution" into the open. In this sense the issue both crystallized the class consciousness of the majority of the white population, clinching the political power of the RF, and intimidated the British government and related interests into renouncing the reformist program and con-stitutional advancement up to 1965.

But if it is true that the *threat* of UDI, combined with the repression of the African Nationalist movement, was enough to consolidate the status quo and to divert the possibility of reforms, what induced the RF government actually to *implement* UDI?

2. SOME ASSUMPTIONS ON UDI

Many reasons for the decision to implement the UDI threat can be found, but at the present stage of documentation none is per se convinc-ing. All we can do is to list a number of possible motives, but any at-tempt to assign weights to these possibilities may be misleading.

A first reason may be traced in the African unrest in the rural areas adduced by Lardner-Burke (the Rhodesian Minister of Law and Order) in order to justify the declaration of a state of emergency over the whole country which was the prelude to UDI. It is not possible to judge to what extent African unrest really threatened a breakdown of law and order since too little of what has been happening over the last year or two in the African rural areas and townships has leaked out through the Rhodesian and foreign press. But if sufficiently widespread unrest had persisted within the African population it is quite possible that the RF government feared that, notwithstanding the strict security measures, the internal situation might explode, upsetting the delicate balance of threats and counterthreats upon which the preservation of the status quo rested.

A second reason is that the threat of UDI was wearing out, both as a catalyst of class solidarity and as an instrument of intimidation. Some African leaders north of the Zambesi were already voicing (for example, at the Commonwealth Prime Ministers' Conference in London at the end of June 1965) the idea that UDI was merely a device to divert attention from more fundamental issues, viz., African constitutional advancement. It may be, therefore, that in want of a substitute for the UDI threat, which was becoming an empty one, the RF government decided to implement it.

The relationship between economic base and superstructure is always one of mutual interdependence. The superstructure can influence the economic base by conditioning the behavior of the members of the various classes. If this is accepted, it is possible that UDI, having been embodied in the ideology of the ruling classes, came to be regarded by the rank and file of the RF not as an instrument of intimidation *vis-à-vis* the reformist groups, and of propaganda in fostering class solidarity within the white population, but as a real solution of the contradictions inherent in the Rhodesian society. Remembering the high degree of control exercised by the rank and file of the RF over the ruling elite, it is reasonable to conclude that the pressure exercised by the former probably represented a powerful spurt for the latter to declare independence unilaterally.

The realism of these three assumptions increases once they are seen in the light of yet another possible explanation. That is, the RF government may have considered that conditions were particularly favorable for the success of the operation. There were no alternatives to white settlers' rule acceptable to the British government and related interest; class consciousness of the white classes was high; and both conditions had been reinforced by the Rhodesian government's policies. In order to assess whether or not the expectations of the RF government were misplaced we must discuss the nature and the chances of success of the retaliatory action undertaken by the British government. But, whether UDI succeeds or not (in the sense to be discussed below), it is difficult to deny that it was a "fair bet."

3. WHITHER RHODESIA?

Let us first examine the chances of success of the retaliatory action undertaken by the British government. In assessing the success of this action what really matters is not so much *the extent to which economic sanctions will hit the Rhodesian economy* but rather *the existence of a mechanism whereby economic hardship (whatever its intensity) can induce the emergence of a political alternative* acceptable to those classes or groups which directly or indirectly share political power in Rhodesia, namely the settlers and the British government. What is acceptable to the British government is determined by a set of circumstances which are largely exterior to the Rhodesian situation; they concern British domestic politics and Britain's international relations in general and in Africa in particular. At any event we may assume in the first place that what is acceptable to the British government is some program of reforms aimed at the development of an African middle class to whom power could *ultimately* (say, in five to six years' time) be transferred according to the traditional pattern followed in granting independence to colonial territories. For the white Rhodesians, on the other hand, UDI has represented an attempt to perpetuate those restrictions on competition which are at the roots of their privileged economic and political position. Reforms aimed at promoting the development of an African middle class will lead to increased African competition in the produce, retail, and skilled labor markets. African advancement would mean a progressive erosion of their social status and of the premium they enjoy over wages and general working conditions in Britain, South Africa, and other white Commonwealth countries—either because it would induce substitution of African for white workers and/or because it would eliminate those restrictions on the supply of their (real or imaginary) skills from which that premium originates. White workers, petty bourgeoisie, and most of the agrarian capitalists are aware that their socioeconomic position *as classes* is based on their control of the political machinery. If and when they think that such control cannot be maintained indefinitely (that is, under present circumstances, that UDI has failed) they will prepare themselves to leave the country.

It is unrealistic to expect the majority of the white Rhodesians to cooperate in bringing about those conditions which would force them to relinquish their present political and economic power. Thus if white unemployment is induced by these sanctions, all the white unemployed can be expected to do is either to emigrate or to put pressure on the party leadership to step up unproductive activities (Army, Police, Civil Service, etc.) in order to absorb them, and to subsidize or force capitalists to keep them in employment. (Of course such a situation would be untenable in the long run, but, as argued below, the long-run effects of sanctions are to a large extent irrelevant.) Other classes within the white population—manufacturing capitalists, some professional groups, and in general all those who are not vulnerable to African competition—are not directly opposed to African advancement. These classes, however, cannot possibly be organized politically in opposition to the present rulers for two main reasons.

In the first place they are numerically insignificant and, though they retain a crucial position in the economic structure of society, their *economic* power cannot be translated into *political* opposition because of the high degree of class consciousness of the overwhelming majority of the electorate. The second reason is probably more fundamental. Though these classes are not directly threatened by African competition, their economic functions are tied to a certain economic base in the sense that the possibility of finding an outlet for their products and services is highly dependent on the given composition and level of demand, which, in turn, is determined by the existing class structure. Though a gradual removal of the shackles on competition would benefit them by improving market conditions in both factors and products market, any major and especially any *sudden* change in the economic base would seriously endanger their economic position. Under conditions of fast economic development such as obtained in the 1950's relatively minor reforms were easily smuggled into the superstructure, and manufacturing capitalism (and related interests) could play an important political role. As economic growth slowed down, population growth outstripping the growth of production, class conflicts hardened, and reforms became impracticable. Under these new circumstances the alternative to the status quo became a radical, revolutionary change of the superstructure but, for the reasons just mentioned, the former was and is preferable to the latter for those groups who had attempted the reformist programs. It follows that a solution of this type cannot be implemented without the prior removal from political power of the white settlers (which can only be achieved through military intervention and subsequent direct rule), since it cannot be expected to be brought about from within the system.

THE MINIMUM ACCEPTABLE

If military intervention and subsequent direct rule are not considered viable in London, then we must assume that, provided some face-saving device is available, the British government is prepared to meet the "minimum" acceptable to the ruling classes in Rhodesia. The "minimum" acceptable to the ruling classes in Rhodesia is the indefinite continuation of their control over the political machinery. This result can be brought about essentially in two ways. In the first place there can be a gradual consolidation of the regime in the political sphere, even though the economic hardship caused by sanctions increases—at least temporarily. Irrespective of the degree of contraction of the economy, what matters most from the regime's point of view is to last long enough, say, a year or two after the declaration, to consolidate itself politically to such an extent that, even if sanctions have not been formally relaxed, loopholes will be more easily found. Furthermore, one can also assume that given a long enough period, a certain readjustment in the pattern of trade and production would take place. One can expect a switch (at least partial) in productive processes which would lessen the economic dependence on Britain and other "hostile" countries, increasing the economy's self-sufficiency and/or dependence on the South African economy. Given the absence within the system of any mechanism that can translate *economic* hardship into *political* opposition to UDI only British military intervention can stop this consolidation. A commitment against such intervention can only mean its tacit acceptance.

The acceptance may even be negotiated. It is clear that the Rhodesian rulers are prepared to make concessions (constitutional or otherwise) provided they are left in control of the political machinery. Whatever the constitutional arrangements, it would then be possible to control administratively, economically, and socially the political evolution of the system—ultimately reverting to an *apartheid* system of one sort or another consistent with the class interests of white workers, petty bourgeoisie, and agrarian capitalists. Any sign of success of the "talks about talks" between British and Rhodesian civil servants, at present (June, 1966) being held in Salisbury, would therefore seem to point to a negotiated, rather than tacit, acceptance of the trend towards apartheid in Rhodesia.

SANCTIONS AND MILITARY INTERVENTION

To sum up, the ability of sanctions to impose economic hardship on the white population should not be denied. Given sufficient determination on the part of the British and Zambian governments, such hardship can be increased at will; there is a limit, of course, determined by the resilience of the economy and the determination—difficult to assess correctly—of the South African government to keep Rhodesia under white settlers' control. What must be questioned is the belief that such hardship will bring about political change in the sense of accepting ultimate African rule. Since it ignores the economic base and superstructure (and especially their interdependence) of the Rhodesian social system this belief is based on naïve analysis. On the other hand, if it is accepted that political change in the desired direction cannot be produced from within the Rhodesian social system, ultimately the British government will have either to intervene militarily in order to produce the change from without, or gradually to accept the status quo. If the first alternative is chosen, it is not clear why military intervention was not carried out in the first place when UDI was declared. Even if the main obstacle was British public opinion, there is no reason to expect this obstacle to disappear. What is more important is that the passing of time is not going to improve the prospects of a bloodless intervention, and this for two main reasons. In the first place a certain confusion of interests was bound to exist in the top and middle ranks of the Army, Police, Judiciary, and Civil Service when UDI was declared. These were in fact inherited by the RF government from the Federal period and to some extent must have retained the "liberal" characteristics of the previous rule. At the time of UDI the presence of a British armed force could have made the choice between "treason and loyalty" a real and not merely a theoretical one, as in effect it became. In the absence of such force the crucial choice was, and is, between supporting the status quo and resigning. As a result of delaying action on the part of the British government, these groups will be increasingly committed to the Smith regime, both through increased commitment of the individuals and through a process of selection and substitution which inevitably accompanies promotions, recruitment, and resignations. From this point of view, therefore, the increased commitment to the regime of the administrative and military apparatus can only reduce the chances of a swift, and possibly bloodless, seizure of power by Britain. Moreover, of course, anti-British feelings among white Rhodesians have hardened since UDI and the introduction of sanctions. These feelings are an expression, in the ideological sphere, of the class consciousness of white Rhodesians. As such they have perfectly rational roots, but they may easily develop emotionally into an autonomous element capable in itself of influencing the behavior of the party's rank and file, the ruling elite, and the white population at large.

If the assumption of naiveté on the part of the British government is not thought to be satisfactory, then the conclusion must be drawn that British government and related interests accept the prospect of Rhodesia ultimately resorting to apartheid.

PROSPECTS OF AFRICAN REVOLUTION

One crucial question has been left out of the discussion so far: the prospects of an African revolution. Can we expect an African revolution to halt the trend towards an apartheid society—which, as we have seen, may be the result of the British government's Rhodesian policy? There are two problems here. What are the chances that an insurrectionary movement will gather momentum? If it did, how would it influence the trend of events outlined above?

Notwithstanding the severe security measures taken by the government, outbursts of violence have already occurred in Salisbury and in some rural areas in the Northern and Eastern parts of the country. The regime, while disclosing acts of violence due to infiltrators from outside the country, has tried its best, often successfully, to conceal any violent activity originating within the country. Whether these activities will gather momentum is difficult to say. The disproportion of forces—in weapons, organization, training, etc.—between the two sides is enormous, being itself a reflection of the class structure of the system. Geographically the country is land-locked and except in the North[60] is surrounded by countries more or less sympathetic to the regime. There are no jungles or mountainous areas except on the borders (the region being a plateau, generally from 4,000 to 5,000 feet above sea-level, enclosed by the Lowveld of the Zambesi and Limpopo valleys to the North and South respectively). What is more important, the Land Apportionment Act, besides its political-economic effects, has segregated the Africans in such a way that, in the urban areas, they can be "sealed off" from the white communities, enhancing the security of the latter. All these factors are handicaps in the organization of revolutionary activity in Rhodesia. Furthermore, Rhodesia (with South Africa) represents the unique situation of a society where, almost literally, all the top and middle ranks of the Army, Police, Civil Service, etc. are occupied by the ruling classes who are easily identified by the color of their skin. Moreover, some units of the armed forces consist exclusively of members of the dominant classes. This factor rules out the possibility of the ruling classes being ousted by any form of *coup d'état* and makes protracted guerrilla warfare of the traditional type unlikely to succeed in directly toppling the regime.

Presumably this is consciously or subconsciously realized by the African population. Unless it lapses into resignation, its widespread discontent will be channelled into terrorist activities.[61] Assuming that the organization of the nationalist movement is being restructured in this sense, a *tendency* for widespread terrorism will most certainly develop with the steady increase (worsened by sanctions) of unemployment.

It is of course possible that such activities could come just at the "right time," adding insecurity to economic hardship, transforming the "creeping" emigration of whites into a "galloping" one, and then setting up a cumulative process of violence and economic hardship the outcome of which is uncertain: intervention from the South, intervention from the North, Britain's or UN's intervention, a combination of these—or no intervention at all.

60. The Zambian government, however, has so far impeded the flow of arms through its country.
61. The distinction between terrorism and guerrilla warfare is based on the fact that the latter is *mainly* directed against regular forces while the former is mainly directed against the civilian population.

Part VII   **AFRICA IN THE WORLD:**
PAN-AFRICANISM AND
NEUTRALISM

The height of the Cold War coincided with the advent of independence for many new nations in Africa and Asia. Recently freed from the political ties of colonialism, wary of a still unknown communism, most of these countries decided to adhere to a policy of "neutralism." Neutralism has had different meanings for different nations at different times. Perhaps George Washington best expressed the common core of interest in 1793 when he declared that the United States, "The First New Nation," would follow a policy of "non-entangling alliances." She would not be drawn into the power struggle of Europe where her own vital interests were not involved; she would mind her own business, and see to her own destiny, and by implication would, of course, welcome aid that was not "entangling." On June 9, 1956, John Foster Dulles denounced neutralism "as an

immoral and short-sighted conception" on the grounds that its practitioners wrongly believed that "a nation can buy safety for itself by
being indifferent to the fate of others." Today, few statesmen or
analysts argue the morality of the problem of neutralism. A more
difficult question centers on the feasibility of relatively poor countries
following an independent course in an increasingly interdependent
world divided into spheres of influence by gigantic superpowers.
What range of choice do even the most seriously and well-inten-
tioned noncommitted have? Will the superpowers tolerate truly
nonaligned states? Have they no interest in the domestic politics of
these countries? Warnings about "inherent communist expansionism"
are countered by the proposition that the Western world seeks to
arrest the social revolution against feudal or quasifeudal regimes that
is sweeping the underdeveloped world because it fears a loss of the
status quo and entrenched colonial or neocolonial interests. One
school of neutralist thought, including Africans as staunchly allied
to the West as Léopold Senghor, argues that the real division in the
world is not between East and West, capitalism and communism, but
between the rich and poor, the capitalist and proletarian *nations*. All
industrialized nations are alike in that they are in a position to exploit
the underdeveloped countries. All the nations of Africa should
therefore band together in their common defense.

Such an undertaking might form the basis of a new type of pan-
Africanism, and demonstrates a possible impetus between neutralism
and some form of broader political unity. Yet pan-Africanism, as
Rupert Emerson's article shows, became a complicated doctrine in
practice, once African leaders became responsible for the affairs of
their own autonomous nation-states. Gone are the days when a small,
virtually free-floating, group of African students and intellectuals
could meet in somebody's apartment in Paris and London and discuss,
with only the clearest commitment to their ideals and each other,
plans for a new African man and a new society of the United States
of Africa. Today, pan-Africanism remains a dream and a vision. Each
country desires to be left alone—to develop its economy, to unify its
own people—neutral even from other African states. Faced with the
hard realities of the postindependence world, the difficulties of economic development, the necessities of facing competing domestic
interests, the complexities of international relations, the establishment
of effecting a state apparatus on simply a country basis, few energies

have been available recently for broader movements. Yet a belief and commitment to pan-Africanism persists. Not all would agree that the new nations of Africa represent the wave of the future, nor would all believe that they have a unique ideological message for mankind. Yet, as the new nations develop in all their variety and complexity, the western civilizations that created the Hiroshima and Auschwitz tragedies may yet learn something new.

Fred L.
Hadsel

AFRICA AND THE WORLD:
NONALIGNMENT RECONSIDERED

African nonalignment was initially formulated and first flourished during the decade between the holding of the Afro-Asian conference at Bandung in 1955 and the failure to hold the "Second Bandung" at Algiers in 1965. Two streams of thought and action contributed principally to African nonalignment—the Asian conferences in the immediate postwar period, where nonalignment, as a term, received general currency, and the African independence movement of the 1950's, which within a few years transformed a largely colonial domain into a generally independent continent. These two streams were like the White and Blue Niles at their confluence at Khartoum. At first, they retained a separate identity, although traveling along the same direction, but fairly soon they largely intermixed, even though they never quite lost the qualities of their separate sources.

The several Asian conferences between 1947 and 1954 were a search for identity on the part of new independent nations and a reaction against colonialism as they had known it during their dependent years. This movement came to a heady fruition in the Bandung Conference of 1955. Thereafter it involved itself more and more with African and other nations—eventually reaching as far west as Cuba and, in due course, becoming entangled with the Sino-Soviet dispute. In the course of this development, it lost whatever Asian cohesiveness it ever had and became a battleground for other powers and other movements.[1]

1. See especially G. H. Jansen, *Nonalignment and the Afro-Asian States* (New York: Frederick A. Praeger, 1966); Cecil V. Crabb, *The Elephant and the Grass: A Study in Nonalignment* (New York: Frederick A. Praeger, 1965); John W. Burton (ed.), *Nonalignment* (London, 1966); *Nonalignment in Foreign Affairs*, *The Annals*, The American Academy of Political and Social Science, Vol. 362 (November 1965).

Reprinted from *The Annals*, Vol. 372 (July 1967), pp. 97–103, by permission of the author and publisher. *The views expressed in this article are entirely personal and are not to be considered as official comments of an official of the Department of State.*

Growth of Political Nonalignment in Africa

During the formative period of Asian nonalignment, the activators of independence in Africa were so deeply enmeshed in their struggle both to achieve leadership within their potential area of authority and to obtain independence from their colonial metropoles, that they initially had neither the time nor the inclination to branch out beyond these immediate goals. However, as the independence movement gained momentum, its leaders instinctively sought cooperation from each other, and out of this pan-Africanism of the 1950's came the desire for still wider association that led to a marriage of the newer African with the older Asian movement. A measure of this expanding association is found in the number of Africans attending such meetings at the beginning and the end of the first decade of African involvement in nonalignment. At Bandung in 1955, four African countries took part while, after the floodtide of independence, twenty-eight African countries were represented at the Cairo Conference in 1964.[2]

Thus, the independence movement of this decade was what in economic jargon is called a "precondition" for the development of African nonalignment. The pan-African movement, then, gave African nonalignment its initial formulation and, in fact, was an important conditioning element throughout this period.[3] For example, Ghana's independence in March 1957 provided its leader, Kwame Nkrumah, the sovereign political base from which to launch the first Conference of Independent African Nations, April, 1958, and the first All African Peoples Conference, December, 1958. Thereafter, conference followed conference in the continent until the meeting at Addis Ababa in May, 1963, which established the Organization of African Unity (OAU). The charter was an amalgam of these various movements. It dedicated the member nations (1) to safeguard their national sovereignty, (2) to eradicate colonialism from the remaining dependent territories of Africa, (3) to support unity among member nations, and (4) to uphold nonalignment in Africa's relations with the rest of the world.

It is impossible for any observer to measure the strength of African devotion to these various principles, which, in any case, merged one into

---

2. African delegations were in the following ratio: Bandung, 1955: 4 of 29; Belgrade, 1961: 10 of 24; and Cairo, 1964: 28 of 47.
3. See especially Colin Legum, *Pan-Africanism: A Short Political Guide* (rev. ed.; New York: Frederick A. Praeger, 1965); S. Okechukwu Mezu (ed.), *The Philosophy of Pan-Africanism* (Washington, D. C.: Georgetown University Press, 1965); and Immanual Wallerstein, *Africa: The Politics of Unity: An Analysis of a Contemporary Social Movement* (New York: Vintage, 1967).

another. It would be logical to assume that the intensity of feeling was probably greatest with respect to national sovereignty and most diffuse with respect to political nonalignment. The problems of national development, continued colonial control, and all-African cooperation were certainly of more immediate interest. Whatever the difference might be with respect to these questions, there was a generally held feeling of mutual endeavor, even brotherhood, in the OAU, which was more tangible than the sentiments recorded at the more infrequent meetings of Africans and Asians. For one thing, the OAU was more active. It held three full assemblies, ten foreign minister meetings, and a number of commission and special meetings in the period 1963–1965, while during the same years the larger Afro-Asian nonaligned group held only two conferences and foundered in two preparatory meetings for the third. For another thing, the OAU soon turned to national and colonial questions. Resolutions dealing with these issues were widely discussed and generally accepted, even though differences on such matters as the pace of African unity were sometimes sharply drawn. After the first meeting, the OAU did not deal with nonalignment as such, and while certain of its resolutions were concerned with issues which related to nonalignment, it tended to concentrate on problems within the continent.

Nevertheless, a number of African leaders developed an extensive interest in nonalignment. President Nasser had taken part in the Bandung Conference, and the other three African heads of state sent senior ministers. Presidents Nkrumah, Touré, Keita, Nyerere, Obote, Ben Bella, and others were increasingly active in nonaligned conferences after their countries achieved independence. At the same time, nonalignment obtained less explicit adherence from other African leaders. In these cases, endorsement ranged from support of particular goals to lip service for political purposes. Finally, a fairly small group of African leaders made it clear to their colleagues that they did not subscribe at all to this point of view, even though their countries were members of the OAU.

It is difficult, even impossible, to try to make an exact count of the views of African leaders on nonalignment during this decade. Governments changed; new problems emerged; attendance at particular meetings was sometimes incomplete. Rather, the events of this first decade of African involvement in the movement showed a wide variation in the degree of acceptance of the ideas making up the doctrine and a similar diversity in the extent of participation in formulating such views in the nonaligned conferences. This is hardly surprising when one considers the range of ideas which, in accumulation, made up the political content of African nonalignment of this period.

Principal Themes of Political Nonalignment

Although the number of African leaders who devoted themselves actively to the propagation of nonalignment was relatively small, no single person was recognized as the high priest of the movement, and many of them were concerned with one or a few of its tenets. While, therefore, it is possible in very general ways to identify the principal themes of nonalignment, it is also necessary to pave any formulation with caveats as to the universality, cohesiveness, and application of these ideas. In short, it is hard to be more than impressionistic or to achieve more than an approximate consensus as to the recurring elements.

First, nonalignment was one formulation of an overriding aspiration, that of preserving the independence of the African nation. By no means the only way this desire could be articulated, nonalignment was nevertheless a call to judge foreign policy primarily on the basis of new-found freedom.

Second, nonalignment performed two very important tasks in the internal politics of African nations whose independence and political stability was not always secure. In states made up of disparate peoples and divergent traditions, nonalignment helped secure the support of these various elements in the body politic by reinforcing the goal of independence in foreign policy. In states where either the anticolonialist or pro-Communist groups were at odds with the government—or with each other—nonalignment became a means of neutralizing these critics of the established leadership.

Third, nonalignment, which was viewed by the skeptics as wishful thinking, was in another sense a supremely realistic assessment of the weakness of small nations in a world of more powerful nations. Proponents of nonalignment in this context argued that the only way for a small nation to maintain its identity was to stay out of the struggle among the giants. In a similar sense, advocates of nonalignment declared that military alliances with the powerful caused small countries to forfeit their independence, and abstention from such alliances was therefore considered the hallmark of the nonaligned.

Fourth, nonalignment could not escape the historical circumstances from which it emerged. Being part of the independence movement and intensely anticolonial in background, nonalignment sometimes emphasized primarily *not* aligning with the former colonial powers of their Western allies. Even after independence, since many colonial administrators, institutions, and connections remained intact, African leaders under pressure to seek further attributes of sovereignty attacked those nationals and nations closest at hand. Hence, Western critics of nonalignment claimed that it, in fact, leaned toward the East. This charge seemed reinforced when one observed the active participation of either the Soviet Union or Communist China, or both, in conferences which were ostensibly non-aligned. Such a climate of controversy not only made "real" nonalignment next to impossible to define, but made a real consensus on the term impossible, even at conferences of the nonaligned.

Fifth, nonalignment provided a welcome basis for cooperation among nations which were otherwise distant from each other in geography, people, or history. In that sense, it was an umbrella under which widely different nations could find a communion of views, such as anticolonialism or disarmament; a common cause, such as economic development or eradication of disease; or confirmation of their fears, especially concerning great-power pressures.

Sixth, nonalignment became a means of cooperation among nations with a view to exercising influence in world affairs which individually or in small groups they could not otherwise achieve. Inherent in this cooperative effort was often a judgment as to the moral right of the nonaligned as against the immorality of power politics as exercised by the great powers of the world. To some observers this appeared to be little more than moralizing based on weakness and was a point of view quickly forgotten when it came to issues closer at home. But to others, this point of view stemmed from an urgent search for human values and a desperate fear that they would be destroyed before they could be achieved.

Other elements were to be found in nonalignment, such as the condemnation of nuclear weapons, the instinctive aversion to military bases, and the danger of external involvement jeopardizing domestic economic growth. Specific situations or particular problems called forth variations in these themes. But like the abstraction of the composite "average man" in public opinion surveys, these six elements were the most common attributes of nonalignment during this decade.

Evolution of Economic Nonalignment in Africa

During the same decade between Bandung and Algiers, African leaders also developed their views with respect to economic nonalignment. More diffuse than its political counterpart, and neither as fully formulated nor as generally endorsed, economic nonalignment became increasingly important in African thinking as this period moved to a close.

Three general reasons account for the different state of economic nonalignment. In the initial surge of independence, the emphasis was more generally placed on political action and political effect. Most African leaders appeared to accept President Nkrumah's admonition of seeking first the political keys to the kingdom of full independence. Moreover, the various conferences dealing with nonalignment tended to emphasize the political more than economic.

Equally important, moreover, was the fact that African nations were already in a special economic relationship with European countries, both individually and with the Commonwealth and European Economic Community. All of them were heavily dependent upon external assistance from the West. It might be within the realm of the practical for many of the African nations to eschew military alliances, but it was obviously impossible for any government to avoid economic agreements with the former metropoles.

Principal Themes of Economic Nonalignment

Under these circumstances, it is understandable that the themes of economic nonalignment developed during the decade between Bandung and Algiers were neither clear-cut nor universally supported. Moreover, they developed more slowly in an era where political considerations predominated.

First—aside from the overriding desire to obtain as much economic assistance as possible—there developed a desire on the part of many African leaders to decrease dependence on a single foreign country. Stimulated in part by criticism from within the country, these leaders tended to equate a greater degree of independence with a larger number of nations giving them assistance. In the first instance this usually meant turning to the United States, whose technical assistance and developmental aid increased to a high point in 1963.

Second, for political reasons as much as economic, there developed a tendency to balance the West against the East. There then began dialogues with the Soviet Union, East European countries, and finally with Communist China. This trend was also attractive to a number of Africans as a direct means of increasing their total help, and it was attractive to some because they hoped to play off one power bloc against the other.

Third, the slogan of "aid without strings" became a part of the doctrine of economic nonalignment. In some cases, this became an emotional reaction against even efforts to make assistance more efficient; in others, this attitude was part of the negotiating process that took place as African countries sought to minimize the burden inherent to obtaining funds for economic development. Whatever the exact rationale, it is clear that some leaders exaggerated the strength of any alleged strings, and a number were certainly fearful lest their independence of political action be compromised by such agreements.[4]

Fourth, there developed among some spokesmen, especially of Sub-Saharan Africa, the point of view that the West had an obligation to assist their economic growth. The colonial powers (including the United States) had taken their manpower during the years of slave trade; they had exported their resources, both mineral and agricultural; and as developed nations they had a duty to help the less developed.

Finally, the preference increased in certain African quarters for multilateral assistance rather than bilateral. These proponents stated that since the United Nations, the International Bank for Reconstruction and Development (IBRD), the International Monetary Fund (IMF), and other specialized agencies were not controlled by any single power, it was better to obtain assistance in that form if at all possible.

The Period of Transition

Toward the end of the decade between Bandung and Algiers, African nonalignment began a transformation which is still under way. This transitional period, however, is too much with us to permit a satisfactory sorting out of the interaction which affected African nonalignment. What we can discuss, instead, are several probable causes of the change we are living through, and certain directions along which African thought seems to be moving. Infallibility in this analysis is clearly impossible.

In the first place, the change was certainly a product of the split between the Soviet Union and Communist China. This split destroyed one of the assumptions of the Third or Nonaligned World—that these countries of Africa and Asia were standing between two giant blocs. In fact this situation recently stimulated the editor of *Jeune Afrique*, the most widely read of francophone journals, to declare that the Third World had become the Second, since the Communist world, which had been the Second, had fallen apart. As the split widened and the competition intensified, the Chinese in particular became more militant in pressing nonaligned countries to join them in attacking the West and the Soviet Union. This not only revealed the hypocrisy of Communist cooperation with nonaligned countries, but it highlighted the futility of trying to get agreement on nonaligned position in particular problems in which Communist China had a stake, such as its border dispute with India.

4. This view reached an extreme point in Kwame Nkrumah's *Neo-Colonialism: The Last Stage of Imperialism* (New York: International Publishers, 1965; London, 1965).

The history of the Afro-Asian People's Solidarity Organization (AAPSO) just before and during this transitional period illustrates some of these points. Originally an organization receiving considerable support from African nationalist movements and governments, AAPSO had become a battleground of the Chinese and Soviets by the time it held its conference at Moshi, Tanganyika, in February, 1963. It had also been receiving less support from African governments, who found that, while the secretariat was located in Africa, it was, in fact, dominated by the two major Communist powers. As AAPSO became more and more a transparent front organization, it became less attractive to many African leaders. Moreover, when AAPSO sponsored the Havana Tri-Continental Conference which was finally held in January, 1966, it became clear to the overwhelming number of African countries that AAPSO's interest in their continent was incidental to its interest in expanding communism.

The greater awareness in Africa of Communist China's militancy during 1965 was another element in the disillusionment with China as a colleague in nonalignment. For example, Chou En-Lai's statement in Dar es Salaam in June 1965 that Africa was ripe for revolution implied a point of view and an apparent willingness to intervene in African affairs that was not appreciated by many African leaders. Equally sobering as an indication of general Chinese Communist philosophy and tactics was the long statement by Marshal Lin Piao in September of the same year. This statement, which was repeatedly broadcast by the Peking radio, placed the underdeveloped world, that is, Africa, within a plan of Communist conquest which, to say the least, contradicted African aspirations for nonalignment.

A dramatic change in the fortunes of nonalignment also occurred in 1965, during the two unsuccessful efforts in June and October to hold the Afro-Asian Conference at Algiers. The issues and maneuvers which accompanied the preliminary meetings of the Standing Committee and the preparatory meetings of the Foreign Ministers involved Sino-Soviet rivalry and Asian politics more than they did issues of African nonalignment. A number of African states had throughout been skeptical concerning the usefulness of the conference; the African Commonwealth nations came out in favor of postponement on the eve of the first attempt in June; and the cross-currents of debate divided even those African countries who attended the October meeting, when postponement was finally accepted by the participants.

It has been argued with some cogency that the failure to hold the Afro-Asian conference in Algiers did not finish off nonalignment, but it did bring to the end the cycle of Afro-Asian conferences, in which the rationale of nonalignment had been developed. It meant the end, for the time being at least, of international meetings such as those in Belgrade

(1961) and Cairo (1964) whose *raison d'être* had been the value and influence which might be derived from international association of nonaligned nations.

In the meantime, there had begun a series of political changes in Africa which within a year would have considerable effect upon the personalities of the continent's leadership. The first occurred in Algeria in June, 1965. During the following winter and spring, the leadership changed in the Congo (K), Dahomey, Central African Republic, Upper Volta, Nigeria, and Ghana. These developments had two principal effects on African nonalignment. First, the changes removed two of the activists among nonaligned leaders, Ben Bella and Nkrumah. Second, as the pattern of leadership changed, there was a perceptible turning of attention away from distant foreign issues to problems of politics in Africa and at home.

Along with the series of political changes in the leadership of Africa, there also developed a new pattern in the issues which preoccupied the African nations. The Congo problem, which had long been a barometer of conflicting African attitudes on the United Nations, the role of metropoles, and the orientation of newly independent African nations, slowly became less acute as an international issue as the rebellion within the country was brought under control and the government at Kinshasa gained acceptability within Africa. Meanwhile, the issues in southern Africa were increasingly concerning the leadership elsewhere in the continent. The most dramatic of these emerging issues was Southern Rhodesia, whose unilateral declaration of independence on November 11, 1965, opened a new phase in the problems of southern Africa. Rhodesia occasioned a special meeting of the OAU Foreign Ministers in December, 1965, and became a principal concern of the organization thereafter. At the same time, it became apparent to most observers that other issues in this part of Africa—the Portuguese territories, Southwest Africa, and South Africa itself—were occupying a larger amount of attention than matters outside the continent.

It would be a serious exaggeration to suggest that after 1965 a clear-cut swing away from political nonalignment took place. Circumstances were too complex to be neatly described, and the responses of the various leaders were inevitably in terms of the problems which were of particular concern to their particular country. One of the most articulate of African leaders, President Nyerere, mirrored the difficulties, dilemmas, and aspirations facing his country in a series of public statements in the summer of 1966, when he emphasized the costs of an independent non-aligned policy, the necessity for developing national economic and political strength, and the need for African cooperation to this end. As far as political nonalignment was concerned, he stressed the view that its enduring elements were protection of independence, friendship with all countries (or nonengagements with any bloc), and adaptation from any source of institutions which contribute to economic development. At the same time, these efforts could only be successful, in his view, when accompanied by cooperation among Africans to settle disputes and to build toward African unity.[5] Other leaders saw the problem differently, thereby confirming the general impression that there was no single response to the changing African scene.

An increasing emphasis on economic development also occurred in this period of transition, although its themes are difficult to identify, even in a tentative manner. It can be said—if not proved—that, proportionately, there was greater concern with economic problems as of the mid-1960's than earlier in the decade. Political independence had run its course for the time being—with the exception of Botswana and Lesotho in 1966—but political independence had not brought the economic growth that the leaders hoped or that many of the people expected. Hence, there was broader realization of the economic difficulties facing Africa and greater recognition that Africa faced a "long haul" in this field of effort. An eloquent description of Africa's needs and one nation's proposals to meet these problems was given by the Kenyan Chairman, Mr. Tom Mboya, at the biennial United Nations Economic Commission for Africa (ECA) conference in Lagos, February, 1967.[6]

The consequences of the greater concern for economic development were numerous, and in their total effect they contributed to reconsideration of views on economic nonalignment which a few years earlier were widely, if not generally, accepted. As African leaders measured the magnitude of problems facing them and felt the continued pressure of their people for improving living conditions, they recognized all the more clearly the fundamental importance of external assistance. Facing a plateau in the overall amount of assistance available from foreign donors, moreover, some African nations began to reconsider their previous positions and, along with this review, to modify some of their views and tactics of nonalignment.

One of the changes in emphasis took place in the attitude of African nations with respect to the European Common Market. The eighteen-nation-association agreement had been signed on July 20, 1963. Discussion for admission as associated members was opened by Nigeria, Uganda, Kenya, and Tanzania during 1965–1966, thus adding to the

5. Julius K. Nyerere, "The Cost of Non-alignment," *Africa Report* (October 1966), pp. 61–65 (Memorandum to TANU of June 9, 1966); "Africa Faces a Dilemma," Speech at the University of Zambia, Lusaka, July 13, 1966; Address delivered at Mogadiscio, Somalia, August 23, 1966.

6. Tom Mboya, "A Development Strategy for Africa: Problems and Proposals," Statement at the Eighth Session of the ECA, Lagos, February 13, 1967.

number of African nations which are seeking economic benefits through a formal association with European countries.

Another change was the higher priority given to commodity agreements, particularly those concerning coffee and cocoa. African countries began to take a more active role in implementing the coffee agreement and in seeking the conclusion of a cocoa agreement. Indicating a wider recognition of the importance of cooperative institutions for the regulation of such crops, the nations directly concerned settled down in 1966 to negotiations necessary to reach a workable solution to the cocoa problem.

A third trend has been a decrease in the suspicions directed against private business as agents of neocolonialism. Not only have a number of states enacted legislation to attract business, but, during the period 1964–1967, they signed some thirteen investment guarantee agreements with the United States and gave other indications of their interest in the cooperation of United States and other firms in their development.

These scattered illustrations, however, point to another trend which also suggests a greater pragmatism. This is the recognition of the role of "self-help" in economic development. Such an emphasis, of course, relates to one of the initial elements of nonalignment, that of achieving real independence. One can argue that "self-help" is a new way of dealing with an old desire.

Throughout most of the period of the rise and modification of nonalignment, African nations had welcomed international cooperation in the field of economic development. The United Nations Economic Commission for Africa, established in 1958, had been more active than its counterparts in other regions of the world. This trend continued during the period of transition with respect to nonalignment. The elements abetting the modification of attitudes towards nonalignment appeared, in this instance, to reinforce what had been gradually developing during previous years. The United Nations Development Program, for example, increased its African activities, especially in the direction of regional river basin projects. The World Bank similarly continued to expand its activities in Africa during the mid-1960's. International institutions were particularly attractive to these countries concerned with nonalignment, since they thought that any political conditions would be avoided by virtue of the nature of the lending agency.[7]

Another development in international organization, however, took place during the mid-1960's, which may have considerable effect in reshaping the African views on economic nonalignment. This was the growth within the United Nations of a common effort on the part of

7. An editorial in the *Ethiopian Herald*, March 29, 1967, is one example of this point of view.

underdeveloped countries to devote more of the United Nations efforts to their problems. This feeling had helped stimulate the holding of the United Nations Conference on Trade and Development (UNCTAD) in 1964. At this conference, some seventy-five of the members from the undeveloped parts of the world grouped themselves together to further their common goal of rapid economic growth. Declaring that a division of the world between the affluent and the impoverished was intolerable, they hailed their unity at the conference as the first step toward achieving development.[8] Both the approach and substance of the seventy-five (now seventy-seven) suggest some of the concerns which underlay earlier nonalignment, but they began developing a far different strategy as they sought to secure greater economic benefits and, therefore, economic independence for the developing nations of the world. The proposal made on several occasions in the past year by President Senghor that these nations meet, possibly in Algiers, to prepare for the next UNCTAD conference, presently planned for 1968, may lead to further steps in this direction. In referring to this meeting as an economic non-aligned conference, President Senghor was adapting an old label to a new situation.

Conclusion

A description which indicates so many strands of development and so much diversity in the patterns of events cannot fail to lead to highly qualified conclusions. Yet it is clear, at the tactical level at least, that certain of the modalities of nonalignment have been discarded. For example, the large conference producing many resolutions has been abandoned for the time being. Moreover, some of the assumptions which gave rise to nonalignment have been called into question. Thus, the fears which metropoles instinctively incited in many newly independent nations are receding into the background as time goes by. In addition, in the balance of attention which every leader must strike on the problems that preoccupy him, those matters closer to home have become proportionately more important than those which stimulated some of the nonaligned pronouncements of previous years. Political stability, relations with nearby nations, and Africa's own tranquility have weighed more importantly than Berlin, Tibet, or Cuba.

That this transformation is not a simple turning within, a sort of African version of isolation, however, is especially clear in the fields of economics. Recognition of the tremendous task of development has

---

8. For one assessment, see Sidney Weintraub, "After the UN Trade Conference: Lessons and Portents," *Foreign Affairs* (October 1964), pp. 37–50.

accentuated the need for national action, self-reliance, and self-help. But it has also stimulated more relations with the outside world, in particular Europe and the Western Hemisphere. It has brought renewed attention to problems of trade and commodities. And, as a long-term trend, it may well lead to a new community of interest among the underdeveloped nations. While any action in conference will be very different from the meetings between Bandung and Cairo, African leaders will nevertheless be dealing with some of the same issues which stimulated the first wave of nonalignment: national independence, economic development, and relations with non-African powers. In such a situation, it is safe to say that the pragmatism which is a significant characteristic of the transitional period through which nonalignment is now going will help to avoid some of the abstraction and unreality which characterized the African movement during its initial decade.

Rupert　　　　**PAN-AFRICANISM**
Emerson

*T*he African scramble for independence has led to
two major political trends which have at least the superficial look of
being contradictory but which may still turn out to be complementary.
One is the consolidation of states, and, it may be, of nations, within the
frontiers traced on the map of Africa with an imperial flourish by the
colonial powers. The other is the unceasing agitation and conferring to
secure some sort of African unity which would bring together within a
common framework either all the African peoples or such more limited
groupings of them as are now prepared to join forces for general or
particular purposes. The unanswered, and still unanswerable, question is
whether the states which have been emerging in such quantities, with
more still to come—twenty-nine African members of the UN at the end
of 1961 as against five in 1955—will serve as the building blocks for a
greater African union or whether they will jealously guard the separate
identity which they have now achieved.

The realist is likely to be tempted to dismiss pan-Africanism as an
idle and romantic dream, unable to make a significant breach in the solid
walls of state sovereignty which Africans are in process of erecting. The
turn of events may well prove him to be correct, but in the interim the
devotion to pan-Africanism is both widespread and charged with emotion. Nkrumah is far from being alone in his repeated insistence that the
independence of particular African states takes on its full meaning only
if all of Africa is free and if African unity is achieved. This sense of a
mutuality of interest in freedom among all African peoples and countries
found virtually no counterpart in the corresponding anticolonial drive
of the Asian peoples, each of which pursued and enjoyed its independence
without significant regard for the others. In the eyes of the believers the
case for African unity rests not only on such utilitarian grounds as the
need to collaborate and to establish a common front against Africa's

Reprinted in abridged form from *International Organization*,
Vol. 6, No. 2 (Spring 1962), pp. 437–456, by permission of
the author and publisher.

enemies but also on the mystique of the conviction that Africans are born to share a common destiny. To the special circumstances of Africa which press toward unity the contention is often added that this is an era of global interdependence in which particularist nationalisms have become anachronistic.

Self-Determination and Territorial Integrity

The present consolidation of African states within the former colonial frontiers runs counter to much of what had been both predicted and desired during the colonial era. It was widely assumed that as soon as Africans came to freedom they would sweep aside the arbitrary boundaries imposed by the imperialists which cut across tribes and overrode the dictates of geography and economics. The continent had been partitioned to meet colonial convenience, but it would now be reshaped to realize its "natural" contours and return to its African essence. The accusation that the colonial powers had arbitrarily divided Africa among themselves rested on indisputable historical evidence; the further accusation, however, that they had broken up pre-existing African unity could be established only by a reconstruction of history. The balkanization of Africa is an old-established matter to which European colonialism only added new dimensions. Furthermore, the fact was normally neglected that while the job might on a number of counts have been much better done, the creation of states of a sensible size to live in the modern world could only be accomplished by a lumping together of tribal peoples who had no heritage of common identity.

The characteristic problem confronting anyone who seeks to estab- lish the political shape of Africa south of the Sahara is that there are no "natural" communities or political entities between the smallest and the most typical expression of African community, and tribe, at one extreme, and the whole of the African continent at the other. A number of African kingdoms and empires which reached beyond a single tribe existed in the past, but they appear to have left only a slight imprint, if any, as far as a continuing sense of community is concerned, although the names of Ghana, Mali, and the like still command respect. Such regional groupings as West or East or Central Africa are not infrequently spoken of, but they generally lack clear definition, could be constituted in a number of different guises, and have no identifiable African past. This is not to deny that unions built on such regional foundations may come into being, but only that, if they do, they will either be new creations or adaptations of cooperative arrangements established under colonial auspices.

The political vehicle to which the Africans south of the Sahara have everywhere entrusted their new found independence is the colonial state, despite the fact that none of these states had any existence prior to their invention by the colonial regimes responsible for them. (This includes Liberia if the Americo-Liberians are substituted for the colonial regime.) In all or most of the countries a great number of the people still have no effective awareness of their "national" stature, as defined by the colonial boundaries, but the political life of the leaders and their follow-ers in the nationalistic movements was led at the level of the colonial territory. As soon as they got down to serious business parties and movements were organized on the basis of the several territories, and the immediate enemy to be overcome was the colonial government, even though at a remote distance behind it there stood the imperial power. During the search for independence each territory had its own party or parties, each concentrating on the political situation of that particular territory and paying relatively little attention to the activities of its neighbors. The one notable exception was in the two big French federa-tions of West and Equatorial Africa, where parties—most notably the *Rassemblement démocratique africain* (RDA)—overflowed the lesser territorial boundaries and operated at a federal level in a number of the countries which have since come separately to sovereign independence. In the postwar years when the RDA flourished it was no doubt a relevant item not only that the federations were in existence but also that much of the political life of the territories centered in Paris and in the National Assembly where they were all represented, thus bringing the African leaders into intimate contact with each other. It seems reasonable to assume that the federal and Parisian ties which were thus built up among the leaders were largely responsible for the fact that since independence the former French colonies have made move after move to regain at least some of the unity which was sacrificed as the individual territories began to exercise the autonomy granted them under the *loi cadre* of 1956. In Lockean terms it might be said that the territorial units with which the leaders had mixed their political labor were the ones which retained political existence as colonialism came to an end; and in the French case this concerned both the twelve separate territories and the two federa-tions they had constituted.

In most instances the transition from colonial status to independence was made in amicable agreement with the controlling power, which meant that the new Africa regimes could take over intact the going con-cerns, as they have been called, of the colonial administrations. Except for the lack of a foreign office and perhaps of a military establishment, the instrumentalities of government were already in operation and needed only to be nudged over to a new posture. The leading African political figures were often already substantially in charge of the affairs of their countries in the last phase of colonialism, and the africanization of the government services was in varying degrees under way. If new constitutions were generally written, they tended to build on the inherited institutions. The more painful transition in the case of Guinea, where France resented the assertion of independence, and the speedy disintegration of the Congo, where no preparation had been made for independence, only underlined the good fortune of the rest.

The universal African acceptance of the practice of concentrating on the going concerns of the inherited colonial territories had worked to undermine the earlier conviction that major realignments of the political boundaries would be necessary. This earlier version found expression in one of the resolutions of the first All-African People's Conference which met in Accra in December, 1958. Speaking up for the unity of Africa and a Commonwealth of Free African States, this resolution

> denounces artificial frontiers drawn by imperialist powers to divide the people of Africa, particularly those which cut across ethnic groups and divide people of the same stock; calls for the abolition or adjustment of such frontiers at an early date; calls upon the independent states of Africa to support a permanent solution to this problem founded upon the wishes of the people.

This doctrine appears to find continued expression in some of the statements and policies of President Nkrumah, in part no doubt as justification for his claim that because of tribal affiliation Togo and parts of the Ivory Coast should be joined to Ghana. Their "liberation" would be a part of the process of doing away with colonialism's evils—although Sylvanus Olympio of Togo and Félix Houphouet-Boigny of the Ivory Coast fail to see it in that light.

A significant reaffirmation of Nkrumah's position appeared in the communiqué which he and President Abdulla Osman of Somalia issued at the conclusion of the latter's visit to Ghana in October, 1961. It will be remembered that Somalia has extensive territorial claims against Ethiopia, Kenya, and French Somaliland, based on the Somalis on the wrong side of the frontiers. The communiqué sees a union of African states as the step which would automatically make obsolete the frontier problems inherited from the colonial regimes, but also recognizes the imperative need to call upon the principle of self-determination as a means of removing the artificial colonial frontiers which were drawn without respect for ethnic, cultural, or economic links.[1]

1. *The Party* (Accra), October 1961 (No. 14), p. 13. When it was reported that Sylvanus Olympio, then Prime Minister of Togoland, was opposed to the

This is not a doctrine which has found favor as the years have gone by. Indeed, as early as April, 1958, the Conference of Independent African States, also meeting at Accra, in demanding respect for the independence, sovereignty, and territorial integrity of African states, took a conservative position very difficult to reconcile with the revolutionary implications of self-determination. Be it noted that this was a conference of *states*, and not of *peoples*, the latter term meaning parties, movements, and other nongovernmental organizations. I have been able to find in the records of the several succeeding African conferences of either states or peoples no repetition of the plea that self-determination should be relied upon to restore Africa to its proper dimensions. The more left-inclined gathering of African states at Casablanca in January 1961 seems to have made no pronouncement on these subjects, except, of course, its call for African unity, but the larger meeting of twenty African states at Monrovia in May 1961 came out firmly for the absolute equality of states, noninterference in internal affairs, respect for sovereignty, and unqualified condemnation of outside subversive action by neighboring states. In this setting self-determination is acceptable only for territories as a whole and not for ethnic pieces of them.

Responsible political leaders everywhere are wary of the principle of self-determination, and African political leaders have good reason to be warier than most. For the reasons which have been suggested above, the African state system as a whole and in its parts is fragile. It has neither the sanction of old-established political entities nor well-knit communities to lend stability to its states. The effective units of community are the tribes, but to open the door to African tribal self-determination would be to move toward a Balkanization which would verge on anarchy, if it did not wholly achieve it. Furthermore, it is generally true that the present leaders seek a modernization of their societies in which the tribal past would play at best only a ceremonial role. To allow the tribes to take over as the dominant elements in the shaping of Africa would be to expose to ruin much of what these leaders have accom-

---

integration of his country with Ghana, the Ghanaian Ministry of Foreign Affairs issued the following statement: "The arbitrary carving out of the African Continent by the imperialist powers during the 'scramble for Africa' in the 19th century resulted in an unnatural and unsatisfactory situation. People of the same ethnic group, indeed sometimes members of the same family, came to be ruled by different powers and were compelled to regard their brothers across the border as foreigners. The Ewes along the Ghana/Togoland border are not the only such victims. The Sanwi, Aowin and Nzema peoples on the Western borders of Ghana are in a similar plight. "The Prime Minister's suggestion is therefore no bid for expansionism. It represents the natural urge of these peoples to achieve the basic ethnic regrouping of the communities which had been violated by the plans of the imperialist powers for domination and exploitation." *Ghana Today* (London), November 25, 1959.

plished and seek to accomplish in the immediate future. The tragic affairs of the Congo, where tribalism partially reasserted itself when the central authority collapsed, stand as a warning as to what may happen.

Given the circumstances of Africa it is eminently comprehensible that there should be a determination on the part of many African statesmen to stand by the existing political structure of the continent even though any one can with ease poke his fingers through the loopholes with which it is riddled. The consolidation and utilization of what presently exists seems a far sounder procedure than an effort to reconstruct the political map of Africa which would run the immediate risk of creating a far worse situation than the one which now exists.

Considerations of this sort led President Olympio to look with a skeptical eye on the pretensions of pan-Africanism and to plead the cause of the present African countries:

> In their struggle against the colonial powers the new African states, arbitrary and unrealistic as their original boundaries may have been, managed at last to mobilize the will of their citizens toward the attainment of national independence. Achieved at great sacrifice, such a reward is not to be cast away lightly; nor should the national will, once unified, be diluted by the formation of nebulous political units.[2]

It is a fair summary of his contention to say that he warned against pursuing a shadowy vision of African unity and counseled instead the use of the tools at hand to tackle "the central task to which we are committed—the earliest possible economic and social betterment of our people." For this purpose, he held, the principle of national sovereignty should be retained, combined with an active policy of cooperation with other African states.

In a similar vein the Abbé Fulbert Youlou, President of the Congo (Brazzaville), is cited as having remarked concerning pan-Africanism that "those who talk about it should start by sweeping up in front of their own hut, before thinking of sweeping up before that of their neighbor."[3]

The Sources of Pan-Africanism

The pan-Africanism which is being pursued simultaneously with the internal consolidation of the new states has many faces and can take on many guises. The simplest and, all in all, perhaps the most satisfactory

2. Sylvanus E. Olympio, "African Problems and the Cold War," *Foreign Affairs,* October 1961 (Vol. 40, No. 1), p. 51.

3. Cited by E. Milcent, "Forces et idées-forces en Afrique Occidentale." *Afrique Documents,* Mai 1960 (No. 51), p. 63.

version of it is the sense that all Africans have a spiritual affinity with each other and that, having suffered together in the past, they must march together into a new and brighter future. In its fullest realization this would involve the creation of "an African leviathan in the form of a political organization or association of states," as Nnamdi Azikiwe, Governor-General of Nigeria and one of the pioneer leaders of African nationalism, recently put it in a speech in which he expressed his conviction that such a leviathan was bound to arise.[4] At lesser levels it might involve an almost infinite variety of regional groupings and collaborative arrangements, all partial embodiments of the continent-embracing unity which is the dream of the true pan-Africanist.[5]

The sources from which pan-Africanism derives are in part obscure and debatable and in part reasonably clearly written on the record.

How much of the claimed sense of common identity is to be attributed to the feeling that all Africans, despite the unmistakable physical differences among them, are members of the same race? Here, as in most other social-political manifestations of the idea of race, what is important is not the unascertainable biological fact of common physical heritage but the belief that there is such a heritage, at least in the sense of distinguishing Africans from the other peoples of the world.

One complication raised by the racial approach is the question as to whether North Africa, Arab and Berber in composition as against the *Afrique noire* south of the Sahara, forms a part of a single continental pan-Africa. If blackness of skin be taken as the principal outward criterion of Africanness, the North African peoples evidently belong in a different category, but the general assumption and practice have been to include North Africa in the pan-African family, despite the fact that it has attachments to the Arab world of the Middle East not shared by sub-Saharan Africans as well as attachments to the broader world of Islam which are shared by only some of the peoples to the south. My own crystal ball suggests that while for some purposes the North African countries will be drawn into continental African groupings, they will continue to have Arabic, Mediterranean, and Muslim affiliations which will keep them from anything approaching total absorption into a conceivable pan-African union.

Even though Africans generally, having been the principal victims of a prior racialism, repudiate a new racialism asserting itself in a pan-African guise, it seems very difficult to escape racial conceptions as one

4. Nnamdi Azikiwe, "The Future of Pan-Africanism," a speech made in London on August 12, 1961, published by the Nigerian High Commission, London.
5. The article by Erasmus H. Kloman, Jr. gives an account of many of the more recent African groupings, *International Organization*, Vol. XVI, No. 2 (Spring 1962).

of the basic elements in pan-Africanism. The concept of *Négritude*, expounded by Aimé Césaire, Léopold Senghor, and others, bases itself explicitly on the people of "Negro race" (incidentally leading into the further demographic question as to the relation of African-descended people through the world to a pan-African or pan-Negro movement). Nkrumah's conception of the African Personality is less obviously tied to racial moorings but it cannot evade the racialist implications which are inherent in any such idea. Senghor overtly brings these implications to the fore in his assertion that

> Négritude is the whole complex of civilized values—cultural, economic, social, and political—which characterize the black peoples, or, more precisely the Negro-African world. . . . the sense of communion, the gift of myth-making, the gift of rhythm, such are the essential elements of Négritude, which you will find indelibly stamped on all the works and activities of the black man.[6]

It is both fruitless and unwise to seek to give to either *Négritude* or African Personality a precise and specific content. Both, like Americanism and other similar concepts, stand as proud symbols of the accomplishments and virtues of a people, to be phrased in large and generous terms. Any effort to define them more closely runs the risk of starting arguments which divide those whom it is sought to unite rather than to bring them together. One key feature of these concepts and of the general trend of African thinking in recent years is that black has become a color to admire and be proud of. The earlier assumption, convenient for the slave owner and white ruler, had been that white represented the superior beings endowed with a high and advanced civilization whereas black stood for the properly servile inferiors who had not progressed beyond the primitive stages of mankind. African nationalism has brought about a transvaluation of values which establishes the African as a person of consequence and the heir of a history and culture, still in process of rediscovery, which have made their contribution to the world. To be black is itself a distinctive bond of unity.

Running through this range of thought and emotion is the conviction that the Africans as a people have been oppressed, exploited, and degraded to a greater extent than any other great mass of mankind in history. No elaborate exposition of the centuries of the slave trade, slavery, and colonialism is needed to point the moral of the African belief that they have been collectively mistreated and that their common identity has been forged in the flames of their common suffering. If all hands have been against them in the past, it is all the more necessary for them

6. Léopold Sédar Senghor, *West Africa*,
November 4, 1961, p. 1211.

now to join forces to ensure that their weakness does not again invite disaster.

In the creation of the conception that the continent forms a single pan-African whole a large role has been played by the Negroes overseas and particularly those in the West Indies and the United States. Having lost the memory of the particular tribes and regions from which they came and being aware of the anonymous unity which slavery had thrust upon them, it was natural that they should look across the Atlantic and see Africa and their fellow Negro brethren as a whole. Many Negro religious figures, teachers, professional men, and others contributed to the stream which flowed toward pan-Africanism, but four names can be singled out as peculiarly significant: E. W. Blyden, who was the distinguished nineteenth-century precursor of later developments; W. E. B. Du Bois, who fathered a series of Pan-African Congresses; Marcus Garvey, who sought to establish a "universal confraternity" and a "central nation" for the Negro race; and George Padmore, who served as a crystallizing center for pan-Africanism in London, influencing many Africans, including Kwame Nkrumah.

The considerable number of African leaders who have been educated or have lived abroad must have experienced a similar inclination toward a pan-African outlook as they were thrown into contact with Africans from many countries and were forced to look at the affairs of their continent through other eyes and from afar.

It seems eminently probable that not only Africa's elements of unity but, perversely, its diversity and heterogeneity as well have had an influence in promoting pan-Africanism. Precisely the instability of African states within their arbitrary frontiers and the lack of any "natural" stopping points between the tribe and continental Africa in the large lend an attraction to the broader view which it might not otherwise have—and which it may cease to have if and when African states achieve the internal consolidation which they are now seeking. The depth and breadth of an exclusive attachment to the new states is inevitably open to question, and it is reasonable to think that some of the ills from which Africa suffers or which potentially threaten it can be better handled on a collective basis than by some forty separate political entities. Thus Gabriel d'Arboussier, Senegalese Minister of Justice, predicting a Union of West African States by 1965, sees as the decisive weapon in the present evolution of Africa the unity which it has not yet achieved but which is imposed on it by its multiple diversities and internal divisions whether they be tribal, religious, ethnic, or territorial.[7]

In particular, the threat of contingent anarchy contained in the fact

7. Gabriel d'Arboussier, "La coopération des états africains et les problèmes inter- nationaux," *Afrique documents*, Mars– Avril 1961 (No. 66), p. 68.

that Africa's tribal structure only accidentally coincides with state frontiers might be greatly eased if larger unions of states could be brought
into being, thus making possible arrangements by which tribes that
straddle boundaries within the union could reestablish some measure of
unity. It is, of course, true that in many parts of Africa boundaries are
sufficiently porous to enable people to move easily back and forth across
them in the interior, but the more states assert their sovereignty the more
the boundaries will seal them off from each other, making formal agreements necessary if tribal and other customary links are to be maintained.
Thus an East African union, for example, of the kind which has been
much discussed recently, could lay the groundwork for a solution or at
least an amelioration of the three-way political partition which has been
imposed on the Somalis and the Masai and perhaps of the problem of the
Kenya coastal strip as well.

The Varieties of Pan-Africanism

To identify the sources of pan-Africanism is a far easier task than to
predict what practical results it is likely to achieve.

The first goal which the pan-Africanists have always set for themselves—the liberation of all of Africa from alien rule—should be reached
shortly with the one great exception of South Africa where the end of
white domination in the peculiarly objectionable form of apartheid is
still not in sight. The two other major areas of difficulty are the Rhodesias with their strong white minorities and the Portuguese territories of
Angola and Mozambique where no effective move has been made to prepare the Africans to manage their own affairs. Failure to achieve speedy
independence and self-government for the African majorities in the great
southern reaches of the continent would be a blow to African aspirations, but it is arguable that nothing could better promote the practical
advance of pan-Africanism than its confrontation by a continued un-
yielding colonialism, perhaps involving new Sharpevilles in the form of
violent suppression of nationalist agitation. The result of such a situation
might well be that Africa's independent states would band more closely
together to furnish aid to their oppressed brethren than they would
otherwise be ready to do.

The first step is to win independence; the second is to knit together
the newly freed peoples. On the face of it, there is a ring of gross im-
probability about the dream that within the foreseeable future a great
leviathan might be created which would embrace all the African states
within a single political structure. Although some sort of collaborative

functional arrangements may conceivably be worked out on an Africa-wide basis, it is likely that any close political union will be limited to regions such as West or East Africa, and that even at the regional level functional collaboration, as, for example, in relation to transport and communications, health and sanitary provisions, and certain economic matters, is much more probable than merging of sovereignties. Furthermore, any strong regional movement or organization would be likely to impair the possibility of realizing a full pan-Africanism. . . .

.   .   .   .

To the regionalism of geography may be added two other categories of regionalism: one of language and the other of ideology.

A regionalism of language finds its principal expression in the efforts of the former French dependencies to regain some of the advantages which came to them as members of the West and Equatorial African federations and to build even more extensive joint enterprises within the ranks of the African peoples *d'expression française*. . . .

.   .   .   .

No corresponding links have been formed among the former British African territories, although those which have come to independence have remained within the Commonwealth—and remained all the more happily with the departure of South Africa from it. . . .

At least until very recently English-speaking Africans and Negroes tended to monopolize both the term "pan-Africanism" and the movements and congresses associated with it.[8] In part, perhaps, this arose from the fact that many of the outstanding French African leaders were for a time drawn to France and to Paris, with the result that they somewhat lost sight of their African heritage. It has also been suggested that France frowned upon pan-African conceptions because their advocates were likely to be precisely those radical nationalists who were pressing most vigorously for modernization and equality: "French repudiation of the goal of independence led to deep suspicion of the goal of unity."[9] Whether or not the French are to be held directly responsible for the breaking up of the federations of West and Equatorial Africa, it is clear

8. "As a movement which was conceived in America and which blossomed in West Africa, pan-Africanism remains essentially an English-speaking movement, a delayed boomerang from the era of slavery as practiced on the West African coast two centuries ago. It is significant that, linguistically and ethnically, most of the American Negroes in North America came from the coastal areas on the Gulf of Guinea, and only a few from the in-terior areas of Senegal and Niger." Paul-Marc Henry, "Pan-Africanism: A Dream Come True," *Foreign Affairs*, April 1959, p. 445. See also T. Hodgkin and R. Schachter, "French-speaking West Africa in Transition," *International Conciliation*, May 1960, p. 432; Philippe Decraene, *Le panafricanisme*, Paris, 1959.

9. Immanuel Wallerstein, *Africa: The Politics of Independence*, New York, Vintage Books, 1961, p. 111.

that they did nothing to encourage their maintenance or reestablishment after 1956.

As independence came in sight, however, French-speaking Africans have demonstrated an increasing interest in associating themselves with the pan-African movements from which they have at all events never been wholly divorced. Particularly for those who, like Senghor, stressed the anachronistic parochialism of nationalism in the contemporary world, the broader horizons of pan-Africa were inevitably appealing, and even the union of Africa was seen as only a stepping-stone to the union of mankind.

Another side of the coin is the accusation which has been leveled by Nkrumah and others against the ex-French states that they are tools of neocolonialism both in allowing the language barriers imposed by imperialism to determine their alignments and in the degree to which they have remained tied to France financially and otherwise. Certainly a number of the territories left behind in the collapse of the two federations seem hopeless experiments in endowing with life artificial political entities which have no prospect of economic and political viability. Their dependence on France for the barest minimum of survival cannot help but raise questions as to the reality of their independence; . . . . it is a plausible speculation that a large share of such coordination as they have achieved between themselves has been the product of activities which have taken place in Paris rather than in one or another African capital.

Casablanca and Monrovia

The two major ideological groupings, which go under the names of the cities in which they originated in 1961, Casablanca and Monrovia, both cut across the linguistic boundaries and thus help to prevent a permanent freezing of the lines dividing the former British and French territories. On a larger scale these two groupings carry on the attack on linguistic solidarity which was initiated with the Ghana-Guinea union in 1958, later extended by the addition of Mali (the ex-French Soudan) after the breakup of the Mali Federation in 1960.

Although it is tempting to read a deep and long-lasting ideological conflict into the split between these two major groups, many observers are inclined to be skeptical of the solidarity of each of the groups within itself and of the depth and sticking power of the ideological divergence. Certainly it is premature to assume that any political situation in Africa has as yet had time to achieve real stability. Both within each of the states

* [N.B. This was written before the 1965–1969 military corps in Mali, Ghana, etc. Ed. Note]

and in the relations between them forces are at work which sharply challenge the existing order and may end by overthrowing it. The series of apparently cordial state visits which the heads of countries in the opposing blocs pay each other, with the consequent communiqués endorsing friendship and African unity, indicate that the ideological lines are far from representing any total separation.

When these cautionary remarks have been made, however, it is essential to recognize that as of now serious cleavages divide the members of the two groups which tend to head in different directions in outlook and policy. Undoubtedly the Casablanca group, of which Guinea, Ghana, and Mali constitute the sub-Saharan members, is more activist, radical, and left-oriented, taking its anticolonialism, its socialism, and its pan-Africanism a good deal more seriously than does the larger and more conservative Monrovia grouping in which Nigeria and Liberia play leading roles and which includes the entire Brazzaville community as well as Ethiopia and Somalia from the other side of the continent. Relations between Guinea, Ghana, and Mali on one side and the Soviet bloc on the other tend to be considerably more intimate than those between the latter and the Monrovia contingent.

The Nkrumah doctrine that African unity must be sought through a merger of sovereignties in a new political kingdom has not found many takers among the African leaders. The reasons for this rejection are not hard to find, among them being the manifest disinclination to accept the proffered headship of Nkrumah himself in a potential African union. This is a difficulty which must be a recurrent one: where strong one-man leadership has established itself, as is so often the case in Africa, it will be a painful process to select from among the leaders of the states which are uniting one to stand out in splendor while the others sink back to subordinate positions. The surrender of the trappings and the more substantial perquisites of sovereignty is not a step which is lightly taken, even for the attainment of African unity. Several of the African leaders have indicated plainly enough that they have not fought the battles for independence in order to abandon it again in favor of someone else's rule. Thus the Prime Minister of Nigeria, with an icy side reference to Nkrumah, remarked that his country had waited one hundred years for freedom and did not propose to throw it away on gaining independence, and Houphouet-Boigny similarly protested that his Ivory Coast had not come to independence in order to be subjected to a backward African country.[10]

10. For Nkrumah, see the New York *Times*, January 14, 1960. For Houphouet-Boigny, see "Les chances de l'Afrique," *Revue politique et parlementaire,* Juillet 1961, pp. 3–11. Nnamdi Azikiwe in 1959 affirmed his confidence in the creation of the United States of Africa, but warned that:

African Harmony and Discord

Deep in the heart of every true believer is the conviction that the principle of the natural harmony of interests applies in his domain. For the pan-Africanist this implies belief in the assumption that, once the affairs of the continent cease to be distorted by the machinations of the colonialist and neocolonialist, African states and peoples will live in harmony with each other. Such a view rests upon the faith that the apparent differences and difficulties between states can be overcome by goodwill since all Africans have common outlooks and desire the unity of their peoples. In actuality the potentialities for conflict among African states are as great as those in other parts of the world; . . . . Three other disputes may be mentioned which seem symptomatic of the kind of troubles which may be coming along as the African states work out their relationships among themselves and establish their own continental balance of power: Morocco's claim to take over Mauritania, the demand of Somalia that the Somali-inhabited portions of Ethiopia and Kenya should be joined to it, and the controversy between Cameroun and Nigeria as to the status of the northern portion of the former British Cameroons. To these must of course be added any number of possible disputes arising from cross-frontier tribal claims, not to mention all the usual subjects which offer fertile fields for disagreement among states.

.   .   .   .

. . . . In a speech delivered by President Modibo Keita of Mali in June 1961[11]. . . . he spoke of his continuing conviction that the countries of Africa can never achieve full independence as long as they remain small and each concentrates on itself alone. Although, he pointed out, the constitution of Mali provides for total or partial abandonment of sovereignty on behalf of a grouping of African states, actual political unification with other states could be undertaken only if there were an identity of views on both international policy and domestic economic policy. Even without such an identity of views, cooperation would be possible with all African states, whatever their political or economic position, but

It would be capital folly to assume that hard-bargaining politicians who passed through the ordeal of victimization and the crucible of persecution to win their independence will easily surrender their newly-won power in the interest of a political leviathan which is populated by people who are alien to one another in their social and economic relations. It has not been possible in Europe or America, and unless Africa can show herself different from other continents, the verdict of history on this score will remain unchallenged and unaltered.

ZIK, *A Selection from the Speeches of Nnamdi Azikiwe*, Cambridge, University Press, 1961, p. 72.

11. Modibo Keita, "The Foreign Policy of Mali," *International Affairs*, October 1961, pp. 435–6.

the conditions for a political merger were much more stringent. President Keita had, of course, been one of the central figures in the collapse of the Mali Federation, whose demise could in good part be attributed to sharp disagreements on both foreign and domestic policy between Senegal and Soudan. It might be added that the more recent divorce of Syria from Egypt, shattering the United Arab Republic, was in part attributable to similar differences in outlook and policy between the two countries.

Which way the African future will turn is still a matter for wide-open speculation. It is evident that strong forces are pulling in a number of different directions, that African states are frequently divided among themselves, and that all African leaders express their devotion to the cause of African unity although with varying interpretations and varying degrees of intensity. Most of them would undoubtedly concur in the verdict of Julius Nyerere, principal architect of Tanganyika's independence, that African nationalism is different from other nationalisms of the past in that "the African national State is an instrument for the unification of Africa, and not for dividing Africa, that African nationalism is meaningless, is dangerous, is anachronistic if it is not at the same time pan-Africanism."[12]

How different African nationalism is remains to be seen. Insofar as precedents are relevant it is clear on the historical record that elsewhere the more parochial nationalist forces have almost always won out over the more broadly integrating supernational forces. It remains the fact that the rediscovery of Africa by the Africans is still only in its opening stages. It is a vast continent which has always been internally divided, and the superimposed colonial divisions worked to prevent the different peoples from establishing any real contact with each other. Pan-African gatherings, United Nations caucuses, and a host of other meetings and interstate visits are bringing at least an upper crust of the African peoples in touch with each other, but it will be long before the colonially-determined lines of transport and communications can be so reconstructed as to open up easy intercourse between the countries.

But perhaps the precedents are not relevant. Times have changed and African nations still have an insubstantiality about them which distinguishes them from their fellows around the globe. Of all the questions which may be asked the most significant is as to the depth and universality of the belief that Africans are born to a common destiny.

12. *World Assembly of Youth Forum,* No. 40, September 1961, p. 14. Most of the leaders would presumably also agree with Nyerere's further contention that only African unity can save the continent from the rival imperialisms of capitalism and communism.

SELECTED BIBLIOGRAPHY

Periodicals Specializing in African Developments

Africa, Journal of the International African Institute

African Abstracts, London

African Affairs, Journal of the Royal African Society

African Digest, London

Africa Report, United States

Africa Today, United States

West Africa, London

Marches tropicaux (*Marches coloniaux*), Paris

Présence africaine, Paris

Journal of Modern African Studies, England

Journal of African History, England

Recommended general studies in paperback dealing with Africa

Adam, Thomas R., *Government and Politics in Africa South of the Sahara*, third ed., Random House, New York, 1964.

Bohannan, Paul D., *Africa and Africans*, Doubleday, New York, 1964.

Burke, Fred G., *Africa's Quest for Order*, Prentice-Hall, Englewood Cliffs, 1963.

Dumont, René, *False Start in Africa*, rev. ed., Praeger, New York, 1969.

Fanon, Frantz, *The Wretched of the Earth*, Grove Press, New York, 1965.

———, *Black Skins, White Masks*, Grove Press, New York, 1968.

Hatch, John, *Africa Today and Tomorrow*, rev. ed., Praeger, New York, 1965.

Hodgkin, Thomas, *Nationalism in Africa*, New York University Press, New York, 1956.

Judd, Peter, (ed.), *African Independence*, Dell, New York, 1963.

Kilson, Martin L. and Rupert Emerson, (eds.), *The Political Awakening of Africa*, Prentice-Hall, Englewood Cliffs, 1965.

Lloyd, Peter C., *Africa in Social Change*, Penguin, Baltimore, 1967.

McCord, William, *The Springtime of Freedom: Evolution of Developing Societies*, Oxford University Press, New York, 1965.

Post, Ken, *The New States of West Africa*, Penguin, Baltimore, 1968.

Shepherd, George, Jr., *The Politics of African Nationalism*, Praeger, New York, 1962.

Spiro, Herbert J., *Africa: The Pri-*

macy of Politics, Random House, New York, 1966.

———, *Patterns of African Development,* Prentice-Hall, Englewood Cliffs, 1967.

Wallerstein, Immanuel, *Africa: The Politics of Unity,* Random House, New York, 1967.

1. Africa's Dual Heritage: Imperialism and Precolonial Greatness

Baulin, Jacques, *The Arab Role in Africa,* Penguin, Baltimore, 1962.

Crowder, Michael, *A Short History of Nigeria,* rev. ed., Praeger, New York, 1966.

Davidson, Basil, *The African Slave Trade,* Little Brown, Boston, 1961.

———, *The Lost Cities of Africa,* Little Brown, Boston, 1959.

Diop, Cheikh Anta, *Anteriorité des Civilisations Nègres,* Présence Africaine, Paris, 1967.

Duffy, James, *Portuguese Africa,* Harvard University Press, Cambridge, 1959.

Fage, J. D., *An Introduction to the History of West Africa,* third ed., Cambridge University Press, New York, 1966.

Gann, Lewis H., and Peter Duignan, *Burden of Empire,* Praeger, New York, 1967.

Harrison-Church, R. J., *West Africa,* rev. ed., Longmans Green & Co., London, 1960.

Hunton, Alphaeus T., *Decision in Africa,* rev. ed., International Publishers, New York, 1960.

Kimble, George, *Tropical Africa,* Vol. I, Doubleday, New York, 1960.

Labouret, Henri, *Africa Before the White Man,* Walker & Co., New York, 1963.

McCall, Daniel F., *Africa in Time Perspective,* Oxford University Press, New York, 1969.

Nkrumah, Kwame, *Neo-Colonialism: The Last Stage of Imperialism,* International Publishers, New York, 1966.

Oliver, Roland, ed., *The Dawn of African History,* second ed., Oxford University Press, New York, 1968.

Oliver, Roland and A. E. Atmore, *Africa Since 1800,* Cambridge University Press, New York, 1967.

Perham, Margery, *The Colonialist Reckoning,* Knopf, New York, 1962.

———, *African Outline,* Oxford University Press, New York, 1966.

Stamp, L. D., *Africa: A Study in Tropical Development,* second ed., John Wiley, New York, 1964.

Suret-Canale, Jean, *Afrique Noire, L'Ere Coloniale,* Editions Sociales, Paris, 1964.

Wiedner, Donald, *A History of Africa South of the Sahara,* Random House, New York, 1962.

Woddis, Jack, *Africa: The Roots of Revolt,* The Citadel Press, New York, 1960.

II. The Struggle for Independence: The Tribe, Tribalism, and the Conditions for Social Development

Ainslie, Rosalynde, *The Press in Africa*, rev. ed., Walker & Co., New York, 1968.

Barber, W. J., *The Economy of British Central Africa*, Stanford University Press, Stanford, 1961.

Bascom, William R. and M. J. Herskovits, (eds.), *Continuity and Change in African Cultures*, University of Chicago Press, Chicago, 1958.

Benveniste, Guy and W. E. Moran, Jr., *Handbook of African Economic Development*, Praeger, New York, 1962.

Bohannan, Paul, (ed.), *African Homicide and Suicide*, Atheneum, New York, 1967.

Busia, Kofi, *The Position of the Chief in the Modern Political System of Ashanti*, International Publications Service, New York, 1968.

Epstein, A. L., *Politics in an Urban African Community*, Manchester University Press, Manchester, 1958.

Fallers, Lloyd, *Bantu Bureaucracy*, University of Chicago Press, Chicago, 1965.

Field, M. J., *Search for Security*, Northwestern University Press, Evanston, 1960.

Fortes, Myer and E. Evans-Pritchard, (eds.), *African Political Systems*, Seabury Press, New York, 1940.

Gluckman, Max, *Custom and Conflict in Africa*, Barnes & Noble, New York, 1964.

Mair, Lucy P., *Primitive Government*, Penguin, Baltimore, 1962.

Meek, C. R., *Land, Law and Custom in the Colonies*, Barnes & Noble, New York, 1946.

———, *Law and Authority in a Nigerian Tribe: A Study in Indirect Rule*, Barnes & Noble, New York, 1968.

Murdock, George P., *Africa, Its People and Their Cultural History*, McGraw-Hill, New York, 1959.

Ottenberg, Simon and Phoebe, *Culture and Societies of Africa*, Random House, New York, 1960.

Wilson, Godfrey and Monica, *The Analysis of Social Change*, Gordian Press, New York, 1968.

III. The Struggle for Independence: The Dynamics of Nationalism

Apter, David, *The Political Kingdom in Uganda*, rev. ed., Princeton University Press, Princeton, 1967.

———, *Ghana in Transition*, rev. ed., Atheneum, New York, 1963.

Arikpo, Okoi, *The Development of Modern Nigeria*, Penguin, Baltimore, 1967.

Breese, Ghald, *Urbanization in Newly Developing Countries*, Prentice-Hall, New Jersey, 1966.

Bretton, Henry, *The Rise and Fall of Kwame Nkrumah*, Praeger, New York, 1966.

Coleman, James, *Nigeria: Background to Nationalism*, University of California Press, Berkeley and Los Angeles, 1958.

Cowan, L. Gray et al., (eds.), *Education and Nation Building in Africa*,

Hargreaves, J. D., *West Africa: The Praeger, New York.*

Former French States, Prentice-Hall, Englewood Cliffs, 1967.

Markovitz, Irving Leonard, *Léopold Sédar Senghor and the Politics of Négritude*, Atheneum, New York, 1969.

Nkrumah, Kwame, *Ghana*, Nelson, London, 1957.

————, *I Speak of Freedom*, Praeger, New York, 1961.

————, *Dark Days in Ghana*, International Publishers, New York, 1968.

Okuma, T., *Angola in Ferment*, Beacon Press, Boston, 1962.

IV. The Consolidation of Power: The Definition of the Political Arena

American Society for African Culture, (ed.), *Pan-Africanism Reconsidered*, University of California Press, Berkeley & Los Angeles, 1962.

Austin, Dennis, *Politics in Ghana*, Oxford University Press, New York, 1964.

Awolowo, Obafemi, *Awo: Autobiography*, Cambridge University Press, 1960.

Azikiwe, Nnamdi, Zik: *A Selection from the Speeches*, Cambridge University Press, New York, 1961.

Bienen, Herbert, *Tanzania: Party Transformation and Economic Development*, Princeton University Press, Princeton, 1967.

Bretton, Henry, *Power and Stability in Nigeria*, Praeger, New York, 1962.

Busia, Kofi, *The Challenge of Africa*, Praeger, New York, 1962.

Carter, Gwendolyn, (ed.), *African One Party State*, Cornell University Press, New York.

————, (ed.), *National Unity and Regionalism in Eight African States*, Cornell University Press, New York, 1966.

Chidzero, B. T. O., *Tanganyika and International Trusteeship*, Oxford University Press, New York, 1961.

Coleman, James S. and Carl Rosberg, Jr., (ed.), *Political Parties and National Integration in Tropical Africa*, University of California Press, Los Angeles and Berkeley, 1964.

Delavignette, Robert, *Freedom and Authority in French West Africa*, International Publishing Service, New York, 1968.

Dia, Mamadou, *The African Nations and World Solidarity*, Praeger, New York, 1961.

Hughes, A. J., *East Africa: The Search for Unity*, Penguin, Baltimore, 1968.

Jahn, Janheinz, *Muntu: An Outline of Neo-African Culture*, Grove Press, New York, 1958.

Kilson, Martin, *Political Change in a West African State*, Harvard University Press, Cambridge, 1966.

Legum, Colin, *Pan-Africanism, A Short Political Guide*, Praeger, New York, 1962.

Lewis, W. H., (ed.), *French Speaking Africa: The Search for Identity*, Walker & Co., New York, 1965.

Lumumba, Patrice, *Congo, My Country*, Praeger, New York, 1962.

Morgenthau, Ruth Schacter, *Political Parties in French Speaking West Africa*, Oxford University Press, New York, 1964.

Padmore, George, *Pan-Africanism or Communism*, 1962.

Rosberg, Jr., Carl and William Friedland, (eds.), *African Socialism*, Stanford University Press, Stanford, 1964.

Sartre, Jean-Paul, *Black Orpheus*, Prèsence Africaine, Paris, n.d.

Segal, Ronald, *African Profiles*, rev. ed., Penguin, Baltimore, 1962.

Senghor, Leopold S., *African Socialism*, Praeger, New York, 1964.

Sigmund, Paul, (ed.), *The Ideologies* of *Developing Nations*, rev. ed., Praeger, New York, 1967.

Sklar, Richard L., *Nigerian Political Parties*, Princeton University Press, Princeton, 1963.

Touré, Sekou, *Toward Full Re-Africanization*, Patrice Lumumba Press, Conakrey, 1959.

Weiss, Herbert, *Political Protest in the Congo*, Princeton University Press, Princeton, 1967.

V. Processes of Encadrement: Bureaucratic Development and Economic Growth

Achebe, Chinera, *Things Fall Apart*, Obolensky, New York, 1959.

———, *Man of the People*, Doubleday, New York, 1966.

Adu, A. D., *The Civil Service in New African States*, Praeger, New York, 1965.

Apter, David, *The Politics of Modernization*, University of Chicago Press, Chicago, 1965.

Davis, Ian, *African Trade Unions*, Penguin, Baltimore, 1966.

Fougeyrollas, Pierre, *Modernisation des Hommes*, Flammarion, Paris, 1967.

Hamon, Leo, (ed.), *Le Role Extra-Militaire de l'Armée dans le Tiers Monde*, Presses Universitaire de France, Paris, 1966.

Hance, A. H., *African Economic Development*, Praeger, New York, 1967.

Hambridge, G., (ed.), *Dynamics of Development*, 1964.

Hapgood, David, *Africa: From Independence to Tomorrow*, Atheneum, New York, 1965.

Hunter, Guy, (ed.), *The New Societies of Tropical Africa*, Praeger, New York, 1964.

Kuper, Leo, *An African Bourgeoisie*, Yale University Press, New Haven, 1965.

Lloyd, P. C., (ed.), *The New Elites of Tropical Africa*, Oxford University Press, New York, 1966.

Mphalale, Eziekiel, *The African Image*, Praeger, New York, 1962.

Nyerere, Julius K., *Freedom and Socialism*, Oxford University Press, New York, 1969.

Sacks, Wulf, *Black Anger*, Grove Press, New York, 1969.

Tutuola, Amos, *The Palm-Wine Drinkard*, 1953.

Zimmerman, L. J., *Poor Lands, Rich Lands: The Widening Gap*, Random House, New York, 1965.

VI. The Politics of Race

Abrahams, Peter, *Tell Freedom*, Knopf, New York, 1954.

Bunting, Ian, *The Rise of the South African Reich*, Penguin, Baltimore, 1964.

John A. Davis and James K. Baker,

Southern Africa in Transition, Praeger, New York, 1966.

First, Ruth, *South West Africa,* Penguin, Baltimore, 1963.

Keatley, Patrick, *The Politics of Partnership,* Penguin, Baltimore, 1963.

Leys, Colin, *European Politics in Southern Rhodesia,* Oxford University Press, New York, 1959.

Lytton, David, *The Goddamn White Man,* Simon & Schuster, New York, 1960.

Marquard, Leo, *Peoples and Policies of South Africa,* fourth ed., Oxford University Press, New York, 1969.

——, *Short History of South Africa,* Praeger, New York, 1968.

Mason, Philip, *Year of Decision: Rhodesia and Nyasaland,* Oxford University Press, New York, 1960.

Mbeki, G., *South Africa: The Peasants Revolt,* Penguin, Baltimore, 1964.

Patterson, Sheila, *The Last Trek: A Study of the Boer People,* Hillary, New York, 1957.

Rosberg, Jr., Carl and John Nottingham, *The Myth of Mau Mau,* Praeger, 1966.

Sacks, B., *Road from Sharpeville,* 1961.

Segal, Ronald, (ed.), *Sanctions Against South Africa,* Penguin, Maryland, 1964.

VII. Africa in the World: Pan-Africanism and Neutralism

Des Africanistes Russe Parlent de l'Afrique, Prèsence Africaine, Paris, 1960.

Barros, R. *African States and the United Nations versus Apartheid,* New York, 1967.

Bowles, Chester, *Africa's Challenge to America,* 1956.

Brzezinski, Z., (ed.), *Africa and the Communist World,* Stanford University Press, Stanford, 1965.

Coleman, James, "America and Africa," *World Politics,* July, 1957.

Crowder, Michael, *Senegal: A Study in French Assimilation Policy,* second rev. ed., Barnes & Noble, New York, 1967.

Goldschmidt, Walter, (ed.), *The United States and Africa,* rev. ed., Praeger, New York.

Hovet, Thomas, *Africa in the United Nations,* Northwestern University Press, Evanston, 1963.

International Political Communities, Anchor Books, Garden City, 1966.

Keita, Mobido, "The Foreign Policy of Mali," International Affairs, October, 1961.

London, Kurt, (ed.), *New Nations in a Divided World,* Praeger, New York, 1963.

McKay, Vernon, *Africa in World Politics,* Harper & Row, New York, 1963.

McKay, Vernon, ed., *African Diplomacy,* Praeger, New York, 1967.

Martin, Lawrence, *Neutralism and Non-Alignment,* Praeger, New York, 1962.

Morgenthau, Hans, "A Political Theory of Foreign Aid," American Political Science Review, June, 1962.

Morison, D., *The USSR and Africa,* Oxford University Press, New York, 1964.

Neumann, Heinzgeorg, "Portuguese Policy in Africa," *International Affairs,* pp. 663–675.

Nielson, M. A., *African Battleline*, Atheneum, New York, 1965.

O'Brien, Connor Cruse, *To Katanga and Back*, Grosset & Dunlap, New York, 1962.

Okigbo, Pius H., *Africa and the Common Market*, Northwestern University Press, Evanston, 1967.

Padelford, Norman and Rupert Emerson, *Africa in the World*, Praeger, New York, 1963.

Padmore, George, *Pan-Africanism or Communism*, 1957.

Phillips, Claude S., *The Development of Nigerian Foreign Policy*, Northwestern University Press, Evanston, 1964.

Quigg, P., (ed.), *Africa: A Foreign Affairs Reader*, New York, Praeger, 1964.

Rothchild, Donald, *Toward Unity in Africa*, Public Affairs Press, Washington, 1960.

Thiam, Doudou, *The Foreign Policy of African States*, Praeger, New York, 1963.

Zartman, I. William, *International Relations in the New Africa*, Prentice-Hall, Englewood Cliffs, 1966.

INDEX

AAC (Anglo American Corporation), 409, 412
AAPSO (Afro-Asian People's Solidarity Organization), 438
Abbot Laboratories, 265
Abeokuta (Nigeria), 70, 74
Addis Ababa Plan, 325
Africa Dances (Gorer), 32
African Chiefs Ordinance (Repeal) Act of 1963, 125*n*
African Chiefs (Special Powers) Ordinance (1957), 125
African Communities League, 195
African Development Bank, 310
African Mineworkers Union, 86
African National Church, 190
African National Congress (ANC), 358–61, 389
African National Congress of the Rhodesias and Nyasaland, 158, 190
African nationalism, 158–98, 228–29, 406*n*, 413, 419–20
  description of, 154–60
  development of, 160–76, 179–98
  external influences on, 180–84
  freedom of activity in, 165
  Mau Mau myth and, 207–12
  nonalignment supported by, 438
  Pan-Africanism and, 445, 450–51, 454, 458
  problems in researching, 176–78
  traditional leadership and, 124–25
African socialism, 3–5, 215–17, 334

  as moderate policy, 277
  TANU's policy of, 266–76
  technological development and, 8, 12
  Weltanschauung opposition and, 4–5
African Trade Unions, 414
"Africanus" (pseudonym), 97–98
Afrifa, Gen. A. A., 264–65
Afrikaans Reformed Churches (Dutch Reformed Churches), 368*n*, 381–85
Afrikaanse Nationale Studentebond (ANSB), 387–88
Afrikaanse Studente Bond (ANS), 388
Afrikaanse Studentebond, 386
Afrikaners (Boers), 352, 355–57
  social structures of, 368–92
Afrique Noire (periodical), 169
Afro-Asian Conference (Algiers, 1965), 431, 438–39
Afro-Asian Conference (Bandung, 1955), 199, 431–33
Afro-Asian People's Solidarity Organization (AAPSO), 438
Afro-Shirazi Party, 189, 345
Agbebi, Majola, 188, 198
Aggrey, J. E. K., 177
Akufo-Addo, Edward, 264
Alafin, 74
Alaké, 70, 74, 76
Alfa Alimou, 103–4
Alfa Bakar Diallo, Chief, 108–9